INDIA

SHOWING ANCIENT PLACE NAMES AND HISTORICAL SITES

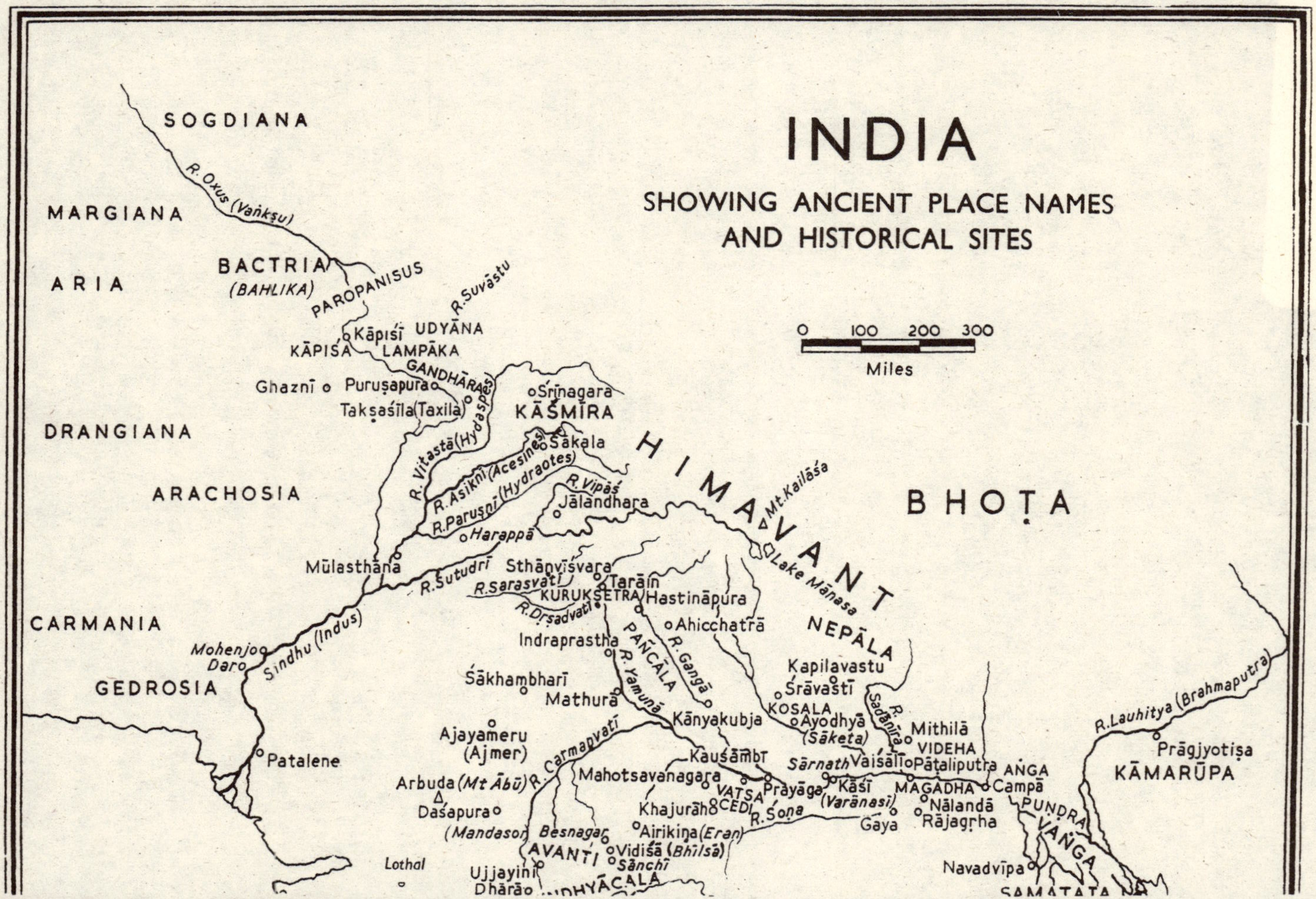

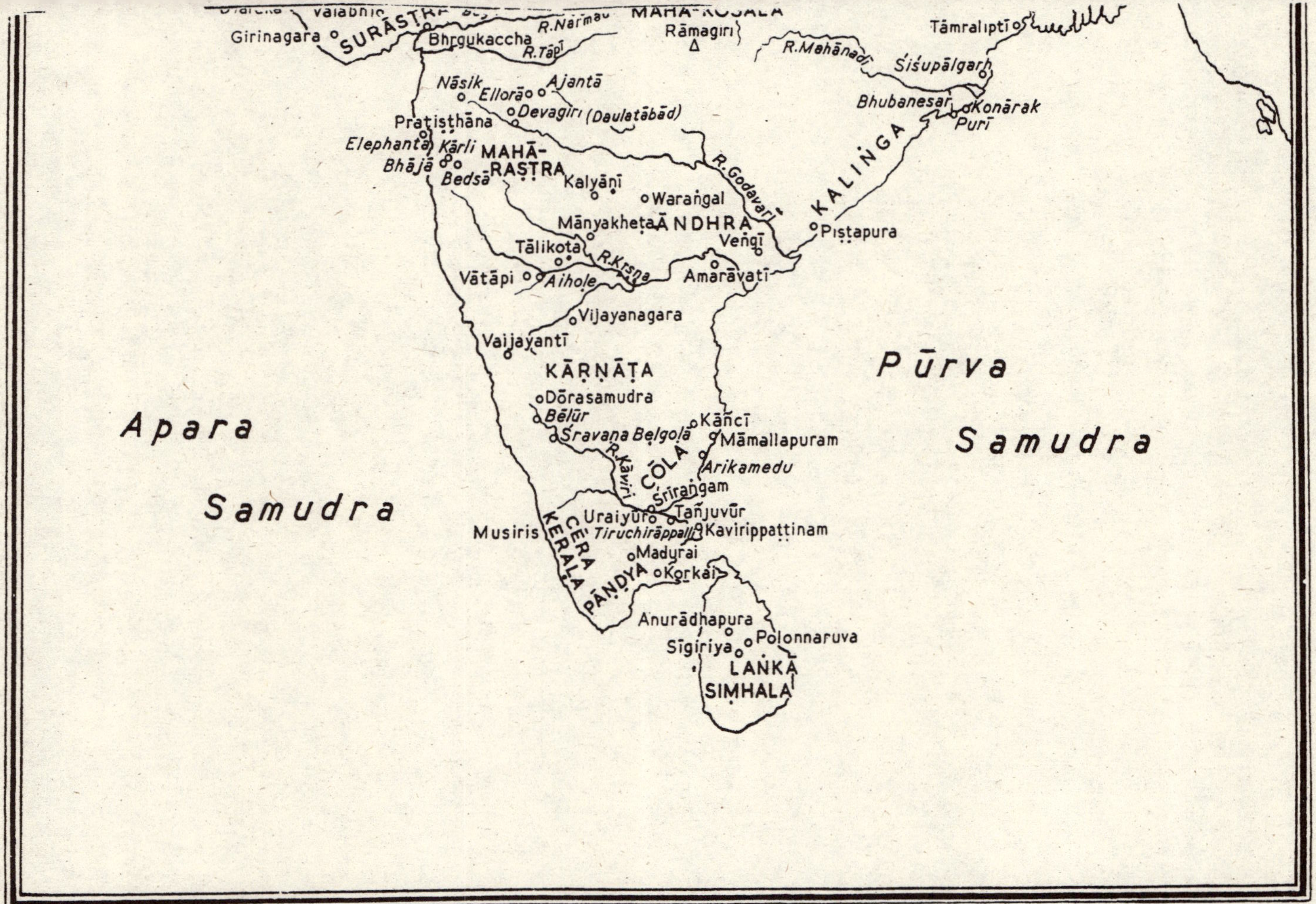
Girinagara
SURĀSTRA
Bhrgukaccha
R.Narmada
R.Tāpī
Rāmagiri
R.Mahānadī
Tāmraliptī
Śiśupālgarh
Bhubanesar
Konārak
Purī
Nāsik
Ellorā
Ajantā
Devagiri (Daulatābād)
Pratisthāna
Elephanta
Kārli
Bhājā
Bedsā
MAHĀ-
RASTRA
Kalyānī
Warangal
R.Godavari
KALINGA
Pistapura
Mānyakheta
ANDHRA
Vengī
Tālikota
R.Krsna
Vātāpi
Aihole
Amarāvatī
Vijayanagara
Vaijayantī
KĀRNĀTA
Pūrva
Samudra
Dōrasamudra
Bēlūr
Śravana Belgola
Kāñcī
Māmallapuram
Apara
Samudra
R.Kāviri
CŌLA
Arikamedu
Śrīrangam
Uraiyūr
Tañjuvūr
Musiris
CĒRA
KERALA
Tiruchirāppalli
Kavirippattinam
Madurai
PĀNDYA
Korkai
Anurādhapura
Polonnaruva
Sīgiriya
LANKĀ
SIMHALA

THE WONDER THAT WAS INDIA

British Museum

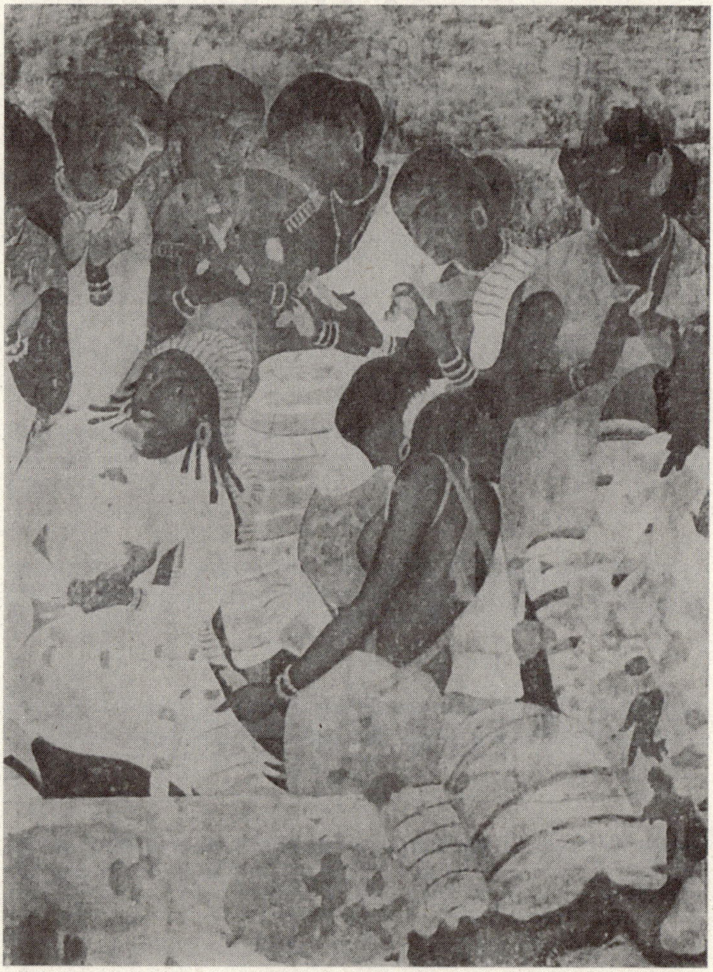

Girl Musicians and Dance. Mural Painting. Bāgh.
7th century

THE WONDER THAT WAS INDIA

Volume One

A survey of the history and culture of the Indian sub-continent before the coming of the Muslims

A. L. BASHAM

Third Revised Edition

PICADOR INDIA

First published in the UK 1954 by Sidgwick & Jackson, London
First published in India 2019 by Picador India
This edition published 2022 by Picador India
an imprint of Pan Macmillan Publishing India Private Limited
707 Kailash Building
26 K. G. Marg, New Delhi 110001
www.panmacmillan.co.in

Pan Macmillan, The Smithson, 6 Briset Street, Farringdon, London EC1M 5NR
Associated companies throughout the world
www.panmacmillan.com

ISBN 978-93-89109-34-4

10

Typeset in Times New Roman by R. Ajith Kumar, New Delhi
Printed in India by Replika Press Pvt. Ltd.

FSC www.fsc.org MIX Paper | Supporting responsible forestry FSC™ C016779

IN MEMORY OF
MY MOTHER
WHO DIED WHILE THIS WORK
WAS IN PROGRESS

"I shall not now speak of the knowledge of the Hindus, ... of their subtle discoveries in the science of astronomy—discoveries even more ingenious than those of the Greeks and Babylonians—of their rational system of mathematics, or of their method of calculation which no words can praise strongly enough—I mean the system of nine symbols. If these things were known by the people who think that they alone have mastered the sciences because they speak Greek they would perhaps be convinced, though a little late in the day, that other folk, not only Greeks but also men of a different tongue, know something as well as they."

The Syrian astronomer-monk
SEVERUS SEBOKHT (*writing A.D. 662*).

FOREWORD

THE publication of this edition of A.L. Basham's *The wonder that was India* marks the golden jubilee of its first publication, in 1954, by Sidgwick & Jackson of London. Basham's book has become a classic in its field. It found a wide readership from the start. In America, for example, the paperback, which was published by Grove Press (1959), sold over 10,000 copies in the first two years. Its readership in South Asia and Europe was increased through the publication of translations in Hindi, Urdu, Punjabi, Telugu, Tamil, Sinhalese, French, German, Spanish, Russian, Polish and Croat.

Arthur Llewellyn Basham (1914–1986), to give his full name, did a B.A. Honours I in Sanskrit language and literature (called "Indo-Aryan Studies") at the School of Oriental and African Studies of the University of London, before taking up a Ph.D. in the history of ancient India, also at SOAS, under L.D. Barnett. His doctoral thesis, on the history and doctrines of the Ajivikas, was subsequently published and remains a very useful overview of the topic.* Basham became a lecturer in the history of India at SOAS in 1948. He taught ancient Indian history there for many years, until 1965, when he moved to Australian National University, retiring in 1980. He taught as a visitor in various universities, before and after retirement, in India, the United States and Mexico. During his long career he had many honours, including honorary degrees from Kurukshetra University and the Nava Nalanda Mahavihara, and the Dr. B.C. Law Gold Medal for Indology of the Asiatic Society, Calcutta, and was president of the 28th International Congress of Orientalists at Canberra in 1971. He died in India while on a fellowship at the Asiatic Society, and is buried in the Old Military Cemetery of All Saints Cathedral in Shillong.

This bare outline of the life does not convey the special quality of the man. Basham was a warm and generous teacher, and a kind of uncle to his students. He had a large number of postgraduate students, most of them from newly independent India and Pakistan, some of them already accomplished scholars, others mere beginners, and all of them unused to English weather, English food, English lodging and English reserve. Basham was anything but reserved, and he lavished time on the improvement of their writings, he backed them in their difficulties with the administration, he gave them practical advice and lent them money in a pinch. Basham used to say that the students—over a hundred of them—were his proudest achievement, and indeed a whole generation of his students filled leading positions in the universities of India, Pakistan and Bangladesh. This

---

*A.L. Basham, *History and doctrine of the Ajivikas: a vanished Indian religion*. London, 1951.

warmth toward his students was of a piece with his warmth of feeling for India, which is so evident in his book.

The book itself, like any book, is the product of the author's life and times, and the special circumstances of its making. The first thing to be said about it has to do with the title, which was imposed upon him by the publisher, and about which Basham was slightly embarrassed. *The wonder that was India* was commissioned as part of a series of books with the titles, *The glory that was Greece*, *The grandeur that was Rome*, *The splendour that was Egypt* and *The greatness that was Babylon*. It was, in other words, part of a series on the ancient civilisations. Basham used to say that he blamed the nineteenth-century American writer Edgar Allen Poe for his florid title. Poe had written, in his poem 'To Helen', in which the classic features of the object of his affection call Poe back to his cultural homeland of the Greek and Roman texts from his vagrant wanderings (to places such as India, perhaps?),

On desperate seas long wont to roam,
Thy hyacinth hair, thy classic face,
Thy Niad airs have brought me home
To the glory that was Greece,
And the grandeur that was Rome.

Thus, Sidgwick & Jackson took the line, 'the glory that was Greece and the grandeur that was Rome' and had the bad idea of multiplying it. The title of Basham's book has spawned yet others, as we may see from the internet, where we may find such titles as *The wonder that is India*, *A wonder of Ancient India*: *the Mahabharata*, *Wandering wonder Ibn Batuta*, and *Neem—the wonder tree of India*.

Each of the books of this series was, like Basham's, a substantial work on an ancient civilisation, written by a scholar with good specialist credentials, well-produced, with over a hundred illustrations and selling at an affordable price—45 shillings. The fact that the series dealt with ancient civilisations explains the past tense of the title: *The wonder that* was *India*. Other civilisations of the series were in some sense extinct, except for that of India, which does not fit the pattern of the others in that regard, and for which the use of the past tense is not really appropriate. It was for this reason that Basham's book is, as the subtitle says, 'A survey of the culture of the Indian sub-continent before the coming of the Muslims'. For Basham the 'coming of the Muslims' meant the coming of Persian language sources, and as he had no Persian he did not feel competent to speak authoritatively about the later period. This suited the publisher's remit. There is no question here of anti-Muslim feeling.

Coming to the substance of the book, we see that it is not a history book in the normal sense of a continuous chronological narrative, but a sort of an encyclopaedia of Indian civilisation, with chapters on prehistory, history, the state, society, everyday life, religion, the arts, language and literature, and the heritage of India. It also contains many short appendices giving very useful summaries of knowledge on particular topics such as cosmology and geography, astronomy, the calendar, mathematics, and the like. It is a synthesis of existing knowledge, not a monograph that breaks new ground or develops a new methodology. But in spite of its essentially pedagogical nature, it has a mission and it has something quite new to say about its topic. Let me specify what the programme of the book was and what was new about it when it appeared.

Like any other book of history we can understand it best by seeing it as the result of the intersection of three things: the author's intellectual formation, the historical period in which it was written, and the prior texts upon which it builds or from which it seeks to distinguish itself.

We begin with the author himself. Basham had an artistic nature, and this expressed itself in a number of ways. He played the piano, and had written some musical compositions while still a teenager. He could draw, and if you look closely at some of the line drawings in this volume you will see a tiny ALB monogram, identifying figures he drew for it. But he was especially fond of literature, and was widely read in poetry and novels in several languages. In fact, Basham had written and published a book of verse and a novel, during the thirties, while still a very young man and before he took up Sanskrit and ancient Indian history. Both his parents were writers, and undoubtedly his love of literature came from them. (His father, a journalist, had served in India during World War I, and Basham learned a few rudiments of Hindustani from him as a boy, so it seems that he also got his interest in India from his father.) It shows clearly in his chapter on literature, which is filled with his own translations from works in Sanskrit, Prakrit and Tamil. A second great interest was in Indian religions. It is striking that the chapter on religion is the longest of the book, and gives a very extensive outline of the topic.

Basham came of age during the thirties, which for a young Englishman was marked by the great depression, the shrinking and near disappearance of liberal democracy—which seemed to have no answers for the problems of the age—from the European continent, the growth of communism and fascism, and the rising tide of the Indian nationalist movement. These form the context of his early writings. Basham's tendencies were anti-imperial, and he strongly favoured Indian independence. He briefly joined the Communist Party, as did many young intellectuals of the period, but it did not suit him and he quit a few months later. During World War II he was a conscientious objector to the war and served in the London fire brigade. Ramachandra Guha has said, 'Inside every thinking Indian there is a Gandhian and a Marxist struggling for supremacy.'* This seems roughly to have been true for Basham. In his case he turned away from the Marxist self he had once tried on, and although he was not in any direct sense a Gandhian he was an admirer of Gandhi and a pacifist.

The historical moment in which Basham wrote this book was very different from the thirties, during which he had his brief career as a writer, or the forties, in which he became an historian. In the fifties the worldwide depression was over,

---

* Ramachandra Guha, *An anthropologist among the Marxists and other essays* (Delhi: Permanent Black, 2001), p. 1.

fascism had been rolled back from Europe and Japan, and India, Pakistan and Ceylon had been made independent of Britain and of one another. It was the period of the massive decolonisation of European empires, led by India and Pakistan. At the time it seemed that every other month another British colony became a newly enrolled member of the newly created United Nations. The British Empire was turned into the British Commonwealth, proposing a continuing but different relation among Britain and its former colonies. *The wonder that was India*, now fifty years old, is only a little younger than the republics that emerged from the break up of British India, and Basham wrote in the immediate aftermath of Partition and Independence. Basham's book is devoted to the project of decolonising Indian history from the British side of the British-Indian relation, much as R.C. Majumdar's multivolume *History and culture of the Indian people*, written entirely by Indian scholars and meant to replace imperial histories of India, did so from the Indian side. Basham signals the place of his book in this new order of things very clearly.

It was written, he tells us, to interpret Indian civilisation to the ordinary Western reader in the light of the growing part being played in world affairs by the three nations that emerged from British India in 1947. Although primarily intended for Westerners, he hoped that it might be of interest to Indian, Pakistani and Sri Lankan readers as well, as the interpretation of a friendly foreigner. He thinks there may be room for a new outline of Indian culture to replace many excellent works now out of print, to further understanding of the civilisation of the new states in the contemporary world. We need now to identify the prior texts and explain Basham's relation to them.

Basham was decidedly in favour of the winding-up of the British Empire, but he was proud of the contributions to Indian history of British scholars such as Sir William Jones and Charles Wilkins, Alexander Cunningham and Sir John Marshall, as he makes explicit in the introduction. Elsewhere he is harshly critical of Vincent Smith, writer of a canonical textbook with an unmistakably imperial message. Basham quite consciously tried to write a book for the new age, and to find a new relation to India for the British scholar, based on appreciation. He is at pains to correct the harshly negative assessment of Indian civilisation that goes back to the times of James Mill's essay 'of the Hindus' in his *History of British India* (1817), Macaulay's infamous 'Minute on education' (1835) and the missionary critique of Hindu society. In doing so Basham adopts the Indophilia of the early Orientalists, before Indophobia had become hegemonic in Britain, upon the publication of Mill's book.* Basham is proposing a new relationship between the 'European student' and Indians, and he finds the materials from which to fashion this new relation in the British Orientalists.

Basham tells us in the preface that his book is to some extent modelled upon *Antiquities of India*, written some forty years previously by his teacher, L.D.

---

*On the Indomania or Indophilia of the early British Orientalists, and the Indophobia of Mill, Hegel and other anti-Orientalists, see Thomas R. Trautmann, *Aryans and British India* (New Delhi: Sage India, 1997).

Barnett. What he does not say so directly, but is evident elsewhere, is that it was written *against* Vincent Smith' s *Early history of India* (1904, 4th edition 1924), a book that had become a standard in Indian schools and universities. Of this book Basham wrote a study remarkable for the severity of his judgment against it. Smith, who had served thirty years in the Indian Civil Service, 'never really came to terms with the land' of India 'or its people', Basham argued.

> The imaginative and intellectual effort demanded in order to see the world through the eyes of a people not nurtured in a culture based on the Bible and the classics was too much for him, if he ever realised the necessity of such an effort. India was always mysterious and remote to him, in parts strangely beautiful, but aloof, utterly foreign, and hence to be feared.

Smith's many remarks derogatory of Indians were not mere propaganda for continued British rule, Basham thought.

> Such gratuitous insults to India's aspirations, which would probably have passed unnoticed in the time of Mill and Elphinstone, but which in Smith's day might have been deliberately calculated to arouse the antagonism of all his Indian readers, are evidence of a sensibility morbidly blunted in this respect; they are likewise evidence of deep-seated fear, and perhaps also of an unexpressed and almost unconscious sense of guilt.

He goes on to suggest a most interesting explanation having to do with the psychodynamics of colonial rule in Ireland, in whose English ruling class Smith grew up.*

Smith's theory of Indian history was that, Indian society being made up of 'mutually repellent molecules' and thus ever on the brink of chaos, Indians were never so happy as when they were held in good order under the rule of a firm but benevolent empire, such as that of the Mauryas, the Guptas, the Mughals or the British. This high-imperial history was the hegemonic text and interpretation that Basham and Majumdar, moving toward one another from different directions, sought to replace. They succeeded.

To these negative stereotypes Basham offers correctives, which readers may find in his introduction to this book. I will not repeat them here, but I will mention a succinct statement of his philosophy of history given a few years after the publication of *The wonder that was India*, in the inaugural lecture he gave on the occasion of his having become professor of the University of London.† The body of the lecture is directed against three supposed patterns of Indian history

---

*A.L. Basham, 'Modem historians of ancient India', in C.H. Philips, ed., *Historians of India, Pakistan and Ceylon,* pp. 260–293 (London: Oxford University Press 1961). Discussion of Vincent Smith begins on p. 266; the quotations are from p. 272.

†A.L. Basham, *The Indian sub-continent in historical perspective: an inaugural lecture delivered on 11 March 1958.* London: School of Oriental and African Studies, University of London, 1958.

that have prevailed in the West: that empires in India cannot last more than a few generations; that Hinduism is uniquely spiritual and other-worldly; and that Indian civilisation has remained essentially the same since the times of the Mauryas and in spite of repeated invasions. In other words, he attacks the commonplace notions of unpolitical India, spiritual India, and unchanging India. This programme of the inaugural lecture provides a key to the structure of *The wonder that was India*.

Thus, the first three chapters of the book, on prehistory, history and the state, are meant to show that, far from being unpolitical and unchanging, India has a dynamic political history and also a set of ideas about time and the state that amount to a historical consciousness. This was a constant theme of Basham's teaching also, which was directed to the political thought of ancient India as well as the narrative history of the state. As to religion, while it is made prominent by being given the longest chapter of the book, at over hundred pages, it is nevertheless but one chapter among many, showing that Basham did not want to collapse the idea of India's civilisation into a history of its religions, as so many writers do. Indeed, in the inaugural lecture Basham asserts his belief that 'the level of religious earnestness in India was at no time higher than in the nineteenth and twentieth centuries' and that the idea of India as exceptionally spiritual is an effect of modern nationalism. Finally, the other chapters, on society, everyday life, the arts, language and literature, and the heritage of India, speak to his conviction that Indians in the mass were passionately engaged with the things of this world in ancient times, and were not world-denying ascetics.

This, then, is the programme of *The wonder that was India*, and of Basham's other writings as well. Readers will judge how well it succeeds in its programme, and to what extent it still speaks to us, fifty years after it first appeared. I believe it has great deal to say to us, and that it says it clearly and beautifully, but as a student of Basham I am not a disinterested witness. I will not attempt to draw the balance of its accomplishment and continuing value, which readers can do for themselves. I will only say that it is the work of a great and good teacher.

Thomas R. Trautmann
University of Michigan, 2004

PREFACE TO THE SECOND EDITION

IN order to explain the aims and purposes with which I wrote this book and the principles which I employed in writing it, I can do no better than quote from the Preface to the first edition:

"As this book is intended for the general reader I have tried, as far as possible, to leave nothing unexplained. And as I believe that civilization is more than religion and art I have tried, however briefly, to cover all aspects of Indian life and thought. Though primarily intended for Westerners I hope that the book may be of some interest to Indian, Pakistani and Sinhalese readers also, as the interpretation of a friendly *mleccha*, who has great love and respect for the civilizations of their lands and many friends among the descendants of the people whose culture he studies. The work may also be of help to students who are embarking on a course of serious Indological study; for their benefit I have included detailed bibliographies and appendices. But, for the ordinary reader, the work is cumbersome enough, and therefore I have not given references for every statement. I have tried to reduce Sanskrit terms to a minimum, but the reader without background knowledge will find definitions of all Indian words used in the text in the index, which also serves as a glossary.

"Sanskrit, Prakrit and Pāli words are transliterated according to the standard system at present used by Indologists; this, with its plethora of diacritic marks, may at first seem irritating, but it is the only sound method of expressing the original spelling and gives a clear idea of the correct pronunciation. Modern Indian proper names are generally given in the most usual spelling* with the addition of marks over the long vowels, to indicate their approximately correct pronunciation. Throughout this work the word "India" is of course used in its geographical sense, and includes Pākistān. Though very inadequately, I have tried to include in the scope of this survey Ceylon, whose culture owed much to India but developed many individual features of its own.

"The translations, except where specified, are my own. I lay no claim to great literary merit for them, and have not been able to reproduce the untranslatable incantation of the originals. In most cases they are not literal translations, since the character of Indian classical languages is so unlike that of English that literal translations are at the best dull and at the worst positively ludicrous. In places I have taken some liberty with the originals, in order to make their purport clearer

---

*Except in a few cases where, to avoid confusion, I have substituted *a* for the more usual *u,* e.g. P*a*njāb, S*a*tlej, etc.

to the Western reader, but in all cases I have tried to give an honest interpretation of the intentions of their authors, as I understand them."

Whatever the shortcomings of *The Wonder that was India*, it has clearly served a useful purpose, and in this I take legitimate pride. Though one of a series of surveys of ancient civilizations intended mainly for the general reader, it has been widely used as a college textbook, not only in England but also in India itself and in America, and it has already encouraged several young men and women in at least three continents to proceed further in the field of Indology. When I submitted the typescript of the first edition to the publishers, I feared that my work fell between two stools, being too dull for the ordinary reader and not sufficiently erudite for the serious student. Perhaps this judgment is a fair one, and the reviewer who referred to the book as a "charnel house of facts" was not far out. Nevertheless, the fact that a new edition is demanded proves that *The Wonder that was India* has met a widespread need, however inadequately.

It is now eights and half years since *The Wonder that was India* first appeared. In that time no very startling new light has been thrown on early India, though the indefatigable work of archaeologists in both India and Pakistan is slowly revealing more of the remains of the prehistoric and historical past of the sub-continent. Recent excavations, however, have not radically altered the general picture of pre-Buddhist India, though they have tended to confirm the suspicion of some Western Indologists and the earnest conviction of many Indians that the culture of this period was by no means as backward as some minimalists have suggested.

Of the historical periods many new and valuable studies have been produced since 1954, and fresh light has been thrown on several aspects of Indian history and culture, but nothing has been written to alter the general outline, and most of the problems of Indology which were outstanding ten years ago remain unsolved. There is as yet no real certainty about the date of Kaniṣka, despite the appearance of new evidence. The dark periods of Indian history between the time of the Buddha and the rise of the Mauryas, and that between the decline of the Kuṣāṇas and the rise of the Guptas, are still almost as dark as ever. In the field of religion many questions, such as those connected with the growth of theistic devotion and Tantricism, are still unanswered. In fact every branch of Indian studies still offers scope for unlimited research.

In preparing this edition I have taken account of several recent archaeological discoveries. The chapter on political life and thought has been considerably revised in the light of the evidence that the *Śukranīti* is a 19th-century production and therefore quite irrelevant. My suspicions about this were confirmed by the work of Dr. L. Gopal (p. 70, n.), to whom I am much indebted. The section on music in Chapter VIII has been largely rewritten on the advice of my colleague Mr. N. Jairazbhoy, who pointed out several mistakes in the original text and gave me the benefit of his own researches in the history of Indian music. My friend Mr. D. Barrett, of the British Museum, has given me valuable advice on the most recent views on the dating of certain important works of art, and the text has been amended accordingly. Various errors and anachronisms have been corrected, and many stylistic lapses, of which the first edition was all too full, have been put right. Some of the illustrations have been replaced by better ones.

In the last ten years several changes have taken place in the state boundaries of India, such as the disappearance of Hyderabad and the division of the former Bombay State into Maharashtra and Gujarat. These changes have been taken into account, and as far as possible I have employed for place names the new official spellings of the Indian Government. In some instances I have done this with considerable misgiving, especially in the case of Vārānasī which seems an unnecessary archaism for Benares; but as this is now the name by which the sacred city is officially referred to in India, and which is likely to become more widely known with the years, it seems right, on balance, that I should use it. Ganges has no real justification except that it is traditionally the name by which the great river is known in Europe and America, so I have no misgivings about substituting the officially accepted Gangā, the name by which the river is known in every Indian language.

Several additions have been made to the bibliography and a few works which were included in the first edition have been omitted. I am quite conscious of the inadequacy of the bibliography as a guide to the serious student. In defence I can only point out that it is meant primarily for the general reader who wishes to go further in one or other branch of Indian studies; the university student will obtain the bibliographical information he requires from his teacher. Certain Continental reviewers have complained of the absence from the bibliography of several important books in French and German. I must make it clear that works in languages other than English have been included only when particularly significant. Few "general readers" in the English-speaking world are able to read lengthy volumes in German, and even those who have some equipment in French are disinclined to use it for such purpose. This is very regrettable, but it is a fact which cannot be ignored. Hence many important Continental works are omitted. If ever a translation is made of this book in French or German it is to be hoped that the bibliography will be adapted to the language concerned.

In conclusion I would again record my gratitude to those who assisted me in one way or another in the writing of the first edition: Dr. F. R. Allchin, Dr. A. A. Bake, the late Dr. L. D. Barnett, Professor J. Brough, Professor A. T. Hatto, Dr. J. R. Marr, Professor A. K. Narain, Professor C. H. Philips, Mr. P. Rawson, Mr. C. A. Rylands, Dr. Devahuti Singhal and Dr. Arthur Waley. I am also grateful to numerous reviewers, some of whose suggestions have been adopted in this edition, and to many friends who have offered helpful advice and criticism.

A. L. BASHAM
London, 1963

PREFACE TO THE THIRD EDITION

THE Second edition of this book was published in New York in 1963, and before it could appear in Britain a paper-back edition was called for, thus making it possible to incorporate further alterations and corrections. No drastic changes have been made in this edition, but a few notes on recent archaeological discoveries have been added. Small emendations and stylistic improvements have been incorporated, and additions have been made to the bibliography.

A. L. BASHAM
Canberra, 1966

CONTENTS

LIST OF ILLUSTRATIONS

PLATES

LINE DRAWINGS AND MAPS

CHRONOLOGY OF PRE-MUSLIM INDIA

Prehistoric Period

B.C.	c. 3000	Agricultural communities in Balūchistān.
	c. 2500–1550	The Harappā Culture.

Protohistoric ("Vedic") Period

c. 1500–900	Composition of the Hymns of the *Ṛg Veda*.
c. 900	The Mahābhārata War.
c. 900–500	Period of the later Vedas, Brāhmaṇas and early Upaniṣads.

"Buddhist" Period

c. 566–486	Gautama Buddha.
c. 546–494	Bimbisāra king of Magadha.
c. 494–462	Ajātaśatru king of Magadha.
c. 362–334	Mahāpadma Nanda, king of Magadha.
327–325	Invasion of Alexander of Macedon.

Mauryan Period

c. 322–298	Candragupta.
c. 298–273	Bindusāra.
c. 269–232	Aśoka.
c. 183	End of Dynasty.

The Age of Invasions

c. 190	Greek Kingdoms in N.-W. India.
c. 183–147	Puṣyamitra Śuṅga.
c. 90	Śakas invade N.-W. India.
c. 71	End of Śuṅga Dynasty.
c. 50 B.C.–A.D. 250	Sātavāhana Dynasty in Deccan.

A.D.	Early 1st century	Kuṣāṇas invade N.-W. India.
	? 78–c. 101	Kaniṣka.
	c. 130–388	Śaka satraps in Ujjayinī.

Gupta Period

320–c. 335	Candra Gupta I.
c. 335–376	Samudra Gupta.
c. 376–415	Chandra Gupta II.

c. 415–454	Kumāra Gupta I.
c. 454	First Hūṇa invasion.
c. 454–467	Skanda Gupta.
c. 495	Second Hūṇa invasion.
c. 540	End of Imperial Gupta Dynasty.
606–647	Harṣa king of Kānyakubja.

MEDIEVAL DYNASTIES OF NORTHERN INDIA*

712	Arabs occupy Sind.
c. 730	Yaśovarman of Kānyakubja.
c. 760–1142	Pālas of Bengal and Bihār.
c. 800–1019	Pratihāras of Kānyakubja.
c. 916–1203	Candellas of Bundelkhand.
c. 950–1195	Kalacuris of Tripurī (Madhya Pradesh).
c. 973–1192	Cāhamāṇas of Ajmer.
c. 974–1238	Caulukyas of Gujarāt.
c. 974–1060	Paramāras of Dhārā (Mālwā).
c. 1090–1193	Gāhaḍavālas of Vārānasī and Kānyakubja.
c. 1118–1199	Senas of Bengal.
1192	Second Battle of Tarāin.

MEDIEVAL DYNASTIES OF THE PENINSULA*

c. 300–888	Pallavas of Kāñcī (Madras State).
c. 550–757	First Cālukya Dynasty, of Vātāpī (W. and C. Deccan).
c. 630–970	Eastern Cālukyas of Veṅgī (Āndhra Pradesh).
757–973	Rāstrakūtas of Mānyakheta (W. and C. Deccan).
c. 850–1267	Cōlas of Tanjore (Madras State).
973–c. 1189	Second Cālukya Dynasty, of Kalyāṇī (W. and C. Deccan).
c. 1110–1327	Hoysaḷas of Dōrasamudra (C. and S. Deccan).
c. 1190–1294	Yādavas of Devagiri (N. Deccan).
c. 1197–1323	Kākatīyas of Warangal (Āndhra Pradesh).
1216–1327	Pāndyas of Madurai (Madras State).
1336–1565	Vijayanagara Empire.
1565	Battle of Tālikota and sack of Vijayanagara.

* The dates given for these dynasties are the periods of their importance. In many cases their existence can be traced both earlier and later.

PRONUNCIATION

MORE detailed notes on the Indian alphabet and its pronunciation are given in App. X, p. 462ff. The following is a rough guide for the general reader.

The vowels *ā*, *ī*, *ū*, *e*, *ai*, *o*, *au* are long, and have approximately the same pronunciation as in Italian, or as the vowels in the English words *calm*, *machine*, *rule*, *prey*, *time*, *go* and *cow*, respectively. *A*, *i*, *u* are short, and equivalent to the vowels in the English words *cut*, *bit* and *bull*. The reader should avoid the temptation to pronounce *a* as in English *sat*. Thus Sanskrit *sama* is pronounced as English *summer*. *Ṛ* is classed as a short vowel, and is pronounced as *ri* in *rich*.

The aspirated consonants *th* and *ph* must never be pronounced as in English *thin* and *phial*, but as in *pothole* and *shepherd*. *C* is pronounced as *ch* in *church*. *Ś* and *ṣ* are both generally pronounced as English *sh* in *shape*. The distinction between the other sub-dotted "retroflex" consonants (*ṭ*, *ṭh*, *ḍ*, *ḍh* and *ṇ*) and the dentals, without dots, is not important to the general reader.

FOOTNOTES AND REFERENCES

NOTES marked with *, ‡, etc, are given at the bottom of the page. Those marked with figures are references only, and are given with classified bibliographies at the back of the book; they may be ignored by the reader who does not intend to pursue the topic further.

I

INTRODUCTION: INDIA AND HER ANCIENT CULTURE

THE LAND OF INDIA

THE ancient civilization of India grew up in a sharply demarcated sub-continent bounded on the north by the world's largest mountain range—the chain of the Himālayas, which, with its extensions to east and west, divides India from the rest of Asia and the world. The barrier, however, was at no time an insuperable one, and at all periods both settlers and traders have found their way over the high and desolate passes into India, while Indians have carried their commerce and culture beyond her frontiers by the same route. India's isolation has never been complete, and the effect of the mountain wall in developing her unique civilization has often been over-rated.

The importance of the mountains to India is not so much in the isolation which they give her, as in the fact that they are the source of her two great rivers. The clouds drifting northwards and westwards in the rainy season discharge the last of their moisture on the high peaks, whence, fed by ever-melting snow, innumerable streams flow southwards, to meet in the great river systems of the Indus and the Gangā. On their way they pass through small and fertile plateaux, such as the valleys of Kashmīr and Nepāl, to debouch on the great plain.

Of the two river systems, that of the Indus, now mainly in Pākistān, had the earliest civilization, and gave its name to India.* More than two thousand years before Christ the fertile plain of the Panjāb ("Five Rivers"), watered by the five great tributaries of the Indus—the Jhelam, Chenāb, Rāvī, Beās and Satlaj—had a high culture, which spread as far as the sea and along the western seaboard at least as far as Gujarāt. The lower Indus, in the region of Pākistān known as Sind, now passes through barren desert, though this was once a well watered and fertile land.

---

* The Indians knew this river as Sindhu, and the Persians, who found difficulty in pronouncing an initial *s*, called it Hindu. From Persia the word passed to Greece, where the whole of India became known by the name of the western river. The ancient Indians knew their sub-continent as *Jambudvipa* (the continent of the *jambu* tree) or *Bhāratavarṣa* (the Land of the sons of Bharata, a legendary emperor) (p. 439f). The latter name has been in part revived by the present Indian government. With the Muslim invasion the Persian name returned in the form *Hindustān*, and those of its inhabitants who followed the old religion became known as *Hindus*. The form *Hindusthān*, popular in modern India, is an Indo-Iranian hybrid with no linguistic justification.

The basin of the Indus is divided from that of the Gangā by the Thar, or desert of Rājasthān, and by low hills. The watershed, to the north-west of Delhi, has been the scene of many bitter battles since at least 1000 B.C. The western half of the Gangā plain, from the region around Delhi to Patnā, and including the *Doāb*, or the land between the Gangā and its great tributary river Yamunā (formerly spelt Jumna, Jamna), has always been the heart of India. Here, in the region once known as *Āryāvarta*, the land of the Āryans, her classical culture was formed. Though generations of unscientific farming, deforestation, and other factors have now much reduced its fertility, this was once among the most productive lands in the world, and it has supported a very large population ever since it was brought under the plough. At its mouth in Bengal the Gangā forms a large delta, which even in historical times has gained appreciably on the sea; here the Gangā joins the Brahmaputra, which flows from Tibet by way of the Valley of Assam, the easternmost outpost of Hindu culture.

South of the great plain is a highland zone, rising to the chain of the Vindhya mountains. These are by no means as impressive as the Himālayas but have tended to form a barrier between the North, formerly called Hindustān, and the Peninsula, often known as the Deccan (meaning simply "South"), a term used sometimes for the whole peninsula, but more often for its northern and central portions. Most of the Deccan is a dry and hilly plateau, bordered on either side by long ranges of hills, the Western and Eastern Ghāts. Of these two ranges the western is the higher, and therefore most of the rivers of the Deccan, such as the Mahānadī, the Godāvarī, the Kistnā or Kṛṣṇā, and the Kāvirī, flow eastwards to the sea. Two large rivers only, the Narmadā and the Tāptī, flow westwards. Near their mouths the Deccan rivers pass through plains which are smaller than that of the Gangā but almost as populous. The south-eastern part of the Peninsula forms a larger plain, the Tamil country, the culture of which was once independent, and is not yet completely unified with that of the North. The Dravidian peoples of Southern India still speak languages in no way akin to those of the North, and are of a different ethnic character (p. 22f), though there has been much intermixture between Northern and Southern types. Geographically Ceylon is a continuation of India, the plain of the North resembling that of South India, and the mountains in the centre of the island the Western Ghāts.

From Kashmīr in the North to Cape Comorin in the South the sub-continent is about 2,000 miles long, and therefore its climate varies considerably. The Himālayan region has cold winters, with occasional frost and snow. In the northern plains the winter is cool, with wide variation of day and night temperature, whereas the hot season is almost intolerable. The temperature of the Deccan varies less with the season, though in the higher parts of the plateau nights are cool in winter. The Tamil Plain is continuously hot, but its temperature never rises to that of the northern plains in summer.

The most important feature of the Indian climate is the monsoon, or "the Rains". Except along the west coast and in parts of Ceylon little rain falls from October to May, when cultivation can only be carried on by carefully husbanding the water of rivers and streams, and raising a winter crop by irrigation. By the end of April growth has practically ceased. The temperature of the plains rises as high as 110°F. (43°C) or over, and an intensely hot wind blows. Trees shed their leaves, grass is almost completely parched, wild animals often die in large numbers for want of water. Work is reduced to a minimum, and the world seems asleep.

Then clouds appear, high in the sky; in a few days they grow more numerous and darker, rolling up in banks from the sea. At last, in June, the rains come in great downpouring torrents, with much thunder and lightning. The temperature quickly drops, and within a few days the world is green and smiling again. Beasts, birds and insects reappear, the trees put on new leaves, and the earth is covered with fresh grass. The torrential rains, which fall at intervals for a couple of months and then gradually die away, make travel and all outdoor activity difficult, and often bring epidemics in their wake; but, despite these hardships, to the Indian mind the coming of the monsoon corresponds to the coming of spring in Europe. For this reason thunder and lightning, in Europe generally looked on as inauspicious, have no terrors for the Indian, but are welcome signs of the goodness of heaven (p. 224).

It has often been said that the scale of natural phenomena in India, and her total dependence on the monsoon, have helped to form the character of her peoples. Even today major disasters, such as flood, famine and plague, are hard to check, and in older times their control was almost impossible. Many other ancient civilizations, such as those of the Greeks, Romans and Chinese, had to contend with hard winters, which encouraged sturdiness and resource. India, on the other hand, was blessed by a bounteous Nature, who demanded little of man in return for sustenance, but in her terrible anger could not be appeased by any human effort. Hence, it has been suggested, the Indian character has tended to fatalism and quietism, accepting fortune and misfortune alike without complaint.

How far this judgement is a fair one is very dubious. Though an element of quietism certainly existed in the ancient Indian attitude to life, as it does in India today, it was never approved by moralists. The great achievements of ancient India and Ceylon—their immense irrigation works and splendid temples, and the long campaigns of their armies—do not suggest a devitalized people. If the climate had any effect on the Indian character it was, we believe, to develop a love of ease and comfort, an addiction to the simple pleasures and luxuries so freely given by Nature—a tendency to which the impulse to self-denial and asceticism on the one hand, and occasional strenuous effort on the other, were natural reactions.

THE DISCOVERY OF ANCIENT INDIA

The ancient civilization of India differs from those of Egypt, Mesopotamia and Greece, in that its traditions have been preserved without a break down to the present day. Until the advent of the archaeologist, the peasant of Egypt or Iraq had no knowledge of the culture of his forefathers, and it is doubtful whether his Greek counterpart had any but the vaguest ideas about the glory of Periclean Athens. In each case there had been an almost complete break with the past. On the other hand, the earliest Europeans to visit India found a culture fully conscious of its own antiquity—a culture which indeed exaggerated that antiquity, and claimed not to have fundamentally changed for many thousands of years. To this day legends known to the humblest Indian recall the names of shadowy chieftains who lived nearly a thousand years before Christ, and the orthodox brāhmaṇ in his daily worship repeats hymns composed even earlier. India and China have, in fact, the oldest continuous cultural traditions in the world.

Until the last half of the 18th century Europeans made no real attempt to study India's ancient past, and her early history was known only from brief passages in the works of Greek and Latin authors. A few devoted missionaries in the Peninsula gained a deep understanding of contemporary Indian life, and a brilliant mastery of the vernaculars, but they made no real attempt to understand the historical background of the culture of the people among whom they worked. They accepted that culture at its face value, as very ancient and unchanging, and their only studies of India's past were in the nature of speculations linking the Indians with the descendants of Noah and the vanished empires of the Bible.

Meanwhile a few Jesuits succeeded in mastering Sanskrit, the classical language of India. One of them, Father Hanxleden, who worked in Kerala from 1699 to 1732, compiled the first Sanskrit grammar in a European tongue, which remained in manuscript, but was used by his successors. Another, Father Coeurdoux, in 1767, was probably the first student to recognize the kinship of Sanskrit and the languages of Europe, and suggested that the brāhmaṇs of India were descended from one of the sons of Japhet, whose brothers migrated to the West. Yet the Jesuits, for all their studies, gained no real understanding of India's past: the foundations of Indology were laid independently, in another part of India, and by other hands.

In the year 1783 one of the most brilliant men of the 18th century, Sir William Jones (1746–94) (pl. IV*a*), came to Calcutta as a judge of the Supreme Court, under the governor-generalship of Warren Hastings, who himself had deep sympathy with both Muslim and Hindu culture. Jones was a linguistic genius, who had already learnt all the more important languages of Europe as well as Hebrew, Arabic, Persian and Turkish, and had even obtained a smattering of Chinese with the aid of the very inadequate material which was available at the time. Before coming to India he had recognized the relationship of European languages to Persian, and had rejected the orthodox view of the 18th century, that all these tongues were derived from Hebrew, which had been garbled at the Tower of Babel. In place of this dogma Jones suggested that Persian and the European languages were derived from a common ancestor which was not Hebrew.

Of the little band of Englishmen who administered Bengal for the Honourable East India Company only one, Charles Wilkins (1749–1836), had managed to learn Sanskrit. With the aid of Wilkins and friendly Bengālī paṇḍits Jones began to learn the language. On the first day of 1784 the Asiatic Society of Bengal was founded, on Jones' initiative, and with Jones himself as president. In the journal of this society, *Asiatic Researches*, the first real steps in revealing India's past were taken. In November 1784 the first direct translation of a Sanskrit work into English, Wilkins's *Bhagavad Gītā*, was completed. This Wilkins followed in 1787 with a translation of the *Hitopadeśa*. In 1789 Jones translated Kālidāsa's *Śakuntalā*, which went into five English editions in less than twenty years; this he followed by translations of the *Gita Govinda* (1792), and the law-book of Manu (published posthumously in 1794 under the title *Institutes of Hindoo Law*). Several less important translations appeared in successive issues of *Asiatic Researches*.

Jones and Wilkins were truly the fathers of Indology. They were followed in Calcutta by Henry Colebrooke (1765–1837) and Horace Hayman Wilson (1789–1860). To the works of these pioneers must be added that of the Frenchman Anquetil-Duperron, a Persian scholar who, in 1786, published a translation of four Upaniṣads from a 17th-century Persian version—the translation of the whole manuscript, containing 50 Upaniṣads, appearing in 1801.

Interest in Sanskrit literature began to grow in Europe as a result of these translations. In 1795 the government of the French Republic founded the École des Langues Orientales Vivantes, and there Alexander Hamilton (1762–1824), one of the founding members of the Asiatic Society of Bengal, held prisoner on parole in France at the end of the Peace of Amiens in 1803, became the first person to teach Sanskrit in Europe. It was from Hamilton that Friedrich Schlegel, the first German Sanskritist, learnt the language. The first university chair of Sanskrit was founded at the College de France in 1814, and held by Léonard de Chézy, while from 1818 onwards the larger German universities set up professorships. Sanskrit was first taught in England in 1805 at the training college of the East India Company at Hertford. The earliest English chair was the Boden Professorship at Oxford, first filled in 1832, when it was conferred upon H. H. Wilson, who had been an important member of the Asiatic Society of Bengal. Chairs were afterwards founded at London, Cambridge and Edinburgh, and at several other universities of Europe and America.

In 1816, Franz Bopp (1791–1867), a Bavarian, on the basis of the hints of Sir William Jones, succeeded in very tentatively reconstructing the common ancestor of Sanskrit and the classical languages of Europe, and comparative philology became an independent science. In 1821, the French Société Asiatique was founded in Paris, followed two years later by the Royal Asiatic Society in London. From these beginnings the work of the editing and study of ancient Indian literature went on apace throughout the 19th century. Probably the greatest achievement of Indological scholarship in 19th-century Europe was the enormous Sanskrit-German dictionary generally known as the St. Petersburg Lexicon, produced by the German scholars Otto Böhtlingk and Rudolf Roth, and published in parts by the Russian Imperial Academy of Sciences from 1852 to 1875. England's greatest contributions to Sanskrit studies were the splendid edition of the *Ṛg Veda*, and the great series of authoritative annotated translations, *Sacred Books of the East*. Both these works were edited by the great German Sanskritist Friedrich Max Müller (1823–1900), who spent most of his working life as Professor of Comparative Philology at Oxford.

Meanwhile the study of ancient Indian culture was proceeding in another direction. The first work of the Asiatic Society of Bengal had been almost entirely literary and linguistic, and most of the 19th-century Indologists were primarily scholars in the classical tradition, working on written records. Early in the 19th century, however, the Bengal Society began to turn some of its attention to the material remains of India's past, as the East India Company's surveyors brought back to Calcutta many reports of temples, caves and shrines, together with early coins and copies of inscriptions in long-dead scripts. By working backwards from the current scripts the older ones were gradually deciphered, until in 1837 a gifted amateur, James Prinsep, an official of the Calcutta Mint and Secretary of the Asiatic Society of Bengal, interpreted for the first time the earliest Brāhmī script and was able to read the edicts of the great emperor Aśoka. Among Prinsep's colleagues in the work of decipherment was a young officer of the Royal Engineers, Alexander Cunningham (pl. IV*b*), the father of Indian archaeology. From his arrival in India in 1831 Cunningham devoted every minute he could spare from his military duties to the study of the material remains of ancient India, until, in 1862, the Indian government established the post of Archæological Surveyor, to which he was appointed. Until his retirement in 1885 he devoted himself to the unravelling of India's past with complete single-heartedness. Though he made no startling discoveries, and though his technique was, by modern archæological standards, crude and primitive, there is no doubt that, after Sir William Jones, Indology owes more to General Sir Alexander Cunningham than to any other worker in the field. Cunningham was assisted by several other pioneers, and though at the end of the 19th century the activities of the Archæological Survey almost ceased, owing to niggardly government grants, by 1900 many ancient buildings had been surveyed, and many inscriptions read and translated.

It was only in the 20th century that archæological excavation on a large scale began in India. Thanks to the personal interest of the Viceroy, Lord Curzon, in 1901 the Archæological Survey was reformed and enlarged, and a young archæologist, John (later Sir John) Marshall (pl. IV*d*), appointed as Director General. For a country of the size of India the Archæological Department was still lamentably small and poor, but Marshall was able to employ a number of expert assistants, and had funds for excavation on a scale more extensive than anything previously attempted. For the first time traces of the ancient cities of India began to come to light— archæology, as distinct from the surveying and conservation of ancient monuments, had begun in real earnest. The greatest triumph of the Archæological Survey of India under Sir John Marshall's directorship was undoubtedly the discovery of the Indus civilization. The first relics of India's oldest cities were noticed by Cunningham, who found strange unidentified seals in the neighbourhood of Harappā in the Panjāb. In 1922 an Indian officer of the Archæological Survey, R. D. Banerjī, found further seals at Mohenjo Daro in Sind, and recognized that they were the remains of a pre-Āryan civilization of great antiquity. Under Sir John Marshall's direction the sites were systematically excavated from 1924 until his retirement in 1931. Digging was interrupted by financial retrenchment, and by the Second World War; but further important discoveries were made at Harappā during the brief directorship of Sir R. E. Mortimer Wheeler just after the war, though the sites are still by no means fully cleared.

Much has yet to be done. Many mounds as yet unexcavated may throw floods of light on the dark places of India's past: unpublished manuscripts of great importance may yet lie mouldering in out-of-the-way libraries. India, Pākistān and Ceylon are poor countries, desperately in need of funds with which to raise the standard of living of their peoples; but with the resources available the archæological departments of all three countries are working to their fullest capacity to reveal the past.

Even in the last century, much valuable work was done by natives of India, especially by such Sanskritists and epigraphists as Drs. Bhāū Dājī, Bhagavānlāl Indrājī, Rājendralāl Mitra, and the great Sir R. G. Bhāndārkar (pl. IV*c*). Now the chief initiative in Indology comes from the Indians themselves. Indians are well on the way to completing the first critical edition of the gigantic *Mahābhārata*, and have started work on the enormous Poona Sanskrit Dictionary, which, when complete, will probably be the greatest work of lexicography the world has ever seen. The Director General of the Archæological Department is now an Indian (Dr. A. Ghosh), and today the Western Indologist cannot hope to be more than the helper and friendly critic of the Asian. In times like these, however, when Asia is reacting against a century and a half of European domination, and a new culture, which will contain elements of East and West in firm synthesis, is in the process of birth, the European student still has a useful role to play in Indology.

THE GLORY OF ANCIENT INDIA

At most periods of her history India, though a cultural unit, has been torn by internecine war. In statecraft her rulers were cunning and unscrupulous. Famine, flood and plague visited her from time to time, and killed millions of her people. Inequality of birth was given religious sanction, and the lot of the humble was generally hard. Yet our overall impression is that in no other part of the ancient world were the relations of man and man, and of man and the state, so fair and humane. In no other early civilization were slaves so few in number, and in no other ancient lawbook are their rights so well protected as in the *Arthaśāstra* (p. 132f). No other ancient lawgiver proclaimed such noble ideals of fair play in battle as did Manu (p. 132). In all her history of warfare Hindu India has few tales to tell of cities put to the sword or of the massacre of non-combatants. The ghastly sadism of the kings of Assyria, who flayed their captives alive, is completely without parallel in ancient India. There was sporadic cruelty and oppression no doubt, but, in comparison with conditions in other early cultures, it was mild. To us the most striking feature of ancient Indian civilization is its humanity.

Some 19th-century missionaries, armed with passages from Hindu and Buddhist scriptures, often taken out of their context, and with tales of famine, disease, and the evils of the Hindu caste and family system, have helped to propagate the widespread fallacy that India is a land of lethargic gloom. The traveller landing at Bombay has only to watch the rush-hour crowds, and to compare them mentally with those of London, to realize that the Indian character is neither lethargic nor unhappy. This conclusion is borne out by a general acquaintance with the remains of India's past. Our second general impression of ancient India is that her people enjoyed life, passionately delighting both in the things of the senses and the things of the spirit.

The European student who concentrates on religious texts of a certain type may well gain the impression that ancient India was a land of "life-negating"* ascetics, imposing their gloomy and sterile ideas upon the trusting millions who were their lay followers. The fallacy of this impression is quite evident from the secular literature, sculpture and painting of the time. The average Indian, though he might pay lip-service to the ascetic and respect his ideals, did not find life a vale of tears from which to escape at all costs; rather he was willing to accept the world as he found it, and to extract what happiness he could from it. Daṇḍin's description of the joys of a simple meal served in a comparatively poor home (p. 396ff) is probably more typical of ancient Indian everyday life than are the Upaniṣads. India was a cheerful land, whose people, each finding a niche in a complex and slowly evolving social system, reached a higher level of kindliness and gentleness in their mutual relationships than any other nation of antiquity. For this, as well as for her great achievements in religion, literature, art and mathematics, one European student at least would record his admiration of India's ancient culture.

* This term, as applied to Indian religion, thought and culture, is that of the great Dr. Albert Schweitzer (*Indian Thought and its Development*, passim).

II

PREHISTORY: THE HARAPPĀ CULTURE AND THE ĀRYANS

PRIMITIVE MAN IN INDIA

LIKE prehistoric Europe, Northern India experienced ice ages, and it was after the second of these, in the Second Interglacial Period, more than 100,000 years before Christ, that man first left surviving traces in India. These are the palaeolithic pebble tools of the Soan Culture, so called from the little river in the Panjāb where they have been found in large numbers. In type they resemble tools widely distributed all over the Old World, from England to Africa and China. In India no human remains have been found in association with the tools, but elsewhere such industries have been shown to be the work of primitive anthropoid types, such as the *Pithecanthropus* of Java and China.

In the South there existed another prehistoric stone industry, which is not conclusively dated, but which may have been the approximate contemporary of that of the Soan Valley. The men of this culture made core tools, especially fine hand axes, formed by striking off flakes from a large pebble, and they evidently had much better command over their material than the Soan men. This Madras Industry, as it is called by the archaeologists, has affinities with similar core tool industries in Africa, western Europe, and southern England, where it has been found in association with a more advanced type of man—a true *Homo sapiens*.

The Gangā Valley is one of the newest parts of the earth's surface, and geologists believe that much of it was still a shallow sea at the time of these two stone-age industries; but there may have been contact between them by way of Rājasthān, for the tools of one culture have been found sporadically in the region of the other. The men who used these palaeoliths must have lived in India for many millennia. Who they were and what became of them we do not know. Their blood may still flow in the inhabitants of modern India, but if the pebble industry of Soan was the work of proto-human anthropoids they must have vanished long ago, like the Neanderthal men in Europe and the Pithecanthropi of the Far East. *Homo sapiens* continued in India, his skill and technical equipment imperceptibly improving down the ages. He learnt to fashion microliths, tiny and delicate stone arrowheads and other implements, which have been found in many parts of India, from the N.-W. Frontier to the extreme south. Similar microlithic industries occur in many parts of the Near East and Africa, but their chronological relationship with the microlithic industry of India is not clear. In parts of the Deccan microliths are often found together with polished stone axes, and it would seem that in the remoter parts of the Peninsula their use was only fully replaced by that of iron tools around the beginning of the Christian age.[1]

THE FIRST VILLAGES

Palaeolithic man was a hunter and food gatherer, and lived in very small communities, which were usually nomadic. In the course of time he learnt to kindle fire, to protect his body from the weather with skin, bark or leaves, and to tame the wild dog which lurked round his campfire. In India, as all over the world, people lived thus for many thousands of years.

Then, very recently in the perspective of geological time, great changes took place in man's way of living. Certainly not much earlier than 10,000 B.C., and perhaps as late as 6000 B.C., man developed what Professor Gordon Childe calls "an aggressive attitude to his environment". He learnt how to grow food crops, to tame domestic animals, to make pots, and to weave garments. Before discovering the use of metal, he taught himself to make well-polished stone implements far in advance of those of the palaeolithic age. Such implements have been found all over India, but mostly in the North-West and in the Deccan, and usually on or near the surface. In much of the country neolithic culture survived long, and many of the wilder hill tribes of the present day have only recently emerged from this stage.

Developed agriculture and permanent villages probably began in the 7th millennium B.C., in the Middle East. In India the earliest remains of settled cultures are of little agricultural villages in Balūchistān and lower Sind, perhaps dating from the end of the 4th millennium.

Classical writers show that when, in 326 B.C., Alexander of Macedon crossed the Indus, the climate of N.-W. India was much as it is today, though perhaps a little moister. The river valleys were fertile and well wooded, though the coastal strip to the west of the Indus, now called the Makrān, and much of Balūchistān, were already dry and desolate. But in 3000 B.C. the climate was very different. The whole Indus region was well forested, providing fuel to burn bricks and food for the wild elephant and rhinoceros, and Balūchistān, now almost a waterless desert, was rich in rivers. This region supported many villages of agriculturists, who had settled in the upland valleys of Balūchistān and in the then fertile plain of the Makrān and the lower Indus.

These people belonged to several cultures, primarily distinguished by different types of painted pottery. Each culture had distinctive features of its own, but all were of the same generic pattern as those of the Middle East. Though their settlements were small, rarely more than a few acres in extent, their material standards were comparatively high. The villagers dwelt in comfortable houses of mud brick with lower courses of stone, and made good pottery, which they painted

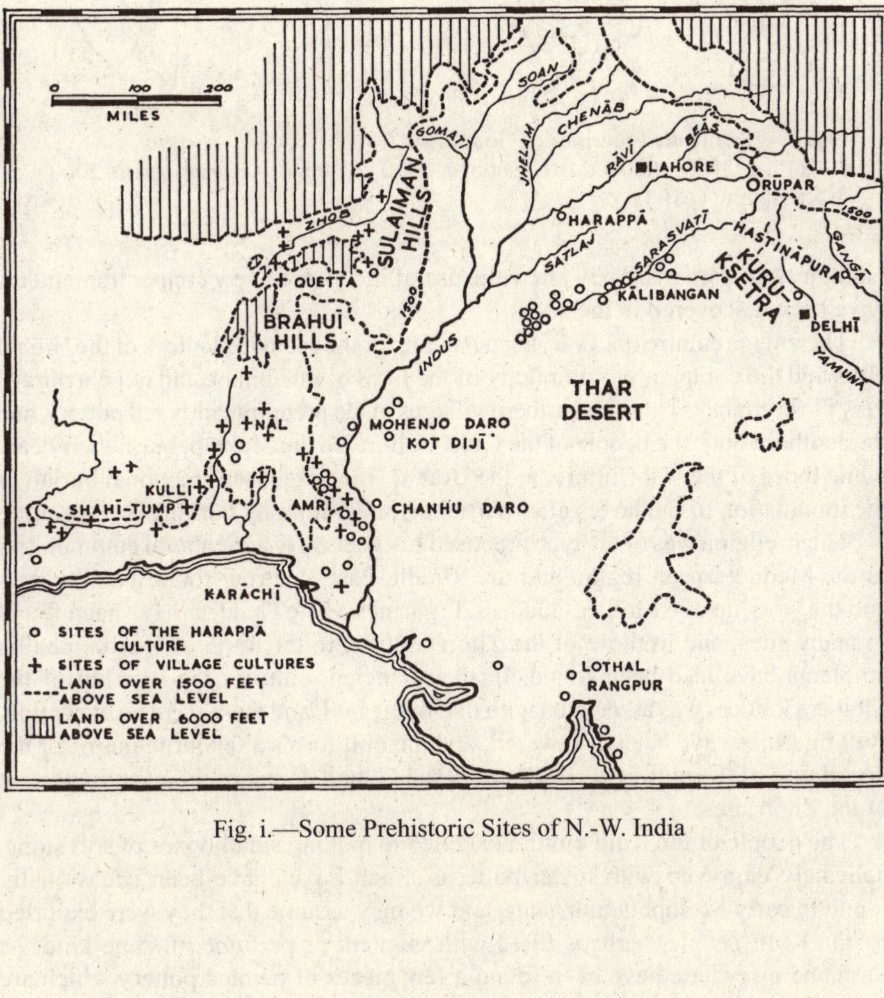

Fig. i.—Some Prehistoric Sites of N.-W. India

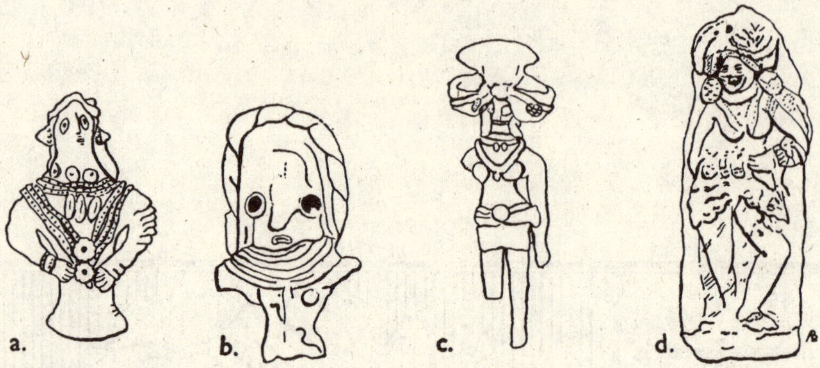

Fig. ii.—Terracotta Figurines of Goddesses.
a. Kullī, c. 2500–2000 B.C. b. Zhob, c. 2500–2000 B.C. c. Harappā, c. 2000 B.C.
d. Kauśāmbi, c. 100 B.C.

with pleasant patterns. They knew the use of metal, for a few copper implements have been discovered in the sites.

The village cultures had varying customs, for the secluded valleys of the Brāhūī Hills and the comparative simplicity of the lives of inhabitants did not encourage very close contact. Thus the northern villages made predominantly red pottery, and the southern buff; the people of the Kullī Culture, in the Makrān, burnt their dead, while those of the Nāl Culture, in the Brāhuī Hills, practised fractional burial, or the inhumation of the bones after partial disintegration by burning or exposure.

Their religion was of the type practised by other early agricultural communities in the Mediterranean region and the Middle East, centring round fertility rites and the worship of a Mother Goddess. Figurines of the Goddess have been found in many sites, and in those of the Zhob Culture, to the north of Quetta, phallic emblems have also been found. In many ancient cultures the worship of the Mother Goddess was associated with that of the bull, and these were no exception. Bull figurines have been discovered, and the bull forms a favourite motif for the decoration of the pottery of Kullī and Rānā Ghundāī, one of the most important of the Zhob sites.

The people of the Kullī culture excelled in making small boxes of soft stone, delicately engraved with linear patterns. Such boxes have been occasionally found in early Mesopotamian sites, and we may assume that they were exported by the Kullī people, perhaps filled with unguent or perfume of some kind. At Susa and elsewhere have been found a few pieces of painted pottery which are evidently imitated from the wares of the Kullī people, who obviously traded with the Middle East. Otherwise there is little evidence of contact. No certainly identifiable Mesopotamian remains have been found in Balūchistān, and there is no trace of objects from the Kullī Culture along the overland route. It seems that the Kullī people made contact with the earliest Mesopotamian civilizations by sea.

THE HARAPPĀ CITY CULTURE

In the early part of the 3rd millennium, civilization, in the sense of an organized system of government over a comparatively large area, developed nearly simultaneously in the river valleys of the Nile, Euphrates, and Indus. We know a great deal about the civilizations of Egypt and Mesopotamia, for they have left us written material which has been satisfactorily deciphered. The Indus people, on the other hand, did not engrave long inscriptions on stone or place papyrus scrolls in the tombs of their dead; all that we know of their writing is derived from the brief inscriptions of their seals, and there is no Indian counterpart of the Rosetta Stone. Several brilliant efforts have been made to read the Indus seals, but none so far has succeeded. Hence our knowledge of the Indus civilization is inadequate in many respects, and it must be classed as prehistoric, for it has no history in the strict sense of the term.

The civilization of the Indus is known to the archaeologist as the Harappā Culture, from the modern name of the site of one of its two great cities, on the left bank of the Rāvī, in the Panjāb. Mohenjo Daro, the second city, is on the right bank of the Indus, some 250 miles from its mouth. Recently, excavations have been carried out on the site of Kālībanga, in the valley of the old River Sarasvatī, now almost dried up, near the border of India and West Pākistān. These have revealed a third city, almost as large as the two earlier known, and designed on the same plan. As well as these cities a few smaller towns are known, and a large number of village sites, from Rupar on the upper Satlaj to Lothal in Gujarāt. The area covered by the Harappā Culture therefore extended for some 950 miles from north to south, and the pattern of its civilization was so uniform that even the bricks were usually of the same size and shape from one end of it to the other. Outside this area the village cultures of Balūchistān seem to have continued much as before.

This great civilization owed little to the Middle East, and there is no reason to believe that it was formed by recent immigrants; the cities were built by people who had probably been in the Indus Valley for several centuries. The Harappā people were already Indians when they planned their cities, which hardly altered for about a thousand years. We cannot fix a precise date for the beginning of this civilization, but certain indications synchronize it roughly with the village cultures of Balūchistān. The site of Rānā Ghundāī produced a stratification which showed, in the third phase of the village's history, a type of pottery with bold designs in black on a red background. From evidence discovered by Sir R. Mortimer Wheeler in 1946 it seems that the city of Harappā was built on a site occupied by people using similar pottery. There is no evidence of the date of the foundation of the other great city of Mohenjo Daro, for its lowest strata are now below the level of the Indus, whose bed has slowly risen with the centuries; though diggings have reached 30 feet below the surface, flooding has prevented the excavation of the earliest levels of the city. Important fresh light on the origins of the Harappā culture has recently been thrown by the excavations at Kot Dijī, opposite Mohenjo Daro a few miles from the left bank of the Indus. Here, below the level of the Harappā

Culture, have been found remains of an earlier culture, with pottery and tools of cruder workmanship. This Kot Dijī culture seems to have been the prototype of the developed city civilization which grew out of it.

Thus the Harappā Culture, at least in the Panjāb, was later in its beginnings than the village cultures, but it was certainly in part contemporary with them, for traces of mutual contact have been found; and some of the village cultures survived the great civilization to the east of them. From the faint indications which are all the evidence we have, it would seem that the Indus cities began in the first half, perhaps towards the middle, of the 3rd millennium B.C.; it is almost certain that they continued well into the 2nd millennium.

When these cities were first excavated no fortifications and few weapons were found, and no building could be certainly identified as a temple or a palace. The hypothesis was then put forward that the cities were oligarchic commercial republics, without sharp extremes of wealth and poverty, and with only a weak repressive organization; but the excavations at Harappā in 1946 and further discoveries at Mohenjo Daro have shown that this idyllic picture is incorrect. Each city had a well-fortified citadel, which seems to have been used for both religious and governmental purposes. The regular planning of the streets, and the strict uniformity throughout the area of the Harappā culture in such features as weights and measures, the size of bricks, and even the layout of the great cities, suggest rather a single centralized state than a number of free communities.

Probably the most striking feature of the culture was its intense conservatism. At Mohenjo Daro nine strata of buildings have been revealed. As the level of the earth rose from the periodic flooding of the Indus new houses would be built almost exactly on the sites of the old, with only minor variations in ground plan; for nearly a millennium at least, the street plan of the cities remained the same. The script of the Indus people was totally unchanged throughout their history. There is no doubt that they had contact with Mesopotamia, but they showed no inclination to adopt the technical advances of the more progressive culture. We must assume that there was continuity of government throughout the life of the civilization. This unparalleled continuity suggests, in the words of Professor Piggott, "the unchanging traditions of the temple" rather than "the secular instability of the court".[2] It seems in fact that the civilization of Harappā, like those of Egypt and Mesopotamia, was theocratic in character.

The two cities were built on a similar plan. To the west of each was a "citadel", an oblong artificial platform some 30–50 feet high and about 400 x 200 yards in area (pl. V). This was defended by crenelated walls, and on it were erected the public buildings. Below it was the town proper, in each case at least a square mile in area. The main streets, some as much as 30 feet wide, were quite straight (pl. VI*a*), and divided the city into large blocks, within which were networks of narrow unplanned lanes. In neither of the great cities has any stone building been found; standardized burnt brick of good quality was the usual building material for dwelling houses and public buildings alike. The houses, often of two or more stories, though they varied in size, were all based on much the same plan—a square courtyard, round which were a number of rooms. The entrances were usually in side alleys, and no windows faced on the streets, which must have presented a monotonous vista of dull brick walls. The houses had bathrooms, the design of which shows that the Harappan, like the modern Indian, preferred to take his bath standing, by pouring pitchers of water over his head. The bathrooms were provided with drains, which flowed into sewers under the main streets, leading to soak-pits. The sewers were covered throughout their length by large brick slabs. The unique sewerage system of the Indus people must have been maintained by some municipal organization, and is one of the most impressive of their achievements. No other ancient civilization until that of the Romans had so efficient a system of drains.

Fig. iii.—Interior of a House of the Harappā Culture
(*By permission Dept. of Archaeology Government of India, and Arthur Probsthain, London.*)

The average size of the ground floor of a house was about 30 feet square, but there were many bigger ones: obviously there were numerous well-to-do families in the Indus cities, which perhaps had a middle class larger and more important in the social scale than those of the contemporary civilizations of Sumer and Egypt. Remains of workmen's dwellings have also been discovered at both sites—parallel rows of two-roomed cottages, at Mohenjo Daro with a superficial area of 20 x 12 feet each, but at Harappā considerably larger; they bear a striking resemblance to the "coolie lines" of modern Indian tea and other estates. At Harappā rows of such buildings have been found near the circular brick floors on which grain was pounded, and they were probably the dwellings of the workmen whose task was to grind corn for the priests and dignitaries who lived in the citadel. Drab and tiny as they were, these cottages were better dwellings than those in which many Indian coolies live at the present day.

The most striking of the few large buildings is the great bath in the citadel area of Mohenjo Daro. This is an oblong bathing pool 39 x 23 feet in area and 8 feet deep, constructed of beautiful brickwork made watertight with bitumen (pl. VI*b*). It could be drained by an opening in one corner and was surrounded by a cloister, on to which opened a number of small rooms. Like the "tank" of a Hindu temple, it probably had a religious purpose, and the cells may have been the homes of priests. The special attention paid by the people of the Harappā culture to cleanliness is hardly due to the fact that they had notions of hygiene in advance of those of other civilizations of their time, but indicates that, like the later Hindus, they had a strong belief in the purificatory effects of water from a ritual point of view.

The largest building so far excavated is one at Mohenjo Daro with a superficial area of 230 x 78 feet, which may have been a palace. At Harappā a great granary has been discovered to the north of the citadel; this was raised on a platform of some 150 x 200 feet in area to protect it from floods, and was divided into storage blocks of 50 x 20 feet each. It was doubtless used for storing the corn which was collected from the peasants as land tax, and we may assume that it had its counterpart at Mohenjo Daro. The main food crops were wheat, barley, peas, and sesamum, the latter still an important crop in India for its seeds, which provide edible oil. There is no clear evidence of the cultivation of rice, but the Harappā people grew and used cotton. It is not certain that irrigation was known, although this is possible. The main domestic animals known to modern India had already been tamed—humped and humpless cattle, buffaloes, goats, sheep, pigs, asses, dogs, and the domestic fowl. The elephant was well known, and may also have been tamed. The Harappā people may have known of the horse, since a few horse's teeth have been found in the lowest stratum of the Balūchistān site of Rānā Ghundāī, probably dating from several centuries earlier than the foundation of Harappā. This would indicate that horse-riding nomads found their way to N.-W. India in small numbers long before the Āryan invasion; but it is very doubtful whether the Harappā people possessed domestic horses themselves, and if they did they must have been very rare animals. The bullock was probably the usual beast of burden.

On the basis of this thriving agricultural economy the Harappā people built their rather unimaginative but comfortable civilization. Their bourgeoisie had pleasant houses, and even their workmen, who may have been bondmen or slaves, had the comparative luxury of two-roomed brick-built cottages. Evidently a well organized commerce made these things possible. The cities undoubtedly traded with the village cultures of Baluchistān, where outposts of the Harappā culture have been traced, but many of their metals and semi-precious stones came from much longer distances. From Saurāshṭra and the Deccan they obtained conch shell, which they used freely in decoration, and several types of stone. Silver, turquoise and lapis lazuli were imported from Persia and Afghānistān. Their copper came either from Rājasthān or from Persia, while jadeite was probably obtained from Tibet or Central Asia.

Whether by sea or land, the products of the Indus reached Mesopotamia, for a number of typical Indus seals and a few other objects from the Indus Valley have been found in Sumer at levels dating between about 2300 and 2000 B.C., and some authorities believe that the land of *Melukka*, reached by sea from Sumer, and referred to in Sumerian documents, was the Indus Valley. Evidence of Sumerian exports to India is very scant and uncertain, and we must assume that they were mainly precious metals and raw materials. The finding of Indus seals suggests that merchants from India actually resided in Mesopotamia; their chief merchandise was probably cotton, which has always been one of India's staple exports, and which is known to have been used in later Babylonia. The recently excavated site at Lothal in Gujarāt has revealed harbour works, and the Harappā people may have been more nautically inclined than was formerly supposed. No doubt from their port of Lothal they were in touch with places farther south, and it is possibly thus that certain distinctive features of the Harappan culture penetrated to South India.

It seems that every merchant or mercantile family had a seal, bearing an emblem, often of a religious character, and a name or brief inscription in the tantalizingly indecipherable script. The standard Harappā seal was a square or oblong plaque, usually made of the soft stone called steatite, which was delicately engraved and hardened by heating (pl. IX). The Mesopotamian civilizations employed cylinder seals, which were rolled on clay tablets, leaving an impressed band bearing the device and inscription of the seal; one or two such seals have been found in Mohenjo Daro, but with devices of the Harappā type. Over 2,000 seals have been discovered in the Indus cities, and it would seem that every important citizen possessed one. Their primary purpose was probably to mark the ownership of property, but they doubtless also served as amulets, and were regularly carried on the persons of their owners. Generally they depict animals, such as the bull, buffalo, goat, tiger and elephant, or what appear to be scenes from religious legend. Their brief inscriptions, never of more than twenty symbols and usually of not more than ten, are the only significant examples of the Harappā script to have survived.

This script had some 270 characters, which were evidently pictographic in origin, but which had an ideographic or syllabic character. It may have been inspired by the earliest Sumerian script, which probably antedates it slightly, but it bears little resemblance to any of the scripts of the ancient Middle East, though attempts have been made to connect it with one or other of them. The most striking similarities are with the symbols used until comparatively recent times by the natives of Easter Island, in the eastern Pacific,[3] but the distance in space and time between the two cultures is so great that there is scarcely any possibility of contact or influence. We do not know what writing media were used, though it has been suggested that a small pot found at the lesser site of Chanhu Daro is an inkwell. Certainly the Harappans did not inscribe their documents on clay tablets, or some of these would have been found in the remains of their cities.

They were not on the whole an artistic people. No doubt they had a literature, with religious epics similar to those of Sumer and Babylon, but these are forever lost to us. The inner walls of their houses were coated with mud plaster, but if any paintings were made on these walls all trace of them has vanished. The outer walls, facing the streets, were apparently of plain brick. Architecture was austerely utilitarian, a few examples of simple decorative brickwork being the only ornamentation so far discovered. No trace of monumental sculpture has been found anywhere in the remains, and if any of the larger buildings were temples they contained no large icons, unless these were made of wood or other perishable material.

But if the Harappā folk could not produce works of art on a large scale they excelled in those of small compass. Their most notable artistic achievement was perhaps in their seal engravings, especially those of animals, which they delineated with powerful realism and evident affection. The great urus bull with its many dewlaps, the rhinoceros with knobbly armoured hide, the tiger roaring fiercely, and the many other animals (pl. IX) are the work of craftsmen who studied their subjects and loved them.

Equally interesting are some of the human figurines. The red sandstone torso of a man (pl. VIII*a*) is particularly impressive for its realism. The modelling of the rather heavy abdomen seems to look forward to the style of later Indian sculpture, and it has even been suggested that this figurine is a product of much later times, which by some strange accident found its way into the lower stratum; but this is very unlikely, for the figure has certain features, notably the strange indentations on the shoulders, which cannot be explained on this hypothesis. The bust of another male figure, in steatite (pl. VII), seems to show an attempt at portraiture. It has been suggested that the head is that of a priest, with his eyes half closed in meditation, but it is possible that he is a man of Mongolian type, for the presence of this type in the Indus Valley, at least sporadically, has been proved by the discovery of a single skull at Mohenjo Daro.

Most striking of the figurines is perhaps the bronze "dancing girl" (pl. VIII*b*). Naked but for a necklace and a series of bangles almost covering one arm, her hair dressed in a complicated coiffure, standing in a provocative posture, with one arm on her hip and one lanky leg half bent, this young woman has an air of lively pertness, quite unlike anything in the work of other ancient civilizations. Her thin boyish figure, and those of the uninspiring mother goddesses, indicate, incidentally, that the canons of female beauty among the Harappā people were very different from those of later India. It has been suggested that this "dancing girl" is a representative of a class of temple dancers and prostitutes, such as existed in contemporary Middle Eastern civilizations and were an important feature of later Hindu culture, but this cannot be proved. It is not certain that the girl is a dancer, much less a temple dancer.

The Harappā people made brilliantly naturalistic models of animals, specially charming being the tiny monkeys and squirrels used as pinheads and beads (pl. IX*g*). For their children they made cattle with movable heads, model monkeys which would slide down a string, little toy carts, and whistles shaped like birds, all of terracotta. They also made rough terracotta statuettes of women, usually naked or nearly naked, but with elaborate head-dresses (fig. ii, c); these are certainly icons of the Mother Goddess, and are so numerous that they seem to have been kept in nearly every home. They are very crudely fashioned, so we must assume that the goddess was not favoured by the upper classes, who commanded the services of the best craftsmen, but that her effigies were mass produced by humble potters to meet popular demand.

Though they had not completely given up the use of stone tools the Harappā people used implements of copper and bronze; but in many respects they were technologically backward in comparison with Mesopotamia. The Sumerians very early invented knives and spearheads with ribs in the middle for extra strength, and axeheads with holes for the shafts; but the blades of Harappā were flat and easily bent, while the axeheads had to be lashed to their handles; only in the topmost levels do we find tools of a better type, which were probably left by invaders. In one respect the Harappā people were technically in advance of their contemporaries—they had devised a saw with undulating teeth, which allowed the dust to escape freely from the cut, and much simplified the carpenter's task. From this we may assume that they had particular skill in carpentry. They made beautiful beads of semi-precious stones and faience, and their pottery, though mostly plain and uninteresting, was well made, and a few specimens are delicately painted (fig. iv).

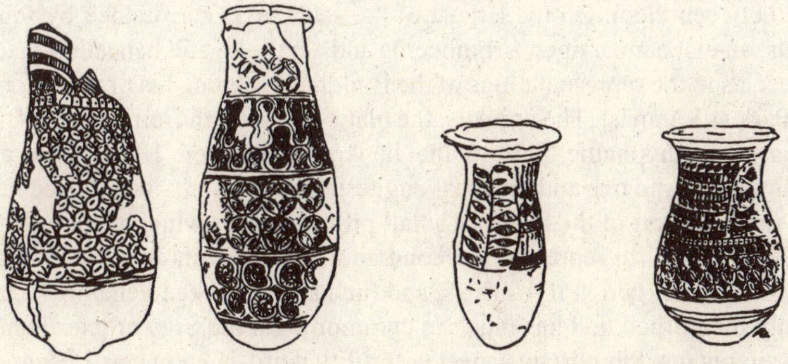

Fig. iv.—Painted Pottery of the Harappā Culture

The men wore robes which left one shoulder bare, and the garments of the upper classes were often richly patterned. Beards were worn, and men and women alike had long hair. The elaborate head-dresses of the Mother Goddess figures probably had their counterparts in the festive attire of the richer women. The goddesses often wear only very short skirts, but on one seal women, perhaps priestesses, are depicted with longer skirts, reaching to just below the knee. The coiffures of the women were often elaborate, and pigtails were also popular, as in present-day India. Women loved jewellery, and wore heavy bangles in profusion, large necklaces, and earrings.

As far as we can reconstruct it from our fragmentary knowledge, the religion of the Harappā people had some features suggesting those characteristics of later Hinduism which are not to be found in the earliest stratum of Indian religious literature. The Mother Goddess, for instance, reappears only after the lapse of over a thousand years from the fall of Harappā. We have seen that she was evidently the divinity of the people, and the upper classes seem to have preferred a god, who also shows features found in later Hinduism. As well as the figurines already mentioned, which may represent divinities, there are a few in terracotta of bearded nude men with coiled hair; their posture, rigidly upright, with the legs slightly apart, and the arms held parallel to the sides of the body but not touching it, closely resembles the stance called by the Jainas *kāyot-sarga*, in which meditating teachers were often portrayed in later times; the repetition of this figure, in exactly the same posture, would suggest that he was a god. A terracotta mask of a horned deity has also been found.

The most striking deity of the Harappā culture is the horned god of the seals (pl. IX*c*). He is depicted on three specimens, in two seated on a stool or small dais, and in the third on the ground; in all three his posture is one well known to later Indian holy men, with the legs drawn up close to the body and the two heels touching, a position quite impossible to the average Westerner without much practice. The god's body is nude, except for many bangles and what appear to be necklaces, and he wears a peculiar headdress, consisting of a pair of horns, which may have been thought of as growing from his head, with a plant-like object between them. On the largest of the seals he is surrounded by four wild animals, an elephant, a tiger, a rhinoceros and a buffalo, and beneath his stool are two deer, as in the representations of the Buddha preaching his first sermon in the Deer-Park at Vārāṇasī. The animals, the plant-like growth from the head, and the fact that he is ithyphallic, indicate that he is a fertility god. His face has a fierce tigerish aspect, and one authority has suggested that it is not meant to be human;[4] to the right and left of the head are small protuberances which were believed by Sir John Marshall to represent a second and third face on either side. Marshall boldly called this god "Proto-Śiva", and the name has been generally accepted; certainly the horned god has much in common with the Śiva of later Hinduism, who is, in his most important aspect, a fertility deity, is known as *Paśupati*, "the Lord of Beasts", and is sometimes depicted with three faces.

Animals played a big part in the religion of the Indus people. Though all the animals shown on the seals may not have been particularly sacred, the bull occurs in contexts which prove that he at least was so; on many seals he stands before a peculiar object which is evidently not a manger, and has no utilitarian purpose, but is a "cult object", probably a table on which corn was grown for fertility rites.[5] On some seals small lines emerge from the table, which may represent the growing corn, no doubt eaten by the sacred bull as part of the ceremony. The bull is usually depicted with a single horn, and has sometimes been referred to as a unicorn, though there is little doubt that the artist was trying to portray a normal bull, whose second horn was concealed by the first. In Hinduism the bull is specially associated with the god Śiva, but he does not seem to have been connected with the "Proto-Śiva" of Harappā, for he is not among the animals surrounding the god on the famous seal. The horns of the "Proto-Śiva" are not those of an ox but of a buffalo. The cow, so revered in later Hinduism, is nowhere depicted.

Certain trees were sacred, as they are in Hinduism today, notably the *pīpal*, which is specially honoured by Buddhists as the species under which the Buddha found enlightenment. One very interesting seal (pl. IX*d*) depicts a horned goddess in a pīpal tree, worshipped by a figure also wearing horns, with a human-headed goat watching the ceremony and a row of seven pigtailed women, probably priestesses, in attendance.

One of the few traces of Sumerian contact is to be found in the seal showing a hero grappling with two tigers (pl. IX*e*)—a variant of a famous Mesopotamian motif in which the hero Gilgamesh is depicted as fighting two lions. The rotund face of the hero, and the peculiar treatment of his hair, suggest that he represents the sun, and that the night-prowling tigers are the powers of darkness.

Phallic worship was an important element of Harappā religion. Many cone-shaped objects have been found, which are almost certainly formalized representations of the phallus. The *liṅga* or phallic emblem in later Hinduism is the symbol of the god Śiva, who is more commonly worshipped thus than as an icon; it is a fair inference that these objects were connected with the ithyphallic "Proto-Śiva" of the seals. It has been suggested that certain large ring-shaped stones are formalized representations of the female generative organ and were symbols of the Mother Goddess, but this is most doubtful.

Until Sir Mortimer Wheeler's work at Harappā in 1946 nothing was known with certainty of the way in which these people disposed of their dead; but from a cemetery then discovered, containing at least 57 graves, it appears that burial was the usual rite. The whole cemetery has not been excavated and the evidence is not yet fully assessed, but it is clear that the dead were buried in an extended posture with pottery vessels and personal ornaments.

Who were the people who built this great civilization? Some Indian historians have tried to prove that they were the Āryans, the people who composed the *Ṛg Veda*, but this is quite impossible. From the skeletal remains so far examined it appears that some of the Harappans were people of the long-headed, narrow-nosed, slender Mediterranean type, found all over the ancient Middle East and in Egypt, and forming an important element of the Indian population at the present day. A second element was the Proto-Australoid, with flat nose and thick lips, related to the Australian aborigines and to some of the wild hill-tribes of modern India. A single skull of Mongolian type has been found, and one of the short-headed Alpine type. The bearded steatite head to which we have referred shows elements of both the latter types, while the bronze dancing girl seems certainly Proto-Australoid. Then as now, N.-W. India was the meeting-place of many races.

The modern South Indian is usually a blend of Mediterranean and Proto-Australoid, the two chief ethnic factors in the Harappā culture; moreover the Harappā religion seems to show many similarities with those elements of Hinduism which are specially popular in the Dravidian country. In the hills of Balūchistān, where the people of the Nāl and Zhob Cultures built their little villages, the Brāhuīs, though ethnically now predominantly Iranian, speak a Dravidian language. Thus it has been suggested that the Harappā folk were Dravidians, and Father H. Heras, one of the authorities who have tried to read their script, has even claimed that their language was a very primitive form of Tamil.

It might be suggested that the Harappā people consisted of a Proto-Australoid element, which at one time may have covered the whole of India, overlaid by a Mediterranean one, which entered India at a very early period, bringing with it the elements of civilization. Later, under the pressure of further invasions, this Mediterranean element spread throughout the sub-continent, and, again mixing with the indigenous peoples, formed the Dravidians. The chief objection to this theory is that the megaliths erected by the early Dravidians in South India have been shown to be not very ancient; a recent theory even holds that the Dravidians came to India from the west by sea as late as the second half of the lst millennium B.C.[6] We can only say with certainty that some of the inhabitants of the Indus cities were of a type widely found further to the west, and that their descendants must survive in the present-day population of India.

It does not follow that the rest of India was wholly ignorant of the Harappā culture. Certain finds of copper implements in the district of Ranchi (S. Bihār) and elsewhere suggest that the peoples of North India learnt the use of metal from Harappā, for the blades are without the strengthening midrib; but the dating of these objects is very uncertain, and they may be much later than the fall of Harappā.

Certain pre-Aryan sites in the western half of northern India also give evidence of Harappān cultural influence on peoples at a lower cultural level. Evidence from places such as Hastināpura, Kauśāmbī and the very recently excavated Atranjī Kherā near Alīgarh, together with Deccan sites like Navdātolī and Nevāsā, show that by the end of the 2nd millennium B.C. there were many settlements whose inhabitants lived in reasonably comfortable conditions, knowing the use of metal. They were apparently illiterate, but far from barbarous, and as our picture of prehistoric India grows more accurate it becomes clear that, even outside the region of the Harappā culture, many peoples in the sub-continent had attained a considerable degree of cultural progress. Even as far east as Bengal there was at least one metal-using settlement in the 2nd millennium—this was at a place now called Pāndu Rājar Dhibī, where a seal and pottery have been found somewhat resembling those of Minoan Crete, though we cannot be sure that this indicates actual contact. This latter site seems to indicate two strata of the population—a comparatively cultured, metal-using element living by the side of another which was still using microliths. The picture of prehistoric India beyond the region of the Harappā culture is rapidly becoming clearer, and in time it may be possible to trace in broad outline the movements of early peoples throughout the sub-continent, and solve many problems at present very obscure.

Whatever the case may be, pre-Āryan India made certain advances in husbandry for which the whole world owes her a debt. Cotton was to the best of our knowledge first used by the Harappā people. Rice was not one of their staple crops, nor was it grown in neolithic China, whose main food crop was millet. Wild rice is known in Eastern India, and it is here, in the swampy Gangā Valley, that it was probably first cultivated by the neolithic contemporaries of the Harappā people. The water buffalo, known to the Harappā people, was a comparatively late arrival in China, and it may have been first domesticated in the Gangetic Plain, though some authorities believe that it originated in the Philippine Islands.

Perhaps the most widely appreciated of prehistoric India's gifts to the world is the domestic fowl. Ornithologists are agreed that all domestic species descend from the wild Indian jungle fowl. The Harappā people knew the domestic fowl, though its remains are few and it is not depicted on the seals. It was probably first tamed by neolithic Indians in the Gangā Valley, whence it found its way by the Burma route to China, where it appears in the middle of the 2nd millennium. The Egyptians knew it at about the same time, as a rare luxury bird.[7] Clearly India, even at this remote period, was not wholly cut off from the rest of the world.

THE END OF THE INDUS CITIES

When Harappā was first built the citadel was defended by a great turreted wall, 40 feet wide at the base and 35 feet high. In the course of the centuries this wall was refaced more strongly than before, though there is no evidence that the city was dangerously threatened by enemies. But towards the end of Harappā's existence its defences were further strengthened, and one gateway was wholly blocked. Danger threatened from the west.

First to suffer were the Balūchistān villages. The earliest level of the site of Rānā Ghundāī shows that bands of horse-riding invaders were present in the region before 3000 B.C., but they soon disappeared, to give way to the peasant culture which occupied the site in the 3rd millennium and was contemporary with the Indus cities. Then, in 2000 B.C. or a little later, the village was burnt, and a new, coarser type of pottery appears—evidently invaders had occupied the site. Soon afterwards came other invaders, using unpainted encrusted pottery. Similar though less complete evidence appears in other North Balūchistān sites, while in South Balūchistān people of an intrusive culture founded a settlement at Shāhī Tump, not far from Sutkagen Dor, which was the most westerly outpost of the Harappā Culture. The Shāhī Tump people used the shaft-hole axe and round copper seals, and replaced the earlier local culture, known to archaeologists as the Kullī Culture. In the last phase of the life of Mohenjo Daro painted pottery and stone vessels resembling those of Balūchistān appear, and this may indicate a large influx of Kullī refugees, who brought their crafts with them.

After the barbarians had conquered the outlying villages the ancient laws and rigid organization of the Indus cities must have suffered great strain. At Mohenjo Daro large rooms were divided into smaller ones, and mansions became tenements; potters' kilns were built within the city boundaries, and one even in the middle of a street. The street plan was no longer maintained. Hoards of jewellery were buried. Evidently the city was overpopulated and law and order were less well kept, perhaps because the barbarians were already ranging the provinces and the city was full of newcomers, whom the city fathers could not force into the age-old pattern of its culture.

When the end came it would seem that most of the citizens of Mohenjo Daro had fled; but a group of huddled skeletons in one of the houses and one skeleton of a woman lying on the steps of a well suggest that a few stragglers were overtaken by the invaders. In this level a fine copper axe has been found, with a very strong shafthole and an adze blade opposite that of the axe—a beautiful tool, adapted both for war and peace, and superior to anything the Harappā people possessed (fig. v). Swords with strengthening midribs also make their appearance. A single pot burial of a man of rather Mongolian type may be that of one of the invaders.

From Harappā comes evidence of a different kind. Here, near the older cemetery of interments, is another cemetery on a higher level, containing fractional burials in pots of men with short-headed Armenoid skulls. A skull of similar type was buried in the citadel itself. At Chanhu Daro, on the lower Indus, the Harappā people were replaced by squatters, living in small huts with fireplaces, innovations which suggest that they came from a colder climate. These people, though unsophisticated in many respects, had superior tools and weapons. Similar settlements were made in Balūchistān at about the same time. Among the scanty remains of these invaders there is clear evidence of the presence of the horse. The Indus cities fell to barbarians who triumphed not only through greater military prowess, but also because they were equipped with better weapons, and had learnt to make full use of the swift and terror-striking beast of the steppes. In other parts of India, however, the impact of the invaders was not immediately felt, and it appears that the Harappā city of Lothal, in Gujarāt, survived long after its parent cities had fallen, and its culture seems to have developed gradually, merging into that of the later period with no sharp break in continuity.

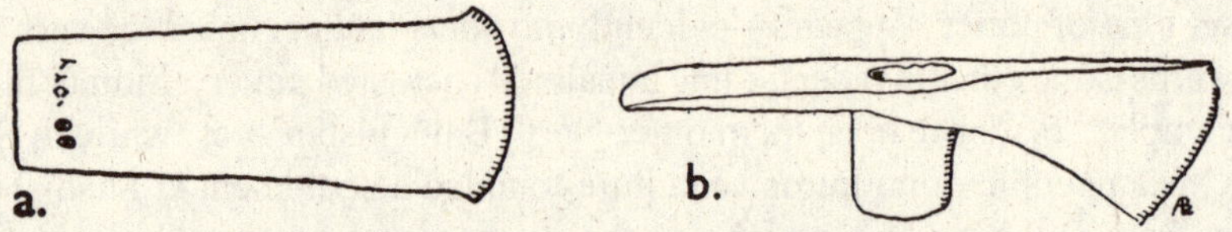

Fig. v.—Axes of the Indus Cities
a. Inscribed unsocketed axe-head. b. Shaft-hole axe-adze

The date of these great events can only be fixed very approximately from synchronisms with the Middle East. Sporadic traces of contact can be found between the Indus cities and Sumeria, and there is some reason to believe that this contact continued under the First Dynasty of Babylon, which produced the great lawgiver Hammurabi. This dynasty was also overwhelmed by barbarians, the Kassites, who came from the hills of Iran and conquered by virtue of their horse-drawn chariots. After the Kassite invasion no trace of contact with the Indus can be found in Mesopotamia, and it is therefore likely that the Indus cities fell at about the same time as the dynasty of Hammurabi. Earlier authorities placed the latter event in the first centuries of the 2nd millennium B.C., but new evidence, which appeared shortly before the outbreak of the Second World War, has resulted in a revised chronology. The fall of the First Babylonian Dynasty is now thought to have taken place about 1600 B.C.

The earliest Indian literary source we possess is the *Ṛg Veda*, most of which was composed in the second half of the 2nd millennium. It is evidently the work of an invading people, who have not yet fully subjugated the original inhabitants of N.-W. India. In his great report on the excavations at Mohenjo Daro, Sir John Marshall maintained that some two centuries or more elapsed between the fall of the Indus cities and the invasion of the Āryans; but the more recent excavations at Harappā and elsewhere, the revision of the chronology of Babylon, and indications in the *Ṛg Veda* itself, have all tended to reduce the gap. Many competent authorities, led by Sir R. Mortimer Wheeler, now believe that Harappā was overthrown by the Āryans. It is suggested that the interments in the later cemetery at Harappā are those of "true Vedic Āryans", and that the forts or citadels which the Vedic war-god Indra is said to have destroyed included Harappā in their number.

There is not enough evidence to say with certainty that the destroyers of the Indus cities were members of the group of related tribes whose priests composed the *Ṛg Veda*, but it is probable that the fall of this great civilization was an episode in the widespread migratory movements of charioteering peoples which altered the face of the whole civilized world in the 2nd millennium B.C.

INDO-EUROPEANS AND ĀRYANS

The invaders of India called themselves *Āryas*, a word generally anglicized into Āryans. The name was also used by the ancient Persians, and survives in the word *Irān*, while *Eire*, the name of the most westerly land reached by Indo-European peoples in ancient times, is also cognate. Here we cannot discuss the many theories on the origin of these people, but can only give that which seems to us most reasonable, and which, we believe, would be accepted by a majority of those who specialize in the subject.

About 2000 B.C. the great steppeland which stretches from Poland to Central Asia was inhabited by semi-nomadic barbarians, who were tall, comparatively fair, and mostly long-headed. They had tamed the horse, which they harnessed to light chariots with spoked wheels, of a much faster and better type than the lumbering ass-drawn cars with four solid wheels which were the best means of transport known to contemporary Sumer. They were mainly pastoral, but practised a little agriculture. There is no evidence that they were in direct contact with the Sumerians, but they had adopted some Mesopotamian innovations, notably the shaft-hole axe. In the early part of the 2nd millennium, whether from pressure of population, desiccation of pasture lands, or from both causes, these people were on the move. They migrated in bands westwards, southwards and eastwards, conquering local populations, and inter-marrying with them to form a ruling class. They brought with them their patrilinear family system, their worship of sky gods, and their horses and chariots. In most of the lands in which they settled their original language gradually adapted itself to the tongues of the conquered peoples. Some invaded Europe, to become the ancestors of the Greeks, Latins, Celts and Tentons. Others appeared in Anatolia, and from the mixture of these with the original inhabitants there arose the great empire of the Hittites. Yet others remained in their old home, the ancestors of the later Baltic and Slavonic people. And yet others moved southwards to the Caucasus and the Iranian tableland, whence they made many attacks on the Middle Eastern civilizations. The Kassites, who conquered Babylon, were led by men of this stock. In the 14th century B.C. there appeared in N.-E. Syria a people called Mitanni, whose kings had Indo-Iranian names, and a few of whose gods are familiar to every student of Indian religion: *Indora*, *Uruvna* (the Vedic god Varuṇa), *Mitira*, and *Naśatiya*. As well as those of the Mitanni, other chiefs in Syria and Palestine had names of Indo-Iranian type.

The marauding tribesmen gradually merged with the older populations of the Middle East, and the ancient civilizations, invigorated by fresh blood and ideas, rose to new heights of material culture; but the peaceful and conservative cities of the Indus valley could neither withstand nor absorb the invaders. The culture which was to succeed that of Harappā was, as we shall see, diametrically opposed to its predecessor. Only after many centuries did some elements of the older civilization, kept alive no doubt by the poorer people and serfs, begin to influence the conquerors.

The Āryan invasion of India was not a single concerted action, but one covering centuries and involving many tribes, perhaps not all of the same race and language. It seems certain that many of the old village cultures of the western hills were destroyed before the cities of the Indus Valley, but otherwise the course of Āryan expansion cannot be plotted, owing to the paucity of material remains. Evidently the invaders did not take to living in cities, and after the fall of Harappā and Mohenjo Daro the Panjāb and Sind became a land of little villages, with buildings of wood and reed the remains of which have long since perished. For centuries after the fall of Harappā this part of India is almost an archaeological blank, which at present can only be filled by literary sources.

THE ĀRYANS IN INDIA. THE PROTO-HISTORIC PERIOD

Among the many peoples who entered India in the 2nd millennium B.C. was a group of related tribes whose priests had perfected a very advanced poetic technique, which they used for the composition of hymns in praise of their gods, to be sung at sacrifices. These tribes, chief of which was that of the Bharatas, settled mainly in East Panjāb and in the region between the Satlaj and the Yamunā which later became known as Brahmāvarta. The hymns composed by their priests in their new home were carefully handed down by word of mouth, and early in the 1st millennium B.C. were collected and arranged. They were still not committed to writing, but by now they were looked on as so sacred that even minor alterations in their text were not permitted, and the priestly schools which preserved them devised the most remarkable and effective system of checks and counter checks to ensure their purity. Even when the art of writing was widely known in India the hymns were rarely written, but, thanks to the brilliant feats of memory of many generations of brāhmaṇs, and to the extreme sanctity which the hymns were thought to possess, they have survived to the present day in a form which, from internal evidence, appears not to have been seriously tampered with for nearly three thousand years. This great collection of hymns is the *Ṛg Veda*, still in theory the most sacred of the numerous sacred texts of the Hindus.

The period of the Vedas, Brāhmaṇas and Upaniṣads is a sort of transition from prehistory to history. If history, as distinct from archaeology, is the study of the human past from written sources, then India's history begins with the Āryans. The *Ṛg Veda*, and the great body of oral religious literature which followed it in the first half of the 1st millennium B.C., belong to the living Hindu tradition. The Vedic hymns are still recited at weddings and funerals, and in the daily devotions of the brāhmaṇ. Thus they are part of historical India, and do not belong to her buried prehistoric past. But they tell us little about the great events of the time, except in irritatingly vague incidental references; even on social conditions their information is scant; only on religion and thought is the historian more fully informed.

Yet from the hymns of the *Ṛg* and *Atharva Vedas*, the sacrificial instructions of the Brāhmaṇas, and the mysticism of the Upaniṣads, the outlines of a culture emerge, though often all too vaguely, and here and there we see the faint wraiths of great sages and tribal leaders, whose importance for their times was such that their names were recorded in sacred literature. Around these phantoms later tradition draped glittering mantles of legend, legend in which many Indians still implicitly believe, and which, in other contexts, is exceedingly important. But when the mantles are removed only vague shadows remain, little more than the names of chieftains who three thousand years ago waged successful war against their enemies. For the period before the time of the Buddha we can only trace the general character of the civilization which produced the Vedic literature and give a brief and tentative sketch of its expansion.

THE CULTURE OF THE *ṚG VEDA*

No real synchronisms are contained in the *Ṛg Veda* itself, to give us any certain information on the date of its composition. Some authorities in the past claimed an exceedingly early date for it, on the basis of tradition and ambiguous astronomical references in the hymns themselves—it was even believed by one very respected

Indian scholar that it went back to 6000 B.C. The discovery of the Indus cities, which have nothing in common with the culture described in the Veda and are evidently pre-Vedic, proves that the hymns cannot have been composed before the end of Harappā. The great development in culture, religion and language which is evident in the later Vedic literature shows that a long period must have elapsed between the time of the composition of the last hymns of the *Ṛg Veda* and the days of the Buddha—perhaps as much as 500 years. It is therefore probable that most of the *Ṛg Veda* was composed between 1500 and 1000 B.C., though the composition of some of the most recent hymns and the collation of the whole collection may have taken place a century or two later.

When the hymns were written the focus of Āryan culture was the region between the Yamunā and Satlaj (*Śutudrī*), south of the modern Ambālā, and along the upper course of the river Sarasvatī. The latter river is now an insignificant stream, losing itself in the desert of Rājasthān, but it then flowed broad and strong, and probably joined the Indus below the confluence of the Satlaj. The Vedic poets knew the Himālayas but not the land south of the Yamunā, and they did not mention the Vindhyas. To the east the Āryans had not expanded far beyond the Yamunā, and the Gangā is mentioned only in one late hymn.

At this time the Āryans had not wholly subjugated the indigenous inhabitants. Though many hymns refer to battles between one Āryan tribe and another, there is, underlying this intertribal rivalry, a sense of solidarity against the *Dāsas* and *Dasyus*, who evidently represent the survivors of the Harappā Culture, and kindred peoples of the Panjāb and the North-West. The Dāsas are described as dark and ill-favoured, bull-lipped, snub-nosed, worshippers of the phallus, and of hostile speech. They were rich in cattle, and dwelt in fortified places called *pur*, of which the Āryan war-god Indra has destroyed hundreds. The main work of destroying the settlements of the Dāsas had been accomplished some time before the composition of the hymns, and the great battles which must then have taken place were already misted over with legend; but the Dāsas were still capable of massing armies of 10,000 men against the invaders.

Other enemies of the Āryans were the *Paṇis*, who are described as wealthy people who refused to patronize the Vedic priests, and who stole the cattle of the Āryans. They were not so strongly hated as the Dāsas, and their settlements seem often to have continued unmolested. It has been suggested that the Paṇis were Semitic traders, but the evidence is so slight that this conclusion cannot be accepted.

The Āryans were not uninfluenced by the earlier inhabitants. In classical Sanskrit the word *dāsa* regularly means "slave" or "bondman", and in the later hymns of the *Ṛg Veda* it was already acquiring that meaning, while the feminine form *dāsī* is used in the sense of "slave-girl" throughout the book; but, though many of the vanquished Dāsas must have been enslaved, some seem to have come to terms with the conquerors, and one Dāsa chief is mentioned as following Āryan ways and patronizing the brāhmaṇs.[8] One result of this contact of Āryan and non-Āryan is evident even in the earliest stratum of the *Ṛg Veda*, the language of which is appreciably affected by non-Indo-European influences. All Indian languages, from Vedic to the modern vernaculars, contain a series of sounds, the retroflex or cerebral consonants, which cannot be traced in any other Indo-European tongues, not even in Old Iranian, which is closely akin to Sanskrit. These sounds must have developed quickly, from the efforts of non-Āryans to master the language of their conquerors. No doubt the invaders often married indigenous women, whose children were bilingual, and after a few generations the Āryans' original language showed the effect of the admixture of aboriginal blood. Numerous words in the *Ṛg Veda* are not connected with any known Indo-European roots, and were evidently borrowed from the natives. Non-Āryan influence on religion and culture must also have been felt very early, and the gradual disappearance of much of the original Indo-European heritage beneath successive layers of non-Āryan innovation can be traced through the early religious literature of India.

The primitiveness of early Āryan society was much exaggerated by some 19th-century Indologists, who thought they found in the highly formalized and rigidly controlled style of the *Ṛg Veda* the first outpourings of the human spirit and an echo of Rousseau's noble savage. In fact even when the earliest hymns were composed the Āryans were not savages, but were on the fringes of civilization. Their military technique was in advance of that of the Middle East, their priestly schools had raised the tribal sacrifice to a fine art, and their poetry was elaborate and formalized. On the other hand they had not developed a city civilization. The complete absence of any words connected with writing in the *Ṛg Veda*, despite its size and the many contexts in which such words might be expected to occur, is almost certain proof that the Āryans were illiterate. They were a people of warlike stockbreeders, organized in tribes rather than in kingdoms. Their culture bears a generic likeness to that of *Beowulf* the earlier Icelandic sagas, and the old Irish prose epics, and was somewhat less advanced than that depicted in the *Iliad*.

The tribes were ruled by chiefs who bore the title *rājā*, a word related to the Latin *rex*. The rājā was not an absolute monarch, for the government of the tribe was in part the responsibility of the tribal councils, the *sabhā* and *samiti*. These two words occur together in many contexts and the distinction between them is not wholly clear—possibly some tribes called their governing body *sabhā* and others *samiti*, while yet others had both assemblies, the first an inner council of a few great men of the tribe and the second a larger gathering of heads of families.[9] These two bodies exerted much influence on the king and their approval was necessary to ensure his accession. Some tribes seem to have had no hereditary chief, but were governed directly by the tribal council, for in one passage[10] we read of kings sitting down together in the assembly, which suggests that, as in some later oligarchic clans, the title of rājā was taken by all the great men of the tribe, who governed it through a folk-moot.

But hereditary kingship was the rule, and the rājā, dwelling in a fine hall, had a rudimentary court, attended by courtiers (*sabhāsad*) and chiefs of septs (*grāmaṇī*). Already he had a general (*senānī*), who was responsible under the king for minor campaigns and cattle-raids against neighbouring tribes. Very important was the chief priest (*purohita*), who by his sacrifices ensured the prosperity of the tribe in peace and its victory in war. Often the purohita appears as a tribal medicine-man, performing magical ceremonies and muttering spells for victory both before and during battle.

The Āryans looked on the king primarily as a leader in war, responsible for the defence of the tribe. He was in no sense divine at this early period, and had no religious functions, except to order sacrifices for the good of the tribe and to support the priests who performed them. The priest-king of some other early cultures had no counterpart in Vedic India. There was no regular revenue system and the king was maintained by the tribute of his subjects and the booty won in battle. If the king had judicial functions, as he certainly had later, there is no reference to them; murder was probably punished by a system of wergeld, as with the Anglo-Saxons and some other early Indo-European peoples, but beyond this we have no information on the administration of justice in the time of the *Ṛg Veda*.

Several chieftains are mentioned by name, and around some of them later tradition has embroidered very unreliable stories, but only one rājā is recorded in the *Ṛg Veda* as performing any deed of historical importance. This is Sudās, king of the Bharatas, the tribe dwelling on the upper reaches of the Sarasvatī River. Three poems of the collection describe the great "Battle of the Ten Kings" at which Sudās defeated a coalition of ten tribes of the Panjāb and the North-West, on the banks of the River Paruṣṇī, the modern Rāvī. The most powerful of these ten tribes was that of the Pūrus, who dwelt on the lower Sarasvatī and were the Bharatas' western neighbours; their king, Purukutsa, was apparently killed in the battle. In the succeeding age we hear no more of either Bharatas or Pūrus, but a new tribe, that of the Kurus, controls the old land of the Bharatas and much of the northern Gangā-Yamunā Doāb. In the traditional genealogy of the Kuru chiefs both Bharata and Pūru occur as names of their ancestors, and they are referred to indiscriminately as "sons of Bharata" and "sons of Pūru". The two tribes no doubt merged as a result of the conquest of one by the other, and this process of fusion, whereby tribes became peoples and nations, must have been going on all through the Vedic period.

When the Āryans entered India there was already a class division in their tribal structure. Even in the earliest hymns we read of the *kṣatra*, the nobility, and the *viś*, the ordinary tribesmen, and the records of several other early Indo-European peoples suggest that a tribal aristocracy was a feature of Indo-European society even before the tribes migrated from their original home. As they settled among the darker aboriginals the Āryans seem to have laid greater stress than before on purity of blood, and class divisions hardened, to exclude those Dāsas who had found a place on the fringes of Āryan society, and those Āryans who had intermarried with the Dāsas and adopted their ways. Both these groups were low in the social scale. At the same time the priests, whose sacrificial lore was becoming more and more complicated, and who therefore required greater skill and training, were arrogating higher privileges to themselves. By the end of the Ṛg Vedic period society was divided into four great classes, and this fourfold division was given religious sanction and looked on as fundamental. This is evident from one of the most important hymns of the collection, in which the four classes are said to have emanated from the dismembered primeval man, who was sacrificed by the gods at the beginning of the world (p. 210f).

The four classes, priest (*brāhmaṇa*), warrior (*kṣatriya*), peasant (*vaiśya*) and serf (*śūdrā*), were crystallizing throughout the period of the *Ṛg Veda*. They have survived to the present day. The Sanskrit word used for them, *varṇa*, means "colour", and suggests their origin in the development of the old tribal class structure through contact with people of different complexion and alien culture. The term varna does not mean, and has never meant, "caste", by which convenient word it is often loosely translated (p. 128).

The basic unit of Āryan society was the family. A group of related families formed a sept or *grāma*, a term which later regularly meant "village", but which in the *Ṛg Veda* usually refers to a group of kinsfolk rather than to a settlement. The family was staunchly patrilinear and patriarchal. The wife, though she enjoyed a respectable position, was definitely subordinate to her husband. Marriage was usually monogamous, and apparently indissoluble, for no reference to divorce or the remarriage of widows occurs in the *Ṛg Veda*.

The Āryans followed a mixed pastoral and agricultural economy, in which cattle played a predominant part. The farmer prayed for increase of cattle; the warrior expected cattle as booty; the sacrificial priest was rewarded for his services with cattle. Cattle were in fact a sort of currency, and values were reckoned in heads of cattle. There is no evidence that they were held sacred at this time—the cow is in one or two places given the epithet "not to be killed", but this may only imply her economic importance. In any case it is quite clear that both oxen and cows were slaughtered for food.

The horse was almost as important as the cow, though mainly for military reasons. The chestnut horses of the Āryans, hamessed to light chariots, must have terrified the people of the Indus Valley, as the horses of the conquistadores terrified the Aztecs and Incas. A few hymns of the *Ṛg Veda* according to the rubric describe a divine horse Dadhikrā, and contain some of the finest lines on the horse in the world's literature, recalling the famous passage in praise of the war-horse in the Book of Job.[11]

"Rushing to glory, to the capture of herds,
swooping down as a hungry falcon,
eager to be first, he darts amid the ranks of the chariots,
happy as a bridegroom making a garland,
spurning the dust and champing at the bit.

"And the victorious steed and faithful,
his body obedient [to his driver] in battle,
speeding on through the mêlée,
stirs up the dust to fall on his brows.

"And at his deep neigh, like the thunder of heaven,
the foemen tremble in fear,
for he fights against thousands, and none can resist him,
so terrible is his charge."[12]

Though there are passages which refer to riding, the horse is more frequently described as the motive power of the chariot. References to this vehicle—a favourite subject for similes and metaphors—are so numerous that it is possible to reconstruct it in considerable detail. It was a light chariot with two spoked wheels, drawn by two horses yoked abreast, and carrying two warriors.

Among other domestic animals the Āryans knew the goat and the sheep, which provided wool, their chief textile. The elephant is only mentioned in late hymns, and was rarely if ever domesticated. A divine bitch, Saramā, plays an important part in a legend which cannot be fully reconstructed, but the dog did not mean as much to the people of the *Ṛg Veda* as it did to a kindred Āryan pastoral people, the ancient Iranians, who made it a sacred animal.

Though stockbreeding receives more attention from the poets, agriculture must also have been important, but it seems to have been looked on as rather plebeian, and therefore was not much referred to. Only one word is used for corn—*yava*, which later meant barley, but at this period may have implied all species of cultivated grain. There are references to ploughing and reaping, and others which have been doubtfully interpreted as showing that the Āryans knew something of irrigation.

The Āryans were a wild, turbulent people and had few of the taboos of later India. They were much addicted to inebriating drinks, of which they had at least two, *soma* and *surā*. Soma was drunk at sacrifices and its use was sanctified by religion (p. 205f). Surā was purely secular, and was evidently very potent; in more than one passage it is mentioned with disapproval by the priestly poets.

The Āryans loved music, and played the flute, lute and harp, to the accompaniment of cymbals and drums. They used a heptatonic scale, similar to our own major scale, which is thought by some to have originated in Sumeria and to have been spread by the Indo-European peoples. There are references to singing and dancing, and to dancing-girls, who may have been professionals.

Besides these amusements the Āryans delighted in gambling. At all times India has loved to gamble. In the remains of the Indus cities numerous dice have been found, and the Āryans have left their own record of their gambling propensities in the beautiful "Gamester's Lament", one of the few predominantly secular poems which by lucky chance have found their way into the *Ṛg Veda* (p. 357ff).

Though they had not developed a city civilization, and did not build in stone or brick, the Āryans were technically well equipped. Their bronze-smiths were highly skilled, and produced tools and weapons much superior to those of the Harappā Culture. They, and the carpenters and chariot-makers, are frequently referred to in the hymns with much respect. There is no good reason to believe that iron was used in India at this period. *Ayas*, one of the terms for metal in the *Ṛg*

Veda, came to mean iron at a later date, and is related to the German word *Eisen* and the English *iron*; but it is also akin to the Latin *aes*, meaning bronze, and it certainly means this metal or copper in the *Ṛg Veda*. No trace of iron has been found in the upper levels of the remains of the Indus Culture, and at this period iron implements were rare, even in the advanced civilizations of Mesopotamia. Iron ore is common enough, but its smelting demands higher skill than the Āryans had developed. At the time of the composition of the *Ṛg Veda* the process of smelting iron was hardly known outside Anatolia, where the Hittite kings tried to keep it a secret. Only at the very end of the 2nd millennium did the use of iron begin to spread widely over the civilized world, and it is very unlikely that it reached India before this time.[13]

As might be expected of a people without cities, the Āryans did not have an advanced economic system. In Mesopotamia the silver shekel, though unstamped, served as a means of exchange, but the Āryans relied for their unit of value and means of barter on the unwieldy cow. The *niṣka*, a term later used for a gold coin, is also mentioned as a sort of currency, but at this time was probably a gold ornament of some kind. There is no evidence of a regular class of merchants or moneylenders, though indebtedness is sometimes referred to.

The religion of the early Āryans, about which we know much more than we do about their everyday life and customs, will be discussed in a later chapter (p. 208ff).

THE LATER VEDIC AGE

Between the composition of the *Ṛg Veda* and the age of the Buddha, when we begin to trace the history of India with comparative clearness, a period of some four or five hundred years elapsed. During this time the Āryans pushed eastwards down the Gangā, and their culture adapted itself to changed conditions. Recently Indian archaeologists have excavated parts of a few sites which belong to this period, such as Hastināpura, Ahicchatrā and Kauśāmbī, the lowest levels of which have been reasonably fixed at between 900 and 600 B.C., the time of the later Vedas.[14] The town of Hastināpura was almost completely destroyed by flood at the end of its existence, and little remains but sherds of painted grey pottery, a few copper implements, and traces of houses of unbaked brick. Kauśāmbī has produced similar pottery, a little iron, and remains of a well made city wall faced with burnt brick, but there is some disagreement among archaeologists as to its dating. The typical pottery has been found from the Sarasvatī Valley in the west to Ahicchatrā, near the upper Gangā, in the east. With these exceptions we have scarcely any direct knowledge of the period, and our only important sources are sacred texts, the later Vedas, Brāhmaṇas and Upaniṣads, which will be treated elsewhere from a religious and literary point of view (p. 210ff).

Besides these contemporary documents there are many legends which seem to refer to this period contained in other sources, notably the Epics and Purāṇas; but these are so overlaid by the accretions of later centuries that no attempt at interpreting them historically has so far won general acceptance, and it may never be possible to sift the fact from the fiction. Even the social conditions described in the narrative portions of the Epics, the stories of which may have been composed in a primitive form at this time, do not always refer to this age, but to the obscure period between the Mauryan and Guptan Empires. Attempts of some earlier authorities to create an "Epic Age" in the history of India, as distinct from the age of the later Vedas, are quite unconvincing. There was no Epic Age, and for our knowledge of this period we may only rely on the literature of the period itself. This, like the *Ṛg Veda*, is wholly religious, and tells us little more than the older source about the history of the time.

One event, not definitely recorded in these contemporary sources, but so strongly remembered that it must have been very important, was the great battle of Kurukṣetra, not far from the modern Delhi. This battle, magnified to titanic proportions, formed the basis of the story of the greatest of India's epics, the *Mahābhārata*. According to the legend the whole of India, from Sind to Assam and from the Himālayas to Cape Comorin, took part in the war, which arose through a dynastic dispute in the great Kuru tribe (p. 364). It is by no means certain that the war was in fact a civil one, and the story has been plausibly interpreted as a muddled recollection of the conquest of the Kurus by a tribe of Mongoloid type from the hills. But certainly a great war took place, and succeeding generations looked on it as marking the end of an epoch. The names of many of the heroes of the *Mahābhārata* may genuinely be those of contemporary chieftains, but we must regretfully record that the story is of less use to the historian even than the *Iliad*, or most of the Norse and Irish saga literature. It compares better with the *Nibelungenlied*, the product of an age very different from that which it purports to describe, and the result of the assimilation of many diverse martial traditions. It is as futile to try to reconstruct the political and social history of India in the 10th century B.C. from the *Mahābhārata* as it would be to write the history of Britain immediately after the evacuation of the Romans from Malory's *Morte d'Arthur*.

According to the most popular later tradition the Mahābhārata War took place in 3102 B.C., which, in the light of all evidence, is quite impossible. More reasonable is another tradition, placing the war in the 15th century B.C., but this is also several centuries too early in the light of our archaeological knowledge. Probably it took place around the beginning of the 9th century B.C.; such a date seems to fit well with the scanty archaeological remains of the period, and there is some evidence in the Brāhmaṇa literature itself to show that it cannot have been much earlier.[15] From this time onwards the centre of culture and political power shifted to the Gangetic Doāb and the Kuru capital, Hastināpura or Āsandīvant. Throughout most of the later Vedic period the Kurus and their neighbours the Pancālas were the greatest and the most civilized of Indian peoples. The names of several Kuru kings have been passed down in legend and two at any rate, Parikṣit and Janamejaya, are mentioned in the literature of the time as mighty conquerors.

Early in this period the Āryans pressed further eastwards, and set up kingdoms in Rosala, to the east of the Doāb, and in Kāśī, the region of Vārāṇasī.* The former, which grew in importance with time, was the realm of Rāma, the hero of the second of the great Indian epics, the *Rāmāyaṇa* (p. 365f). For all his later fame the literature of the period ignores Rāma and his father Daśaratha completely, so we must conclude that both were comparatively insignificant chieftains, whose exploits were by chance remembered, to be elaborated and magnified by later generations of bards until, around the beginning of the Christian Era, they received their final form. It is not even certain that Rāma was a king of Kosala at all, for the earliest version of the legend that we possess makes him a king of Vārāṇasī, which was for a time a kingdom of some importance, but was conquered by Kosala towards the end of this period.

Another important kingdom was Videha, to the east of the River Gandak and north of the Gangā. One of the Brāhmaṇas[16] tells that once the fire-god Agni moved eastwards, burning up the earth, until he came to the River Sadānīrā (the modern Gandak), where he stopped. In his wake followed a chieftain from the River Sarasvatī, Videgha Māthava. Before his arrival no Āryan would cross the Sadānīrā, because the purifying fire-god had not burnt the land on its eastern bank; but Agni instructed Videgha to carry him over, and thus the land of Videha was Āryanized, and took its name from that of its first colonizer. The legend is important because it is the only significant account of the process of colonization in an approximately contemporary source. In the progress of Agni, burning up the earth, we see not only the gradual eastward expansion of the Āryan fire cult, but also the clearing of jungle and waste by burning, as bands of migrating warrior peasants founded new settlements.

Though Rāma is ignored in the literature of the period his traditional father-in-law, Janaka king of Videha, is more than once mentioned and is clearly a historical figure. He was a great patron of the hermits and wandering philosophers who propagated the new mystical doctrines of the Upaniṣads, and he himself took part in their discussions. By the time of the Buddha the kingdom of Janaka had disappeared, and his capital city, Mithilā, had lost its importance. The kingdom was replaced by the tribal confederacy of the Vṛjjis, headed by the Licchavis, who may have been Mongols from the hills, but were more probably a second wave of Āryan immigrants.

South of Videha, on the right bank of the Gangā, was the region known as Magadha, then of little account. It was not wholly Āryanized, but bands of nomadic renegade Āryans called *vrātyas*, who did not follow the Vedic rites, roamed the land with their flocks and herds. Only in the time of the Buddha, under the great king Bimbisāra, did Magadha begin to show the energy and initiative which were to lead to the setting up of the first great Indian empire. To the east of Magadha, on the borders of the modern Bengal, the small kingdom of Aṅga had arisen, while, beyond Aṅga, Bengal and Assam were still outside the pale of Āryan civilization.

---

* Until recently known as Benares or Banaras. The old Sanskrit form of the name has now been officially revived.

Thus the texts of the period are mainly concerned with the region from the Yamunā eastwards to the borders of Bengal. The area south of the Gangā receives little attention, and it has been reasonably suggested that the main line of Āryan penetration was not down the river, the banks of which were then probably thick swampy jungle, but along the Himālayan foothills. Expansion was not wholly confined to the north of the Gangā, however. Contemporary literature has little to say about the rest of Northern India, but conditions at the time of the Buddha were such that it must have been colonized some time previously, and this is confirmed by tradition. On the Yamunā the tribe of the Yādavas had settled in the region of Mathurā, while further down the river the kingdom of Vatsa was ruled from its capital of Kauśāmbī, very important in later times. By the end of this period the Āryans had advanced down the Chambal River, had settled in Mālwā, and had reached the Narmadā where there was an important city, Mahiṣmatī. Probably parts of the N.-W. Deccan were also under Āryan influence. According to the Epic tradition Saurāshtra was colonized by a branch of the Yādavas, led by the great hero Kṛṣṇa, and, though the association of Kṛṣṇa with the story is probably unhistorical (p. 267f), the legend may be founded on fact.

While the Āryans had by now expanded far into India their old home in the Panjāb and the North-West was practically forgotten. Later Vedic literature mentions it rarely, and then usually with disparagement and contempt, as an impure land where the Vedic sacrifices are not performed. It may have been once more invaded by Indo-Iranian tribes who did not follow the orthodox rites.

The culture of the later Vedic period was materially much in advance of that of the *Ṛg Veda*. The Āryan tribes were by now consolidated in little kingdoms, which had not wholly lost their tribal character, but had permanent capitals and a rudimentary administrative system. The old tribal assemblies are still from time to time referred to, but their power was waning rapidly, and by the end of this period the king's autocracy was in most cases only limited by the power of the brāhmaṇs, the weight of tradition, and the force of public opinion, which was always of some influence in ancient India. Here and there the old tribal organizations succeeded in adapting themselves to the changed conditions, and *gaṇas*, or tribal republics, survived for many centuries in outlying districts; but political divisions based on kinship were giving place to those based on geography, and in many parts of India the tribes were rapidly breaking up. This, and the strong feeling of insecurity which it caused, may have been an important factor in the growth of asceticism and of a pessimistic outlook on the world, which is evident throughout this period.

If the popular assemblies had lost power, another element in the state was rising in influence—the *ratnins*, or "jewel bearers", the relatives, courtiers and palace officials of the king, who were looked on as so important that at the king's consecration special sacrifices were performed to ensure their loyalty. The list of ratnins includes the purohita, or chief priest of the palace, the general, the chamberlain, the king's charioteer, and various other influential palace servants. Two of the ratnins, the *saṃgrahitṛ* and *bhāgadugha*, have been explained as treasurer and revenue-collector respectively, but these interpretations are almost certainly false, and we have no clear evidence of a developed revenue system at this time.[17]

The period saw a great development of the sacrificial cult, which took place *pari passu* with rising royal pretensions. Much of the Brāhmaṇa literature is devoted to instructions for the meticulous performance of certain royal sacrifices not mentioned in the *Ṛg Veda*; among these were the lengthy *rājasūya*, or royal consecration, and the *vājapeya*, or "drink of strength", a sort of rejuvenation ceremony, which not only restored the vital forces of a middle-aged king, but raised him from the status of a simple rājā to that of a *saṃrāṭ* a complete monarch free of all allegiance and with lesser kings subordinate to him. Most famous and significant of these sacrifices was the *aśvamedha*, or horse-sacrifice, wherein a specially consecrated horse was set free to roam at will for a year, followed by a chosen band of warriors. Chieftains and kings on whose territory the horse wandered were forced to do homage or fight, and if it was not captured by a neighbouring king it was brought back to the capital and sacrificed at the end of the year. It was the ambition of every important king to perform a horse-sacrifice, and the evil effects of the sacrifice on inter-state relations were felt to the end of the Hindu period.

By now the Āryans had nearly all the equipment of a civilization of the ancient type. Where the *Ṛg Veda* speaks only of gold and copper or bronze the later Vedic texts also mention tin, lead, silver and iron.* The importance of iron, harder and cheaper than bronze, for clearing forests of hard tropical timber needs no stressing. Its introduction must have greatly accelerated the rate of Āryan expansion. The elephant was tamed, though little used in war. The Āryans now cultivated a large range of crops, including rice, and they understood something of irrigation and manuring.

Specialized trades and crafts had appeared. In place of the few craftsmen in the *Ṛg Veda* many are now referred to, including jewellers, goldsmiths, metal-workers, basketmakers, ropemakers, weavers, dyers, carpenters and potters. Various types of domestic servant are mentioned, and a rudimentary entertainment industry existed, with professional acrobats, fortune-tellers, flute-players and dancers, while there are also references to usurers and merchants.

Though Āryan culture had by now made great advances there is still no mention of coined money or writing, both of which were certainly used in India before the time of the Mauryas. Coinage may have been introduced towards the end of the 6th century B.C., through Persian influence, but it is doubtful whether we should accept the negative evidence of later Vedic literature to show that writing was wholly unknown, for this literature was intended for a limited audience of priests, who had developed a unique system of memory training, and who may well have looked on writing as an objectionable innovation. There is evidence in

---

* "Black bronze" is referred to in the *Yajur Veda*, and a little iron has been discovered at an early level at Kauśāmbī, but no iron has been found in the remains of Hastināpura at this level. Recently iron has been found in very early levels at Atranjī Kherā (U.P.) and Pāndu Rājar Dhibī (Bengal). The view that iron was hardly known in India until the 6th century has now little to commend it.[18]

the literature itself of faint contacts with Mesopotamia, notably in the Indian flood legend (p. 265), which first appears at this time and which bears some similarity to that of Babylon. After a break of many centuries Indian merchandise was again finding its way to Mesopotamia, and it is possible that Semitic merchants, or Indian merchants returning from the West, brought an alphabetic system of writing, which was gradually taken up by the learned and adapted to the phonetics of Indian speech, to become the *Brāhmī* script of Mauryan times (p. 348f)

The most important developments of this age were religious, and will be considered elsewhere (p. 212ff). Culturally the period of the later Vedic literature saw Indian life and thought take the direction which it has followed ever since. The end of this shadowy age, with its kings growing in power, its priests arrogating to themselves ever greater privileges, and its religious outlook rapidly changing, marks the beginning of the great period of India's culture in which the pattern of her society, religion, literature and art gradually assumed something of its present shape.

III

HISTORY: ANCIENT AND MEDIEVAL EMPIRES

SOURCES OF HISTORY

AT the courts of ancient Indian kings careful records were kept of the events of chief importance to the realm, but unfortunately these archives are completely lost to us. In the 12th century A.D. a Kashmīrī poet, Kalhaṇa, thought fit to write the history of his native land in verse, but his "River of Kings" (*Rājataraṅgiṇī*), although of great value for the study of the history of Kashmīr, has little to tell us about India as a whole, and there is no good evidence that similar chronicles were composed elsewhere. The Ceylon Chronicle (*Mahāvaṃsa*) is primarily a history of Buddhism in Ceylon, though it gives reliable information on political history. It is perhaps unjust to maintain that India had no sense of history whatever, but what interest she had in her own past was mainly concentrated on the fabulous kings of a legendary golden age, rather than on the great empires which had risen and fallen in historical times.

Thus our knowledge of the political history of ancient India is often tantalizingly vague and uncertain, and that of the medieval period, which we may take as beginning in the 7th century A.D., is often but little more precise. History must be pieced together from passing references in texts both religious and secular, from a few dramas and works of fiction purporting to describe historical events, from the records of foreign travellers, and from the many panegyrics or other references to reigning monarchs and their ancestors which have been found carved on rocks, pillars and temple walls, or incorporated as preambles to the title-deeds of land grants; the latter, fortunately for the historian, were usually engraved on copper plates (pl. LXXXVII). The early history of India resembles a jigsaw puzzle with many missing pieces; some parts of the picture are fairly clear; others may be reconstructed with the aid of a controlled imagination; but many gaps remain, and may never be filled. Few dates before the middle ages can be fixed with certainty, and the history of Hindu India, as far as we can reconstruct it, is almost completely lacking in the interesting anecdotes and vivid personalities which enliven the study of the past for professional and amateur historians alike. Moreover there is much disagreement among competent authorities on many important topics.

As our knowledge is so vague and unsatisfactory the reader may well suggest that the political history of Hindu India should be left to the expert; here, however, we cannot agree with him. Too many Indologists have studied Indian religion, art, language and literature in a political and historical vacuum, and this has tended to encourage the widespread fallacy that ancient Indian civilization was interested almost solely in the things of the spirit. However defective our knowledge may be, we have ample evidence to show that great empires rose and fell in India, and that, as in religion, art, literature and social life, so in political organization India produced her own system, distinctive in its strength and weakness. Therefore some knowledge of her political history is essential for a true understanding of her ancient civilization.

THE AGE OF THE BUDDHA

It is in the 6th century B.C. that Indian history emerges from legend and dubious tradition. Now for the first time we read of great kings, whose historicity is certain and some of whose achievements are known, and from now on the main lines of India's political development are clear. Our sources for this period, the Buddhist and Jaina scriptures, are in many respects inadequate as historical documents. Their authors cared little for political affairs; like the Vedas, these texts were passed down by word of mouth for centuries, but, unlike the Vedas, they evidently grew and altered with time. Yet they contain authentic reminiscences of historical events, and, though composed independently in different languages, they partially confirm one another.

The age in which true history appears in India was one of great intellectual and spiritual ferment. Mystics and sophists of all kinds roamed throughout the Gangā Valley, all advocating some form of mental discipline and asceticism as a means to salvation; but the age of the Buddha, when many of the best minds were abandoning their homes and professions for a life of asceticism, was also a time of advance in commerce and politics. It produced not only philosophers and ascetics, but merchant princes and men of action.

By now the focus of civilization had shifted eastwards, and four great kingdoms, outside the earlier area of brāhmaṇic culture, had eclipsed the old land of the Kurus in both political and economic importance; these were Kosala, Magadha, Vatsa and Avanti, of which the first three have been located in the last chapter and the fourth was approximately equivalent to the region later known as Mālwā. Of the four we know most about Kosala and Magadha, the chief scenes of the activities of the Buddha and of Mahāvīra, the founder of Jainism. Kosala, the home of the legendary Rāma, was already in decline. Her king, Prasenajit (in Pāli, Pasenadi), was indeed still a mighty monarch, ruling an area little smaller than France; but from fleeting references in the Buddhist scriptures it seems that he was inefficient, and squandered his time and wealth on holy-men, both orthodox and heretical. His kingdom, which was infested by robbers, was loosely controlled through tribal chieftains and vassal kings.

Bimbisāra of Magadha, on the other hand, was a man of a different stamp. The sources show us a resolute and energetic organizer, ruthlessly dismissing inefficient officers, calling his village headmen together for conferences, building roads and causeways, and travelling over his kingdom on tours of inspection. In general he seems to have been a man of peace, and to have kept on good terms with the kingdoms to the west of him, exchanging courtesies even with the king of far-off Gandhāra on the upper Indus. His one conquest was that of the little kingdom of Aṅga, on the borders of the modern Bengal. Campā, the capital city of Aṅga, was already of considerable commercial importance, for it was a river port from which ships would sail down the Gangā and coast to South India, returning with jewels and spices which were already much in demand in the North. Although Aṅga was Bimbisāra's only conquest, he seems also to have gained control of part at least of the district of Kāśī (Vārānasī), as the dowry of his chief queen, who was the sister of Prasenajit of Kosala. His capital was Rājagṛha, some sixty miles to the south-east of the modern Patnā.

Bimbisāra was deposed, imprisoned and murdered about 494 B.C.—some seven years before the death of the Buddha—by his son, Ajātaśatru. Soon after usurping the prosperous kingdom built up by his father, the parricide went to war with his aged uncle Prasenajit, and gained complete control of Kāśī. Just after this Prasenajit, like Bimbisāra, was deposed by his son, and died. The new king, Virūḍhaka (in Pāli, Viḍūḍabha), then attacked and virtually annihilated the little autonomous tribe of the Śākyas, in the Himālayan foothills, and we hear no more of the people which produced the greatest of Indians, the Buddha. Probably Virūḍhaka, like Ajātaśatru of Magadha, had ambitions of empire, and wished to embark on a career of conquest after bringing the outlying peoples, who had paid loose homage to his father, more directly under the control of the centre; but his intentions were unfulfilled, for we hear no more of him except an unreliable legend that he was destroyed by a miracle soon after his massacre of the Sākyas. A little later his kingdom was incorporated in Magadha.

On concluding his war with Prasenajit Ajātaśatru turned his attention to the tribal confederation of the Vṛjjis, on the north bank of the Gangā, which had often caused trouble by raiding Magadhan territory. After a protracted war he occupied their chief city, Vaiśālī, and annexed their lands. The chief element of the confederation, the tribe of the Licchavis, succeeded in preserving its identity, however, and survived at least until the 4th century A.D., when it was again influential in the politics of Eastern India. The early stages of Ajātaśatru's war with the Vṛjjis took place around the time of the Buddha's death, in about 486 B.C.

The accounts of the reigns of Bimbisāra and Ajātaśatru give evidence of a definite policy, aimed at the control of as much of the course of the Gangā as possible. It seems that they were the first Indian kings to conceive the possibility of a far-flung empire. Tradition indeed tells of earlier emperors who controlled the whole land from coast to coast, but these very shadowy figures are almost certainly the exaggerations of later story-tellers, inspired by the memory of the mighty Mauryas. There is little doubt that the legendary emperors, such as Rama, do represent historical figures of the days before the Buddha, but they were probably small tribal chieftains only powerful in comparison with their fellows. For the traditions of their immense conquests we have no historical evidence whatever.

If there was any source of the inspiration of the two great kings of Magadha it must have been the Achaemenid Empire of Persia, whose founder, Cyrus the Great (558–530 B.C.), came to the throne about sixteen years before the accession of Bimbisāra, and proceeded rapidly to build up the greatest empire the world had then seen. At this time the city of Takṣaśilā, in the North-West, was already a centre of learning and trade. Young men from Magadha were sent there to finish their education, and Bimbisāra was in diplomatic contact with Puṣkarasārin (in Pāli, Pukkusāti), king of Gandhāra, whose kingdom probably included Takṣaśilā. In an inscription of about 519 B.C. Darius I, the third of the Achaemenid emperors, claims possession of Gandhāra, and in a slightly later inscription he also claims *Hindush*, or "India", which, according to Herodotus, became the twentieth satrapy of the Persian Empire. The extent of the Persian province of Hindush is not certain, but it probably included much of the Panjāb. It is hardly likely that the kings of Magadha were ignorant of what was happening in the North-West, and perhaps their expansionist policy was in part inspired by the example of the Persians.

The scriptures of the Buddhists and Jainas give us little information on the events which took place after the deaths of the founders of the two sects, and therefore we know scarcely anything about the latter part of Ajātaśatru's reign. There is evidence that he fought Pradyota, king of Avanti, and that for a time at least the fortunes of war did not favour him; but he certainly succeeded in creating the most powerful empire India had yet known, controlling both banks of the Gaṅgā from Vārānasī to the borders of Bengal, which was still beyond the pale of Āryan civilization. In the succeeding century and a half Magadha continued to expand, for, when the curtain is again lifted on India's past in the 4th century B.C., Pāṭaliputra (now Patnā), the new capital of Magadha, controls all the Gaṅgā basin; the rest of Northern India, with the exception of Rājasthān, Sind, the Panjāb and the North-West, is part of the Magadhan Empire, and the other kingdoms are either annihilated or reduced to insignificant vassalage.

ALEXANDER AND THE MAURYAS

In the middle of the 4th century B.C., Mahāpadma Nanda was emperor of Magadha. He was an unpopular upstart, but, as far as can be gathered from the few references to him, he was an energetic and ambitious king, who succeeded in gaining control of Kaliṅga (the modern Orissā and the northern coastal strip of Āndhra Pradesh), and perhaps of other parts of the Deccan. His death seems to have been followed by a disputed succession, which coincided with important events in the North-West. Out of the confusion of the times emerged the greatest and most powerful of India's many empires.

In 330 B.C. Alexander of Macedon defeated Darius III, the last of the Achaemenids, and set out to subdue the whole of the former Persian Empire, which had long ceased to exercise effective control over its remoter provinces. In the decisive battle of Gaugamela Alexander had already met Indian troops, for a small contingent of soldiers from the west of the Indus, with fifteen elephants, had fought with Darius. Over a hundred years earlier Greeks had already measured swords with Indians, for, according to Herodotus, a detachment of Indians fought in the Persian army at Plataea.

After a long campaign in Bactria, the region watered by the River Oxus on the borders of the modern Soviet Union and Afghānistān, Alexander crossed the Hindu Kush and occupied the district of Kābul. Then, fiercely but unsuccessfully resisted by the hillmen, he descended the Kābul Valley and reached the Indus, which he crossed in the spring of 326. Omphis* king of Takṣaśilā (known to classical writers as Taxila), had already submitted, and the city offered no resistance. Beyond the Jhelam, however, lay the territory of the most warlike king of the Panjāb, Porus† for fear of whom Omphis had willingly thrown in his lot with Alexander. It was only with great difficulty, after a surprise crossing of the Jhelam, that the Macedonians succeeded in defeating the troops of Porus, who was captured. Porus was a very tall and handsome man, whose courage and proud hearing made a great impression on the Greeks; when brought before his conqueror he was found to have received nine wounds, and he could barely stand; but when Alexander asked him how he wished to be treated he boldly replied: "As befits me—like a king!" Alexander was so impressed by his captive that he restored him to his kingdom as a vassal and, on the retreat of the Greek forces, left him in charge of the Panjāb.

After the defeat of Porus Alexander continued his advance, subduing numerous tribes and petty kingdoms; but at the Beās he was forced to turn back, for his generals feared mutiny if his troops were made to advance further into unknown country. Alexander returned across the Panjāb and fought his way down the Indus, often meeting stiff opposition from the martial tribes. At the mouth of the Indus the army divided, part returning to Mesopotamia by sea, and part, led by Alexander himself, by land, along the coast through the desolate Makrān. After much hardship both detachments reached the Euphrates, together with a smaller body which had been sent back earlier by way of Arachosia (the modern Kandahār). There is no doubt that Alexander intended to retain control of his Indian conquests, for he left garrisons behind him and appointed satraps to govern the conquered territories. But revolts in the Indian provinces and the sudden death of Alexander in 323 B.C. made the Macedonian position in India untenable, and the last of Alexander's generals, Eudamus, left the North-West in 317.

Although the Greeks had known something of India before the invasion of Alexander, their knowledge was mostly of the nature of fantastic travellers' tales. Now for the first time Greeks and Indians came into close contact. It is clear from classical accounts of Alexander's campaign that the Greeks were not unimpressed by what they saw of India. They much admired the courage of the Indian troops,

---

*This is the name as given by classical sources. It probably represents the Sanskrit *Āmbhi*.

†Probably the Sanskrit *Paurava*, which would connect Porus with the old Kuru tribe of whose ruling family this was a cognomen.

the austerity of the naked ascetics whom they met at Takṣaśilā, and the probity and simplicity of the tribes of the Panjāb and Sind.

The immediate effects of the invasion were slight. Greek colonies were established in Bactria, Afghanistan and N.-W. India. Some of these prospered, for about seventy years later Greek was still the principal language spoken around Kandahār if we are to judge from the Greek inscriptions of Aśoka discovered there in recent years.

The kingdoms and tribes of the North-West were disorganized and overthrown, but Alexander made so small an impression upon India that in the whole of her surviving ancient literature there is no reference to him. In later centuries the Indians came to know the Greeks, but of Greek influence in India at this time there is scarcely a trace. However, it may be that the invasion, and the political vacuum created in the North-West by Alexander's retreat, had indirect effects of the utmost importance.

Classical sources speak of a young Indian named Sandrocottus— identical with the Candragupta Maurya of Indian sources—who sided with the Greeks. Plutarch states that Sandrocottus advised Alexander to advance beyond the Beās and attack the Nanda emperor, who was so unpopular that his people would rise in support of an invader. The Latin historian Justin adds that later Sandrocottus offended Alexander by his boldness of speech, and the conqueror ordered that he should be put to death; but he escaped, and after many adventures succeeded in expelling the Greek garrisons and gaining the throne of India. Whether or not these stories are true, it is reasonable to believe that the emperor Candragupta Maurya, who rose to power soon after Alexander's invasion, had at least heard of the conqueror, and perhaps derived inspiration from his exploits.

Both Indian and classical sources agree that Candragupta overthrew the last of the Nandas and occupied his capital, Pāṭaliputra; the latter add that after Alexander's retreat Candragupta subdued the North-West, driving out the Greek garrisons. It is not clear which of these operations was first undertaken, and, with the annoying uncertainty of much ancient Indian history, estimates of the date of Candragupta's accession vary within a decade (324–313 B.C.); but though the detailed history of his rise to power is uncertain, it is evident that he was the chief architect of the greatest of India's ancient empires. According to all Indian traditions he was much aided in his conquests by a very able and unscrupulous brāhmaṇ adviser, called variously Kauṭilya, Cāṇakya and Viṣṇugupta; indeed in the play *The Minister's Signet Ring*, a work of the 6th century A.D., which purports to describe the last stages of Candragupta's triumph over the Nanda (p. 393), the king is depicted as a weak and insignificant young man, the real ruler of the empire being Cāṇakya. The minister is the reputed author of the *Arthaśāstra*, or "Treatise on Polity", a very valuable source of information on state administration. The text as we have it at present is certainly not the work of Kauṭilya (p. 69), but it is very valuable nevertheless, and contains genuine Mauryan reminiscences.

Soon the Greeks were again at the doors of India. Alexander's general Seleucus Nicator had succeeded in gaining control of most of the Asiatic provinces of the shortlived Macedonian Empire, and turned his attention to the East. About 305 B.C. he met Candragupta in battle, and seems to have suffered the worst of the engagement, for he failed in his attempt to recover Alexander's Indian provinces, and was compelled to yield parts of what is now Afghānistān to Candragupta, receiving in exchange only 500 elephants. The peace was concluded by a matrimonial alliance, the exact nature of which is uncertain;[1] but it is not impossible that the successors of Candragupta had Greek blood in their veins.

Seleucus sent an ambassador, Megasthenes, to reside at the Mauryan court at Pāṭaliputra, and the envoy wrote a detailed account of India which became the standard textbook on the subject for later classical writers. Unfortunately no manuscript of Megasthenes' description of India has survived, but many Greek and Latin authors made abundant use of it, and from their works it may be partially reconstructed. The record of Megasthenes, though by no means as complete and accurate as might be wished, is of great importance as the first authentic and connected description of India by a foreign traveller. It is evident from a comparison of the fragments of Megasthenes with the *Arthaśāstra* that the Mauryan empire had developed a highly organized bureaucratic administration, which controlled the whole economic life of the state, and that it had a very thorough secret service system, which was active among all classes from the highest ministers to the submerged tenth of the towns.

Megasthenes much admired the Emperor Candragupta for his energetic administration of justice, which he presided over personally in open *darbār*.* He dwelt in great luxury in an enormous palace at Pāṭaliputra, which, though built wholly of wood, was of unbelievable beauty and splendour; but his life was not a happy one, for he was in constant fear of assassination, an ever-present danger to many Indian kings, and very stringent precautions were taken for his security. The capital was a large and fine city, surrounded by a wooden wall; it was controlled by an administrative board of thirty members, who regulated in detail the whole social and economic life of the people. Megasthenes noticed the existence of caste, though his classification of the population in seven endogamous groups is certainly erroneous (p. 128).

According to Jaina tradition Candragupta abdicated the throne, became a Jaina monk, and fasted to death, in the manner of Jaina saints, at the great Jaina temple and monastery of Śravaṇa Belgolā, in the modern Mysore. Whatever the truth of this legend, he was succeeded after a reign of twenty-four years by his son Bindusāra, about whom little is known except that he was in touch with Antiochus I, the Seleucid king of Syria. According to Athenaeus, Bindusāra requested of the Greek king a present of figs and wine, together with a sophist. Antiochus sent the figs and wine, but replied that Greek philosophers were not for export. This quaint little story seems to indicate that Bindusāra, like many other Indian kings, shared his attentions between creature comforts and philosophy, but he was certainly

---

*This word is strictly an anachronism, as it is Persian and was introduced by the Muslims, but it is better known and less ambiguous than the equivalent Sanskrit word, *sabhā*.

energetic enough to hold the great empire intact, and it is even probable that he added to it in the Deccan. He was succeeded about 269 B.C., probably after a short interregnum, by his son Aśoka, the greatest and noblest ruler India has known, and indeed one of the great kings of the world.

According to Buddhist sources Aśoka usurped the throne, killed all possible rivals, and began his reign as a tyrant, but this story is not borne out by Aśoka's own inscriptions, which are the oldest surviving Indian written documents of any historical significance. They consist of a series of edicts engraved in very similar form on rocks and pillars at widely scattered points all over India (fig. vi), and form a unique monument to a great king's memory. The edicts are in part inspired by Achaemenid precedent, but their contents are very different from the great inscriptions of Darius I, for instance, which glorify the emperor, catalogue his conquests, and enumerate the peoples and tribes under his sway. Aśoka's edicts are in the nature of official pronouncements of policy, and instructions to his officers and subjects. They contain many personal touches, and the drafts were probably composed by the emperor himself.

They tell us that when the king had been consecrated eight years he underwent a complete change of heart, and embarked on a new policy. In Aśoka's own words:

> "When the King, Priyadarśī* Beloved of the Gods, had been consecrated eight years, Kaliṅga was conquered. 150,000 people were thence taken captive, 100,000 were killed, and many more died. Just after the taking of Kaliṅga the Beloved of the Gods began to follow Righteousness, to love Righteousness, to give instruction in Righteousness. When an unconquered country is conquered, people are killed, they die, or are made captive. That the Beloved of the Gods finds very pitiful and grievous.... Today, if a hundredth or a thousandth part of those who suffered in Kaliṅga were to be killed, to die, or to be taken captive, it would be very grievous to the Beloved of the Gods. If anyone does him wrong it will be forgiven as far as it can be forgiven. The Beloved of the Gods even reasons with the forest tribes in his empire, and seeks to reform them. But the Beloved of the Gods is not only compassionate, he is also powerful, and he tells them to repent, lest they be slain. For the Beloved of the Gods desires safety, self-control, justice and happiness for all beings. The Beloved of the Gods considers that the greatest of all victories is the victory of Righteousness, and that [victory] the Beloved of the Gods has already won, here and on all his borders, even 600 leagues away in the realm of the Greek king Antiyoka, and beyond Antiyoka among the four kings Turamaya, Antikini, Maga and Alikasudara, and in the South among the Cōlas and Pāṇḍas and as far as Ceylon."[2]

* "Of Gracious Mien", Aśoka's throne name. It is now certain that this is to be looked on as a proper name and not as a title, for the recently discovered Greek inscription of Aśoka at Kandahār renders it as Πιοδασσης, instead of translating it into Greek.

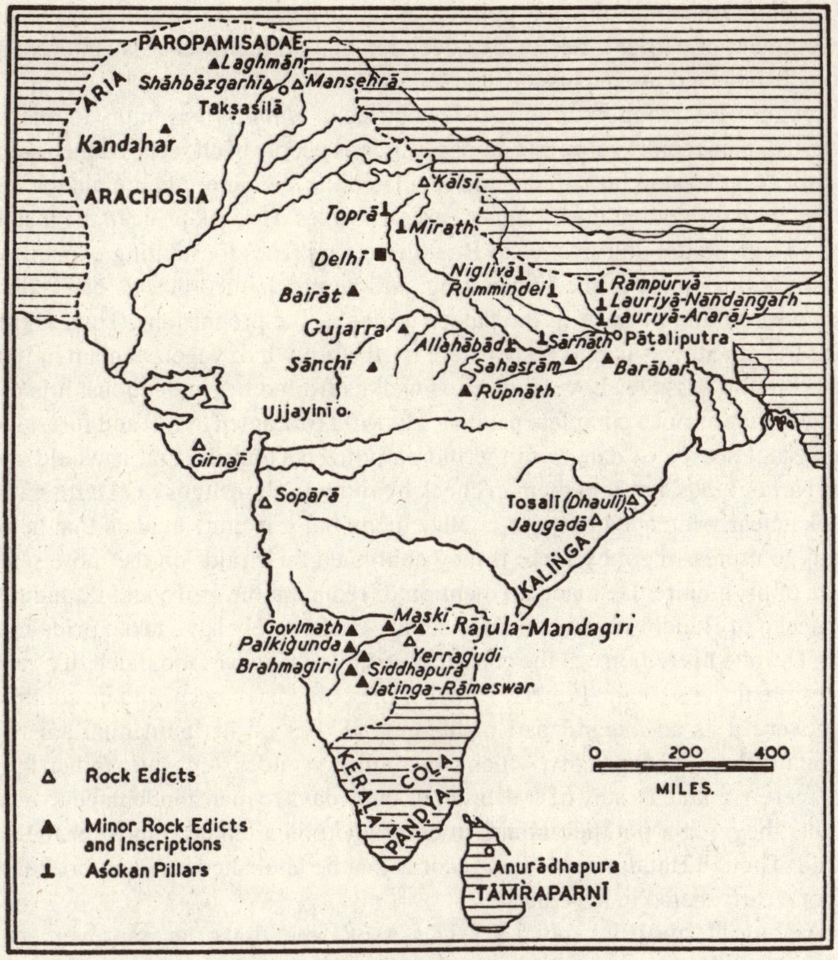

Fig. vi. The Empire of Aśoka
(The pillars originally at Mirath and Toprā are now at Delhi)

Thus we see that the keynote of Aśoka's reform was humanity in internal administration and the abandonment of aggressive war. In place of the traditional policy of territorial expansion he substituted conquest by Righteousness (as we here inadequately translate the very pregnant word *dharma*). He claims to have won many victories by this method, even among the five Hellenic kings whose names, loosely disguised by Indianization, are to be read in the above extract—Antiochus II Theos of Syria, Ptolemy II Philadelphus of Egypt, Antigonus Gonatas of Macedonia, Magas of Cyrene and Alexander of Epirus. It seems that Aśoka believed that, by setting an example of enlightened government, he might convince his neighbours of the merits of his new policy and thus gain the moral leadership of the whole civilized world. He by no means gave up his imperial ambitions, but modified them in accordance with the humanitarian ethics of Buddhism.

In domestic affairs the new policy was felt in a general relaxation of the stern government of earlier times. Asoka declared that all men were his children, and more than once reproved his local govemors for their failure to apply this precept thoroughly. He strongly supported the doctrine of *ahimsā* (non-injury to men and animals), then rapidly spreading among religious people of all sects, banned animal sacrifices, at least in his capital, and regulated the slaughter of animals for food, completely forbidding the killing of certain species. He took pride in the fact that he had substituted pilgrimages to Buddhist holy places for hunting expeditions, the traditional sport of the Indian king, and he proclaimed that he had reduced the consumption of meat in the palace to negligible proportions. Thus Aśoka's encouragement was in part responsible for the growth of vegetarianism in India.

From the passage above quoted, as well as from other indications, it is clear that Aśoka was not a complete pacifist. The wild tribesmen of hill and forest were a constant source of danger to the more civilized villagers, and it would seem that earlier kings had kept them in check by ruthless campaigns of extermination. Aśoka clearly intended to try to civilize them, but it is quite evident that he was ready to repress them by force if they continued their raids on the more settled parts of his empire. He made no mention of reducing the army, and if, under the influence of Buddhism, he had done so, he would surely have taken pride in the fact. Despite his remorse at the conquest of Kaliṅga, he was too much of a realist to restore it to its original rulers, whoever they may have been, and he continued to govern it as an integral part of his empire. For all his humanitarianism he maintained the death penalty, which was abolished under some later Indian kings, and merely granted a stay of execution of three days to men condemned to death, so that they might put their affairs in order and prepare their minds for the next world. Though Buddhist tradition records that he abolished judicial torture, this is not clearly stated in his edicts.

Among his positive social services Aśoka mentions the improvement of communications by planting fruit trees along the roads to provide shade and food, digging wells at intervals, and setting up rest-houses for weary travellers. He developed the cultivation of medicinal herbs, which, with other drugs, were supplied to men and animals alike. To ensure that his reforms were put into effect he inaugurated a new class of official, the "Officers of Righteousness" (*dharma-mahāmātra*), who, taking their instructions direct from the centre, were ordered to investigate the affairs of all the provinces, to encourage good relations between man and man, and to ensure that the local officials carried out the new policy. Thus Aśoka's reforms tended to centralization rather than devolution.

It is evident that, after his change of heart if not before, Aśoka's personal religion was Buddhism, and some authorities believe that he actually entered the Buddhist order. But the inscriptions show that he was no metaphysician, and indeed he probably had little interest in or understanding of the finer points of Buddhism. Although he never mentions the Buddhist *nirvāṇa*, he speaks frequently of heaven; and he seems to have held the naive belief that, as a result of the growth of morality through his reforms, the gods had manifested themselves on earth, a phenomenon which had not occurred for many years previously.[3] In fact the *Dharma* officially propagated by Aśoka was not Buddhism at all, but a system of morals consistent with the tenets of most of the sects of the Empire and calculated to lead to peace and fellowship in this world and heaven in the next. Aśoka's metaphysical presuppositions were not distinctively Buddhist, but were evidently those traditional in India at the time. A streak of puritanism in the Emperor's character is to be inferred from the edict banning rowdy popular fairs and allowing religious gatherings only.

Aśoka's Buddhism, though enthusiastic, was not exclusive. More than once he declared that all sects were worthy of respect, and he dedicated artificial caves to the sect of Ājīvikas, who were among the chief rivals of the Buddhists. His relations with the Buddhist clergy seem to have been erastian, for he had no compunction in prescribing passages of scripture which the order was specially to study, and he instructed local officers to ensure that all ill-behaved Buddhist monks were unfrocked. It was in Aśoka's reign that Buddhism ceased to be a simple Indian sect and began its career as a world religion. According to tradition a great council of the Buddhist clergy was held at Pāṭaliputra, at which the Pāli canon was finally codified, and after which missions were sent throughout the length and breadth of India and beyond.

Tradition unanimously ascribes the conversion of Ceylon to Mahendra (in Pāli, Mahinda), Aśoka's son, or in some sources his brother, who had become a Buddhist monk. Though the relationship of the apostle of Ceylon to Aśoka is very doubtful, there can be no doubt of his historicity, or of that of King Devānampiya Tissa, his first convert. Though Āryans may have settled in Ceylon more than two centuries before this time, it was only now that the culture of the island began to develop, under the fertilizing influence of Buddhism. The Ceylon Chronicle, which, being nationalist in its sympathies, is not likely to be false in this particular, implicitly admits that Tissa was loosely subordinate to Aśoka, since it states that he underwent a second consecration and was converted to Buddhism on Aśoka's instructions. Thus at least one of Aśoka's "victories of Righteousness" outside his empire was successful; his attempts at the moral conquest of the Hellenic kings certainly ended in failure, for there is no reference to his embassies in any classical source, and if they reached their destinations they can have had little effect on the ambitious successors of Alexander.

To the modern student Aśoka towers above the other kings of ancient India, if for no other reason than that he is the only one among them whose personality can be reconstructed with any degree of certainty. But even Aśoka is not as clear a figure as we would wish, and his policy has been the subject of varied judgements. Critics have accused him of ruining the Mauryan Empire, either by antagonizing the brāhmaṇs or by sapping the martial spirit of the ruling classes.[4] We cannot accept either of these accusations. It appears that the old Emperor, who died about 232 B.C., somewhat lost grip in his latter years,[5] and the succession was disputed by his sons. The Empire began to fall apart on his death, when the governors of the great provinces, usually members of the royal family, established their virtual independence. The successors of Aśoka were lesser men than he, and little is known of them but their names.

The Aśoka of the Buddhist legends is, in the words of a 19th-century authority, "half monster and half idiot",[6] his humanity and practical benevolence overlaid by the accretion of monkish legends of later centuries; but the king of the rock and pillar inscriptions comes alive, as a real man, and a man far ahead of his times. Aśoka was by no means an other-worldly dreamer, but every inch a king, a little naive, often rather self-righteous and pompous, but indefatigable, strong-willed and imperious. It is with good reason that the Indian Republic has adopted for the device of its state seal the capital of an Aśokan column (pl. XXIII*a*).

THE AGE OF INVASIONS

For some fifty years Mauryan kings continued to rule in Magadha until, about 183 B.C., Puṣyamitra Śuṅga, a brāhmaṇ general of Bṛhadratha, the last Mauryan king, succeeded in gaining power by a palace revolution. Puṣyamitra was a supporter of the orthodox faith, and revived the ancient Vedic sacrifices, including the horse-sacrifice; but the flourishing state of Buddhism at this period is attested by the remains at Bhārhut, and the stories of his persecution of Buddhist monks are probably much exaggerated by sectarian tradition. The kingdom of the Śuṅgas was by no means a closely-knit centralized empire, like that of the Mauryas, but one of a type which was to become normal in Hindu India and which may be loosely termed feudal (p. 82ff). Its centre was in Vidiśā (E. Mālwā), which at most times seems to have been directly controlled by the king, whose domains were surrounded by a circle of vassal states small and great, in varying degrees of subservience. but some evidently autonomous enough to issue their own coins. Beyond the realm of Puṣyamitra much of the old Mauryan Empire was now independent, and little is known of the condition of Magadha, the former centre of culture and power.

The inspiration of the Mauryas was soon almost forgotten. Later the Guptas tried to build an empire of a more centralized type, and directly controlled much of North India for over a hundred years, but, with this major exception and a few minor ones, all later Hindu imperialism was of the quasi-feudal type, loose and unstable. The memory of Aśoka's renunciation of further conquest was soon forgotten, and aggressive war again became the sport of kings, and was looked upon by theorists as a normal activity of the state. In general the history of post-Mauryan India is one of the struggle of one dynasty with another for regional dominance, and the political, though not the cultural, unity of India was lost for nearly two thousand years.

Puṣyamitra is mentioned in several sources, and his name is recorded in one brief inscription, referring to an obscure descendant.[7] He did not take regal titles, but was throughout his reign referred to by the simple epithet *senapati*, or "general". Agnimitra, his son, who seems to have been king during his father's lifetime, is known from Kālidāsa's drama *Mālavikā and Agnimitra*, while his grandson Vasumitra is recorded in the same source as having defeated the Greeks. An inscription on a column at Besnagar (pl. X*c*), near Bhīlsā, records that a Śuṅga king Bhāgabhadra received an ambassador named Heliodorus from a Greek king of Takṣaśilā, Antialcidas. Otherwise the Śuṅgas are mere names recorded, usually in garbled form, among the muddled king-lists of the *Purāṇas*, religious texts dating from Gupta times onwards.

Meanwhile on India's north-western borders events which were to have a profound effect both on her own history and on that of Asia generally were taking place. A series of invasions, all inadequately documented, brought the whole of what is now West Pākistān, Mālwā and Saurāshtra, much of Uttar Pradesh and Rājasthān, and even for a while part of Western Mahārāshtra under the control of alien kings.

The first invaders were the Bactrian Greeks. Small colonies of Asiatic Greeks had been settled in Bactria by the Achaemenids, and these were strengthened by settlements established by Alexander and Seleucus Nicator. About the middle of the 3rd century B.C. Diodotus, the govemor of Bactria, declared himself independent of the Seleucid Empire, and the Iranian province of Parthia became independent at about the same time. Diodotus was succeeded by his son, also named Diodotus, who was soon overthrown and replaced by a usurper, Euthydemus. Euthydemus came to terms with the Seleucid emperor Antiochus III, who had vainly attempted to regain the lost province; with his flank now secure, he began to expand over the Hindu Kush, and gained a foothold on the N.-W. Frontier, which had probably already broken away from the Mauryan Empire. Early in the 2nd century B.C. Demetrius, the son and successor of Euthydemus, pressed further into India. He and his successors occupied most of the Indus Valley and the Panjāb, and led great raids far into the Gangā Valley, at least one of which, perhaps led by King Menander, reached Pāṭaliputra. Soon the home domains of the Bactrian Greeks were wrested from them by another usurper, Eucratides, but descendants of Euthydemus continued to rule in the Panjāb and parts of the North-West. Then the Eucratids were also tempted to try their fortunes beyond the mountains, and gained control of the Kābul Valley and the district of Takṣaślā. The Greek domains in India were divided into several petty kingdoms, those of the Kābul Valley and the N.-W. Frontier chiefly ruled by kings of the line of Eucratides, and those of the Panjāb under the line of Euthydemus.

Little is known of the history of the Greeks in India, and their fortunes can only be faintly reconstructed from their remarkable coins (pl. LXXXIV), most of which bear legends in Greek on the obverse and in Prākrit on the reverse. From now on, however, the *Yavanas* (a term borrowed by India through the Persian from the Greek 'Ιάονες) are mentioned from time to time in Indian literature. Through the Greco-Bactrian kingdoms Western theories of astrology and medicine began to enter India, and perhaps the development of the Sanskrit drama was in part inspired from this source. More than one Indian tradition speaks of great Yavana raids. One of the Greek kings of the Panjāb is specially remembered by Buddhism as the patron of the philosopher-monk Nāgasena; this was Milinda, or Menander, who ruled at Śākala (?Siālkot), and whose long discussions with the sage are recorded in a well-known Pāli text, the *Questions of Milinda*. Menander is said to have become a Buddhist, but the Besnagar column, to which we have already referred, shows that the Greeks also sometimes supported the orthodox creeds, for it was erected by the ambassador Heliodorus in honour of the early Vaisnavite deity Vāsudeva. Thus some of the Greeks, while not completely merging with the local population, soon felt the influence of Indian ways of thought and made many compromises with Indian culture. The author of the law-book of Manu, writing probably a century or two later than Heliodorus, describes the Yavanas as degenerate kṣatriyas, or members of the warrior class, and thus gives them a place in Hindu society.

The Greco-Bactrian kingdoms, however, did not long survive. Bactria itself was occupied by the Parthians early in the second half of the 2nd century B.C., and the Greeks were confined to their possessions in India and Afghānistān. Then fresh invaders appeared from the north. A complex chain of causes, climatic and political, led to new movements of the peoples of Central Asia. The consolidation of the Chinese Empire under the great emperor Ch'in Shih Huang Ti (247–210 B.C.), the building of the Great Wall of China, and perhaps also the drying up of the Central Asian pasture lands, had driven large bands of nomads westwards, from the confines of China to the region east of the Caspian. Soon a nomadic people, called by the Chinese Yüeh-chih, was hearing heavily on the Scythian tribesmen on the borders of Bactria. The Scyths, whom India was to know as Śakas, were driven by pressure from the north and east to attack Bactria, which they occupied, soon to be followed by the Yüeh-chih. The Śakas moved on from Bactria to attack first the Parthian rulers of Iran and then the Greeks in India. By the middle of the lst century B.C. only a few petty Greek chiefs still ruled in India, and the power of the Śakas reached as far as Mathurā. The Śakas continued the earlier practice of issuing coins with inscriptions in Greek and Prākrit. The earliest of their kings known to have ruled in India was Maues (? c. 80 B.C.).

Towards the end of the 1st century B.C. a line of kings with Iranian names, usually known as Pāhlavas, gained the brief suzerainty of N.-W. India. One of them, Gondophares, is worthy of mention as the ruler to whose kingdom St. Thomas is said to have brought India's first knowledge of Christianity (p. 301). Some authorities have cast doubt on the truth of the legend, maintaining that Gondophares' date was too early for him to have been St. Thomas's contemporary;[8] but at any rate he was important enough for his fame to reach the West, and that St. Thomas preached in India is by no means impossible. Gondophares was perhaps responsible for the extinction of the last of the Greek kings, Hermaeus, whose line had held out in Kabul against the Śakas.

The Pāhlavas were in turn conquered by the Yüeh-chih. The racial affinities of these people are uncertain; physically they were of Turkish type, but, like the Śakas, appear to have spoken an Iranian language. For a century or more they dwelt in Bactria and the neighbouring regions of Central Asia, divided into autonomous tribes, until control was consolidated in the hands of Kujūla Kadphises of the tribe of the Kuṣāṇas. At some time in the first half of the lst century A.D. Kujūla led his warriors over the mountains, and he and his son Vīma Kadphises between them gained control of N.-W. India.

Vīma Kadphises was succeeded, probably after a short interregnum, by Kaniṣka, who ruled all the western half of Northern India at least as far as Vārāṇasī, and whose dominions in Central Asia were very extensive. The Chinese annals speak of a Kuṣāṇa king, either Kaniṣka or one of the Kadphises, demanding the hand of a princess of the imperial house of Han in marriage, and being soundly defeated for his arrogance by the great general Pan Ch'ao, who at the end of the 1st century A.D. carried Chinese arms as far as the Caspian.

This period was a very significant one in the history of Buddhism, and Kaniṣka is remembered in Northern Buddhist tradition as a great patron of the faith. Numerous remains testify to the importance and popularity of Buddhism at the time, and it was now that it began to spread to Central Asia and the Far East. Some intimations of the Indian religion had already reached China, but it exerted no real influence until now, when the Kuṣāṇa and Chinese empires were in close contact. The period is also noteworthy for the Gandhāra school of art, which was influential not only in India but also, indirectly, in the Far East (p. 324f).

The date of Kaniṣka, like the chronology of the whole Śaka-Kuṣāṇa period, is very uncertain, and estimates of the year of his accession have varied from 58 B.C. to A.D. 248. At present opinions of most competent authorities are divided between A.D. 78 and 144. The former date is that of the foundation of one of the most widespread Indian systems of dating, later known as the Śaka Era. Kaniṣka was not, strictly speaking, a Śaka, but the term was very loosely applied, and he is known to have founded an era. Though the date A.D. 78 fits well with other Indian evidence, certain complicated synchronisms, mainly based on non-Indian sources, suggest that he reigned some decades later than this, and the question cannot be finally settled until new evidence appears. The successors of Kaniṣ ka continued to reign in N.-W. India, but their empire was soon much reduced. About the middle of the 3rd century Vāsudeva, one of Kaniṣka's successors, was soundly defeated by Shāpur I of the new Sāsānian dynasty of Persia, and from now on the North-West came much under Iranian influence.

Meanwhile new kingdoms had been set up in the Peninsula. In Orissā a great conqueror, Khāravela, appeared in the latter half of the 1st century B.C.; he raided far and wide over India and was a great patron of Jainism; but his empire was short-lived, and we know nothing of his successors. At about the same time an important kingdom arose in the N.-W. Deccan from the ruins of that of the Mauryas—the kingdom of the Sātavāhanas or Āndhras, centred on Pratiṣṭhāna (modern Paithān). This survived for 300 years or more, until the 3rd century A.D., its power often reaching beyond the Narmadā into Mālwā and, in the 2nd century A.D., from coast to coast. Traditionally the first Sātavāhana king, Sīmuka, put an end to the last insignificant Śuṅgas and to the Kāṇva kings, who reigned for a short time in part of the old Śuṅga Empire. For a while, around the beginning of the 2nd century A.D., the Sātavāhanas were driven from the N.-W. Deccan by invading Śakas of the clan of Kṣaharāta, whose great satrap Nahapāna left a number of inscriptions; but the Sātavāhanas, under the greatest of their rulers, Gautamīputra Sātakarnin, recovered their lands about A.D. 130, and nothing more is heard of the Kṣaharātas.

Another Śaka dynasty, generally known as the "Western Satraps", gained control of Gujarāt and Mālwā at about the same time, and ruled until soon after A.D. 388, at its height governing much of Rājasthān and Sind. The greatest king of this line was Rudradāman, who has left the earliest important inscription in correct Sanskrit, a long panegyric which records his martial exploits and his reconstruction at Girnar in Saurāshṭra of a great artificial lake, which had been excavated under Candragupta and improved in the time of Aśoka. This inscription is among the earliest certainly dated records of ancient India, and proves that Rudradāman was reigning in A.D. 150.

At this time the Dravidian South first begins to appear in the light of history. Traditionally the Tamil country has always been divided into three kingdoms—Cōla (the Coromandel Coast), Kerala or Cēra (Malabār), and Pāṇḍya (the southern tip of the Peninsula). These three are mentioned by Aśoka as the scenes of his "victories of Righteousness" beyond his own dominions, and numerous rough inscriptions indicate that Buddhist and Jaina ascetics visited the Tamil land before the beginning of the Christian era. In the earliest stratum of Tamil literature, which was probably composed in the early centuries A.D., we find the three kingdoms in a state of almost continual warfare. Their kings, and the many lesser chieftains who are also mentioned, seem to have been more bloodthirsty than those of the North, and the literature contains hints of massacres and other atrocities such as are rarely heard of in Sanskrit literature; one passage even suggests cannibal feasts after battle.[9] The ancient Tamil, by no means perfectly Āryanized, was a man of very different stamp from his gentle and thoughtful descendant. Wild and ruthless, delighting in war and drink, worshipping fierce gods with bacchanalian dances, passionate in love, he compares strikingly with the grave and knightly warriors of the Sanskrit epics, which were probably receiving their final form at the time when the poems of the Tamil anthologies were being written. A few centuries were to alter the picture somewhat, and the next stratum of Tamil literature shows a much deeper penetration of Āryan ideals and standards, but a streak of ruthlessness and disregard for individual life is evident in the Dravidian character down to the fall of Vijayanagara.

Very early the Tamils took to the sea. Even in the 2nd century B.C. they twice invaded Ceylon, the first time soon after the death of the great king Devānampiya Tissa, and the second a little later. The latter invasion resulted in the long occupation of the whole of the northern half of the island by the Tamil king Eḷāra, who was expelled with great difficulty by the Sinhalese national hero, King Duṭugāmuṇu (in Pāli, Duṭṭhagāmaṇi) (161–137 B.C.). Tamils probably found their way to S.-E. Asia at about the same time, and in the 1st century A.D. were in close contact with Egypt and the Roman Empire, through the flourishing trade with the West (p. 135ff).

THE GUPTAS AND HARṢA

We know little of events in North India after the decline of the Kuṣāṇas, but it seems that by the 3rd century A.D. all India east of the Panjāb and Mālvā was in the hands of small Indian kings and tribal chiefs. Some authorities have depicted the great Gupta emperors as liberators of India from the foreign yoke, but it seems that by this time the invaders had become thoroughly Indianized, and that their expulsion was the work of the little known predecessors of the Guptas.

In A.D. 320 there arose a new Candra Gupta* whose successors in great measure restored the splendour of the Mauryas. He owed his rise to power largely to his marriage with a princess Kumāradevī of the tribe of the Licchavis, who now reappear on the scene, eight centuries after their defeat by Ajātaśatru. From the prominence given to the Licchavi princess in the genealogies of later Gupta kings, and the minting of special coins to commemorate her marriage to Candra Gupta (fig. xxiv*a*, p. 383), it seems that the Licchavis had profited by the absence of a strong central control to establish a new kingdom, and were very influential in Magadha at the time. Candra Gupta I possessed fairly large domains, including the regions of Magadha and Kosala.

Under his successor, Samudra Gupta (c. A.D. 335–316), Pāṭaliputra once more became the centre of a great empire. Samudra's power reached from Assam to the borders of the Panjāb. He aimed at the establishment of a closely knit empire of the Mauryan type, for in his great Allahābād inscription he is said to have "violently uprooted" no less than nine kings of Northern India, and to have annexed their kingdoms to his own. The martial tribes of Rājasthān, however, merely rendered him homage, as did several kingdoms on his frontiere, while in the Eastern Deccan, where Samudra led a successful expedition as far as Kāñcī (Kānchīpuram, Conjeeveram), the defeated kings were reinstated on giving homage and tribute, and probably heard little more of their titular overlord.

Samudra Gupta's main effort was in the direction of the west, where the Śakas had ruled for over 200 years and the land was enriched by the lucrative western trade. From their capital of Ujjayinī (modern Ujjain) the Śakas still controlled Mālwā and Gujarāt, and were a power to be reckoned with. Though Samudra's inscription makes a vague reference to his receiving homage from "the Śaka Lords", it is probable that he did not measure swords with them, or if he did was unsuccessful, for it is unlikely that he would have allowed them to remain independent if he could have prevented it. There is indeed a story that on his death the Śakas actually succeeded in shaking the Gupta Empire, and forced a weak king, Rāma Gupta, to conclude a dishonourable peace. Most authorities reject the story, and deny the historicity of Rāma Gupta, but the discovery of copper coins hearing this name tends to strengthen our belief that it has a basis of fact.[10]

---

* We divide the name into its two component parts to distinguish this king and Candra Gupta II from Candragupta Maurya. In Sanskrit the names are identical but the Gupta emperors evidently looked on the latter element of their names as a surname.

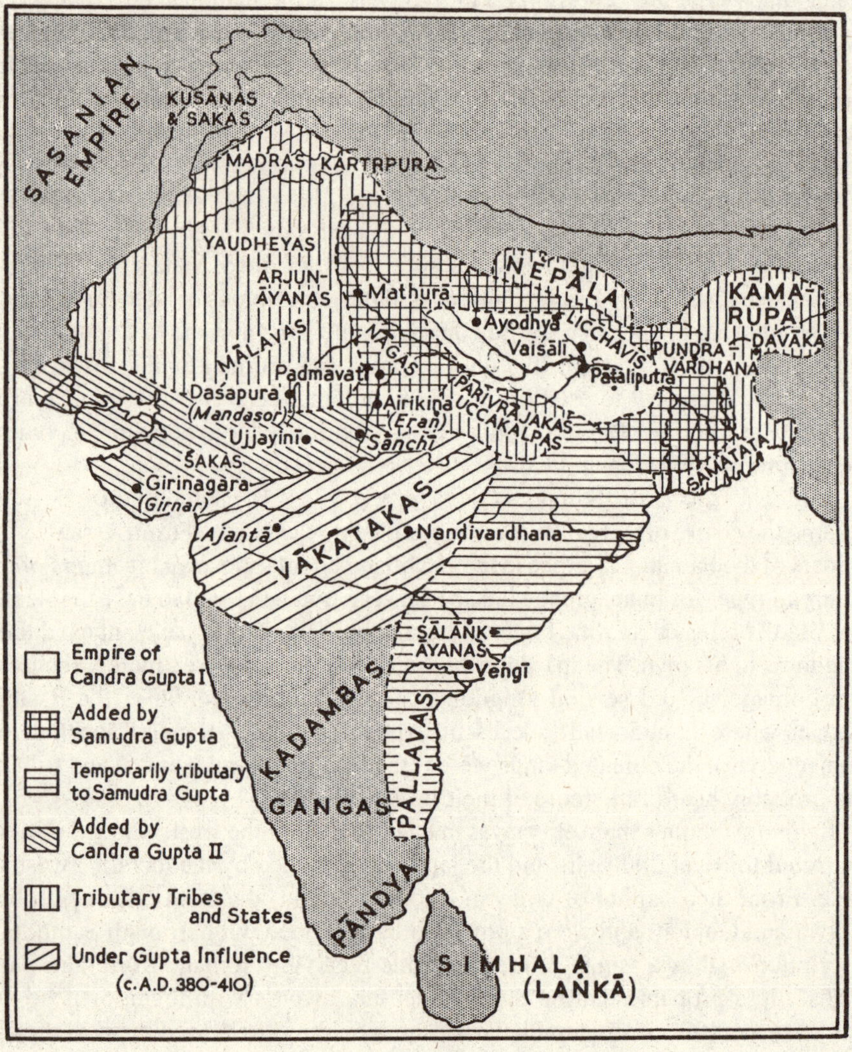

Fig. vii. The Gupta Empire

It was Candra Gupta II (c. 376–415), the son of Samudra and younger brother of the shadowy Rama Gupta, who finally defeated the Śakas, soon after A.D. 388. Thus he became the paramount sovereign of all Northern India, with the exception of the North-West; and he had some control over much of the Northern Deccan, thanks to the marriage of his daughter Prabhāvatī with Rudrasena, king of the Vākāṭakas, who ruled a large kingdom in the modern Madhya Pradesh, Mahārāshtra and north-western Āndhra Pradesh. Rudrasena died young, and his widow reigned until her sons came of age. It is evident from Prabhāvatī's charters that during her regency the Vākāṭaka court was much under Gupta influence.

The reign of Candra Gupta II perhaps marks the high watermark of ancient Indian culture. Later Indian legend tells of a great and good King Vikramāditya, who drove the Śakas out of Ujjayinī and ruled over all India, which was most prosperous and happy beneath his sceptre. Vikramāditya was certainly one of the titles of Candra Gupta II, and the legend seems therefore to refer to him. The only important discrepancy is that the traditional Vikramāditya is said to have founded the Vikrama Era, the most important of India's many systems of dating, which is still current in North India, and which commences in 58 B.C.; thus legend places him some 400 years too early. Kālidāsa, the greatest of India's poets and dramatists, is traditionally associated with Vikramāditya, and the internal evidence of his works points to the fact that he wrote at about this time.

The prosperity and happiness of Candra Gupta's empire is attested by another foreign traveller, unfortunately not as observant and informative as Megasthenes. This was Fa-hsien, a Chinese monk who came to India in order to obtain authentic copies of the Buddhist scriptures. The account of his travels gives much information about temples and monasteries and repeats many Buddhist legends, but only a few passing phrases mention social conditions, and nothing at all is said about Candra Gupta himself, although Fa-hsien was in India for some six years of his reign. The pilgrim did, however, note the peacefulness of India, the rarity of serious crime, and the mildness of the administration. He stated that it was possible to travel from one end of the country to the other without molestation, and without the need of passports. In his remarks on social custom he noted that all respectable people were now vegetarians, meat eating being confined to low castes and untouchables, in regard to whom he gives us the earliest clear reference to "pollution on approach". He found Buddhism still flourishing, but theistic Hinduism was very widespread.

The record of Fa-hsien shows that India had changed much since the days of Megasthenes, some 700 years earlier. The mild ethics of Buddhism and Jainism had gradually leavened Indian society, which was now more gentle and humane than in the days of the Mauryas. In place of the old sacrificial Brāhmaṇism, Hinduism had appeared, in form not very different from that of recent centuries. Soon harsher and more primitive elements were to re-emerge, but in the best days of the Gupta Empire Indian culture reached a perfection which it was never again to attain. At this time India was perhaps the happiest and most civilized region of the world, for the effete Roman Empire was nearing its destruction, and China was passing through a time of troubles between the two great periods of the Hans and the T'angs.

Candra Gupta II was succeeded by his son Kumāra Gupta I (c. 415–454), who, like Samudra Gupta, performed the Vedic horse-sacrifice which, at least in theory, might only be performed by great conquerors. There is no evidence, however, that he added to his realm, although for most of his reign he preserved it intact. But in the last years of Kumāra Gupta I the empire suffered a severe blow; as with many other important events of early Indian history, details are annoyingly absent, but it is clear that among the chief enemies with whom the Guptas had to contend were new invaders, called in India the Hūṇas. They were a Central Asian people, known to Byzantine writers as Hephthalites or White Huns, and it is usually considered that they were a branch of the great group of Turko-Mongol peoples who were threatening Europe at about the same time; certain modern scholars, however, claim that they were in no way related to the Huns of Attila, but were of Iranian stock.[11] The Hūṇas had occupied Bactria some time before, and now, like the earlier Greeks, Sakas and Kuṣāṇas, they crossed the mountains and attacked the plains of India; it is probable that kindred Central Asian tribes came in their train.

Once more Western India was the prey of fierce raiders, who were with the greatest difficulty kept at bay by the Emperor's son, Skanda Gupta. During the war with the Hūṇas Kumāra Gupta died, and Skanda Gupta (c. 454–467) assumed power, though not born of the chief queen and therefore not the regular heir to the throne. He succeeded in re-establishing the Gupta Empire, and by the end of 455 it was again at peace; but he reigned for little more than twelve years, and on his death the great days of the Guptas were over. The empire continued, but central control weakened, and local govemors became feudatory kings with hereditary rights. To the west of Vārāṇasī the Gupta emperors now exercised little more than titular control.

At the close of the 5th century fresh Hūna inroads occurred, and this time were even more difficult to repel. The empire was disunited, and no strong man of the calibre of Skanda Gupta came forward to drive out the invader. For some thirty years, from A.D. 500 onwards, Western India was in the hands of Hūṇa kings, two of whom, Toramāṇa and his son Mihirakula, were apparently mighty monarchs. The latter is remembered by the 7th-century Chinese traveller Hsüan Tsang as a fierce persecutor of Buddhism, and in Kashmīr, one of the centres of his power, memories of his sadistic tyranny were still alive in the 12th century, when they were recorded by the historian Kalhana. Mihirakula seems to have been driven from the plain of the Gangā by Narasimha Gupta, who had the cognomen Bālāditya, by which name he is remembered by Hsüan Tsang; about 530 Mihirakula was also defeated in Western India, this time by Yaśodharman, an energetic king of Mandasor, who built a large kingdom which did not survive his death. Though Mihirakula apparently retained his hold on Kashmīr and parts of the North-West, Hūṇa power never again seriously threatened India, and the

Hūṇas soon lost their individuality.

These incursions were the death-blow of the Gupta Empire, which by A.D. 550 had completely vanished. A new Gupta line, probably not related to the great one, ruled in Magadha until the 8th century. North of the Gangā another kingdom, that of the Maukharis, rose to prominence, and first gave importance to the city of Kānyakubja, the modern Kanauj, which until the coming of the Muslims was to be the cultural centre of Northern India and its largest and most prosperous city. In Gujarāt a line of Gupta feudatories, the Maitrakas, became strong and independent. Evidently all semblance of political unity had again vanished. It is at this time that we first hear of the Gurjaras, a new people who were to provide one of the strongest dynasties of the Middle Ages. The invasions of the Hūṇas destroyed or dispersed the older martial tribes of Rājasthān and their places were taken by newcomers, either acclimatized invaders or indigenous tribes from the hills, from whom most of the Rājput clans of the Middle Ages were descended.

The centre of interest now shifts for a time to Sthāṇvīśvara (modern Thānesar), in the watershed of the Satlaj and the Yamunā, which is so important for India's security, and where so many decisive battles have been fought. Here a local king, Prabhākaravardhana of the family of Puṣyabhūti, had grown in power as a result of successful raids on Western India and against the Hūṇas, who still held parts of the Panjāb. His mother was a princess of the second Gupta line, and his daughter, Rājyaśrī, was married to the Maukhari king Grahavarman. Thus Prabhākaravardhana kept on good terms with his neighbours in the east, while he gathered strength in the west. But the Guptas and Maukharis were hereditary enemies, and at about the time of Prabhākaravardhana's death war broke out between them. Rājyavardhana, the new king of Sthāṇvīśvara, hurried to the support of the Maukharis, while the Guptas had the assistance of Śaśāṇka, the king of Bengal. In the war both Grahavarman of Kānyakubja and Rājyavardhana of Sthāṇ vīśvara were killed. The former died without an heir, and the two kingdoms were combined under Harsavardhana or Harṣa, the second son of Prabhākaravardhana and the brother-in-law of Grahavarman.

Harṣa ascended the throne in 606 at the age of sixteen, and in the forty-one years of his reign he succeeded in partially restoring the glories of the Guptas. Some of his fame is due to the fact that, in comparison with most other early Indian kings, his reign is remarkably well documented. The poet Bāṇa, who was patronized by Harṣa, has left a florid account of the events leading up to his rise to power (p. 448ff), while in the latter part of his reign India was visited by another Chinese pilgrim, Hsüan Tsang, who wrote a very valuable description of India, which, unlike the account of Megasthenes, has survived intact. While his main purpose, like that of Fa-hsien, was to obtain Buddhist manuscripts and visit sacred sites, Hsüan Tsang was less other-worldly than the earlier pilgrim, and he was in close touch with Harṣa, whom he much admired and who gave him an honoured place at his court. His work is therefore of much greater historical value than that of Fa-hsien.

Although Harṣa gained control of most of Northern India, from Gujarāt to

Bengal, his empire was feudal in structure. Outside the immediate domains of Kānyakubja and Sthāṇvīśvara many of the old kings retained their thrones. Śaśāṇka, the fierce anti-Buddhist king of Bengal who overran Magadha at the time of Harṣa's accession, was driven back to his own domains and his kingdom fell to Harsa, but Deva Gupta, the king who had been chiefly responsible for the downfall of Harṣa's brother-in-law Grahavarman Maukhari, was replaced by a relative, Mādhava Gupta, and the Maitraka king of Gujarāt, after being defeated by Harṣa, was allowed to retain his throne as a vassal. Harṣa controlled his great empire by ceaselessly travelling from province to province, both in his own domains and in those of his feudatories, who seem to have spent much time in attendance on their overlord. When he died without heirs it is not surprising that his empire fell to pieces.

Harṣa seems to have been a man of great gifts and intense energy. As Candragupta by Megasthenes, he is described by Hsüan Tsang as hearing the complaints of his humbler subjects with unwearying patience, not in his audience hall, but in a small travelling pavilion by the roadside. He loved pomp, however, and in his progresses he was accompanied by a tremendous train of attendants, courtiers, officials, Buddhist monks, and brāhmaṇs. He was a loyal and warm friend, and, if we can believe the sources, fantastically generous to those whom he favoured. He loved philosophy and literature, and in his leisure found time to write three very competent dramas (p. 393).

His empire was very extensive. Even Bhāskaravarman, the king of remote Assam, attended his court, and if not technically feudatory to him was much under his influence. It would seem that Bhāskaravarman assisted Harsa against Śaśāṇ ka at the beginning of his reign, and the two kings were lifelong friends. Only in the Deccan Harṣa could make no progress. Here he attacked the Cālukya king Pulakeśin II, but was thoroughly defeated, and could never again pass the Narmadā.

Hsüan Tsang shows that Buddhism was definitely declining in India at this time, although in the latter part of his reign Harṣa fell increasingly under its influence. Now certain elements of later Hinduism, of which there are few traces in the time of the Guptas, were strongly in evidence. The growth of tantric cults (p. 295) and of such practices as widow-burning (p. 162f) shows that a cultural decline had already set in. Law and order were not as well maintained as in Gupta times, for, in contrast to Fa-hsien, who was so impressed by the peaceable and law-abiding state of India, Hsüan Tsang was twice robbed by bandits in Harṣa's domains, and on one occasion was nearly sacrificed to the goddess Durgā by river pirates, in the very heart of the empire.

THE MIDDLE AGES IN THE NORTH

The history of the succeeding centuries is a rather drab story of endemic warfare between rival dynasties. It can be followed in some detail, thanks to the numerous inscriptions and copper-plate charters of the period, but the detail is monotonous and uninteresting to all but the specialist.

On Harṣa's death there was great confusion. A usurper, Aruṇāśva, temporarily seized Kānyakubja, and attacked Wang Hsüan-ts'ê, who had come with a small detachment of troops as ambassador to Harṣa from the Chinese emperor T'ai-tsung. Wang escaped with his little force and gathered an army from Tibet, Nepal and Assam; with the aid of this he captured Aruṇāśva, who was taken back to China to end his days in attendance on the T'ang Emperor. After this Bhāskaravarman of Assam extended his power westwards, and occupied part of Magadha. Meanwhile the second Gupta dynasty revived, and Ādityasena Gupta was the most important monarch of the latter half of the 7th century, and one of the last great Indian kings to perforal the Vedic horse-sacrifice. Early in the 8th century an upstart named Yaśovarman established an empire at Kānyakubja, which for a while controlled much of the North, but which soon fell to Lalitāditya, one of the few kings of Kashmīr to play an important part in the politics of the Gangetic Plain. In the following two centuries two great dynasties, the Pālas of Bihār and Bengal, and the Gurjara-Pratihāras of Kānyakubja, divided the hegemony of most of Northern India between them.

The Pālas of Eastern India were the first to gain the ascendancy, and for a while, in the early part of the 9th century, were the masters of Kānyakubja. The long reign of the great king Dharmapāla (c. 770–810) marks the apogee of Pāla power; by the time of his death control of Kānyakubja was lost, but his successor, Devapāla (c. 810–850), was still a very important king and was in diplomatic contact with the Śailendra kings of Sumātra. The Pāla kings are chiefly notable for their patronage of Buddhism, which, in a rather corrupt form, flourished in their dominions during the three centuries of their rule. It was from the Pāla empire that Buddhism was introduced into Tibet, where, combined with many native beliefs, it survives to the present day.

In the 9th and 10th centuries the Gurjara-Pratihāras, who probably originated in Rājasthān, were masters of Kānyakubja and were the most powerful kings of Northern India. They successfully resisted the Arabs, who in 712 had occupied Sind and who for over a century made frequent attacks on their eastern neighbours. The two most powerful Pratihāra kings, Mihira Bhoja (c. 840–885) and Mahendrapāla (c. 885–910), pushed back the Pālas, and were overlords of most of Northern India as far as the borders of Bengal. But they were weakened by the repeated invasions of the Rāṣṭrakūṭas of the Deccan, who temporarily occupied Kānyakubja in 916. These persīstent raids from the south seem to have turned the attention of the Pratihāra kings away from the North-West, where new forces were gathering which were ultimately to overthrow Hindu India. Though they regained their capital after its occupation by the Rāṣṭrakūṭas, the Pratihāras never regained their strength, and throughout the 10th century their feudatories grew more and more influential at the expense of their former masters.

In Afghānistān a line of Turkish chieftains had established a powerful kingdom at Ghaznī, and began to look covetously at the rich plains of India. In 986 one of their amirs, Sabuktigīn, made his first attack on the most important king of N.-W.

Fig. viii. India in the early 11th century, A.D.
(Names in parentheses are of dynasties which were feudatory at the time, but became important later)

India, Jayapāla; in a second raid he occupied Peshāwar. In 997 he was succeeded by his son Mahmūd, who soon embarked on a deliberate policy of raiding the rich and divided kingdoms of India. In 1001 he defeated and captured Jayapāla, who committed suicide. Jayapāla's son Ānandapāla formed a league of Hindu princes against the invader, but the unwieldy and disunited Indian forces, basing their strategy and tactics on ancient precepts and relying on the unpredictable morale of the fighting elephant, were defeated near Peshāwar by the smaller and more mobile Muslim army, and the whole of India lay open to the invader. Between 1001 and 1027 Mahmūd made seventeen great raids on India. The whole western half of the land felt the force of the *Turuṣkas*; palaces and temples were looted and desecrated, and enormous caravans of booty and slaves were taken back to Ghaznī. The raids reached as far as the great shrine of Somnāth in Saurāshtra and the kingdom of the Candellas in Bundelkhand. Among India's great cities Kānyakubja and Mathurā were captured and plundered.

Mahmūd did not remain in India, however, for, though Muslim chroniclers depict him as a staunch propagator of Islām, intent on converting the infidel and bringing India under the control of the true faith, his expeditions were for the purpose rather of plunder than of conquest. But the N.-W. Frontier and the Panjāb were annexed to his kingdom, as were the Arab kingdoms of Sind, which had long ceased to be a menace to the rest of India. After the sack of Kānyakubja the great Pratihāra dynasty, which had been losing power for a hundred years, soon disappeared. Its last important king, Rājyapāla, was defeated and dethroned by his neighbour Vidyādhara the Candella, whose kingdom had formerly been tributary to the Pratihāras and who profited by their discomfiture at the hands of the Muslims to extend his own power; but Vidyādhara himself was too weak to resist Mahmūd effectively, and was forced to pay him tribute

For about a century and a half Northern India retained its independence. In Vārānasī and Kānyakubja a new ruling family, the Gāhaḍavālas, managed to build a fairly prosperous kingdom. In Rājasthān the dynasty of the Cāhamānas rose in prominence and power. The influence of the Candellas of Bundelkhand grew with the fall of the Pratihāras. In Gujarāt there ruled the prosperous line of the Caulukyas or Solāṇkīs, much under the influence of Jainism. In Mālwā the Paramāra dynasty flourished under King Bhoja (1018–1055), famous in legend, who was an accomplished scholar and a great builder of dams and artificial lakes for irrigation (p. 168f). Madhya Pradesh was in the hands of the Kalacuri dynasty. In Bengal the Pālas were replaced by the Senas, who were strong supporters of orthodox Hinduism, and who inaugurated something of an anti-Buddhist reaction.

Thus Northern India, in the twilight of Hindu independence, was hopelessly divided. As well as the main dynasties whose names we have mentioned there were many lesser lines, theoretically tributary to the greater, but virtually independent in their own territories and always ready to revolt against their overlords. The conservative kings of India had learnt no lessons from Mahmūd's raids. They were still incapable of serious co-operation, and their enormous armies were slow and unwieldy. At the end of the 12th century the three chief kings of Northern India—Pṛthvīrāja Cāhamāna, Jayaccandra Gāhaḍavāla, and Paramardīdeva Candella*—were in a state of tripartite war.

A new Turkish ruling house supplanted the line of Mahmūd in Afghānistān. In 1173 Ghiyās-ud-dīn of Ghor annexed Ghaznī. His younger brother, Shihāb-ud-dīn, usually known as Muhammad of Ghor, proceeded to conquer the Ghaznavid possessions in the Panjāb and Sind, and then turned his attention to the Hindu states. The initiative in resistance came from Pṛthvīrāja, who patched up his quarrels and prepared to meet the invader. In 1191 the Hindu army met Muhammad at Tarāin, not far from Thānesar, which had once been the capital of the great Harṣa. The invaders were defeated, but in the following year they returned with a larger force. This time the mounted archers of the Muslims overpowered the Hindu army and Pṛthvīrāja was defeated and killed. He is remembered to this day by the Rājputs as a model of chivalry and courage, and is the hero of many folk ballads.

Muhammad returned home, and left the work of conquest to his generals. The chief of these, Qutb-ud-dīn Aibak, occupied Delhī, an important city of the Cāhamāna kingdom, and made it his headquarters. Another general, Muhammad ibn Bakhtiyār, pressed on down the Gangā and overran Bihār, where he put many Buddhist monks to the sword. He then occupied Bengal with little difficulty. The Candella kingdom of Bundelkhand fell in 1203. In 1206 Muhammad, who had succeeded his brother as sultan of Ghor, was assassinated and his general Qutb-ud-dīn, a manumitted slave, became the first sultan of Delhi.

In Rājasthān and other outlying districts Hindu kingdoms continued, sometimes paying tribute to the more energetic sultans but often virtually free, while regions with sharply defined natural boundaries, such as Kashmīr, Nepāl, Assam and Orissā, retained their autonomy. These kingdoms had always been in effect independent, only occasionally rendering tribute and homage to the greater kings of the Plains, and in general they had little political effect on India as a whole, and were little affected by it politically. From now on, until the 18th century, Muslim rulers dominated Northern India, and the great days of Hindu civilization were at an end.

THE MIDDLE AGES IN THE PENINSULA

While in Northern India Hindu culture declined somewhat after the Gupta age, in the Deccan it flourished and advanced. By this time Āryan influence had penetrated the whole of the Peninsula, and the contact of Āryan and Dravidian produced a

* These names are often met in their Hindi forms: Prithvītrāj or Pithorā Chāuhān, Jaichand Gāharwār, and Parmāl Candel.

vigorous cultural synthesis, which in turn had an immense influence on Indian civilization as a whole.

Power was generally centred on two foci, one in the Western Deccan and the other in the Cōla country, the Coromandel coast. The political history of the medieval Deccan is largely concerned with the struggles between the dynasties controlling these two centres. Many lesser kingdoms also existed, however, often tributary to the larger ones but sometimes rising to considerable power.

In the Northern Deccan the Vākāṭakas vanished at about the same time as the Guptas, and in the middle of the 6th century the west and centre of the Peninsula came under the control of the Cālukya Dynasty, ruling from Vātāpi (now called Bādāmi) in Mysore. Its greatest king, Pulakeśin II (c. 609–642), was the approximate contemporary of Harṣa, whom he successfully resisted, only to be defeated at the end of his reign by Narasiṃhavarman, the Pallava king of Kāñcī (Kanchīpuram). The Pallavas, who had been ruling since the 4th century, were great temple builders (p. 313), and seem to have much encouraged the growth of Āryan institutions in the South.

In the 7th century the Cālukyas divided into eastern and western branches, and in the following century the western branch was replaced by the Rāṣṭrakūṭas of Mānyakheṭa (modern Mālkhed in Mysore), whose martial efforts were largely directed against the North, and who made many raids beyond the Narmadā. A revived Cālukya line, ruling from Kalyāṇī, replaced the Rāṣṭrakūṭas in 973, and controlled the Deccan until the end of the 12th century, when their empire was divided between the Yādavas of Devagiri in the Northern Deccan, the Kākatīyas of Warangal in the Telugu-speaking areas of the east, and the Hoysaḷas of Dōrasamudra in Mysore.

The Pallavas of Kāñcī persisted with declining fortunes to the end of the 9th century, when their territories were annexed by the Cōla kings of Tānjuvūr (Tanjore), Āditya I (c. 870–906), and Parāntaka I (c. 906–953). The Cōla kingdom, one of the three great kingdoms of Tamil tradition, had been virtually submerged by the Pallavas for centuries. Now it rose again, and for some 300 years ruled the Coromandel Coast and much of the southern part of the Peninsula, giving a large measure of security to its people and supporting a flourishing social and cultural life. The most notable of the Cola kings were Rājarāja I (985–1014) and Rājendra I (1014–1042), in whose reigns the power of the dynasty reached its zenith. The former conquered Ceylon, and the latter carried his power by land to the mouth of the Gangā, and sent out a great naval expedition, which occupied parts of Burma, Malaya and Sumātra. This was perhaps despatched with the intention of suppressing the piratical activities of the Indonesian kings, who interfered with the flourishing trade between South India and China. The Cōla hold on S.-E. Asia does not appear to have lasted long, however, and Rājendra's naval expedition is unique in the annals of India.

The Cōla held Northern Ceylon until soon after 1070, when they were expelled by the Sinhalese king Vijayabāhu I (1070–1114). From now on the Cōla power declined, and the Pāṇḍya kings of Madurai were continually attempting to regain their independence, while pressure from the Cālukyas increased. Vijayabāhu of Ceylon inaugurated a period of success and prosperity for the island, which culminated in the reign of Parākramabāhu I (1153–1186), the greatest of Sinhalese kings (pl. LX*a*), whose splendour can be seen in the remains of his capital, Polonnaruva, whither the seat of government had been transferred from the earlier capital of Anurādhapura at the time of the Tamil invasions. Parākramabāhu for a while turned the tables on the Tamils, and Sinhalese troops, profiting by the Pāṇḍyan rebellions against the Cōlas, attacked the Indian coast and even temporarily occupied Madurai.

Though their power declined, the Cōlas long maintained the central part of their empire, the region around Kāñcī and Tānjuvūr. The political stability and freedom from attack afforded by their efficient government greatly encouraged Tamil culture, and the large number of donative inscriptions of this period testifies to a flourishing economy. Administratively the Cōla Empire is remarkable for the influence exerted by local autonomous bodies; village and district councils, under the supervision of the central government, introduced an element into the structure of the state which, if not democratic, was at least popular (p. 91).

The Cōlas fell in the 13th century, when their territory was shared by the Hoysaḷ as of Mysore and the revived Pāṇḍya dynasty of Madurai. Now the Deccan was soon to feel the force of Islām, which was already the master of Northern India. In the reign of the able sultan of Delhi, Alā'-ud-dīn Khaljī (1296–1515), a series of brilliant raids led by the eunuch general Malik Kāfūr, a converted Hindu, crushed the Deccan kingdoms, and for a time a Muslim sultanate was set up even in Madurai, in the extreme south.

The Dravidians were not finally subjugated, however. In 1336, within a few years of Malik Kāfūr's raids, an independent Hindu kingdom was founded at Vijayanagara, on the Tuṅgabhadrā River. This kingdom, after desperately resisting the Bahmanī sultans of the Northern Deccan, established its hegemony over the whole Peninsula from the Kṛṣṇā River southwards. Learning something of military strategy from their Muslim enemies, the kings of Vijayanagara maintained their independence until the middle of the 16th century, and, in a reduced form, even later. Of the splendour and affluence of their capital we have European accounts, from the Italian Nicolo dei Conti, who visited India in the early 15th century, and from the Portuguese travellers Paes and Nuniz, who about a hundred years later made contact with the kingdom of Vijayanagara from the recently established Portuguese settlement of Goa. All were impressed by the splendour of the capital and the wealth of the court.

The great king Kṛṣṇa Deva Rāya (1509–1529) (pl. LXXI), had he lived longer, might have driven the Muslims from the Deccan altogether. Of him Paes wrote in terms rarely used by a European traveller of an oriental monarch:

> "He is the most feared and perfect king that could possibly be, cheerful of disposition and very merry; he is one that seeks to honour foreigners, ...

asking about all their affairs whatever their condition may be. He is a great ruler and a man of much justice, but subject to sudden fits of rage. ... He is by rank a greater lord than any, by reason of what he possesses in armies and territories, but... he has nothing compared to what a man like him ought to have, so gallant and perfect is he in all things."[12]

Paes, in the reign of Kṛṣṇa Deva Rāya, remarked on the prosperity of the people and the cheapness of provisions; but Nuniz, the second Portuguese traveller, who visited Vijayanagara in the reign of Kṛṣṇa's successor Acyuta (1529–42), was less impressed, and stated that the underlings of the king were overbearing and the common people much oppressed. It is evident that the beneficient regime of Kṛṣṇa Deva Rāya was not continued after his death. His successors were weaker men than he, and embroiled themselves unnecessarily in the intrigues of the Muslim sultanates of the Northern Deccan, relying on the prestige gained for them by their more powerful predecessor. In 1565 the *de facto* ruler of Vijayanagara, Rāma Rāja, was utterly defeated at Tālikoṭa by a coalition of Deccan sultans, the great city was mercilessly sacked, and the greatness of the empire was at an end.

This was the last important Hindu kingdom of the older type. That of the Marāthās, which arose in the Western Deccan in the late 17th century and was the most forceful element in Indian politics in the 18th, lies beyond our province.

The ultimate importance of this period in the history of the Peninsula was cultural and religious. Jainism was once very strong in Mysore and other parts of the South, and often, under royal patronage, it became virtually the state religion. But in the Tamil country at this period a new ecstatically devotional theism arose, looking for inspiration rather to hymns in the vernacular than to the Vedas or earlier sacred texts in Sanskrit. This was subsequently to set the standard for the popular religion of the whole of India, through the work of missionary theologians who travelled all over the sub-continent in the later middle ages. The work and influence of the great medieval Dravidian saints and philosophers will be discussed in another chapter.

This brief outline of the political history of Hindu India shows that she produced many bold adventurers and imperious conquerors. As our following chapter tells, they were ruthless in gaining and retaining power, and looked on war as a normal political expedient. Except during the Mauryan period political unity was unknown, and the highly organized and tightly controlled administration of the ancient Indian state had no counterpart in inter-state relations, where endemic anarchy was only mitigated by a tradition of fair play in warfare, which was by no means always followed. Here, and in the conservatism of the medieval period, lay the great weakness of Hindu India, which made her a prey to successive invaders. Of these the wild tribes of Central Asia were rapidly assimilated, but the Muslims, with their rigidly codified religion, were too much for even the omnivorous Hindu culture to digest. Interaction between the two religions and ways of life indeed took place, and once at least a *modus vivendi* was almost reached (p. 432). It is not wholly surprising, however, that, when India began to reassert herself, two nations should have replaced the single British Rāj; but all impartial students must regret that the unity of the Indian sub-continent has been once more lost, and trust that India and Pākistān may soon forget the bitterness born of centuries of strife, in co-operation for the common welfare of their peoples.

PLATE I

Max Hürlimann, "Indien", Atlantis Verlag, Zürich

The Plains. Irrigation near Chingleput, Madras.

PLATE II

(a) The Jungle. Western Ghāts

Max Hürlimann, "Indien", Atlantis Verlag, Zürich

(b) The Hills. Amarnāth, Kashmīr

Ministry of Information and Broadcasting, New Delhi

(c) The Deccan Plateau. Fortress of Devagiri

A. L. Basham

PLATE III

(a) Irrigation. The "Sea of Parākrama", Polonnaruva, Ceylon

A. L. Basham

A. L. Basham

(b) The Edge of the Plain. Site of Rājagrha, Bihār

(c) The Gangā, Vārānasī

A. L. Basham

PLATE IV

Pioneers of Indology

From the painting by Sir Joshua Reynolds, by courtesy of the Earl of Spencer

Sir William Jones

Institution of Royal Engineers

Sir Alexander Cunningham

Bhāndārkar Institute, Poona

Sir R. G. Bhāndārkar

Sir John Marshall

Sir John Marshall

PLATE V

Crayon Drawing by Alan Sorrell. Festival of Britain Trustees

Mohenjo Daro. A Hypothetical Reconstruction

PLATE VI

Dept. of Archaeology, Government of India

(a) "First Street", Mohenjo Daro

Dept. of Archaeology, Government of India and Messrs. Arthur Probsthain, London

b) The Great Bath, Mohenjo Daro

PLATE VII

Dept. of Archaeology, Government of India and Messrs. Arthur Probsthain, London

Statuette of a Bearded Man, Mohenjo Daro

PLATE VIII

Messrs. Faber & Faber, Royal Academy Trustees and Museum of Central Asian Antiquities, New Delhi

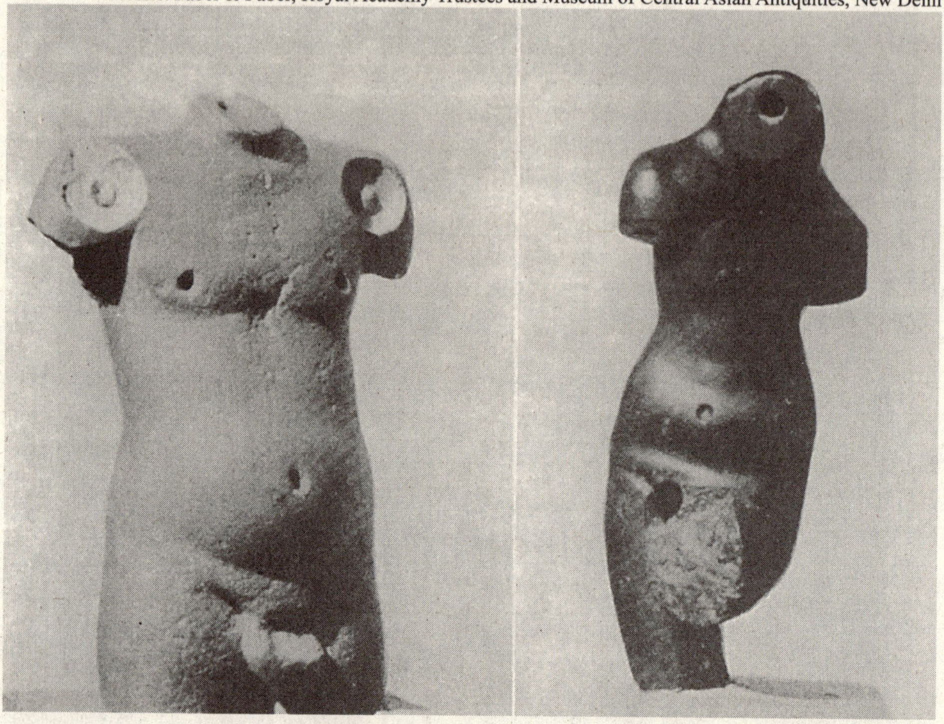

(a) Male Torsos, Harappā

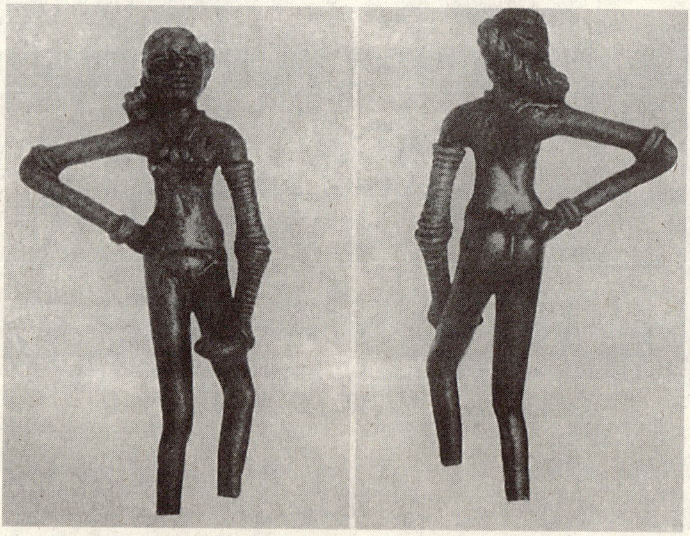

Dept. of Archaeology, Government of India and Messrs. Arthur Probsthain, London

(b) Bronze Statuette of a Girl, Mohenjo Daro

PLATE IX

(a–f) Seals of the Harappā Culture

Dept. of Archaeology, Government of India and Messrs. Arthur Probsthain, London

a) Bull with Cult-object

b) Humped Bull

c) Horned God with Animals

d) Worship of a Tree-goddess

e) Hero Grappling with Tigers

f) Fight between Horned Man (Tree-god?) and Horned Tiger

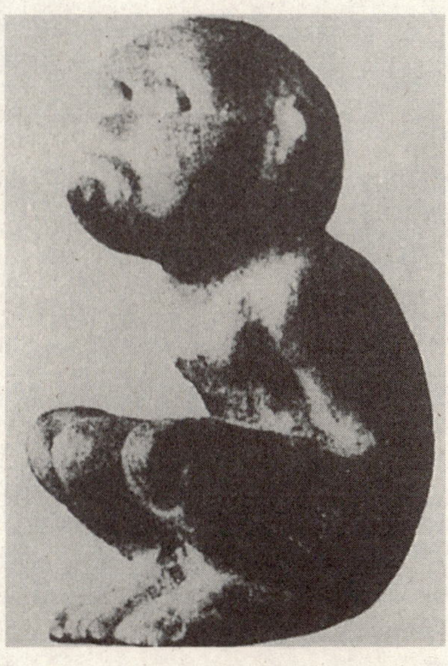

(g) Monkey. Harappā Culture

PLATE X

Dept. of Archaeology, Government of India and Messrs. Arthur Probsthain, London

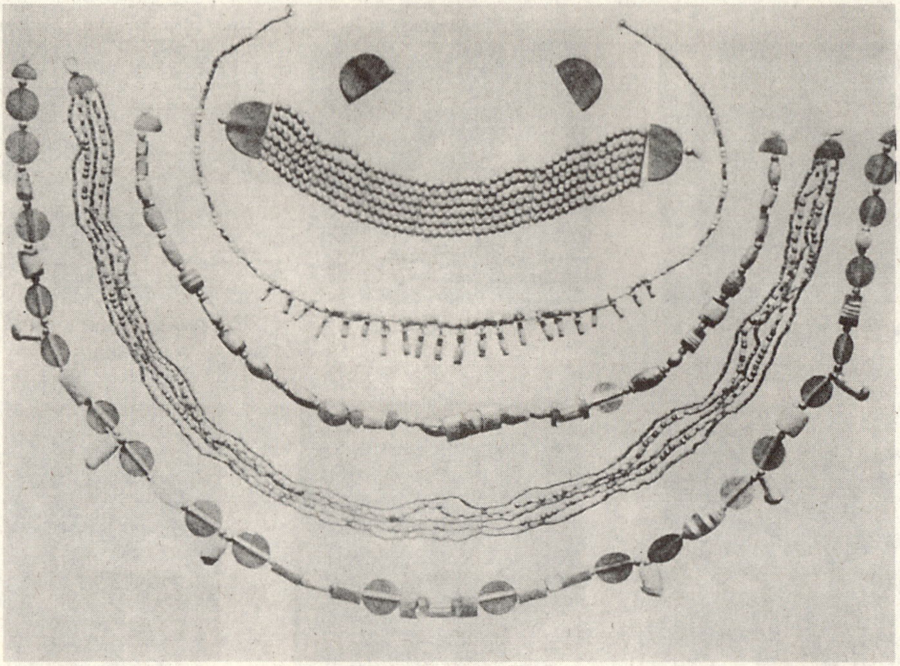

(a) Jewellery, Mohenjo Daro

Dept. of Archaeology, Government of India

(b) Mauryan Column, Lauriyā Nandangarh, Bihār

A. L. Basham

(c) The Column of Heliodoras, Besnagar, M.P.

PLATE XI

Dept. of Archaeology, Government of India

(a) Aerial View of the site of Śiśupālgarh. Approximately 1 mile square. 1st–2nd century A.D.

A. L. Basham

b) The Great Stūpa, Sānchī, M.P. 2nd-1st century B.C.

A. L. Basham

a) Dhamekh Stūpa, Sārnāth, near Banarās, with foundations of monasteries. Gupta period

A. L. Basham

b) The Great Stūpa, Nālandā

A. L. Basham

c) Remains of Monasteries, Nālandā

A. L. Basham

d) Corner Turret, Great Stūpa, Nālandā

Professor B. Rowland Harvard University

The Great Caitya-hall, Kārlī, Bombay, c. 1st century B.C. – 1st century A.D.

PLATE XIV

Dept. of Archaeology, Government of India

(a) Façade of Cave XIX, Ajantā. Gupta Period

A. L. Basham

(b) The Caves of Ajantā

PLATE XV

Kailāsanātha Rock-temple, Ellorā. 8th Century A.D.

Max Hürlimann, "Indien", Atlantis Verlag, Zürich

a) General View

A. L. Basham

b) Column (*dhvajastambha*) in the Courtyard

A. L. Basham

c) Pillar

PLATE XVI

Fogg Art Museum, Harvard University

(a) Shore Temple, Māmallapuram. End of 7th Century A.D.

b) Temple, Somnāthpur, Mysore

IV

THE STATE: POLITICAL LIFE AND THOUGHT

SOURCES

FROM the days of Plato and Aristotle European thought has turned its attention to such questions as the origin of the state, the ideal form of government, and the basis of law, and politics has long been looked on as a branch of philosophy. India also thought about such questions, but she had no schools of political philosophy in the Western sense. The problems which form the stock-in-trade of the European political philosopher are answered in Indian texts, but in a take-it-or-leave-it manner, with little discussion; often indeed the only argument in favour of a proposition is the citation of an old legend, used much as Plato's adaptations of older myths to reinforce his theories.

Though India had no formal political philosophy, the science of statecraft was much cultivated, and a number of important textbooks on this topic have survived. *Daṇḍanīti*, the administration of force, or *rājanīti*, the conduct of kings, was a severely practical science, and the texts cursorily dismiss the more philosophical aspect of politics, but give comparatively detailed advice on the organization of the state and the conduct of governmental affairs. The later Vedic literature tells us something, incidentally, about political life and thought in the pre-Buddhist period, and we can gather much from the Pāli scriptures of Buddhism; but the earliest and most important textbook specifically devoted to statecraft is the *Kauṭilīya Arthaśāstra*, which is attributed to Kauṭilya, the famous minister of Candragupta Maurya (p. 44). Some authorities still maintain the full authenticity of the work, but there are grave objections to this view. The text refers to people and places (notably China) which do not seem to have been known to the Indians in the 4th century B.C. It does not use much of the official terminology employed in the Aśokan inscriptions or in the Pāli scriptures, but it contains many governmental terms which apparently did not become popular until post-Mauryan times. Yet it is certainly pre-Guptan, and is, we believe, the elaboration of a Mauryan original which was perhaps the work of Kautilya himself. Whatever its age, the *Arthaśāstra* gives very detailed instructions on the control of the state, the organization of the national economy, and the conduct of war, and it is a most precious source-book for many aspects of ancient Indian life.

The next important source, in chronological order, is the great epic, the *Mahābhārata*, of which the twelfth book, known as the *Śānti Parvan*, is a collection of many disparate passages on statecraft and human conduct, inserted into the body of the epic in the early centuries of the Christian era. Other passages on statecraft are found elsewhere in the *Mahābhārata*, and in the second of the great epics, the *Rāmāyaṇa*. The large body of literature generally called *Smṛti*, giving instruction in the Sacred Law, is very important in this connexion, and will be discussed later (p. 113f); especially significant is the seventh section of the lawbook ascribed to the primeval sage Manu, probably composed early in the Christian era.

From the Gupta period and the Middle Ages a number of political texts survive, the most important of which are the *Nītisāra* ("Essence of Politics") of Kāmandaka, perhaps written during the Gupta period, and the *Nitivākyāmṛta* ("Nectar of Aphorisms on Politics") of Somadeva Sūri, a Jaina writer of the 10th century.* These repeat much that has been said before, but here and there contain original ideas. Besides sources specifically dealing with political life and thought, ancient Indian literature as a whole, from the *Ṛg Veda* onwards, yields much information, and inscriptions of one kind and another are extremely valuable in this connexion.

The texts do not discuss wholly impossible utopias; their advice is often pedantic, but usually more or less feasible. However, it is not likely that any king conducted his affairs wholly on textbook lines, and there is ample evidence that the recommendations of the experts were not always put into effect. The reader must always bear in mind that in the texts on statecraft and Sacred Law the authors describe things not as they were in fact, but as they believed they ought to be. Probably in no kingdom of ancient India, not even in that of the Mauryas, was the influence of the state quite so all-pervading as in the system envisaged by the *Arthaśāstra*, though its author evidently based his precept upon current practice. Similarly the vicious punishments laid down by Manu for religious crimes (for example a śūdra who "arrogantly teaches brāhmaṇs their duty" shall have boiling oil poured in his mouth and ears[1]) are the suggestions of a fanatic and were rarely if ever put into practice. Moreover the texts are permeated with pedantry, and show the passion for sterile classification to which the Indian pandit has often been prone. It is unlikely that the more energetic and self-reliant rulers worried overmuch about the *Arthaśāstra's* discussion of different schools of thought on such questions as whether it is better to acquire a wild and rebellious but prosperous country, or a pacific but poor one. Many errors have been made by historians through their uncritical acceptance of these political texts as giving an exact picture of things as they were.

KINGSHIP

The earliest legend about the origin of kingship occurs in the *Aitareya Brāhmaṇa*,[2] one of the later Vedic texts, perhaps of the 8th or 7th century B.C. This tells how the gods and demons were at war, and the gods were suffering badly at the hands of their enemies. So they met together and decided that they needed a *rājā* to lead

* The Nītiśāstra of Śukra has now been shown with practical certainty to be a work of the early 19th century, perhaps written for the benefit of a Marāthā prince subordinate to the East India Company (L. Gopal, BSOAS xxv, pp. 524-56). It is ignored in this book.

them in battle. They appointed Soma* as their king, and the tide soon turned in their favour. This legend suggests that in the earliest times kingship in India was thought to be based upon human need and military necessity, and that the king's first duty was to lead his subjects in war. A little later the *Taittirīya Upaniṣad*[3] repeats the story, but in a significantly altered form; the discomfited gods did not elect their ruler, but sacrificed to the high god Prajāpati, who sent his son Indra to become their king. At this stage the king was still thought of as primarily a leader in war—"they who have no king cannot fight" says the text—but kingship was already given divine sanction and the king of the immortals, who was the prototype of all earthly kings, held his office by the appointment of the Most High.

Even at this time, before the days of the Buddha, the king was exalted far above ordinary mortals through the magical power of the great royal sacrifices. The Royal Consecration (*rājasūya*), which in its full form comprised a series of sacrifices lasting for over a year, imbued the king with divine power. In the course of the ceremonies he was identified with Indra "because he is a kṣatriya and because he is a sacrificer",[4] and even with the high god Prajāpati himself.[5] He took three steps on a tiger's skin, and was thus magically identified with the god Viṣṇu, whose three paces covered earth and heaven. The chief priest addressed the gods with the words: "Of mighty power is he who has been consecrated; now he has become one of yours; you must protect him."[6] The king was evidently the fellow of the gods, if not a god himself.

The magical power which pervaded the king at his consecration was restored and strengthened in the course of his reign by further rites, such as the *vājapeya*, in essence a sort of rejuvenation ceremony, and the horse-sacrifice (*aśvamedha*, p. 43), which not only ministered to his ambition and arrogance, but also ensured the prosperity and fertility of the kingdom. Implicit in the whole brāhmaṇic ritual was the idea of the king's divine appointment, and though the rājasūya was replaced in later times by a simplified *abhiṣeka*, or anointment, the ceremony still had this magical flavour.

But the centre of brāhmaṇic culture was the Gangā-Yamunā Doāb. If among the Kurus and Pañcālas, who were the chief tribes of this region, the king was hedged about with divine mystery, elsewhere his status may have been less exalted, for the Buddhists had their own legend of the origin of kingship, which involved no heavenly prototype but looked back to a primitive social contract.[7] The story of this is put into the mouth of the Buddha himself, and, whether or not it is really his, it certainly represents the thought on the subject in the eastern part of India in the centuries following the Buddha's death, for the Jainas, who appeared at about the same time and in the same region, had a somewhat similar legend.[8]

In the early days of the cosmic cycle mankind lived on an immaterial plane, dancing on air in a sort of fairyland, where there was no need of food or clothing, and no private property, family, government or laws. Then gradually the process

* Probably this is an early priestly emendation for Indra, who figures as king of the gods in other contexts.

of cosmic decay began its work, and mankind became earthbound, and felt the need of food and shelter. As men lost their primeval glory distinctions of class (*varṇa*) arose, and they entered into agreements one with another, accepting the institutions of private property and the family. With this theft, murder, adultery, and other crime began, and so the people met together and decided to appoint one man from among them to maintain order in return for a share of the produce of their fields and herds. He was called "the Great Chosen One" (*Mahāsammata*), and he received the title of rājā because he pleased the people. The derivation of the word *rājā* from the verb *rañjayati* ("he pleases") is certainly a false one, but it was widely maintained and is found even in non-Buddhist sources.

The story of the Mahāsammata gives, in the form of a myth worthy of Plato, one of the world's earliest versions of the widespread contractual theory of the state, which in Europe is specially connected with the names of Locke and Rousseau. It implies that the main purpose of government is to establish order, and that the king, as head of the government, is the first social servant, and ultimately dependent on the suffrage of his subjects. Thus in ancient Indian thought on the question of the origin of monarchy two strands are evident, the mystical and the contractual, often rather incongruously combined.

In thought, if not in practice, it was the mystical theory of kingship which carried most weight with succeeding generations. The author of the *Arthaśāstra* had no illusions about the king's human nature, and seems to have had little time for mysticism, but he recognized that legends about the origin of kingship had propaganda value. In one place he advises that the king's agents should spread the story that, when anarchy prevailed at the dawn of the aeon, men elected the mythical first king Manu Vaivasvata to kingship.[9] He thus encourages a contractual theory. In the same passage, however, he states that the people should be told that, as the king fulfils the functions of the gods Indra (the king of the gods) and Yama (the god of death) upon earth, all who slight him will be punished not only by the secular arm but also by heaven. When the king harangues his troops before battle he is advised to tell them that he is a paid servant just as they are;[10] but at the same time he is told to go to the length of having his secret agents disguised as gods, and allowing himself to be seen in their company, in order that his simpler subjects may believe that he mixes with the gods on equal terms.[11] Asoka and other Mauryan kings took the title "Beloved of the Gods" (*Devānampiya*), and, though they seem not to have claimed wholly divine status, they were no doubt looked on as superior semi-divine beings.

In the period of the later Vedas, though there is no evidence that a really large Indian kingdom existed at the time, the possibility of a realm reaching to the sea was recognized, perhaps as a result of what Indians had heard of Babylonia or Persia. With the Mauryas the possibility was realized, and, though they were soon almost forgotten, they left behind them the concept of the Universal Emperor (*cakravartin*), which was incorporated into Buddhist tradition, and, blended with later Vedic imperialist ideas, was taken over by orthodox Hinduism.* Just as Buddhas appear from time to time in the cosmic cycle, heralded by auspicious omens and endowed with favourable signs, to lead all living beings along the road to enlightenment, so do Universal Emperors appear, to conquer all Jambudvīpa and rule prosperously and righteously. The concept of the Universal Emperor was also known to the Jainas, and in the Epics numerous kings of legend, such as Yudhiṣṭhira and Rāma, are said to have been *digvijayins*, conquerors of all the four quarters. The Universal Emperor was a divinely ordained figure with a special place in the cosmic scheme, and as such was exalted to semi-divine status. The tradition was an inspiration to ambitious monarchs, and in the Middle Ages some even claimed to be Universal Emperors themselves.

Fig. ix. A Cakravartin

After a relief from the stūpa of Jagayyapeta on the lower Krishnā c. 200–100 B.C. On his proper right the wheel, symbolizing universal empire, and his chief queen. On his left the chief minister and the crown prince. At his feet the imperial elephant and horse.

The invasions of the Greeks, Śakas and Kuṣāṇas brought new influences from West and East. Their kings, following the practice of the orientalized Seleucids and other rulers of the Middle East, took the semi-divine title *trātāra*, equivalent to the Greek σωτήρ (saviour); they were not satisfied with the simple title of *rājā*, which had served Aśoka, but were "great kings" (*mahārāja*) and "kings of kings"

* This interpretation of the data is open to question, but seems to me the most feasible explanation of the *Cakkavattisīhanāda Sutta (D.N.,* 3, 58ff), probably the oldest occurrence of the Cakravartin concept. This text either inspired Aśoka or was inspired by him, and the very late character of the Sutta rather suggests the latter.

(*rājātirāja*) on the Persian model. The Kuṣāṇas, perhaps from the influence of China, where the emperor was the Son of Heaven, took the further title "Son of the Gods" (*devaputra*). Later, from Gupta times onwards, every important king would take some such title as "Great King of Kings, Supreme Lord" (*mahārājādhirāja-paramabhaṭṭāraka*), while even the title mahārāja was used only for small vassal kings.

With these influences at work the doctrine of royal divinity was explicitly proclaimed. It appears first in the Epics and the Lawbook of Manu. The latter declares in dignified language:

"When the world was without a king
    and dispersed in fear in all directions,
the Lord created a king
    for the protection of all.

"He made him of eternal particles
    Of Indra and the Wind,
Yama, the Sun and Fire,
    Varuṇa, the Moon, and the Lord of Wealth*

"And, because he has been formed
    of fragments of all those gods,
the king surpasses
    all other beings in splendour.

"Even an infant king must not be despised,
    as though a mere mortal,
for he is a great god
    in human form."[12]

To the ideal of the Universal Emperor was added the inspiration of such brāhmaṇic ceremonies as the horse-sacrifice, which apparently fell into desuetude under the Mauryas, but was revived by the Śuṅgas and was performed by many later kings both in north and south. Even comparatively feeble and petty monarchs managed to perform horse-sacrifices of some sort, and claimed the exalted status of the emperors of legend. After the time of the Guptas these sacrifices became rare, however—the last we have been able to trace took place in the Cōla Empire in the 11th century[13]—but the tradition of royal divinity continued. Kings referred to their divine status in their titles and panegyrics, and they were regularly addressed by their courtiers as *deva*, or god. The Cōla kings and some others were even worshipped as gods in the temples.

In the period between the Mauryas and Guptas anarchy frequently prevailed. Mass lawlessness, riot, pillage and rape were widespread. Raiding bands of invaders from the North-West penetrated far into the heart of India, and some

* The god Kubera (p. 276).

brāhmaṇs even believed that the end of the aeon was drawing near and that the world would soon be destroyed. It was then that an almost pathological dread of anarchy (*mātsya-nyāya*, literally "the way of the fishes", of whom the stronger eat the weaker) grew in the minds of Indian thinkers. In the words of the *Rāmāyaṇa*:

> "Where the land is kingless the cloud, lightning-wreathed
> and loud-voiced, gives no rain to the earth.
>
> "Where the land is kingless the son does not honour his father,
> nor the wife her husband.
>
> "Where the land is kingless men do not meet in assemblies,
> nor make lovely gardens and temples.
>
> "Where the land is kingless the rich are unprotected,
> and shepherds and peasants sleep with bolted doors.
>
> "A river without water, a forest without grass,
> a herd of cattle without a herdsman, is the land without a king."[14]

Passages such as this, which may be paralleled in many sources, further assisted in strengthening the royal prestige, and it is in their light that we must read later legends on the origin of kingship.

There is a very ancient story of a first man, Manu, who combined the characteristics of Adam and Noah in Hebrew tradition (p. 265). This story appears in many forms and versions, one of which, found in the *Mahābhārata*,[15] tells that at the beginning of this period of cosmic time, when greed and wrath had disturbed human relations, men inflicted untold misery upon one another. As in the Buddhist legend, they agreed to respect each other's life and property, but they had no confidence in their contracts, and so they approached the high god Brahmā to help them; he nominated Manu, here apparently thought of not as a man but a god, to be their first king. Some such legend as this was in the mind of the author of the Laws of Manu, when he composed the passage we have quoted. Variants of this story occur in other parts of the *Mahābhārata* and elsewhere, some making the first king Virajas, the son of the god Viṣṇu, and depicting him as imposed on mankind by the gods, without any suggestion of a contract or of human intervention of any kind.[16] All adapt the earlier legends to stress the divine status of the king, and his divine appointment to the kingly office. With the exception of a few Rājput families which claimed descent from the fire-god Agni, nearly all medieval Indian kings traced their genealogies back to Manu, either through his son Ikṣvāku or his daughter Ilā; descendants of Ikṣvāku are referred to as of the solar, and those of Ilā as of the lunar line. Despite the growth of royal pretensions through the centuries the claims of the king did not go unchallenged, and in practice his divinity often made little difference to the body politic. Divinity was cheap in ancient India. Every brāhmaṇ was in a sense a god, as were ascetics with a reputation for sanctity. Householders sponsoring and financing sacrifices were in theory raised to divinity, at least for the duration of the ceremony, while even sticks and stones might be alive with inherent godhead. Moreover the gods were fallible and capable of sin. If the king was a god on earth he was only one god among many, and so his divinity might not always weigh heavily upon his subjects. The Buddhists and Jainas explicitly denied the king's godhead, and one court poet at least, Bāṇa, who was patronized by the great Harṣa, had the temerity to reject the whole rigmarole of royal divinity as the work of sycophants who befuddled the minds of weak and stupid monarchs, but did not fool the strong and the wise.[17] The king was usually held in great awe and respect, but it is doubtful if he was ever treated with quite the same abject serviliry as were, for instance, the more psychopathic Roman or Chinese emperors.

Though the king was an autocrat, not limited by constitutional controls, there were many practical checks on his sovereignty. The king's function was not conceived in terms of legislation, but of protection, and this involved the protection not only of his subjects from invasion, but also of the order of society, the right way of life for all classes and ages (*varṇāśrama-dharma*, p. 138), as laid down in the sacred texts. If he infringed sacred custom too blatantly he incurred the hostility of the brāhmaṇs, and often of the lower orders also. In such a case his fate was pointed out to him in many a cautionary tale, the most common of which was that of the legendary Veṇa. This king apparently took his divinity too seriously, for he forbade all sacrifices except to himself, and confused society by enforcing inter-class marriages. The divine sages (*ṛṣis*) remonstrated with him, but Veṇa continued in his evil courses. At last the exasperated sages beset him in a body and slew him with blades of sacred grass (*kuśa*), which miraculously tumed to spears in their hands. This story, repeated in several sources, must have been a continual warning to the secularly-minded king who was tempted to flout the Sacred Law. No doubt many headstrong kings succeeded in breaking it with impunity, but the recognition of the moral justification of revolt against an impious king must always have acted as some check on his autocracy. More than one great dynasty, such as the Nandas, Mauryas and Śuṅgas, fell as a result of brāhmaṇic intrigue. The *Mahābhārata* explicitly sanctions revolt against a king who is oppressive or fails in his function of protection, saying that such a ruler is no king at all, and should be killed like a mad dog.[18]

The brāhmaṇs and the Sacred Law were not the only checks on the king. All textbooks on statecraft recommend the king to listen to the counsel of his ministers, who are advised to be fearless in debate, and more than one king was overthrown through the intrigues of his councillors. Another and very important check was public opinion. The Vedic rājā was limited by popular or semi-popular assemblies, and though these disappeared in later times kings were invariably advised to keep a finger on the pulse of public feeling, and never to offend it too blatantly. The Buddhist Jātaka stories (p. 235), which are certainly not historical but which reflect conditions in Northern India well before the beginning of the Christian Era, give more than one instance of kings deposed by mass revolt. In the legend of Rāma (p. 365f), who was held up as an ideal king to later Hindu rulers, the hero exiles his beloved wife Sītā, though he is himself convinced of her innocence, on hearing the news that his subjects suspect her chastity, and fear that her presence in the palace will bring misfortune on the nation. At the very end of our period the great king of Vijayanagara, Kṛṣṇa Deva Rāya (p. 67), remitted a marriage tax because it was not popular.[19] The Indian town mob was dangerously inflammable, and the king who seriously outraged popular opinion did so at his own peril. Most textbooks insist that he must at all costs keep the masses contented.

Nevertheless ancient India had her supporters of passive obedience. The *Mahābhārata*, which, as we have seen, in places expressly allows revolt against a wicked king, elsewhere states that any king is better than none. The dread of anarchy was a potent factor in preserving even a weak and oppressive king on his throne.

> "A man should first choose his king, then his wife,
>   and only then amass wealth;
> for without a king in the world
>   where would wife and property be?"[20]

THE ROYAL FUNCTION

The idea of a body politic, of the state as an organism transcending its component parts, though it appears in a rather vague form, does not seem to have taken any great hold on ancient Indian thought. A classification popular with the theorists enumerates seven elements of sovereignty* which are called *aṅgas*, meaning limbs or parts of the human body. Such weak analogies carried little weight, however. Society, the age-old divinely ordained way of Indian life, transcended the state and was independent of it. The king's function was the protection of society, and the state was merely an extension of the king for the furtherance of that end.

The king's function involved the protection not only of his kingdom against external aggression, but also of life, property and traditional custom against internal foes. He protected the purity of class and caste by seeing to it that those who broke caste custom were excommunicated; he protected the family system by punishing adultery, and ensuring the fair inheritance of family property; he protected widows and orphans by making them his wards; he protected the rich against the poor by suppressing robbery; and he protected the poor against the rich by punishing extortion and oppression. Religion was protected by liberal grants to learned brāhmaṇs and temples, and frequently to heterodox sects also. The duty of protection was often little more than the preservation of the *status quo*, but it was nevertheless onerous, and involved positive duties, such as developing irrigation, relieving famine, and generally supervising the economic life of the realm.

The ideal king was a paragon of energetic beneficence. Aśoka was not the

* Some manuscripts of the *Arthaśāstra* significantly add an eighth—the enemy.

only king in India to proclaim that all men were his children, or to take pride in his ceaseless activity. The *Arthaśāstra*, despite its advocacy of every dishonest expedient for the acquisition and maintenance of power, puts the kingly duty in simple and forceful language, setting an ideal such as few ancient civilizations can boast of. Comparing the king and the ascetic it says:

> "The king's pious vow is readiness in action,
> his sacrifice, the discharge of his duty.
>
> "In the happiness of his subjects lies the king's happiness,
> in the welfare of his subjects, his welfare.
> The king's good is not that which pleases him,
> but that which pleases his subjects.
>
> "Therefore the king should be ever active,
> and should strive for prosperity,
> for prosperity depends on effort,
> and failure on the reverse."[21]

Elsewhere the *Arthaśāstra* suggests a routine time-table for the king which allows him only four and a half hours' sleep and three hours for eating and recreation, the rest of the day being spent in state affairs of one kind or another. No doubt such a programme was rarely kept in practice, but it at least shows the ideal set before the king. Candragupta Maurya is said by Megasthenes to have listened to the petitions of his subjects even while in the hands of his masseurs, while his grandson Aśoka ordered that important business was to be set before him at all times, even when he was in his harem. In all sources the king is told that he must be prompt in the administration of justice and always accessible to his people. The swarms of guards, ushers, and other officials who surrounded the king's person must often have demanded bribes, and otherwise have obstructed the access of the subject to his sovereign, but the best of Indian kings at all times have made the public audience or darbār an important instrument of government.

Nearly all the foreign travellers who visited India during our period were much impressed by the pomp and luxury of the Indian king. Their impressions are confirmed by indigenous sources. The king's splendid palace was controlled by a chamberlain, who had a large staff of palace servants of both sexes; the spiritual life of the court was cared for by the chaplain or *purohita*, and many lesser brāhmaṇs; while numerous astrologers, physicians, poets, painters, musicians and learned men dwelt in the purlieus of the palace and enjoyed royal patronage. An important figure in early days, though he is not referred to in the inscriptions of later times, was the *sūta*, who combined the functions of royal charioteer, herald and bard, and was often the friend and confidant of the king. Another member of the royal entourage was the *vidūṣaka*, known to us chiefly from the Sanskrit plays, who corresponded approximately to the court jester of medieval Europe.

Many kings were almost constantly on the move, touring their kingdoms with enormous trains of troops, courtiers, wives, concubines and servants. On such tours business was combined with pleasure—hunts were arranged and famous shrines visited, but also recalcitrant vassals were chastised and local grievances investigated. Many inscriptions on stone and copper, from the days of Aśoka onwards, record the munificence of pious kings to religious foundations and brāhmaṇs while on such tours.

Kings were expected to patronize art, letters and learning. Like most men of the upper classes they were literate, and often devoted much of their leisure to hearing the recitations of their court poets. Some were themselves competent writers, and numerous works ascribed to royal authors have survived. Samudra Gupta was a famous musician, and on some of his coins is depicted as playing the harp (fig. xxivf*b*, p. 383).

Despite the injunctions of the *Arthaśāstra* the king often found time for other less intellectual pursuits. Hunting was usually among the chief of his pleasures, and though the doctrine of non-injury discouraged it a tacit exception was made in the case of kings and nobles. Kings are often referred to as gambling with their courtiers, and sometimes as indulging in drinking bouts, not only with the court but also in the privacy of the harem with the queens and concubines. The textbooks reprobate all these amusements, which are reviewed in the *Arthaśāstra*, whose author quaintly quotes the opinions of various earlier authorities on their comparative perniciousness.

The harem (*antaḥpura*) was in charge of an official (*kañcukin*), usually not a eunuch as in many other ancient civilizations, but an elderly man, who is generally depicted in literature as a benevolent and fatherly friend both of the king and his ladies. From the plays and stories dealing with this aspect of palace life, the ladies of the harem, whether queens or concubines, seem to have been fairly well treated, though both they and the king often went in some fear of the chief queen (*mahiṣī*), whose power in the harem was very great and was often wielded rather harshly over the lesser queens and concubines.

Ideally a royal family was of the kṣatriya or warrior class, but in practice this was often not the case. The Śuṅgas and Kāṇvas were brāhmaṇs, as were several other Indian dynasties; the family of Harṣa is said by Hsüan Tsang to have been of the vaiśya, or mercantile class; while the Nandas, and perhaps even the Mauryas, sprang from the despised śūdras. In practice the aphorism "whoever rules is a kṣatriya" was applied, and after a few generations kingly families from the lower orders were quietly assimilated into the martial class.

Kingship was normally reserved for the male, though a few small Orissan ruling families in the Middle Ages seem regularly to have permitted a daughter to inherit the throne. Diddā, the wicked 10th-century queen of Kashmīr, managed to retain control of the state by acting as regent for her sons, and putting them to death one after the other before they reached their majorities. The benevolent queen of the Kākatīyas of Warangal, Rudrammā (c. 1259–1288), governed by a legal fiction, drafting her state documents in the masculine gender. Queens did, however, act as regents during their sons' minorities, as in the case of Diddā and Prabhāvatī Guptā (p. 57), and royal ladies sometimes wielded much power in the state. Thus Rājyaśrī, widow of Grahavarman the last Maukhari king of Kānyakubja, regularly took a seat of honour beside her brother Harṣa, and shared in state deliberations. Women in politics were often to be found in the medieval kingdoms of the Peninsula; for instance Akkādevī, sister of the Cālukya king Jayasiṃha II (1015–1042), was a provincial governor, and Kundavai, the elder sister of the great Cōla Rājarāja I, seems to have played a role similar to that of Rājyaśrī. Women even sometimes took part in war—Akkādevī fought battles and superintended sieges, while Umādevī, queen of the Hoysala king Vīraballāla II (1173–1220), led two campaigns against recalcitrant vassals.

Succession was normally by primogeniture but exceptions might often occur, for the Sacred Law did not allow a diseased, maimed or seriously infirm prince to ascend the throne, and the line could not pass through such a prince. Thus in the *Mahābhārata* legend (p. 361) the Pāṇḍava princes were quite within their rights in claiming the throne from the blind Dhṛtarāṣṭra. Moral perversity might also exclude a prince from succession. "A wicked son, though an only one," says the *Arthaśāstra*, "should never ascend the throne".[22] Kings sometimes nominated their successors, overriding the claims of their eldest sons if these were given to evil courses. Thus Samudra Gupta was nominated by his father Candra Gupta I, against other claimants, at a great darbār, after which the old king apparently abdicated; and similar instances can be found. The absence of a strict rule of primogeniture was the cause of dynastic disputes, and hence undoubtedly led to the weakening of empires.

Princes were trained with great care, and the heir to the throne (*yuvarāja*) was often associated with his father in government. This custom was widespread, and was especially strong with the invaders from the North-West and with the Cōlas, whose crown princes issued charters in their own names and acted independently of their fathers while the latter were still on the throne. The Śakas and Pāhlavas often inscribed the name of the ruling king on the obverse of their coins, while that of the sub-king was given on the reverse.

Princes might be a great source of danger to their parents.

According to a Buddhist tradition Magadha was ruled from Ajātaśatru onwards by five parricides in succession, which suggests that at the time this region of India followed the widespread primitive custom of putting the king to death when his vital powers failed, a practice of which the ritual nature was not remembered by succeeding generations. Kings are warned against the intrigues both of sons and wives, "for princes, like crabs, eat their own parents".[23] The activities of the princes should be strictly controlled, and they should be constantly spied upon, to ensure that they would not revolt against their fathers.

The prince's impatience to acquire his patrimony was often gratified by the voluntary abdication of an elderly king—a practice approved by precept and tradition. Examples of such abdication may be found at all times and in all parts of India. Sometimes the abdication was followed by religious suicide. Several kings, the most notable being Candragupta Maurya, are said to have resigned their thrones and slowly starved themselves to death under the influence of Jainism. Others passed straight to heaven by drowning in a sacred river. Of such kings the most famous was the Cālukya Someśvara I (c. 1042–1068), who, when his powers began to fail, waded into the holy Tuṅgabhadrā and drowned himself to the sound of religious music, while his courtiers lined the banks. In some of the medieval principalities of Kerala the ritual suicide of the king became a regular institution.

Other systems of inheritance prevailed in a few cases. Thus the throne of the Śaka satraps of Ujjayinī passed not to the king's son but to his younger brother, and only when all the brothers were dead did the eldest son of the eldest brother inherit. There are indications that brother-to-brother succession was not wholly unknown elsewhere in India, and it was almost regularly followed in Ceylon. This system prevailed in China under the Shang dynasty (c. 1500–1100 B.C.), and was also followed by many Central Asian tribes; it is still known in East Africa.

In the early days of the Cēra kingdom of Kerala inheritance was through the male line, but about the 12th century a matrilinear system became regular, according to which the heir to the throne was the son not of the king, but of his eldest sister. This system, called *Marumakkattāyam*, continued in Cochin and Travancore until very recent times, both for royal succession and the inheritance of estates. Perhaps it existed in Kerala at an early period, but was dropped by the upper classes for a while under brāhmaṇical influence, to be revived in the course of centuries. Other traces of matrilinear succession can be found in ancient India, notably in the very common use of metronymics in royal titles, but it was not regularly followed in any important kingdoms.

If the king died with no heir to the throne much power was wielded by the magnates of the realm, for the courtiers, nobles, ministers, religious leaders and wealthy merchants would sometimes meet together and choose a king. Thus the nobles of Kānyakubja invited Harṣa to assume the throne when Grahavarman died childless. Gopāla, the founder of the Pala line of Bengal and Bihār, was chosen as king by the great men of the land. A further example is the appointment of the boy Nandivarman (735–797) as the Pallava king of Kāñcī by an assembly of nobles and ministers. The Kashmīr Chronicle provides other instances.

QUASI-FEUDALISM

Authorities differ on the definition of a feudal system. Some would confine the term to a complex structure of contractual relations covering the whole of society from king to villein, such as that which prevailed in medieval Europe. Others use the term so loosely that they apply it to any system where political power is chiefly in the hands of landowners. Most non-Marxist historians would prefer the narrower definition, according to which ancient India never had a true feudal system. Something very like European feudalism did evolve among the Rājputs after the Muslim invasions, but this is outside our period. Ancient India had, however, a system of overlordship which was quasi-feudal, though it was never as fully developed as in Europe and it rested on a different basis.

In the later Vedic period there were already lesser chiefs tributary to the greater. Terms in these texts like *adhirāja* and *saṃrāṭ*, often loosely translated "emperor", seem actually to imply lordship over a number of feudatories. Magadhan imperialism aimed at a centralized realm, though even in Mauryan times vassal chiefs existed in the more remote regions of the empire. With the fall of the Mauryas the typical large kingdom had a central core of directly administered territory, and a circle of vassal kingdoms subordinate in varying degrees to the emperor. These vassals had vassals of their own in petty local chieftains calling themselves rājās. The Indian system differed from that of Europe in that the relations of overlord and vassal were not regularly based on contract, whether theoretical or otherwise, and ancient India had nothing quite comparable to the European manor, though institutions of a somewhat similar type were beginning to develop at the very end of our period.

When decisively defeated in battle a king might render homage to his conqueror and retain his throne. Thus vassals usually became so by conquest rather than by contract, though the *Arthaśāstra* advises a weak king to render voluntary homage if necessary to a stronger neighbour. This state of affairs was supported by the Epics and Smṛti literature, which discouraged outright conquest. "Lawful conquest" (*dharmavijaya*) did not involve the absorption of the conquered kingdom, but merely its reduction to vassal status. Though many later kings, such as Samudra Gupta, ignored the Sacred Law and incorporated conquered kingdoms into their empires, custom was against this practice.

The amount of control exercised by the overlord varied greatly. Ideally the vassal was expected to pay regular tribute to his emperor, and to assist him with troops and funds in war. He attended the overlord's court on ceremonial occasions, and the panegyrics of powerful medieval kings regularly mention the jewels of many splendid turbans glittering like the waves of the sea, as the vassals bow before their lord. In his charters the vassal was expected to mention the name and title of his overlord before his own. In some cases a resident representative of the overlord was stationed at the vassal's capital. The vassal's sons might be educated with the princes of his master, and serve as pages, and his daughters might be demanded for the imperial harem. Often a vassal acted as a minister of his suzerain, or a minister or favourite might be set up as a vassal king by his master. Hence in the medieval period the status of minister often merged with that of vassal, and the provincial governor, holding office at the king's pleasure, tended to become a feudatory king or chief in his own right.

The great vassal (*mahāsāmanta*) was always very powerful, and had his own administration and army. Among the many threats to the security of a king the revolting vassal was one of the most dangerous. The history of the Western Deccan offers typical examples. Here, from the 6th century onwards, the Cālukya dynasty held sway; a vassal, Dantidurga Rāṣṭrakūṭa, overthrew it and established his own dynasty about 753, and the Cālukyas were reduced to insignificant vassalage; but some 200 years later they profited by the weakness of the Rāṣṭrakūṭas to regain the hegemony, which they maintained until the end of the 12th century, when their vassals, the Yādavas, Kākatīyas and Hoysaḷas, shared their domains between them.

In fact the suzerain's hand weighed very lightly on the more powerful and remoter tributaries, and many claims to homage and tribute amounted to very little. Samudra Gupta, for instance, even claimed the king of Ceylon, Śrī Meghavarṇa, as his vassal; but it is clear from a reliable Chinese source that the claim was based merely on the reception of a Sinhalese mission hearing gifts and requesting permission to erect a Buddhist monastery at the sacred site of Gayā.

The lesser chiefs, on the other hand, had little more power than the lords of the manor in medieval Europe, though they claimed the proud title of rājā. In this connection an interesting story is told in an inscription at Dūdhpānī, in S. Bihār, dating from the 8th century A.D.

> Three merchant brothers were returning from the port of Tāmralipti to their home in Ayodhyā with a caravan of merchandise and provisions, and rested for the night at a village called Bhramaraśālmalī. Meanwhile the local king, Ādisiṃha, passed by on a hunting expedition, with a large train of followers, and, as was the custom, he demanded food and fodder of the villagers. But they were suffering from a temporary shortage, and could scarcely meet this demand. So they sent a deputation to the merchants, who at their request gave the king provisions from their own stock. The king found the companionship of the eldest brother, Udayamāna, very agreeable, and so he and his brothers became members of Ādisiṃha's court. One day Udayamāna revisited the village of Bhramaraśālmalī, and the villagers, remembering his former kindness, asked him to become their king. King Ādisiṃha approved the request, and so the merchant Udayamāna became rājā of Bhramaraśālmalī, while his two brothers were made kings of adjoining villages.[24]

This little story illustrates another means whereby quasi-feudal relations arose. After the Mauryan period it became usual for kings to pay their officers and favourites not with cash, but with the right to collect revenue from a village or a group of villages. Such a right often carried other privileges, and usually made the recipient the intermediary between king and taxpayer. It greatly encouraged the tendency towards devolution, instability, and inter-state anarchy.

OLIGARCHIES AND REPUBLICS

Though monarchy was usual in ancient India, tribal states also existed, which were governed by oligarchies. The term "republic" is often used for these bodies and, though it has been criticized by some authorities, it is quite legitimate if it is remembered that the *gaṇas*, or tribes, were not governed like the Republic of India by an assembly elected by universal suffrage. The Roman Republic was not a democracy, but it was a republic nevertheless, and the evidence shows that in some of these ancient Indian republican communities a large number of persons had some say in the government.

Vedic literature gives faint indications of such tribes at a very early date (p. 29), and the Buddhist scriptures recognize the existence of many republics, chiefly in the foothills of the Himālayas and in N. Bihār. These were mostly tributary to the greater kingdoms, but exercised internal autonomy. One such people was the tribe of the Śākyas, who dwelt on the borders of modern Nepāl, and to whom the Buddha himself belonged. Though in later legend the Buddha's father, Śuddhodhana, is depicted as a mighty king living in great pomp, he was in fact a tribal chief, depending on the support of a large assembly of householders, who gathered regularly to discuss tribal politics in a meeting hall (in Pāli, *santhāgāra*).

The most powerful non-monarchical state at this time was the Vṛjjian confederacy, of which the chief element was the tribe of the Licchavis and which long resisted the great Ajātaśatru. According to a rather dubious Buddhist tradition the Licchavis had no less than 7707 rājās, a term which must have covered all the heads of families of the tribe who were eligible to take part in the tribal assembly. Jaina sources tell of an inner council of thirty-six tribal chieftains controlling the affairs of the Licchavis, Mallas and allied tribes in their war with Ajātaśatru. The whole confederation had a rājā-in-chief, an executive head who, like the rājā of the Śākyas, seems to have held office for life and often to have passed on his position to his heir.

It has been reasonably suggested that the organization of the Buddhist clergy, which is said to have been laid down by the Buddha himself, is modelled on the constitution of one of these republican tribes, perhaps the Śākyas. Buddhist monastic affairs were managed by a general meeting of the monks, with a regular system of procedure and standing orders not very different from that of the business meeting of a present-day society. The Buddhist chapter differed from the modern committee, however, in that decisions normally needed the unanimous consent of the assembled monks. Differences which could not be settled were referred to a committee of elders.

In the Buddha's day the free tribes were standing up with difficulty to the internal pressure of changing social and economic conditions and to the external pressure of the rising kingdoms of Eastern India. We have seen that both the Śākyas and the Vṛjjis were conquered at about the time of the Buddha's death, the former never to rise again (p. 40). The Buddha himself, though a friend of kings, seems to have had a deep affection for the old republican organization, and in a remarkable passage he is said to have warned the Vṛjjis shortly before his death that their security depended on maintaining their traditions and holding regular and well attended folk-moots.

Western India did not feel the force of imperialism as strongly as the east, and here republican tribes survived for much longer. Several such peoples are mentioned in the classical accounts of Alexander's invasion, and the *Arthaśāstra* devotes a whole chapter to the means whereby such tribes may be reduced to vassalage by an ambitious king—the main method being to sow dissension between the leading tribesmen so that the tribal assembly loses its unanimity and the tribe is divided against itself. Such a procedure, according to a Buddhist legend, was employed by Ajātaśatru's wily minister Varṣakāra to weaken the Vṛjjis before invasion. The *Arthaśāstra* probably refere ironically to the martial arrogance and practical ineptitude of the republics when it states that the members of seven named tribes "make a living by their title of rājā".[25]

The *Mahābhārata* takes full cognisance of the existence of republican can tribes in Western India, and their survival until the 5th century A.D. is attested by numerous coins and a few short inscriptions. Perhaps the most important western republic was that of the Yaudheyas in Northern Rājasthān, which issued numerous coins, hearing the inscription "Victory to the Yaudheya tribe"; one of their official seals has been found, with the proud legend, "Of the Yaudheyas, who possess the magic spell of victory"; and one fragmentary Yaudheya inscription survives. This mentions the chief of the tribe, whose name has unfortunately been worn away by the weathering of the stone; he has the regal title of maharaja, but he is also called *mahāsenāpati*, or general-in-chief, and he is "placed at the head of the Yaudheya people".[26]

The Mālava tribe may be the same as the Malloi described by Greek historians as living in Panjāb at the time of Alexander. If so, the tribe moved south during the centuries, for its coins are found in Rājasthān, and it gave its name to Mālwā, the region around Ujjayinī, north of the Narmadā. Some brief 3rd-century inscriptions at Nandsā in Rājasthān refer to the Mālava Śrīsoma, who "supported the ancestral yoke of government", and whose position was therefore hereditary.[27] It is probable that the Mālavas founded the era later known as the Era of Vikrama, for several early inscriptions refer to this as "the Era handed down by the Mālava tribe".

Most of these western tribes became tributary to the Guptas after Samudra Gupta's great conquests in the 4th century (p. 54). After this we hear little more of them, and they probably vanished as a result of the Hūṇa invasions. We know scarcely anything about their organization, which may have been loosely feudal, with a large number of petty chieftains more or less subordinate to a single head, who held office with their consent and could do little without their help. In any case modern India may take legitimate pride in the fact that, though she may not have had democracies in the modern sense, government by discussion was by no means unknown in her ancient civilization.

COUNCILLORS AND OFFICIALS

"A single wheel cannot turn", says the *Arthaśāstra*, rather inaccurately, "and so government is only possible with assistance. Therefore a king should appoint councillors and listen to their advice."[28] At the head of affairs was a small body of elder statesmen, whom the king was advised to choose with the utmost care. The size of this privy council (*mantri-pariṣad*) varied, and the authorities suggest figures ranging from seven to thirty-seven; we have little evidence of its size in practice, but it seems more often to have approached the smaller of these figures than the larger.

The council was not a cabinet in the modern sense, but an advisory body with few corporate functions. Thus the king is in one place advised to lay his most secret plans before only one member of the council, to avoid leakage. The council's purpose was primarily to advise and aid the king, and not to govern; but it was no mere rubber-stamping body, for all authorities urge that councillors should speak freely and openly, and that the king should give full consideration to their advice.

In fact the council often exerted great powers. It might transact business in the king's absence, and the Aśokan inscriptions show that it might make minor decisions without consulting him. The Śaka satrap Rudradāman (p. 53) referred the question of rebuilding the Girnar dam to his councillors, who advised against it, so that he was forced to undertake the work against their advice, apparently at the expense of the privy purse and not of public funds. The Kashmīr Chronicle gives one case of a privy council deposing the king, and another of its vetoing the king's nomination of his successor.

At its meetings the council took the strictest precautions to preserve complete secrecy, for agents of the king's enemies at home or abroad were constantly in search of information. The texts advise that women, notoriously unreliable, and even talking birds such as parrots and mynahs, whose vocal powers were much overestimated in ancient India, should be excluded from the vicinity of the council chamber.

Though the *Arthaśāstra* advises the king to appoint ministers by merit alone it would seem that in later times most of the privy councillors, and indeed of the whole civil service of the kingdom, enjoyed their positions by virtue of inheritance. Candella inscriptions show that a line of five generations of councillors held office during the reigns of seven generations of kings, and there are many similar examples.

Sometimes a minister succeeded in obtaining complete control of a kingdom, and the king became a mere puppet. This tendency was exemplified in later times in the Marāthā state, where the descendants of Śivājī were completely eclipsed by the *Peshwās*, or hereditary ministers, and a similar state of affairs prevailed in Nepāl until quite recently. In ancient India there were many cases of ministerial usurpation and of ministers who became de facto rulers under weak kings. The aged Rāma Rāja of Vijayanagara (p. 67), who lost the battle of Tālikoṭa and thus brought about the end of the last great empire of Hindu India, was not the legal king, but the hereditary minister of the insignificant Sadāśiva, who was later murdered by Rāma Rāja's brother.

The functions of the councillors were not always sharply defined or delimited, and terminology varied considerably. There seems usually to have been a chief counsellor, the *mantrin* par excellence, often called "great counsellor" (*mahāmantrin*). With orthodox kings the *purohita* or court chaplain was very influential, and one source even suggests that before coming to a final decision the king should deliberate privately with him.[29] The treasurer and chief tax-collector (called in the *Arthaśāstra sannidhātṛ* and *samāhartṛ* respectively), were important, as was the "minister of peace and war" (*sāndhivigrahika*), a title which does not appear until Gupta times. This minister approximated to the foreign secretary of the modern state, but had more definite military functions and often accompanied the king on campaign. The *prāḍvivāka*, or chief judge and legal advisor, seems to have been important in medieval Hindu kingdoms, and the *senāpati*, or general, was always influential, while the *mahākṣapaṭalika*, or chief record keeper and secretary, no doubt attended the council meetings.

In theory neither the king nor his council were legislative bodies in the modern sense of the term. The royal decrees (*śāsana*) which they promulgated were not generally new laws, but orders referring to special cases. Dharma and established custom were usually looked on as inviolable, and the king's commands were merely applications of the Sacred Law. Heterodox kings, however, did from time to time issue orders which were in the nature of new laws, the most notable case being Aśoka.

To transmit the royal decrees a corps of secretaries and clerks was maintained, and remarkable precautions were taken to prevent error. Under the Cōlas, for instance, orders were first written by scribes at the king's dictation, and the accuracy of the drafts was attested by competent witnesses. Before being sent to their recipients they were carefully transcribed, and a number of witnesses, sometimes amounting to as many as thirteen, again attested them. In the case of grants of land and privileges an important court official was generally deputed to ensure that the royal decrees were put into effect. Thus records were kept with great care, and nothing was left to chance; the royal scribes themselves were often important personages.

Councillors and high officials in general are often referred to in early sources as *mahāmātras*, and from Gupta times onwards as *kumārāmātyas*, or "princely ministers"; the latter epithet seems to have been a title of honour. There was no high degree of specialization, and councillors, like modern cabinet ministers, often changed their posts. All of them, even aged ministers of the brāhmaṇ class, might perform military functions. In some sources they are divided into two groups—deliberative officials (*matisaciva* or *dhīsaciva*), and executive officials (*karmasaciva*). The former were councillors, while the latter approximately corresponded to high-ranking civil servants of modern times.

Of the seven occupational classes into which Megasthenes divided all the inhabitants of India, two were connected with the government; the last of the seven, "those who deliberate on public affairs", must represent the councillors, while the penultimate class of "overseers" (ἐπισκοποι) are the *adhyakṣas* or superintendents of the *Arthaśāstra*. As well as most of the officials we have mentioned this text enumerates many others—the superintendents of crown lands, of forests, of forest-produce, of state herds, of waste lands, of the treasury, and of mines, the chief goldsmith, the comptroller of state granaries, and the superintendents of commerce, of tolls and customs, of state spinning and weaving workshops, of slaughter houses, of passports, and of shipping. Military requirements were cared for by the superintendents of the armoury, of cavalry, of elephants, of chariots, and of footmen, all of whom seem to have been rather civil than military officials, as far as it is possible to draw a dividing line between them in ancient India. The less reputable amusements of the populace were controlled by the superintendents of liquor, of gaming, and of prostitutes. Aśoka inaugurated a further class of official called *dharma-mahāmātras*, or ministers of Righteousness, whose duty was to supervise the affairs of all religious bodies, and to ensure that the officials followed the Emperor's new policy; this class of official existed under different titles in some later empires, as did officers who administered the great royal donations to religious establishments.

Thus in Mauryan times every aspect of the life of the individual was watched over, and as far as possible controlled, by the government. Though no later state developed the same degree of control as did the Mauryas, the ideal of the *Arthaśāstra* did not wholly disappear. The government not only regulated the economic life of the country, but also took an important part in it. All mines, which term for the ancient Indian included pearl fisheries and salt pans, were owned by the state, and were either worked directly with the labour of criminals or serfs, or let out to entrepreneurs, from whom the king claimed a percentage of their output as royalty. The produce of the forests, from elephants to firewood, was the property of the state. There were large state farms, cultivated either by direct labour or on a share-cropping basis, the products of which went to the state granaries. The state owned manufactories for spinning and weaving, which were staffed by indigent women, rather like the houses of industry under the Elizabethan poor-law. Munitions of war were made in state arsenals, and ships were built in state shipyards, to be let out to fishermen and merchants. In fact there was no question of *laissez-faire* in ancient India.

This highly organized bureaucracy was much tied up with "red tape". The *Arthaśāstra*[30] suggests that departments should be headed by more than one chief, to prevent excessive peculation, and to ensure that no one individual grew too powerful; the text adds that officials should be transferred frequently and states that no government servant should be allowed to take any decision without reference to his superior, except in emergency.

The *Arthaśāstra* envisages the payment of the many officials of the state in cash, and gives a lengthy tariff of salaries.[31] This is very obscure, however, since bare figures are quoted, without specifying the type of coin or the period of payment. The period was probably a month, and the coins were *paṇas*, apparently of silver. In any case the list makes it clear that the crown servant of ancient India, like the Indian civil servant of modern times, enjoyed a standard of life much above that of his less fortunate fellows. The chief councillor, the purohita, the heir apparent, the chief queen, the queen-mother, the king's preceptor, and the chief sacrificial priest of the palace received 48,000 panas monthly, while at the lower end of the scale even palace workmen, attendants and bodyguards received sixty. In contrast to these a labourer on the crown lands received only one and a quarter pana and provisions.[32] The last figure is so low that we cannot but believe that the coin referred to by the *Arthaśāstra* was a silver one, otherwise a single copper cooking pot would cost more than the labourer's annual wage.

These data apply to the Mauryan age, or to the period immediately following it. Later it became usual for kings to reward their officers by grants of the revenue of a village or district, a system not unknown even in earlier times, and which, as we have seen, helped in the development of the quasi-feudal system of medieval India.

LOCAL ADMINISTRATION

The ancient Indian kingdom was divided into provinces and these into divisions and districts, all with very variable terminology. In the Maurya and Gupta periods the provincial governor was appointed directly by the king, and was usually a member of the royal family. In later times his status was often hereditary and he approximated to a vassal king. We can see the development of this process in a series of inscriptions from Western Bengal, issued by the governors of the Gupta emperors in the 5th and 6th centuries A.D.[33] Here we read of three successive generations of governors, of whom the first, Cirātadatta, is merely an *uparika*, a viceroy; with the decline of the central administration under Budha Gupta his successors call themselves *uparika-mahārāja*, and are well on the way to becoming kings, holding office by birth rather than by appointment. Numerous independent dynasties did in fact arise through provincial governors growing too strong for their masters.

District governors were not usually appointed from the centre, but by the provincial governors. Like the District Officers of the Indian Civil Service, they combined judicial and administrative functions. At this level, in some parts of India at least, the government was assisted by a council, for from the Gupta inscriptions already mentioned we find that the decisions of the district officer were made after consultation with a body of leading residents which included the chief banker, the chief caravan leader, the chief craftsman, and the chief scribe. These members of the council were no doubt heads of guilds or castes, and probably held office by hereditary right. In the Peninsula, especially under the Cōlas, similar district councils existed, and had even wider powers, levying local taxes and exercising judicial functions with the concurrence of the representative of the central government.

Cities too had their councils. Megasthenes' description of the government of Pāṭaliputra by a committee of thirty members divided into six sub-committees is not exactly confirmed elsewhere, and some doubts have been cast on his accuracy. But some cities issued their own coinage, and must therefore have had considerable local autonomy. Councils existed in small towns and large villages in various parts of India, especially the Cōla country, where they were very vigorous.

In general the most important element in city administration was the governor (*nāgaraka*, *purapāla*). His chief responsibilities were revenue collection, and the preservation of law and order by means of police, secret agents and troops, which were stationed in the chief towns under a captain (*daṇḍanāyaka*), who might be the governor himself. The watchmen or police were sometimes fierce and oppressive, and among the privileges given to brāhmaṇ villages by benevolent kings immunity from entry by police was one of the most valued.

The system of government envisaged by the *Arthaśāstra* involved a careful check on the movements and activities of all the inhabitants of the city through petty officials called *gopa*, probably often working in a part-time capacity, who were responsible for the collection of revenue, and the supervision of forty households each. These men not only kept careful note of the births, deaths, income and expenditure in the families under their charge, but even of the visitors they received and of any important developments in the households. The information obtained by the gopa was passed on to the town office and permanently recorded, and similar records were kept in the villages. We cannot be sure that the system advocated by the *Arthaśāstra* was ever wholly put into effect, but Megasthenes confirms that registers were maintained and the movements of strangers carefully supervised. It would seem, in fact, that conditions in the larger Mauryan cities approximated to those of a modern police state, with the open supervision of the gopas supplemented by a vigorous secret service.

The city governor had other, more positive duties. He was responsible for the cleanliness of the streets and precautions against fire. His duties also involved the prevention or alleviation of such disasters as famine, flood and plague. Thus the last record we have of the Girnar dam tells how it broke, and was reconstructed by the local city governor, Cakrapālita, in 455, during the reign of Skanda Gupta.[34] Cakrapālita, the son of the provincial governor Parṇadatta, is praised in the inscription commemorating the rebuilding of the dam in terms which are evidently formal panegyric, but certain passages are quite unexpected, and depict the city governor as a popular figure on the most friendly terms with the citizens. In any case, these verses show us the ideal set before the local official in Gupta times, and are therefore very significant.

"He caused distress to no man in the city,
    but he chastised the wicked.
Even in this mean age
    he did not fail the trust of the people.
He cherished the citizens as his own children
    and he put down crime.
He delighted the inhabitants
    with gifts and honours and smiling conversation,
and he increased their love
    with informal visits and friendly receptions."

VILLAGE ADMINISTRATION

At all times the village was the unit of government. In the South, and occasionally in the North, districts were classified according to the number of villages they were supposed to contain, for instance the *Gangāvādi 96,000* or the *Nidgundige 12*. The number of villages supposed to exist in the larger units is evidently exaggerated, but it must be remembered that almost any settlement, even a tiny group of huts in a jungle clearing, qualified for the name of *grāma*; but a grama might also contain as many as 1,000 families, and there was no clear dividing line between a village and a town.

From pre-Mauryan times collectors were appointed over groups of villages, and in the villages themselves two elements, which survive to the present day, represented the last link in the chain of governmental control. These were the village headman and the village council.

The headman's was normally a hereditary position, though he was frequently looked on as the king's representative, to be replaced at his pleasure. He was usually one of the wealthier peasants, and was remunerated with tax-free land, dues in kind, or both. In the larger villages he was a very important functionary, with a small staff of village officials, such as an accountant, a watchman and a toll-collector. These offices too were often passed from father to son, and were remunerated in the same way as that of the headman.

In some sources the headman seems an oppressive local tyrant. The *gāmabhojaka*, who appears in numerous Pāli Jātaka stories, is not so much the representative of his people and one of their number as a squire, with wide powers over the villagers, fining them for minor offences and expelling them for serious ones. In more than one passage in this source we read of villagers appealing to the king for protection against wicked headmen. Usually, however, the headman appears rather as the champion of the villagers. He was responsible for the defence of the village, and in the South, where the village council received greater recognition, this was his most important function. Villages were liable to raids from neighbouring kingdoms, or from the wild tribesmen of hill and jungle. In less settled times bandits roamed the country in large gangs, and Āryans and Dravidians alike had a very ancient tradition of cattle-raiding. When the central government was weak, village feuds and cattle-raids might lead to pitched battles. All over the Deccan are to be found "hero-stones" (*vīragal*) recording the death of a village warrior, often the headman, "while defending the cattle". By medieval times the headman seems often to have been incorporated into the quasi-feudal system. The merchant Udayamāna (p. 82f), for instance, though dignified by the title of rājā, was in fact little more than a village headman.

The village council is rarely referred to, though it certainly existed all over India. In most kingdoms it was not recognized as part of the state machine. One lawbook gives it a brief mention,[35] and states that its powers derive from the king, but this is certainly a false interpretation. There is no evidence that the rights of the village council ever depended on the delegation of royal power. It was independent of the government and continued to function, whatever dynasty was ruling the district. Southern kings, however, seem increasingly to have given it recognition, and hence in the Cōla empire it played an important part in administration.

We have no record of the composition of the village council in the North, where in later times it traditionally consisted of five of the most respected villagers, including the headman. Indeed no northern Indian source gives any clear indication of the existence of village councils at all, until after the Muslim invasion, and it is possible that they did not even exist at the time in the Gangā Valley.

Southern councils were constituted according to local custom. In some villages of the Western Deccan all householders attended the village meeting, although they may have had chiefs who formed an inner council. Elsewhere villages were governed by committees, often chosen by lot. In the Cōla kingdom at Uttaramērūr, a large village inhabited by brāhmaṇs (*agrahāra*), a number of inscriptions from the 10th century onwards throw much light on local politics. The village was divided into thirty wards or sections, each of which had a representative on the council, chosen annually by lot. The council was divided into five sub-committees, the first three of which were responsible for gardens and orchards, tanks and irrigation, and the settlement of disputes respectively, while the functions of the last two are uncertain. Members were unpaid, and could be removed from office for misconduct. The right to sit on the council was limited by a property qualification of a house and a small plot of land. Membership was confined to men between the ages of thirty-five and seventy, and those who had served for a year were ineligible for reappointment for another three years.

The two latter features of the Uttaramērūr constitution are also found in the constitutions of other village councils of which records survive. All seem to have been closed both to youth and old age, and in some the minimum age was as high as forty. Most had checks on the reappointment of retiring members, no doubt to avoid corruption and to prevent any individual from growing too influential. In one case even close relatives of a retiring member were debarred from membership for five years, and in another the retiring member could not be reappointed for ten years.

These Southern councils not only arbitrated in disputes and managed social affairs outside the jurisdiction of the government, but were responsible for revenue collection, assessing individual contributions and negotiating the village's collective assessment with the king's representative. They had virtual ownership of the village's waste land, with right of sale, and they were active in irrigation, road-building, and other public works. Their transactions, recorded on the walls of village temples, show a vigorous community life, and are a permanent memorial to the best side of early Indian politics.

PUBLIC FINANCE

All ancient Indian authorities on statecraft stress the importance of a full treasury for successful government, and India had evolved a regular system of taxation before the Mauryan period. At all times the basic tax was that on land, usually called *bhāga* or "share", which was a fixed proportion of the crop. The figure generally given in the Smṛti literature is one sixth, but Megasthenes gives it as one quarter, while the *Arthaśāstra* suggests one quarter or even one third for fertile lands; there is some reason to believe that one quarter was the proportion generally levied even in the mild reign of Aśoka. The tax was usually paid in kind, and the Jātakas refer to the royal officers measuring out grain on the threshing floor for conveyance to the king's granary; but settlements similar to those of later times, when tax was fixed in advance on the basis of the estimated yield of the land, were also known. In the middle ages, especially in the South, many villages had commuted their land tax for an annual cash payment.

Numerous exemptions and remissions were granted; thus land brought newly under the plough was not taxed fully for five years, while the tax might be wholly or partially remitted in times of bad harvest. Remissions might also be given to a village embarking on a collective irrigation project or some other enterprise in the public interest. Generally the tax was levied on the gross yield, but sometimes an allowance was made to cover the requirements for consumption and seed until the next harvest, and some medieval Indian assessments seem to have been levied on the net yield only.

According to the Sacred Law women, children, students, learned brāhmaṇs and ascetics should not be taxed in any form, and many grants of tax-free land were made to brāhmaṇs and temples; but in practice even religious establishments often paid tax, though at a lower rate than the ordinary peasant. At the other extreme, classes which society in general disliked often had to pay extra taxes, especially in the South; these included those who followed objectionable trades, such as leather workers, and followers of heterodox faiths, such as Muslims and Ājivikas (p. 259ff).

As well as the basic land tax several other taxes fell upon the cultivator, such as fixed annual cash payments, and dues for the use of water from a tank or canal owned by the king. Taxes were paid on cattle and other livestock, and on all kinds of agricultural and dairy produce. Peasants in South India often paid house taxes, and taxes were also levied on shops and necessary industrial equipment such as looms, potters' wheels and oil presses. Many of these lesser taxes were the perquisites of the local council, and were devoted to the needs of the village.

According to the *Arthaśāstra* merchants travelling from place to place paid small road tolls which were collected by an officer called *antapāla*, who was responsible for the upkeep of the road and its safety. If we are to believe the text these taxes formed a sort of insurance, for the antapāla was expected to make good any loss suffered by the merchants from thieves. It is doubtful whether this system was regularly adopted in later times, when kingdoms were less well organized, but something like it must have prevailed in the Mauryan period. Tolls on a varying *ad valorem* tariff were also levied at the city gates on incoming merchandise. The *Arthaśāstra* suggests that essential goods such as grain, oil, sugar, pots and cheap textiles should be taxed at one-twentieth of their value, and other goods at rates varying from one fifteenth to one fifth. Various market dues were also levied, but the ten per cent sales tax recorded by Megasthenes is nowhere mentioned in an Indian source.

All craftsmen were expected to devote one or two days' work per month to the king, but this tax was probably often commuted to a sort of income tax on average daily earnings. There was also liability to forced labour (*viṣṭi*), though this did not always fall very heavily upon the masses. Services in labour and gifts of provisions were expected by the king and his officers when on tour, and this might put small rural communities into serious difficulties (p. 83). Such obligations of forced labour and service prevailed in some Indian states until very recent times.

So complex a system of taxation could not be maintained without surveying and accountancy. The Jātaka stories refer to local officers as "holders of the [surveyor's] cord" (*rajjugāhaka*), and the officers called in the Aśokan inscriptions *rajjūka* may have been the same; Megasthenes records that the land was thoroughly surveyed. Land was only transferred to a new owner after reference to the local land records, and this fact, with the names of the record keepers who had certified its transferability, was often noted in the copper-plate title deeds. The better organized kingdoms evidently kept full and up-to-date records of land ownership corresponding to the English Domesday Book. Unfortunately they were written on perishable materials, and all have long since vanished.

Taxation was burdensome, especially in times of bad harvest or under rapacious kings. There are numerous references in Jātaka stories to the harsh exactions of local officers, and to peasants emigrating en masse from the villages to escape crushing taxes. In medieval South Indian inscriptions we read of something like the rent-strikes of later times, and of a whole village council being imprisoned for failure to pay the land tax. One inscription records an appeal to the Cōla emperor Rājarāja I, in protest against the looting of a village in punishment of tax default; in this case the king upheld the action of his local officers. A defaulting taxpayer was liable to eviction, though he might be given a year's grace or more in case of real need.

The textbooks on statecraft invariably stress the danger of unduly heavy taxation. Nobody can hold honey in his mouth without tasting some of it, and it is to be expected that local officers will claim more tax than their due, but really extortionate collectors are a great danger to the king's safety. Certain admirable general principles are laid down in our sources—taxation should never act as a check on trade and industry; the king should tax as a bee sucks honey, without hurting the flower; taxes should be fixed so as always to allow a profit to the taxpayer; articles of commerce should not be taxed more than once; increases in taxation should not be imposed without due warning. No doubt the better monarchs tried to maintain these principles in their fiscal policy.

Taxation was theoretically justified as a return for the protection granted by the king. In the story of the primeval king Manu (p. 75), it is said that when Brahmā first appointed him he demurred, fearing that he would be responsible for the sins of the people; but men were so direly in need of government that they promised that their sins would be upon their own heads, and undertook to give Manu a share of their crops and herds if he would protect them. The Buddhist story of the first king (p. 71) records a similar promise as part of the contract. Generally it is stated that the king is only entitled to tax his people if he protects them, and thus he obtains in addition a share of the religious merit acquired by them, especially by his brāhmaṇ subjects; if he fails in his duty he has no moral right to receive tax, and reaps a share of all the demerit accruing to his subjects.

On the other hand more than one source speaks of the king as the owner of all the land and water in his kingdom; the corollary of this proposition would be that the tax on crops and the other products of the earth was a sort of rent in return for tenancy. That this idea, as well as the doctrine of taxation in return for protection, underlay ancient Indian practice, is evident from the fact that the king had the right to evict defaulting peasants, that he claimed the reversion of the property of those dying without heirs, that he sometimes demanded a fee comparable to the medieval European heriot before a holding was transferred to the heirs of a dead householder, and that he was the owner of treasure trove. Manu speaks of the king as ultimate lord (*adhipati*) of the land,[36] and therefore entitled to his share of treasure and minerals. Bhattasvāmin, the medieval commentator on the *Arthaśāstra*, declares bluntly that the king is lord of land and water, but that other things are the property of individual householders.[37] His statement is borne out by several other sources, and by the record of Megasthenes. More than one legend tells of kings giving away or trying to give away their kingdoms, as though they were personal property.

A few sources, however, reject the idea of the king's ultimate ownership of the land. Thus in a Jātaka story a king tells his mistress that he cannot give her his kingdom, for he is not its owner. When a legendary king, Viśvakarman Bhauvana, gave land to the priests, the goddess of earth rose up in person and rebuked him, saying that he had no right to give her away. A medieval commentator, probably basing his statement on this old story, says that kings cannot give away land, because it is owned in common.[38] The 16th-century jurist Nīlakaṇṭha states that land is the property of its owner, and kings have only the right to tax it; he adds that a gift of land does not imply a gift of the soil itself, but only of the right to make use of it.[39]

The attempts of some scholars to prove that the idea of the royal ownership of land never existed in ancient India seems to have sprung from the implicit presupposition, perhaps ultimately derived from the *laissez-faire* social philosophy of Herbert Spencer, that there was something primitive and shameful in such a conception. It is noteworthy that those authorities who denied royal ownership most forcibly were also those who overstressed the democratic element in the ancient Indian way of life. Such patriotic scholars as Dr. K. P. Jāyaswāl, writing when India's independence had not been achieved, did much to give her people faith in themselves, and therefore may have served a practical purpose. Now, with a free India, there can be no excuse for attempting to force the interpretation of texts whose meaning is perfectly obvious, in order to try to prove that the king laid no claim to ownership of the land and water of his domains. On this question, as on many others, ancient Indian opinion differed,[40] but our sources show that the majority of thinkers on the subject favoured the doctrine of royal ownership.

Whatever the theory, we may assume that in practice the royal ownership weighed lightly on the peasant who paid his taxes regularly; but the *Arthaśāstra* suggests that not only tax defaulters but also peasants who failed to cultivate their holdings efficiently should be evicted, though we have no evidence that this was regularly done.

The system which we have outlined was followed with many variations in normal times throughout pre-Muslim India; but in emergencies whips might be changed for scorpions. According to the theorists a king in serious financial straits was justified in adopting the most drastic and oppressive measures, rather than lose his throne. He might raise taxes indefinitely, levy forced loans and benevolences from wealthy people, resume grants and immunities promised in perpetuity, confiscate the hoarded wealth of goldsmiths and even rob religious establishments, especially those of heterodox sects. There is good evidence from the Kashmir chronicle and elsewhere that kings did sometimes go to these extreme lengths. In fairness, however, it must be pointed out that the theorists give as justifiable motives for such extortion not only danger from external and internal enemies, but the hunger of the poor through famine, flood or plague.

We know much about the income of the Indian king, but comparatively little about his expenditure. Much of the income of the state was stored, and the wealth of even small kingdoms is attested by foreign travellers and by the records of the booty obtained by Muslim invaders. According to accepted theory a well-stocked treasury was the king's chief source of strength, and no kingdom could function properly without it. The effect of this doctrine was certainly bad. The great reserves of precious metals and jewels, never touched except in direst emergency, were economically useless, and the treasury of a king was inevitably the target of the greed of his neighbours. The royal treasures, the existence of which was reported by early Muslim travellers, were important factors in encouraging the invasions which ultimately destroyed Hindu India.

LEGAL LITERATURE

With the passage of time the sacrificial instructions of the Brāhmaṇas became obscure, and a new group of texts was composed to elucidate them. These were *Śrauta Sūtras*; the term *sūtra* literally means "thread", but it was used with a secondary meaning of a manual of instruction in the form of brief aphorisms; the whole title may be paraphrased as "Manuals Explaining the Scriptures ". A little later were composed *Gṛhya Sūtras* dealing with domestic religious ceremonies, and finally manuals of human conduct, the *Dharma Sūtras*. A set of three sūtras, one on each of these topics, attributed to the same legendary sage, was called a *Kalpa Sūtra*. The Dharma Sūtras are our earliest sources for Hindu law, the most important being those attributed to Gautama, Baudhāyana, Vasistha and Apastamba. They were probably mainly composed between the 6th and the 2nd centuries B.C., but in some respects they look back to earlier times, while they contain later interpolations. The first three seem to have been written in a more westerly part of India than the early Buddhist scriptures, with which they are approximately contemporary, and the *Āpastamba* may have been composed in the Northern Deccan.

Later, from the early centuries of the Christian era onwards, the prose sūtras, including several now lost to us, were expanded and remodelled in verse form.

These revisions are the *Dharma Śāstras* ("Instructions in the Sacred Law"). The latter term is sometimes used for the Dharma Sūtras also, but most modern authorities reserve it for the longer versified texts of later days. There are numerous Dharma Śāstras, the earliest of which is that of Manu, probably composed in its final form in the 2nd or 3rd century A.D. Other important Dharma Śāstras are those of Yājñavalkya, Viṣṇu and Nārada, which date from the Gupta period and the Middle Ages, and there are numerous others of less importance, some preserved in a fragmentary form. Manu is still largely concerned with human conduct generally, but the works of his successors approach more and more closely to purely legal textbooks.

The Sūtras and Śāstras taken together are known as *Smṛti* ("remembered"), as distinct from the earlier Vedic literature, which is *Śruti* ("heard"), and which was believed to have been directly revealed to its authors, and therefore of greater sanctity than the later texts. Thus the *Mānava Dharma Śāstra*, or lawbook of Manu, is often known as the *Manu-Smṛti*. The Epics and Purāṇas were also looked on as Smṛti, and contain much legal lore. In fact hundreds of verses in Manu are also to be found in the *Mahābhārata*, and were probably not plagiarized, but inherited from a common source.

Many medieval jurists wrote lengthy commentaries on the Smṛti literature. Of these the most important was Vijñāneśvara, who wrote at the court of the great Cālukya emperor Vikramāditya VI (c. 1075–1127). His *Mitākṣarā*, a commentary on the lawbook of Yājñavalkya, played a very important part in forming the civil law of modern India. Other important jurists of the middle ages were Hemādri (c. 1300), and Jīmūtavāhana (12th century), whose treatise on inheritance (*Dāyabhāga*), part of a great compilation called *Dharmaratna*, has also influenced later Indian law.

It cannot be too strongly stressed that the whole Smṛti literature is the work of brāhmaṇs, who wrote from their own point of view. The *Arthaśāstra*, written from a more secular angle, differs from the Smṛtis in many particulars. It is certain that the advice of the Smṛtis was not regularly followed in many ancient kingdoms, though it became increasingly authoritative with time. The statements of the Smṛtis must as far as possible be checked by comparison with the *Arthaśāstra* and by passing references to law and custom in general literature, inscriptions, and the writings of foreign travellers.

THE BASIS OF LAW

Though we know very little about the legal system of the Ṛg Vedic period it is clear that the idea of a divine cosmic order already existed. *Ṛta*, the regularity of the universal process, was perhaps the forerunner of the later concept of *Dharma*. The latter word, etymologically akin to the English word "form", is untranslatable, and had many meanings. In the Aśokan inscriptions and some other Buddhist sources it seems to have the broad general meaning of "righteousness"; but in legal literature it may perhaps be defined as the divinely ordained norm of good conduct, varying according to class and caste. In this context we translate it as the "Sacred Law".

As well as Dharma there are, according to the textbooks, other bases of law: contract, custom and royal ordinance. The earlier religious lawbooks gave little attention to these, but their importance increased with time. It was recognized that, owing to the decadence of the age, Dharma was not now known in its fullness and purity and therefore supplementary sources of law were needed. Generally Dharma was thought to override all other bases of law, but the *Arthaśāstra* and one other lawbook[41] maintain that the royal ordinance overrides the others, a doctrine which we must ascribe to the totalitarianism of the Mauryas, and which few later jurists would have supported.

The king's duty of protection was chiefly the protection of Dharma, and as protector of Dharma he was Dharma incarnate. From Aśoka onwards kings sometimes assumed the title *Dharmarāja*, which was also one of the names of Yama, the god of death and the departed. Both Yama and the king maintained the Sacred Law by punishing evil-doers and rewarding the righteous.

Another concept, much in evidence in some sources, was that of *Daṇḍa*. The primary meaning of this word is "a stick", from which its secondary meanings may be easily inferred. In varying contexts it may be translated as "military force", "coercion", "punishment", "a fine", or simply "justice". Human nature was evil and corrupt. In the benighted age in which most ancient Indian writers on law and morals believed themselves to be living mankind could only be disciplined to observe the Sacred Law by fear of punishment. In the stem words of Manu:

> "If the king did not inflict punishment
> untiringly on evil-doers
> the stronger would roast the weaker,
> like fish upon a spit. ...
>
> "The whole world is controlled by punishment,
> for a guiltless man is hard to find. ...
>
> "Where dark and red-eyed Punishment
> walks the land, destroying sinners,
> the people are not harassed,
> if he who inflicts it is discerning."[42]

The king's responsibility for maintaining Dharma by means of Daṇḍa was not taken lightly. Impartial administration of justice brought him the same spiritual reward as Vedic sacrifices. Kings failing in their duty suffered in Hell. Even delay in justice was visited with dire penalties, for a legendary king called Nrga was reborn as a lizard, because he kept two litigants waiting in a dispute over a cow. Some sources declared that it was incumbent upon a king to restore the full value of stolen articles to the plaintiff, if the thief could not be brought to justice. Moreover, the king was believed to incur the demerit of criminals not brought to book, and to suffer in the next life accordingly, while from the secular point of view the king who perverted justice or was negligent in its administration was in danger of losing his throne.

CRIME

Megasthenes speaks of the Indians as remarkably law-abiding, and states that crime was very rare; similar evidence is given by Fa-hsien and by medieval Arab travellers, though Hsüan Tsang paints a somewhat less favourable picture. The impressions of foreign travellers are not wholly confirmed by Indian sources, however, and a profound sense of the insecurity of life and property underlies much of the legal literature.

In the earlier part of the period with which we deal, a process was going on in some ways comparable to that which is now taking place in parts of Africa. Uncivilized or semi-civilized tribes were breaking up under the pressure of Āryan Culture; even as early as Mauryan times villages were often overpopulated; many poor folk from the country and the hills drifted to the towns, as they are doing at the present day, and found life even more difficult than in their old surroundings. Some of these unfortunate and uprooted people provided the submerged tenth of habitual criminals which seems to have existed in all ancient Indian cities. In order to suppress crime the *Arthaśāstra* advises the imposition of a stringent curfew from about two and a half hours after sunset to the same time before dawn. Later sources speak of castes of professional thieves who had raised stealing to the status of a fine art, and who made use of written manuals on their profession.

Crime was equally rampant in the countryside, where the existence of large robber bands is attested from the time of the Buddha onwards. Hsüan Tsang gives the earliest account of hereditary bandits who robbed their victims and murdered them as a religious duty, like the later thugs. Trading caravans were heavily guarded, but were nevertheless frequently plundered by highwaymen. Thus ancient India was faced with a very serious crime problem, though the evidence of most of the foreign travellers suggests that the best ancient Indian kings managed to cope with it. Crime was suppressed through the local officers and garrison commanders, who had large staffs of police and soldiers, as well as secret agents who served as detectives. Watchmen kept guard through the night in city and village, and in some medieval kingdoms special officers (*duḥsādha-sādhanika*) were deputed to track down and apprehend bandits.

ADMINISTRATION OF JUSTICE

In the small kingdoms to which the early Dharma Sūtras refer the king might be the sole source of justice and indeed his own executioner, striking down condemned thieves with his mace; but in general the administration of justice was delegated, the king's court being reserved for appeals and serious crime against the state.

In medieval kingdoms, the councillor called Prāḍvivāka, the king's chief legal adviser, was responsible for justice and might also himself act as a judge.

The composition of the courts varied with time and place, but the evidence indicates that ancient India preferred a bench of magistrates to a single judge. A Jātaka story tells of a bench of five magistrates, all of whom, incidentally, are corrupt, while the *Arthaśāstra* advises that a court with a bench of three magistrates be set up for every ten villages, with higher courts in districts and provinces. Manu suggests a bench consisting of the Prāḍvivāka and three lesser judges, while the drama called "The Little Clay Cart" (p. 393) contains a scene in a court of justice, presided over by a chief judge, here called *adhikaraṇika*, a wealthy merchant (*śreṣṭhīn*), and a representative of the caste of scribes (*kāyastha*). The title given to the chief judge is derived from *adhikaraṇa*, "a government office", and suggests that he was an official who combined judicial and administrative functions; the two other magistrates were evidently leading citizens, who served on the bench as do our justices of the peace.

Though judicial corruption is often referred to, the standards set for judges and magistrates are very high; they are to be learned, religious, devoid of anger, and as impartial as humanly possible. To prevent bribery it is suggested that no private interviews should be allowed between judges and litigants until cases are settled. The *Arthaśāstra* advises that the honesty of judges should be periodically tested by agents provocateurs, while the *Viṣṇu Smṛti* prescribes banishment and forfeiture of all property for a judge found guilty of corruption or injustice—the most severe penalty a brāhmaṇ could incur under the Sacred Law.

False witness was generally looked on with great abhorrence, and, besides various temporal penalties, it incurred a hundred unhappy rebirths in future lives. In serious criminal cases evidence might be accepted from all sources, but in civil law only certain witnesses were qualified; generally women, learned brāhmaṇs, government servants, minore, debtors, persons with criminal records, and persons suffering from physical defects could not be called on to give evidence, while the evidence of low-caste people was not valid against persons of higher caste. Several tests, some very sound psychologically, are laid down to assess the veracity of witnesses.

Where the accused was open to grave suspicion not amounting to certainty he might be tortured to elicit confession. The tortures enumerated for this purpose are not all of the most extreme type, and include various forms of whipping. Brāhmaṇs, children, the aged, the sick, lunatics and pregnant women were theoretically exempt from torture, while only light torture was prescribed for women.

Another means of ascertaining guilt was the ordeal, which could be used in both civil and criminal cases, and in certain forms is still sometimes resorted to to settle disputes out of court. Ordeals are little mentioned in early texts, but they seem to have grown more popular in later times. The Smṛti writers apparently distrusted ordeals, and generally limited their application to cases in which there was no concrete evidence on either side. Several ordeals are mentioned, however, including ordeals by fire and immersion similar to those known in medieval

Europe, and possibly having a common Indo-European origin in the remote past. Specially interesting is the ordeal of the ploughshare, in which the accused man had to touch a red-hot iron ploughshare with his tongue; if he was not burned he was deemed innocent—psychologically a fairly sound test of his own confidence in the result, since if he had a guilty conscience his salivary glands would not function properly, and his tongue would be burnt.

Megasthenes remarked that the Indian was not inclined to litigation, and he may have been correct, though the same could not be said of India of more recent times. In any case, though there were many brāhmaṇs learned in law they never constituted a class of professional pleaders, and those who did not serve on the bench presumably used their knowledge to settle cases out of court. There is evidence, however, that by the end of our period a class of lawyers, in the modern sense, was beginning to develop, for some late textbooks allow litigants to employ proxies, who are to be rewarded with a share of the money involved, while one source grants to any learned brāhmaṇ the right to give his views on a case from the body of the court.[43]

PUNISHMENT

The penalties imposed for criminal offences developed from two very ancient customs, the wergeld and the religious penance imposed for ritual offences. The influence of both can be clearly traced in the system of punishment followed in later times.

The early Sūtras laid down fines for the punishment of murder—1,000 cows for killing a kṣatriya, 100 for a vaiśya, and 10 for a śūdra or a woman of any class; the killing of a brāhmaṇ could not be expiated by a fine. The cattle were handed to the king, who passed them on to the relatives of the slain man, a bull being added as the king's perquisite. Later sources lose sight of the true nature of the fines as means of buying off the vengeance of the family of the dead man, and lay down that the cattle are expiatory gifts, to be given to the brāhmaṇs. But the wergeld left its mark on the legal system in the form of the fines, which, with or without other punishment, are a special feature of ancient Indian justice. Fines ranging from a small copper coin to the confiscation of all property were levied, and could atone for all but the most serious crime. They were an appreciable source of income to the state, and many medieval charters, giving revenue rights over a village or district, specifically include the right to receive the fines levied at the local court. A condemned person who could not pay his fine was reduced to bondage until it was paid by his labour.

The Smṛti writers rarely mention imprisonment, but all other sources show that it was common. Aśoka was proud of the many gaol-deliveries which he had ordered in the course of his reign; according to a later tradition he is said to have maintained in his unreformed early years a prison in which the most fiendish tortures were inflicted, and from which no prisoner came out alive.[44] Hsüan Tsang mentions imprisonment as the usual form of punishment under Harṣa.

Forced labour in the state mines and elsewhere is mentioned as a punishment in the *Arthaśāstra*, and no doubt amounted to imprisonment of a very severe type. Mutilation and torture were common penalties for many crimes, and numerous forms are described by legal writers. Such punishments were often looked on rather as penances, and the idea of religious penance was never completely absent from the thought of the pious authors of the Smrtis, in considering the punishment of crime. It was generally believed that by undergoing punishment in this life the criminal escaped the evil consequences of his crime in the next.

The death penalty is laid down in many forms and for many crimes. Unlike the early Sūtras the *Arthaśāstra* prescribes it for murder, even as a result of a duel or quarrel, if the injured man dies within seven days. Hanging is the penalty for spreading false rumours, house-breaking, and stealing the king's elephants and horses. Those who plot against the king, force entry into the king's harem, aid his enemies, create disaffection in the army, murder father, mother, son, brother or an ascetic, or commit serious arson, are to be burnt alive. Beheading is the penalty laid down by the *Arthaśāstra* for wilful murder or stealing a herd of cattle. The man who deliberately breaks a dam is to be drowned in the same dam. Women murdering their husbands or children, killing others by poison, or committing arson are to be torn apart by oxen. Civilians stealing military supplies are to be shot to death with arrows. These are some of the many forms of execution suggested by the *Arthaśāstra*. This text is comparatively lenient towards sexual crime, but Manu also prescribes death in various unpleasant forms for most types of adultery and sexual assault. Even the benevolent Aśoka, for all his distaste for the taking of life, did not abolish the death penalty (p. 48). The usual form of execution, little mentioned in the textbooks on law but often referred to in general literature, was impalement.

Nevertheless it is evident that some opinion definitely opposed the death penalty, and the question is considered from both sides in a remarkable passage in the *Mahābhārata*.[45] Here the argument against capital punishment and heavy penalties in general is not based, as might be expected, on the doctrine of non-violence, which in no way forbade either capital punishment or war, but rests wholly on humanitarian considerations. In most cases mutilation, long imprisonment and execution result in untold suffering for many innocent people, especially for the wife and family of the criminal. The argument is quickly refuted—in this dark age the innocent must suffer with the guilty, in order that society may be protected, anarchy avoided, and men enabled to pursue the Sacred Law in peace.

Humanitarian ideas, probably encouraged by Buddhism, were effective in Gupta times in moderating the fierce punishments of earlier days. Fa-hsien records that the death penalty was not imposed in Northern India, but most crime was punished by fines, and only serious revolt by the amputation of one hand. The Chinese traveller may have exaggerated, but his testimony at least suggests that executions were rare. Hsüan Tsang 200 years later, reported that prisoners were not executed under Harsa, but were left to rot in dungeons. In later times there is good evidence that capital punishment was inflicted, and criminals often became the victims of human sacrifice, but in the medieval period we read of sentences which, even by modern standards, seem surprisingly mild. Thus a Cōla inscription records the gift of 96 sheep to endow a perpetual lamp in a temple, the donor being a man who had stabbed an army officer to death; this was apparently the only penalty he suffered. Other South Indian instances can be found of murderers being let off with comparatively small penances of this nature. It would seem that here the blood feud had by no means disappeared, and if a murderer could appease the enmity of his victim's family the court would let him off lightly. Killing in self-defence was justified in law, as was the stealing of small quantities of food to stave off starvation.

In later times the lives of many animals were protected by law, especially that of the cow. The story of the Cōla king who ordered the execution of his own son for the accidental killing of a calf is certainly a legend, and we need not believe that Kumārapāla (c. 1143–1172), the Jaina king of the Caulukya dynasty of Gujarāt, so strictly enforced non-violence that heavy fines were inflicted on people who killed fleas, but these stories show the climate of opinion in medieval India. In the later period the wanton killing of a cow was among the most serious of crimes.

The legal system envisaged by the Smṛtis would impose graduated punishment according to class. Thus a brāhmaṇ slandering a kṣatriya should, according to Manu, pay a fine of fifty panas, but for slandering a vaiśya or a śūdra the fines are only twenty-five and twelve paṇas respectively. For members of the lower orders who slander their betters the penalties are much more severe. Similar gradations of penalty according to the class of the offender are laid down for many crimes, and the equality of all before the law was never admitted in ancient India, and was quite contrary to most Indian thought. If the *satnatā*, which Aśoka instructed his officials to employ in their judicial dealings,[46] means equality the case is unique; it is probable that the word implies no more than consistency, or perhaps mildness. It is hardly likely that even Aśoka was bold enough to introduce so drastic a change in the administration of justice—one which no other ancient lawgiver, Indian or otherwise, would have agreed to.

In the later Vedic period some brāhmaṇs claimed to be above the law altogether. At the proclamation of the king at the end of the royal consecration ceremony the chief officiating brāhmaṇ turned to the assembled multitude and cried "Here is your king, O Kurus—for us, our king is [the god] Soma". At all times the priestly class demanded many privileges in law. According to most orthodox sources the brāhmaṇs were exempt from execution, torture, and corporal punishment, the worst penalty that could be imposed on them being the humiliation of losing their topknot (p. 138), followed by confiscation of property and banishment. But the Smṛti of Kātyāyana allows the execution of a brāhmaṇ for procuring abortion, the murder of a respectable woman, and the theft of gold, while the *Arthaśāstra* admits it for sedition, and also sanctions the branding of brāhmaṇs. In "The Little Clay Cart" the hero, though a brāhmaṇ, is threatened with torture and sentenced to death, and there is much other evidence that the brāhmaṇs did not always obtain the privileges which they claimed.

In fairness to the Hindu legal system, we must note that it did not always work in favour of the brāhmaṇ. Manu lays down that as the penalty for theft the śūdra should pay a fine equal to eight times the value of the stolen goods, while the vaiśya, kṣatriya and brāhmaṇ should pay sixteen, thirty-two and sixty-four times the value respectively. The upper classes were expected to follow higher standards of conduct than the lower, and their thefts were correspondingly more heinous.

As well as the royal courts there were other tribunals which could arbitrate in disputes and deal with minor crime. These were the councils of villages, castes and guilds, whose validity as judicial bodies for their members was fully recognized in the legal literature. They could punish offenders by fines and excommunication, the latter a very serious penalty indeed, and they probably played as important a part in the life of the community as did the king's courts. Unfortunately we have little knowledge of their procedure.

THE SECRET SERVICE

Perhaps the least pleasant feature of political life in ancient India was the espionage system. The most detailed picture of the working of this secret service is given in the *Arthaśāstra*, the author of which devotes two chapters to its organization, and refers to it throughout his treatise. The text visualizes a country riddled from top to bottom with secret agents or spies. They were organized through "institutes of espionage" to which they delivered information, sometimes in cipher, and from which they received their orders. These institutes were not responsible for the whole organization of espionage, however, for there were special spies, directly subordinate to the king or a high minister, and employed to spy on the ministers themselves.

The spies might be recruited from any walk of life, and might be of either sex. Brāhmaṇs unable to make a living by their learning, merchants fallen on evil days, barbers, astrologers, humble servitore, prostitutes, peasants—all might be enrolled as secret agents. A special class of spy was the *satṛ*, an orphan trained from childhood for the work, and usually masquerading as a holy-man or a fortune-teller, two professions whose members, being specially trusted by the public, could gain access to information which others might find difficulty in obtaining. A further class was that of the desperado, recruited from professional prize-fighters; the main duty of such an agent was the assassination of those enemies of the king for whom a public trial was not expedient, but he also performed other secret deeds of daring and violence on behalf of his master.

The ancient Indian secret service has incurred much criticism, some of which is not wholly fair. Probably no government at any time has been able to function without secret agents of some sort, if only honest detectives for the suppression of crime, and every ancient civilization had its spies, though perhaps not so thoroughly organized as those envisaged in the *Arthaśāstra*. The ancient Indian spy system was not quite comparable to the secret political police of some modern states, since its function was by no means confined to the suppression of criticism and sedition, and it was looked on not as a mere machiavellian instrument for maintaining power, but as an integral part of the state machinery.

Certainly one of the spy's chief duties was protecting the king's power. He sought out sedition, whether in the brothel or in the palace of the crown-prince. He served as agent provocateur, to test the loyalty of high ministers, generals and judges. In the territory of enemies, whether potential or actual, he not only obtained information on the strength and plans of the king's foes but also encouraged sedition, and plotted the assassination of the enemy king and his ministers. He also acted as a detective for the suppression of crime. For this purpose he frequented, in disguise, taverns, brothels and gambling dens, listened to the conversation of men in their cups, and carefully watched those who seemed abnormally affluent.

But he had also other duties of a more positive character. He was an important means of keeping a finger on the pulse of public opinion. In the story of Rāma (p. 365f) it is a spy who informs the king that his subjects suspect Sītā's chastity. The secret service, in fact, kept the king in touch with his people. It was also a means of maintaining the king's popularity. One of the spy's duties was to spread stories favourable to the king, to praise him in public, to argue with those who criticized the administration, and in general to spread propaganda in the king's favour. There is no reason to believe that mild criticism of the king or his administration was normally punished. The ancient Indian secret service might no doubt, in the hands of an unjust king, be a very evil thing, but under a just administration it had positive and useful functions, and was not a mere instrument of repression.

HINDU MILITARISM

The rule of law in personal, family and class relations was a fundamental element of ancient Indian thought, but in the sphere of international affairs there was no real conception of its possibility. A few enlightened people recognized the evil effects of the warfare which afflicted the Indian sub-continent during most of its history, but their message was generally unheard. Aśoka was possibly the only ancient Indian king who finally broke with the tradition of aggression, though his spirit can perhaps be heard in certain passages in Buddhist texts, and many ordinary people must have echoed his sentiments. In several passages of the *Mahābhārata*, notably in the famous *Bhagavad Gitā*, the evil and cruelty of war are referred to, and it is suggested that the life of the solider is a sinful one. But such arguments are only put forward to be demolished by counter-arguments, most of which are based on the necessities of this dark age of the world and on the dangers of anarchy. Positive condemnations of war are rare in Indian literature.

In one story the Buddha himself is depicted as intervening in a tribal war between the Śākyas and their neighbours the Koliyas, and persuading the contestants to come to terms. In the beautiful *Dhamtnapada*, an early collection of Buddhist verse, we read:

Victory breeds hatred,
for the conquered sleep in sorrow;
above victory or defeat
the calm man dwells in peace.[47]

Buddhism was specially popular with the mercantile classes, who stood to lose much from constant warfare, and the passing and rare references to the evils of war in Buddhist texts may in part represent the mild protest of the vaiśyas against the continual campaigning which interfered with their trading ventures. In any case war was generally accepted as a normal activity of the state, even by Buddhist kings. The doctrine of non-violence, which in medieval India had become very influential and had made most of the respectable classes vegetarian, was never at this time taken to forbid war or capital punishment. It was only in modern times that Mahātmā Gāndhī reinterpreted it in this sense.

The intense militarism of ancient India did not lead to the building of a permanent empire over the whole sub-continent. In this respect the early history of India contrasts strikingly with that of China, where, from the 3rd century B.C., a single empire was the rule and division the exception. In India the Mauryas succeeded in creating a unified empire for a century, and in the heyday of the Guptas much of North India was under one sceptre, but at other times numerous factors prevented the unification of the recognized cultural unit of Bhāratavarṣa, which so many ambitious monarchs desired.

One of these factors was the mere size of the land, but the Chinese emperors conquered equal difficulties. Another reason for the failure of Indian empire builders was that, for all the wise counsel of the *Arthaśāstra*, no king of India was able to develop a bureaucracy capable of functioning without a strong guiding hand; in China the examination system and the ethics of Confucius ensured that those incharge of affairs would usually be men of character and intellect, if rather pedantic and conservative. In India the hereditary tendency and reliance on the King's favour produced a ministerial cadre of perhaps lower quality. But one of the main factors which prevented the unification of India was the martial tradition itself.

For the post-Mauryan king the idea of empire was something very different from that to which the West is accustomed. According to the *Arthaśāstra* there are three types of conquest: righteous conquest, conquest for greed, and demoniac conquest.* The first is conquest in which the defeated king is forced to render homage and tribute, after which he or a member of his family is reinstated as a vassal. The second is victory in which enormous booty is demanded and large portions of enemy territory are annexed. The third involves the political annihilation of the conquered kingdom and its incorporation in that of the victor.

* In Sanskrit: dharmavijaya, lobhavijaya, and asuravijaya. Aśoka used the term dharmavijaya, "conquest by Righteousness", in a very different sense.

The two latter types are generally disapproved of by all sources except the *Arthaśāstra*. Thus the *Mahābhārata* declares:

> "A king should not attempt
> to gain the earth unrighteously,
> for who reveres the king
> who wins unrighteous victory?
> Unrighteous conquest is impermanent,
> and does not lead to heaven."[48]

The idea of "righteous conquest" or "conquest according to the the Sacred Law" may have developed among the Āryans soon after their occupation of North India, as an expression of their solidarity against the dark-skinned natives. It is evident, though not explicitly stated, in later Vedic literature. The kings of Magadha from Bimbisāra onwards ignored it, and annexed territory without compunction; but the doctrine that war should be waged for glory and homage rather than sordid aims such as wealth and power grew in importance with the fall of the Mauryas, and was accepted by the medieval quasi-feudal order. "Demoniac conquest" still took place from time to time, notably under the Guptas, but "righteous conquest" was the ideal which Hindu kings were expected to follow, and it is evident that they usually did so. War became the sport of kings— a sport which was often very profitable and always very serious, in which the shame of defeat might well only be expunged by suicide, but a sport nevertheless. The Peninsula, inheriting a fierce Dravidian tradition never completely submerged by Āryan influence, had a more realistic approach; here conquest with annexation was more common, as well as ruthlessness towards captives and non-combatants, but even the South was not unaffected by the ideal of the "righteous conquest".

In most of the texts on statecraft we read of the "six instruments of policy" (*ṣāḍguṇya*): peace, war, waiting for the enemy to strike the first blow, attack, alliance, and "double policy" or making peace with one enemy and continuing war with another.* The list is a stock one, and gives a further example of the delight of the Indian theorist in pedantic classification, but it is nevertheless significant. Peace is only one of the six categories; the others are aspects of war in all its branches. The *Arthaśāstra* quotes an earlier authority, Vātavyādhi, as disagreeing with the sixfold classification, and maintaining that statecraft involved only two aspects, peace and war.[49] Of this view the text strongly disapproves; pacific relations are straightforward and obvious, while war is complex and highly developed. It is significant that one of the words commonly used for enemy, *para*, has the simple primary meaning of "other".

At all times conquest was the chief ambition of the Indian king. Even Aśoka,

* In Sanskrit: sandhi, vigraha, āsana, yāna, saṃśraya, and dvaidhībhāva. The terms are somewhat differently interpreted in different sources.

who abjured aggressive war, did not give up the hope of conquest (p. 46). The position is succinctly put by the *Arthaśāstra*: "The king who is weaker than 'the other' should keep the peace; he who is stronger should make war."[50] The same aphorism is repeated in many other sources, in slightly varying forms, but a difference of attitude is apparent as we leave the Mauryan recollections of the *Arthaśāstra* for the later texts, the outlook of which reflects memories of the later Vedic age, adapted to the often anarchic conditions of the period between the Mauryas and Guptas.

For the earlier source war is a "continuation of policy by other means". Its purpose is not glory, but wealth and power, and the passage we have quoted, defining the three types of conquest, is, we believe, either a sop to conventional doctrine or a later interpolation, for it is inconsistent with the tenor of the book. The whole work is written for a king who aspires to become an emperor on the Mauryan model, and such a king is not advised to embark on war lightly. There are many other ways of gaining power, intrigue and assassination among them, and these should always be resorted to in preference to war, which should only be looked on as a last resort. If a king suffers decisive defeat he must submit, in the hope that he will be allowed to retain his throne as a vassal and will ultimately again achieve independence and conquer his former overlord. The *Arthaśāstra* says nothing about fair play in battle, and evidently looks on conquest of the demoniac variety as the most profitable and advisable. Though in one passage, not in keeping with the main tenor of the work, it suggests allowing the conquered king to remain as a vassal, it ends on a note of humanitarian imperialism. The victor must do everything in his power to conciliate the conquered people; if their economy has suffered badly from the war, taxes must be remitted; ministers of the defeated king must be won round, and law and order restored as quickly as possible; when in the conquered country the king should wear local dress and follow local customs. Evidently, from the point of view of the *Arthaśāstra*, the main motive of war is gain and the building up of a great empire.

The more orthodox texts take a different attitude. For them the major motive of war is glory, not gain. War is not merely a means to an end, but part of the warrior's *dharma* and good for its own sake. As soon as a king has established himself on the throne he should, as a matter of course, attack his neighbours. Rules of fair fighting are laid down, which are not heard of in the *Arthaśāstra*. For the later sources, such as Manu, a battle was ideally a gigantic tournament with many rules: a warrior fighting from a chariot might not strike one on foot; an enemy in flight, wounded or asking quarter might not be slain; the lives of enemy soldiers who had lost their weapons were to be respected; poisoned weapons were not to be used. Homage and not annexation was the rightful fruit of victory.

These rules were not always kept. The heroes of the *Mahābhārata* infringe them many times, even at the behest of their mentor Kṛṣṇa, and the infringements are explained and pardoned by recourse to casuistical arguments of expediency and necessity. The rules of war could only be maintained strictly by a king certain of victory or certain of defeat. Where chances were narrow the claims of self-preservation inevitably made themselves felt. But the chivalrous rules of war, probably based on very old tradition, and codified in their present form among the martial peoples of Western India in post-Mauryan times, must have had some effect in mitigating the harshness of war for combatant and non-combatant alike. It is doubtful if any other ancient civilization set such humane ideals of warfare.

Together with these rules, the later texts introduce the conception of military honour, which is not found in the realistic *Arthaśāstra*, except in the form of propaganda to maintain the morale of the troops. Flight is the deepest of shames; the soldier slain in flight incurs the guilt of his lord, and suffers proportionately in the after-life, but the soldier slain while fighting to the last passes straight to heaven. Such ideals culminated in the *jauhar*, the final holocaust which was the fate of many a medieval Rājput king with his family and bodyguard, the women and children burning alive in the inner chambers of the fort while the men fought to the last on the battlements.

The live dog was no longer thought to be better than the dead lion, in so far as the spirit of the Epics permeated Hindu life. But the *Arthaśāstra* was not wholly forgotten, and not every king of medieval India was willing to sacrifice himself and his family when defeat stared him in the face. As well as kings who resisted the Muslim invaders to the last there were many who tried to buy them off, and who retained diminished kingdoms under the suzerainty of the hated *Mleccha*.

In this political climate it is not surprising that inter-state relations were of the most machiavellian character. The basic concept which governed the relations of one king with another was the doctrine of the "circles" (*maṇḍala*), which, like many other concepts, was pedantically elaborated by the theorists on statecraft. The king on whose territory the circle is centred is known as "he who desires conquest" (*vijigīṣu*). The king whose territory adjoins that of the would-be conqueror is "the enemy" (*ari*)—"when he is in trouble he must be attacked, when he has little or no help he may be uprooted, otherwise he must be harassed and weakened".[51] Beyond the enemy lies "the friend" (*mitra*) the natural ally of the conqueror. So far the system of circles is simple and obvious, but the theorists enlarged it further. Beyond the friend is "the enemy's friend" (*arimitra*), and beyond him "the friend's friend" (*mitra-mitra*). The opposite frontier of the conqueror's kingdom provides a further series of potential foes and allies, the "heel-seizer" (*pārṣṇigraha*), who is an ally of the conqueror's enemy and is liable to attack the conqueror in the rear, the "defender" or rearward friend (*ākranda*), the heel-seizer's ally (*pārṣṇigrahāsāra*), and the rearward friend's friend (*ākrandāsāra*). The main purport of this enumeration is clear—a king's neighbour is his natural enemy, while the king beyond his neighbour is his natural ally. The working of this principle can be seen throughout the history of Hindu India in the temporary alliances of two kingdoms to accomplish the encirclement and destruction of the kingdoms between them.

In such conditions diplomatic relations were not thoroughly organized, and there is no evidence of a system of permanent ambassadore. Relations between one court and another were maintained by envoys (*dūta*), who resided at the court to which they were sent only while transacting the business in hand. As in most civilizations, the person of the envoy was inviolable, and it was thought that a king slaying an envoy would be reborn in hell with all his councillors.

Megasthenes states that peasants would till their fields peacefully even when a battle was raging nearby, but this is probably too optimistic a generalization. Devastation of the crops to weaken the enemy was quite legitimate according to the textbooks, and, although there was a strong feeling that the lives of non-combatants should be respected, this rule was not always kept. In any case, except in favoured times and localities the peasant was never altogether safe from raiders, and, though the wholesale sacking of cities was not common in ancient India, the townsman could rarely feel secure against the looting and exactions of enemy occupation. Conditions in Hindu India were not unlike those in medieval Europe, where there was a broad and recognized cultural unity accompanied by inter-state anarchy resulting in perpetual warfare. In Europe, however, the well-organized and centralized Roman Church often acted as a pacifying element in the situation; in India Hinduism, which had no all-embracing super-national organization, rather encouraged inter-state anarchy by incorporating many martial traditions into the Sacred Law.

MILITARY ORGANIZATION AND TECHNIQUE

The ancient Indian army contained more than one type of soldier, and troops are sometimes classified into six categories: hereditary troops, forming the backbone of the army; mercenaries; troops provided by corporations (*śreṇi*); troops supplied by subordinate allies; deserters from the enemy; and wild tribesmen, used for guerilla fighting in hill and jungle. Of this list the third category is obscure, but it perhaps refers to the private armies maintained by merchant guilds for the protection of their caravans and trading posts, which might be loaned to the king. In medieval Ceylon the corporation of Kerala merchants called *Maṇigrāma* (p. 194), like the Honourable Company in 18th century India, became an important and often a decisive factor in the island's politics through its private army. The fierce mercenaries of Kerala (Malabār) and Karṇāṭa (Mysore) found ready employment in the armies of many Indian and Sinhalese kings throughout out the Middle Ages.

Of the four great classes the kṣatriya was the warrior par excellence, and no doubt most of the hereditary troops considered themselves to belong to this class, but all classes took part in war. Brāhmaṇs holding high military rank are mentioned in the Epics and in many medieval inscriptions, and their participation in war is expressly permitted in some texts. The lower orders fought also, but usually as auxiliaries or subordinates.

In the early Vedic period all free men were no doubt liable to military service by tribal custom, but, with the strengthening of caste ideas, the liability vanished in most parts of India. There is no evidence of general conscription in any major Indian kingdom from the Mauryas onwards, though the *Arthaśāstra* mentions villages which provided troops in lieu of taxes, and such villages of warriors existed in the quasi-feudal Middle Ages; the martial character of the tribes of N.-W. India, Rājasthān, and parts of the Western Deccan, seems to have altered little from the earliest times, despite numerous invasions and changes of overlord, and it survives to the present day; among such people most able-bodied men took part in war.

The traditional divisions of the Indian army were four: elephants, cavalry, chariots and infantry; some sources add other categories, such as navy, spies, pioneers and commissariat, to bring the total up to six or eight. Of these elements the most important, from the point of view of contemporary theory, was the first.

Elephants employed in war are first definitely mentioned in the Buddhist scriptures, where it is said that king Bimbisāra of Magadha owned a large and efficient elephant corps. They were trained with great care and attention, and, marching in the van of the army, acted rather like tanks in modern warfare, breaking up the enemy's ranks and smashing palisades, gates, and other defences (p. 409f); a line of elephants might also act as a living bridge for crossing shallow rivers and streams. Elephants were often protected by leather armour, and their tusks tipped with metal spikes. The Chinese traveller Sung Yün, who visited the kingdom of the Hūṇas in the early 6th century, speaks of fighting elephants with swords fastened to their trunks, with which they wrought great carnage, but there is no confirmation of this practice in other sources. As well as the mahout the elephant usually carried two or three soldiers, armed with bows, javelins and long spears, and advanced with a small detachment of infantry to defend it from attack.

The great reliance placed on elephants by Indian tacticians was, from the practical point of view, unfortunate. Though fighting elephants might at first strike great terror in an invading army unused to them, they were by no means invincible. Just as the Romans found means of defeating the elephants of Pyrrhus and Hannibal, so Greeks, Turks and other invaders soon lost their fear of the Indian fighting elephant. Even the best trained elephant was demoralized comparatively easily, especially by fire, and when overcome by panic it would infect its fellows, until a whole squadron of elephants, trumpeting in terror, would turn from the battle, throw its riders, and trample the troops of its own side. The pathetic Indian faith in the elephants' fighting qualities was inherited by the Muslim conquerors, who, after a few generations in India, became almost as reliant on elephants as the Hindus, and suffered at the hands of armies without elephants in just the same way.

Cavalry, though important, was not up to the standard of that of many other early peoples, and the weakness of their cavalry was an important factor in the defeat of Indian armies attacked by invaders from the North-West; the decisive victory of Alexander over Porus in 326 B.C. and that of Muhammad of Ghor over Pṛthvīrāja in A.D. 1192 were both largely due to superior, more mobile cavalry. Mounted archers were a special danger to Indian armies.

The chariot as a vehicle of war disappeared soon after the commencement of the Christian era. In the Vedic period it was the major fighting arm, and it retained this importance in the Epic stories. The *Arthaśāstra* and other evidence shows that in Mauryan times it was still widely used in war, and early sculpture depicts a few fighting chariots; but by Gupta times the chariot was little more than a means of transport. The light two-horsed chariot of the Vedic period, carrying only a driver and a warrior, developed into a larger and more cumbrous vehicle. Four-horsed chariots are mentioned by classical sources, and are depicted at Sānchī and elsewhere, with horses yoked abreast and carrying four men.

Fig. x.—Royal Warriors (after a terracotta plaque from Ahicchatrā, U.P. *c*. 6th century A.D.)

There are several references to ships being used for military purposes, but little evidence that Indian kings had a real conception of the value of sea-power, or of naval warfare. Ships were chiefly used for conveying troops, usually along the great Indian rivers; but the Cālukya king Pulakeśin II employed a navy to besiege Purī, not far from the modern Bombay (p. 466, n), and the two great Cōla kings, Rājarāja I and Rājendra I (p. 65), developed a positive maritime policy and evidently had a regular navy. The Sinhalese conqueror Parākramabāhu I (p. 66) is said to have invaded Burma by sea. Ships of war were used to put down the many pirates who infested the Indian Ocean, and Arab writers of the Middle Ages show that the petty chiefs of the West Coast themselves organized pirate fleets; but, with the exception of the Cōlas, it is doubtful if any Indian king possessed a navy in the modern sense.

The infantry, though little mentioned in the texts, must at all times have been the real backbone of the army. An élite corps, a sort of Pretorian Guard, existed in most kingdoms. In the medieval South this royal guard was pledged to defend the king's person to the death, and its loyalty was confirmed by a ceremonial meal eaten with the king on his accession. The privilege of eating with the king conferred on the guardsmen a sort of nobility, and they are mentioned by Marco Polo as "Companions of Honour".

The *Arthaśāstra* envisages a corps of physicians to care for the wounded, ready in the rear with drugs, bandages, and other equipment. The existence of such a corps, and of a staff of horse and elephant doctors attached to the army, is confirmed by other sources. The same text mentions the employment of women to cook for the troops in the rear of the battle.

According to most theorists the basic unit of the Indian army was the *patti*, a sort of mixed platoon consisting of one elephant, one chariot, three horses, and five foot-soldiers. Three pattis constituted a *senāmukha*, three senāmukhas a *gulma*, and so on up to the "complete army" (*akṣauhiṇī*), of 21,870 pattis. The exaggerated precision of this list is another example of the pedantry which beset most ancient Indian writing on practical matters, and there is no good evidence that the army was regularly divided in this way, with all arms intermixed. Other sources speak of commands rising in units of ten, and the *Arthaśāstra* mentions a unit consisting of 45 chariots, 45 elephants, 225 horses, and 675 footmen; five of these detachments formed a full battle array (*samavyūha*), resembling the Roman legion in size. The *Arthaśāstra* allows wide variation in these numbers according to the availability of resources and the requirements of the situation.

The Indian army was usually a very large one. Classical accounts state that the forces of the last Nanda king consisted of 20,000 cavalry, 2,000 chariots, 200,000 footmen, and a number of elephants variously given as 3,000, 4,000, or 6,000. Plutarch records that Candragupta Maurya overran India with 600,000 men. Hsūan Tsang states that at the beginning of his career Harṣa had 5,000 elephants, 20,000 cavalry, and 50,000 footmen, which were increased to 60,000 elephants and 100,000 cavalry at the height of his power. The 9th-century Arab traveller Al Mas'ūdī says that the Pratihāra king Mahendrapāla had four armies of 800,000 men each, while the Cōla king Rājarāja I is said to have invaded the kingdom of the Cālukyas with an army of 900,000. All this evidence is far from reliable, but it is noteworthy that estimates of the size of medieval armies are considerably larger than those of armies of the earlier period, and this may bear some relation to fact. Fully mobilized, and including auxiliaries and non-combatants, it is not impossible that the total fighting force of a larger medieval kingdom numbered well over a million.

According to Megasthenes the Mauryan army was organized under a committee of thirty, divided into sub-committees which controlled the corps of infantry, cavalry, chariots, elephants, navy, and commissariat. This system seems to be modelled on Megasthenes' description of the city government of Pāṭaliputra (p. 89), and is not confirmed by any other source. The *Arthaśāstra* describes the army as organized under a number of superintendents, with a general (*senāpati*) at the head of all military affairs. Medieval armies often had numerous generals, with a "great general" (*mahāsenāpati*) in supreme command. The general was always a very important figure in the realm, and often a member of the royal family. He took orders direct from the king, who was expected to take command in major engagements, even when aged. Kings often fought in the van of the battle, but the cautious *Arthaśāstra* advises them to direct operations from the rear. Below the general were numerous captains (*nāyaka*, *daṇḍanāyaka*), who, in the medieval period, often approximated to a feudal nobility. Regiments, divisions and squadrons were recognized by distinguishing standards, and often had a definite corporate life. In medieval South India we hear of the troops of a regiment subscribing to a fund for the dependants of a comrade killed in battle, and there are records of religious donations made by regimental subscription.

The arms of ancient India were not appreciably different from those of other early civilizations. Efforts have been made by some scholars, not all of them Indian, to show that firearms and even flying machines were known, but this is certainly not the case. The one clear reference to firearms occurs in the text on polity ascribed to Śukra, which is in fact a product of the 19th century (p. 72, n). The mysterious and magical weapons of the Epics, slaying hundreds at a blow and dealing fire and death all around them, must be the products of the poet's imagination. If India had had firearms her Greek, Chinese and Arab visitors would certainly have recorded the existence of such wonders, and also, *a fortiori*, of the marvellous aerial pavilions described in the *Rāmāyaṇa*, early Tamil texts, and elsewhere, the making of which was quite beyond the technical ability of any ancient civilization.

In fact the Indians possessed the ancient world's equipment of artillery—ballistas (probably not known before Mauryan times), battering rams and other siege engines. The inspiration for the wonderful weapons of the poets may have come from the incendiary missiles, fireballs, fire-arrows and the like, which were a special feature of Indian military equipment, though disapproved of as unfair by the Smṛi writers. The *Arthaśāstra* especially stresses the value of incendiarism in war, and even suggests the use of birds and monkeys to carry fire to the enemy's rooftops. It gives brief formulae for the composition of inflammable material, and these are clear enough to show that this was not gunpowder.

The usual Indian bow in Mauryan times was some five or six feet long, and often made of bamboo; it shot long cane arrows. According to classical accounts it was a very powerful instrument, which was rested on the ground and steadied with one foot, but the bows of the few archers shown in early sculpture are raised from the ground. Poisoned arrows were known and used, though condemned in religious texts. The less cumbersome composite bow, often made of horn (*śārṅga*), was also known, and became more popular in later times. Swords were of various types, the most dangerous being the *niṣtriṃśa*, a long two-handed slashing sword. Lances and javelins were among the usual equipment of the Indian soldier, and included a special long lance (*tomara*) used in fighting from the backs of elephants. Iron maces and battle-axes were also used. Terracotta slingstones have been found in the remains of the Indus cities, and the sling was used in later times, though it does not seem to have been an important weapon.

The warriors depicted in early sculpture (pl. XXIV) are only lightly defended with armour, but the use of armour of metal or leather developed as a result of the influx of invaders from the North-West, and in the Middle Ages coats of mail became more usual, together with armour for horses and elephants. Shields of bent cane covered with leather, or of metal, were regularly used, sometimes protecting the whole body. Helmets are not often depicted until the Middle Ages, and it would seem that the Indian soldier relied mainly on the thick folds of his turban to protect his head.

Fortification was an important branch of military science, but nearly all the fortresses of pre-Muslim India have been so developed and adapted in later times that they no longer give a true picture of ancient Indian military architecture. An important exception is the long wall of rough-hewn stone protecting the site of the ancient Rājagṛha, the capital of Bimbisāra of Magadha, which probably dates back to the Buddha's day. Recently the revetted brick-faced wall of the old city of Kauśāmbl has been uncovered by Indian archaeologists. This, probably first constructed before the time of the Buddha, was from time to time enlarged and strengthened, until it became a rampart of imposing height and thickness. Another example is Śiśupālgarh in Orissā, where a small section of the city ramparts dating from pre-Gupta times, has been excavated. It was a workmanlike brick wall, set on an earthwork and probably surrounded by a moat.

The ideal *durga*, or fortified city, as described in the *Arthaśāstra*, was circled by three very wide moats, within which was an earthwork, covered with spiny shrubs, and surmounted by a wall thirty-six feet high, with numerous square towers and roofed balconies for archers. With this may be compared Megasthenes' description of the defences of Pāṭaliputra, which is said to have had a mighty wooden wall, with 570 towers and 64 gates. The *Arthaśāstra* advises against the use of wood for fortifications, owing to its liability to fire and rot, but archaeology bears out Megasthenes, for the remains of some of the gigantic timbers of the wall of Mauryan Pāṭaliputra have been excavated near the modern Patnā. The defences of Śiśupālgaṛh were certainly smaller and less elaborate (pl. XI*a*).

Fig. xi.—A Siege (from a relief at Sānchī, *c.* beginning of Christian era)

The most important surviving pre-Muslim fortress is Devagiri (modern Daulatābād), the capital of the Yādava kings of the Northern Deccan until its capture by the troops of Ala'-ud-dīn Khaljī in 1312. The outer fortifications have mostly been replaced and developed by later Muslim rulers, but the citadel, on an almost inaccessible hill, (pl. II*c*), still contains the corridors cut by the Hindu kings through the solid rock, which were virtually the only means of reaching the summit and are a memorial to the engineering skill of medieval India.

In sieges the attackers relied mainly on close investment and the reduction of their enemy by starvation and thirst, but capture by storm was not unheard of, and mining was regularly employed. The word for a mine or underground tunnel was *suranga*, borrowed from the Greek word σῦριγξ, which had the same secondary meaning; from this we may infer that the Indians learned something of siegecraft from the Greco-Bactrian kings.

The Indian army was slow and ponderous. The *Arthaśāstra* declares that a good army can march two *yojanas* a day, while a bad army can march only one. The yojana, like the medieval English league, is an uncertain measure of distance, varying from four to ten miles; but internal evidence shows that the author of the *Arthaśāstra* had in mind a yojana of about five miles. Thus a march of ten miles per day was the most that could be expected even of a well-trained and efficient army. This is not surprising, when we read of its complex and cumbrous organization.

The army dwelt in an enormous camp which was in fact a temporary city, with quarters for the king, for the king's harem, and for camp followers, merchants and prostitutes. The king and his chief officers took many members of their families with them on campaign, including a representative selection of their wives and concubines, and probably, on later analogy, the lower ranks did likewise. The Rāṣṭrakūṭa king Amoghavarṣa (817–877) was actually born in camp, while his father Govinda III was campaigning in the Vindhyas. This large body of non-combatants not wholly subject to army discipline must have appreciably slowed the pace of the army and impaired its efficiency. One theorist disapproved of taking women on campaign,[52] but it seems that his advice was rarely if ever followed.

The *Arthaśāstra* envisaged strict discipline in the camp; it was to be thoroughly guarded and policed, and exit and entry were to be controlled by a rigorous system of passes. In fact it was probably less well organized than this source suggests, especially in later times, when the secret of detailed organization, which the Mauryas possessed and the *Arthaśāstra* reflects, was largely lost. Bāṇa's vivid description of Harṣa's army striking camp (p. 399f) does not suggest a very efficient quartermaster's department, though the confusion which he describes may have been more apparent than real.

The *Arthaśāstra* gives much advice on the preliminaries of battle, but unfortunately says little on the actual conduct of the fighting, for which we must turn to the exaggerated accounts of the Epics and other sources.

Battle was a great religious rite, the highest sacrifice of the warrior, and as such was not entered without proper preliminaries. The day and time of giving battle were chosen with great care by astrologers, whenever this was possible, and purificatory rites were performed on its eve. Before battle the troops were harangued by brāhmaṇs, and by the king himself, and were encouraged with promises of booty and glory, with the certainty of heaven for the slain.

The *Arthaśāstra* advises the employment of heavy infantry in the centre, with light infantry, chariots and cavalry on the wings. The elephants were generally concentrated in the centre, while the archers took up positions behind the spearmen. Descriptions of battles are usually turgid, and overlaid with fanciful and supematural elements; but it is clear that at most times great emphasis was placed on single combat between picked warriors. Though the mass fighting of the rank and file must often have played a decisive part in the encounter, it is given little notice in the literature which is our only source of information. For the ordinary soldier courage and morale depended on the leader. Only the noble or the élite warrior could be relied on to fight to the last, and there is more than one account of an army fleeing in panie when its chief was killed or wounded.

The *Arthaśāstra* suggests that a price should be put on every enemy head, varying according to rank from twenty paṇas upwards; this would not encourage the giving of quarter, but the massacre of prisoners was unusual, and it is very strongly deprecated in the Smṛti texts. Captives were usually released on payment of ransom, and those who could not pay, which category probably included most of the common soldiers, were enslaved; but their enslavement was usually temporary, and they were released when they had paid their ransom by their labour.

From these notes it will be seen that inter-state relations and war were the weakest aspects of Indian polity. The kingdoms of medieval Hindu India, incapable either of empire building or of firm alliances, and maintaining enormous unwieldy armies which were continuously at war, indeed produced their heroes, but they were quite incapable of withstanding the Turks, whose military science was not over-burdened by pedantic theory or ancient tradition.

PLATE XVII

A. A. Bake

(a) A Corner of the Temple, Somnāthpur

A. A. Bake

(b) Frieze, Somnāthpur

J. R. Marr

(c) Guardian Deity (Dvārapāla), Hoysaleśvara Temple, Halebīd, Mysore. 12th century A.D.

PLATE XVIII

J. R. Marr

J. R. Marr

(a) and (b) Temple of Bēlūr, Mysore. 12th century A.D.

J. R. Marr

(c) Pilaster, Temple of Śrīrangam. 16th century A.D.

PLATE XIX

(b) Sculpture on the South Gateway, Great Temple, Madurai. 17th Century A.D.

(a) North Gateway, Temple of Chidambaram. 16th Century A.D.

(c) Suchindram, Kerala. A Typical South Indian Temple. 17th Century A.D.

PLATE XX

(a) Buddhist Temple, Bodh Gayā, Bihār. 5th–6th century A.D.

Ministry of Information and Broadcasting, New Delhi

(b) Liṅgarāja Temple, Bhubanesar, Orissā. 11th century A.D.

Ministry of Information and Broadcasting, New Delhi

(c) Kandāriya-Mahādeo Temple, Khajurāho. *c.* A.D. 1000

PLATE XXI

A. Nawrath, "Glories of Hindustan", Metheun & Co., London

(a) A Wheel of the Sun's Chariot. Temple of Sūrya, Konārak, Orissā. 13th Century A.D.

Dept. of Archaeology, Government of India

(b) City Gateway, Dābhoī, Barodā. 11th century A.D.

Max Hürlimann, "Indien", Atlantis Verlag, Zürich

(c) Chapel of the Temple of Neminātha, Mt. Ābū, Rajasthan. 13th Century A.D.

PLATE XXII

Max Hürlimann, "Indien", Atlantis Verlag, Zürich

Ceiling, Temple of Ādinātha, Mt. Ābū

PLATE XXIII

(a–b) Capitals of Mauryan Pillare

Dept. of Archaeology, Government of India

a) Sarnaāth

Dept. of Archaeology, Government of India

b) Rāmpurvā, Bihār. (now in the National Museum, New Delhi)

(c–e) Relief Medallions, Bhārhut (now in the Indian Museum, calcutta)

c) The Dream of Queen Mayā

(d) The merchant Anathapindaka buys the Jetavana grove by covering it with square coins (right) and presents it to the Buddhist order (left)

PLATE XXIV

Warrior, Bhārhut (now in the Indian Museum, Calcutta)

PLATE XXV

Yakṣī, Bhārhut (now in the Indian Museum, Calcutta)

(a) Yaksī, bearing a chaurī. Dīdārganj, Bihār. ?1st Century B.C. (now in the Patna Museum)

(b) Liṅgam, Guḍimallam, Madras. 1st century B.C.

PLATE XXVII

A. L. Basham

(a) Architraves of the East Gateway, Sānchī, M.P.. End of the 1st century B.C.

Dept. of Archaeology, Government of India

(b) Corner of East Gateway (front), Sānchī

PLATE XXVIII

Architraves of North Gateway, Sānchī

Top: Illustration of the Jātaka story of the Six-tusked Elephant

Middle: The demon hosts of Māra (left centre) tempt the Buddha, symbolized by the vacant throne under the Bodhi Tree on the left

Bottom: The story of Vessantara, told from right to left: (i) Vessantara and his family in a hut in the forest; (ii) he gives away his two children; (iii) he gives away his wife; (iv) he is reunited with his family.

PLATE XXIX

Trustees and Indian Museum, Calcutta

(a) Yakṣī with Bird and Cage, above, a lady at her toilet. Mathurā, 1st–2nd century A.D.

Trustees and Indian Museum, Calcutta

(b) Bacchanalian Scene. Curzon Museum, Mathurā

PLATE XXX

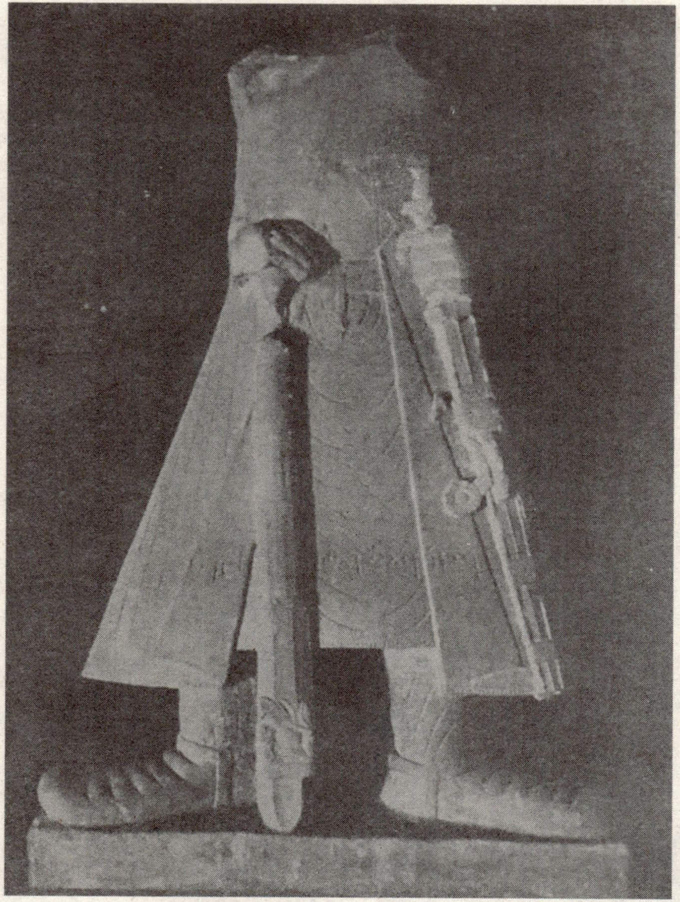

Dept. of Archaeology, Government of India

a) Headless Statue of Kaniṣka, Mathurā

Messrs. Faber & Faber, Royal Academy Trustees and Curzon Museum, Mathurā

b) Head of a Kuṣāṇa King, Mathurā

PLATE XXXI

Dept. of Archaeology, Government of India

(a) Indo-Corinthian Capital, Jamālgarhī, Peshāwar. 1st–2nd century A.D.

Dept. of Archaeology, Government of India

(b) The Buddha Preaching, Gandhāra School

Victoria & Albert Museum. Crown Copyright

(c) Head of the Buddha, Gandhāra School

PLATE XXXII

British Museum

(a) Oarsmen (river or marine deities), Gandhāra School

Major–General H. L. Houghton

(b) City Goddess, Chārsaddā, Peshāwar. Gandhāra School

V

SOCIETY: CLASS, FAMILY AND INDIVIDUAL

LAWS OF CLASS AND STAGE OF LIFE

OFTEN and in many contexts we read of "the *Dharma* of class and stage of life" (*varṇāśrama-dharma*), which in the golden age of the remote past was self-evident and uninfringed, but which is now vague, misunderstood and partly forgotten, and which the brāhmaṇs interpret and the king preserves and enforces. The implication of this phrase is that Dharma is not the same for all. There is indeed a common Dharma, a general norm of conduct which all must follow equally, but there is also a dharma appropriate to each class and to each stage in the life of the individual. The dharma of men of high birth is not that of humbler folk, and the dharma of the student is not that of the old man.

This thoroughgoing recognition that men are not the same, and that there is a hierarchy of classes, each with its separate duties and distinctive way of life, is one of the most striking features of ancient Indian sociology. Criticisms of the pretensions of the higher classes were heard from time to time, and equalitarian propositions were occasionally put forward, but in general this concept has held its ground from the end of the Ṛg Vedic period to the present day.

THE FOUR GREAT CLASSES

We have seen that by the end of the Ṛg Vedic period the fourfold division of society was regarded as fundamental, primeval, and divinely ordained (p. 26). The four varnas of India developed out of very early Āryan class divisions, for some stratification existed in many Indo-European communities, and ancient Iran had four *pištras* or classes, comparable in some respects to those of India. In India this stratification grew more rigid when, in the Vedic period, a situation arose rather like that prevailing in South Africa today, with a dominant fair minority striving to maintain its purity and its supremacy over a darker majority. Tribal class-divisions hardened, and the dark-skinned aboriginal found a place only in the basement of the Āryan social structure, as a serf with few rights and many disabilities. Soon the idea of varṇa had become so deeply embedded in the Indian mind that its terminology was even used for classification of precious commodities such as pearls, and of useful materials like timber. Theoretically all Āryans belonged to one of the four classes, with the exception of children, ascetics and widows, who were outside the system.

Varṇa came to the Dravidian South comparatively late, for the earliest Tamil literature shows a society divided into tribal groups with little sense of the precedence of one over the other. Succeeding centuries saw the gradual hardening of class, until South Indian brāhmaṇs became even stricter in their ritual observances and South Indian untouchables even more debased than those of the North.

A sharp distinction was made between the three higher classes and the śūdra. The former were twice-born (*dvija*), once at their natural birth and again at their initiation, when they were invested with the sacred thread and received into Āryan society* (p. 139f). The śūdra had no initiation, and was often not looked on as Āryan at all. The fourfold division was in theory functional. Manu[1] lays down that the duty of the brāhmaṇ is to study and teach, to sacrifice, and to give and receive gifts; the kṣatriya must protect the people, sacrifice, and study; the vaiśya also sacrifices and studies, but his chief function is to breed cattle, to till the earth, to pursue trade and to lend money; the śūdra's duty is only to serve the three higher classes—and "it is better", Manu adds elsewhere,[2] "to do one's own duty badly than another's well". This epigram, elaborated so beautifully in the *Bhagavad Gītā*, was the leading theme of most Indian social thought; for each man there was a place in society and a function to fulfil, with its own duties and rights.

This was the ideal, but though in the Middle Ages it was perhaps approached it has never been wholly reached. The precepts of the texts which lay down the laws for the conduct of the four classes were rarely fully carried out in practice, and were often blatantly infringed. The texts, which we have already discussed (p. 96f), were written by brāhmaṇs and from the brāhmaṇic point of view, and represent conditions as the brāhmaṇs would have liked them to be. Thus it is not surprising that they claim the utmost honour for the priestly class and exalt it above measure.

The brāhmaṇ was a great divinity in human form.[3] It was thought his spiritual power could instantly destroy the king and his army, if they attempted to infringe his rights. In law he claimed great privileges (p. 103), and in every respect he demanded precedence, honour and worship. Even the Buddhist scriptures, though they do not admit the more extravagant brāhmaṇical claims and regularly exalt the kṣatriya over the brāhmaṇ, recognize his greatness, if he is pious and sincere.

These Buddhist sources show us two types of brāhmaṇ. There were learned brāhmaṇs, performing all the rites of the Āryan and receiving great respect; but there were also village brāhmaṇs, who made much of their living by fortune-telling and magic, and who were less honoured. For all the rigidity of the class system the brāhmaṇs soon lost their racial purity, and it has even been suggested that, as Āryan culture expanded, schools of aboriginal sorcerers and medicine men managed to obtain a footing in the brāhmaṇic order, just as aboriginal chiefs were certainly

---

*In later texts the term "twice-born" was often reserved for brāhmaṇs, but strictly it applies to kṣatriyas and vaiśyas also, if they have been initiated.

assimilated to the warrior class. Thus, it may well be, the proto-Hinduism of the Harappā culture was ultimately assimilated to the Āryan faith.

Of professional priests there were various types and classes. In the earliest times we read of the semi-legendary *ṛsis*, or seers, who composed the Vedic hymns, while the sacrificial ritual demanded a number of priests (*ṛtvij*) with specialized duties—invokers (*hotṛ*), cantore (*udgātṛ*), and priests to perform the manual operations of the ceremony (*adhvaryu*). The term *brāhmaṇa* meant originally "one possessed of *brahman*", a mysterious magical force of the type widely known to modern anthropologists by the Melanesian word *mana*. It was first applied to the specially trained priest who superintended the whole sacrifice, and was ready to counteract with his magic spells any evil influence caused by minor errors of ritual. By the end of the Ṛg Vedic period the term was used for all members of the priestly class.

There were other divisions within the order. The brāhmaṇs of the later Vedic period were divided into exogamous septs (*gotra*), a system which was copied in part by other classes and has survived to the present day (p. 132ff). Later the brāhmaṇ class formed many castes, linked together by endogamy and common practices. A further division was the *śākhā* or branch, based on the recension of the Vedic texts accepted as authoritative by the family in question.

Often the brāhmaṇ lived under the patronage of a king or chief, and was provided for by grants of tax-free land, farmed by peasants, who would pay their taxes to the brāhmaṇ instead of to the king; but there were also land-owning brāhmaṇs, who cultivated large estates by hired labour or serfs. The religious brāhmaṇ might have a high post at court, and the purohita's* importance in the state has already been noted (p. 87). Other brāhmaṇs might earn a competence as teachers of the Veda, and of other branches of learning.

At all times many brāhmaṇs led truly religious lives. Kālidāsa's *Śakuntalā* gives a charming picture of a settlement of such pious brāhmaṇs, living simply but not too austerely in huts in the forest, where even the wild deer were unafraid of the gentle hermits, and the woodland was for ever perfumed with the fragrance of their sacred fires. Such brāhmaṇ colonies were supported by the gifts of kings and chiefs and of the peasants of the neighbourhood. Other brāhmaṇs became solitary ascetics, while in the Middle Ages brāhmaṇ monastic orders were founded, rather on the Buddhist model.

But the varied religious activity of ancient India did not provide a livelihood for more than a few of the brāhmaṇs. The Smṛti literature contains special sections on "duty when in distress" (*āpad-dharma*), which carefully define what a man may legitimately do when he cannot earn a living by the calling normally followed by his class, and by these provisions brāhmaṇs might pursue all manner of trades and professions. Many were employed in important government posts, and several royal families were of brāhmaṇ origin. Generally the lawbooks disapproved

---

* This term was extended to mean a family priest, who performed the many rites and ceremonies of Hinduism for a family or group of families, and has survived in this sense to the present day.

of brāhmaṇs engaging in agriculture, because it inflicts injury on animals and insects, but this rule was often ignored. A brāhmaṇ was forbidden to trade in certain commodities—among them cattle and other animals, slaves, weapons, and spirituous liquor—and his lending money at interest was also disapproved of, though Manu[4] allowed him to lend at low interest to "wicked people", by whom he probably meant those who did not maintain Āryan rites. But though the brāhmaṇ kept these rules rigidly, he would nevertheless find many trades and professions open to him.

Opinions differed as to whether a brāhmaṇ engaged in a secular profession was worthy of the respect accorded to the practising member of his class, and no clear ruling is laid down. Manu, the most authoritative of the Smrtis, is uncertain on this point, and in different parts of the text diametrically opposed views are given.[5] As far as can be gathered from general literature the special rights of the brāhmaṇ were usually only granted to those who lived by sacrifice and teaching. Cārudatta, the poor brāhmaṇ hero of the play "The Little Clay Cart" (p. 103), receives scurvy treatment at the hands of the court, probably because he is a brāhmaṇ by birth only, and not by profession.

For all his prestige, the brāhmaṇ was often the butt of satire. Even in the *Ṛg Veda*[6] the croaking of frogs at the beginning of the rainy season is compared to the monotonous reciting of the priests, though here no sarcasm may be intended. There can be no other good explanation of a remarkable passage in the early *Chāndogya Upaniṣad*,[7] which describes a vision of the sage Vaka Dālbhya, wherein dogs move round in a circle—each holding the tail of the preceding dog in its mouth—"just as the priests do when about to sing praises"; and then, repeating the very sacred syllable *Ōm*, they sing: "*Om!* let us eat! *Ōm!* let us drink! *Ōm!* may the gods Varuṇa, Prajāpati and Savitṛ bring us food!" Another early reference to the gluttony of brāhmaṇs occurs in the *Aitareya Brāhmaṇa* in an interesting passage which describes the other three classes from the point of view of the warrior; here the brāhmaṇ is "a receiver of gifts, a drinker of soma, an eater of food, to be expelled at will". The *vidūṣaka*, the fool of Sanskrit drama (p. 78), an amiable but gluttonous figure of fun, is invariably a brāhmaṇ.

There are, however, few frontal attacks on brāhmaṇical pretensions, even in the literature of the Buddhists, who came nearest to an anti-brāhmaṇical point of view; but one brief Buddhist tract, the "Diamond Needle" (*Vajrasūci*), ascribed to Aśvaghoṣa, of the lst or 2nd century A.D., attacks the claims of the priesthood, and indirectly the whole class system, with vigorous dialectical skill. The claims of the brāhmaṇ were, in fact, often ignored, and not wholly unchallenged.

The second class was the ruling one, the members of which were in the Vedic period called *rājanya*, and later *kṣatriya*. The theoretical duty of the kṣatriya was "protection", which included fighting in war and governing in peace (p. 77f). In early times he often claimed precedence over the brāhmaṇ; this claim is implicit in the *Aitareya Brāhmaṇa* passage which we have quoted, the inclusion of which in a brāhmaṇical scripture is hard to account for. According to Buddhist tradition, in times when the brāhmaṇs are the highest class Buddhas are born in that class, while when kṣatriyas are the highest they are born as kṣatriyas. The historical Buddha was a kṣatriya, and his followers evidently had few doubts about class priorities. Where the names of the four classes are mentioned together in the Pāli scriptures that of the kṣatriya usually comes first.

A strong king was always a check on brāhmaṇic pretensions, just as the brāhmaṇs were a check on the pretensions of the king. Tradition speaks of many anti-brāhmaṇical kings who came to evil ends, and the legend of Parasurāma, who destroyed the whole kṣatriya class for its impiety (p. 266), must contain a recollection of fierce strife between the two classes in pre-Buddhist times. After the Mauryan period the brāhmaṇ's theoretical position was established throughout most of India, but in fact the kṣatriya was often still his equal or superior.

The martial class of ancient India, from great emperors to petty chiefs, was recruited from all races and ranks, and all the invaders of India down to the coming of the Muslims were given a place in the social order in this way. Manu[9] describes the warlike peoples on the fringes of Āryan civilization, including the Greeks (*Yavana*), the Scyths (*Śaka*), and the Parthians (*Pahlava*), as kṣatriyas who had fallen from grace through their neglect of the Sacred Law, but who could be received once more into the Āryan fold by adopting the orthodox way of life and performing appropriate penitential sacrifices. This provision might be applied to almost any conquering people, and the Rājputs, in later times the kṣatriyas *par excellence*, were no doubt largely descended from such invaders.

The kṣatriyas claimed and received certain privileges. They continued old customs not in keeping with orthodoxy, with such persistence that the brāhmaṇic lawgivers were forced to give them legal status. Thus marriage by capture was permitted to the kṣatriya, as were the clandestine liaison and the *svayaṃvara*, at which a girl chose her husband from among the assembled suitors (p. 145f). Like the brāhmaṇs, they did not always live by fulfilling their ideal function. The rules of *āpad-dharma* applied to them also, and there are many records of men of warrior stock becoming merchants and craftsmen.

In Vedic times the *vaiśya*, or mercantile class, though entitled to the services of the priesthood and to the sacred thread of initiation, was but a poor third to the brāhmaṇs and kṣatriyas. In the *Aitareya Brāhmaṇa* passage to which we have referred the vaiśya is described as "paying tribute to another, to be lived on by another, to be oppressed at will". Other passages in early brāhmaṇic literature show him as a wretched and down-trodden cultivator or petty merchant, who is of no interest to his betters except as a source of profit.

According to Manu[10] the special duty of the vaiśya was keeping cattle, which were made over to his charge at the creation of the world. The class evidently originated in the ordinary peasant tribesman of the *Ṛg Veda*, but long before the lawbook ascribed to Manu was composed vaiśyas had many other activities. The śūdras, the humblest of the four classes, had by now taken to agriculture, and Manu admitted many other legitimate vaiśya occupations besides cattle rearing and farming. The ideal vaiśya had expert knowledge of jewels, metals, cloth, threads, spices, perfumes, and all manner of merchandise—he was, in fact, the ancient Indian business-man.

Though the Brāhmaṇa literature gives the vaiśya few rights and humble status, the Buddhist and Jaina scriptures, a few centuries later in date and of more easterly provenance, show that he was not always oppressed in practice. They mention many wealthy merchants living in great luxury, and powerfully organized in guilds. Here the ideal vaiśya is not the humble taxpaying cattle-breeder, but the *asītikoṭivibhava*, the man possessing eight million *paṇas*. Wealthy vaiśyas were respected by kings and enjoyed their favour and confidence. It was they, rather than the kṣatriyas, who chiefly favoured the rising unorthodox religions of Buddhism and Jainism. They formed by this time, at least in the regions of Magadha and Kosala, a true bourgeoisie, no doubt small in number, but very important. Numerous inscriptions from Śuṅga times onwards record the great donations of vaiśya merchants and skilled craftsmen to religious causes, especially to Buddhism, and show that they were prosperous and influential.

If the vaiśya, according to the *Aitareya Brāhmaṇa*, was to be oppressed at will, the lot of the *śūdra* was even more unfortunate. He was "the servant of another, to be expelled at will, to be slain at will"— but the latter phrase may be interpreted "to be beaten at will", and the import of the whole passage seems to be satirical.

Śūdras were not "twice-born". For them there was no initiation into full Āryan status, and they were not regularly considered Āryans, though the *Arthaśāstra* in its chapters on slavery[11] specifically mentions them as such. The śūdra was in fact a second-class citizen, on the fringes of Āryan society. The word śūdra is of doubtful etymology, and occurs only once in the *Ṛg Veda*; it was perhaps originally the name of a non-Āryan tribe, which became subordinate to the conquerors, and the beginnings of the śūdra class may be accounted for in this way, though it certainly included other elements. As the rigidity of brāhmaṇic observances increased, groups which refused to accept orthodox custom, or clung to old practices which were no longer respectable, fell to the rank of śūdras. There are today castes which themselves claim to be kṣatriyas, but which are branded by the brāhmaṇs as śūdras because they adhere to customs which have long become objectionable, such as meat eating or the remarriage of widows. Persons born illegitimately, even when of pure high-class blood, were counted as śūdras.[12]

Śūdras were of two kinds, "pure" or "not-excluded "(*aniravasita*) and "excluded" (*niravasita*). The latter were quite outside the pale of Hindu society, and were virtually indistinguishable from the great body of people later known as untouchables. The distinction was made on the basis of the customs of the śūdra group in question and the profession followed by its members. According to the brāhmaṇical textbooks the chief duty of the pure śūdra was to wait on the other three classes. He was to eat the remnants of his master's food, wear his cast-off clothing, and use his old furniture. Even when he had the opportunity of becoming wealthy he might not do so, "for a śūdra who makes money is distressing to the brāhmaṇs".[13] He had few rights, and little value was set on his life in law. A brāhmaṇ killing a śūdra performed the same penance as for killing a cat or dog.[14] The śūdra was not allowed to hear or repeat the Vedas. A land where śūdras were numerous would suffer great misery.

Thus the textbooks give small hope of happiness to the wretched śūdra, who could do little but serve his betters in unpleasant and servile tasks, and whose only hope was rebirth in a higher social class; but there is good evidence that śūdras did not always live the humble and wretched life laid down for them in the Sacred Law. There is mention of śūdras engaged in manufacture and commerce, and by Mauryan times many śūdras were free peasants.[16] The śūdra had a place of sorts in the Hindu fold, and was encouraged to imitate the customs of the higher classes. Though he might not hear the Vedas, the Epics and Purāṇas were open to him, and he had a part in the devotional religion which became more and more popular from post-Mauryan times onwards and ultimately eclipsed the older cults; in the *Bhagavad Gītā* the lord Kṛṣṇa himself promises full salvation to those śūdras who turn to him.[16] From the point of view of most medieval sects, class and caste were affairs of the body rather than of the spirit, and verses expressing the fundamental equality of all men are to be found in Dravidian devotional literature and in vernacular religious literature of later times. Theoretically Buddhism and Jainism made no class distinctions in religious affairs. As we have seen, śūdra kings were not unknown, and many śūdras, despite the injunctions of the lawbooks, must have been prosperous.

UNTOUCHABLES

Below the śūdras were the early representatives of the people who were later called untouchables, outcastes, depressed classes, or scheduled castes. Buddhist literature and the early Dharma Sūtras show that several centuries before Christ there already existed groups of people who, though serving the Āryans in very menial and dirty tasks, were looked on as quite outside the pale. Sometimes they were called the "fifth class" (*pañcama*), but most authorities rejected this term, as if to insist that they were to be excluded from the Āryan social order altogether.

Numerous groups of these people are mentioned, by names which are non-Āryan in origin, and were probably those of aboriginal tribes which came under the sway of the advancing Āryans. Chief of these groups was the *caṇḍāla*, a term which came to be used loosely for many types of untouchable. The caṇḍāla was not allowed to live in an Āryan town or village, but had to dwell in special quarters outside the boundaries. Though some caṇḍālas had other means of livelihood, in theory their main task was the carrying and cremation of corpses, and they also served as executioners of criminals.

According to the lawbooks the caṇḍāla should be dressed in the garments of the corpses he cremated, should eat his food from broken vessels, and should wear only iron ornaments. No man of higher class might have any but the most distant relations with a caṇḍāla, on pain of losing his religious purity and falling to the caṇḍāla's level. By Gupta times caṇḍālas had become so strictly untouchable that, like lepers in medieval Europe, they were forced to strike a wooden clapper on entering a town, to warn the Āryans of their polluting approach.

Certain classes of outcastes or untouchables seem to have gained their unenviable position through the growth of the sentiment of non-violence—for instance the *niṣāda*, who was a hunter, the fishing caste called *kaivarta*, and the leather worker (*kārāvara*). The *pukkusa** who appears as a sweeper in Buddhist literature, may have fallen in status because members of his class made and sold alcoholic liquor. More difficult to account for are such base classes as the basket-maker (*veṇa*) and the chariot-maker (*rathakāra*). In early Vedic times the latter was a most respected craftsmen, but soon fell to the status of an impure śūdra or outcaste.

By the beginning of the Christian era the outcastes themselves had developed a caste hierarchy, and had their own outcastes. Manu[17] mentions the *antyāvasāyin*, a cross between a caṇḍāla and a niṣāda, who was despised even by the caṇḍālas themselves. In later India nearly every untouchable group imagined that some other group was lower than itself, and this stratification evidently began quite early.

Even the lot of the untouchable was not altogether without hope. Though he was denied access to the temples and the comforts of orthodox religion, Buddhist monks preached to him, and the more enlightened wandering ascetics would give him instruction. The untouchable dying in defence of brāhmaṇs, cows, women, and children secured a place in heaven. Orthodox texts contain frequent warnings on the evils which arise when śūdraṣ and outcastes grow too powerful, and this would seem to show that even a caṇḍāla might occasionally become influential.

Another class of untouchable was the *mleccha*, a word commonly used for outer barbarians of whatever race or colour. As an invader he was loathed, but once he had come into contact with Indian ways and was less strange and forbidding his status might improve. In fact it was not blood which made a group untouchable, but conduct. Generally there was no chance of an individual rising in the social scale, but for a group this was possible, over a number of generations, by adopting more orthodox practices and following the rules of the Smṛtis. Thus the Indian class system was always somewhat fluid.

CONFUSION OF CLASS

An early legend tells of Viśvāmitra, a kṣatriya who, by penance and piety, became a brāhmaṇ and a seer (*ṛṣi*) to boot; but as time went on such raising of one's rank in the social scale became more and more difficult, and finally virtually impossible, though convenient fictions sometimes permitted kings and chiefs of low status to find legendary kṣatriya ancestors and advance in the class hierarchy. While it became difficult for the individual to rise, it grew progressively more easy for him to fall. Every breach of the manifold regulations of one's class entailed

* This is the Pāli form; the Sanskrit is *paulkasa*.

impurity and outcasting, either permanent or temporary. The lawbooks give long lists of penances for the restoration of the unfortunate offender, ranging from trivial ones, such as bathing or touching Gangā water, to others so rigorous that they must usually have resulted in the death of the penitent. Secular literature, however, tells many stories of high-class people infringing the rules of purity without doing penance, and no doubt the more sophisticated townsman often took his class responsibilities lightly.

The continual injunctions to the king to ensure that "confusion of class" (*varṇa-saṃkara*) did not take place indicate that such confusion was an ever-present danger in the mind of the orthodox brāhmaṇ. The class system was indeed a very fragile thing. In the golden age the classes were stable, but the legendary king Veṇa (p. 76), among his many other crimes, had encouraged miscegenation, and from this beginning confusion of class had increased, and was a special feature of the *Kali-yuga*, the last degenerate age of this aeon, which was fast nearing its close. The good king, therefore, was advised to spare no effort to maintain the purity of the classes, and many dynasties took special pride in their efforts in this direction.

Before the tightening of the social system in the Middle Ages confusion of class was comparatively frequent, and some forms of interclass marriage were expressly permitted. The type of marriage known to anthropologists as hypergamous, when the husband is of higher class than the wife, was by no means disapproved of; on the other hand hypogamous marriage, when the wife's status was higher than that of the husband, was always frowned on. The former was "in accordance with the direction of the hair" (*anuloma*), smooth and natural, while the latter was "against the hair", or "brushing the wrong way" (*pratiloma*). This distinction is to be found in other societies; for instance in Victorian England the peer who married an actress rarely incurred the same scora and ostracism as the lady who married her groom.

The earlier legal literature permitted *anuloma* or hypergamous marriage, provided that a man's first wife was of his own class. Generally brāhmaṇs were forbidden to take śūdra wives, but one lawbook allowed even this,[18] and Bāṇa, the 7th-century poet, who was a brāhmaṇ, had a stepbrother by a śūdra mother. Various mixed classes, many of them the forerunners of later castes, were said to be the products of marriages of this type, and their members were not looked on as in any way unclean, but enjoyed a position intermediate between that of the two parents. Of the groups thought to have descended from hypergamous marriage only the niṣāda, in theory a cross between a brāhmaṇ and a śūdra woman, was thought to be impure.

Hypogamous or *pratiloma* marriage, on the other hand, produced offspring whose status was lower than that of either parent. Thus the caṇḍālas were believed to have descended from marriages between śūdras and brāhmaṇ women. The only exceptions were the class of charioteers, or *sūtas*, thought to have sprung from the hypogamy of kṣatriyas and brāhmaṇs, and the bards or *māgadhas*, descended from vaiśya fathers and kṣatriya mothers, both of whom were well respected. The complex system of sub-classes low in the social scale, out of which the Indian caste system developed, was believed to be wholly the result of "confusion of class". This tradition was accepted by early Indologists, but, as we shall see, is completely unfounded.

CASTE

Relations between classes and social groups in later Hinduism were governed by rules of endogamy (marriage was only legitimate within the group), commensality (food was only to be received from and eaten in the presence of members of the same or a higher group), and craft-exclusiveness (each man was to live by the trade or profession of his own group, and not take up that of another). Megasthenes noted seven endogamous and craft-exclusive classes in India—philosophers, peasants, herdsmen, craftsmen and traders, soldiers, government officials and councillors. His sevenfold division is certainly false, but he gives evidence to show that in Mauryan times class barriers were already hardening. Even in the Gupta period, however, the regulations were by no means rigid. Hypergamous inter-marriage was recognized, the rule of craft-exclusiveness was often ignored, or circumvented by the convenient escape clauses of *āpad-dharma* (p. 121), and in the earlier lawbooks the brāhmaṇ was permitted to accept food from any Āryan. It was only in late medieval times that it was finally recognized that exogamy and sharing meals with members of other classes were quite impossible for respectable people. These customs, and many others such as widow-remarriage, were classed as *kalivarjya*—customs once permissible, but to be avoided in this dark *Kali* age, when men are no longer naturally righteous.

In this chapter we have so far hardly used the word which in most minds is most strongly connected with the Hindu social order. When the Portuguese came to India in the 16th century they found the Hindu community divided into many separate groups, which they called *castas*, meaning tribes, clans or families. The name stuck, and became the usual word for the Hindu social group. In attempting to account for the remarkable proliferation of castes in 18th- and 19th-century India, authorities credulously accepted the traditional view that by a process of intermarriage and subdivision the 3,000 or more castes of modern India had evolved from the four primitive classes, and the term "caste" was applied indiscriminately to both *varṇa* or class, and *jāti* or caste proper. This is a false terminology; castes rise and fall in the social scale, and old castes die out and new ones are formed, but the four great classes are stable. They are never more or less than four, and for over 2,000 years their order of precedence has not altered. All ancient Indian sources make a sharp distinction between the two terms; *varṇa* is much referred to, but *jāti* very little, and when it does appear in literature it does not always imply the comparatively rigid and exclusive social group of later times. If caste is defined as a system of groups within the class which are normally endogamous, commensal and craft-exclusive, we have no real evidence of its existence until comparatively late times.

Caste is the development of thousands of years, from the association of many different racial and other groups in a single cultural system. It is impossible to show its origin conclusively, and we can do little more than faintly trace its development, since early literature paid scant attention to it; but it is practically certain that caste did not originate from the four classes. Admittedly it developed later than they, but this proves nothing. There were subdivisions in the four classes at a very early date, but the brāhmaṇ gotras, which go back to Vedic times, are not castes, since the gotras are exogamous, and members of the same gotra are to be found in many castes.

Perhaps the first faint trace of caste is to be found in the careful cataloguing of trades and professions in later Vedic literature, as if their members were looked on almost as distinct species. In the Pāli scriptures many groups of traders and craftsmen are described as living apart; thus we read of villages of brāhmaṇs, potters, hunters and robbers, and of separate quarters in the towns for different trades and professions. Many trades were organized in guilds, in which some authorities have seen the origin of the commercial castes; but these trade groups cannot be counted as fully developed castes. A 5th-cenury inscription from Mandasor[19] shows us a guild of silk-weavers emigrating in a body from Lāṭa (the region of the lower Narmadā) to Mandasor, and taking up many other crafts and professions, from soldiering to astrology, but still maintaining its guild-consciousness. We have no evidence that this group was endogamous or commensal, and it was certainly not craft-exclusive; but its strong corporate sense is that of a caste in the making. Hsüan Tsang, in the 7th century, was well aware of the four classes, and also mentioned many mixed classes, no doubt accepting the orthodox view of the time that these sprang from the intermarriage of the four, but he shows no clear knowledge of the existence of caste in its modera form.

To the present day the life of the lower orders is much more affected by caste than by varṇa—it is not being a vaiśya or a śūdra, but being an *ahīr*, a *kāyasth*, or a *sonār* which matters—and corporate feeling is centred around the caste group, whether based on region, race, profession or religion. The same strong corporate sense existed among the Mandasor silk weavers, and evidence of its existence at an even earlier date can be gathered from many sources. Indian society developed a very complex social structure, arising partly from tribal affiliations and partly from professional associations, which was continuously being elaborated by the introduction of new racial groups into the community, and by the development of new crafts. In the Middle Ages the system became more or less rigid, and the social group was now a caste in the modern sense. Professor J. H. Hutton has interpreted the caste system as an adaptation of one of the most primitive of social relationships, whereby a small clan, living in a comparatively isolated village, would hold itself aloof from its neighbours by a complex series of taboos, and he has found embryonic caste features in the social structure of some of the wild tribes of present-day India. The caste system may well be the natural response of the many small and primitive peoples who were forced to come to terms with a more advanced economic and social system. It did not develop out of the four

Āryan varṇas, and the two systems have never been thoroughly harmonized.

By the end of our period many of the present-day caste groups were already in existence. Even the brāhmaṇ class was much subdivided into endogamous groups, often based on locality and race, with many different practices. The Rājputs were divided into clans which, if not regularly endogamous, were castes of a sort, and the vaiśyas, śūdras and untouchables had evolved hundreds of castes. They were governed by local committees of elders, usually hereditary, who had the power to expel members and regulate caste rules, and whose decisions, from the time of the *Arthaśāstra* onwards, had the force of law.

After the large joint family, the caste provided social security, helping destitute members and caring for widows and orphans. A man expelled from his caste was also automatically expelled from his family, unless the whole family accompanied him in his social ostracism. He was lost to society, and could only consort with the lowest of the low. Though he might manage to retain some of his former wealth he was isolated, a tree torn up by the roots. Permanent loss of caste was the greatest catastrophe, short of death and the major chronic diseases, which could happen to a man.

Early Tamil literature gives no evidence of caste, but the growth of Āryan influence and the development of a more complex political and economic structure produced a system in some ways more rigid than that of the North. By the Cōla period an important feature of South Indian caste structure had appeared, and this has survived to the present day. In the Dravidian country groups claiming to be kṣatriyas were few, other than the ruling families, and vaiśyas were equally rare. Nearly the whole of the population were brāhmaṇs, śūdras or untouchables, and the śūdra castes, which formed the mass of the people, were divided into two great caste groups, known as the right and left hands. The great animosity and rivalry which still exists between these groups is at least a thousand years old. On the right are the trading castes, some weaving castes, musicians, potters, washermen, barbers, and most of the cultivating and labouring castes; on the left are various castes of craftsmen, such as weavers and leather workers, cowherds, and some cultivating castes. We have no evidence of how this strange bisection of society arose.

Hypergamy never wholly disappeared. In Kerala, where matrilinear succession has continued almost to modern times, men of the great brāhmaṇ caste of Nambūdiris have regularly married the women of the dominant secular caste, the Nayyars. In Bengal the Rāḍhī caste of brāhmaṇs and the important and respectable castes of scribes (*kāyastha*) and doctors (*vaidya*) are divided into subcastes, which are hypergamous. The system is known as "kulīnīsm", from the name of the highest subcaste of the brāhmaṇs (*kulina*); it was by tradition imposed by the Bengal king Ballāla Sena (l2th century), but is no doubt a survival from much earlier times.

The institution of caste, independent of the government and with social ostracism as its most severe sanction, was a powerful factor in the survival of Hinduism. The Hindu, living under an alien political order imposed from above, retained his cultural individuality largely through his caste, which received most of the loyalty elsewhere felt towards king, nation and city. Caste was so strong that until recent years all attempts at breaking it down have ended in failure. Equalitarian religious reformers of the late Middle Ages, such as Basava, Rāmānand, and Kabīr, tried to abolish caste among their followers; but their sects soon took on the characteristics of new castes, and in some cases divided into castes within themselves. The Sikhs, despite the outspoken sentiments of their *gurus* and the adoption of rites such as the ritual meal eaten in common, deliberately intended to break down caste prejudice, did not overcome caste feeling. Even the Muslims, for all their equalitarian faith, formed caste groups. The Syrian Christians of Kerala early divided into sections which took on a caste character, and when in the 16th century Roman Catholic missionaries began to make converts in South India their flocks brought their caste prejudices with them, and high-caste converts held themselves aloof from those of the lower orders.

Only in the last fifty years has the caste system shown real signs of breaking down, thanks to the many inventions of the West not designed for use in a society divided into watertight compartments, the spread of Western education, growing national sentiment, and the intensive propaganda of enlightened leaders. The process is not yet complete, and it will be many years before all trace of caste feeling is eradicated; but when Mahātmā Gāndhī, in many ways socially conservative, persuaded his followers to sweep their own floors and clean their own latrines he sounded the death knell of the old Hindu social order, which, for all its faults, has preserved the identity of Indian society through centuries of foreign domination.

SLAVERY

Megasthenes declared that there were no slaves in India. He was certainly wrong, but Indian slavery was milder than the form to which he had been used, and slaves were much less numerous than in the civilizations of the West; hence he may not have recognized the *dāsa* as a slave. There was no caste of slaves; though the *Arthaśāstra* declares that servitude is not in the nature of the Āryan (in which term the humble śūdra is explicitly included), an individual of any class might in certain circumstances become a slave, although most slaves were no doubt of low caste.

The word *dāsa* originally meant a member of the peoples conquered by the Āryans in their first invasions of India. Its later connotation no doubt developed from the reduction to bondage of the many dāsas captured in battle, and here we find the probable origin of Indian slavery. The *Mahābhārata* declares that it is a law of war that the vanquished should be the victor's slave,[20] and the captive would normally serve his captor until ransomed. But there were several other classes of slaves in later times. Children born of slaves normally became the slaves of their parents' masters. Slaves might be bought, given away, or mortgaged. A free man might sell himself and his family into slavery in times of dire distress. He might also be reduced to slavery for crime or debt, but in these cases his servitude might be only temporary. All these types of slavery are recognized in the Smṛti literature and elsewhere.

As in other slave-owning civilizations, the slave might become an important man, and there are even references in stories to slaves serving as royal counsellors. Slaves might sometimes perform work of economic importance, such as agriculture or mining, but they were usually domestic servants or personal attendants. The slave was, in fact, a subordinate member of his master's household. His maintenance was his master's responsibility, and if he died sonless it was incumbent on the master to perform funeral and commemorative rites for the welfare of his soul. According to most lawbooks a slave's property ultimately belonged to his master, and he might be bought, sold, loaned or given away; but masters had no rights over the lives of their slaves, and were not allowed to abandon them in old age, as was done in many other ancient civilizations. "A man may go short himself or stint his wife and children, but never his slave, who does his dirty work for him."[21] Some lawbooks even limited the right of a master to give corporal punishment to his slave. "A wife, a son, a slave, a servant or a younger brother may, when they do wrong, be beaten with a rope or a cane, but only on the back and not on the head. If a man beats them otherwise he should be punished as a thief."[22] The manumission of a slave was commended by the textbooks as a pious act, and in any case a person enslaved for debt became free when he had paid the debt with his labour.

The *Arthaśāstra*, in many ways more liberal than the religious lawbooks, lays down regulations appreciably milder than those we have outlined. The sale of children into slavery is explicitly forbidden except in dire emergency. Slaves are entitled to own and inherit property, and to earn money freely in their spare time. Slaves of the upper classes cannot be forced to perform defiling duties. The chastity of slave-girls is protected—the master who rapes a slave-girl must set her free and pay her compensation, and if she has a child by her master, even with her own consent, both mother and child become free. A promise made by a man in dire necessity to sell himself and his family into slavery is not binding.

The humane regulations of the *Arthaśāstra*, probably unique in the records of any ancient civilization, are perhaps survivals of Mauryan laws, and it is therefore not surprising that Megasthenes declared that there was no slavery in India. India, unlike some other ancient civilizations, was never economically dependent on slavery; the labourer, farm worker and craftsman were normally free men, and the *latifundia* of the Roman magnate had no counterpart in India. Slave markets are not mentioned in early sources, and though provision was made for the sale of slaves they do not seem at first to have been a regular article of commerce. In the early centuries of the Christian era, however, there was trade in slave-girls between India and the Roman empire in both directions, and slave markets existed in the 16th-century Vijayanagara empire.

There are numerous references in literature to slaves being badly treated by their masters, and the slave's lot must have been often a very unhappy one; but he was probably better off in India than in most parts of the ancient world. Indeed in many contexts it would seem that the word dāsa implies rather a bondsman or serf than a chattel slave.

GOTRA AND *PRAVARA*

The Hindu social order was complicated by other features which had no original relationship to class or caste, but were roughly harmonized with them. These were the institutions of *gotra* and *pravara*, which were in existence in late Vedic times, and probably earlier, and are very important to the orthodox brāhmaṇ to this day.

The original meaning of *gotra* is "a cowshed", or "a herd of cows"; in the *Atharva Veda*,[23] the word first appears with the meaning of "a clan", which it has retained with a special connotation. Some ancient Indo-European peoples, such as the Romans, had exogamous clans as well as generally endogamous tribes. It may well be that the gotra system is a survival of Indo-European origin which had developed specially Indian features.

Gotra as it existed in historical times was primarily a brāhmaṇic institution, adopted rather half-heartedly by other twice-born classes and hardly affecting the lower orders. All brāhmaṇs were believed to have descended from one of the ṛṣi, or legendary seers, after whom the gotras were named. The religious literature generally speaks of seven or eight primeval gotras, those of Kaśyapa, Vasiṣṭha, Bhṛgu, Gautama, Bharadvāja, Atri and Viśvāmitra. The eighth gotra, that of Agastya, is named after the sage who is said to have taken the Vedic religion beyond the Vindhyas, and who is a sort of patron saint of the Dravidians. His name may have been added to those of the original seven as the South became progressively Āryanized. These primeval gotras were multiplied in later times by the inclusion of the names of many other ancient sages.

Though the gotras perhaps evolved from local units within the Āryan tribe they had quite lost their tribal character by historical times, and brāhmaṇs from the furthest parts of India and of different caste groups might have the same gotra. The chief importance of gotra was in connexion with marriage, which was forbidden to persons of a common gotra.

The position was further complicated by *pravara*. In the brāhmaṇ's daily worship he mentioned not only the name of the founder of his gotra, but also the names of certain other sages who were believed to be the remote ancestors of his family. The formula generally contained three or five names, and set up a further bar to marriage, for the same names would occur in the pravaras of families of other gotras. According to the custom of some gotras marriage was impossible with a member of another gotra having one pravara name in common, while others barred intermarriage only when there were two common names in the pravaras. Thus matrimonial choice was much restricted, especially when in the Middle Ages the endogamous caste system was fully established.

The social prestige of the brāhmaṇs led to the respectable classes adopting a gotra system of some sort. Kṣatriyas and vaiśyas took the same gotra names as the brāhmaṇs; their gotras, however, were not based on the claim to descent from an ancient sage, but merely on the gotra of the family of brāhmaṇs which traditionally performed their domestic rituals. As imposed on non-brāhmaṇic families the system was quite artificial. Non-brāhmaṇ families were also expected to take the pravaras of their domestic priests, but this rule counted for little. The real gotras of the kṣatriyas and vaiśyas were secular (*laukika*) ones, founded by legendary eponymous ancestors. Legal literature takes little note of these secular gotras, but numerous references in inscriptions show that the term was used in the sense of "sept" or "clan", and that many non-brāhmaṇ gotras existed which do not occur in the lists of any of the lawbooks.

Early lawgivers take a comparatively liberal view of breaches of gotra regulations. A man marrying a woman of the same gotra must perform a *cāndrāyaṇa* penance, a severe fast of a month's duration, and henceforth maintain his wife as he would a sister;[24] no stigma attaches to the child of such a marriage. With ruthless logic, however, later jurists declare that this rule applies only to inadvertent marriage within the gotra; when the relationship is known the sin is equivalent to that of incest.

THE FAMILY

The Indian family was, and usually still is, a joint one—that is to say a close link was maintained between brothers, uncles, cousins and nephews, who often lived under one roof or group of roofs, and who owned the immovable property of the line in common. Like the European and Semitic family, it was patriarchal and patrilinear. The father was head of the house and administrator of the joint property, and, except in Kerala (p. 150f), the headship descended in the male line.

The ancient Indian family included parents, children, grand-children, uncles and their descendants, and various collaterals on the male side. It might include adopted children, and unless poor it would also possess a varying number of servants, domestic serfs, and clients; a brāhmaṇ family might in addition find room for a number of students, who were engaged in a lengthy course of training under the head of the house and were treated as members of the family. Thus, especially in a polygamous society where girls were married very young, it formed a very large group.

The family, rather than the individual, was looked on as the unit of the social system; thus the population of a given region was generally estimated in families rather than in heads. The bonds of family were such that relationships within the group were often blurred or lost sight of; for instance a son might commonly refer to all his father's wives indiscriminately as his mothers, and the distinction between brother and paternal cousin was not always made clearly—even today the same word is used for both.

The group was bound together by *śrāddha*, the rite of commemorating the ancestors, at which balls of rice called *piṇḍa* were offered (p. 153). Sons, grandsons and great-grandsons of the deceased joined together in śrāddha, and three generations of the dead were believed to participate in the benefits of the ceremony. Thus the dead and the living were linked together by this rite, which, like the ancestor worship of the Chinese, was a most potent force in consolidating the family. Śrāddha defined the family; those who were entitled to participate in the ceremony were "co-pindas" (*sapiṇḍo*), members of the family group. The rite, which is still practised, goes back to Vedic times.

This deep sense of family solidarity led, as might be expected, to nepotism and various other abuses, and today the joint family system is beginning to weigh heavily on the younger generations; but it gave a measure of social security to its members. In distress a man could rely on his sapindas, and the ne'er-do-well cousin or the indolent good-for-nothing uncle, living in a corner of the family home in comparative comfort while adding little or nothing to the family fortunes, was probably just as common a figure in ancient India as he is today.

Though a powerful and awe-inspiring figure, the paterfamilias was not usually an arbitrary tyrant; his power, like that of the king, was somewhat limited by Sacred Law and custom. The jurists differed on the question of his rights over the family property. In modern times there are two great schools of family law, called after the legal texts on which they are based *Mitākṣarā* and *Dāyabhāga* (p. 97f); most families of Bengal and Assam follow the rules of Dāyabhāga, while the rest of India generally follows Mitākṣarā. According to the latter school sons and grandsons have a right in the family property even before the death of the paterfamilias, who is little more than a trustee and manager on behalf of the family, without the right to give property away so as to impoverish his dependents. Dāyabhāga maintains that sons only obtain rights over the property on the death of the father, but even this school recognizes that he is not an outright owner, but only a steward for his descendants. Both schools existed in medieval times, and represent codifications of much earlier practices.

At a very early time fathers may have had absolute rights over their children, for certain ancient and popular stories remind us of the Hebrew legends of Abraham and Isaac and of Jephthah's daughter. The most famous of these is the story of Śunaḥśiepa.

> King Hariścandra of Ayodhyā was childless, and vowed that if he had a son he would sacrifice him to the god Varuṇa. Soon a son was born to him, and named Rohita; but Hariścandra was naturally disinclined to perform his share of the bargain. In punishment Varuṇa afflicted him with dropsy. After some years Hariścandra decided to sacrifice Rohita, who was now a youth, but the son refused to give his life for the sake of his father's health, and fled to the forest, where he lived for six years.
>
> One day Rohita met a brāhmaṇ, Ajīgarta, and bought his second son Śunaḥśepa for a hundred cows, as a substitute for himself. Varuna agreed to accept the sacrifice of Śunaḥśepa in place of Rohita, and the brāhmaṇ boy was sent to the court of Hariścandra to be prepared for sacrifice. Ajigarta agreed to earn another two hundred cows by binding his son to the sacrificial stake and slaying him. The sacrifice was made ready, and Śunaḥśepa was led to the slaughter; he commenced to sing hymns in praise of the gods, and his

devotion was such that Varuna was moved to compassion. Hariścandra was cured of his disease, and Śunaḥśepa lived to become a great and famous sage.

Another well-known story of the same tenor is that of Naciketas, the interlocutor of the *Kaṭha Upaniṣad*.

> The brāhmaṇ Vājaśravasa gave away all his wealth to priests performing ing sacrifices on his behalf, having promised to give up all that he possessed. His son, Naciketas, saw that he still had one possession, and asked "Dear Father, to whom will you give me? "The father made no reply, but when Naciketas repeated the question a third time he said angrily, "I shall give you to Death!"
>
> Naciketas obediently went to the palace of Yama, the god of the dead, but found that he was not at home; only after he had waited for three nights did the god return. Yama so regretted his impoliteness in keeping a guest waiting for so long that he offered Naciketas three boons. With the first the boy was restored to life, and his father pacified; with the second he learnt the secret of the fire sacrifice; and with the third he obtained from Yama full knowledge of the mystery of life after death, which makes up the body of the poem.

Certain early legal texts do allow a father to give away, sell or abandon his son,[25] and the legends we have mentioned would confirm that this was done,* but other sources positively forbid such actions.[26] The father's right over the life of his child is nowhere explicitly admitted, but the *Arthaśāstra* looks on the killing of a son as among the most heinous forms of murder; on the other hand even parricide is permissible in self-defence.

Left to itself, a joint family would tend to increase in size until it became so large as to be unmanageable; hence the Sacred Law made provision for its break-up. The partition of a large joint family was favoured by the lawyers, since thus more domestic rites would be performed and the gods receive more honour and bless the land more readily. Commonly partition took place on the death of the paterfamilias, when the property was divided among the sons. There was no provision for wills in ancient India, and the eldest son received no special inheritance, except sometimes a very small weightage amounting to one twentieth of a share. The partition was not necessarily postponed until the father's death. It regularly occurred if he renounced the world to become an ascetic, and under the Mitākṣarā system it might take place even without his consent by agreement among the sons, if he was senile, incurably diseased, had taken to evil courses, or was otherwise incapable of managing the family affaire. Individual sons, like the Prodigal in the Gospel, might demand their share and leave the family, though this was not wholly approved, and was virtually impossible under the Dāyabhāga system.

In the partition minute rules, varying somewhat with different authorities, were laid down as to the shares to be received by other relatives when there were no

---

* Compare also the Buddhist legend of Vessantara (p. 252).

sons. Most authorities rejected the rights of women to inherit; but Yājñavalkya[27] lays down an authoritative list of priority in inheritance, which places the wife, followed by the daughters, immediately after the sons. The right of a wife to inherit if no sons were living was accepted by the Mitākṣarā school, which was chiefly based on Yājñavalkya.

The joint family property did not include the individual possessions of the members; at least from medieval times onwards personal earnings, gifts, and so on were generally thought to belong to the member of the family who earned them. This was, however, probably a late concept. Manu[28], for instance, states that the property of a son, wife or slave belongs to the head of the household, and the same precept is repeated by some other early lawgivers; the rights of the paterfamilias, it would seem, tended to grow less with time.

THE FOUR STAGES OF LIFE

We have seen that for the theorist society involved two concepts; one of these was class, or *varṇa*, while the other was stage of life, or *āśrama*. This was a later idea than that of class, and was evidently more artificial. Just as Āryan society was divided into four classes, so the life of the individual Āryan was divided into four stages; on his investiture with the sacred thread, when he put his childhood behind him, he became a *brahmacārin*, leading a celibate and austere life as a student at the home of his teacher; next, having mastered the Vedas, or part of them, he returned to his parental home and was married, becoming a householder (*gṛhastha*); when, well advanced in middle age, he had seen his children's children and had thus surely established his line, he left his home for the forest to become a hermit (*vānaprastha*); by meditation and penance he freed his soul from material things, until at last, a very old man, he left his hermitage and became a homeless wanderer (*sannyāsin*), with all his earthly ties broken.

This scheme, of course, represents the ideal rather than the real. Many young men never passed through the first stage of life in the form laid down, while only a few went beyond the second. Many of the hermits and ascetics of ancient India were not old men, and had either shortened or omitted the stage of householder. The series of the four stages is evidently an idealization of the facts, and an artificial attempt to find room for the conflicting claims of study, family life, and asceticism in a single lifetime. It is possible that the system of the *āśramas* was evolved partly as a counterblast to the unorthodox sects such as Buddhism and Jainism, which encouraged young men to take up asceticism and by-pass family life altogether, a practice which did not receive the approval of the orthodox, though in later times provision was made for it. Despite their artificiality, however, the four stages of life were an ideal which many men in ancient India attempted to follow, and thus they deserve our consideration. Moreover they serve as a framework round which we can model the life of the individual.

According to the scheme of the four stages life began not with physical birth, but with the second birth, or investiture with the sacred thread. Thus the child was not a full member of the Āryan community, but nevertheless his existence was hedged around with religious rites, which began even before his birth. Few religions can have marked the course of the life of their members with so many rites and ceremonies as Hinduism. According to the texts on the subject there were some forty ceremonies (*saṃskāra*), which covered the whole life of a man from his conception to his death; some of these were of great importance, and were performed by all respectable members of the Āryan community, while others were often neglected by the less pious.

THE CHILD

Of the various saṃskāras, or personal ceremonies, in the life of the pious Hindu the first three took place before birth: these were *garbhādhāna* to promote conception, *puṃsavana*, to procure a male child, and *sīmantonnayana*, to ensure the safety of the child in the womb. The birth ceremony (*jātakarma*) took place before the cutting of the umbilical cord, and involved the whispering of sacred spells (*mantra*) in the baby's ear, placing a mixture of honey and ghee in his mouth, and giving him a name, to be kept secret by his parents until his initiation. At birth the child and his parents were ritually impure, and therefore were not entitled to take part in ordinary religious ceremonies until after some ten days, when the child was given his public name and the period of impurity ceased. Minor rites of infancy, not always looked on as particularly sacred, were the ear-piercing ceremony, and the *niṣkramaṇa*, when the child was taken out of the house and shown the sun for the first time.

More important was the first feeding of solid food (*annaprāśana*). In the child's sixth month he was given meat, fish or rice (in later times usually the latter) mixed with curds, honey and ghee, to the accompaniment of Vedic verses and oblations of ghee poured on the fire. The tonsure (*cūḍākarma*) took place in the third year, and was confined to boys; with various rites the child's scalp was shaved, leaving only a topknot which, in the case of a pious brāhmaṇ, would never be cut throughout his life. Another ceremony, not looked on as of the first importance, was carried out when the child first began to learn the alphabet.

Many of these ceremonies are now rarely if ever practised in their full form, and it is doubtful if every ancient Indian family, even of the higher classes, performed them regularly, especially in the case of girls. Their number, however, shows the importance of the child in the life of his parents. From the earliest hymns of the *Ṛg Veda* sons were looked on as great blessings. At least one son was almost essential, to perform funeral rites for his father and thus ensure his safe transit to the other world. Adopted sons were but poor substitutes for true sons, and their efficacy at śrāddha ceremonies was dubious. Thus there were strong religious reasons for the pro-creation of children. The intense family feeling of Hindu India enhanced the desire for sons, without whom the line would disappear.

Girls, on the other hand, were incapable either of helping their parents in the other world or of perpetuating the line, for on marriage, according to orthodox theory, they became members of their husbands' families. The necessity of providing them with dowries also lessened their desirability. There were thus very practical reasons why girls should be unwanted, and in a civilization so heavily weighted in favour of the male it is surprising that there is little evidence of the exposure or infanticide of girls. Rājput families in later times certainly often destroyed their infant girls, and the same may well have been done by the very poor at all periods; but no special reference is made to exposure or infanticide in the early legal texts. In the best Indian families daughters, though their birth may have been regretted, were cared for and petted just as sons were.

The general impression obtained from the literature is that in ancient India the child's life was a happy one. Maxims of the type of "Spare the rod and spoil the child" are rare or non-existent. The small child of ancient India was generally pampered, humoured, and allowed a degree of freedom which few children in Europe obtained until modern times. The loving descriptions of children in poetry nearly always show them as the spoilt darlings of their parents. Thus Kālidāsa:

> "With their teeth half-shown in causeless laughter,
> and their efforts at talking so sweetly uncertain,
> when children ask to sit on his lap
> a man is blessed, even by the dirt on their bodies."[29]

The speaker of this verse is a great king, and it shows us even the little children of princes playing naked in the dust, and loved with tenderness by their elders.

But the undisciplined life of the small child soon came to an end. For the poor child there was work to do almost as soon as he could walk, and for the wealthier there were lessons. Normally a boy began to learn the alphabet in his fourth or fifth year. In the richer homes tutore were maintained for the children of the family, but in the Middle Ages education was also given at village schools attached to temples. Though women's education was never looked on as essential, girls were by no means neglected, and well-bred women were usually literate.

The curriculum of the child's early studies seems always to have included reading and elementary arithmetic, but at this stage of his life he was not a full member of the Āryan community, and his formal schooling had not yet commenced. Only on his investiture with the sacred thread was he ready to learn the Vedas and embark on a detailed course of study calculated to equip him for his ancestral calling.

INITIATION

The great rite of *upanayana*, the second birth whereby a boy became a full member of his class and of society, was confined to brāhmaṇs, kṣatriyas and vaiśyas. The śūdras and lower orders could not undergo it, and were never allowed to hear or learn the most sacred of the scriptures. The ideal age for the ceremony varied according to class—eight for a brāhmaṇ, eleven for a kṣatriya, and twelve for a vaiśya.

It was a very ancient rite, going back to times before the Āryans divided into Indian and Iranian branches, for the Zoroastrians had a similar ceremony, a form of which is still practised by the modern Pārsīs. The kernel of the ceremony was the investing of the boy, clad in the garments of an ascetic and with a staffin his hand, with the sacred thread (*yajñopavīta*), which was hung over his left shoulder and under his right arm, and which he was expected to wear continuously from that day forward. It was a cord of three threads, each of nine twisted strands, made of cotton, hemp or wool for brāhmaṇs, kṣatriyas and vaiśyas respectively, and it had great religious significance, as it still has for the orthodox. Its removal or defilement involved its owner in humiliation and ritual impurity, which could only be expunged by rigorous penance.

The ceremony also included the whispering of the *Gāyatrī* in the ear of the initiate by the officiating brāhmaṇ. This is a verse from a hymn of the *Ṛg Veda*,[30] addressed to the old solar god Savitṛ, and it is still looked on as the most holy passage of that most holy text. It is repeated in all religious rites and ceremonies, and has a position in Hinduism rather like that of the Lord's Prayer in Christianity, except that the Gāyatrī may only be uttered by the three higher classes.

Tát Savitúr vdreṇiatṃ
bhárgo devásya dhīmahi,
dhíyo yó nah pracodáyāt.

Let us think on the lovely splendour
of the god Savitṛ,
that he may inspire our minds.

Probably even before the Christian era many kṣatriyas and vaiśyas had ceased to perform the initiation ceremony in the full form, for the term "twice-born", applying to all who had undergone the ceremony, became more and more looked on as a synonym of brāhmaṇ. Some non-brāhmaṇ castes, however, maintain the ceremony to the present day, and it is still performed in orthodox brāhmaṇ families. Normally the initiation was confined to boys, though in Vedic times girls were also sometimes initiated.

In this initiation ceremony there was little or no trace of overt sexual symbolism, and it was never thought of, like circumcision and other initiation ceremonies among more primitive peoples, as a rite fitting the initiate for sexual life. The initiated boy was still a minor, but he had taken the status of an Āryan, and it was now his duty to master the religious lore of the Āryans in order to prepare himself for the rōle of a householder. As a *brahmacārin* or religious student he had as yet several years of celibacy before him.

EDUCATION

According to the ideal of the sacred texts, the training of the brahmacārin took place at the home of a brāhmaṇ teacher (*guru*). In some early sources the guru is depicted as a poor ascetic, and it is one of the student's duties to beg food for his teacher, but this rule seems not to have been regularly followed. The student was, however, expected to treat his master with the utmost reverence, ministering to all his needs and obeying all his commands implicitly.

Among the first lessons of the student was the performance of *sandhyā*, the morning, noon and evening devotions, Which included reciting the Gāyatrī, restraint of the breath, sipping and sprinkling water, and pouring libations of water to the sun, which was looked on rather as a symbol of the special deity of the worshipper, whether Viṣṇu or Śiva, than as the Sungod himself. These rites were incumbent upon all the twice-born, and in various forms are still performed.

The main subject of study was the Veda, and long hours were devoted to its mastery. The teacher would instruct the few students seated on the ground about him by rote, and for many hours daily they would repeat verse after verse of the Vedas, until one or more was mastered. Sometimes, to ensure correctness, the hymns were taught in more than one way, first with the words connected, then in their isolated form (*padapāṭha*), and then with the words interwoven in *ab*, *bc*, *ed* pattern (*kramapāṭha*), or in even more complicated ways. This remarkable system of mnemonic checks and the patience and brilliant memories of many generations of teachers and students preserved the Vedas for posterity in much the same form as that in which they existed nearly a thousand years before Christ.

The boys in the guru's home did not confine their attention wholly to the Vedic texts. There were other fields of study, notably the "Limbs of the Veda", or subsidiary sciences necessary for its proper understanding. These six *vedāhgas* consisted of: *kalpa*, the performance of sacrifice; *śikṣā*, correct pronunciation, or phonetics; *chandas*, metre and prosody; *nirukta*, etymology, the interpretation of obscure words in the Vedic texts; *vyākaraṇa*, grammar; and *jyotisa*, astronomy, or the science of the calendar. Moreover in post-Vedic times teachers would often instruct their students in the six schools of metaphysics, or in that school which they specially favoured. Those versed in the Sacred Law would expound it to their students, while others would teach special secular subjects, such as astronomy, mathematics or literature.

The writers of Smṛti envisaged all young men of the upper class as undergoing this training. Such was not the case—in fact it is doubtful if more than a small proportion of young men ever went through a full course of Vedic education. Princes and the sons of chiefs and nobles were trained in arms and in all the manifold sciences needed to fit them for government, while most boys of the lower orders probably learnt their trades from their fathers. The Buddhist scriptures, however, show that there was a form of apprenticeship, and the lawbooks lay down rules governing it.

Certain cities became renowned for their learned teachers, and achieved a reputation comparable to that of the university cities of medieval Europe. Chief among these were Vārāṇasī and Takṣaśilā, which were already famous in the time of the Buddha; later, around the beginning of the Christian era, Kāñcī acquired a similar reputation in the South. Vārāṇasī, then usually called Kāśī, was particularly renowned for its religious teachers, but Takṣaśilā, in the far North-West, laid more emphasis on secular studies. The Buddhist Jātaka tales show that young men from all over the civilized part of India sought education in this city, through which a trickle of Iranian and Mesopotamian influence found its way to India. Among the famous learned men connected with Takṣaśilā were Pāṇini, the grammarian of the 4th century B.C. (p. 343), Kauṭilya, the brāhmaṇ minister of Candragupta Maurya, and traditionally the chief master of the science of statecraft, and Caraka, one of the two great masters of Indian medical science.

Though it was the ideal of the Smrtis that a small number of students should study under a single teacher, it seems that veritable colleges existed at these "university towns". Thus we read of an establishment at Vārāṇasī with 500 students and a number of teachers, all of whom were maintained by charitable donations. Ideally, again, the teacher asked no fee; the students repaid him for his teaching by their reverent service, and only at the end of their studies was he presented with a gift, traditionally a cow. Manu, however, makes it quite clear that there were venal teachers who were willing to teach the Vedas for money.[31] A Jātaka story tells of a teacher of Takṣaśilā who made his ordinary pupils wait on him all day, while those who paid fees were treated like his own children. At Takṣaśilā the rules of the Smṛti were also relaxed in another respect, for we read of married students, who did not live in their masters' houses but had homes of their own and only visited their teachers for lectures.

With Buddhism and Jainism education centred not on the teacher's home, but on the monastery. Every monastery might give training to postulants, but quite early in the history of these two religions certain establishments acquired a special reputation as centres of learning. In the Middle Ages some developed into true universities. The most famous of these was the Buddhist monastery of Nālandā in Bihār, which, founded in Gupta times, remained the most famous teaching centre of medieval Buddhism until it was pillaged by the invading Muslims. Our knowledge of the day-to-day life of Nālandā depends chiefly on Hsüan Tsang, who shows us the monastery in the 7th century as full of intellectual activity. Under its aged and saintly abbot, Śīlabhadra, Nālandā did not confine itself to training Buddhist novices, but also taught the Vedas, Hindu philosophy, logic, grammar and medicine. It would seem that the student population was not confined to the Buddhist order, but that candidates of other faiths who succeeded in passing a strict oral examination were admitted.

According to Hsüan Tsang, Nālandā was supported by the revenues of an enormous estate of one hundred villages, and by the alms of many patrons, including the great Harsa himself; it provided free training for no less than 10,000 students, who had a large staff of servants to wait on them. The remains of Nālandā, however, belie Hsüan Tsang (pl. XII). The monastery consisted of a very large complex of buildings, but it could hardly have accommodated a thousand monks in anything like the comfort described by the Chinese traveller.

Many other Buddhist monasteries all over the country, and Jaina monasteries in the West and South, served as centres of learning, as did their Christian counterparts in medieval Europe. In the Middle Ages a Hindu monasticism developed, and the *mathas* of the Hindu orders also became centres of learning.

MARRIAGE

Ideally studenthood lasted for twelve years, though it might be terminated when the student had mastered one Veda. A few very earnest students took vows of perpetual celibacy, and continued religious studies throughout their whole lives. Normally, however, the young man in his early twenties would return home, to resume the everyday life of his class. He would take a ritual bath, and reward his teacher according to the means of his family. From now on he was a *snātaka* ("one who has bathed"), and he might enjoy normal worldly pleasures, eat any kind of food usually eaten by his class, and wear fine clothes and jewellery, which he put on at a special homecoming ceremony (*samāvartaṇa*).

It was generally thought advisable for a snātaka to marry as soon as possible, for unless he had taken a vow of religious celibacy marriage and the procreation of children were a positive duty. Marriage had three main purposes: the promotion of religion by the performance of household sacrifices; progeny, whereby the father and his ancestors were assured of a happy after-life and the line was continued; and *rati*, or sexual pleasure.

The normal religious marriage was and still is arranged by the parents of the couple, after much consultation and the study of omens, horoscopes, and auspicious physical characteristics. The couple were usually of the same class and caste, but of different gotras and pravaras if they were of high class. Rules of prohibited degrees were very strict, especially in Northern India, where, even in a caste which disregarded gotra, marriage was forbidden between persons with a common paternal ancestor within seven generations or a maternal ancestor within five. In the Deccan, however, this rule was not strictly followed, and there are records of cousin-marriage even in ruling families.

Though in early times it was usual for girls to be fully adult before marriage, the Smrtis recommend that while a husband should be at least twenty a girl should be married immediately before puberty. So philoprogenitive had Hindu orthodoxy become that it was even declared that a father who did not give his daughter in marriage before her first menstruation incurred the guilt of one procuring abortion (a very grave sin, worse than many kinds of murder) for every menstrual period in which she remained unmarried.[32] The general view was that the ideal marriage was one in which the bride was one third the age of the groom—thus a man of twenty-four should marry a girl of eight.[33]

The marriage of boys, whether before or just after puberty, is nowhere suggested, but the ideal of a rigorous period of studentship before marriage is always maintained. The child-marriage of both parties, which became common in later times among well-to-do families, has no basis at all in sacred literature, and it is very doubtful whether the child-marriage of girls was at all common until the late medieval period. The heroines of poetry and fiction are apparently full grown when they marry, and the numerous inscriptions which throw much light on the customs of the time give little or no indication of child-marriage. Ancient Indian medical authorities state that the best children are produced from mothers over sixteen, and apparently recognize the practice of child-marriage as occasionally occurring, but disapprove of it.[34]

The reasons for the development of child-marriage cannot be given with certainty. Some have suggested that the fear of marauding Muslims encouraged parents to marry their daughters in childhood and to confine their wives more strictly in their homes; but both these customs existed in pre-Muslim times, so this cannot be the only reason. It may in part be due to the growing religious insistence on the necessity of progeny, but this was strong at all times. The sexuality of the Indian character may have played some part in it. A woman was thought to be naturally libidinous; an unmarried girl attaining puberty would proceed to find a lover, however strictly her parents guarded her; once she had lost her virginity she would become unmarriageable and the parents would have the choice of the disgrace and expense of maintaining an unmarried daughter indefinitely, or the even greater disgrace of casting her out to become a beggar or a prostitute. From the point of view of her parents a daughter was a serious economic liability, and this may have encouraged the custom.

Religious marriage was solemnized by very complicated ceremonies, the expenses of which fell on the family of the bride, and, with the dowry, were a very heavy burden to her father and family. To this day Hindu parents will often involve themselves in crippling debts in order to marry their daughters. Though the rules for the wedding ceremony laid down in different textbooks vary in details, the rite differed little from that of the present day, or from the marriage ceremony of the *Ṛg Veda*. The bridegroom, decked in great finery and attended by a train of friends and relatives, proceeded to the bride's home and was received by her father with a *madhuparka*, an auspicious ceremonial drink of honey and curds. Usually the ceremony was held in a gaudy temporary pavilion in the courtyard of the house. Bride and groom entered the pavilion separately, and sat on either side of a small curtain. To the accompaniment of sacred verses muttered by the officiating brāhmaṇ the curtain was removed, and the couple saw one another, often for the first time. The bride's father stepped forward, and formally gave her to the groom, who promised that he would not behave falsely to her in respect of the three traditional aims of life—piety, wealth and pleasure. Next, offerings of ghee and rice were made in the sacred fire. The groom grasped the bride's hand while she offered grain in the fire, round which he then led her, usually with their garments knotted together, after which she trod on a millstone. The couple next took seven steps together, the bride treading on a small heap of rice at each step.

Finally they were sprinkled with holy water and the main part of the ceremony was completed.

As described above the rite seems comparatively simple, but it was complicated by the recitation of many *mantras*, or Vedic and other verses believed to have magical and spiritual efficiency. Even at this stage the marriage ceremony was not completely over. The newly married pair returned to the bridegroom's house, where a further sacrifice to the domestic fire was performed. In the evening it was incumbent upon them to look at the Pole Star, a symbol of faithfulness. For three nights the couple were expected to remain continent; in some texts they are allowed to sleep together with a staff between them, but others instruct them to sleep apart on the ground. On the fourth night the husband performed a rite to promote conception, and the marriage was consummated.*

The length and solemnity of this ceremony will give some idea of the importance and sanctity of marriage in the eyes of ancient Indian lawgivers; but the form of marriage which we have described, though now regular among respectable Hindus, was not the only one known to ancient India, and a marriage might be considered binding even when the religious ceremony had not been performed. The textbooks enumerate eight types of marriage, named after various gods and supernatural beings:

(1) *Brāhma*, marriage of a duly dowered girl to a man of the same class by the ceremony described above.
(2) *Daiva*, when a householder gives a daughter to a sacrificial priest as part of his fee.
(3) *Ārṣa*, in which, in place of the dowry, there is a token bride-price of a cow and a bull.
(4) *Prājāpatya*, in which the father gives the girl without dowry and without demanding bride-price.
(5) *Gāndharva*, marriage by the consent of the two parties, which might be solemnized merely by plighting troth. This form of marriage was often clandestine.
(6) *Āsura*, marriage by purchase.
(7) *Rākṣasa*, marriage by capture.
(8) *Paiśāca*, which can scarcely be called marriage at all—the seduction of a girl while asleep, mentally deranged, or drunk.

Of these eight forms the first four were generally approved, and were permissible to brāhmaṇs; these were religious marriages, and were indissoluble. The other forms were looked on with varying degrees of disfavour by the pious. *Gāndharva* marriage, which often might amount to no more than a liaison, was

* The secular Kāmasūtra even advises the postponement of consummation for ten days (below, p. 148).

surprisingly respected. Some doubts existed as to whether it was possible to brāhmaṇs, but it was certainly allowed to the warrior class and the lower orders. It forms the basis of many romantic stories, and has given rise to one of the stock figures of later poetic convention—the *abkisārikā*, the girl who secretly leaves her father's home by night to meet her lover at the appointed trysting place.

Āsura marriage, in which the bride was bought from her father, was looked on with disfavour by all the sacred texts, though the *Arthaśāstra* allows it without criticism. There is evidence that marriage by purchase, as well as the orthodox marriage with dowry, existed even in Vedic times, but it was not a true Āryan custom and was only allowed as a sop to the evil propensities of man. *Rākṣasa* marriage, or marriage by capture, was practised especially by warriors. The most famous example, according to later tradition, was the marriage of Pṛthvīrāja Cāhamāna, the last great Hindu king of North India, with the daughter of Jayaccandra of Kānyakubja, whom he carried off as a not unwilling captive. Epigraphy and tradition record several other instances. *Paiśāca* marriage was universally reprobated. The names of the last three types are derived from those of demons, of which the *piśāca* was the lowest and most repulsive. This form of marriage, according to the lawbooks, was not fitted for the higher classes, and could only be allowed on suffrance to the lower orders.

Some authorities have tried to explain away the less reputable forms of marriage, and to prove that they were non-existent or very rare; but it is hardly likely that the lawgivers would have admitted these forms, of which they wholeheartedly disapproved, if they had not had a solid basis in ineluctable social custom. It would seem that, with surprising realism, the jurists recognized a wide range of relationships, so that the girl seduced by her lover's promises or carried off by raiders would have some legal claim to wifely status, and her child some degree of legitimacy. No doubt among the upper classes most marriages were of the first type, and any of the other forms might be solemnized later by religious rites and thus raised in status.

A special form of the gāndharva marriage was the *svayaṃvara* or "self-choice". The law books lay down that if a girl is not married by her parents soon after attaining puberty she may choose her own husband, and evidently marriage by the choice of the bride sometimes took place. Epic literature shows that more than one form of svayaṃvara was practised. Princess Sāvitrī toured the country in her chariot in search of a suitable mate, until she found Satyavant, the woodcutter's son. Damayantī chose her husband Nala at a great ceremony, at which she passed along the assembled ranks of her suitors until she found the man of her choice. Another form of svayaṃvara was that by which Rāma won Sītā, at a great archery contest. We have references to the performance of svayaṃvaras as late as the 11th century, for Vikramāditya VI, the great king of the Cālukyas, is said to have obtained brides by this method. The svayaṃvara was normally concluded by the performance of the rites of religious marriage, and later legal commentators maintain that no form of marriage is complete without the religious ceremony, at least in an abridged form.

With the long marriage ceremony completed the householder might devote himself to the three ends of life, a classification commonly found in both religious and general literature. The three are: *dharma*, gaining religious merit through following the Sacred Law; *artha*, gaining wealth by honest means; and *kāma*, pleasure of all kinds. The three were of descending order of importance, and it was thought that where the interests of one end conflicted with those of another the higher should have priority. The two latter ends need little explanation, but for the high class Indian the first involved numerous religious duties, notably the performance of birth, marriage, funeral, and other ceremonies, and the regular carrying out of the "Five Great Sacrifices" (*pañca-mahāyajña*).

The greatness of these sacrifices lay not in their expense or complexity, but in their importance. They were to be performed daily and consisted of:

(1) *Brahmayajña*, the worship of Brāhmaṇ, the World-Spirit, by reciting the Vedas.
(2) *Pitṛyajña*, the worship of the ancestors, by libations of water and periodical śrāddhas.
(3) *Devayajña*, worship of the gods, by pouring ghee on the sacred fire.
(4) *Bhūtayajña*, the worship of all things living, by scattering grain and other food on the threshold for animals, birds, and spirits.
(5) *Puruṣayajña*, the worship of men, by showing them hospitality.

Ideally the five great sacrifices should be performed thrice a day, at the sandhyās, or periods of worship at sunrise, noon and sunset.

SEXUAL RELATIONS

Though the learned brāhmaṇs who composed the Smṛti literature and prescribed canons of behaviour for the Indian layman were puritanical in many respects, they did not disparage physical love. Of the three ends of life the third, pleasure, though less important than the other two, was a legitimate branch of human activity, for which provision had to be made in the scheme of existence. In its broadest sense the word *kāma* means desire of every kind and its fulfilment, but, like such English words as "desire" and "passion", it usually had a sexual connotation. Of all legitimate pleasures sexual pleasure was thought to be the best.

The literature of Hindu India, both religious and secular, is full of sexual allusions, sexual symbolism, and passages of frank eroticism. The preoccupation with such themes increased in the Middle Ages, when the process of cosmic creation was figured as the union of god and goddess, and images of closely embracing couples (*maithuna*) were carved on the walls of temples. Some religious sects even introduced ritual intercourse as part of their cult and a potent aid to salvation. But the exaggerated sexual religiosity of the later Middle Ages was only an expression of the vigorous sexuality which was to be found in Indian social life at all times. Sexual activity was indeed a positive religious duty, for the husband was told to have intercourse with his wife within a period of eight days at the close of every menstruation.

The Indian passion for classification, though it did not result in the emergence of experimental science, led to the development of rather pedantic schools on many aspects of human activity, including sexual relations. On this topic a number of textbooks survive, the most important and earliest of which is the *Kāmasūtra*, attributed to the sage Vātsyāyana and written in the early centuries of the Christian era, or perhaps in the Gupta period. This remarkable work gives, as may be imagined, detailed instructions on erotic technique, aphrodisiac recipes and charms, and incidentally much very valuable information about the life of the ancient Indian. From texts such as this, and from many passages in courtly literature, we may learn much about the sexual life of the upper classes.

Sexuality was not looked on as a mere vent for the animal passions of the male, but as a refined mutual relationship for the satisfaction of both parties. The sophisticated townsman for whom the *Kāmasūtra* was written was advised to consider the satisfaction of his mistress as well as his own, for she was as passionate as himself, and it was even said by some that her pleasure in sex was greater than his. Love-play was manifold and thoroughly classified; thus the *Kāmasūtra* defines no less than sixteen types of kiss. There was much tenderness in lovemaking, though it often culminated in very violent embraces; it was a favourite poetic convention to describe lovers of both sexes, whether married or single, as displaying the tokens of their passion to their confidential friends, in the form of the marks of nails and teeth.

The erotic preoccupations of ancient India are made very evident in art and literature. The ideal of feminine beauty in ancient India differed very greatly from the matronly type of the Greeks, or the slender more boyish type of modern Europe and America. The Indian ideal, thick-thighed, broad hipped, but very slender-waisted, and with heavy breasts, seems evidently chosen for physical satisfaction. The poets loved to describe their heroines in terms of luxurious frankness. They did, however, observe certain conventional restraints. The preliminaries of sexual intercourse are treated, and it is recollected in tranquillity in general terms, but the act itself is rarely if ever described in detail until a very late period. Such detailed descriptions occur in vernacular poetry, but the poets of India's greatness preferred to leave something at least unsaid.

As an example of the better side of Indian sexual life we quote from the *Kāmasūtra*:

> "For the first three days after their marriage husband and wife should sleep on the floor and abstain from intercourse.... For the next seven days they should bathe to the sound of music, adorn themselves, dine together, and pay their respects to their relatives and to the other people who attended their wedding. ... On the evening of the tenth day the husband should speak gently to his wife ... to give her confidence.... Vātsyāyana recommends that a man should at first refrain from intercourse, until he has won over his bride and gained

her confidence, for women, being gentle by nature, prefer to be won over gently. If a woman is forced to submit to rough handling from a man whom she scarcely knows she may come to hate sexual intercourse, and even to hate the whole male sex … or she may grow to detest her husband in particular, and will then turn to another man."[35]

Vātsyāyana then gives a detailed example of the courtship of a newly married bride by her husband, which would win the approval of most modern psychologists.

The erotic life of ancient India was generally heterosexual. Homosexualism of both sexes was not wholly unknown; it is condemned briefly in the lawbooks, and the *Kāmasūtra* treats of it, but cursorily and with little enthusiasm. Literature almost ignores it. In this respect ancient India was far healthier than most other ancient cultures. Another unpleasant feature of ancient civilizations, the eunuch, was also rare, though not completely unknown. Castration, whether of men or animals, was disapproved of, and harems were generally guarded by elderly men and armed women.

DIVORCE

From the point of view of the Sacred Law a marriage was indissoluble, once the seven steps had been taken together. Even if not consummated it could not be annulled, and divorce was quite impossible. An errant wife lost most of her rights, but her husband was still responsible for her bare maintenance if it was demanded, and she was not entitled to remarry. The lawbooks vary in their attitude to the adulterous wife; generally if she had wilful intercourse with a man of base caste her lot was hard; Manu[36] and some other sources even lay down that she should be torn apart by dogs. But the adulteress who strayed with a man of higher caste was more fortunate; most authorities agree that she should be made to wear dirty clothes, sleep on the ground, and eat only enough food barely to sustain life until her next menstruation; thereafter she might be restored to her husband's bed and her old position in the household.

Though the religious lawbooks leave no room for divorce, the *Arthaśāstra*[37] shows that it was possible in early times, at least in marriages not solemnized by religious rites. In this case divorce was allowed by mutual consent on grounds of incompatibility, and one party might obtain divorce without the consent of the other if apprehensive of actual physical danger from his or her partner. The *Arthaśāstra* would allow divorce even after religious marriage if a wife had been deserted by her husband, and lays down waiting periods of from one to twelve years, which vary according to circumstances and class.[38] These provisions, however, do not appear in later lawbooks, and were probably forgotten by Gupta times, when divorce became virtually impossible for people of the higher classes. Among many lower castes, however, divorce is still permitted by custom, and this must also have been the case in earlier days.

POLYGAMY

The ordinary people of India, as of every other part of the world, were generally monogamous, though even in the time of the *Ṛg Veda* polygamy was not unknown. Kings and chiefs were almost invariably polygamous, as were many brāhmaṇs and wealthier members of the lower orders.

In ordinary circumstances polygamy was not encouraged by the earlier legal literature. One Dharma Sūtra[39] definitely forbids a man to take a second wife if his first is of good character and has borne him sons. Another later source states that a polygamist is unfit to testify in a court of law.[40] The *Arthaśāstra*[41] lays down various rules which discourage wanton polygamy, including the payment of compensation to the first wife. The ideal models of Hindu marriage are the hero Rāma and his faithful wife Sītā, whose mutual love was never broken by the rivalry of a co-wife. However, polygamous marriages are so frequently mentioned that we may assume that they were fairly common among all sections of the community who could afford them.

A husband was told to treat his wives alike, but this was a rule which could hardly be enforced by law and was usually a psychological impossibility. Tied to her husband's home, the first wife often felt bitterly the happiness of her rival.

> "Grief of the man who loses all his wealth,
>   and of him whose son is slain;
> grief of a wife who has lost her lord,
>   and of him whom the king has made captive;
> grief of a childless woman,
>   and of him who feels the breath of a tiger at his back;
> grief of the wife whose husband has married another woman,
>   and of one convicted by witnesses in court—
> these griefs are all alike."[42]

Several of the courtly dramas deal with the jealousy of the king's senior wife towards the latest object of her lord's affections, but they invariably end on a happy note, with the acceptance by the old queen of her younger rival. Polygamous households were not necessarily unhappy, and the first wife might console herself, if she had male children, with the knowledge that she was the chief wife, the mistress of the household, entitled to the first place beside her husband at the family rites.

If polygamy was common, its reverse, polyandry, was not wholly unknown, though it was impossible for ordinary people of respectable class in most parts of India. "For brother to take the wife of brother," writes one legal text, "is a great sin, though in other lands it is even known to marry a girl to an entire family".[43] The *locus classicus* of ancient Indian polyandry is the *Mahābhārata*, where the heroes, the five Pāṇḍava brothers, share their wife Draupadī in common. This is certainly a part of the original story, and its truth must have been very widely believed by the people of early India, for otherwise the priestly editors of the Epic would undoubtedly have invented four sisters of Draupadī, to match the five brothers and thus to satisfy orthodox prejudices. Lawyers were hard put to it to explain this abnormal matrimonial arrangement, but it is well known among the Mongolian hill tribes to this day, and also among certain low castes in the Deccan. There are a few other references to polyandry here and there in Indian literature.

Among the Nayyars of Kerala a practice prevailed until comparatively recent times, no doubt a survival of remote antiquity, which was different from the group marriage of the Himālayan tribes, and was connected with the local matrilinear family system. A girl was married, as a sop to Āryan convention, to a man hired for the purpose; the marriage was not consummated and she might never see her husband again. She remained in the family home, and the fact of her marriage was published; when it became known, she was courted by the eligible men of the neighbourhood, from whom she chose her true husband, often a Nambūdiri brāhmaṇ, who was accepted without ceremony. The children of the union took their mother's name, and the inheritance passed through her line, though the eldest male of the family acted as head of the house. The husband had no rights over his wife's family at all, and might take less interest in his children than did their maternal uncle. He might be discarded by the mother of his children and replaced by another suitor, though real promiscuity on her part was frowned upon. The Kerala system of *marumak-kattāyam* shows that the pattern of matrimonial relations had more variety than allowed by the legal texts.

In his efforts to produce a son a man might without slur on his character take a second wife, if his first was barren, and so on indefinitely; indeed in these circumstances polygamy was a religious duty. If the husband was sterile or impotent he had to take further measures. In the last resort he would appoint a close relative, usually a brother, to produce offspring on his behalf. From several stories in the Epics and elsewhere it appears that holy men of special sanctity were also often in demand for this purpose, and practices of this kind are said to take place occasionally even at the present day.

Similarly if the husband died without producing male issue his brother might act on his behalf. This practice of levirate (*niyoga*) was well known in many ancient societies, and references to it are common in early Indian legal literature. Before the beginning of the Christian era, however, it began to be disapproved of, and medieval writers include it among the forbidden *kalivarjya* customs, which were permitted in earlier ages.

OLD AGE AND DEATH

According to the letter of the Sacred Law, when a householder's hair turns white and he sees his sons' sons he should become a hermit, either leaving his wife to the care of his children or taking her to the forest with him. There, living in a little hut on the alms of villagers or food collected from the wilds, he should perform regular rites at his sacred fire and study the Upaniṣads, in order to raise his soul above earthly things. He may add to his hardships by deliberate self-mortification. "In summer he should sit exposed to the heat of five fires, in the rainy season he should live under the sky, in winter he should wear wet clothes, and so he should gradually augment his hardships."[44] This is the stage of life of the *vānaprastha*, the forest hermit.

Before death there is yet another stage through which to pass. When all last attachments to worldly things have passed away the hermit may leave his forest retreat, give up the performance of all ceremonies, and become a homeless wanderer (*sannyāsin*), with nothing but a staff, a begging bowl, and a few rags of clothing:

"He should not wish to die,
nor hope to live,
but await the time appointed,
as a servant awaits his wages....

"He must show no anger
to one who is angry.
He must bless the man who curses him ...
He must not utter false speech.

'Rejoicing in the things of the spirit, cairn,
caring for nothing, abstaining from sensual pleasure,
himself his only helper,
he may live on in the world, in the hope of eternal bliss."[46]

We must not imagine that more than a small proportion of elderly men followed these drastic means of achieving salvation. For the ordinary man the status of householder was enough, and he was content with the hope of a long period of conditioned bliss in heaven, followed by another happy birth on earth—the fate assured to the householder who fully maintained the rites and ethics of the Āryan. But the number of elderly men who took up asceticism was considerable, and the desire of adult and married sons to obtain control of the family property no doubt encouraged the asceticism of their parents. Even today it is not unusual for an elderly man to follow the course laid down by the ancient sages and to end his days in asceticism, though nowadays his hermitage may be a hut in the family compound, or a secluded room in his old home.

As a man was born in impurity so he died in impurity. Nearly all ancient peoples had a horror of contact with a corpse, and India was no exception. No doubt the idea of ritual impurity originated in a very primitive belief in demons, but it survived in the advanced civilization of classical India, when its basis was no longer properly recognized. According to the Sacred Law mourners must avoid all close contact with outsiders for fear of carrying pollution; they must submit to rigid dietary restrictions, and sleep on the ground; and they must not shave their hair, or worship the gods. The caṇḍālas, who have the duty of laying out and shrouding the body and carrying it to the cremation ground, are the most inauspicious of creatures and the lowest of the low.

The funeral ceremonies (*antyeṣṭi*) were the last of the many sacraments which marked the stages of a man's life. According to the most favoured Āryan custom the corpse was carried to the burning ground as soon as possible after death, followed by the mourners, the eldest leading; it was cremated, to the accompaniment of sacred texts; the mourners circumambulated the pyre, not in the auspicious clockwise direction but anti-clockwise; then they bathed in the nearest river, tank or lake, and returned home, this time led by the youngest. On the third day after the cremation the charred bones of the dead were gathered up and thrown into a river, preferably the Gangā.

For ten days after the cremation libations of water were poured for the dead, and offerings of rice-balls (*piṇḍa*) and vessels of milk were made for him. On death a man's soul became a miserable ghost (*preta*), unable to pass on to the World of the Fathers or to a new birth, and liable to do harm to the surviving relatives. With the performance of the last antyeṣṭi rite on the tenth day it acquired a subtle body with which to continue its journey, speeded on its way and nourished in the after-life with the pindas offered at periodical śrāddha ceremonies. With the tenth day, the mourners ceased to be impure, and resumed their normal lives.

This funeral ceremony was that followed by the upper classes in ancient India, and is no different from that of present-day Hinduism. There were other funeral customs, however. The Harappā people buried their dead, while the early Āryans did not throw the charred remains into a river but buried them, in the case of important people under a large barrow. Small children, whose bodies do not carry the same impurity as those of their elders and who are not full members of the Āryan community, are still often buried, as are ascetics and members of some low castes in South India. These customs have probably survived from very early days. In most literary references the *śmaśāna*, or cremation ground, is described as covered with putrefying corpses and haunted by dogs and vultures, rather than as the scene of cremation. The descriptions of such places show that many people in ancient India did not cremate their dead, but, like the Zoroastrians of Persia, merely abandoned their bodies to the wild beasts. No doubt economic considerations played a big part in this practice, especially in those parts of the country where timber was scarce; even to this day the poorer Indians must be content with exiguous funeral pyres, and their corpses are often not completely burnt.

WOMEN

A woman, according to most authorities, was always a minor at law. As a girl she was under the tutelage of her parents, as an adult, of her husband, and as a widow, of her sons. Even under the liberal rules of Buddhism a nun, however advanced in the faith, was always subordinate to the youngest novice among the brethren. Early lawbooks assessed a woman's wergeld as equivalent to that of a śūdra, whatever her class.

Most schools of law allowed a woman some personal property (*strīdhana*) in the form of jewellery and clothing. The *Arthaśāstra* allowed her also to own money up to 2,000 silver panas, any sum above this being held by her husband in trust on her behalf.[41] The husband had certain rights over his wife's property; he might sell it in dire emergency, and he might restrain her from giving it away wantonly, but for practical purposes it was her own, and when she died it passed not to her husband or to her sons, but to her daughters. Thus the property rights of women, limited though they were, were greater than in many other early civilizations. In fact women sometimes possessed more than was usually allowed to them by the rules of *strīdhana*. Jaina tradition mentions a potter-woman of the town of Śrāvastī who owned a pottery with one hundred potter's wheels. Her status is nowhere mentioned, and it may be that she was a widow, for we have seen that some legal schools allowed a widow to inherit when there were no sons.

Women could at all times take up a life of religion, though of course they could not officiate as priests. A few Vedic hymns are ascribed to women seers, and among the voluminous Buddhist scriptures is a whole collection of poems ascribed to the nuns of the early church; many of these are of great literary merit (p. 458). The *Bṛhadāraṇyaka Upaniṣad*[46] tells of a learned lady, Gārgī Vācaknavī, who attended the discussions of the sage Yājñavalkya and for a time so nonplussed him with her searching questions that he could only jestingly reply, "Gārgī, you mustn't ask too much, or your head will drop off!" References occur here and there in later texts to girls occasionally attending the lectures of gurus, and mastering at least part of the Vedas. By the time of the Smṛtis, however, around the beginning of the Christian era, Vedic knowledge was closed to women, although the heterodox sects still catered for them. The tāntric sects of the Middle Ages, who worshipped feminine divinities, gave women an important place in their cult and instituted orders of female ascetics.

In general, however, women were not encouraged to take up a life of religion or asceticism. Their true function was marriage, and the care of their menfolk and children. But the better class laywomen seem to have been educated, and there are several references to works of Sanskrit poetry and drama by women authors, of which some fragments survive. In Tamil the early poetess Avvaiyār has left work of much merit, and a splendid martial ode describing the great victory of the early Cōla king Karikālan at Veṇṇi is ascribed to an unnamed potter's wife.[47] The ladies of Sanskrit courtly literature are often described as reading, writing, and composing songs, and they seem to have been well versed in the arts of the time. Though from medieval times until very recent years the arts of music and dancing were looked on as quite unfit for respectable Indian girls, and were practised only by low-caste women and prostitutes, this was not the case in ancient days, when well-to-do girls were taught singing and dancing, as well as other ladylike arts such as painting and garland-making.

In Muslim times the Hindus of Northern India adopted the system of *parda*, by which from puberty to old age women were carefully screened from the sight of all men but their husbands and close relatives. Though such a system did not exist in ancient India the freedom accorded to married women has often been exaggerated by authorities anxious to show that the more objectionable aspects of later Hindu custom had no place in India's ancient culture. Certainly the *Ṛg Veda* depicts young men and unmarried girls mixing freely, and gives no evidence that married women were in any way secluded, but this text belongs to a time which had long passed in the great days of Hindu culture. Kings, at any rate, kept their womenfolk in seclusion. The detailed instructions of the *Arthaśāstra* make it quite clear that the *antaḥpura* or royal harem was closely guarded, and that its inmates were not allowed to leave it freely. It was certainly not so strictly secluded as in later Muslim communities, however, for early Arab travellers remarked that queens were often to be seen in Hindu courts without veils, and many other references show that, though screened from the general public and carefully watched, the royal ladies were not completely inaccessible, as in the Muslim system.

The women of the upper classes also were kept at a distance from the opposite sex. The *Arthaśāstra*,[37] in many ways more liberal than the religious lawbooks, lays down quite stringent rules for the punishment of immodest wives. A woman who insolently takes part in games, or drinks, against her husband's wishes, is to be fined three panas. If she leaves her home without his permission to visit another woman she is to be fined six panas; if she visits a man the fine is twelve; while if she goes on such errands by night the fine is doubled. If she leaves the house while her husband is asleep or drunk she is to be fined twelve panas. If a woman and a man make gestures of sexual import to one another, or converse facetiously in secret, the woman is to be fined twenty-four panas and the man twice that sum. If their conversation takes place in a suspicious place, lashes may be substituted for panas and "in the village square a caṇḍāla shall give her five lashes on each side of the body". Thus the husband had almost unlimited rights over his wife's movements.

Elsewhere the *Arthaśāstra* gives evidence of a different kind to show that even in Mauryan times the freedom of high-class women was considerably restricted by custom. In the instructions to the king's Superintendent of Weaving we are told that the staff of the royal weaving and spinning establishments should be made up of indigent women—a motley collection, including widows, cripples, orphans, beggar-women, women who had failed to pay fines and were compelled to work them off, and broken-down prostitutes. These were all of low class, and worked under male overseers.[48]

It might happen that sometimes a better-class woman fell on evil days, and was compelled to earn a living in this way. She was catered for, however, in a different manner. If she could still afford to employ a maid, the maid might fetch the yarn from the weaving shop, and bring it back in the form of cloth; but if the lady was compelled to fetch and deliver her own material stringent precautions were laid down so that her modesty should in no way be offended. She was to go to the weaving shop in the dim light of dawn, when she would not be easily seen. The official who received her work should only use a lamp to examine its workmanship; if he looked her in the face, or spoke to her about anything other than her work, he incurred the fine known as "the first amercement", from forty-eight to ninety panas. It is evident from these instructions that upper-class women, though their faces were unveiled, were not normally seen in public without their menfolk.

There were certainly wide differences of custom however. Girls of good class and marriageable age are described in story as visiting temples and taking part in festivals without guardian or chaperone. Early Tamil literature, more popular in character than that of the Āryan North, makes many references to the free association of young men and women. Early sculpture gives the same impression. At Bhārhut and Sānchī wealthy ladies, naked to the waist, lean from their balconies to watch processions, and scantily dressed women in the company of men worship the Bodhi Tree, under which the Buddha gained enlightenment. We may conclude that, while a woman's freedom was generally much restricted, it was rarely completely taken away.

A wife, however, had little initiative. Her first duty was to wait on her husband, fetching and carrying for him, rubbing his feet when he was weary, rising before him, and eating and sleeping after him.

"She should do nothing independently
even in her own house.
In childhood subject to her father,
in youth to her husband,
and when her husband is dead to her sons,
she should never enjoy independence....

"She should always be cheerful,
and skilful in her domestic duties,
with her household vessels well cleansed,
and her hand tight on the purse-strings....

"In season and out of season
her lord, who wed her with sacred rites,
ever gives happiness to his wife,
both here and in the other world.

"Though he be uncouth and prone to pleasure,
though he have no good points at all,
the virtuous wife should ever
worship her lord as a god."[49]

Passages of this type are frequent in literature of a religious and semi-religious type, and stories of obedient and faithful wives are numerous. The great models of Indian womanhood are Sītā, who faithfully accompanied her husband Rama into exile and endured great hardships and temptations for his sake (p. 365f), and

Sāvitrī, who, like the Greek Alcestis, followed her husband Satyavant when he was being carried away by the death-god Yama, and so impressed the god with her loyalty that he released her lord. A medieval tale gives an even more striking example of wifely fidelity:

> A woman was holding her sleeping husband's head in her lap, as they and their child warmed themselves in winter before a blazing fire. Suddenly the child crawled towards the fire, but the woman made no attempt to save it from the flames, since thus she would wake her lord. As the baby crawled further into the flames she prayed to the fire-god Agni not to hurt him. The god, impressed by her obedience, granted her prayer, and the child sat smiling and unharmed in the middle of the fire until the man awoke.[50]

Though the early Indian mind, prone to exaggeration, perhaps overdid the necessity of wifely obedience, her status was not without honour.

> "The wife is half the man,
> the best of friends,
> the root of the three ends of life,
> and of all that will help him in the other world.
>
> "With a wife a man does mighty deeds...
> With a wife a man finds courage.
> A wife is the safest refuge....
>
> "A man aflame with sorrow in his soul,
> or sick with disease, finds comfort in his wife,
> as a man parched with heat
> finds relief in water.
>
> "Even a man in the grip of rage
> will not be harsh to a woman,
> remembering that on her depend
> the joys of love, happiness, and virtue.
>
> "For woman is the everlasting field,
> in which the Self is born."[51]

Passages like these, showing the honour and esteem in which women were held, are quite as numerous as those which stress their subservience. Everywhere it is stated that a woman should be lovingly cherished, well fed and cared for, and provided with jewellery and luxuries to the limits of her husband's means. She should never be upbraided too severely, for the gods will not accept the sacrifice of the man who beats his wife. The ancient Indian attitude to women was in fact ambivalent. She was at once a goddess and a slave, a saint and a strumpet.

The latter aspect of her character is frequently brought out in semi-religious and gnomic literature. Women's lust knows no bounds:

"The fire has never too many logs,
the ocean never too many rivers,
death never too many living souls,
and fair-eyed woman never too many men."[52]

No one man can satisfy a libidinous woman's cravings; unless constantly watched she will consort with every stranger, even with a hunchback, a dwarf or a cripple (p. 365), and in the last resort will have recourse to Lesbian practices with members of her own sex. Her deception is as all-embracing as her lust, and she is incorrigibly fickle.

Moreover, women are quarrelsome and given to pique. They quarrel with one another, with their parents, and with their husbands. The henpecked husband, as we show elsewhere (p. 410f), was well-known in ancient India. Many verses in medieval anthologies depict the emotion of *māna*, an untranslatable word implying a mixture of anger, wounded pride and jealousy. Early Tamil literature contains a whole class of poems describing the efforts of the husband to cairn his wife's anger, roused by his attentions to a rival, usually a prostitute. If Sītā, the heroine of the *Rāmāyaṇa*, is invariably meek and compliant before her lord, Draupadī of the *Mahābhārata* can round on her five husbands and reproach them in no uncertain terms. The Mauryan kings were guarded by amazons trained in the use of sword and bow, and the Greeks were impressed by the ferocity with which the women of some of the Panjāb tribes aided their menfolk in resisting Alexander. In later times women sometimes took part in war (p. 80), and the tradition was continued among the Rājputs until quite recently; there are numerous records of masterly and war-like widows resisting the enemies of their husbands—the last being the famous Rānī of Jhānsī, whose part in the Sepoy Revolt has made her a national heroine of modern India.

PROSTITUTION

Ancient India contained one class of women who were not bound by the rules and restrictions which limited the freedom of the high-caste wife. These were the prostitutes (*veśyā*, *gaṇikā*). There were certainly many poor and cheap prostitutes, who would end their days in beggary, or as menials and work-women; but the typical prostitute of literature was beautiful, accomplished and wealthy, enjoying a position of fame and honour comparable to that of the Aspasias and Phrynes of classical Greece.

As in Greece, the higher class hetaira was an educated woman. The authorities on erotics demand that, as well as in the art immediately essential to her profession, she should be thoroughly trained in "the sixty-four arts". These formed a stock list, which included not only music, dancing and singing, but also acting, the composition of poetry, impromptu and otherwise, flower-arrangement and garland-making, the preparation of perfumes and cosmetics, cooking, dress-making and embroidery, sorcery, conjuring and sleight of hand, the composition of riddles, tongue-twisters and other puzzles, fencing with sword and staff, archery, gymnastics, carpentry and architecture, logic, chemistry and mineralogy, gardening, training fighting cocks, partridges and rams, teaching parrots and mynahs to talk, writing in cipher, languages, making artificial flowers, and day modelling.

It is hardly likely that the prostitute did in fact study all the arts of this rather bizarre list, but it shows what was expected of her. If she mastered those arts most suited to her profession a brilliant future awaited her. "A courtesan of a pleasant disposition, beautiful, and otherwise attractive, who has mastered the arts … has the right to a seat of honour among men. She will be honoured by the king and praised by the learned, and all will seek her favours and treat her with consideration."[53] The literature of the Middle Ages fully bears out this statement.

Typical of such accomplished courtesans was Ambapālī, the hetaira of Vaiśālī, famous in Buddhist legend. Much that is said of this lady is certainly legendary, but it gives a significant indication of the status of the better type of courtesan in ancient India. Ambapālī was immensely wealthy, highly intelligent, and famous throughout the civilized portion of India. She was one of the most treasured possessions of her city, and mixed on equal terms with princes. On his last journey to the Hills, as he passed through Vaiśālī, the Buddha accepted her invitation to dine in preference to that of the city fathers, who wished to give him a civic reception. Ambapālī is said to have become a Buddhist nun, and one of the most beautiful poems of the Pāli canon is attributed to her (p. 409).

The prostitute was protected and supervised by the state. The *Arthaśāstra*[54] suggests the appointment of a Superintendent of Prostitutes who should be responsible for the care and supervision of the palace courtesans, the inspection of brothels, and the collection of two days' earnings from each prostitute every month, as tax to the government. Teachers and trainers of prostitutes were to be given encouragement by the state. As in all other societies, around the prostitute congregated men of doubtful character, either outside the law or on its borderline—thieves, rogues, pseudo-magicians, and confidence tricksters of all kinds. The texts on statecraft recommend that for this reason special watch should be kept on brothels and that prostitutes should be enlisted in the secret service. This fact was noted by Megasthenes, who remarked that the spies did much of their work with the help of prostitutes. From the example of the play "The Little Clay Cart" it would seem that a prostitute might become an honest woman by marriage, for here the heroine, the high-souled courtesan Vasantasenā, ultimately becomes the second wife of the brāhmaṇ hero Cārudatta.

The position of the courtesan merged with that of the concubine. Kings and chiefs retained in their palaces numerous prostitutes, who were salaried servants, and who often had other duties to perform, such as attending on the king's person. The status of these women is somewhat obscure, but apparently they were not only at the service of the king, but also of any courtier on whom he might choose temporarily to bestow them, and thus they were not on a par with the regular inhabitants of his harem. Prostitutes of this type accompanied the king wherever he went, and even awaited him in the rear when he went into battle.

Another type of prostitute pursued her trade in an odour of sanctity. In the Middle Ages the god in his temple was treated like an earthly king; he had his wives, his ministers and attendants, and all the paraphernalia of a court—including his attendant prostitutes. These were often the children of mothers of the same profession, born and reared in the temple precincts, but they might be daughters of ordinary citizens, given in childhood to the god as pious offerings. They attended on the god's person, danced and sang before him, and, like the servants of an earthly king, were at the disposal of the courtiers whom he favoured, in this case the male worshippers who paid their fee to the temple.

We have no evidence of temple prostitution in very early times, though it certainly existed in other ancient civilizations, and it has been suggested, without valid evidence in our opinion, that it was known in the prehistoric Indus cities (p. 16). The earliest record of religious prostitution comes from a cave at Rāmgarh, in the Vindhya hills some 160 miles south of Vārāṇasī; this cave contains two significant Prākrit inscriptions in a script which shows that they were written not long after the days of Aśoka. The first of these is in verse:

> "Poets, the leaders of lovers,
> light up the hearts which are heavy with passion.
> She who rides on a seesaw, the object of jest and blame,
> how can she have fallen so deep in love as this?"

And then, in prose:

> "The excellent young man Devadinna the painter loved Sutanukā, the slave-girl of the god."[55]

The enamoured Sutanukā is referred to by the word later regularly used for a temple prostitute—*devadāsī*—and was evidently something of the kind herself. There are no other clear references to devadāsīs in early sources, however, and we must assume that they were rare until the Middle Ages. Temple prostitution was most common in the South, where it survived until recent times. The wild fertility cults of the early Tamils involved orgiastic dancing, and their earliest literature shows that prostitution was common among them; thus religious prostitution came naturally to the Dravidian. Many inscriptions and charters of the medieval South commemorating donations to temples refer specially to devadāsīs; for instance a general of Vikramāditya VI Cālukya, named Mahādeva, is recorded as founding a temple in memory of his late mother, with quarters for the most beautiful temple-prostitutes in the country.[56] In his eyes, and in those of his contemporaries, there was no incongruity in such a memorial.

Prostitution, though in many contexts honoured and respected, was much disapproved of by the Smṛti writers, whose works contain passages of warning against the evils of prostitution reminiscent of those in the Jewish Book of Proverbs. Manu and some other texts class the harlot and gambler with the thief and blackmailer, and declare that brāhmaṇs must never consort with prostitutes, on pain of very heavy penances. One source even maintains that the murderer of a prostitute commits no sin and should incur no punishment at law.[57] But, as we have noticed in many other cases, the secular attitude differed very greatly from the religious ideal, and here it was the secular view which prevailed. By the Middle Ages the brāhmaṇs who propounded the Sacred Law might themselves be attached to temples with hundreds of prostitutes on their staffs.

WIDOWS

In general a widow could not remarry. By medieval times this rule was applied so strictly in the upper classes that it included even girls widowed in childhood, whose marriages had not been consummated. Moreover, the custom of *niyoga*, which gave the childless widow a chance to conceive a son by her brother-in-law (p. 151), passed into desuetude in the early centuries of the Christian era.

All evidence shows, however, that the remarriage of widows was fairly common in earlier times. The *Arthaśāstra* admits its possibility. In the famous old story of Nala and Damayantī, the hero, who has long been parted from his wife, is reunited with her by the subterfuge of her announcement that she presumes his death and plans to hold a second svayamvara. One or two of the minor authorities permit a woman's remarriage if her husband disappears, dies, becomes an ascetic, is impotent, or loses caste;[58] but some later commentators explain away these awkward references by the easy fiction of *kali-varjya* (p. 128), and all agree with Manu: "nowhere is a second husband permitted to respectable women".[59] Thus the practice of widow remarriage, together with many other healthy old customs, gradually disappeared among the higher classes.

In those families which adhered to the letter of the law the lot of the widow was very hard. She was to all intents and purposes an ascetic, sleeping on the ground, and eating only one simple meal a day, without honey, meat, wine or salt, wearing no ornaments or coloured garments, and using no perfumes. In medieval times widows were also expected to shave their hair. The widow had to maintain this austere regimen to the end of her days, in the hope of being remarried to her former husband in the next life; her time was spent in prayer and other religious rites on his behalf, and any breach of her ascetic discipline not only made her liable to a very unhappy rebirth, but also endangered the welfare of the soul of her departed husband, who might suffer in the after-life for the shortcomings of his other half on earth.

Moreover a widow was inauspicious to everyone but her own children. Wherever she went her presence cast a gloom on all about her. She could never attend the family festivals which played so big a part in Hindu life, for she would bring bad luck on all present. She was still a member of her husband's family, and could not return to that of her father. Always watched by the parents and relatives of her lord, lest she broke her vows and imperilled the dead man's spiritual welfare, shunned as unlucky even by the servants, her life must often have been miserable in the extreme.

In these circumstances it is not surprising that women often immolated themselves on their husbands' funeral pyres, a practice noticed with much disapprobation by European travellers and only put down in the last century. The word *satī* (written *suttee* by older English writers) means "a virtuous woman", and the word was erroneously applied by early British officials and missionaries to the satī's self-immolation.

The history of the custom takes us back to the earliest cultures. Many ancient peoples buried or burnt a man's widows, horses, and other cherished possessions with his corpse, in order that he might have all that he loved and needed in the other world. We know that such practices were followed by the kings of Ur, and also by the ancient Chinese and some early Indo-European peoples. One of the funeral hymns of the *Ṛg Veda* shows that in the earliest form of the cremation rite known to us the widow lay down beside the dead man, and his bow was placed in his hand; the bow was removed, and the wife called on to return to the land of the living.[60] This practice must look back to a time long before the composition of the hymn, when the wife was actually burnt with her husband.

The earliest datable notice of the self-immolation of the satī occurs in Greek accounts of Alexander's invasion. One or two cases are mentioned in the Epics, but these are rare enough to show that the custom was uncommon at the time of their composition. Early Smṛti literature allows it, but in general does not strongly emphasise it. The first memorial to a satī is found at Eran, near Sagar in Madhya Pradesh, where a brief inscription engraved on a pillar in A.D. 510 records the tragic passing of a hero and his wife in short verses of un-Indian simplicity, which suggest the epitaphs of the Greek Anthology:

> "Hither came Bhānu Gupta, the bravest man on earth,
> a great king, a hero bold as Arjuna;
> and hither Goparāja followed him,
> as a friend follows a friend.
>
> "And he fought a great and a famous battle,
> and passed to heaven, a god among chieftains.
> His wife, loyal and loving, beloved and fair,
> followed close behind him into the flames."[61]

It is known that the nomads of Central Asia practised this custom, and it may have received some stimulus from their invasions. In any case, from this time onwards it became more common, and there are numerous satī-stones all over

India, commemorating the many faithful wives who followed their slain lords in death.

Criticisms of the custom were not unknown. It was condemned by the humane poet Bāṇa, in the 7th century, and by the tantric sects, which even declared that the woman burning herself on her husband's pyre went straight to hell. But some medieval writers roundly declare that the satī, by her self-immolation, expunges both her own and her husband's sins, and that the two enjoy together 35 million years of bliss in heaven.

The living cremation of the satī was always in theory voluntary, but, if we are to judge from later analogy, social and family pressure may have made it virtually obligatory on some high-caste widows, especially those of the warrior class. The 15th-century traveller Nicolo dei Conti states that as many as three thousand of the wives and concubines of the kings of Vijayanagara were pledged to be burnt with their lord on his death.*

The widow was, as we have seen, an inauspicious encumbrance to her husband's family, and might seriously endanger the welfare of his soul by the least breach of her vows. In a polygamous household the objection to widows would be correspondingly multiplied. The widow herself, if she had no young children, might well prefer even a painful death, in the hope of reunion with her husband, to a dreary life of hunger, scorn, and domestic servitude. It is thus not surprising that satīs were so common in medieval Hindu society.

* South Indian kings were often accompanied in death not only by their wives, but also by their ministers and palace servants. There are also numerous records of royal officers giving their lives in sacrifice to a god for the prosperity of a king and his kingdom.

VI

EVERYDAY LIFE: THE DAILY ROUND IN CITY AND VILLAGE

THE VILLAGE

WE have no certain means of assessing the population of ancient India, since the detailed registers which were kept in many kingdoms have long since vanished. One authority has suggested that during the medieval period the total population of the Sub-continent was between 100 and 140 million,[1] a figure which seems reasonable, although based on very slender evidence. But whatever India's population in ancient and medieval times, it was certainly mainly rural. At the present day it is said that 85 per cent of India's total population dwell in villages, and we may be sure that the proportion in the past was no less, but probably more. The average man in ancient India was a countryman.

Fig. xii.—A village (from a relief at Amarāvatī. *c.* 2nd century A.D.)

No one who has travelled from Delhi to Calcutta by train could fail to be impressed by the monotony of the great Gangetic Plain. The shabby little villages, often very close together, are punctuated only by rivers and canals. They have a few trees on their outskirts, and here and there a small grove divides one from another. Otherwise there is nothing to be seen between the villages but little fields separated by narrow footpaths and occasional rough roads. But this was not the case in ancient times.

Even when the first Englishmen set up their trading stations in Madras, Bombay and Calcutta there were more trees in the countryside; and in the earlier period India was much better afforested. Hsüan Tsang's account of India shows that, in the 7th century, dense jungle lined the banks of the Gangā for many miles on end. The countryside was wilder than it is today. The tiger, now rare except in certain districts, roamed the length and breadth of the land. In the West the lion, now almost extinct, was common. Herds of wild elephants, carefully preserved by kings, were numerous in regions where they are now unknown. The foothills of the Vindhyas and the Ghāts, now in many places almost denuded of larger trees by centuries of woodcutting and many generations of browsing goats, were richly forested. In fact the age-old agricultural techniques of India had not yet exhausted her soil, and her peasants had not yet torn up her forests, though in some places, notably Magadha (South Bihār) and parts of the Tamil country, this process was almost complete by the Middle Ages, if not before.

The Indian village differed very little from that of the present day, but while most villages in the North are now open and undefended, in earlier times they were usually walled or stockaded, as they are still in many parts of the Deccan. The village was a cluster of huts, small and large, often grouped round a well or a pond, near which was a small open space with a few trees. In earlier times villages often had clubrooms, which served as rest-houses for travellers and as centres of social life; later the place of these halls was taken by the village temples. The villagers formed a self-conscious community, and often had an energetic communal life. We quote from a Jātaka story.

> "One day they stood in the middle of the village to transact village business, and they ... [decided to] do good works; so they would get up betimes, and go out with knives, axes and crowbars. With their crowbars they rolled away the stones on the four highways; they cut down the trees which caught the axles of their carts; they levelled the irregularities [of the roads]; they built an embankment and dug tanks; they made a village hall; they showed charity and kept the [Buddhist] commandments."[2]

This vigorous corporate life continued into the Middle Ages. Tamil inscriptions show that the village councils (p. 91) took an active interest in the communal welfare, dug and renewed reservoirs, made canals, improved the roads, and cared for the village shrines. This strong sense of the community was one of the chief factors in the survival of Hindu Culture.

Most of the villagers were free peasants, and their land was to all intents and purposes their own, though the king claimed its ultimate ownership (p. 94f). The lot of the peasant was hard, though perhaps poverty was not so grinding as it later became, and agricultural indebtedness was certainly less heavy. Most peasant holdings were small, and were usually worked by the owner and his family; but there were a few large farmsteads, the owners of which cultivated their estates with hired labour. Kings too had large demesnes, worked by serfs and labourers, who in Mauryan times received one and one quarter paṇa per month with maintenance.[3] Other land was let out by the owners to share-croppers in return for one half of the crop.

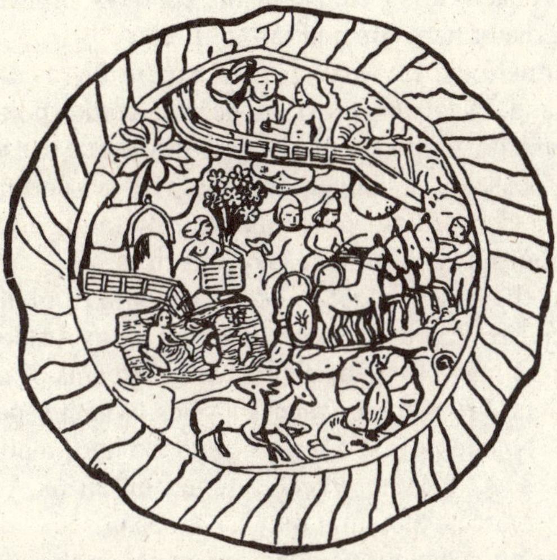

Fig. xiii.—Country scene (from a terracotta plaque found at Bhītā, near Allahābād.? 1st century B.C.)

These landless labourers existed in the Indian village at least from Mauryan times, and probably earlier, their state an unhappy and despised one. Illness, famine, idleness, or some other cause would sometimes compel a peasant to sell his holding, or result in his eviction for non-payment of tax, and he would be reduced to shame and penury as a casual labourer. But this process, whereby land tended to become concentrated in the hands of a few landowners, was more than counteracted by the Indian joint family system. On the death of the head of the house there was usually a partition of the family lands, and thus a few generations might see the break-up of a large estate. A real class of squires or large farmers never appeared in Hindu India.

To heavy taxation, forced labour, and the visitations of the king and his officers, were added periodical dearths and famines to afflict and impoverish the peasant. Though Megasthenes declared that famine was unknown in India, he certainly wrote in this particular from inadequate knowledge. References to famine, with its attendant horrors, are fairly common in ancient Indian literature (p. 394). Indeed a great famine is said to have occurred not long after Megasthenes left India, at the end of the reign of Candragupta Maurya. The more energetic and conscientious kings did what they could to prevent and relieve famine. The *Arthaśāstra* even suggests that a king is justified in confiscating the hoarded wealth of his richer subjects in order to feed the hungry. The state granaries would be opened in emergency, the charity of religious establishments and private persons was no doubt of some help; but with such poor communications local famine might be even more severe than it is now. There is reason to believe that rainfall was rather heavier than in recent years, and the pressure of population on the means of subsistence was not as great as it has now become. Hence outbreaks of dearth and famine were probably less frequent in ancient days, but when they did occur they caused even greater hardship and loss of life.

Throughout our period there was a gradual expansion of cultivation as a result of pressure on the land. The *Arthaśāstra*[4] suggests a positive policy of colonization, clearing of waste, and development of new villages, while the Jātaka stories show us groups of hardy peasants from overpopulated villages cutting new settlements from the jungle, and even tell of whole villages emigrating *en masse* to the wilds to escape the attentions of extortionate tax-collectors.

In the flat plains the land was cut by canals running from the great rivers, and dotted with artificial reservoirs (usually referred to in Anglo-Indian jargon as "tanks"), which were made by damming smaller streams or enlarging lakes by stopping their outlets. From these water-supplies, whether natural or artificial, water was raised by counterpoised "sweeps", and fed into smaller channels which watered the fields. The "Persian wheel", tumed by an ox, is nowhere clearly mentioned in early sources, though it may have been used.

Irrigation works, often of enormous size, were undertaken by beneficent kings as a religious and social duty. The most famous of these reservoirs was that of Girnar, the history of which has come down to us, thanks to two inscriptions on the site (pp. 63, 105). We do not know when the great embankment, over 100 feet thick at the base, finally crumbled. Probably the largest achievement of Indian irrigation until recent years was the lake at Bhojpur, near Bhopāl, built in the middle of the 11th century by Bhoja Paramāra, the king of Dhārā. This too has vanished; the embankment was breached by the Muslims in the 15th century, and has never been restored; but it is evident from those traces which remain that the lake originally covered no less than 250 square miles.[5] In the extreme north of India we read of Suyya, a great engineer in the service of king Avantivarman of Kashmīr (9th century), who "made the streams of Indus and Jhelam flow according to his will, like a snake-charmer his snakes". In the south, at the end of our period, Paes saw the building of a mighty tank at Vijayanagara, the embankment of which, he says, was a crossbow-shot wide. The first efforts at its construction were unsuccessful, so King Kṛṣṇa Deva Rāya ordered a great human sacrifice of prisoners to appease the gods, and finished the work with the labour of 20,000 men.

Most of the larger irrigation works of Hindu India have now vanished, but in Ceylon ancient reservoirs of enormous size still exist (pl. III*a*), though the canal systems which they served have largely disappeared, and are only now being repaired. After many centuries of neglect, recent govemments, both in India and Ceylon, have begun to redevelop the irrigation systems without which tropical agriculture cannot flourish, and which were among the first concerns of kings of ancient times.

AGRICULTURE AND STOCKBREEDING

The staple corn crops of ancient India were, as they are today, wheat and barley in the cool north and elsewhere as winter crops, rice in the irrigated plains, and millet in the dryer lands, such as parts of the Deccan, where rice would not grow well. Among other crops sugar cane was widely grown, and sugar exported to Europe, while leaf vegetables and gourds of various kinds were cultivated nearly everywhere, as was the sesamum, much valued for its edible oil. Numerous types of peas, beans and lentils were grown throughout the sub-continent. South India, especially Kerala (Malabār), grew many spices, particularly pepper, cardamom, ginger and cinnamon, which were carried all over India and exported to Europe. The Himālayan foothills produced the precious saffron. Cotton was at all times the staple textile crop.

Of fruits pride of place was taken by the mango, which was grown in orchards and much valued. The small Indian banana, or plantain, was also grown in damper parts of the land. The coconut was a comparatively late importation from S.-E. Asia, and is not mentioned in early sources, though it was well known in the Middle Ages. In the coastal areas grew palmyra and talipot palms, which provided India's chief writing material, and also the alcoholic drinks now known as toddy and arrack. Another valued palm was the areca, whose hard, slightly narcotic nut, broken up, mixed with lime and other ingredients, and wrapped in the leaf of the betel vine, formed the *tāmbūla*, or chewing quid, which was introduced into Northern India from the South early in the Christian era, and has ever since been a most popular source of post-prandial solace to the Indian. The date palm was grown in the dryer regions of the West, but is little mentioned in literature. The sour fruit of the tamarind was widely used to flavour curry. The grape, introduced from Persia with the almond and walnut, was cultivated in the Western Himālayas. Sandal and other trees which mostly grew in the South provided much-prized fragrant woods.

The Greek travellers were very impressed by the fertility of India's soil and the energy and ability of her cultivators. The modern traveller's impressions are diametrically opposite, but the Greeks judged Indian agriculture by standards lower than ours, and the soil was less exhausted then than it is now. The Greeks found it a great source of wonder that India produced two crops a year. In the wetter parts of the land the two crops might even grow without irrigation, while in the plains a summer crop of rice was raised during the monsoon, and a second irrigated crop in the dry season.

Ancient India knew the use of manure, and the *Arthaśāstra* lays down several rules for the management of the king's farms which indicate a well-developed agricultural technique. The Indian peasant has until very recently been so conservative in his methods that we may assume that the ordinary villagers of ancient days cultivated the land much as do those of the present day, ploughing with shallow wooden ploughs drawn by oxen, harvesting with sickles, threshing with oxen, and winnowing by tossing their corn in the wind.

The basic livestock of the peasant were cattle, used for ploughing, transport and food. Villages employed a communal cowherd, who drove the cattle, branded with their owners' marks, to the waste beyond the ploughed fields every morning, and returned with them at dusk. We have no means of comparing the yield of the cattle of ancient days with that of their scraggy modern counterparts, but as there was more pasture and waste it may have been better. Milk and curd were important articles of diet, as was ghee (*ghṛta*), which is butter clarified by heating, which will keep indefinitely in a hot climate.

The inviolability of the cow was of slow growth. Though there seems to have been some feeling against the killing of cows even in Vedic times, Aśoka did not forbid the slaughter of cattle, and oxen, at any rate, were killed for food even later. But the *Arthaśāstra* refers to the existence of herds of aged, diseased and sterile cattle,[6] and it therefore appears that even before the Christian era they were normally allowed to die a natural death, at least in some parts of the country. The same work suggests that those who kill cattle should be put to death, but from the context it is clear that this prescription applies only to killers of beasts stolen from the royal herds.

As well as cattle owned by cultivating peasants there were large herds belonging to professional herdsmen, who led a semi-nomadic life in the wilder parts of the country. One important tribe of these people, the Ābhīras, who dwelt in widely scattered localities of South Rājasthān, Mālwā and Sind around the beginning of the Christian era, was perhaps responsible for the development of the cult of Kṛṣṇa in his pastoral aspect, and Ābhīra chiefs set up a short-lived kingdom in the N.-W. Deccan on the ruins of the Sātavāhanas.

Other domestic animals included the buffalo, second only to the ox as a beast of burden and the favourite victim of sacrifices to the goddess Durgā, whose cult became very popular in the Middle Ages. The goat was bred widely, as was the sheep in the cooler districts. The fine goats' wool fabric of Kashmīr was known and used widely in Northern India, and heavier sheep's and yaks' wool blankets were exported in small quantities from the hills to the Northern Plains, where the winter nights are usually cold enough to make their comfort pleasant. The domestic pig was also known, though it did not play a very important part in rural economy.

Horses were bred chiefly in Sind and the North-West. They would not breed well in the Deccan, and were regularly imported by sea from Sind, Persia and Arabia to the ports of Western India. The horse was always a luxury animal, used chiefly by the warrior class. For the ordinary people the chief means of conveyance was the ox, of which certain varieties could draw carts at a considerable pace. The kings of Vijayanagara delighted in watching races of light carts to which an ox and a horse were yoked abreast.

The elephant was certainly tamed by the time of the Buddha. It rarely breeds in captivity, and therefore it had to be hunted and captured alive. Special forest tracts were designated as elephant preserves, inhabited by trackers, hunters and tamers, in the employ of the king. Generally the ownership of elephants was confined to kings and chiefs, and peasants living in the vicinity of elephant forests must have cursed the depredations of these beasts, which would frequently leave the jungle to raid the clearings.

The camel is not often mentioned, but it was certainly known and used as a beast of burden in the dryer parts of the country, and by the Middle Ages was also found in the Deccan. Some medieval dynasties employed the camel in war. The mule and the ass were other common beasts of burden.

The half-wild pariah dog was as common in early India as it is today, and dogs were also used in hunting. In the hills a special breed of large dog, perhaps resembling the modern Tibetan mastiff, was famous beyond the bounds of India. The Persian emperor Artaxerxes I (465–424 B.C.) is said by Herodotus to have exempted the inhabitants of four Babylonian villages from taxation in return for their breeding Indian dogs for war and hunting. These dogs were also known in the Egypt of the Ptolemies. The dog is only once mentioned with respect and affection in Indian literature, and was rarely if ever treated as a pet. The exception occurs in the *Mahābhārata*, where the five Pāṇḍava brothers and their wife Draupadī take their dog with them on their final pilgrimage to heaven, and the eldest brother Yudhiṣṭhira refuses to enter without his faithful friend. It has been suggested that the episode shows Iranian influence, for with the Zoroastrians the dog was a sacred animal. The domestic cat is rarely mentioned.

The hunting leopard or cheetah (*citraka*) is only referred to as a wild beast until the Middle Ages, and similarly the hawk was not tamed in early times. Hawking and hunting with cheetahs did not become popular among the ruling classes until the 11th century, and the custom may have been learnt from the Muslims.

The fowl was known, though eggs played but a small part in the diet of early India. The peacock, in earlier times, was certainly used as food, and was the favourite dish of the emperor Aśoka,[7] until he adopted a vegetarian diet. We read of whole villages of peacock-rearers, who supplied their birds to kings and wealthy people, at first largely for food, but later chiefly for ornament. Several other ornamental fowl, especially the ruddy sheldrake or brahmany duck (*cakravāka*), were kept in the parks of the rich, and parrots and mynahs were very popular as pets, especially with ladies, who are referred to as devoting long hours to teaching the birds to talk.

Silkworms were bred and reared, chiefly in Bengal and Assam. It has been suggested by some that silk was known even in Vedic times, and silk-making moths were certainly indigenous to India; but it is probable that silk made from the cocoons of domesticated worms was first introduced to India from China by way of the Burma Road, in the second half of the 1st millennium B.C. The earliest certain references to silk are found in the Buddhist scriptures, and in the *Arthaśāstra*, where it is called *cinapaṭṭa*, "the Chinese cloth". In the 2nd century B.C. the Chinese traveller Chang K'ien found that Chinese silk was imported into Bactria by way of India, and this suggests that even at this time the Indians had not yet fully mastered the art of spinning and weaving fine silks, which they certainly did later. Besides the silkworm another insect of commercial importance was the lac-insect, which provides both the resin used for shellac (and in India for articles of ornament), and also the dye known as lake.

THE WILD TRIBES

In the Himālayan foothills and the remoter parts of the Vindhyas and the Deccan wild tribes still exist. Most of them are now partly civilized and Hinduized, but some, though happy folk, knit together by tribal custom into solid, self-supporting and self-sufficient communities, still preserve vestiges of ferocious and barbaric tradition. The Gonds of the Eastern Deccan offered human sacrifices at their fertility ceremonies until well into the last century, the victims often being unfortunate villagers kidnapped from the more civilized settlements, while head-hunting among the Nāgas of Assam is even now not completely stamped out.

At one time, of course, practically the whole of India was inhabited by such peoples, and in ancient and medieval times they were more numerous and occupied a wider area than at present. From the earliest invasions they waged a losing battle against the advancing culture of the Āryans, and at all times they were a source of danger to the outposts of civilization in the vicinity of their lands. The brief statement of Aśoka's policy towards the forest tribes (p. 46) throws a flood of light on the ruthless policy of earlier kings towards them. Many primitive peoples were exterminated and many more lost their identity in the course of the growth of Hindu civilization; but some accepted the suzerainty of their civilized overlords, and retained their ancestral lands. The *Arthaśāstra* mentions such people as useful in time of war. Many of these tribes came more and more under the influence of Āryan ways, and their tribal cults were roughly assimilated to Hinduism by wandering brāhmaṇs. Such tribes were undoubtedly the ancestors of many lower Hindu castes of later times. Some primitive tribes may well have learnt enough from the Āryans to become powerful, and it has been reasonably suggested that more than one important medieval dynasty originated in such a way.

At all times, however, uncivilized tribal peoples continued to exist in the outlying districts in virtual independence, perhaps occasionally paying tribute in kind to the representative of their overlord. The last great king of Hindu India, Kṛṣṇa Deva Rāya of Vijayanagara, mentioned them in a brief textbook on government in Telegu, the *Āmuktamālyada*. When the forest folk multiplied in the kingdom, he wrote, they caused no little trouble to the king and his subjects; but, like Aśoka, he advocated fair and honest treatment towards them. "If the king grows angry with them, he cannot wholly destroy them, but if he wins their affection by kindness and charity they serve him by invading the enemy's territory and plundering his forts."[8]

At all times the wild tribesmen were a danger to the settled villagers in the outlying parts of the country. In medieval literature, both in Sanskrit and the Dravidian vernaculars, are references to these wild raiders pillaging crops, herds and houses, and capturing victims for human sacrifice. The area of their operations was slowly pushed back, and as more and more primitive tribes were assimilated to the Hindu order they became gradually less dangerous; but throughout the period covered by this book they were a source of fear in many parts of India, the bogey-men with which mothers frightened their naughty children. No doubt many of the characteristics of the demons and malevolent spirits of Hindu mythology, Nāgas, Yakṣas, Rākṣasas and the like, were acquired from the wild tribes (p. 278f).

THE TOWN

By the time of the Buddha, there were small towns all over North India, and some, such as Kāśī (Vārāṇasī) and Kauśāmbī, had an antiquity of centuries; but even at this time large cities were few. According to an ancient tradition, at the time of the Buddha's "Great Decease" the disciple Ānanda said that he regretted that his master was to die in so small a town as Kuśinagara, and mentioned the six cities which he considered important enough for a Buddha to die in: Śrāvastī, Campā, Rājagṛha, Sāketa (later generally known as Ayodhyā), Kauśāmbī, and Kāśī. These were evidently the greatest cities of the 5th century B.C., but their sites are still not wholly excavated, and we have no good means of judging their size, except in the case of one of them. This is Rājagṛha, the walls of which still remain, and show that the fortified area had a perimeter of twenty-five miles. The whole area was not built upon, but Rājagṛha was a garden city, with a central core, and houses in the suburbs surrounded by extensive parks and fields.

Pāṭaliputra in the time of the Mauryas, according to Megasthenes, was a long narrow city, stretching nine miles along the bank of the Ganga, and reaching only one and a half miles inland. It was no doubt mainly built-up, unlike Rājagṛha, which covered a larger area but must have had a smaller population. At the end of our period Paes states that Vijayanagara was larger and more populous than Rome and contained 100,000 houses, from which we may infer that its population was at least half a million, and probably more.

At the time of writing several excavations have been made at various Indian city sites, but only one such site, and that not representative, has been excavated sufficiently to reveal the pian of the city. This is Takṣaśilā, where two cities have been discovered, one dating from the time of the Achaemenid kings of Persia and the other from the Greco-Bactrian period. Both were built on either side of a broad main street, and the larger houses of both had central courtyards, in the manner traditional in India from the days of the Harappā Culture; but in other respeets the two were very different. The first city, known to archaeologists as Bhīr Mound, shows no trace of town planning; on the irregular and crooked main street opened a maze of narrow alleys, ramifying in all directions at the whim of many private builders. The second city, known as Sirkap, had a fine main street some twenty feet wide, running due north and south, with lesser roads running off it at right angles and at regular intervals; it was evidently strictly planned.

Fig. xiv.—An ancient Indian city, *c.* 2nd–lst century, B.C. (based on the evidence of contemporary sculpture). (Reproduced from Percy Brown's "Indian Architecture (Buddhist and Hindu period)," published by D. B. Taraporevala Sons & Co. Ltd., Bombay)

However we cannot attribute the layout of Sirkap wholly to the orderly Greeks. Two thousand years before their arrival in India the cities of Mohenjo Daro and Harappā had been laid out on similar regular lines, and there is little doubt that other Indian cities were carefully planned. It was by no means uncommon for a powerful king to build a wholly new capital, and this would give much scope to the town-planner. The *Arthaśāstra*[9] gives detailed instructions for the establishment of such a new city. It advises a square gridiron plan, divided into wards or sectors by six main roads, three running north and south, and three east and west. The chief temples were to be located in the centre, and different classes of the community were to be segregated in separate wards. The fortified city of Śiśupālgarh was certainly built as an almost exact square of nearly a mile on each side (pl. XI*a*), but it has not been sufficiently excavated to ascertain whether the street plan conformed to the *Arthaśāstra's* scheme.[10] It is possible that the northern city of Ahicchatrā in Uttar Pradesh did so approximately, but here again the excavated portions are not sufficient to tell with certainty.

The city had two foci, the palace and the temple. Of ancient Indian palace architecture we know little; the fragments of the highly polished columns of the Mauryan palace at Pāṭaliputra, and a large building at Takṣaśilā which may have been a palace, are all that have survived except from a very late period; but from this and other evidence it would seem that the palace was usually situated in or near the centre of the city, and that it was often defended by fortifications as a sort of citadel.

Temples have survived better, though we have no Hindu temples from pre-

Gupta times. In the temple the religious sentiments of the people were largely concentrated. From the temple came the great and splendid religious processions which filled and still fill the heart of the ordinary Hindu with almost superhuman exaltation. In the medieval period the temple, especially if it was a great and famous temple in one of the sacred cities,* was itself a city in miniature (fig. xv). It was enormously wealthy, and a source of wealth to the town from the many pilgrims who visited it. Such a temple was a great landowner, with many employees, including priests, musicians, attendants, and dancing girls for the temple services, a staff of scribes and accountants, and many craftsmen and labourere. Often the temple maintained schools and refuges for sick men and animals; it dispensed charity to beggars, and relieved the poorer citizens in time of distress and famine. Like the medieval European monastery it might grant land and privileges to its servants in princely wise. The great temple, especially in the Deccan, was a corporate body which often played a bigger part in the life of the ordinary citizen than did the civil government. The larger Buddhist and Jaina monasteries were equally influential in their own districts, though they were usually located outside the big cities.

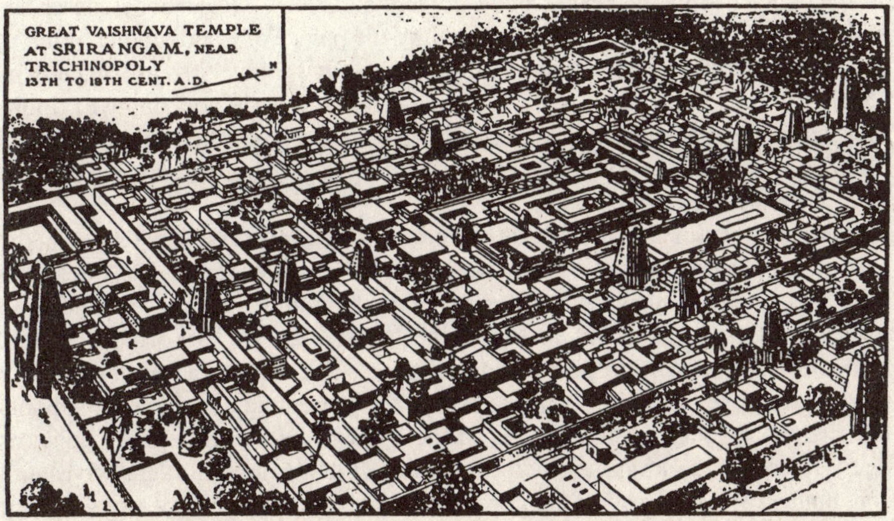

Fig. xv—The temple of Śrīraṅgam. 13th–18th centuries, A.D. (Reproduced from Percy Brown's "Indian Architecture (Buddhist and Hindu Period)", published by D. B. Taraporevala Sons & Co. Ltd., Bombay)

From literary sources, and from the evidence of sculpture and painting, we can get some idea of the houses of the wealthy, which probably did not differ greatly,

*These are traditionally seven: Ayodhyā, Mathurā, Māyā (Hardwār, in northern Uttar Pradesh, where the Gangā meets the Plain), Kāñcī (Conjeeveram), Ujjayinī (Ujjain), Dvāravatī (Dwārkā in Saurāshtra), and of course Kāśī (Vārāṇasī); but others were almost equally sacred, notably Prayāga (Allahābād), Madurai, and Purī (Orissā).

except in size, from the palaces of kings. The typical larger town house was one of several storeys; three-storeyed buildings seem to have been quite common, and there are literary references to houses of seven and even eleven storeys, though the latter at least are hardly credible. Down to Gupta times most houses, from palaces to small cottages, were built with barrel-vaulted roofs, with gable-ends and often ornate finials (fig. xiv). Roofs were both thatched and tiled. Later the high barrel-vaulted roof gave way to a flatter type, with overhanging eaves. Larger houses of later times usually had raised terraces or flat roofs on which the members of the household slept in hot weather. In historical times houses were not, like the houses of the Indus cities, closed in by bare walls, but had windows and balconies overlooking the street. In the medieval period the balconies were often screened with lattices, so that the ladies of the household might see without being seen, but the balconies of houses depicted at Bhārhut and Sānchī have no such screens. The walls were whitewashed, and, as today, might be decorated with painted pictures and ornamentation, both on the flat and in stucco relief. The usual larger house had a square courtyard surrounded by a veranda, behind which were the living quarters. Bathrooms are mentioned in literature, sometimes with running water, probably diverted from a nearby stream.

The ancient Indian greatly loved flowers and trees. Megasthenes describes with wonder the beautiful parks surrounding the palace of Candragupta Maurya, and many references in Sanskrit literature show that wealthy citizens had gardens attached to their houses, and often larger parks in the suburbs containing pavilions in which they spent much of their leisure. There are references in poetry to artificial hillocks (*krīḍāśaila*), which suggest that landscape gardens of the Japanese type were sometimes laid out.

As in all hot climates an expanse of water was an almost essential feature of the garden, and the parks of the wealthy contained artificial lakes and pools, often with fountains, and with steps leading down to them for bathing. A further refinement, for cooling the air in the hot season, was the "water-machine"(vāriyantra), which, from the description of the poet Kālidāsa,[11] seems to have been a sort of revolving spray, rather like that used to water lawns at the present day. In the bathing pools the citizens would cool themselves in the hot weather, and literature contains many references to kings and heroes playing in the water with their wives and concubines. We also read of subterranean chambers at one end of such bathing tanks,[12] cooled by the water surrounding them on all sides, in which the tired bather might rest. Another feature of the pleasure garden which was looked on as almost indispensable was a swing, in which adults of both sexes took delight. Gardens were watered by channels which led from the main tank to the trees and flower beds.

Specially loved were flowering trees, which are very frequently mentioned in poetry, especially the *aśoka* (*Saraca indica*), a smallish tree hearing a mass of lovely scarlet or orange blossoms, which, it was said, would only flower if kicked by a beautiful woman; other favourites were the tall pale-flowered *śirīṣa* (*Albizzia spp.*), the fragrant, orange-flowered *kadamba* (*Anthocephalus cadamba*), and the red *kiṃśuka* (*Butea frondosa*); the banana (*kadalī*) was grown for ornament as well as for its fruit. Bushes and creepers were also much loved, especially the jasmine, of which there were many varieties, and the white *atimukta* (*Hiptage madablota*); other popular trees were the *campaka* (*Michelia champaca*), with very fragrant yellow flowers, and the hibiscus, or China rose (*japā*). Most beloved of all flowers, and the subject of much religious and other symbolism, was the lotus or water-lily in its many varieties. This beautiful flower the poets never tired of mentioning, giving it dozens of synonyms and epithets. The rose, common enough in North India today, was apparently unknown, and was probably introduced by the Muslims.

As well as the private gardens of the rich there were public gardens and parks, often mentioned in story. In the vicinity of most cities were groves which were the favourite resorts of the townspeople. Aśoka took pride in the fact that he had planted such groves for the recreation of man and beast, and some other kings are recorded as having followed his example.

Of the life and homes of the city poor we are told little in literature, but the cottages here and there depicted in early sculpture are, like the larger houses, barrel-roofed, and apparently one-roomed. We must assume that the poorer folk dwelt, as they do today, in huts made of wood, reed or mud brick, and thatched with straw. Many no doubt had no homes at all, but slept in odd corners of the city with their few possessions around them.

Efforts were made by the more energetic authorities to provide some amenities for the poorer citizens. The *Arthaśāstra* suggests that a public well should be provided for every ten families. The same text recommends a fixed tariff of fines for leaving rubbish in the streets, and stringent precautions against fires; every home was to keep elementary fire-fighting equipment in readiness, and on an outbreak of fire all able-bodied citizens in the neighbourhood were liable to be called on to help put out the flames. The city authorities were to provide drainage for surface water, and fines were to be imposed for blocking the drains.[13] We cannot tell how far these recommendations were put into practice, but it is hardly likely that they had no basis whatever in fact.

Undoubtedly the most remarkable description of an ancient Indian city is contained in the early Tamil poem *The Garland of Madurai*, (*Maduraikkāñji*) said to have been written in honour of a 2nd century Pāṇḍyan king Neduñjeliyan, but was probably composed a century or two later. After a long panegyric on the king, the poet describes the various regions of his kingdom, and concludes with an account of his capital city, Madurai. This is too long to quote, but we must at least summarize this part of the lovely poem, which has a realism rare in the literature of the North.

The poet enters the city by its great gate, the posts of which are carved with images of the goddess Lakṣmī, and which is grimy with ghee, poured in oblation upon it to bring safety and prosperity to the city it guards. It is a day of festival, and the city is gay with flags, some, presented by the king to commemorate brave deeds, flying over the homes of captains, and others waving over the shops which sell the gladdening toddy. The streets are broad rivers of people, folk of every race, buying and selling in the market-place or singing to the music of wandering minstrels.

A drum beats, and a royal procession passes down the street, with elephants leading to the sound of conchs. A refractory beast breaks his chain, and tosses like a ship in an angry sea until he is again brought to order. Chariots follow, with prancing horses and fierce-looking footmen.

Meanwhile stall-keepers ply their trades, selling sweet cakes, garlands of flowers, scented powder and betel quids. Old women go from house to house, selling nosegays and trinkets to the womenfolk. Noblemen drive through the streets in their chariots, their gold-sheathed swords flashing, wearing brightly-dyed garments and wreaths of flowers. From balconies and turrets the many jewels of the perfumed women who watch the festival flash in the sunlight.

The people flock to the temples to worship to the sound of music, laying their flowers before the images and honouring the holy sages. Craftsmen work in their shops—men making bangles of conch shell, goldsmiths, cloth-dealers, coppersmiths, flower-sellers, vendors of sandalwood, painters and weavers. Foodshops busily sell their wares—greens, jak-fruit, mangoes, sugar candy, cooked rice and chunks of cooked meat.

In the evening the city prostitutes entertain their patrons with dancing and singing to the sound of the Iute (*yāḷ*), so that the streets are filled with music. Drunken villagers, in town for the festival, reel in the roadways, while respectable women make evening visits to the temples with their children and friends, carrying lighted lamps as offerings. They dance in the temple courts, which are clamorous with their singing and chatter.

At last the city sleeps—all but the goblins and ghosts who haunt the dark, and the bold housebreakers, armed with rope ladders, swords and chisels, to break through the walls of the mud houses. But the watchmen are also vigilant, and the city passes the night in peace.

Morning comes with the sound of brāhmaṇs intoning their sacred verses. The wandering bards renew their singing, and the shopkeepers busy themselves opening their booths. The toddy-sellers again ply their trade for thirsty morning travellers. The drunkards reel to their feet and once more shout in the streets. All over the city is heard the sound of opening doors. Women sweep the faded flowers of the festival from their courtyards. Thus the busy everyday life of the city is resumed.[14]

The ancient Indian city was a source of pride to its inhabitants. One of the most memorable records of such pride is contained in the 5th century Mandasor inscription of the guild of silk-weavers, already mentioned in another connexion (p. 124). This commemorates the building and subsequent repair by the guild of a splendid temple of the Sun. A poem recording the event was composed "with great care" by one Vatsabhaṭṭi, probably a local hack-poet commissioned for the occasion, and was engraved on stone as a perpetual memorial. No doubt echoing the thought of his patrons, Vatsabhaṭṭi writes in glowing terms of his city,

"Where the water-lilies are ever shaken by tremulous ripples,
and the geese seem to be shut in a cage of pollen,
    blown from the lotuses which shine in the lakes,
bent by the weight of their own stamens;

"Where the groves are adorned with trees
    bowed under the burden of blossoms,
and with bee-swarms, drunk with honey,
    and with women ever-singing;

"Where lovely women dwell
    in houses a-flutter with flags,
most purely white, most lofty,
    like fair hills of cloud that glitter with the vine of the lightning;

"Where other mansions, adorned with groves of swaying bananas,
    lovely as the high peak of Mount Kailāśa,
shine with their long roof-ridges and pavilions,
    loud with the noise of music, and gay with pictures."

And so the poet in fanciful language describes the beauty of the city, the goodness of the local king, the benevolence of the guild, and the splendour of the new temple, until he concludes:

"As the moon the clear heavens,
    as the *kausttibha** the breast of Viṣṇu,
this fairest of temples adorns
    our wholly noble city."[15]

THE MAN ABOUT TOWN

We can learn much about the life of the Greek and Roman bourgeoisie from literature and archaeological remains; but the comparable literature of India is less realistic, and there is no Indian counterpart of Pompeii. Nevertheless there is enough evidence to reconstruct the life of the well-to-do young Indian in some detail from secular literature, among our most important sources being the treatise on erotics, the *Kāmasūtra* (p. 147), which was composed to instruct him in one of his chief recreations.

His room, we are told,[16] should contain a pleasant and soft bed, with a pure white coverlet, a decorated canopy, and two pillows, one at the foot and the other at the head. The room should also have a divan at the head of which perfumes, unguents, flowers, and pots of collyrium should be kept on a little table. On the floor nearby should be placed a cuspidor, to receive the red expectoration caused

* magical jewel, one of the god's insignia.

by betel chewing, and a chest for ornaments and clothes. On the wall should hang a lute (*viṇā*), and the room should also contain a drawing table, a few palm-leaf books, a round seat and a gaming-board. Attached to the house should be an aviary, a garden containing swings, an arbour of climbing plants, and a grass bank on which the owner might sit in the shade with his guests.

Rising in the morning the man about town washes, cleans his teeth, anoints his body with unguents and perfume, puts collyrium on his eyes, dyes his lips with red lac, and looks at himself in the mirror. Then he chews a betel quid to sweeten his breath. He baths every day, rubs his body with oil every other day, shaves his face every fourth day, and his whole body every fifth or tenth day. He eats three meals daily. Much of his time is spent in charming, graceful idleness. He amuses himself by teaching his parrots and mynahs to talk, or by watching fighting cocks, quails or rams; he converses with the parasites who surround him. In the hotter weather he takes an afternoon nap.

He had many intellectual pleasures however. He was not merely a patron and passive admirer of the arts, but was encouraged by society to be himself creative. He should know something of the sixty-four arts (p. 158f). He might be a poet in his own right, and some of the surviving Sanskrit poetry is not the work of professionals. Large gatherings were often held under the patronage of kings or wealthy men for the recitation of poetry, and smaller groups would often meet together for the same purpose, either at the home of one of the group or at the house of a courtesan. These literary parties are mentioned in the *Kāmasūtra* as among the chief pleasures of the educated man. The members of such circles might form regular social clubs, and "should stand together in time of trouble as in prosperity,...and hospitably entertain newcomers to their group".[17] The ancient Indian, like his modern descendant, was usually an extrovert, delighting in the company of his fellows, and warm-hearted in his friendships. The immense stress laid in sacred literature on the duty of hospitality encouraged and gave religious sanction to the social propensities of the time.

Sometimes literary parties were held in the open air, in the gardens and groves about the town, and might be diversified with cock-fighting and bathing. The educated man might also be a painter; his sanctum, as we have seen, contained a painting-board or easel, and the *Kāmasūtra* even suggests that he should have a special room for sculpture, wood-carving and day modelling.

AMUSEMENTS

The amusements of the ancient Indian townsman were by no means all creative or intellectual. Numerous festivals, participated in by rich and poor alike, divided the Hindu year, and were marked by merrymaking and processions. The most popular festival in early times was the Festival of Spring, in honour of Kāma, the Love-god, who, though he played only a small part in the thought of the theologians, was evidently a very popular divinity. At this festival even respectable citizens forgot their caste restrictions, and paraded the streets scattering red powder over their neighbours, squirting them with coloured water, and playing all kinds of practical jokes. The festival still survives under the name *Holī*, though the Love-god now plays no part in it. It is clearly the survival of a primitive and bloody fertility ceremony; but even at its earliest appearance the grim significance of the red powder seems to have been lost, and it was a sort of Hindu saturnalia, a time of universal merrymaking and licence of all kinds.

Though much reprobated by the brāhmaṇ authors of the Smṛti literature, gambling was popular at all times and among all classes except the more rigidly religious people. Six-sided dice have been found in the Indus cities, and the "Gamester's Lament" of the *Ṛg Veda* testifies to the popularity of gambling among the early Āryans (p. 356ff).

The word *akṣa* in the context of gambling is generally roughly translated "dice", but the *akṣas* in the earliest gambling games were not dice, but small hard nuts called *vibhīṣaka* or *vibhīdaka*; apparently players drew a handful of these from a bowl and scored if the number was a multiple of four. Later, oblong dice with four scoring sides were used; like the European gamester the Indian employed a special terminology for the throws at dice: *kṛta* (cater, four), *treta* (trey), *dvāpara* (deuce), and *kali* (ace). So important was gambling in the Indian scheme of things that these four terms were applied to the four periods (*yuga*) of the aeon (p. 282). Gambling played a small but significant part in the ritual of the royal consecration ceremony, and the gambling hall attached to the king's palace in the later Vedic period had some magical or religious significance, though its import is not wholly clear. Among the chief men of the realm, whose loyalty was confirmed by a special ceremony at the consecration of the king (p. 36), was the *akṣavāpa*, or thrower of nuts or dice, evidently the organizer of the royal gambling parties. The plot of the *Mahābhārata* hinges round a great gambling tournament, at which Yudhiṣṭhira lost his kingdom to his wicked cousin Duryodhana, and the Epic tells a similar story in the episode of Nala. The *Arthaśāstra*[16] advocates the strict control of gambling, which it would confine entirely to officially-managed gaming houses, financed by a tax of five per cent of the stakes and a charge for the hire of dice to gamblers, who were to be forbidden to use their own. Stringent fines were laid down for cheating.

With the dice were played board games, similar to our children's games such as ludo, which involved a combination of chance and skill. By the early centuries of the Christian era one of these, played on a board of sixty-four squares (*aṣṭapāda*), had developed into a game of some complexity, with a king-piece, and pieces of four other types, corresponding to the corps of the ancient Indian army—an elephant, a horse, a chariot or ship, and four footmen. The original game needed four players, and their moves were controlled by the throw of the dice. As the game was played with pieces representing military forces, and its strategy suggested that of campaigning armies, it was known as *caturaṅga*, or "four corps". In the 6th century the game was learnt by the Persians, and when Persia was conquered by the Arabs it quickly spread all over the Middle East, under the name *shatranj*, the Persian corruption of *caturaṅga*. It developed into a game for two persons, each with two "armies", the king of one army becoming the "general" or "minister" of the other, and the use of dice to control the moves was given up. It is not quite certain whether these improvements were made in India or Persia, but the latter is more probable.

The game was learnt by the crusaders from the Muslims, and soon spread over Europe. By the Middle Ages it had almost attained its modern form as chess, the "general" of the Muslim game becoming the queen. Thus the world's most intellectual game is the product of three cultures, each of which contributed something to its finished form.

Organized outdoor games were not common, except among children and young women, who are sometimes referred to as playing ball, like Nausicaa in the *Odyssey*. A form of polo, introduced from Central Asia, became popular among warriors in the Middle Ages, though it is little mentioned in literature, and a kind of hockey was also played. But, in general, ancient India did not put such stress on athletics as did the Mediterranean world. Chariot racing is mentioned as early as the *Ṛg Veda*, and bullock racing was popular in the late medieval period. Boxing and wrestling are often referred to, but were not generally the hobbies of respectable young men, but the preserve of low-caste professional pugilists, who performed for the amusement of an audience. The archery contest, however, was a much-loved amusement of the warrior class, and vivid descriptions of such contests occur in the Epics.

Classical sources refer to gladiatorial displays at the court of Candragupta Maurya, and in the medieval Deccan duelling became frequent. The Portuguese traveller Nuniz writes that if two nobles of Vijayanagara quarrelled they would fight to the death in the presence of the king and his court.[19] Despite the growth of the doctrine of non-violence throughout our period, animal fights were always very popular. The favourite animals to be pitted against each other were the fierce little Indian quail (*lāvaka*), the cock and the ram; we also read of fights between bulls, buffaloes and elephants (pls. LXXVII, LXXVIII*b*).

One form of animal contest confined to the Dravidian South was the bullfight, of which we have a vivid description in an early Tamil poem.[20] This sport did not closely resemble the Spanish bullfight, where the scales are heavily weighted against the bull, for here the bull appears to have had the advantage. The fights were popular among herdsmen, who entered the arena unarmed, and "embraced the bull" in an attempt to master it, rather like the cowpunchers of an American rodeo. They made no attempt to kill the bull, and it was not previously irritated, but the bullfight was evidently a sport of great danger, for the poem contains a gory description of a victorious bull, his horns hung with the entrails of his unsuccessful opponents. The bullfight was looked on as an ordeal to test the manhood of young men, since it is stated that the girls who watched the performance would choose their husbands from among the successful competitors in a sort of Tamil svayaṃvara. Though Tamil literature gives no evidence of this, the bullfight had certainly some ritual significance, and was connected with the fertility of the crops. A similar sport was practised as part of a religious ceremonial by the ancient Cretans, and this fact, like many others, links the Tamils with the earliest civilizations of the Mediterranean world. Wrestling with young steers is still a favourite pastime of some pastoral peoples of India.

Many of the amusements of ancient India were provided by professional entertainers. As well as those who practised highly developed arts such as drama, music and dancing, there were others who travelled through town and village, diverting the ordinary folk who could not fully appreciate the nuances of the more sophisticated art forms. We read of musicians, bards, acrobats, jugglers, conjurors and snake-charmers, popular then as now. As well as the courtly theatre there was a folk-drama, occasionally referred to in literature, which portrayed scenes of mythology and legend in dance, song and mime, and from which the Sanskrit drama developed.

CLOTHES AND ORNAMENTS

The garments worn from Vedic times onwards did not fundamentally differ from those worn by Hindus in later times. Like most ancient peoples living in hot climates Indians usually wore lengths of cloth, draped around the body and over the shoulders, and fastened with a belt and pins. The lower garment (*paridhāna*, *vasana*) was usually such a cloth, fastened round the waist with a belt or string (*mekhalā*, *raśanā*); and the upper garment (*uttariya*) was another such length, draped shawl-wise over the shoulders. The latter garment was often discarded in the home, or in hot weather, especially by the lower orders. A third garment (*prāvāra*) was also worn, draped like a mantle or cloak, in the cold season.

This was the general garb of both sexes, as it is today, and varied only in the size and pattern of the cloths and in the manner of wearing them. Sometimes the lower garment was of very small proportions, or a mere loincloth (pl. LXXIV), but the lower garments of the rich often reached almost to the feet. In early sculpture the lower garment is depicted as elaborately pleated in front, and held with a long girdle, the end of which hangs down in front of the garment between the legs (pl. XXVI*a*). In some sculptures the girdle appears to have been the end of the cloth itself, which might also be thrown over the shoulders in the manner of the present day *sārī*. Sometimes the end of the cloth was drawn between the legs and fastened at the back in the manner of the *dhotī*.

Though all these garments were unstitched the art of sewing was not unknown, and women are often depicted wearing jackets or bodices (*colaka*, *kañcuka*) (pl. LXXX). With the invasions of the Śakas and Kuṣāṇas from Central Asia trousers were introduced, and were in vogue among the ruling classes at least until Gupta times, for the Gupta kings are often shown on their coins as wearing them (fig. xxiv, p. 383). Kuṣāṇa kings are shown on their coins, and in the remarkable headless statue of Kaniṣka (pls. XXXa, LXXXIV*e*), wearing long quilted coats, quilted trousers, and boots of typically Central Asian type, which must have been as uncomfortable in the average temperature of India as the thick European clothing worn by the pioneers of the East India Company. The wearing of shirts and trousers seems to have been quite common in medieval Kashmīr and the North-West. In medieval South India goddesses and queens were often depicted as wearing what seem to be light close-fitting trousers. The cloth used for all these garments varied from wool, worn in the Northern winters, to diaphanous silks and muslins, which showed the limbs of the wearer. The paintings of Ajantā and Bāgh show that they were often dyed or otherwise patterned with gay stripes and checks.

In most parts of India footwear was primarily used to protect the feet against the scorching earth of the Indian summer, but in the Himālayas felt boots of Central Asian pattern were worn. On their heads men usually wore turbans, which were fastened in many elaborate patterns (pl. XXIIL*e*). In early times, at least on festive occasions, women wore large and complicated headdresses of a type not seen nowadays, but by the Gupta period they are usually depicted either bare-headed, or wearing head-veils or simple tiara-like headdresses. Orthodox brāhmaṇs shaved the whole head with the exception of the topknot, which was never cut, but with other classes both sexes usually allowed their hair to grow long. The most popular coiffure with women was a large bun at the nape of the neck, often ornamented with a fillet or string of jewels (pl. LXII*e*). The pigtail, most common at the present day, though attested in the Harappā culture and mentioned in literature, does not often appear in sculpture until the medieval period.

There is some controversy on the character of women's dress in ancient India. Throughout our period women are depicted in painting and sculpture as naked to the waist, while on the other hand the great physical modesty of modern Hindu womanhood is common knowledge. James Fergusson, one of the first serious students of ancient Indian sculpture, declared categorically that until the Muslim conquest Hindu women exposed their breasts in public without the least shame.[21] This conclusion has, however, been controverted.[22]

It is asserted that, like the Greeks and Romans, the Indian artist and sculptor followed a tradition of showing the female form in a state of semi-nakedness, when this had no counterpart in real life. The objection, however, is hardly valid. When portraying real life, rather than mythology or figure studies, the classical artist usually draped his women. In the early sculptures of Bhārhut and Sānchī, on the other hand, there is scarcely a woman with covered breasts, even among the crowds in the very realistic reliefs of Indian city life. References to bodices in literature are numerous, and women with covered breasts do sometimes appear in painting and sculpture; but in the Northern Plains and the hillier parts of the Deccan the weather is quite cool for several months of the year, and the use of bodices may have been due rather to climate than to modesty. In Kerala, where many old customs survived long, it was quite normal until comparatively recent times for women of the Nayyar caste to appear in public naked to the waist, and the same is true of the island of Bali, which adopted Hindu culture early in the Christian era. In some literary sources there are references to married women wearing veils, but there is no evidence that these were normally more than head-coverings, or that they concealed the form of the wearer. It is only in late medieval literature that clear expressions of the need of strict physical, as distinct from mental, modesty are found. Women in ancient India were considerably restricted in their activities, and a high standard of modesty was demanded of those of the higher classes (p. 154f); but it is clear that their ideas of propriety in dress were very different from those of their descendants.

If clothes were simple and few, ornaments were complex and many. Gold, silver and precious stones of every available kind were always in demand for personal adornment. Women wore jewelled ornaments on their foreheads, and along the partings of their hair. Earrings were worn by both sexes, and the ears were stretched by heavy and large ornaments, as is done by women in the Tamil country districts to this day. Ornate necklaces were worn, and wide girdles of linked gold with hanging ropes of pearls. Bangles and armlets were popular from the days of the Harappā Culture onwards, and anklets, often set with little tinkling bells, or with their hollows filled with rattling pebbles, were as popular then as now. Nose ornaments, without which Indian women of the older generation felt positively undressed, are nowhere mentioned or depicted, and their use can only have been widely adopted after the Muslim conquest. The few surviving pieces, and the representations of jewellery in sculpture and painting, show that the Indian jeweller attained very high standards in his art (pl. LXXXI*b*). It would seem that the early Indian, like his modern counterpart, would often save his money by investing it in jewellery for his wife and himself. Even the poorer people, who could not afford gold or gems, loaded themselves with ornaments of silver, brass, glass and painted pottery, and all classes adorned their hair, ears and necks with the beautiful flowers which India provides in abundance.

Cosmetics were used by both sexes. Chief among these was a paste made of finely ground dust of sandalwood, often coloured with lac and other dyes, which was smeared over the whole body or applied in patterns. It was believed to cool the skin in the hot season. Collyrium or eye-salve (*añjana*), usually made of black powdered antimony, was very popular, and, as well as enhancing the beauty of the eye, was thought toprevent ophthalmia. Vermilion (*sindūra*), lac (*lākṣā*) and a yellow pigment called *gorocana* were used to mark the beauty-spot on the forehead (*tilaka*), which might often be large and ornate, and which is still popular with Indian ladies. The lips, the tips of the fingers and toes, and the palms and soles of the feet were often dyed red with lac. Though exposed parts of the body were often painted with complicated patterns there is no clear evidence of tattooing, which is popular nowadays in many parts of India.

FOOD AND DRINK

When Fa-hsien visited India in the early 5th century he reported that no respectable person ate meat, the consumption of which was confined to low castes. He probably exaggerated, but certainly by this time many Hindus of the higher classes were vegetarians. The growth of vegetarianism was of course linked with the doctrine of non-violence, which was already old at the time of Fa-hsien. It was known in the days of the Upaniṣads and was elaborated by Buddhism and Jainism, which were largely responsible for the gradual disappearance of the greater Vedic sacrifices at which large numbers of animals were killed and eaten. The reign of Aśoka is a landmark in the development of vegetarianism, for he encouraged it by his own example, and forbade outright the killing of many animals. But the *Arthaśāstra* accepts meat-eating as quite normal, and lays down rules for the management of slaughterhouses and the maintenance of the purity of meat.[23] It was only with the growth of Mahāyāna Buddhism and the new Hinduism that strict vegetarianism became widespread. Even then hunting and meat-eating were practised by the warrior class, and the tantric cults of the Middle Ages restored the practice of sacrifice and meat-eating in a new form. Medical texts, even of a late period, go so far as to recommend the use of both meat and alcohol in moderation, and do not forbid the eating of beef. It is doubtful if complete vegetarianism has ever been universal in any part of India, though in many regions it was and still is practised by most high-caste Hindus. With the prohibition of meat-eating some religious texts included that of eating garlic and onions, the objection to which arose for obvious reasons, and was never given a real religious basis; but it is doubtful if this ban ever had any great effect until a very late period, except on pious brāhmaṇs.

There are several references to the science of cookery (*sūpaśāstra*), which was not disdained even by kings, but no ancient textbook on cookery has survived. From passages in literature we know that ancient Indian cookery did not differ much from that of the present day. Meat and vegetables alike were seasoned in curries and eaten with rice, boiled or fried. With the curry and rice flat cakes of flour, the modern *chapātī*, were eaten, and water, milk, or curd were drunk. The favourite cooking medium was ghee, in which the food was fried and which was poured liberally over the dish; poorer folk often substituted for ghee the oil of sesamum or mustard. Certain foods very widespread in India nowadays are, however, 16th or 17th century importations, brought from America by the Portuguese. The most surprising of these is the chilli or red pepper, so characteristic of South Indian cooking. The brinjal or egg plant is another 17th century innovation, as are, of course the potato and the sweet corn or maize. Fruit and sweetmeats of many kinds were as popular as they are today, but many of the Indian sweets eaten nowadays, such as the *jalebī*, are Muslim importations.

In modern Hinduism there is a strong taboo on the drinking of alcoholic beverages, and most of those who drink regularly are either very Westernized in their ways or of low caste. The moral objection to alcohol is very ancient, but it was long before the ban became widespread, except among brāhmaṇs. Though Aśoka discouraged meat-eating his edicts say nothing about drinking, and it is therefore evident that he had no strong moral objections to it, though Buddhism counts the drinking of spirits as one of the five cardinal sins (p. 251). In Aśoka's day Buddhism was apparently more lax in this respect than it later became. The lawbooks condemned drinking, and Fa-hsien stated that respectable Indians did not drink, but drinking and drunkenness are so frequently mentioned in literature, especially in that of the Tamils, that it is clear that religious precept was not regularly followed in this particular. Only in the 12th century do we find

Kumārapāla, the Jaina king of Gujarāt, forbidding the production and sale of liquor throughout his kingdom.

The *Arthaśāstra* advises the manufacture of liquor in government controlled breweries, and gives several brief and cryptic recipes,[24] which show that there were many alcoholic drinks, some of which are not popular nowadays; among these were rice beer (*medaka*), a sort of spiced beer made of flour (*prosannā*), wood-apple wine (*āsava*), *maireya*, a liquor made of raw sugar, the bark of the *meṣaśṛṅga* tree, and pepper, and mango wine (*sahakār asurā*). Wine from grapes was made in the North-West, and exported in small quantities to the rest of India. In the South, toddy, the fermented sap of the palmyra or coconut, was the staple alcoholic liquor, and is frequently mentioned in early Tamil literature. The *Arthaśāstra*, perhaps reflecting Mauryan conditions, suggests the appointment of a "superintendent of liquor", not only to control the sale and consumption of alcoholic drinks but also to organize their manufacture. The text advises the stringent control of private brewing and of taverns. Tavern-keepers are to be instructed to make their establishments well-furnished and comfortable, and to prevent their patrons from over-indulgence; the text even suggests that they should indemnify customers for any loss sustained while under the influence of liquor, and pay a fine into the bargain. Unlike most other oriental traders tavern-keepers, according to the *Arthaśāstra*, were not to be allowed to build their premises close together, thus discouraging the ancient Indian equivalent of "pub-crawling"; the text also suggests the complete prohibition of the consumption of alcohol "off the premises". The taverns were often the haunts of criminals, and the king's spies were advised to keep a watchful eye on them. The *Arthaśāstra* evidently recognizes drinking as an evil which cannot be wholly forbidden, but which must be strictly controlled.

ECONOMIC LIFE

It has often been said that ancient Indian society was not an acquisitive one. Admittedly the brāhmaṇs, who claimed moral and spiritual leadership, set themselves ideals of dignified austerity, but these ideals were not always followed in practice. A brāhmaṇ who attained a good local reputation for the efficient performance of sacrifices and domestic ceremonies might amass considerable wealth, and if patronized by a king he might become really rich. Corporations of such brāhmaṇs often lived on the proceeds of large agricultural estates (*agrahāra*), transferred to them by kings, and there are accounts of brāhmaṇ landowners who enjoyed great wealth. Other brāhmaṇs, not sufficiently trained to teach the Vedas or to sacrifice, obtained high posts in government service, or even became wealthy by trade. We have seen (p. 147), according to the doctrine of the three aims of life, the place of wealth in the Hindu scheme of things was well established.

In most early Indian literature the world is viewed from the angle of the well-to-do. Poverty, it is more than once said, is living death; to serve another for one's keep is a dog's life, and not worthy of an Āryan. From the time of the *Ṛg*

Veda, which contains many prayers for riches, worldly wealth was looked on as morally desirable for the ordinary man, and indeed essential to a full and civilized life. The ascetic who voluntarily abandoned his wealth performed an act of renunciation which entitled him to the utmost respect. Though by this renunciation he assured himself of spiritual advancement, and was well on the way to salvation (*mokṣa*), the fourth and ultimate aim of existence, the ascetic's life was not that of the ordinary man, and the theoretical classification of the four stages of life (p. 149f) gave ample scope in the second stage to the householder, who was indeed encouraged to build up the family fortunes, and to spend part of them at least on the pleasures of the senses. Thus the ideals of ancient India, while not perhaps the same as those of the West, by no means excluded money-making. India had not only a class of luxury-loving and pleasure-seeking dilettanti, but also one of wealth-seeking merchants and prosperous craftsmen, who, if less respected than the brāhmaṇs and warriors, had an honourable place in society.

Though the basis of ancient Indian industry was at all times the individual craftsman, aided chiefly by members of his own family, larger manufactories, worked chiefly by hired labour, were by no means unknown. The Mauryan state owned not only spinning and weaving workshops (p. 155f), but also shops for the manufacture of weapons and other military supplies, employing salaried craftsmen. The larger mines were also owned and worked by the state. But though the economic order approximated to a sort of state socialism in the time of the Mauryas, it always left scope for the individual producer and distributor. We read here and there of private producers who had far transcended the status of the small home craftsman, and who manufactured on a large scale for a wide market. Thus an early Jaina text[25] tells of a wealthy potter named Saddālaputta who owned 500 potters' workshops and a fleet of boats which distributed his wares throughout the Gangā valley; there are a few other references which confirm that large scale production for a wide market was not unknown in ancient India, though such industrialists as Saddālaputta were no doubt comparatively rare.

A form of industrial organization on a larger scale than the individual craftsman, and probably more common than the entrepreneur, was the workmen's co-operative group, perhaps comparable to the pre-revolutionary Russian *artel*; such groups are mentioned in the Pāli Jātaka stories and elsewhere as carrying out large scale enterprises such as the building of temples and houses. Their existence tended to encourage division of labour; thus one man would fashion the shaft of an arrow, a second would fix the flights, and a third would make and fix the point. Rules are laid down in the lawbooks for the punishment of breach of contract by such co-operatives or their individual members.

Much of the work of the craftsman was sold at the door of his workshop direct to the purchaser. Normally each craft or trade was concentrated in a separate street or bazaar, where the craftsman had his workshop, stall and home. The testimony of Megasthenes, corroborated by the *Arthaśāstra*, shows that in Mauryan times prices were regulated by market officials. The latter text suggests that, as a further effort at maintaining a just price, government officers should buy on the open market when any staple commodity was cheap and plentiful, and release stocks from government stores when it was in short supply,[26] thus bringing down the price and making a profit for the king into the bargain. We have no definite evidence that this idea was ever put into effect, but it is striking that ancient Indian political theorists anticipated by over 2,000 years the plans put forward by the Food and Agriculture Organization of the United Nations for maintaining a stable level of prices of staple commodities on a world-wide scale.

GUILDS

As well as the state, another element did much to control prices and standards of work. This was the guild (*śreṇi*), a form of industrial and mercantile organization which played as big a part in the economy of ancient India as it did in that of most other ancient or medieval civilizations. There are faint and uncertain references to some sort of guild organization even in Vedic literature, but by the time of the composition of the Buddhist scriptures guilds certainly existed in every important Indian town, and embraced almost all trades and industries—we even read of a guild of thieves.

The guild united both the craftsmen's co-operatives and the individual workmen of a given trade into a single corporate body. It fixed rules of work and wages, and standards and prices for the commodities in which its members dealt, and its regulations had the force of law and were upheld by the king and government. Over its own members the guild had judicial rights, which were recognized by the state. A guild court could, like a caste council, expel a refractory member, a penalty which would virtually preclude him from practising his ancestral trade and reduce him to beggary. We read in Buddhist literature of guild courts settling quarrels between members and their wives, and the rules of the Buddhist order lay down that a married woman may not be ordained a nun without the consent of her husband and his guild. Thus the guild had power not only over the economic, but also over the social life of its members. It acted as guardian of their widows and orphans, and as their insurance against sickness. Its powers and functions in this respect were very similar to those of caste councils in more recent times, and, though some authorities would disagree with us, we cannot but conclude that the guilds played an important part in the evolution of trade castes.

The guild was headed by a chief, usually called the "Elder" (*jyeṣṭhaka*, in Pāli *jeṭṭhaka*), who was assisted by a small council of senior members. The office of Elder was usually hereditary and held by one of the richest members of the guild. In the Pāli scriptures the Elder is invariably described as a very wealthy man, often with much influence at the palace, and counselling the king himself. The guilds had a corporate life, symbolized, as in medieval Europe, by the possession of banners, and also of *chaurīs*,* the ceremonial yak's tail fly-whisks which were insignia of nobility. These and other emblems were sometimes granted by royal

* The usual Hindi word. In Sanskrit *camara*.

charter, and were carried in local religious processions by the guildsmen. Some guilds, again like those of medieval Europe, had their own militias, which served as auxiliaries of the king's armies in time of need (p. 110).

All over India are to be found inscriptions recording the donations of guilds to religious causes of all kinds, the most famous being that of the Mandasor silk-weavers, to whom we have already referred. The guilds must have had considerable funds to make such large donations, and no doubt their members paid regular subscriptions which were augmented by fines levied on those who transgressed the guild law. There are references in the legal literature to guilds acting as bankers, accepting deposits, and lending money at interest to merchants and others. They would often act as trustees of religious endowments; the pious would pay a sum of money to a guild, on condition that it would maintain a perpetual lamp in a temple or provide new robes annually for the monks of a Buddhist monastery. Inscriptions recording such acts of benevolence are quite numerous, and no doubt the guilds, while duly carrying out their part of the agreement, profited from such transactions.

The corporate spirit of the guild gave the better type of craftsman and merchant a degree of self-respect which he would not otherwise have found. There is more than one record of riots and affrays between different guilds and trade groups; this was specially the case in the medieval Deccan, where guild and caste often overlapped in function or were virtually synonymous, and the strange division of right and left hand castes led to much friction (p. 130). The fact that more than one guild of the same craft is occasionally recorded in the same place suggests that guilds sometimes broke up.

TECHNICAL ACHIEVEMENT

At all times the work of the Indian craftsman, however primitive and simple his tools, has been admired for its delicacy and skill, and the technical achievement of ancient India was far from negligible. Her spinners and weavers could produce semi-transparent silks and muslins of extreme thinness, which are clearly depicted in sculpture (pl. XXXVI*b*), and which were much in demand in the Roman Empire. Unlike ancient Greece and medieval China, India developed no true ceramic art; indeed from the aesthetic point of view no pottery of historical times is as good as the simply patterned but well designed wares of the prehistoric North-West (fig. iv); but the bright hard polish of the type of pottery usually called "northern black polished ware" is a very creditable technical achievement. In the working of stone on a large scale India's skill is attested by the enormous monolithic columns of the Mauryan period. Many of these bear Aśoka's inscriptions, but it is not certain that they were made and erected by him; some may have existed before his time. All are made of sandstone from the same quarry at Chunār, about twenty-five miles south-west of Vārāṇasī. Some thirty columns have been found in many parts of Northern India, from Sānchī in the south to the Nepālese Tarāī in the north. Their sculptured capitals are great as works of art, but as evidence of Indian technological achievement the columns are even more significant. Weighing as much as fifty tons and measuring some forty feet, they were carved from single blocks of stone, given a polish of wonderful hardness and lustre, and often transported many hundreds of miles to their present positions. The process of their manufacture, polishing and transport has not yet been fully explained, and the secret was apparently lost soon after the Mauryan period, when the school of craftsmen who worked the Chunār sandstone vanished. Though many fine examples of later stone carving have come down to us, some much more impressive artistically than the Mauryan columns, it is doubtful whether India ever again showed such complete mastery of the handling of enormous pieces of stone.

Fig. xvi.—Carting a Pillar (from an engraved sketch on the wall of the medieval fortress of Raichūr, in Mysore). (Reproduced by permission of the Archaeological Department, Government of India)

The Iron Pillar of Meharaulī, near Delhī, is even more remarkable, though of little artistic value and less immediately impressive than the Mauryan columns. It is a memorial to a king called Candra, who was probably Candra Gupta II (c. 376–415), and it now stands not far from the famous Qutb Mīnar, one of the greatest monuments of Muslim India, though it was originally erected on a hill near Ambālā. It is over twenty-three feet high, and consists of a single piece of iron, of a size and weight which could not have been produced by the best European ironfounders until about one hundred years ago. As with the Mauryan columns we have no clear evidence of how it was made, but it must have demanded immense care and labour, and great technical proficiency in preparing and heating the metal. The metallurgical skill of ancient India is further attested by the fact that this pillar, though it has weathered the torrential rains of over 1,500 monsoons, shows no sign of rusting. This is not due to the fact that the Indians had discovered some form of stainless steel alloy, for the column is of iron almost chemically pure. Several suggestions have been put forward to account for the remarkable durability of the Iron Pillar, but no wholly satisfactory explanation has been given. The theory, confidently proposed in a scientific journal,[27] that the dry atmosphere of Delhi is a sufficient cause is quite inadequate, for Delhi is very humid during the rainy season, when ordinary iron quickly rusts. Since the process of oxidization demands a catalyst, it may be the great purity of the metal which has preserved the Iron Pillar so long, as another memorial to India's technical skill.

TRADE AND FINANCE

A money economy only existed in India from the days of the Buddha. That coinage was introduced from the west cannot be proved with certainty, but the earliest clear references to coined money are found in texts looking back to a period shortly after the foundation of the Achaemenid Empire in Persia; this was the first great empire to mint an official coinage, and for a time it controlled the Panjāb. The Babylonians and Assyrians managed with unstamped silver shekels, but the Achaemenid emperors adopted stamped coinage from Lydia and the Greek cities of Asia Minor, which had already employed it for a century or two. If India did not learn the use of coinage from the Persians she invented it independently, but the coincidence is too striking to make this seem probable, especially as one of the earliest Indian words for a coin, *karṣa* (also a small weight) is of Persian origin.

The earliest Indian coinage* consisted of flat pieces of silver or bronze, of irregular shape but fairly accurate in weight. They bore no inscriptions but a number of punch-marks, the significance of which is not finally established, but which probably included the emblems of kings who minted the coins, and control marks of local officials and merchants. Inscribed coins were not regularly minted in India until the 2nd century B.C., and though literary evidence suggests that gold coinage may have existed earlier the oldest surviving gold coins, other than one or two very rare specimens, are those of Vīma Kadphises of the 1st century A.D. As well as the three usual metals, coins of nickel were minted by some of the Greco-Bactrian kings, while the Sātavāhanas of the Deccan made coins of lead, and various alloys are attested. Small purchases were regularly paid for in cowry-shells (*varāṭaka*), which remained the chief currency of the poor in many parts of India until recent times.

The concept of legal tender never seems to have taken root in Hindu India, and coins were often current far beyond the borders of the kingdoms which minted them. Some important dynasties, such as the Pālas of Bengal, did not regularly mint coins but relied on those of other states. Coins circulated less rapidly than they do nowadays, and might be current for centuries; thus the *Periplus of the Erythrean Sea*, a Greek text of the end of the 1st century A.D., notices that the coins of Menander, who ruled in the Panjāb at least two centuries earlier, were current in the port of Barygaza (Bhṛgukaccha, the modern Broach, at the mouth of the Narmadā), which was probably at least 500 miles from Menander's kingdom. Foreign currency circulated freely. In the North-West, Athenian drachms, as well as local imitations, were current before the invasion of Alexander, and Achaemenid, Seleucid, Parthian, Roman, Sāsānian and Islāmic coins were used at different periods. In the South numerous hoards of Roman imperial coins have been found.

Though there is no evidence of a highly organized financial machinery of cheques, drafts and letters of credit, usury was widespread, and moneylending, except by brāhmaṇs, did not incur the reprobation of Hindu moralists, as it did that

* For further information on coinage see Appendix, p. 506f.

of medieval Christianity and Islām. Even in the *Ṛg Veda* we read of indebtedness (p. 357), and the earliest Dharma Sūtras lay down rates of interest and regulations governing debts and mortgages. The just rate of interest is generally given as 1¼ per cent, per month, or fifteen per cent, per year. Later commentators interpret this as applying only to secured loans, and in practice rates of interest were often much higher. Manu[28] and some other lawgivers lay down a sliding scale of interest for unsecured loans, according to the class of the debtor: brāhmaṇs 24 per cent., kṣatriyas 36 per cent., vaiśyas 48 per cent., and śūdras 60 per cent, per year. The *Arthaśāstra*[29] gives, beside the "just rate", three other rates of interest, inadequately defined, but apparently applicable to short-term loans for commercial ventures: the normal commercial rate, 5 per cent. per month; the rate for merchants travelling through forests (overland caravan traders), 10 per cent. per month; and the rate for seafaring merchants, 20 per cent. per month. These enormous rates of interest, 60, 120, and 240 per cent. per year respectively, are measures of both the profit and the risk of ancient Indian commerce.

Humane regulations on indebtedness are laid down in the *Arthaśāstra* and some other legal texts. Interest payments should cease when the total interest paid equals the principal. Loans advanced on securities used by the creditor for his own profit (e.g. beasts of burden) should be free of interest. Husbands are responsible for their wives' debts, but not wives for those of their husbands. But the later lawbooks provide many escape clauses and sometimes completely set aside these earlier injunctions. Debtors might be imprisoned, or enslaved by their creditors until they had worked off their debts. We read of debtors, dogged everywhere by their creditors, at last committing suicide in desperation. The immense expense of the family ceremonials of Hinduism, periodic dearth, the dowering of daughters, and many other factors, worked then as now to drive the less fortunate into debt, and, then as now, the Indian creditor might be a hard man.

We have seen that trade guilds acted as bankers, both receiving deposits and issuing loans. The king or his local officer might make loans to peasants to relieve dearth, or to encourage the cultivation of waste lands and the development of irrigation. The larger temples also sometimes served as bankers, and in the South the village communes occasionally made loans to peasants. There were many professional bankers and moneylenders, however, the *śreṣṭhins* (in Pāli, *seṭṭhi*).*

The śreṣṭhin was not merely a moneylender or banker, but usually a merchant as well. At all times until the coming of the Europeans banking in India was a by-product of trading, and most śreṣṭhins had other sources of income besides moneylending. They appear as leading members of guilds, often fabulously wealthy. Though the craftsman frequently sold his wares direct to the consumer the peasants' surplus products were largely in the hands of middlemen, and a class of large merchants, as distinct from small traders and pedlars, existed at least from the time of the Buddha. In the Jātaka stories we read of śreṣṭhins

* The word literally means "chief". It has survived in the North Indian seth and the Dravidian chetti or setti.

cornering grain, and buying at their own price the products of craftsmen who are virtually their employees. The term śreṣṭhin seems sometimes to have been a title of honour, held only by merchants of wealth and consequence. In the Buddhist scriptures we read of chief śreṣṭhins, honoured by kings, and with places in the royal councils. Under the Guptas the chief banker or śreṣṭhin was sometimes a member of the local advisory council which aided the district officer in controlling local affairs (p. 89).

Though in early literature and inscriptions the śreṇis or guilds seem to have been chiefly organizations of producers, there were also guilds or companies of merchants. Such merchant corporations became very important in the medieval Deccan, and had branches in many cities. One such was the *Vīravalañjigar*, freely translated "the Company of Gentlemen Merchants", which had members in every important city of the Peninsula and was controlled by a central council at Aihoḷe, in Mysore. The company known as *Maṇigrāma* functioned not only in Southern India but also in Ceylon, where it hired out its mercenaries to the Sinhalese kings.

Co-operative ventures both in production and distribution were well known in Hindu India, but they were normally carried out by temporary associations of craftsmen and merchants, and these merchant companies were in no way comparable to the modern joint stock company. These companies may from time to time have undertaken corporate ventures, but the normal function of the mercantile companies was not trading itself, but protecting, furthering and regulating the activities of their members. Overland caravans, though consisting of carts and pack animals owned and led by individual merchants, would be organized and controlled by officers of the company and guarded by the company's mercenaries. They played a similar part in maritime trade, and probably owned warehouses and "factories", where their members might store their wares in safety. Members travelling to strange cities would receive help from officers of the local branch, and, like the craft guilds, the mercantile companies no doubt helped members who fell on hard times, prevented adulteration, undercutting and other malpractices, and represented their members at the king's court.

CARAVANS AND TRADE-ROUTES

By the time of the Buddha recognized trade-routes covered most of Northern India, and by Mauryan times similar routes existed in the Peninsula. Among the chief of these was one which ran from the Gangā port of Tāmraliptī, not far from the modern Calcutta, up the river to the old city of Campā, and thence through Pāṭaliputra and Vārāṇasī to Kauśāmbī, whence a branch went to the port of Bhṛgukaccha on the mouth of the Narmadā by way of Vidiśā and Ujjayinī. From Kauśāmbī the main trunk road passed along the south bank of the Yamunā to Mathurā, from which a branch crossed the modern Rājasthān and the Thar Desert to the port of Patala, near the mouth of the Indus. The main route passed on by the modern Delhī and crossed the five rivers of the Panjāb by way of Śākala (? Siālkot) to the north-western city of Takṣaśilā, whence it continued up the Kābul Valley and on into Central Asia. The great cities to the north of the Gangā and Yamunā were linked to the trunk route by recognized branch roads. Though its course has varied somewhat through the centuries this has always been the main artery of Northern India. The Mauryan emperors cared for this great road, which was marked with milestones and provided with wells and rest-houses at regular intervals.

The main route to the South went from Ujjayinī to the city of Pratisthāna, in the N.-W. Deccan, the capital of the Sātavāhana empire around the beginning of the Christian era. Thence it passed across the Deccan Plateau to the lower Krishnā, and went on to the great southern cities of Kāñcī (Conjeeveram) and Madurai. A network of roads developed early in the Christian era from this old route, linking all the more important cities of the Peninsula. Contact between North and South by way of the east does not at first seem to have been close or frequent, but routes from Pāṭaliputra to Orissā must have existed before the Mauryan period. In the more unsettled times after the Mauryas the wild uncivilized forests of Central India much discouraged travel, and the western route was the most important until at least the Gupta period.

The larger rivers crossed en route by these roads were not bridged. Indian engineering, though very competent in many respects, seems never to have mastered the art of bridging a wide river; but regular ferry services, in Mauryan times regulated by the State, were maintained at every important crossing.

Seventeenth century European visitors to the Mughal Empire were impressed by the badness of the roads, which were atrocious even by the low Western standards of the time. As road builders the Indians never equalled the Romans, but the references in Aśoka's inscriptions, the *Arthaśāstra* and elsewhere, show that under more energetic governments roads were well maintained, and conditions under the Mughals may not have been typical of earlier times.

In the rainy season, roughly corresponding to the European summer, the roads were practically impassable; rivers in spate could not be ferried, and all travelling ceased; even the thousands of wandering religious mendicants, who walked the length and breadth of India from one shrine to another, would settle down until the rains had passed, in the precincts of a temple, the outhouse of a kindly patron, or a cave near a village. But at other times of the year, especially in the cool, bright winter, when the weather of Northern India resembles a rainless late May in England, long caravans of rumbling bullock carts and pack animals—oxen, asses, mules and camels— travelled the dusty roads.

The roads were dangerous to the merchant-caravans. Many of the trade routes linking centres of civilization passed through dense jungle, and over hills where wild tribes dwelt. There were whole villages of professional robbers, ready at all times to waylay the merchant. Other dangers were incurred from wild beasts—tigers, elephants and snakes in particular—and the remoter parts of the country were the reputed haunts of demons of many malevolent kinds. In these circumstances merchants preferred to share their perils together, and we read of as many as 500 men travelling in caravan. Pāli literature tells of bands of professional caravan guards, who would undertake to give guidance and safe conduct over a specified route, and who seem to have been a regular feature of the caravan trade, at least where the merchant corporations did not provide their own guards. If the *Arthaśāstra*'s instructions on the duties of the *antapāla* (p. 93) have any relation to facts it would seem that the Mauryan kings did much to safeguard the roads, and the same is true of many other important dynasties; but the danger that beset caravans from thieves is attested by many stories, and by the enormous rate of interest which the *Arthaśāstra* permits on loans to finance long distance trading ventures.

The caravan leader (*sārthavāha*) was an important figure in the commercial community, and the Gupta copper-plates of Northern Bengal (p. 89) show that the chief caravan leader of a locality might occupy an important place on the district council. Another figure associated with the caravan trade was the land-pilot (in Pāli, *thalaniyyāmaka*), whose existence is attested in the Pāli scriptures; he guided caravans through deserts and waste places, steering by the stare.

The major rivers were used to carry both goods and passengers in vessels large and small. The Gangā served as the artery of the Great Plain, but the Indus and the rivers of the Deccan were also important as trade routes. Like the land routes they were full of dangers: river pirates were numerous, while in some rivers sandbanks and in others submerged rocks were a peril to the navigators.

Luxury articles formed the chief objects of long-distance trade— spices, sandalwood, gold and gems from the South, silks and muslins from Bengal and Vārāṇasī, musk, saffron and yaks' tails from the Hills; but these were not the only merchandise of the caravans. Many regions had to import metal. The chief source of iron in India was South Bihār, and control of the route from the iron producing areas around the modern Rānchī to the Gangā may well have been one of the chief factors in the early rise of Magadhan power. Copper was mined and smelted in various parts of the Deccan, in Rājasthān, and in the Western Himālayas. Salt, an absolute necessity in a hot climate, was imported from the sea coast, and from various rock-salt deposits, notably in the Salt Range in the Panjāb. Certain foodstuffs were articles of long-distance commerce: sugar was carried to cooler and dryer regions where the cane would not grow well, and rice was exported as a luxury food to parts of the North-West.

SEA-TRADE AND OVERSEAS CONTACTS

Whether or not the Āryans of the Ṛg Vedic period knew the sea, by the time of the Buddha or soon after Indian sailors had probably circumnavigated the subcontinent, and perhaps made the first contacts with Burma, Malaya and the islands of Indonesia. In the early centuries of the Christian era maritime trade became most vigorous, especially with the West, where the Roman Empire demanded the luxuries of the East in great quantities. With the fall of the Roman Empire the trade with the West declined somewhat, though it was maintained by the Arabs, and improved gradually with the rising material standards of medieval Europe. Before the time of the Guptas contact was made by sea between South India and

China, and as trade with the West declined that with China increased, the Chinese demand for Indian spices, jewels, perfumes, and other luxury commodities continuing down to the present day.

Certain over-enthusiastic Indian scholars have perhaps made too much of the achievements of ancient Indian seafarers, which cannot compare with those of the Vikings, or of some other early maritime peoples. Much of the merchandise exported from India was carried in foreign bottoms, and though Indian literature mentions ships taking 1,000 passengers this seems an exaggeration. The largest Indian ship known to Pliny, who obtained some accurate information about the maritime trade of the Indian Ocean, measured 3,000 *amphorae*, or only seventy-five tons. In the 5th century Fa-hsien, who had no reason not to tell the truth in this respect, travelled from Ceylon to Java in a ship carrying 200 people, which is the largest complement of passengers and crew attested in a reliable source relating to early India. The few illustrations of ships surviving from this period give little impression of size, though one, at Ajantā, is of a three-master (fig. xvii); and the vessels so vigorously and realistically depicted on the friezes of the great Buddhist temple of Borobudur in Java, all seem comparatively small, the largest containing only fifteen people. All have steadying outriggers, like the fishing boats of present-day South India and Ceylon, and all are steered by large oars—the rudder was unknown in our period.

Normally the timbers of ancient Indian ships were not nailed or riveted, but lashed together; this was done to avoid the imaginary danger of magnetic rocks, for the technique of nailing a ship's timbers was certainly known in India in the medieval period. In fact sewn or lashed timbers were more resilient than nailed ones, and could stand up better to the fierce storms of the monsoon period and the many coral reefs of the Indian Ocean.

Fig. xvii.—A ship, *c.* 6th century, A.D. (From Cave II Ajantā).
(By permission of the Oxford University Press)

An early Jātaka story[30] tells of ships sailing from the port of Bhrgukaccha to a place called Baveru, which must be Babylon. The Pāli *Questions of Milinda*, probably of the 1st century A.D., mentions the possibility of a merchant sailing to Alexandria, Burma, Malaya or China. A story of the 6th or 7th century tells of a merchant's son who sailed to "the Island of the Black Yavanas"[31], which must surely be Madagascar or Zanzibar. These records indicate the known limits of Indian seafaring.

The chief ports of ancient India were on the West Coast—Bhrgukaccha, already mentioned, Supāra, not far from the modern Bombay, and Patala, on the Indus delta. Hence coastal shipping plied to the South and to Ceylon. There is evidence that the direct route across the Indian Ocean from the Red Sea was used, at least occasionally, in pre-Christian times, but most ships sailing to India would follow the coastline. With the growth of commerce in the first century A.D., however, it became usual for ships to cross the Indian Ocean, taking advantage of the monsoon winds. In the East the Gangā Basin was served by the river port of Campā, from which ships sailed down to the sea and coasted to the South and Ceylon. By Mauryan times, with the eastward expansion of Āryan culture, Tāmraliptī became the main seaport of the Gangā basin, and Campā lost its importance. From Tāmraliptī ships not only sailed to Ceylon, but, probably from before the beginning of the Christian era, to South-East Asia and Indonesia.

The merchants and seamen of Roman Egypt knew India well, and there survives a remarkable seaman's guide, compiled in Greek by an anonymous author towards the end of the lst century A.D., *The Periplus of the Erythrean Sea*. From the *Periplus*, Ptolemy's *Geography*, of the following century, and the early Tamil poems which look back to this period, we learn much of the trade of the Tamil lands. Here many flourishing ports are mentioned, the three chief ones being Muśiri, known to the Greeks as Musiris.in the Cēra country (Kerala), Korkai, in the land of the Pāṇḍyas, not far from the modern Tuticorin, and Kāvirippaṭṭinam, the chief port of the Cōla country, at the mouth of the Kāviri.

The Tamil kings did much to develop their harbours and encourage sea-trade. We read of lighthouses, and wharves where "the beautiful great ships of the Yavanas" discharged their merchandise to be examined by customs officials, stamped with the king's seal, and stored in warehouses. Kāvirippaṭṭinam, now a decaying fishing village silted up by the river mud, had an artificial harbour, built, according to a late Sinhalese source, by soldiers captured by the great King Karikālan in a raid on Ceylon.[32]

At this time Socotra had a considerable Indian colony, and the name of the island may be of Indian origin.* Indian merchants were met by Dion Chrysostom in Alexandria. One such merchant, crossing the desert from the Red Sea to the Nile on his way to Alexandria, left a brief inscription in a temple at Redesiye; "Sophon the Indian does homage to Pan for a good journey".[33] "Sophon" probably represents some such Indian name as Subhānu, and Pan was no doubt identified

* *Sukhatara-dvipa*, "The Most Pleasant Island", the landfall for ships crossing the Indian Ocean.

in the merchant's mind with Kṛṣṇa, who was also a god of flocks and herds, and played a rustic flute. It is evident that the author of this inscription was much Hellenized.

As well as merchants, we read of Indian fortune-tellers, conjurors and prostitutes in Rome, while mahouts often accompanied their elephants to the West. There are records of several embassies from Indian kings to the Caesars. The earliest of these is said by Strabo to have been sent by the king of the Pāṇḍyas, and was met by Augustus at Athens about 20 B.C. This mission included an ascetic called Zarmanochegas (Skt. Śramaṇācārya), who, growing tired of a life of earthly bondage, burnt himself to death at Athens. It has been suggested that when St. Paul wrote "though I give my body to be burned, and have not charity, it profiteth me nothing", he had in mind this incident of some sixty or seventy years earlier, of which he had heard from his Athenian colleagues. The theory is of course fanciful, but not wholly impossible. Later embassies are recorded as having been sent to Claudius (from Ceylon), Trajan, Antoninus Pius, Julian the Apostate and Justinian. The latter emperor of Constantinople had an Indian cook.

The main requirements of the West were spices, perfumes, jewels and fine textiles, but lesser luxuries, such as sugar, rice and ghee were also exported, as well as ivory, both raw and worked. A finely carved ivory statuette of a goddess or *yakṣī* has been found in the ruins of Herculaneum (pl. LXXXV*b*). Indian iron was much esteemed for its purity and hardness, and dyestuffs such as lac and indigo were also in demand. Another requirement was live animals and birds; elephants, lions, tigers and buffaloes were exported from India in appreciable numbers for the wild beast shows of Roman emperors and provincial governors, though these larger beasts went mainly overland through the desert trading city of Palmyra; smaller animals and birds, such as monkeys, parrots and peacocks, found their way to Rome in even larger quantities as pets of wealthy Roman ladies. The Emperor Claudius even succeeded in obtaining from India a specimen of the fabulous phoenix, probably a golden pheasant, one of the loveliest of India's birds.

In return for her exports India wanted little but gold. Pottery and glassware from the West found their way to India, and many sherds of Arretine and other wares, mass-produced in Western factories, have been found in the remains of a trading station at Arikamedu, near Pondicherry.[34] There was some demand for wine, and the Western traders also brought tin, lead, coral and slave-girls. But the balance of trade was very unfavourable to the West, and resulted in a serious drain of gold from the Roman Empire. This was recognized by Pliny, who, inveighing against the degenerate habits of his day, computed the annual drain to the East as 100 million sesterces, "so dearly do we pay for our luxury and our women".[36] The drain of gold to the East was an important cause of the financial difficulties in the Roman Empire from the reign of Nero onwards. Not only gold, but coinage of all types was exported to India; Roman coins have been found in such quantities in many parts of the Peninsula and Ceylon that they must have circulated there as a regular currency.

There is good evidence that subjects of the Roman Empire, if not actual

Romans, settled in India. There is mention of a temple of the Emperor Augustus at Musiris but this is probably a mistake, caused by the similarity of the name of the Roman emperor to that of Agastya, the legendary sage (*ṛṣi*) who is said to have brought Āryan culture to South India (p. 279). Early Tamil literature contains several references to the Yavanas, who were employed as bodyguards by Tamil kings, or as engineers, valued for their knowledge of siegecraft and the construction of war-engines. While the term Yavana was often used very vaguely, and, from its original meaning of "a Greek", came to be applied to any Westerner, it is by no means impossible that the Yavanas of South India included fugitives from the Roman legions in their number.

Contacts between India and the West are testified in language. Even a few Hebrew words are believed by some to be of Indian origin—notably *koph*, "monkey" (Skt. *kapi*) and *tukki*, "peacock", (Tamil *togai*). Though the details of the Book of Kings may not be historically accurate the statement that the navy of Tharshish brought to King Solomon gold and silver, ivory, apes and peacocks[36] shows that the Hebrews received commodities from India at an early period. It has been suggested that the land of Ophir, from which King Hiram of Tyre brought gold, precious stones and "almug" trees to Solomon,[37] was Supāra, the ancient port near Bombay; this suggestion is strengthened by the fact that in the Septuagint, the Greek version of the Old Testament, the word occurs as Σωφάρα; the almug trees may have been sandal, one of the Sanskrit words for which is *valguka*, from which the Hebrew word may be derived. Indian loan-words in Greek and Latin are nearly all of articles of trade: precious stones, such as σμάραγδος, emerald (Skt. *marakaṭa*)* and βήρυλλος, beryl (Skt. *vaidurya*)†; spices, such as ζιγγίβερις, ginger (Skt. *śṛṅgavera*) and πιπέρι, pepper (Skt. *pippali*); foodstuffs, such as σάκχαρον, sugar (Skt. *iarkara*) and όρυζα, rice (Tamil *ariśi*); and κάρπασος, cotton (Skt. *karpāśa*) as well as several others. Dubious is the suggested etymology of the word ἐλέφας, elephant, from the Sanskrit *ibha*, meaning elephant, with the Semitic definite article *al* or *el* prefixed.

Greek loan-words in Sanskrit include several connected with mathematics and astronomy, of which some are common, and have passed into the vernaculars of India: *horā*, an hour (ὥρα), *kendra*, centre (κενδρον) and *koṇa*, angle (γωνία); two coins, *dramma* (δραχμη) and *dīnāra* (from the Latin *denarius*, through the Greek); and two words connected with war, *suraṅga*, a mine (p. 115), and *kampana*, a camp (a rare word used in Kashmīr, and borrowed from Latin through Greek); of words connected with writing *melā*, ink (μέλαν), and *kalama*, pen (Κάλαμος) are certain borrowings, though there are synonyms of purely Indian origin for both these words. The derivation of *pustaka*, book, from the Greek πύξινον is no longer supported by competent authorities.

The Chinese in the Middle Ages demanded many of the same commodities as the Westerners, but they had more to offer in exchange. Though the Indians

* These two words are perhaps borrowed from a common Middle Eastern source.

† Same as above.

made splendid silks and muslins of their own they were ready to buy the stuffs of China, and Chinese porcelain found a market in South India and Ceylon, as did the pottery of the Muslim World, numerous sherds of which have been found.

Though maritime trade did not cease it became more and more the affair of foreign merchants. Indians never wholly abandoned the sea, but by the time of the Muslim invasion travel to foreign lands was believed to bring grave impurity upon members of the upper classes, and this, according to some authorities, could never be expunged.[38] This religious objection to sea travel was a measure of the growing fear of and distaste for the sea, which in some degree existed at all times. Though Indian mariners were resourceful and by no means lacking in courage, sailing the sea was always depicted as hateful and desperately perilous. By the Middle Ages the Arabs and Chinese had outstripped the Indians in the art of ship construction, and it became more profitable for the merchant to sell his wares to foreign middlemen than to take them abroad himself. The Muslim invasions encouraged xenophobia, and the people who had planted their colonies from Socotra to Borneo became, with religious sanction, a nation of landlubbers.

PLATE XXXIII

Scenes from the Life of the Buddha, Gandhāra

British Museum

(a) The Conversion of the Buddha's Half-brother, Nanda

Messrs. Faber & Faber, Royal Academy Trustees and Central Museum, Lahore

(b) A Pious Laywoman, Viśākhā, Repulses a Naked Ascetic

PLATE XXXIV

Messrs. Johnston & Hoffman, Calcutta

Dampati Couples (representing Donors). Relief from the Buddhist Cave-temple, Kārlī
c. 2nd century A.D.

PLATE XXXV

Medallion Reliefs from Amarāvatī

Government Museum, Madras

(a) The Buddha tames the made elephant, Nālagiri. On the left, Nālagiri runs amok; on the right, he bows at the Master's feet

Government Museum, Madras

(b) Demigods carry the Buddha's alms-bowl to heaven

Messrs. Faber & Faber, Royal Academy Trustees & British Museum

(c) Gautama leaves his palace for the forest

PLATE XXXVI

A. Nawrath, "Glories of Hindustan", Metheun & Co., London

(b) Standing Buddha, Mathurā. Gupta Period

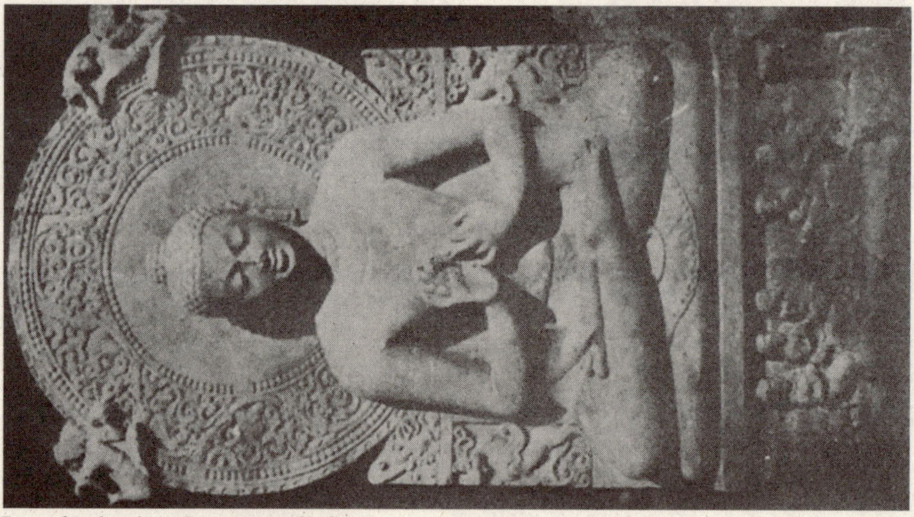

(a) Seated Buddha, Sārnāth. Gupta Period.

Dept. of Archaeology, Government of India

PLATE XXXVII

Gupta Sculpture

Dept. of Archaeology, Government of India

(a) Sūrya, the Sun-god. Pillar capital, Pāwayā, Gwālior

Dept. of Archaeology, Government of India

b) Girl Dancer and Musicians. Lintel slab, Pāwayā

A. L. Basham

c) Viṣṇu as a boar rescues the earth from the cosmic ocean. Colossal rock-sculpture, Udayagiri, Bhīlsā, M.P.

PLATE XXXVIII

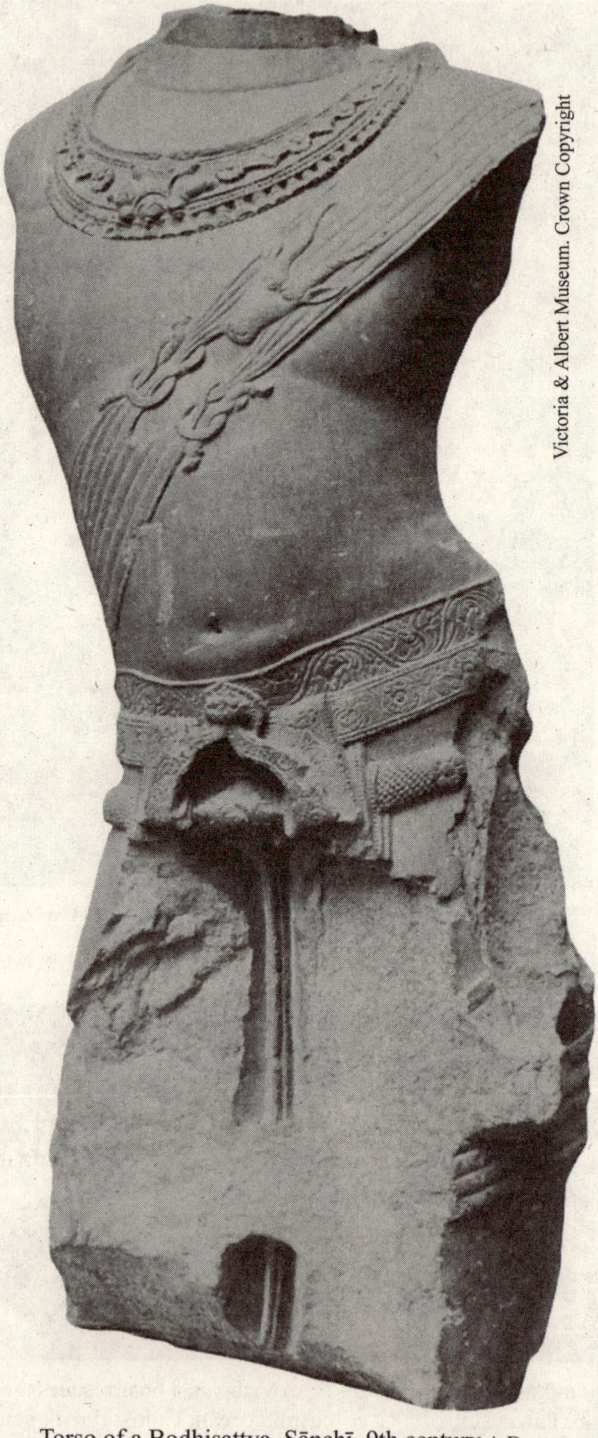

Victoria & Albert Museum. Crown Copyright

Torso of a Bodhisattva, Sānchī. 9th century A.D.

PLATE XXXIX

British Museum

(a) Śiva as Ascetic Dancing with Dwarf (*Gaṇa*) Musicians. Wood-carving, N.W.F.P. Early Medieval.

Messrs. Faber & Faber, Royal Academy Trustees & Central Museum, Lahore

(b) Head of Girl, Ushkur, Kashmīr. *c*. 6th century A.D.

PLATE XL

Dept. of Archaeology, Government of India

Viṣṇu, Ceiling Slab, Aihoḷe, Mysore. 7th century A.D.

PLATE XLI

Musée Guimet, Paris

(a) The Descent of Gangā, Colossal Rock-sculpture, Māmallapuram. 7th century

Fogg Museum of Art, Harvard University

(b) Detail from the Descent of Gangā. A snake-spirit (nāga) swims in the sacred river. To the right, two demi-gods, and a cat, playing the ascetic in order to lure mice

PLATE XLII

Dept. of Archaeology, Government of India

(a) The Pallava King Mahendravikramavarman and two Queens, Māmallapuram, Madras. 7th century A.D.

Dr. Denman Ross

(b) Durgā destroying the Buffalo-demon, Mahisa. Māmallapuram. 7th century A.D.

PLATE XLIII

A. L. Basham

(a) Lovers. Pallava style.
Isurumuniya, Anurādhapura, Ceylon.
c. 7th century A.D.

A. L. Basham

(b) The Demon Rāvaṇa shakes
Mt. Kailāsa, on which sit Śiva and
Pārvatī. Ellorā. 8th century A.D.

Dept. of Archaeology, Government of India

(c) Śiva-Trimūrti. Colossal Rock-sculpture. Elephanta Island, near Bombay.
8th–9th century A.D.

PLATE XLIV

British Museum

Caṇḍī, a form of Durgā. N. India. Medieval.

PLATE XLV
Medieval Sculpture from Nālandā

A. L. Basham

(a) Bodhisattva Teaching

Dept. of Archaeology, Government of India

(b) A Tāntric Buddhist Snake-Goddess

Dept. of Archaeology, Government of India

(c) Head of a Girl

PLATE XLVI

Medieval Sculpture from Nālandā

Raymond Burnier, "Hindu Medieval Sculpture", La Palme, Paris

Lovers (*Maithuna*). Khajurāho, M.P. 10th–11th century A.D.

PLATE XLVII

Raymond Burnier, "Hindu Medieval Sculpture", La Palme, Paris

Apsaras. Khajurāho. 10th–11th century A.D.

PLATE XLVIII

Raymond Burnier, "Hindu Medieval Sculpture", La Palme, Paris

Viṣṇu. Khajurāho. 10th–11th century A.D.

VII

RELIGION: CULTS, DOCTRINES AND METAPHYSICS

(1) THE RELIGION OF THE VEDAS

Gods of the Ṛg Veda

THE earliest civilized inhabitants of India worshipped a Mother Goddess and a horned fertility god; they had sacred trees and animals, and ritual ablutions apparently played an important part in their religious life. Beyond this much has been said and written about the religion of the Harappan people, but in the absence of intelligible texts any efforts at further defining it are very speculative. The salient features of Harappan religion appeared again in a new form at a much later date, and we must assume that it never died, but was quietly practised by the humbler people, gradually developing from contact with other doctrines and cults, until it gathered enough strength to reappear, and largely to overlay the old faith of the Āryan rulers of India.

We have much knowledge of the religion of the early Āryans from the 1028 hymns of the *Ṛg Veda*, which is the oldest religious text in the world still looked on as sacred, and which was probably composed between 1500 and 900 B.C. The *Ṛg Veda* is a collection of hymns for use at the sacrifices of the aristocratic Āryan cult. The three later Vedas, the *Sāma*, *Yajur* and *Atharva*, are of somewhat different character. The *Sāma Veda* is almost useless to the historian, being a collection of certain verses of the *Ṛg Veda* arranged for liturgical purposes. The *Yajur Veda*, compiled a century or two later than the *Ṛg Veda*, contains sacrificial formulae in prose and verse to be pronounced by the *adhvaryu*, or priest who performed the manual part of the sacrifice. It exists in various recensions (*saṃhitā*), which are of two types, the "Black" giving the formulae with rubricated instructions, and the "White" adding detailed instructions in a lengthy appendix called a *Brāhmaṇa*. The *Atharva Veda* consists mainly of magical spells and incantations in verse, and was certainly compiled after the *Ṛg* and *Tajur*. It possesses, however, an atmosphere of simple animism and sympathetic magic, and seems to reflect a lower cultural level than that of the *Ṛg Veda*, deriving from the plebeian religion of the Āryans and containing many non-Āryan elements. The massive Brāhmaṇas, which are looked on as appendices to the Vedas, and the mystical *Āraṇyakas* and *Upaniṣads*, which are in turn appendices to the Brāhmaṇas, complete the literature generally known as Vedic. The material in the Brāhmaṇas looks back in the main to the period between c. 800 and 600 B.C., and the earliest Upaniṣads overlap with the latest Brāhmaṇas, though some Upaniṣads are certainly of much more recent date. The religion of the people who composed this literature was not that of later India, and many scholars refer to it as Brāhmaṇism or Vedism, to distinguish it from Hinduism, to which it bears a relation similar to that between the sacrificial Judaism of the temple and the later Judaism of the synagogue.

Much of the *Ṛg Veda* is imperfectly understood; the oldest exegetical work on it, the *Nirukta* (Etymology) of Yāska, perhaps dating from 500 B.C., shows that at a very early period the brāhmaṇs had forgotten the true meaning of many obsolete words. But the broad outlines of the religion of the *Ṛg Veda* are clear enough. The chief objects of worship were the *devas*, a word cognate with the Latin *deus*. The root from which this word is derived, *div*, is connected with brightness and radiance, and the devas by connotation were "the shining ones". The early gods of the Āryans, like those of the the Greeks, were chiefly connected with the sky and were predominantly male. A few goddesses occur in the *Ṛg Veda*; for instance *Pṛthvī*, a vague and rarely mentioned personification of the earth, *Aditi*, a mysterious and tenuous figure, the great mother of the gods, *Uṣas*, the goddess of the dawn, to whom a number of lovely hymns were addressed, *Rātri*, the spirit of the night, who has a beautiful hymn to herself (p. 355), and *Araṇyāni*, the Lady of the Forest, a nature goddess of little importance who is praised in one very late hymn (p. 356); none of these, however, played a significant part in the cult.

At a remote period the ancestors of the Āryans, Iranians, Greeks, Romans, Germans, Slavs and Celts had similar, if not identical, beliefs; but by the time the Āryans had entered India their religion had developed far from the old Indo-European faith. The great father god of the Indo-European peoples, who appears in Greek as *Zeus* and in Latin as *Ju-piter*, was known to the Āryans as *Dyaus*, the personified heavens, but his star had already set. Father Heaven was often mentioned as the parent of other divinities, but few hymns were composed in his honour, and he was eclipsed by his children.

From the point of view of the Āryan warrior the greatest god was Indra, who fulfilled the dual function of war-god and weather-god. Though his name was different he had many of the characteristics of the Greek Zeus and the Germanic Thor. As Indra *tonans* he rode at the head of the Āryan host and destroyed the fortresses of the Dāsas; as Indra *pluvius* he slew the evil dragon Vṛtra who held back the waters, and thus he brought rain to the parched land (p. 353ff). Indra was associated with storm and thunder, and, like Zeus and Thor, his hand bore the thunderbolt (*vajra*), with which he destroyed his enemies. He was a rowdy amoral deity, fond of feasting and drinking. One hymn, according to the usual interpretation, shows us the drunken Indra bragging in his cups, though it may well represent the feelings of a worshipper who has drunk liberally of the sacred drink *soma*:

"Like wild winds
the draughts have raised me up. Have I been drinking soma

"The draughts have borne me up,
as swift steeds a chariot. Have I ...?

"Frenzy has come upon me,
as a cow to her dear calf. Have I ...?

"As a carpenter bends the seat of a chariot
I bend this frenzy round my heart. Have I ...?

"Not even as a mote in my eye
do the five tribes count with me. Have I ...?

"The heavens above
do not equal one half of me. Have I ...?

"In my glory I have passed beyond the sky
and the great earth. Have I ...?

"I will pick up the earth,
and put it here or put it there. Have I ...?"[1]

With Indra in his course across the sky rode the bright host of *Maruts*, singing martial songs as they aided the war-god in his battles. They were the lesser spirits of the storm, conceived on the analogy of the host of Āryan warriors charging into battle beside their leader. The Āryans evidently had many legends in which Indra was the protagonist, but none of them can be reconstructed in detail from the cryptic allusions of the hymns. Two of Indra's traits connect him with Indo-European mythology, for they were applied to various gods and heroes throughout ancient Europe—he was a dragon-slayer (p. 353), and a wild rider of the storm. The former feature of his character may have been a very early borrowing from Mesopotamia.

Several gods were associated with the sun. *Sūrya* (the common word for sun) drove across the sky in a flaming chariot, like the Greek Helios. *Savitṛ*, the Stimulator, was another solar god, a beautiful verse in whose honour is the most holy of all the verses of the Veda (p. 140). *Pūṣan* too was in some measure a solar god, driving daily across the sky, but his main function was that of guardian of roads, herdsmen and straying cattle. *Viṣṇu*, a god connected in part with the sacrifice, also had solar characteristics, covering the earth in three paces, a trait which he retained in later Hinduism, when his importance greatly increased. On the fringes of the solar pantheon was *Sūryā*, the sun-god's daughter, who seems never to have been worshipped, but merely served to connect her two husbands, the *Aśvins* ("Horsemen" also called *Nāsatyas*), with the sun; these are described as driving across the sky in their three-wheeled chariot, but in the hymns they are not closely associated with natural phenomena. They are twins—a fact which connects them with the Greek Dioscuri and twin gods of pre-Christian Baltic mythology. The Aśvins appear chiefly as helpers of men; among their many good deeds they are said to have rescued shipwrecked mariners, provided artificial legs for the maimed, and found husbands for old maids.

The fire-god, *Agni* (which means simply "fire", and is related to the Latin *ignis*), was the object of much primitive mysticism and speculation. He was the god of the priest, who dealt with him at the fire-sacrifice; he was also the god of the home, for he dwelt in the domestic hearth; he was the intermediary between gods and men, for he consumed the sacrifice and carried it to the gods. He dwelt in the waters of heaven in the form of lightning, and on earth in many forms. He was hidden in the fire-sticks, with which the sacrificial fire was kindled and which were personified as his parents. Agni, in fact, was here, there and everywhere. Was there only one Agni, or were there many Agnis? How could Agni be one and many at the same time? Questions like these are asked in the *Ṛg Veda*, and show the earliest signs of the tendency towards monism, which was to bear fruit in the Upaniṣads.

Soma was a divinity of special character. Soma was originally a plant, not certainly identified, from which a potent drink was produced, which was drunk only at sacrifices, and which caused the most invigorating effects, as we have seen from the hymn quoted above. The Zoroastrians of Persia had a similar drink, which they called *haoma*, the same word as soma in its Iranian form; the plant identified with *haoma* by the modern Pārsīs is a bitter herb, which has no specially inebriating qualities, and which is therefore not the soma of the Veda. The drink prepared from the plant can scarcely have been alcoholic, for it was made with great ceremony in the course of the sacrifice, when the herb was pressed between stones, mixed with milk, strained and drunk on the same day. Sugar and honey, which produce fermentation, were not usually mixed with it, and the brief period between its brewing and consumption cannot have been long enough for the generation of alcohol in appreciable quantity. The effects of soma, with vivid hallucinations and the sense of expanding to enormous dimensions, are rather like those attributed to such drugs as hashish. Soma may well have been hemp, which grows wild in many parts of India, Central Asia and South Russia, and from which modern Indians produce a narcotic drink called *bhang*.

Like many ancient peoples the Indians connected the growth of plants with the moon, with which Soma, the king of plants, was later identified. So important was the god Soma considered by the ancient editors of the *Ṛg Veda* that they extracted all the hymns in his honour and placed them in a separate "book" (*maṇḍala*), the ninth of the ten which constitute the whole. He was the special god of the brāhmaṇs, who referred to him as their "king" or patron deity. He is sometimes even called the king of the gods, but by the ordinary Āryan it is doubtful if he was so highly esteemed.

Varuṇa, second only to Indra in importance, was a god of a type rather different from the others. He is known as an *Asura*, a term, also applied to certain lesser gods, which in later Hinduism came to mean a class of demons, but which was in Persia adopted by the reformer Zarathuštra in its local form as part of the title of the great god of light, Ahura Mazda. Just as the shadowy Dyaus represents the high god of the Indo-European peoples before their separation, so Varuna may have been the high god of the Indo-Iranians before the two peoples divided, one to settle in N.-W. India and the other in the Persian highlands. The name is connected by some authorities with the shadowy Greek heaven-god Uranus. At the time of the composition of the Veda, Varuṇa's prestige was waning before that of Indra, but he retained some importance for many centuries.

Varuṇa was first and foremost a king—not a boisterous tribal war-lord, like Indra, but a mighty emperor, sitting in a great palace in the heavens, often with associated gods around him. Most important of these was *Mitra*, a god with some solar characteristics, but mainly connected with vows and compacts. Mitra was represented in the Zoroastrian pantheon, and, under his Greco-Iranian name Mithras, was widely worshipped in the Roman Empire in early Christian times. Around Varuna sat his scouts or spies (*spaś*), who flew all over the world and brought back reports on the conduct of mortals.

Varuṇa was the guardian of *Ṛta*, the cosmic order, a concept which was perhaps the highest flight of Ṛg Vedic thought. The world takes its regular course, day follows night and season succeeds season, because of Ṛta; man must live according to Ṛta; in later days "non-ṛta" (*anṛta*) became one of the commonest words for untruth and sin. Ṛta depended on Varuṇa, who was sometimes looked on as its maker, and was thus a sort of creator-god.

Of all the Āryan gods Varuṇa was ethically the highest. He was always aware of the deeds of men, and was omnipresent, in the theistic as opposed to the pantheistic sense. Two men, even in the most secret of places or at the ends of the earth, cannot make plans alone—a third person, Varuṇa, is always there.[2] The worshipper approached Varuṇa in a spirit different from that in which he prayed to the other gods, most of whom were lively, cheerful fellows, whom men need not fear if they offered regular sacrifices. Varuṇa was so pure and holy that the mere performance of sacrifice would not ensure his favour, for he abhorred sin, or that which was not conformable to Ṛta. The idea of sin included many purely ritual sins and breaches of taboo, but it also certainly included lying, which Varuṇa and Mitra particularly loathed, and evil deeds prompted by anger, drink, gambling, and the influence of wicked men. When he sang to Varuṇa the cheerful Vedic poet often put on sackcloth and ashes, and prayed to his deity with fear and trembling, for Varuṇa was the severe punisher of sin. Not only did Varuṇa punish the sins of the individual but, like the Yahweh of the Old Testament, he visited the sins of his ancestors upon him, and his ubiquity ensured that there was no escape for the sinner. He caught and bound evil-doers in his snares, so that they became diseased, especially with dropsy, and when they died they descended to the "House of Gay", apparently a sort of gloomy subterranean Sheol, very different from the happy "World of the Fathers", the Āryan heaven.

So humble was the worshipper in Varuṇa's presence, so conscious of weakness, guilt and shortcoming, that on reading the hymns to Varuṇa one is inevitably reminded of the penitential psalms of the Old Testament. It has been suggested that Varuṇa owes much of his character to Semitic influence—certainly not to the Jews, for the penitential psalms were composed after the hymns to Varuṇa, and as far as we know the early Hebrews never came in contact with the Āryans, but perhaps to the Babylonians, who often approached their gods in a similar penitential spirit. We quote a typical hymn to Varuṇa; it is obviously the prayer of a man afflicted with dropsy.

> "Let me not go to the House of Clay, O Varuṇa!
> Forgive, O gracious Lord, forgive!
> When I go tottering, like a blown-up bladder,
> forgive, O gracious Lord, forgive!
>
> "Holy One, in want of wisdom I have opposed you.
> Forgive, O gracious Lord, forgive!
> Though in the midst of waters, thirst has seized your worshipper.
> Forgive, O gracious Lord, forgive!
>
> "Whatever sin we mortals have committed
> against the people of the gods,
> if, foolish, we have thwarted your decrees,
> O god, do not destroy us in your anger!"[3]

Yama, lord of the dead, was a sort of Adam, the first man to die, who became guardian of the World of the Fathers, where the blessed dead, those who have performed the rites of the Āryans, feast joyfully forever.

Rudra (perhaps meaning "the Howler"), like Varuṇa, had a dangerous side to his character, but, unlike Varuṇa, was quite amoral. He resembled the Greek Apollo in that he was an archer-god, whose arrows brought disease. Like Indra he was associated with the storm, but he lacked Indra's popular and genial character. He was a remote god, dwelling in the mountains, and was generally an object of fear, invoked to ward off his arrows of plague and disaster. He had, however, a beneficent aspect, for he was guardian of healing herbs, and as such might give health to those whom he capriciously favoured.

There were many other gods, such as *Tvaṣṭṛ*, the Vedic Vulcan, *Aryaman*, guardian of compacts and marriage, and *Vāyu*, the wind-god, who, though important, cannot be described here. There were also demigods of various kinds, among them *Viśvedevas*, a vague group of indeterminate deities, the *Maruts*, or storm-spirits, already mentioned, *Ṛbhus*, gnomes who worked in metal, *Gandharvas*, divine musicians, originally a single divinity but later looked on as many, and the lovely *Apsarases*, comparable to the nymphs of Greece, who might become the mistresses of gods and men.

No Homer or Hesiod attempted to construct a definitive genealogy of all these gods; their relationships are usually vague, and there is no tidy scheme of precedence among them. Each god must have had his own special devotees and priests, and the *Ṛg Veda* is the result of an imperfect syncretism of many tribal beliefs and cults. Already in the latest stratum of the Vedic hymns gods are equated or paired together, and there are doubts as to which god is really the greatest. In one hymn[4] this important question is asked as a refrain to every verse—"Whom, then, shall we honour with our oblations?"; later theologians were so puzzled by this that they decided that there was a god called *Ka* (Who?), to whom the hymn was addressed.

Sacrifice

The centre of the Āryan cult was sacrifice. The cult of the domestic hearth existed in many ancient Indo-European communities, and small domestic sacrifices, performed by the head of the house, must have been as important in the days of the *Ṛg Veda* as they were in later Hinduism, but the earliest texts describing them are the *Gṛhya Sūtras* (p. 97) of a much more recent period. The *Ṛg Veda* is rather concerned with great sacrifices, paid for by chiefs and wealthier tribesmen. They were already complex rites involving much preparation, the slaughter of numerous animals, and the participation of several well-trained priests.

The main purpose of the sacrifice was the gratification of the gods in order to obtain boons from them. The gods descended to the sacred straw (*barhis*) on the sacrificial field, drank and ate with the worshippers, and duly rewarded them with success in war, progeny, increase of cattle and long life, on a *quid prō quo* basis. The solemn Varuṇa and the grim and unpredictable Rudra are exceptional in the Vedic pantheon. Most of the gods were good natured. Guilt-offerings and thank-offerings, of the kind offered by the ancient Hebrews, are almost unheard of in the Veda.

Nevertheless the ceremony must have had its element of awe and wonder. The worshippers, inebriated with soma, saw wondrous visions of the gods; they experienced strange sensations of power; they could reach up and touch the heavens; they became immortal; they were gods themselves. The priests, who alone knew the rituals and formulae whereby the gods were brought to the sacrifice, were masters of a great mystery. With these ideas, which are explicitly stated in the hymns, went others less obvious. Often in the *Ṛg Veda* we read of a mysterious entity called *brahman*; in many contexts brahman is the magical power in the sacred utterance (*mantra*), but sometimes it has a wider connotation, and implies a sort of supernatural electricity, known to students of primitive religion as *mana*. The possessor of brahman, by a common process of secondary word formation in Sanskrit, became known as *brāhmaṇa** the tribal priest and magician. In later Vedic times the connection of brahman with speech became more and more pronounced, and the brāhmaṇ's magic was thought to lie in the words he uttered. The words and syllables of the Veda were analysed, and, though the texts were still unwritten, the letters of the alphabet were recognized and

* In the Edda the god Wodan, in order to obtain magic power, is sacrificed by himself to himself.

personified as eternal divinities. The metres used in the Veda were also thought of as gods. Later certain syllables were believed to be particularly holy, notably *ŌM* (the *praṇava*), which contains the essence of the Vedas and is pregnant with the utmost power and mystery.

A second conception, which is hinted at in many hymns of the *Ṛg Veda*, and becomes prominent in the latest stratum, is also widely known in primitive religions—the mystical identification of god, victim and sacrificer. From these ideas the sacrifice obtained an even greater importance in the scheme of things than it had had at the time of the composition of the earlier parts of the *Ṛg Veda*. By the end of the period it was widely believed that the universe itself arose from a primeval sacrifice.

Though Varuṇa may sometimes have been looked on as a sort of creator, and there are suggestions of Indra's having fulfilled the same function (p. 353), there is no clearly defined creator-god in the main body of the *Ṛg Veda*. By the end of the Ṛg Vedic period, however, such a god had developed, whether wholly from the speculations of the brāhmaṇs or from non-Āryan influences. This god was *Prajāpati*, "the Lord of Beings", often identified with *Brahmā*, the masculine form of the neuter *brahman*. Prajāpati was thought of as a primeval man (*puruṣa*), who existed before the foundation of the universe. The man was sacrificed, presumably to himself, by the gods, who apparently were his children. From the body of the divine victim the universe was produced. The "Hymn of the Primeval Man", in which this first cosmic sacrifice is described, bristles with obscurities, but its purport is quite clear.

"When the gods made a sacrifice
with the Man as their victim,
Spring was the melted butter, Summer the fuel,
and Autumn the oblation.

"From that all-embracing sacrifice
the clotted butter was collected.
From it he* made the animals
of air and wood and village.

"From that all-embracing sacrifice
were born the hymns and chants,
from that the metres were born,
from that the sacrificial spells were born.

"Thence were born horses,
and all beings with two rows of teeth.
Thence were born cattle,
and thence goats and sheep.

* Presumably "the Man" Prajāpati himself, who survived his own dismemberment.

"When they divided the Man,
    into how many parts did they divide him?
What was his mouth, what were his arms,
    what were his thighs and his feet called?

"The brāhmaṇ was his mouth,
    of his arms was made the warrior,
his thighs became the vaiśya,
    of his feet the śūdra was born.

"The moon arose from his mind,
    from his eye was born the sun,
from his mouth Indra and Agni,
    from his breath the wind was born.

"From his navel came the air,
    from his head there came the sky,
from his feet the earth, the four quarters from his ear,
    thus they fashioned the worlds.

"With Sacrifice the gods sacrificed to Sacrifice—
    these were the first of the sacred laws.
These mighty beings reached the sky,*
    where are the eternal spirits, the gods."[5]

By this time a new attitude to the sacrifice had developed, and the rite had become a supernal mystery. By means of it the priests mystically repeated the primeval sacrifice, and the world was born anew. Without regular sacrifices all cosmic processes would cease, and chaos would come again. Thus the order of nature was on ultimate analysis not dependent on the gods at all, but on the brāhmaṇs, who by the magic of the sacrifice maintained and compelled them. The brāhmaṇ was more powerful than any earthly king or any god; by his accurate performance of sacrifice he maintained all things, and was therefore the supreme social servant; by the slightest variation of ritual he could turn the sacrifice against his patrons and destroy them, and was therefore the most dangerous of enemies. This is the basic doctrine of the *Brāhmaṇas*, and it prevailed in many Āryan communities in North India from about 900 B.C. onwards, and left its mark on Hinduism in the exaltation of the brāhmaṇ, In this period many of the old gods of the *Ṛg Veda* lost their greatness, and became comparatively unimportant, while others rose in popularity, notably Viṣṇu and Rudra; the latter was already sometimes called by the epithet *Śiva*, "the Propitious", originally a deprecatory euphemism.

---

* It is not clear who are the mighty beings referred to. They are not the gods themselves, and the last verse may be a later addition.

New Developments of Doctrine

As Āryan culture pressed further down the Gangā it absorbed new ideas about the after-life. In the *Ṛg Veda* the fate of the dead seems to have been finally decided when they died—they went either to the "World of the Fathers" or to the "House of Clay", where they remained indefinitely. But in one late hymn[6] it is suggested in cryptic language that they might pass to the waters or remain in plants. This may be a reference to metempsychosis in the crude form believed in by many primitive peoples, according to which the souls of the dead pass to animals, plants or natural objects before being reborn in a human body. The *Brāhmaṇa* literature, which had lost the optimism of the *Ṛg Veda*, recognized the possibility of death even in heaven.

In the *Bṛhadāraṇyaka Upaniṣad*[7] the first form of the doctrine of transmigration is given. The souls of those who have lived lives of sacrifice, charity and austerity, after certain obscure peregrinations, pass to the World of the Fathers, the paradise of Yama; thence, after a period of bliss, they go to the moon; from the moon they go to empty space, whence they pass to the air, and descend to earth in the rain. There they "become food, … and are offered again in the altar fire which is man, to be born again in the fire of woman", while the unrighteous are reincarnated as worms, birds or insects. This doctrine, which seems to rest on a primitive belief that conception occurred through the eating by one of the parents of a fruit or vegetable containing the latent soul of the offspring, is put forward as a rare and new one, and was not universally held at the time of the composition of the Upaniṣad. Even in the days of the Buddha, transmigration may not have been believed in by everyone, but it seems to have gained ground very rapidly in the 7th and 6th centuries B.C. Thus the magnificently logical Indian doctrines of *saṃsāra*, or transmigration, and *karma*, the result of the deeds of one life affecting the next, had humble beginnings in a soul theory of quite primitive type; but even at this early period they had an ethical content, and had attained some degree of elaboration.

In whatever way the doctrine of transmigration was developed it involved belief in the repeated passage of the soul from life to life, either for all eternity or for an inestimably long time. It linked all forms of life into a single system. The gods themselves must pass away, and be replaced by other gods. As one Indra died, another was born. The souls of the departed, though now in bliss, would sooner or later pass to new abodes. Animals, insects, and according to some sects plants, all lived under the same law. With remarkable imaginative insight some sages taught that even water, dust and air were filled with minute animalculæ, and that these too had souls which were the same, in essence, as those of men. The whole of life thus passed through innumerable changes.

It was generally, though not universally, thought that these changes were determined by conduct. As one behaved in the present life so one's status in the scale of existence would in future be exalted or abased, and one's lot would be happy or wretched. This doctrine of *karma* (literally "deed") soon became fundamental to most Indian thought. It provided a satisfactory explanation of the mystery of suffering, which has troubled many thoughtful souls all over the world, and it justified the manifest social inequalities of the Āryan community.

To the ordinary man such a doctrine might not appear distasteful, and the fact that it quickly obtained almost universal acceptance shows that it met in great measure ancient India's spiritual needs. Indeed in many respects the idea of saṃsāra, which offers infinite potentialities of new experience to the soul, and which holds out hope even to the humblest of living things and the most evil of beings, might seem more attractive than the traditional static heaven and hell of the West. But to many earnest people the thought of transmigration was not pleasant. Death was always terrible, and the prospect of having to die innumerable times was not a happy one. Life, even when devoid of the major sorrows, was drab and inadequate, while continual rebirth seemed monotonously boring. The growth of the doctrine of transmigration coincided with the development of pessimistic ideas. Rebirth in heaven was not enough—a way had to be found to escape the cycle of birth and death altogether. It was found, to the satisfaction of the best minds of the times, in mystical knowledge, achieved by much meditation and asceticism.

Asceticism

In a late hymn of the *Ṛg Veda*[8] we read of a class of holy men different from the brāhmaṇs, the "silent ones" (*munis*), who wear the wind as a girdle, and who, drunk with their own silence, rise on the wind and fly in the paths of the demigods and birds. The muni knows all men's thoughts, for he has drunk of the magic cup of Rudra, which is poison to ordinary mortals. Another class of early ascetic, much mentioned in the *Atharva Veda*,[9] was the *vrātya*. This term, in its later broad meaning, implied an Āryan who had fallen from the faith and no longer respected the Vedas; but the vrātya of the *Atharva Veda* was a priest of a non-Vedic fertility cult, which involved ritual dancing and flagellation. He travelled from place to place in a cart, with a woman whom he prostituted, and a musician who performed for him at his rites. The status and nature of the vrātyas are still not wholly clear, but it is evident that great efforts were made to convert them to the Āryan faith and to find room for them in the orthodox cult, and they were probably one of the chief sources of the new doctrines and practices.

By the time of the Upaniṣads asceticism had become very widespread, and it was through the ascetics, rather than the orthodox sacrificial priests, that the new teachings developed and spread. Some ascetics were solitary psychopaths, dwelling in the depths of the forests, and suffering self-inflicted tortures of hunger, thirst, heat, cold and rain. Others dwelt in "penance-grounds" on the outskirts of towns, where, like some of the less reputable holy-men of later times, they would indulge in fantastic self-torture, sitting near blazing fires in the hot sun, lying on beds of thorns or spikes, hanging for hours head downwards from the branches of trees, or holding their arms motionless above their heads until they atrophied.

Most of the new developments in thought, however, came from ascetics of less rigorous discipline, whose chief practices were the mental and spiritual exercises of meditation. Some of these dwelt alone on the outskirts of towns and villages, while others lived in huts, under the leadership of an elder. Others wandered, often in large groups, begging alms, proclaiming their doctrines to all who wished to listen, and disputing with their rivals. Some were completely naked, while others wore simple garments.

The original motive of Indian asceticism was the acquisition of magical power. The brāhmaṇs claimed this already, by virtue of their birth and training, but there were other types of power, obtainable by other means. By the time of the Upaniṣads faith in the cosmic mystery of the sacrifice had perhaps begun to wane, even among the brāhmaṇs themselves. Though sacrificial mysticism did not immediately disappear the rite once more came to be thought of as a means of obtaining prosperity, long life, and rebirth in heaven, rather than of sustaining the cosmos. Indeed the wealthy patrons of sacrifices had probably always had the former as their main motive. In the eastern parts of the Gangā Basin Brāhmaṇism was not so deeply entrenched as in the west, and older non-Āryan currents of belief flowed more strongly. The sacrificial cult did not wholly meet the needs of these lands, where firmly founded kingdoms were growing in power and material civilization was rapidly progressing.

The ascetic, even though his penance was of the most severe type, rose far above the heights achieved by the sacrificial priest. Once he had inured his body to pain and privation immeasurable joys awaited him. The hermit of the lower type had much to look forward to even on the material plane, in the form of honour and respect which as an ordinary man he could never hope for, and complete freedom dom from worldly cares and fears. This sense of freedom, of a great load lifted from one's shoulders by casting aside one's family and possessions, is evident in many passages of calm joy in the religious literature of India. But there were greater incentives to asceticism than these. As he advanced in his self-training the hermit acquired powers beyond those of ordinary mortals. He saw past, present and future; he mounted the heavens, and was graciously received at the courts of the gods, while divinities descended to earth and visited him in his hermitage. By the magical power acquired through his asceticism he could work miracles—he could crumble mountains into the sea; if offended, he could burn up his enemies with the glance of his eye, or cause the crops of a whole people to fail; if respected, his magical power could protect a great city, increase its wealth, and defend it from famine, pestilence and invasion. In fact the magic potency formerly ascribed to the sacrifice now began to be attributed to asceticism. In the succeeding age the idea that the universe was founded and maintained through sacrifice slipped into the background; in its place it was widely believed that the cosmos depended on the penances of the great god Śiva, meditating for ever in the fastnesses of the Himālayas, and on the continued austerities of his human followers.

If ascetism had its charms even for the less spiritual, they were still greater for the questing souls who took to a life of hardship from truly religious motives.

As his mystical exercises developed his psychic faculties, the ascetic obtained insight which no words could express. Gradually plumbing the cosmic mystery, his soul entered realms far beyond the comparatively tawdry heavens where the great gods dwelt in light and splendour. Going "from darkness to darkness deeper yet" he solved the mystery beyond all mysteries; he understood, fully and finally, the nature of the universe and of himself, and he reached a realm of truth and bliss, beyond birth and death, joy and sorrow, good and evil. And with this transcendent knowledge came another realization—he was completely, utterly, free. He had found ultimate salvation, the final triumph of the soul. The ascetic who reached the goal of his quest was a conqueror above all conquerors. There was none greater than he in the whole universe.

The metaphysical interpretation of the ascetic's mystical knowledge varied from sect to sect, but the fundamental experience was the same, and, as has been many times pointed out, was not appreciably different from that of the Western saints and mystics, whether Greek, Jewish, Christian or Muslim. But Indian mysticism is unique in its elaboration of techniques for inducing ecstasy, and in the complex metaphysical systems built upon interpretations of mystical experience. Where in other religions mysticism is of varying importance, in those of India it is fundamental.

The great development of asceticism and mysticism soon became too strong for the more earthbound and materialistic Brāhmaṇism to ignore. Places were found for the hermit and the wandering ascetic in the Āryan social structure by the formula of the four stages of life (p. 137f), which first appear in the Dharma Sūtras. Accounts of the discussions and teachings of some of the more orthodox of the early mystics were collected and added to the Brāhmaṇas as Āraṇyakas and Upaniṣads. A little later short treatises of mystical character were composed in verse, and also appended to the Brāhmaṇas as Upaniṣads. Later still a system of mystical training, often known as *yoga* ("union") (p. 285ff), was accepted as an orthodox element of the Hindu system. Indian religion had taken a new direction.

It has been suggested that the development of ascetic and mystical doctrines, especially in the heterodox systems of Buddhism and Jainism, represents a reaction of the warrior class to the pretensions of the brāhmaṇs and to the sterility of the sacrificial cult. This, however, is certainly not the whole truth. Buddha and Mahāvīra, the founder of Jainism, were kṣatriyas; they proclaimed the futility of sacrifice, and more than one passage in the Buddhist scriptures may be interpreted in an anti-brāhmaṇic sense. But many of the teachers of the new doctrines were themselves brāhmaṇs. The Upaniṣads, which represent the thought of the more orthodox mystics, in no way oppose sacrifice, but maintain its qualified validity; and passages speaking respectfully of brāhmaṇs are quite as frequent in the Buddhist scriptures as those which disparage them.

There was certainly some opposition to brāhmaṇic pretensions, and dissatisfaction with the sacrificial cult; but behind this, and the growth of pessimism, asceticism and mysticism, lay a deep psychological anxiety. The time of which we speak was one of great social change, when old tribal units were breaking up. The feeling of group solidarity which the tribe gave was removed, and men stood face to face with the world, with no refuge in their kinsmen. Chieftains were overthrown, their courts dispersed, their lands and tribesmen absorbed in the greater kingdoms. A new order was coming into being. "[Great heroes and mighty kings] have had to give up their glory; we have seen the deaths of [demigods and demons]; the oceans have dried up; mountains have crumbled; the Pole Star is shaken; the Earth founders; the gods perish. I am like a frog in a dry well"; so speaks a king in one of the Upaniṣads.[10] Despite the great growth of material civilization at the time the hearts of many men were failing them for fear of what should come to pass upon earth. It is chiefly to this deep feeling of insecurity that we must attribute the growth of pessimism and asceticism in the middle centuries of the first millennium B.C.

Speculation and Gnosis

Asceticism was not merely a means of escape from an unhappy and unsatisfying world; it had a positive aspect, for it was in part inspired by a desire for knowledge, for the wisdom which the four Vedas could not give. Thus the growth of asceticism is not only a measure of the psychological uncertainty of the times, but also of their thirst for knowledge. It is not just to India to stigmatize her ancient wisdom as mere "life-negation".

All through the first millennium B.C. intelligent minds in India were striving for convincing explanations of the cosmic mystery. In the latest phase of the *Ṛg Veda* poets began to wonder about creation, which was not adequately explained by the current mythology. As we have seen, creation was thought of by some as the effect of a primeval sacrifice. It was also suggested that it was due to a sort of sexual act;[11] elsewhere the world was said to have originated in a "Golden Embryo" (*Hiraṇyagarbha*),[12] the prototype of the Cosmic Egg (p. 439) of later Hindu mythology. In one hymn the poet states that the world arose from warmth (*tapas*, later usually meaning penance or asceticism), and then rather regretfully admits that he is not sure of this hypothesis, and suggests that perhaps even the high god Prajāpati does not know the truth.

This wonderful "Hymn of Creation", one of the oldest surviving records of philosophic doubt in the history of the world, marks the development of a high stage of abstract thinking, and it is the work of a very great poet, whose vision of the mysterious chaos before creation, and of mighty ineffable forces working in the depths of the primeval void, is portrayed with impressive economy of language.

> "Then even nothingness was not, nor existence.
>   There was no air then, nor the heavens beyond it.
> What covered it? Where was it? In whose keeping?
>   Was there then cosmic water, in depths unfathomed?

"Then there were neither death nor immortality,
nor was there then the torch of night and day.
The One breathed windlessly and self-sustaining.
There was that One then, and there was no other.

"At first there was only darkness wrapped in darkness
All this was only unillumined water.
That One which came to be, enclosed in nothing,
arose at last, born of the power of heat.

"In the beginning desire descended on it—
that was the primal seed, born of the mind.
The sages who have searched their hearts with wisdom
know that which is is kin to that which is not.

"And they have stretched their cord across the void,
and know what was above, and what below.*
Seminal powers made fertile mighty forces.
Below was strength, and over it was impulse.

"But, after all, who knows, and who can say
whence it all came, and how creation happened?
The gods themselves are later than creation,
so who knows truly whence it has arisen?

"Whence all creation had its origin,
he, whether he fashioned it or whether he did not,
he, who surveys it all from highest heaven,
he knows—or maybe even he does not know."[13]

In the centuries succeeding the composition of the *Ṛg Veda*, however, speculation was mainly concerned with the symbolism of the sacrifice.

"Dawn is the head of the sacrificial horse, the sun its eye, the wind its breath, fire its mouth; the year is the body of the sacrificial horse, heaven its back, the sky its belly, earth its chest, the four quarters its sides … the seasons its limbs, the months and fortnights its joints; days and nights are its feet, the stars its bones, the heavens its flesh. Its half-digested food is sand, its bowels the rivers, its liver and lungs the mountains, its hair plants and trees. When the sun rises it is the horse's fore-quarters, when it sets it is its hind-quarters. When the horse shakes itself it lightens; when it kicks, it thunders; when it makes water, it rains. Sound is its voice."[14]

* My translation of this obscure verse is very free.

The symbolism of the sacrifice was carried much further than this. Every word or action of the ritual was identified with some aspect of the cosmos. The intellectual ingenuity spent on this process of finding *pratīkas* or symbols must have been considerable, but it was largely sterile. Yet the questing spirit of the "Hymn of Creation" never wholly disappeared, and in the 6th century B.C. it bore fruit in a great wave of thought which was to alter the whole religious life of India.

The early Upaniṣads and the scriptures of Buddhism and Jainism, all of which look back to the 7th or 6th centuries B.C. (though the latter were much later in their final composition), show that there existed a bewildering variety of speculations and theories on the origin of the universe, the nature of the soul, and kindred problems. Some of these were accepted by one or other brāhmaṇic school and incorporated into orthodox belief. Others were the germinal bases of heterodox sects, two of which survive to this day, but most of which have long since vanished, and are only remembered in passing references in the scriptures of their opponents.

Among the more orthodox teachings we find creation ascribed to the self-consciousness of the primeval Person (*Puruṣa*, i.e. Prajāpati), who felt fear, loneliness, and the need of companionship. The Person divided himself, and produced a wife. This couple, taking the forms of animals and men, created the whole universe.[15] The idea of creation by a cosmic sexual act was one which played a great part in later religious thought. The theme is repeated in various forms in later Vedic literature, in some of which *tapas*—the power derived from asceticism—is an essential feature in the process of creation—a significant shifting of emphasis from the older theory that the world depended on a primeval sacrifice.

Other more heterodox teachers put forward naturalistic and atheistic cosmogonic theories. Some believed that the world began as water; others postulated fire, wind, or ether (*ākāśa*, p. 499) as the ultimate basis of the universe. For some the universe was based neither on a deity nor even on an impersonal entity, but on a principle— fate (*niyati*), time (*kāla*), nature (*svabhāva*), or chance (*saṃgati*). It was suggested that the world developed not by the intervention of god or forces external to it, but by a process of internal evolution or "ripening" (*pariṇāma*). Some teachers, like the Buddha, taught that speculation on first causes was a futile waste of time. There were out-and-out pyrrhonists, denying the possibility of any certain knowledge at all, and materialists, who rejected the existence of the soul and all other immaterial entities, while some teachers proclaimed that the world was made of eternal atoms. The intellectual life of India in the 7th and 6th centuries B.C. was as vigorous and pullulating as the jungle after rains.

The propogators of these doctrines, even of materialism and scepticism, were nearly all ascetics, though the literature of the time mentions more than one king who took a keen interest in the new ideas. Chief of these philosopher kings were Janaka of Videha and Ajātaśatru of Kāil (Vārāṇasī), both of whom probably lived in the 7th century B.C. The forest hermits (*vānaprastha*) seem to have departed less far from Vedic orthodoxy than the wanderers (*parivrājaka*), who maintained a bewildering variety of doctrines. It was chiefly among the former that the literature of the Upaniṣads developed.

The term Upaniṣad means literally "a session", sitting at the feet of a master who imparts esoteric doctrines. There are said to be 108 Upaniṣads altogether, but many of these are late sectarian works of little importance. The earlier Upaniṣads, like the great *Bṛhadāraṇyaka* and the *Chāndogya*, are in prose and consist of a series of short expositions of some aspect of the new doctrines, often in the form of question and answer. The Upaniṣads of somewhat later composition, like the *Kaṭha* and the *Śvetāśvatara*, are in verse, and their contents are more closely integrated. Though the speculations of the Upaniṣads differ very considerably, their main purport is the same. One entity, often called *Brahman*, the term used in the *Ṛg Veda* to mean the magic of the sacred word (p. 209), fills all space and time. This is the ground beyond and below all forms and phenomena, and from it the whole Universe, including the gods themselves, has emerged.

The great and saving knowledge which the Upaniṣads claim to impart lies not in the mere recognition of the existence of Brahman, but in continual consciousness of it. For Brahman resides in the human soul—indeed Brahman *is* the human soul, is *Ātman*, the Self. When a man realizes this fact fully he is wholly freed from transmigration. His soul becomes one with Brahman, and he transcends joy and sorrow, life and death. In sleep a man's spirit is set free; it wanders through the universe as a bird or a god, it becomes a king or a brāhmaṇ. Beyond dreaming is dreamless sleep, where the soul's experiences are such that they cannot be expressed; and beyond this again is Brahman. When he reaches Brahman, man is free.

In their struggle to express the inexpressible the sages of the Upaniṣads used imagery of every kind. Sometimes the idea of the soul is rather primitive, and it is described as a tiny manikin in the heart; sometimes it is said to be the breath, or a mysterious fluid which flows in the veins; but sometimes it is thought of as quite incorporeal and immeasurable:

> "'Fetch me a fruit of the banyan tree.'
> "'Here is one, sir.'
> "'Break it.'
> "'I have broken it, sir.'
> "'What do you see?'
> "'Very tiny seeds, sir.
> "'Break one.'
> "'I have broken it, sir.'
> "'Now what do you see?'
> "'Nothing, sir.'
> "'My son,' the father said, 'what you do not perceive is the essence, and in that essence the mighty banyan tree exists. Believe me, my son, in that essence is the Self of all that is. That is the True, that is the Self. And you are that Self, Śvetaketu!'"[16]

Here the soul is the inmost self of the being, in no sense material, though ideas of a sort of soul-stuff, a subtle matter of which the soul was composed, persisted, especially among the Jainas. The term *Ātman* came to mean indiscriminately "soul" and "self", which lends a certain ambiguity to many passages in the Hindu scriptures.

The identity of the souls of the individual and the universe is reiterated throughout the Upaniṣadic literature, with varying emphasis, and with differing interpretations of the nature of the identity and the character of the universal soul. *Tot tvam asi*, "you (the individual) are that (universal essence)", the words of the father to the son in the passage we have quoted, is the leading theme of the Upaniṣads. The one eternal undifferentiated essence, above good and evil, is in a condition of consciousness which is beyond deep sleep (*suṣupti*), but is yet awake and living. Though it fills the whole of space, by a mysterious verity which defies logic but is proved by experience it dwells in the core of the human heart. It is generally thought of as uniform and impersonal, and the word Brahman is of neuter gender. Thus all the multifariousness and incoherence of the universe is explained away, and reduced to a single entity.

> "'Put this salt in water, and come to me in the morning.'
> "The son did as he was told. The father said: 'Fetch the salt.' The son looked for it, but could not find it, because it had dissolved.
> "'Taste the water from the top,' said the father. 'How does it taste?'
> "'Of salt,' the son replied.
> "'Taste from the middle. How does it taste?'
> "'Of salt,' the son replied.
> "'Taste from the bottom. How does it taste?'
> "'Of salt,' the son replied.
> "Then the father said: 'You don't perceive that the one Reality (*sat*) exists in your own body, my son, but it is truly there. Everything which is has its being in that subtle essence. That is Reality! That is the Soul! And you are that, Śvetaketu!'"[17]

The Universal Essence is sometimes defined in purely negative terms. "The Self can only be described as 'Not this, not this'. It is incomprehensible, imperishable, ... unattached, ... unfettered, ... it does not suffer, ... it does not fail."[18] But, despite the negations of this passage, the sage Yājñavalkya, to whom it is attributed, could not escape giving the Universal Essence a degree of personality, and in one place almost identified it with the High God.

> "That great unborn Self, comprised of knowledge, is ... the ether in the heart. In that is the ruler and lord, the king of all things. He grows no greater by good deeds, nor smaller by evil deeds, but he is the lord of all things, the king of all things, the protector of all things."[19]

In the verse Upaniṣads the World Spirit is described rather as a god than as a cosmic essence.

"He encircles all things, radiant and bodyless,
unharmed, and untouched by evil,
All-seeing, all-wise, all-present, self-existent,
he has made all things well for ever and ever."[20]

In the Upaniṣad from which this is taken the World Spirit is referred to as *Īśa*, "the Lord". The *Kaṭka Upaniṣad* calls the Spirit "the Person" (*Puruṣa*), reminding us of the divine victim of the primeval sacrifice from which the world was born. In one passage the World Spirit is mentioned with fear and dread, recalling that earlier felt for the god Varuṇa:

"All things whatever, the whole world,
produced [from Brahman] tremble in its breath.
It is a great terror, an upraised thunderbolt.
They who know this become immortal.

"From terror [of Brahman] the Fire burns.
From terror [of Brahman] the Sun shines.
From fear of Brahman Indra, and the Wind,
and Death as the fifth all run away."[21]

The *Śvetāśvatara Upaniṣad*, which is later than those previously mentioned, describes the World Spirit in completely theistic terms. It is no longer an impersonal essence, but a creator god—in fact the god Rudra, or Śiva. Rudra may be reached not only by meditation and penance, but also by devotion and worship.

"The snarer, who rules alone in his might,
he who governs the world in his power,
is always one and the same,
though all else rise and decay....

"There is one, Rudra alone, ...
who rules the world in his might.
He stands behind all beings, he made all the worlds,
and protects them, and rolls them up at the end of time.

"The Lord lives in the faces of all beings,
in their heads, in their necks.
He lives in the inmost heart of all,
the all-pervading, all-present Śiva."[22]

This brings us very near to the religious atmosphere of the *Bhagavad Gītā*, the most exalted and beautiful of India's religious poems, which teaches a fully-fledged theism and is part of the more recent Hinduism rather than of the old Brāhmaṇism, which slowly changed from a religion of sacrifice to one of devotion.

Ethics of the Upaniṣads

In general the Upaniṣads proclaim salvation by knowledge or realization rather than by faith or works. Their ethics are fundamentally pragmatic. Good and evil are resolved in the all-pervading Brahman, and are relative terms only. From the point of view of the seeker after truth, that is good which leads him to the realization of Brahman, and evil the reverse. Thus anything which discourages the meditative life is ultimately bad, and among the most serious of these obstacles are selfish desires. In more than one context it is said that the universe came into existence through a primeval desire of the World Soul; to attain bliss the hermit must, so to speak, restore the state of things before creation. The normal values of the world, sacrifice, benevolence, and even asceticism, are only good in so far as they lead the soul upwards.

> "There are three branches of the Law. Sacrifice, study and charity are the first, austerity is the second, and to dwell incelibacy in the house of one's teacher … is the third. By all these one only reaches the worlds of the blessed, but the man who is fixed in Brāhmaṇ finds immortality."[23]
>
> "The wise men of old did not want children. 'What should we do with children,' they said, 'when we have Brahman and the world besides?' And they conquered their desire for sons and wealth and the heavenly worlds, and wandered about as beggars. … He who knows [the mystery of Brahman] becomes calm, restrained, satisfied, patient and confident, and he sees himself in the [Great] Self, sees all things as the Self.… Evil does not overcome him, but he overcomes evil. … Free from evil, free from decay, free from hatred, free from thirst, he becomes a [true] brāhmaṇ."[24]

Occasionally it is suggested, especially in the later Upaniṣads, that all desires whatever are incompatible with the saving knowledge.

> "When all desires which cling to the heart
> fall away
> then the mortal becomes immortal,
> and in this life finds Brahman.
>
> "When all the earthly ties of the heart
> are sundered,
> then the mortal becomes immortal.
> This is the end of all instruction."[25]

A life of ascetism was not absolutely necessary to salvation—even kings are said to have realized Brahman while still ruling—but the saving knowledge was at best very hard to obtain, and doubly difficult for one whose mind was full of material cares and desires. All pleasure was therefore suspect.

"The good is one thing and the pleasant another.
Both, with their different ends, control a man.
But it is well with him who chooses the good,
while he who chooses the pleasant misses his mark."[26]

Though often rather negative, the ethical attitude of the Upaniṣads is neither unmoral nor antinomian. He who has not ceased from evil conduct will never obtain Brahman. Here and there are passages of high ethical value among the reiterated mystical similes and parables of the texts. Thus honesty is highly extolled.

"Satyakāma son of Jabālā said to his mother: 'Mother, I want to be a student. What is my family?'

"'I don't know your family, my dear,' she said. 'I had you in my youth, when I travelled about a lot as a servant—and I just don't know! My name is Jabālā, and yours is Satyakāma, so say you are Satyakāma Jabālā.'*

"He went to Gautama Hāridrumata, and said: 'I want to be your student, sir. May I come?'

"'What is your family, my friend?' he asked.

"'I don't know my family, sir,' he answered. 'I asked my mother, and she said that she had me in her youth, when she used to travel about a lot as a servant. … She said that as she was Jabālā and I was Satyakāma I was to give my name as Satyakāma Jabālā.'

"'Nobody but a true brāhmaṇ would be so honest!' he said. … 'Go and fetch me fuel, my friend, and I will initiate you, for you have not swerved from the truth.'"[27]

A further fine ethical passage occurs in the form of a legend in the *Bṛhadāraṇyaka Upaniṣad*. We quote this passage partly because an allusion to it must have puzzled many readers of T. S. Eliot.[28]

"The threefold descendants of Prajāpati, gods, men and demons, were once students at the feet of their father. When they had finished their training the gods said: 'Sir, tell us something [good for our souls]'. He uttered the syllable DA, and then asked them whether they had understood.

"'We understood', they answered. 'You told us *DAmyata* (be self-controlled).' 'Yes,' he said, 'you understood indeed!'

---

* A patronymic, which would give the impression that the boy was the son of a man named Jabālā.

"Then the men asked him, and he uttered the same syllable DA, and then asked them whether they had understood. 'We understood,' they answered. 'You told us *DAtta* (give).' 'Yes,' he said, 'you understood indeed!'

"Then the demons asked him, ... and he uttered the same syllable DA, and then asked them whether they had understood. 'We understood,' they answered. 'You told us *DAyadhvam* (be merciful).' 'Yes,' he said, 'you understood indeed!'

"And the blessed voice of the thunder ever repeats DA DA DA*— be self-controlled, give, be merciful. So these three should ever be taught—self-control, charity and mercy."[29]

Perhaps the highest ethical flight of the Upaniṣads occurs in the instructions said to have been given by Yājñavalkya to his favourite wife before taking up the life of an ascetic. Remembering the double meaning of the word *ātman*, "self" or "soul", the passage may be read in two ways, but the context shows that the Higher Self is intended. This Higher Self, the World Soul, the mystic recognizes in all things, and loves them for their participation with himself in the unity of the spirit. The passage is too long to quote in full, but we paraphrase its most important parts.

"Yājñavalkya had two wives, Maitreyī and Kātyāyanī. Maitreyi knew something of the World Soul, but Kātyāyanī only knew what every woman knows. When he wished to enter on another phase of life Yājñavalkya said: 'Maitreyī, I am leaving home. Let me make a settlement on you and Kātyāyanī.'

"Maitreyī asked: 'My lord, if I owned the whole earth and all its wealth, should I be immortal?'

"'No,' Yājñavalkya replied, 'your life would be the life of the wealthy, and there is no prospect of immortality in wealth.'

"Maitreyī said: 'Of what use to me are things which will not give me immortality? Give me rather your knowledge, my lord.'

"'Lady,' he replied, 'you are truly dear to me, and now you are even dearer. So if you like I will teach you. Listen carefully!

"'A husband is not dear for love of the husband—a husband is dear for love of the Self. Similarly wife, sons, wealth, cattle, priests and warriors, worlds, gods, the Vedas, everything—none of them are dear in their own right, but all are dear for love of the Self.

"'Truly you can see and hear and perceive and know the Self, Maitreyī.

And when you have seen, heard, perceived and known the Self you will know all things.

"'Where there seems to be a duality of self and not-self one sees, smells, tastes, perceives, hears, touches and knows something other. But when all is

*A traditional onomatopæic expression of the sound of thunder.

the Self there is no consciousness of anything other than Self. ... Thus Maitreyī I have instructed you—this is immortality!'

"When he had said this Yājñavalkya went away."[30]

(ii) Buddhism

The Buddha

While the doctrines of the Upaniṣads found a place in the brāhmaṇic system, there were other teachings which could not be harmonized with orthodoxy, but were fostered and developed by heterodox sects. Chief among the teachers of such doctrines was the man who at the end of the sixth and the beginning of the fifth century B.C. established a community of yellow-robed followers, and was known by them as the *Buddha*, the Enlightened or Awakened. Even if judged only by his posthumous effects on the world at large he was certainly the greatest man to have been born in India.

The traditional story of the Buddha, like those of most saints and heroes of ancient days, has suffered much at the hands of higher criticism. The story of his birth and early life appears only in the later books of the Buddhist Scriptures, and many of the references to him in those parts of the canon which purport to give his teachings verbatim are by no means reliable. Even the "Sermon of the Turning of the Wheel of the Law", which is said to be the first sermon preached after the Buddha's enlightenment, and which is the basic teaching of all Buddhist sects, is of dubious authenticity, and in the form in which we have it is not among the earliest parts of the canon. Much doubt now exists as to the real doctrines of the historical Buddha, as distinct from those of Buddhism. One eminent authority suggested that they differed but little from the teachings of the Upanisadic sages,[31] while another held that he rejected the doctrine of transmigration, and taught merely the almost self-evident truism that one generation is affected by the deeds of the preceding one.[32] We here discuss, however, not the life of the Buddha, but what his later followers believed about his life, and not what he taught, but what Buddhism taught.

Certain facts about the Buddha's life are reasonably certain. He was the son of a chief of the Śākyas, a small tribe of the Himālayan foothills. He became an ascetic, and propounded a new doctrine which gained the support of numerous disciples. After many years of teaching in the kingdoms of Kosala and Magadha and in the tribal lands to the north of the Gangā, he died at the age of eighty at some time between the years 486 and 473 B.C., probably nearer the former date than the latter. The story of his life as told by his followers is far more vivid and colourful than this dry outline, and it is infinitely more important, for it has influenced countless millions throughout the whole of Asia east of Afghānistān.

One night Mahāmāyā,* chief queen of Śuddhodhana, king of the Śākyas,

* Throughout this section and generally in this book we employ Sanskrit forms of Buddhist names

dreamt that she was carried away to the divine lake Anavatapta in the Himālayas, where she was bathed by the heavenly guardians of the four quarters of the universe. A great white elephant holding a lotus flower in his trunk approached her, and entered her side (pl. XXIII*c*). Next day the dream was interpreted for her by wise men—she had conceived a wonderful son, who would be either a Universal Emperor (p. 72f) or a Universal Teacher. The child was born in a grove of sāl trees called Lumbinī, near the capital of the Śākyas, Kapilavastu, while his mother was on the way to her parents' home for her confinement. At birth he stood upright, took seven strides, and spoke: "This is my last birth—henceforth there is no more birth for me."

The boy was named Siddhārtha, at a great ceremony on the fifth day from his birth. His *gotra* name was Gautama (in Pāli, Gotama) by which he is commonly referred to in Buddhist literature. The soothsayers prophesied that he would become a Universal Emperor, with the exception of one, who declared that four signs would convince him of the misery of the world, and he would become a Universal Teacher. To prevent this prophecy coming true King Śuddhodhana resolved that he should never know the sorrows of the world. He was reared in delightful palaces, from whose parks every sign of death, disease and misery was removed. He learned all the arts that a prince should learn, and excelled as a student. He married his cousin Yaśodharā, whom he won at a great contest at which he performed feats of strength and skill which put to shame all other contestants, including his envious cousin Devadatta.

But for all his prosperity and success he was not inwardly happy, and for all the efforts of his father he did see the four signs foretold, which were to decide his career, for the gods knew his destiny, and it was they who placed the signs before him. One day, as he was driving round the royal park with his faithful charioteer Channa, he saw an aged man, in the last stages of infirmity and decrepitude—actually a god, who had taken this disguise in order that Siddhārtha Gautama might become a Buddha. Siddhārtha asked Channa who this repulsive being was, and when he learned that all men must grow old he was even more troubled in mind. This was the first sign. The second came a little later, in the same way, in the form of a very sick man, covered with boils and shivering with fever. The third was even more terrible—a corpse, being carried to the cremation-ground, followed by weeping mourners. But the fourth sign brought hope and consolation—a wandering religious beggar, clad in a simple yellow robe, peaceful and calm, with a mien of inward joy. On seeing him Siddhārtha realized where his destiny lay, and set his heart on becoming a wanderer.

Hearing of this King Śuddhodhana doubled his precautions. Siddhārtha was made a virtual prisoner, though still surrounded with pleasures and luxuries of all kinds; his heart knew no peace, and he could never forget the four signs. One morning the news was brought to him that Yaśodharā had given birth to a son, but

---

and terms, for the sake of consistency. The reader who goes on to more detailed study may meet them in their Pāli forms, as used by the Sthaviravāda Buddhists.

it gave him no pleasure. That night there were great festivities, but when all were sleeping he roused Channa, who saddled his favourite horse Kaṇṭhaka, and he rode off into the night, surrounded by rejoicing demigods, who cushioned the fall of his horse's hoofs so that no one should hear his departure (p. 405, and pl. XXXV*c*).

When far from the city he stripped off his jewellery and fine garments, and put on a hermit's robe, provided by an attendant demigod. With his sword he cut off his flowing hair, and sent it back to his father with his garments by the hand of Channa. The horse Kaṇṭhaka dropped dead from grief when he found that he was to be parted from his master, and was reborn in one of the heavens. Thus Siddhārtha performed his "Great Going Forth" (*Mahābhinṣkramaṇa*) and became a wandering ascetic, owning nothing but the robe he wore.

At first he begged his food as a wanderer, but he soon gave up this life for that of a forest hermit. From a sage named Ālāra Kālāma he learned the technique of meditation, and the lore of Brahman as taught in the Upaniṣads; but he was not convinced that man could obtain liberation from sorrow by self-discipline and knowledge, so he joined forces with five ascetics who were practising the most rigorous self-mortification in the hope of wearing away their karma and obtaining final bliss.

His penances became so severe that the five quickly recognized him as their leader. For six years he tortured himself until he was nothing but a walking skeleton. One day, worn out by penance and hunger, he fainted, and his followers believed that he was dead. But after a while he recovered consciousness, and realized that his fasts and penances had been useless. He again began to beg food, and his body regained its strength. The five disciples left him in disgust at his backsliding.

One day Siddhārtha Gautama, now thirty-five years old, was seated beneath a large pipal tree on the outskirts of the town of Gaya, in the realm of Bimbisāra king of Magadha. Sujātā, the daughter of a nearby farmer, brought him a large bowl of rice boiled in milk. After eating some of this he bathed, and that evening, again sitting beneath the pipal tree, he made a solemn vow that, though his bones wasted away and his blood dried up, he would not leave his seat until the riddle of suffering was solved.

So for forty-nine days he sat beneath the tree. At first he was surrounded by hosts of gods and spirits, awaiting the great moment of enlightenment; but they soon fled, for Mara, the spirit of the world and of sensual pleasure, the Buddhist devil, approached. For days Gautama withstood temptations of all kinds (pl. XXXVIII). Māra, disguised as a messenger, brought news that the wicked cousin Devadatta had revolted, thrown Śuddhodhana into prison, and seized Yaśodharā, but Gautama was not moved. Māra called his demon hosts, and attacked him with whirlwind, tempest, flood and earthquake, but he sat firm, cross-legged beneath the tree. Then the tempter called on Gautama to produce evidence of his goodness and benevolence; he touched the ground with his hand, and the Earth itself spoke with a voice of thunder: "I am his witness".

Māra then tried gentler means of shaking Gautama's resolve. He called his three beautiful daughters, Desire, Pleasure and Passion, who danced and sang before him, and tried every means of seduction. Their wiles were quite ineffectual. They offered him Universal Empire; but he was unmoved.

At last the demon hosts gave up the struggle and Gautama, left alone, sank deeper and deeper into meditation. At the dawning of the forty-ninth day he knew the truth. He had found the secret of sorrow, and understood at last why the world is full of suffering and unhappiness of all kinds, and what man must do to overcome them. He was fully enlightened—a Buddha. For another seven weeks he remained under the Tree of Wisdom (*bodhi*), meditating on the great truths he had found.

For a time he doubted whether he should proclaim his wisdom to the world, as it was so recondite and difficult to express that few would understand it; but the god Brahmā himself descended from heaven and persuaded him to teach the world. Leaving the Tree of Wisdom, he journeyed to the Deer Park near Vārāṇasī (the modern Sārnāth), where his five former disciples had settled to continue their penances.

To these five ascetics the Buddha preached his first sermon, or, in Buddhist phraseology, "set in motion the Wheel of the Law". The five were so impressed with his new doctrine that they gave up their austerities and once more became his disciples. A few days later a band of sixty young ascetics became his followers, and he sent them out in all directions to preach the Buddhist Dharma. Soon his name was well known throughout the Gangā Plain, and the greatest kings of the time favoured him and his followers. He gathered together a disciplined body of monks (called *bhikṣus*, or in Pāli *bhikkhus*, literally "beggars"), knit together by a common garb, the yellow robes of the order, and a common discipline, according to tradition laid down in detail by the Buddha himself. Many stories are told of his long years of preaching. He returned to Kapilavastu, and converted his father, wife and son Rāhula, as well as many other members of the court, including his cousin Devadatta, whose heart remained full of jealousy. At the request of his foster-mother and aunt, Kṛṣā-Gautamī, he allowed with much misgiving the formation of a community of nuns. Devadatta grew so jealous of him that once he even tried to kill the Buddha, by arranging for a mad elephant to be let loose in his path; but the beast, impressed by the Buddha's gentleness and fearlessness, calmly bowed at his feet (pl. XXXV*a*). He averted a war between the Śākyas and the Koliyas, by walking between the assembled armies and convincing them of the uselessness and evil of bloodshed. He went alone to the camp of a notorious bandit, Aṅgulimāla, and converted him and his followers from their evil ways.

Though according to legend his life was attended by many wonders, the earliest traditions record few miracles accomplished by the Buddha himself. Once he is said to have performed feats of levitation and other miracles at Śrāvastī, as a result of a challenge from rival teachers, but he sternly forbade the monks to imitate him, and there is no record of his healing the sick by supernatural means. One touching story of the Buddha is interesting in this connexion, since it contrasts strikingly with the Gospel stories of the miracles of Jesus. A woman, stricken with grief at the death of her only son, and hearing that the Buddha was in the vicinity, brought the child's corpse to him in the hope that he would restore it to life. He asked her first to go to the nearby town and bring a handful of mustard seed from a family in which no one had died. She went from house to house, but of course could find no such family, until at last she understood the inevitability of death and sorrow, and became a nun.

For eight months of the year the Buddha and his followers would travel from place to place, preaching to all and sundry. For the four months of the rainy season, roughly corresponding to the English summer, they would stop in one of the parks given to the Buddhist order by wealthy lay followers, living in huts of bamboo and reed—the first form of the great Buddhist monasteries of later times. For over forty years his reputation grew and the *Saṅgha* (literally Society, the Buddhist Order) increased in numbers and influence. With the exception of the conspiracy of Devadatta he suffered no persecution, though a few of his followers were maltreated by their religious opponents. His ministry was a long, calm and peaceful one, in this respect very different from that of Jesus.

The end came at the age of eighty. He spent the last rainy season of his life near the city of Vaiśālī, and after the rains he and his followers journeyed northwards to the hill country which had been the home of his youth. On the way he prepared his disciples for his death. He told them that his body was now like a worn-out cart, creaking at every joint. He declared that he had made no distinction between esoteric and exoteric teaching, but had preached the full doctrine to them.* When he was gone they were to look for no new leader—the Doctrine (*Dharma*) which he had preached would lead them. They must rely on themselves, be their own lamps, and look for no refuge outside themselves.

At the town of Pāvā he was entertained by a lay disciple, Cunda the smith, and ate a meal of pork.† Soon after this he was attacked by dysentery, but he insisted on moving on to the nearby town of Kusinagara (Pāli, Kusinārā). Here, on the outskirts of the town, he lay down under a sāl tree, and that night he died. His last words were: "All composite things decay. Strive diligently!" This was his "Final Blowing-out" (*Parinirvāṇa*). His sorrowing disciples cremated his body, and his ashes were divided between the representatives of various tribal peoples and King Ajātaśatru of Magadha.

The Growth of Buddhism

According to tradition a great gathering of monks met at the Magadhan capital of Rājagṛha soon after the Buddha's death. At this council Upāli, one of the chief disciples, recited the *Vinaya Piṭaka*, or rules of the Order, as he recalled having

* We cannot, of course, rely on the verbatim accuracy of the account of the Buddha's death, and this passage[33] may be an interpolation directed against early heterodox schools which claimed to possess secret teachings of the Buddha. It is equally possible, however, that it refers to the teachers of the Upaniṣads, who kept their most secret doctrines for their closest disciples.

† Most modern Buddhists claim that the last meal was of truffles, and the Pāli phrase *sūkala-maddava,* "sweetness of pigs", is certainly ambiguous.[34] But early commentators took it to mean a choice cut of pork.[35]

heard the Buddha give them. Another disciple, Ānanda, who bears a position in Buddhism similar to that of St. John in Christianity, recited the *Sutta Piṭaka*, the great collection of the Buddha's sermons on matters of doctrine and ethics. Though there may have been a council of some sort, the story as it stands is certainly untrue, for it is quite evident that the scriptures of Buddhism grew by a long process of development and accretion, perhaps over several centuries.

A second general council is said to have been held at Vaiśālī, one hundred years after the Buddha's death. Here schism raised its head, ostensibly over small points of monastic discipline, and the Order broke into two sections, the orthodox *Sthaviravādins* (Pāli *Theravādī*) or "Believers in the Teaching of the Elders", and the *Mahāsaṅghikas* or "Members of the Great Community". The tradition of the second council is as dubious as that of the first, but it at least records that schism began very early. The minor points of discipline on which the Order divided were soon followed by doctrinal differences of much greater importance.

Numerous such differences appeared at the third great council, held at Pāṭaliputra under the patronage of Aśoka, which resulted in the expulsion of many heretics and the establishment of the Sthaviravāda school as orthodox. At this council it is said that the last section was added to the Pāli scriptures, the *Kathāvatthu* of the *Abhidhamma Piṭaka*, dealing with psychology and metaphysics. In fact many of the works of this part of the canon are of later composition, and the details of the account of the council are suspect, but the record shows that by this time widespread differences had developed within the Order.

Meanwhile great changes were taking place in the constitution of Buddhism. Some modern authorities believe that the Buddha had no intention of founding a new religion, and never looked on his doctrine as distinct from the popular cults of the time, but rather as transcending them—a sort of super-doctrine, which would help his followers further along the road to salvation than Brāhmaṇism or Upaniṣadic gnosis. This view is, in our opinion, very questionable. Though the traditions of Buddhism give little evidence of direct antagonism between Buddhists and brāhmaṇs at this early period there was much antagonism between Buddhists and other heterodox sects, such as Jainas and Ājīvikas. These sects did not merely wrangle over doctrinal points, but carried on vigorous propaganda among laymen for their support. We believe that even in the days of the Buddha himself the Order consciously tried to build up a following of layfolk, who would pay to the Buddha their chief if not their only homage. The enormous gifts which so many wealthy people are said to have made to the Order are no doubt exaggerated, but the tradition is more probably partly true than wholly false, and at least some of the wealthy merchants who so liberally supported the new teachings must have looked upon themselves as lay Buddhists.

Whatever its position in the Buddha's lifetime, 200 years later Buddhism was a distinct religion. Aśoka classified all the religions of his empire under five heads; the (Buddhist) *Sangha*, the Brāhmaṇs, the Ājīvikas, the Nirgranthas (or Jainas), and "other sects". He further declared that, while he gave his chief patronage to the Buddhists, he honoured and respected them all, and called on his subjects to do likewise.[36]

By Aśoka's time India was covered with *vikāras*, which were both monasteries and temples. In becoming a religion Buddhism borrowed and adapted much from the popular beliefs of the time. Its simple ritual was in no way based on sacrificial Brāhmaṇism, but on the cult of *caityas*, or sacred spots. These were often small groves of trees, or single sacred trees, on the outskirts of villages, and might also include tumuli, such as those in which the ashes of chiefs were buried. These caityas were the abodes of earth-spirits and genii who, to the simpler folk, were more accessible and less expensive to worship than the great gods of the Āryans. The Jaina scriptures show that unorthodox holy-men often made their homes in or near the caityas, no doubt in order to obtain alms from visitors; and the Buddha is said to have respected these local shrines, and to have encouraged his lay followers to revere them.

Soon after the Buddha's death many communities of monks gave up the practice of constant travel except in the rainy season, and settled permanently on the outskirts of towns and villages, often near the local caityas. With time many of these little monasteries grew in size and importance.

It was the cult of the caitya that Buddhism made its own. According to tradition *stūpas* or tumuli were built by the recipients over the divided ashes of the Buddha. Other stūpas, containing the remains of locally revered monks and ascetics of other denominations, rose up all over India in succeeding centuries. Aśoka unearthed the ashes of the Buddha from their original resting places and divided them still further, rearing stupas for them all over India. The sacred grove or tree of the old popular cult became the Bodhi Tree, a pīpal planted near the stūpa to commemorate the Buddha's enlightenment, an object of great reverence. The original Bodhi Tree of Gayā, under which the Buddha sat, became an object of pilgrimage, and cuttings of it were carried as far as Ceylon. One feature of the Buddhist Cult which has now vanished is the column, perhaps the survival of a phallic emblem or megalith. Such columns existed in many ancient Buddhist monasteries, but their place in the cult is not clear. Temples proper or shrine-rooms do not appear to have been erected until the beginning of the Christian era, when the Buddha began to be worshipped in the form of an image.

His simpler followers evidently raised the Buddha almost to divinity even in his lifetime, and after his death he was worshipped in his symbols—the stūpa, recalling his parinirvāṇa, and the tree, recalling his enlightenment. The worship consisted of circumambulation in the auspicious clockwise direction, and prostrations, with offerings of flowers. Though the more intelligent monks may have recognized his true status, for the ordinary believer he was the greatest of the gods. This is not surprising, for to this day Indians feel and show the utmost respect for those whom they consider holy. It is rather a matter of surprise that it was only 500 years after the Buddha's death that a theology developed which gave full recognition to this state of affairs.

With the support of Aśoka Buddhism greatly expanded, spreading throughout India and to Ceylon. There is some doubt as to how far the doctrine had developed at this time, but at least a rudimentary canon existed, though perhaps not yet committed to writing. The great Buddhist holy places—the Lumbinī Grove at Kapilavastu where the Buddha was born, the Tree of Wisdom at Gayā where he gained enlightenment, the Deer Park near Vārāṇasī where he preached his first sermon, and the grove near Kuśinagara where he died—were visited by many pilgrims, including Aśoka himself. Though there is a tradition of cruel persecution under Puṣyamitra Śuṅga the faith continued to grow. Of all the religious remains of between 200 B.C. and A.D. 200 so far discovered in India those of Buddhism outnumber those of Brāhmaṇism, Hinduism and Jainism together. The old stupas were enlarged and beautified with carved railings, terraces and gateways. All classes of the community, kings, princes, merchants and craftsmen, made donations to the Order, which are recorded in numerous inscriptions. Though the individual monk was bound by his vows to own no property except bare necessities, and to touch no silver or gold, the monasteries grew rich on the alms of the faithful. The revenues of whole villages were alienated to them by pious kings, and even the individual monks began to take their vows of poverty lightly, for more than one inscription records donations made to the Order by ordained members of it.

Though there is little evidence of strong sectarian animus within the Order, sects already existed, and the scriptures had been codified in more than one recension. It is possible that much of the Pāli canon of the Sthaviravādins, in the form in which we have it, emanates from the great monastery on a hilltop near the modern village of Sānchī, the remains of which are among the finest relics of early Buddhism.

Another very important sect, the *Sarvāstivādins*, was strong in the region of Mathurā and in Kashmīr. It was in Kashmīr, according to a tradition preserved in China, that, under the patronage of Kaniṣka (1st-2nd century A.D., p. 61f), a fourth great council was held, at which the Sarvāstivādin doctrines were codified in a summary, the *Mahāvibhāṣā*. It was chiefly among the Sarvāstivādins, but also in the old schism of the Mahāsaṅghikas, that new ideas developed, which were to form the basis of the division of Buddhism into the "Great" and "Lesser Vehicles" (*Mahāyāna* and *Hinayāna*). The brāhmaṇs and their lay supporters had by now largely turned from the older gods, whom they worshipped with animal sacrifices, towards others, who were worshipped with reverent devotion. In N.-W. India the rule of Greeks, Śakas and Kuṣāṇas in turn had thrown open the gates to the West, and ideas from Persia and beyond entered India in greater strength than before. In these conditions teachers of the early Christian centuries gave to Buddhism a wholly new outlook. They claimed to have found a new and great vehicle which would carry many souls to salvation, while the Sthaviravādins and kindred sects had but a small one. The Great Vehicle soon became popular in many parts of India, for it fitted the mood of the times and the needs of many simple people better than did the Lesser Vehicle, which then began to lose ground. In Ceylon, however, the Lesser Vehicle resisted all the attacks of the new sects and thence it was later taken to Burma, Thailand and other parts of South-East Asia, where it became the national religion.

The Great Vehicle, on the other hand, itself soon divided by various schisms, was carried by a succession of Indian monks to China and thence to Japan. By the time of the Guptas it predominated, and Hsüan Tsang, in the 7th century, found the Lesser Vehicle almost extinct in most of India, and only flourishing in a few parts of the West; evidently it had ceased to make a strong emotional appeal in the India of early Hinduism. Buddhism as a whole was already declining. In many places great monasteries were in ruins, and places of pilgrimage almost deserted. But the faith was still important, and had thousands of monks and many prosperous monasteries. Chief of these was Nālandā (p. 143), which, under the patronage of kings of the Pāla line, remained a centre of Buddhist piety and learning until the Muslim invasion. From Nālandā the missionary monk Padmasambhava went forth to convert Tibet to Buddhism in the 8th century, while pilgrims from as far afield as China and South-East Asia visited it to learn the pure doctrine. At this time the general standards of culture in North India were declining. From the end of the Gupta period onwards Indian religion became more and more permeated with primitive ideas of sympathetic magic and sexual mysticism, and Buddhism was much affected by these developments. A third vehicle, "the Vehicle of the Thunderbolt" (*Vajrayāna*), appeared in Eastern India in the 8th century, and grew rapidly in Bengal and Bihār. It was this form of Buddhism, modified by primitive local cults and practices, which was finally established in Tibet in the 11th century, as a result of missions sent from the great Vajrayāna monastery of Vikramaśīla, in Bihār.

Anti-Buddhist persecution was not wholly unknown at this time. In the 6th century the Hūṇa king Mihirakula destroyed monasteries and killed monks. A fanatical Śaivite king of Bengal, Śaśāṅka, in the course of an attack on Kānyakubja at the very beginning of the 7th century, almost destroyed the Tree of Wisdom at Gayā. There are other less reliable accounts of persecution, but it is certain that this was not the main cause of the disappearance of Buddhism from India. A more important factor was the revived and reformed Hinduism, which began to spread northwards from the Tamil country from the 9th century onwards, when the great theologian Śaṅkara travelled the length and breadth of India disputing with the Buddhists. Behind him he left an organized body of Hindu monks to carry on his work. The new form of devotional Hinduism made a very vigorous appeal to the ordinary man, and the persistent tendency of Hinduism to assimilate, rather than to attack, was always at work.

As early as the Gupta period Buddhist monks often took part in Hindu processions. The Buddhist family, which gave its chief support to the local monastery, would at all times rely on the services of brāhmaṇs at births, marriages and deaths. If for a time Buddhism became to all intents and purposes a separate religion, denying the Vedas, the ordinary layman might not see it in that light. For him Buddhism was one of many cults and faiths, by no means mutually exclusive, all of which led to salvation, and all of which were respectable and worthy of honour. Thus, in medieval North India, the Buddha came to be looked on as the ninth of the ten incarnations of the great god Viṣṇu, (p. 269), and Buddhism gradually lost its individuality, becoming a special and rather unorthodox Hindu sect, which, like many others, did not survive. Hinduism, relying for its strength mainly on independent brāhmaṇs and ascetics and on domestic ceremonies, suffered from the Muslim invasion but was not seriously weakened by it. Buddhism, by now mainly concentrated in large monasteries and already rapidly declining in influence, could not stand up to the change. In the first rush of the Muslim advance down the Gangā Nālandā and other great monasteries of Bihār were sacked, libraries were burnt, and monks were put to the sword. Most of the survivors fled to the mountains of Nepāl and Tibet, but some Buddhist monasteries still survived in Bihār and East Bengal. An illuminated Buddhist manuscript contains a colophon stating that it was prepared in Bihār in the 15th century.[37] This is our last record of Indian Buddhism, until its revival in recent years.

The Lesser Vehicle

According to Sinhalese tradition the Pāli canon of the Sthaviravādin school was committed to writing in Ceylon, in the reign of King Vaṭṭagāmaṇi (89–77 B.C.), after it had been finally established at a great council of Sinhalese monks. If we are to believe tradition it had already been sifted and codified at the three councils of Rājagṛha, Vaiśālī and Pāṭaliputra, and had been passed down by word of mouth for some four centuries by teachers who had not the strict mnemonic system of the Vedic schools. As late as the 5th century A.D. written scriptures were rare, and the pilgrim Fa-hsien was hard put to it to find a good copy of the *Vinaya Piṭaka*. Probably even the codification of the canon in Ceylon did not wholly end the process of accretion and interpolation.

At the same time as the canon old commentaries in Sinhalese Prākrit were also committed to writing. These were translated into Pāli, and no doubt considerably altered and expanded, by the great doctor Buddhaghosa, who worked in Ceylon in the 5th century. The original commentaries have completely vanished, and some have doubted whether they ever existed, but it is certain that Buddhaghosa had access to many early traditions not recorded elsewhere.

As it stands today the Pāli canon of the Sthaviravādins, including the scriptures, commentaries and semi-canonical texts, would fill a fair-sized bookcase. It consists of three sections called "baskets" (*piṭaka*), from the fact that the long strips of prepared palm-leaf on which the texts were written were originally stored in baskets. These three are known as the *Vinaya* ("Conduct"), *Sutta** ("Sermon") and *Abhidhamma* ("Metaphysics") *Piṭakas*.

The *Vinaya Piṭaka* contains pronouncements attributed to the Buddha, laying down numerous rules for the conduct of the Order. With each rule the

---

* The Pāli form. The Sanskrit is *Sūtra*. As the Sthaviravādins regularly used Pāli, Pāli forms of names and terms are generally employed in this section, except where the Sanskrit form is better known.

circumstances which led the Buddha to propound it are given, and thus the *Vinaya* contains much early traditional matter.

The largest and most important of the "Three Baskets" is the *Sutta Piṭaka*, which is divided into five "Groups" (*Nikāya*):

(1) *Dīgha* (Long) *Nikāya*, a collection of long sermons ascribed to the Buddha, with accounts of the circumstances in which he preached them.
(2) *Majjhima* (Medium) *Nikāya*, shorter sermons.
(3) *Saṃyutta* (Connected) *Nikāya*, collections of brief pronouncements on kindred topics.
(4) *Aṅguttara* (Graduated) *Nikāya*, a collection of over 2,000 brief statements, arranged rather artificially in eleven sections, according to the number of topics treated in each statement. Thus Section Two contains a discussion on the two things which a man should avoid, Section Three, one on the trinity of thought, word and deed, and so on.
(5) *Khuddaka* (Minor) *Nikāya*, miscellaneous works in prose and verse, some very ancient, but certainly added to the canon later than the four other Nikāyas. Among the contents of the Khuddaka are the *Dhammapada* ("Verses on Virtue"), the *Theragāthā* and the *Therīgāthā* ("Hymns of the Elder Monks and Nuns), which contain some of India's greatest religious poetry, and the *Jātaka*, a collection of over 500 poems, briefly outlining folktales and other stories, which were originally intended to be told in the words of a narrator. The tales are told in full in a prose commentary attributed to Buddhaghosa, which is invariably published with the verses. Many of the tales are secular, and they do not all convey a very exalted message, but they have all been given an odour of sanctity by being ascribed to the Buddha, who is said to have told them as recollections of his previous births as a *Bodhisattva*, a being destined to become a Buddha. These racy and vivid stories are great as literature, and will be considered elsewhere in that aspect (p. 404ff). They are an invaluable source of social history.

The third Piṭaka, *Abhidhamma*, consists of some drily pedantic works on Buddhist psychology and metaphysics of little interest except to the specialist. It is certainly later than the other two Piṭakas.

As well as the canon and its many commentaries there are several semi-canonical works. Chief of these is the "Questions of Menander" (*Milinda-pañha*), an account of the discussions of the Greco-Bactrian king and the monk Nāgasena, which is written with such literary and dialectical skill that it has been suggested, without much evidence, that the author knew something of Plato. Of a different character are the verse chronicles which tell the history of Buddhism in Ceylon, and give valuable information on political and social history also. Of these, the earliest, *Dīpavaṃsa* (the "Island Chronicle") dates from the 4th century A.D., and has no literary merit, but the *Mahāvaṃsa* ("Great Chronicle"), of the following century, contains passages of beauty and vigour (p. 409f). It was continued as the *Cūlavaṃsa* ("Lesser Chronicle") by a succession of monks down to the fall of the kingdom of Kandy to the British at the beginning of the 19th century and we understand that a further appendix has recently been added, bringing it down to the present day.

The basic propositions of this great body of literature are not meta-physical but psychological. Sorrow, suffering, dissatisfaction, and all the manifold unpleasantnesses which are referred to by the word *dukkha*, are inherent in life as it is ordinarily lived; they can only be eliminated by giving up "thirst" (*taṇhā*, often translated "craving"), which includes personal ambition, desire, longing, and selfishness of all kinds. According to orthodox teaching the cause of this "thirst" is the innate but mistaken conviction of individuality— that there is in each living being a permanent core, an ego or soul. While this doctrine was subscribed to at a very early period by all Buddhist sects some modern authorities deny that it was propounded by the Buddha, and claim that he merely taught the abandonment of selfhood and individualism on the lower plane of everyday life, but maintained the existence of an eternal soul. This proposition we find hard to believe, despite certain apparent inconsistencies in the Pāli scriptures. If we can place any reliance at all upon the legend of the Buddha's life, the knowledge gained under the Tree of Wisdom was startlingly original, and not a mere rehash of the lore of the Upaniṣadic sages with a comparatively slight shifting of emphasis.

Whatever the Buddha's original doctrine, there can be no question about the fundamental teaching of Buddhism, the kernel of which is contained in the "Sermon of the Turning of the Wheel of the Law" (*Dhammacakkapavattana Sutta*), which the Buddha is said to have preached to his first disciples at Vārāṇasī. This contains the "Four Noble Truths", and the "Noble Eightfold Path", which are accepted as basic categories by all Buddhist sects. We give it in a somewhat abridged form.

> "Thus I have heard. Once the Master was at Vārāṇasī, at the deer park called Isipatana. There the Master addressed the five monks:
>
> "'There are two ends not to be served by a wanderer. What are those two? The pursuit of desires and of the pleasure which springs from desires, which is base, common, leading to rebirth, ignoble and unprofitable; and the pursuit of pain and hardship, which is grievous, ignoble and unprofitable. The Middle Way of the Tathāgata* avoids both these ends; it is enlightened, it brings clear vision, it makes for wisdom, and leads to peace, insight, full wisdom and Nirvāṇa. What is this Middle Way? … It is the Noble Eightfold Path—Right Views, Right Resolve, Right Speech, Right Conduct, Right Livelihood, Right Effort, Right Recollection and Right Meditation. This is the Middle Way. …
>
> "'And this is the Noble Truth of Sorrow. Birth is sorrow, age is sorrow, disease is sorrow, death is sorrow, contact with the unpleasant is sorrow,

* "He who has thus attained"—one of the titles of the Buddha

separation from the pleasant is sorrow, every wish unfulfilled is sorrow—in short all the five components of individuality are sorrow.

"'And this is the Noble Truth of the Arising of Sorrow. [It arises frorm] thirst, which leads to rebirth, which brings delight and passion, and seeks pleasure now here, now there—the thirst for sensual pleasure, the thirst for continued life, the thirst for power.

"'And this is the Noble Truth of the Stopping of Sorrow. It is the complete stopping of that thirst so that no passion remains, leaving it, being emancipated from it, being released from it, giving no place to it.

"'And this is the Noble Truth of the Way which Leads to the Stopping of Sorrow. It is the Noble Eightfold Path—Right Views, Right Resolve, Right Speech, Right Conduct, Right Livelihood, Right Effort, Right Recollection and Right Meditation.'"[38]

Though there are many difficulties in interpreting the finer points of this short sermon its main message is quite clear—sorrow (remembering that the Pāli word *dukkha* covers a far wider range of feeling than the English word with which we translate it) is inherent in ordinary life; it is due to craving for individual satisfaction; it can only be stopped by stopping that craving; and this can only be done by taking a middle course between self-indulgence and extreme asceticism and leading a moral and well-ordered life.

This very simple doctrine was developed in various rather pedantic forms, most important of which was the "Chain of Dependent Origination" (*Paṭicca-samuppāda*), a series of twelve terms, repeated in more than one passage of the Pāli scriptures, commented on again and again by ancient and modern scholars, and perhaps not fully understood by anybody. Out of Ignorance arises Imagination, thence Self-consciousness, thence Name and Form (i.e. corporeal existence), thence the Six Senses,* thence Contact, thence Feeling (or Emotion), thence Craving, thence Attachment, thence Becoming, thence Rebirth, and thence all the manifold ills that flesh is heir to.

The mechanics of this doctrine are indeed obscure, but it shows that the craving which, according to the Buddha's first sermon, is at the bottom of human misery is ultimately due to ignorance—a sort of cosmic ignorance which leads to the delusion of selfhood. The ignorance primarily concerns the fundamental nature of the universe, which has three salient characteristics—it is full of sorrow (*dukkha*), it is transient (*anīcca*), and it is soulless (*anatta*).

The universe is sorrowful. Buddhists would not claim that there is no happiness in the world, but that in some form or other sorrow is inevitable in every aspect of life. "As the ocean has only one flavour, the flavour of salt," the Buddha is purported to have said, "so has my doctrine only one flavour—the flavour of emancipation [from sorrow]."[39] In ordinary existence sorrow cannot be long avoided.

* The sixth being thought.

The universe is transient. There is no abiding entity anywhere. In this Buddhism has much in common with the teaching of Heraclitus. Every being or object, however stable and homogeneous it may appear, is in reality transient and composite. Man, who thinks himself to be eternal and individualized, is actually a compound of five psychosomatic elements—Body, Feelings, Perceptions, States of Mind, and Awareness. These five vary from minute to minute and there is no permanent substratum to them. The old man is evidently not the same person as the baby in arms of seventy years ago, and similarly he is not the same as the man of a moment ago. At every instant the old man vanishes, and a new man, caused by the first, comes into being, though a specious continuity is given by the chain of cause and effect which links one with the other. Buddhism knows no being, but only becoming. Everything is resolved into momentary configurations of events.* The universe is in continuous flux, and all idea of permanence is part of the basic ignorance out of which sorrow springs.

Thus there is no immortal soul. The universe is soulless. In transmigration nothing passes over from one life to another—only a new life arises as part of the chain of events which includes the old. Even the gods are soulless and the World Soul of the Upaniṣads is an illusion. The Buddhism of the Lesser Vehicle is therefore a religion without souls and without God. No Buddhist teacher was rash enough to deny the existence of the gods outright, but they were thought of as beings in no way supernatural or different from man except in their greater happiness and power. In his search for salvation the true Buddhist by-passed them, for they could neither help nor hinder him greatly, and they would in any case do what they were able to assist him if he kept to the Middle Way.

On these premisses the machinery of transmigration—a doctrine which was taken over by Buddhism from the general beliefs of the time—is hard to explain. If nothing passes from life to life the newborn being cannot be thought of as in any way connected with the being who has died, and whose actions have conditioned his present state. Yet the new being suffers as a result of the actions of the old one. This objection was often raised by the opponents of Buddhism, and was countered by the analogy of the flame of a lamp, which might kindle a flame in another lamp and then be extinguished. If this simile was unconvincing, it was pointed out that the old man, though not, on ultimate analysis, the same person as the young one, suffered illness as a result of the excesses of his youth, and so one being might suffer as a result of the evil done by an earlier being who was part of the chain of cause and effect leading up to his present existence. Terms like "individual", "person", and so on were merely convenient labels for a series of separate momentary events which continued indefinitely, just as "chariot" was a convenient label for a collection of pieces of wood and metal put together in a certain manner.

The only stable entity in Sthaviravāda Buddhism was *Nirvāṇa* (in Pāli, *Nibbāna*), the state of bliss reached by the Buddhas and *Arhants*, or perfected beings. Nirvāṇa is difficult to understand for one who has not experienced it,

* Called *dharmas*, the term here used in a special sense.

and some early Western scholars believed that it implied complete annihilation. A statement attributed to the Buddha: "I have not said that the Arhant exists after death, and I have not said that he does not exist ... because ... this is not edifying, neither does it tend to supreme wisdom"[40] would suggest that Nirvāṇa was believed to be a state neither of being nor of annihilation. The Aristotelian Law of the Excluded Middle was never strictly applied in Indian thought, and a third state, transcending both being and not-being, would not be considered an impossibility. If the whole world was in a state of flux and Nirvāṇa was a state of rest this too did not present an insuperable paradox, for Nirvāṇa was outside the universe; it underlay it, but was not part of it.

Such a concept is not very different from that of the World Soul of the Upaniṣads, and, far from being looked on as a state of annihilation, Nirvāṇa was sometimes described in brilliantly colourful language—"a glorious city, stainless and undefiled, pure and white, unaging, deathless, secure and calm and happy".[41] Nirvana has no definite location, but it may be realized anywhere and at any time, while still in the flesh. The man who finds it never again loses it, and when he dies he passes to this state for ever, in his *parinirvāṇa*, his "Final Blowing Out".

The doctrines which we have described are those of the Sthaviravādin sect of the Lesser Vehicle, which is the only surviving sect of that branch of Buddhism, and is today dominant in Ceylon, Burma, Thailand, Cambodia and Laos. Other sects of the Lesser Vehicle have now quite disappeared, though they survived longer in India itself than the Sthaviravādins. Chief among these was the sect of the *Sarvāstivādins* (They who say "All is"), who had a canon in Sanskrit, and who differed from the Sthaviravādins in their view that the constituents of phenomena (*dharmas*) are not wholly momentary, but exist for ever in a latent form. Another important sect was that of the *Sautrāntikas*, who maintained that our knowledge of the outside world is only a feasible inference, and who were well on the way to the idealism of some schools of the Great Vehicle. A fourth sect, the *Sammitīyas*, even went so far as to reject the doctrine of soullessness and to postulate a sort of soul in the *pudgala* or person, which passes from life to life. These early sects of Buddhism probably gave much encouragement to the evolution of Indian philosophy, as distinct from mystical thought.

Though the Buddha is said to have disapproved of speculation on the origin and end of the world, Buddhists of the Lesser Vehicle devised a cosmological scheme, based largely on prevalent Indian ideas, which accounted for the existence of the world without the intervention of a creator.

As in all Indian cosmologies the universe is cyclic. Over an enormous period of time (*mahākalpa*) it goes through a process of evolution and decline, only to evolve once more. The cycle is divided into four great periods (*asaṅkhyeya*). In the first man declines, and at last everything is destroyed except the highest heaven; the good go to this heaven, and the sinners to the hells of other universes, which may at that time be passing through different stages. The second period is one of quiescence. In the third period evolution again begins. The good karma of the beings in the highest heaven begins to fail, and the "World of Form", a lower heaven, evolves. A great being dies in the highest heaven and is reborn in the World of Form as the god Brahmā. As he is the only living thing therein he is lonely. But other beings follow him from the highest heaven to the lower. As Brahmā was the first to be born in the World of Form, and their birth agrees with his wīshes, he imagines that he is the creator of the other gods, and of all the world, which actually comes into existence through cosmic law. Meanwhile the earth develops, as well as other earths. The first men are fairy-like beings, but gradually they degenerate and become earthbound (p. 71). The fourth period is one of continuation, marked only by a regular pattern of comparative advance and decline, forming a series of lesser cycles within the greater one. This process is repeated for all eternity, but one great cycle is not exactly like the next. There are "Buddha cycles" and "empty cycles", and we are fortunate that we live in a Buddha cycle, in which four Buddhas (Krakucchanda, Kanakamuni, Kāśyapa, and Śākyamuni*) have taught and a fifth (Maitreya) is yet to come.

The Evolution of the Great Vehicle

It is nowhere claimed in the Pāli scriptures that the Buddha was in any way supernatural. His supreme insight was gained by his own efforts, after many ages of striving in many different births. But his birth, enlightenment and death were cosmic events of the highest importance, and his greatness was such that he was revered even by the mighty gods Brahmā and Śakra (an epithet of Indra commonly used by the Buddhists), not to speak of the myriads of lesser deities inhabiting earth and heaven. He is reported to have said that whoever had faith in him and love for him was assured of a rebirth in heaven,[42] a prospect which, as we know from Aśoka's inscriptions, was much more intelligible and desirable to the ordinary man than the rarefied and indescribable Nirvāṇa.

When the Buddha died, according to orthodox theory, the chain of his existence was broken. He finally entered the Nirvāṇa which he had realized at his enlightenment, and ceased to be an individual, or to affect the universe in any way. Just before his death he had told his disciples to rely on the Doctrine for leadership. But soon after his death, if not before, his followers evolved the "Three Jewels", which form the basic profession of faith of Buddhism, and which every Buddhist, both monastic and lay, repeats to this day: "I go for refuge to the Buddha; I go for refuge to the Doctrine (*Dharma*); I go for refuge to the Order (*Saṅgha*)." Though the theorists might explain away the first of the Three Jewels, on the obvious interpretation "going for refuge to the Buddha" implied that the Master, as distinct from his teaching, was in some way still present and able to help his followers.

The Buddha himself probably taught that he was the last of a long succession of earlier Buddhas, who had lived before him. According to tradition these former Buddhas were revered even in the historical Buddha's lifetime. By Mauryan times their cult was widespread, and was patronized by Aśoka. In the end the orthodox Sthaviravādin school counted no less than twenty-five Buddhas, not to speak of

* "The Sage of the Śākyas", a title of Gautama Buddha.

a large number of *pratyeka-buddhas*, who had found the truth for themselves without guidance, but had not taught it to the world.

The carvings of the stupas of Bhārhut and Sānchī, executed in the 2nd and 1st centuries B.C., depict crowds of adoring worshippers reverencing the symbols of the Buddha. A little later sculptors began to carve images of the Buddha himself, and within a few generations all Buddhist sects took to worshipping images. Buddhism kept up with the times, and by the Middle Ages, even in the shrines of the Lesser Vehicle, the Buddha was worshipped just as a Hindu god, with flowers, incense, waving lamps, and deep devotion.

Among the doctrines of Zoroastrianism, which has strongly influenced other religions both East and West, is that of the Saviour (*Šaošyant*), who at the end of the world will lead the forces of good and light against those of evil and darkness. Under the invading rulers of N.-W. India Zoroastrianism and Buddhism came in contact, and it was probably through this that the idea of the future Buddha became part of orthodox belief. If there had been Buddhas before Gautama there would be Buddhas after him. By the time of the "Questions of Menander", around the beginning of the Christian era, the cult of the future Buddha, Maitreya, was widespread among all Buddhist sects.

According to the older conceptions the Buddha wrought many deeds of kindness and mercy in a long series of transmigrations as a *Bodhisattva*, before achieving his final birth as the Sage of the Śākyas; but, since Maitreya and other unnamed Buddhas after him are yet to come, there must be Bodhisattvas existing at present in the universe, who are working continuously for the welfare of all things living. The Jātaka stories show that Bodhisattvas can be incarnated as men, or even as animals; but the more advanced Bodhisattvas, who have the greatest power for good, must be divine beings in the heavens.

Though neither omniscient nor almighty these celestial Bodhisattvas might be adored and prayed to without any misgiving, for it was part of their mission to answer prayer. The Bodhisattva doctrine, a logicai development from the older Buddhism, thus peopled the heavens with mighty forces of goodness, and presented Buddhism with a new mythology. It was this which formed the hallmark of the Mahāyāna, the Great Vehicle.

The Great Vehicle

According to the older doctrine the Bodhisattva works in wisdom and love through many lives so that he may become a Buddha, and ordinary believers are encouraged to follow his example and win Nirvāṇa as quickly as possible. Yet, since the Bodhisattva is a being of immeasurable charity and compassion, surely while one suffering individual remains in the toils of transmigration he will not leave him without help and enter Nirvāṇa, where he can be of no further service to the world. So, quite logically, in the schools of the Great Vehicle the Bodhisattva was thought of not as a being who was soon to become a Buddha, but as one who would bide his time until even the smallest insect had reached the highest goal. The old ideal of the Arhant, the "Worthy" who achieved Nirvāṇa and would be reborn no more, began to be looked on as rather selfish. Instead of striving to become Arhants men should aim at becoming Bodhisattvas, and by the spiritual merit which they gained assist all living beings on the way to perfection.

The idea of transference of merit is a special feature of the teaching of the Great Vehicle. According to the Lesser Vehicle a man can only help another on the Way by example and advice. Each being must be a lamp unto himself, and work out his own salvation. But the belief in transference of merit spread very widely, even affecting the sects of the Lesser Vehicle. The numerous Buddhist dedicatory inscriptions throughout India often contain some such phrase as: "May it be for the welfare of [the donor's] mother and father and of all living beings."

Moreover, the Bodhisattva was thought of as a spirit not only of compassion but also of suffering. In more than one source we read the vow or resolve of the Bodhisattva, which is sometimes expressed in almost Christian terms:

> "I take upon myself ... the deeds of all beings, even of those in the hells, in other worlds, in the realms of punishment. ... I take their suffering upon me, ... I bear it, I do not draw back from it, I do not tremble at it, ... I have no fear of it, ... I do not lose heart. ... I must bear the burden of all beings, for I have vowed to save all things living, to bring them safe through the forest of birth, age, disease, death and rebirth. I think not of my own salvation, but strive to bestow on all beings the royalty of supreme wisdom. So I take upon myself all the sorrows of all beings. I resolve to bear every torment in every purgatory of the universe. For it is better that I alone suffer than the multitude of living beings. I give myself in exchange. I redeem the universe from the forest of purgatory, from the womb of flesh, from the realm of death. I agree to suffer as a ransom for all beings, for the sake of all beings. Truly I will not abandon them. For I have resolved to gain supreme wisdom for the sake of all that lives, to save the world."[43]

The idea of the Suffering Saviour may have existed in some form in the Middle East before Christianity, but features like this are not attested in Buddhism until after the beginning of the Christian era. The Suffering Bodhisattva so closely resembles the Christian conception of the God who gives his life as a ransom for many that we cannot dismiss the possibility that the doctrine was borrowed by Buddhism from Christianity, which was vigorous in Persia from the 3rd century A.D. onwards.

The universe of the Great Vehicle contains numerous Bodhisattvas, chief of whom, from the earthly point of view, is *Avalokiteśvara* ("The Lord who Looks Down"), also called *Padmapāṇi* ("The Lotus-Bearer") (pl. LXXII). His special attribute is compassion, and his helping hand reaches even to *Avīci*, the deepest and most unpleasant of the Buddhist purgatories. Another important Bodhisattva is *Mañjuśrī*, whose special activity is to stimulate the understanding, and who is depicted with a naked sword in one hand, to destroy error and falsehood, and a book in the other, describing the ten *pāramitās*, or great spiritual perfections, which are the cardinal virtues developed by Bodhisattvas.* *Vajrapāṇi*, a sterner Bodhisattva, is the foe of sin and evil, and like the god Indra bears a thunderbolt in his hand. The gentle *Maitreya*, the future Buddha, is worshipped as a Bodhisattva. Also worthy of mention is *Kṣitigarbha*, the guardian of the purgatories, who is thought of not as a fierce torturer but rather as the governor of a model prison, doing his best to make life tolerable for his charges, and helping them to earn remission of sentence. Though the Great Vehicle agrees in theory with the Lesser that the world is full of sorrow, it is fundamentally optimistic. The world contains much good as well as evil, and there is help for all who ask. Every living thing, from the humblest worm upwards, is in a sense a Bodhisattva, for most schools of the Great Vehicle maintain implicitly or explicitly that ultimately all beings will attain Nirvāṇa and become Buddha.

The Great Vehicle was not content with creating this pantheon of noble and beneficient Bodhisattvas. Probably developing from the old heresy of the Mahāsaṅghika school (p. 230) the idea arose that Gautama Buddha had not been a mere man, but the earthly expression of a mighty spiritual being. This being has three bodies; a Body of Essence (*Dharmakāya*), a Body of Bliss (*Sambhogakāya*), and a Created Body (*Nirmāṇakāya*), and of these only the last was seen on earth. The Body of Essence eternally penetrates and permeates the universe; it is the ultimate Buddha, of which the other two bodies are emanations, more or less unreal. The Body of Bliss exists in the heavens, and will continue until the final resolution of all things in the Body of Essence. The Created Body was a mere emanation of the Body of Bliss. This reminds us of the Docetic heresy in Christianity, and it is possible that Docetism and the doctrine of the Three Bodies owe much to a common gnostic source in the Middle East.

The Buddha's Body of Bliss is the presiding deity of the most important Mahāyāna heaven, Sukhāvatī, the "Happy Land", where the blessed are reborn in the buds of lotuses, which rise from a lovely lake before the Buddha's throne. This divine Buddha is usually called *Amitābha* (Immeasurable Glory) or *Amitāyus* (Immeasurable Age). He too shares the compassion of the Bodhisattva, for, though he enjoys endless and infinite bliss, he maintains an interest in his world, and especially in his heaven. At his touch the lotuses open to give birth to the blessed, who are nourished and grow through the food of his word. According to some Chinese and Japanese sects whoever calls on his name, however sinful he may have been, is assured of rebirth in his heaven. Amitābha is, in fact, a Father in Heaven. He, the historical Gautama Buddha, and the Bodhisattva Avalokiteśvara are closely associated, and play a bigger part in Mahāyānist thought than do other Buddhas and Bodhisattvas, because they are chiefly concerned with this region of the universe and this period of cosmic time, but there are many other heavenly

* Charity *(dāna)*, good conduct *(śīla)*, forbearance *(kṣānti)*, courage *(vīrya)*, meditation *(dhyāna)*, insight *(prajñā)*, "skill in knowing what means to take" (to help beings to achieve salvation) *(upāyakauśalya)*, resolution *(praṇidhāna)*, power *(baia)*, and knowledge *(jñāna)*. In some lists only the first six are mentioned. Much mysticism surrounded the idea of the Prajñāpāramitās, especially in the Vajrayāna School.

Buddhas, presiding over other heavens and other universes. All are emanations of the primal Body of Essence, which is no other than the Brahman, the World Soul or Absolute of the Upaniṣads, in different guise. The Body of Essence is sometimes referred to in later Buddhist writings as *Ādi Buddha*, "the Primeval Buddha", and is also described as "the Void" (*Śūnya*), "the True" (*Tattva*), "Wisdom" (*Bodhi*), or "the Womb of those who Attain the Goal" (*Tathāgatagarbha*). Moreover it is Nirvāṇa. The final state, which the Sthaviravādin school found so difficult to describe in words, was for most sects of the Great Vehicle not really different from the mystical union with the absolute Brahman of the Upaniṣads. The wheel turned full circle, and the mystical monism which early Buddhism so strongly opposed found its way into later Buddhism, but with a new terminology.

Most Buddhist sects of both Vehicles had their own versions of the Piṭakas, but, with the exception of the Pāli Piṭakas of the Sthaviravādins, these have not survived in entirety, and in the schools of the Great Vehicle their place was largely taken by later texts, mostly written in the early centuries of the Christian era. These are in Sanskrit, which became the official language of the Great Vehicle in India, though in other parts of Asia it tended to prefer the local tongue. Many of these texts are ostensibly sermons of the Buddha, but of much greater length than those of the Sutta Piṭaka; hence they were known as *Vaipulya Sūtras* ("Expanded Sermons").

Among the earliest Mahāyāna texts is the *Lalitavistara*, a flowery narrative of the life of the Buddha, containing much more of the supernatural and the marvellous than the Pāli account; this text was utilized by Sir Edwin Arnold for *The Light of Asia*, a lengthy poem on the Buddha's life which enjoyed much popularity at the end of the last century, and is still readable, though its style has somewhat dated. Other important scriptures are the *Saddharmapuṇḍarika* ("The Lotus of the Good Law"), a long series of dialogues of considerable literary merit; the *Vajracchedika* ("Diamond Cutter"), containing very subtle metaphysical writing; the *Sukhāvativyūha*, describing the glories of Amitābha and his paradise; the *Karaṇḍavyūha*, glorifying Avalokiteśvara; and the *Aṣṭasahasrikaprajñāpāramitā*, a work describing the spiritual perfections of the Bodhisattvas (p. 243, n). Literature on this latter subject was considerable. As well as these sacred texts the Great Vehicle produced much religious poetry and a great deal of sectarian philosophical literature, some of very high merit.

The Sthaviravādin commentators were perhaps hampered by the Buddha's injunctions against unnecessary speculation, and, though they could on occasion argue very logically, they produced comparatively few works of systematic philosophy. The Great Vehicle, on the other hand, produced many. It had two chief philosophical schools, the *Mādhyamika* and the *Yogācāra*.

The *Mādhyamika* ("Intermediate") School, so called because it took a line midway between the uncompromising realism of the Sarvāstivādins and the idealism of the Yogācāra, looked back to one of India's greatest philosophers, Nāgārjuna, who according to tradition was a contemporary of Kaniṣka, and whose *Mādhyamika Kārikā* formed the basic text of the school. We have seen that in almost all Buddhist sects the universe was believed to be a flux of momentary but interdependent events (*dharma*). Nāgārjuna showed by very subtle arguments that on final analysis the cosmic flux was unreal, as was the consciousness which perceived it and which was itself part of the flux. Therefore Samsāra, the immeasurably long process of transmigration, did not really exist. If the world of change was unreal, its contrary, Nirvāṇa, was also unreal. There was therefore no difference between Saṃsāra and Nirvāṇa, which were one and the same in their common nonentity. In fact if all things were equally unreal, they were on ultimate analysis one and the same. The One Thing which alone had real existence could have no predicate; it was therefore called by Nāgārjuna "Emptiness", or "the Void" (*Śūnyatā*).

This philosophical nihilism did not lead Nāgārjuna and his followers to scepticism or agnosticism. Though nothing but the Void was wholly real, the world and all that it contained, from Amitābha downwards, had a qualified practical reality; and the great Void underlying all the universe was, in fact, the Body of Essence itself, the Primeval Buddha, Nirvāṇa. Final immeasurable bliss was here and now for all who would perceive it—not something remote and cold, but the very breath of life, nearer and more real than one's own heart. "The life of the world is the same as Nirvāṇa ...", said the Mādhyamikas, "and really there is no difference between them at all".[44]

The *Yogācāra* ("Way of Union") or *Vijñānavādin* School completely rejected the realism of the Lesser Vehicle, and maintained a thorough-going idealism, not even allowing the qualified realism of the Mādhyamikas. The world was built by the consciousness, and had no more reality than a dream. The only reality was "Suchness "(*Tathātā*), also called *Dharmadhātu* (freely translated "the Raw Material of Phenomena"), which was equivalent to Nāgārjuna's Void. The Yogācāra school, though perhaps less influential than the Mādhyamika, produced many important philosophers and logicians. Chief of these were Asaṅga, a monk of Peshāwar of the 4th or 5th century, whose *Sūtrālaṅkāra* is the earliest text of the school, Vasubandhu, the younger brother of Asaṅga, and the great logicians Dignāga and Dharmakīrti. Among the most important writings of Yogācāra is the *Laṅkāvatāra Sūtra*, a lengthy text of great subtlety.

The Vehicle of the Thunderbolt

Quite early in the history of the Great Vehicle feminine divinities found their way into the pantheon. One such was Prajñāpāramitā, the Perfection of Insight, the personification of the qualities of the Bodhisattva. Later the Buddhas and Bodhisattvas, who were thought of as male, were, like the gods of Hinduism, endowed with wives who were the active aspect, the "force" or "potency" (*śakti*) of their husbands. The god was believed to be as transcendent and aloof, while the goddess was active in the world; thus the god might be best approached through the goddess. The productive activity of the divine was thought of in terms of sexual union, an idea as old as the *Ṛg Veda*. With the spread of these ideas sexual symbolism, and even sexual intercourse as a religious rite, were incorporated into the teachings of some schools of both Hinduism and Buddhism.

With these ideas was combined a new magical mysticism. The Lesser Vehicle taught that release was obtained by the gradual loss of individuality through self-discipline and meditation; the Great Vehicle added that the grace and help of the heavenly Buddhas and Bodhisattvas assisted the process. The followers of the new teachings taught that it could be best attained by acquiring magical power, which they called *vajra* ("thunderbolt", or "diamond"). Hence the new school of Buddhism was called *Vajrayāna*, "the Vehicle of the Thunderbolt".

Even the Sthaviravādins taught that the monk who reached a high stage of detachment and mental training acquired supernatural powers. At all times there were free-lance Buddhist monks, who did not live regularly in monasteries under orthodox discipline, and who attempted feats of sorcery and necromancy, such as the Buddha is said to have condemned. It was perhaps among these free-lances that the ideas of the new Vehicle developed, to be codified and given dignity under the Pāla kings of Bengal and Bihār. Even in the 7th century Hsüan Tsang found certain monasteries permeated with magical practices.

The chief divinities of the new sect were the "Saviouresses" (*Tārās*), the spouses of the Buddhas and Bodhisattvas. There were also a host of lesser divinities, many called by the names of demons, such as "outcaste women" (*mātaṅgīs*), "demonesses" (*piśācīs*), "sorceresses" (*yoginīs*), and "she-ghouls" (*ḍākinīs*). The Buddhas and Bodhisattvas with their Tārās were approximated to the less amiable members of the Hindu pantheon, and were often depicted with many arms in ferocious poses.

As in the days of the *Brāhmaṇas*, it was thought that these deities should be compelled rather than persuaded. The textbooks outlining the means (*sādhana*) of doing this were called *Tantras*, and hence the new cult is often referred to as tantric. By pronouncing the right formula (*mantra*) in the correct manner, or by drawing the correct magical symbol (*yantro*), one might force the gods to bestow magical power on the worshipper and lead him to the highest bliss. Among the many formulae of tantric Buddhism one is specially famous—the "Six Syllables" (*Ṣaḍakṣarā*), *Ōm maṇi padme hūm*, still written and repeated thousands of times daily in Tibet. This phrase: "Ah! the jewel is indeed in the lotus!", may be sexual in its original significance, mystically repeating the divine coitus of the heavenly Buddha and Prajñāpāramitā, and of Avalokiteśvara and his Tārā.

Tantric Buddhism did not neglect the techniques of mental training which were part of all the chief religions of India, but their direction was altered. Their primary purpose now was to obtain supernormal power. The meditations of the Vajrayāna were often positively psychopathic. The practitioner of the system might so hypnotize himself as to imagine that he was reborn from the womb of a Tārā, to kill his father the Buddha and take his place. In sexual union with a female devotee he and his partner would become Buddha and Tārā, or he himself might become Tārā. In the sexual rites of tantric Buddhism all taboos were lifted. Even incest was permitted, for what was sin to the ignorant was virtue to the initiate, and so as well as ritual copulation meat and alcohoh were indulged in at the tantric covens. These things were, however, done under strict control, and only by initiates at sacred ceremonies. Like the Bengali tantricist of later times the Vajrayāna initiate might in his ordinary life be a normal man, whose occasional religious debauchery served as a catharsis to his evil psychological propensities and was of real help to him in leading the good life as he understood it.

The Buddhist Order

Membership of the Buddhist Order was not restricted by caste, but slaves, soldiers, debtors, and other persons under obligation or in tutelage might not enter it without the permission of their superior. Novices might be admitted from the age of eight upwards, but they could only qualify for full membership of the Order after a long course of study, at the minimum age of twenty. The rites of admission were simple, involving putting on the three yellow or orange robes of the Order, ceremonially shaving the head, and pronouncing the Three Jewels (p. 240) and the "Ten Precepts". The latter form a sort of Buddhist decalogue:

(1) "I accept the precept to refrain from harming living beings.
(2) "I accept the precept to refrain from taking what is not given.
(3) "… from evil behaviour in passion.
(4) "… from false speech.
(5) "… from *surā*, *meraya* and *majjā* (alcoholic drinks), which cause carelessness.
(6) "… from eating at forbidden times (i.e. after midday).
(7) "… from dancing, singing, music and dramatic performances.
(8) "… from the use of garlands, perfumes, unguents and jewellery.
(9) "… from the use of a high or broad bed.
(io) "… from receiving gold and silver."

These precepts were not lifelong vows, but earnest resolves. They were repeated regularly, and if any monk felt that he could no longer honestly maintain them he might leave the Order quite freely, though public opinion tended to frown on the backslider. The vows were often taken for a definite duration only, as is still done in Burma, where boys on leaving school often spend some months in a monastery in preparation for adult life. In this the Buddhist Order sharply contrasts with Christian monasticism.

Of the ten vows the first did not originally involve complete vegetarianism, though it came to do so in many Buddhist communities. A monk might eat meat if the animal providing it was not specially killed for his benefit. The third vow, for the monk, meant absolute celibacy. The fifth was generally taken to mean abstention from all intoxicants. By the sixth, a monk might eat no solid food after midday; this, in a warm climate and for a man not engaged in strenuous work, was no very great hardship, especially as the monk might take sweetened beverages at any time. In colder climates, such as that of Tibet, monks often take an evening meal, which is looked on as medicine. The seventh rule was not taken to include singing and music for liturgical or other religious purposes. The tenth was interpreted very liberally in many monasteries. Strictly a monk might own only eight "requisites"—three robes, a waist-cloth, an alms-bowl, a razor, a needle, and a cloth to strain his drinking-water in order to save the lives of any animalculæ it might contain. In fact he often owned much more than this by the convenient fiction, not unknown in some Christian religious communities, that his property belonged to the Order, from which he had it on loan.

The monk had to beg his food from door to door every morning, taking it back to his monastery for his midday meal. As the monasteries became wealthy, however, the begging round was often reduced to a mere formality, or dropped altogether.

While the Buddhist monk resembled his Christian counterpart in his vows of chastity and poverty, he took no vow of obedience. Each novice or junior monk had his preceptor, and was expected to treat him with great respect, but the monk was essentially a free member of a community of free men. There was no central authority to regulate the many monasteries and enforce uniformity; each was a law unto itself, guided only by the precepts of the Master as it had received them and as it interpreted them. The constitution of the monastery had elements of democracy about it. The chief monk or abbot was not appointed from above or nominated by his predecessor, but held office by the suffrage of all the monks in the monastic parish. The day-to-day business of the monastery was managed by a committee of elder monks, and important decisions, such as the admission or expulsion of members, could only be made by the committee and not by the chief. Important business was discussed at meetings of the whole monastery in chapter (p. 84).

The monks assembled every fortnight on the evenings of the full and new moons for *upavasatha* (in Pāli, *uposatha*), an act of general confession. The long list of monastic rules (*Prātimokṣa*, in Pāli *Pātimokkha*) from the *Vinaya Piṭaka* was read, and each monk confessed any breaches of which he had been guilty during the preceding fortnight. If his fault was serious his case was referred to a committee of elders, which might impose penance or expel him from the Order. The ceremony concluded with the preaching of sermons, to which the pious layfolk of the vicinity listened.

The daily life of the monk was chiefly spent in study and religious exercises, but he was expected to take his share in the work of the monastery, cleaning his cell, and sweeping the courtyard and the monastic buildings, while the elder monks devoted much of their time to teaching the novices. Among the most important of the monk's spiritual exercises were the Four Sublime Moods (*Brahmavihāra*), in which, sitting quietly cross-legged, he endeavoured to fill his mind with the four cardinal virtues of Buddhism—love, pity, joy, and serenity—and to consider all living beings in the light of these virtues. A fifth mood was that of impurity, in which he considered all the vileness and horror of the world and of the life of the flesh. For those more advanced in sanctity there were more exalted meditations, which brought the monk very near to the realization of Nirvāṇa.

One aspect of the monk's mental discipline which deserves mention is the seventh element of the "Noble Eightfold Path" (p. 237)— "Right Recollection". He was taught to train himself to be continually aware of what he was doing, observing himself, as it were, all the time. It was taught that every act must be fully conscious, and distraction, carelessness, and lack of consideration were serious faults. When he ate, the monk should be aware of the nature of the act, its purpose, and the transience of the body which he fed, and similarly with every act throughout the day. No doubt few but the most advanced monks were able to keep up this state of "Right Recollection" continuously.

At one time India possessed numerous Buddhist nunneries, though now monastic life in Buddhism is largely confined to men, except in Tibet. The nuns wore yellow robes and shaved their heads like the monks, and their discipline was very similar. Though strict rules were laid down for preserving the respectability of the two branches of the Order, which often dwelt in adjoining establishments, accusations of immorality were sometimes levelled against them by their religious opponents, and these accusations may have had some foundation. The sexual activity of tantric Buddhism, of course, did not constitute a breach of the vows when performed in accordance with the rites of the sect.

Buddhist Ethics and Morality

Buddhism inculcates a high system of ethics. The Noble Eightfold Path, whereby a man attains Nirvāṇa, is not merely a matter of belief or knowledge, but also one of conduct, and the Four Cardinal Virtues of Buddhism (p. 248) are more positive in character than the non-violence and abstinence of the Upaniṣads.

The chief of these virtues, love (Pāli, *mettā*, Sanskrit, *maitrī*), is somewhat less tinged with emotion than the comparable virtue in Christianity. The term is derived from the word *mitra*, "a friend", and might be translated "friendliness", "good will" or "benevolence". Nevertheless the Buddhist scriptures contain passages which describe *mettā* with a passion which recalls the famous words of St. Paul on the virtue of charity.

> "May every living being, weak or strong, large or small, seen or unseen, near or far, born or yet unborn—may every living thing be full of joy.
>
> "May none deceive another, or think ill of him in any way whatever, or in anger or ill-will desire evil for another.
>
> "Just as a mother, as long as she lives, cares for her only child, so should a man feel all-embracing love to all living beings.
>
> "He should feel boundless love for all the world, above below and across, unrestrained, without enmity. Standing, walking, sitting or lying down, … he should be firm in the mindfulness of love. For this is what men call the Sublime Mood."[45]

In this connexion the following extract is interesting, for it recalls a well-known verse of the Sermon on the Mount.

> "A man buries a treasure in a deep pit, thinking: 'It will be useful in time of need, or if the king is displeased with me, or if I am robbed or fall into debt,

> or if food is scarce, or if bad luck befalls me.'
>
> "But all this treasure may not profit the owner at all, for he may forget where he hid it, or goblins may steal it, or his enemies or even his kinsmen may take it when he is not on his guard.
>
> "But by charity, goodness, restraint and self-control man and woman alike can store up a well-hidden treasure—a treasure which cannot be given to others,* and which robbers cannot steal. A wise man should do good—that is the treasure which will not leave him."[46]

Though the passages quoted above cannot be dated with precision they are certainly pre-Christian, and there is no possibility of Christian influence.

The vow of the Bodhisattva, which we have already quoted (p. 241f), gives sufficient indication of the ethics of the Great Vehicle, which teaches an impassioned altruism scarcely to be found elsewhere in the literature of the non-Christian world.

Though the Buddhist virtue of *mettā* seems often rather a state of mind than a spur to benevolent action, the view that faith without works is dead is sometimes expressed, notably in the story of the Buddha and the sick monk. As the Master was going on a round of inspection, visiting the monks in their cells, he found one who was sick with dysentery, and who had fallen from his bed and lay in his own ordure. With his own hands the Buddha washed the sick man from head to foot, laid him comfortably on his bed, and gave a new rule to the Order:

> "Brethren, you have no mother or father to care for you. If you do not care for one another who else will do so? Brethren, he who would care for me should care for the sick."[47]

Though this precept applies primarily to the Order of monks, it was no doubt under the influence of such teachings that Aśoka established free dispensaries, and that Buddhist monks have at all times studied medical lore, and treated laymen as well as their own fellows.

The Buddhist scriptures were chiefly written for and addressed to the monks and nuns of the order, but a number of passages gave special instruction to the layman, and the first five of the "Ten Precepts" (p. 247f) were binding on the lay community. According to the first of these no Buddhist could follow the profession of hunter or butcher. The resolve not to take life was generally interpreted as permitting lawful warfare and the sentencing of criminals to death, and did not preclude Buddhists from eating meat, if provided by non-Buddhist butchers. But Buddhism tended to encourage mildness and vegetarianism, and somewhat discouraged the militarism which prevailed at most periods in ancient India (p. 104f). The second precept, not to take what is not given, included abstention not only from theft, but also from sharp practice in business.

---

*The doctrine of the Sthaviravādin School. In the Great Vehicle merit can be transferred (p. 242).

For the laymen the third precept did not, of course, involve absolute celibacy, but permitted lawful marriage. It was usually interpreted as forbidding unnatural sexuality and extra-marital relations. Buddhism laid down no hard and fast rules on the questions of marriage and divorce, and at the present day in Buddhist countries marital laws are largely influenced by local custom. The fourth precept, forbidding false speech, was taken to include lying, perjury and slander, while the fifth forbade alcoholic drinks. Modern Buddhists often put a rather liberal interpretation on this rule, and the same may have been done in ancient days, for in one sermon the Buddha is said to have classed only the first four sins as "vices of action", and to have included drinking among the six less reprehensible "openings for the swallowing up of wealth", the others being roaming the streets at unseasonable hours, frequenting festivals, gambling, keeping bad company and idling.

This sermon, the most important Buddhist text on Jay morality, is the "Address to Sigāla",[48] in which the Buddha gives instruction to a young layman on his relations with his fellow men, and on the duties of parents and children, teachers and pupils, husbands and wives, and friends. It breathes a spirit of warm affection and fellowship, not raised to an exalted spiritual level but of an everyday practical type. The text is too long to quote, and we can only summarize some of its instructions.

> Husbands should respect their wives, and comply as far as possible with their requests. They should not commit adultery. They should give their wives full charge of the home, and supply them with fine clothes and jewellery as far as their means permit. Wives should be thorough in their duties, gentle and kind to the whole household, chaste, and careful in housekeeping, and they should carry out their work with skill and enthusiasm.
>
> A man should be generous to his friends, speak kindly of them, act in their interests in every way possible, treat them as his equals, and keep his word to them. They in turn should watch over his interests and property, take care of him when he is "off his guard" (i.e. intoxicated, infatuated, or otherwise liable to commit rash and careless actions), stand by him and help him in time of trouble, and respect other members of his family.
>
> Employers should treat their servants and workpeople decently. They should not be given tasks beyond their strength. They should receive adequate food and wages, be cared for in time of sickness and infirmity, and be given regular holidays and bonuses in times of prosperity. They should rise early and go to bed late in the service of their master, be content with their just wages, work thoroughly, and maintain their master's reputation.

Precepts such as these, which are implicit in the teaching of other religions, are nowhere else so clearly and unequivocally expressed. Specially noteworthy are the duties of husbands to wives and of masters to servants, which seem to anticipate twentieth century ideas on the rights of women and employees.

Among the most important vehicles of Buddhist ethical teaching are the Jātaka stories. These are mostly of secular origin, and many merely inculcate shrewdness and caution in everyday life, as do Æsop's fables (e.g. that given in full on p. 405f). Others teach generosity and self-abnegation in morbidly exaggerated forms, for instance the tale of King Śivi (known also in Hinduism), who ransomed a pigeon from a famished hawk with flesh cut from his own thigh. Many modern readers may well find the very popular story of Prince Viśvāntara (Pāli, Vessantara) distasteful. This prince gave away so much of his royal father's treasure that he was banished with his wife and children in a carriage drawn by four horses. As he left, he gave away the carriage and horses for the asking, and settled in a hut in the forest with his family. Soon he gave his children to a wandering ascetic who needed them to do his begging for him, and finally he disposed of his wife in similar manner. But all ended happily, for those who had asked him for his most precious possessions were gods in disguise who had decided to test his generosity, and he was at last restored to his family and his patrimony (pl. XXVIII). But many old Buddhist stories are of the highest ethical quality, such as that of the monkey who saved the lives of his fellows from the king's archers at the risk of his own by making himself a living bridge over the Gangā, or that of the noble parrot who laid down his life for his friends in a futile attempt to quench a forest fire by drops of water scattered from his wings.

(III) JAINISM AND OTHER UNORTHODOX SECTS

Jainism

Among the many unorthodox teachers who were contemporary with the Buddha was Vardhamāna, known to his followers as *Mahāvira* ("the Great Hero"). Jainism, the "Religion of the Conquerors" (*jinas*), which he founded, had a history very different from that of Buddhism. It succeeded in establishing itself firmly, and in some places became very influential, but it never spread beyond India. Unlike Buddhism, there were no fundamental changes and developments in Jaina doctrine. But though the history of Jainism is less interesting than that of Buddhism, and though it was never so important, it survived in the land of its birth, where it still has some two million adherents, mostly well-to-do merchants.

The legends of Vardhamāna Mahāvīra are less attractive than those of the Buddha and are even more formalized and unreliable, but as he is referred to in the Buddhist scriptures as one of the Buddha's chief opponents his historicity is beyond doubt. He was born about 540 B.C. and was the son of Siddhārtha, a chief of the clan of Jñātrikas, the associates of the Licchavis of Vaiśālī; his mother, Triśalā, was the sister of the Licchavi chief Ceṭaka, and thus, like the Buddha, he was wholly the product of the oligarchic martial clans which were a powerful political force at the time. Though he was educated as a prince, and married and had a daughter, his real interest lay in the quest for salvation. At the age of thirty, when his parents were dead, he left his home for a life of asceticism. At first he followed the practices of an ascetic group called the *Nirgranthas* ("Free from

Bonds"), which had been founded some 200 years earlier by a certain Pārsva. The term Nirgrantha was later used for the members of the order which Mahāvīra founded, and Pārśva was remembered as the twenty-third of the twenty-four great teachers or *Tirthaṅkaras* ("Ford-makers") of the Jaina faith.

For over twelve years Vardhamāna wandered from place to place, begging his food, meditating, disputing, and subjecting his body to austerities of all kinds. At first he wore a single garment which he never changed, but after thirteen months he laid this encumbrance aside, and the rest of his life was spent in complete nudity. For some six years his hardships were shared by another ascetic, Gośāla Maskarīputra, but ultimately the two quarrelled, and Gośāla left Vardhamāna to found the sect of Ājīvikas.

In the thirteenth year of his asceticism Vardhamāna found full enlightenment and Nirvāṇa; he became a "Worthy" (*Arhant*), a "Conqueror" (*Jina*), a "Ford-maker". He soon gained a great reputation and a large band of followers, and for thirty years he taught in the Gangetic kingdoms, patronized by the very kings who also patronized the Buddha. He survive the death of his chief rival, Gośāla, and probably also that of the Buddha, and died of self-starvation at the age of seventy-two in the little town of Pāvā, near the Magadhan capital Rājagṛha. There are conflicting traditions about the date of his death, which was probably in 468 B.C.

For some two centuries the Jainas remained a small community of monks and lay followers, less important than the rival sect of the Ājīvikas. According to a strongly held Jaina tradition Candragupta Maurya joined their order as a monk on his abdication, and it seems certain that there was an accession of strength in Maurya times. A serious famine at the end of Candragupta's reign led to a great exodus of Jaina monks from the Gangā Valley to the Deccan, where they established important centres of their faith.

Out of this migration arose the great schism of Jainism, on a point of monastic discipline. Bhadrabāhu, the elder of the community, who led the emigrants, insisted on the retention of the rule of nudity which Mahāvīra had established. Sthūlabhadra, the leader of the monks who remained in the North, allowed his followers to wear white garments, owing to the hardships and confusions of the famine. Hence arose the two sects of the Jainas, the *Digambaras* ("Space-clad", i.e. naked), and the *Śvetāmbaras* ("*White-clad*"). The schism did not become final until the 1st century A.D., and there were never any fundamental doctrinal differences; later most monks of the naked sect took to wearing robes in public, but the division has persisted down to the present day.

According to tradition an oral sacred literature had been passed down from the days of Mahāvīra, but Bhadrabāhu was the last person to know it perfectly. On his death Sthūlabhadra called a great council at Pāṭaliputra, and the canon was reconstructed as best possible in twelve *Aṅgas*, or sections, which replaced the fourteen "former texts" (*Pūrvas*). This canon was accepted only by the Śvetāmbaras; the Digambaras claimed that the old canon was hopelessly lost, and proceeded to devise new scriptures for themselves, some of which are still unpublished. The texts of the Śvetāmbara canon were finally settled and reduced to writing at a council at Valabhī in Gujarāt in the 5th century A.D. By this time the texts had become very corrupt and one of the Aṅgas had been completely lost, while new material had been added to the original canon in the form of the twelve *Upāṅgas*, or minor sections, and various lesser works. In the Middle Ages a great body of commentarial literature was written both in Prākrit and Sanskrit, and there were many able philosopher monks, who interpreted the scriptures of the sect. Some monks turned their attention to secular literature and other branches of learning, apparently without losing their piety. One of the last great poets in Sanskrit, Nayacandra, of the 14th century (p. 383f), was a Jaina monk, as was Mallinātha, the author of the standard commentary on the poems of Kālidāsa. We owe much to the Jaina monks' love of literature. To copy a manuscript, even a secular one, was considered a work of great religious merit, and thus the old Jaina monasteries of Western India have preserved many rare and otherwise unknown texts, some of which have still to be published and many of which are of non-Jaina origin.

In the period between the Mauryas and the Guptas Jainism can be traced from Orissā in the East to Mathurā in the West, but in later times it was chiefly concentrated in two regions—Gujarāt and parts of Rājasthān, where the Śvetāmbara sect prevailed, and the central part of the Peninsula, the modern Mysore, where the Digambaras were dominant. The Gangā Valley, the original home of Jainism, was little affected by it.

The Śvetāmbaras found much support among the chiefs of Western India, and gained a position of great prominence during the reign of the Caulukya king Kumārapāla, who ruled Gujarāt in the 12th century. Under the guidance of a great Jaina scholar, Hemacandra, Kumārapāla is said to have instituted a Jaina reformation; but on his death the sect lost much of its influence, and though it still flourished it never again became so important. Similarly in the South the Digambaras had great influence in the early Middle Ages, thanks to the patronage of kings, but this influence gradually diminished as that of devotional Śaivism and Vaiṣṇavism grew. There are traditions, which some have doubted but which we believe to have a basis of fact, that the Jainas were sometimes severely persecuted. But although Jainism declined it never disappeared.

Though the Jaina scriptures are comparatively late in their final form, there is little divergence in fundamentals between the two great Jaina sects; thus it seems that the basic teachings of both are very ancient indeed, and are essentially those of Mahāvīra himself. Jainism, like Buddhism, is fundamentally atheistic in that, while not denying the existence of the gods, it refuses them any important part in the universal scheme. The world, for the Jaina, is not created, maintained or destroyed by a personal deity, but functions only according to universal law.

The universe is eternal. Its existence is divided into an infinite number of cycles, each consisting of a period of improvement (*utsarpiṇī*), and one of decline (*avasarpīṇī*). Each period is to all intents and purposes like the last, containing twenty-four *Tirthaṅkaras*, twelve Universal Emperors (*Cakravartins*), both classes being included in the total of sixty-three Great Men (*Śālāka-puruṣas*), who live at regular intervals in the cycle. At the peak period men are of enormous size and reach a tremendous age. They have no need of laws or property, for wishing-trees (*kalpa-vṛkṣa*) give them all they need for the asking. At present the world is rapidly declining. The last Tīrthankara of this age has passed to final Nirvāṇa, and gradually true religion will be lost—Mahāvīra in his omniscience even gave his followers the name and address of the last Jaina of this æon. The process of decline will continue for 40,000 years, when men will be dwarfs in stature, with a life of only twenty years, and will dwell in caves, having forgotten all culture, even to the use of fire. Then the tide will turn, and they will begin to improve again, only to decline once more, and so on for all eternity. Unlike the cosmology of the Buddhists and Hindus, that of the Jainas involves no cataclysms of universal destruction.

The universe functions through the interaction of living souls (*jivas*, literally "lives"), and five categories of non-living entities (*ajiva*): "ether" (*ākāśa*), the means or condition of movement (*dharma*), the means or condition of rest (*adharma*)*, time (*kāla*), and matter (*pudgala*). Souls are not only the property of animal and plant life, but also of entities such as stones, rocks, running water, and many other natural objects not looked on as living by other sects.

The soul is naturally bright, all-knowing and blissful. There are an infinite number of souls in the universe, all fundamentally equal, but differing owing to the adherence of matter in a fine atomic form. This subtle matter, quite invisible to the human eye, is *karma*, the immaterial entity of other systems interpreted materialistically. The naturally bright soul becomes dulled and clouded over by karmic matter and thus acquires first a spiritual and then a material body. The obfuscation of the soul is compared to the gradual clouding of a bright oily surface by motes of dust. Karma adheres to the soul as a result of activity. Any and every activity induces karma of some kind, but deeds of a cruel and selfish nature induce more, and more durable, karma than others. The karma already acquired leads to the acquisition of further karma, and thus the cycle of transmigration continues indefinitely.

On these premisses transmigration can only be escaped by dispelling the karma already adhering to the soul and by ensuring that no more is acquired. This is a slow and difficult process and it is believed that many souls will never succeed in accomplishing it, but will continue to transmigrate for all eternity. The annihilation (*nirjarā*) of karma comes about through penance, and the prevention (*saṃvara*) of the influx (*aśrava*) and fixation (*bandha*)† of karma in the soul is ensured by carefully disciplined conduct, as a result of which it does not enter in dangerous quantities and is dispersed immediately. When the soul has finally set itself free it rises at once above the highest heaven to the top of the universe, where it remains in inactive omniscient bliss through all eternity. This, for the Jainas, is Nirvāṇa.

Though Jaina philosophers developed their doctrines, and evolved a theory of

* Like the Buddhists the Jainas gave to these familiar terms very special connotations, the full discussion of which is beyond the scope of this work. *Dharma* is a sort of secondary space which permits movement, as water permits a fish to swim; *adharma* is a tertiary space which permits rest.

† We quote these four Sanskrit terms as, *with jīva* (souls), *ajīva* (the five categories mentioned earlier), and salvation (*mokṣa*), they constitute the seven fundamental categories *(tattva)* of Jainism.

epistemology of great subtlety (p. 456f) and a remarkable view of space and time suggesting the world picture of relativity physics, their fundamental teachings remained essentially unaltered. Mahāvīra and the twenty-three other Tīrthaṅkaras were adored in the same way as the Buddha and the Hindu gods, but Jainism never compromised in its atheism, and there was no development in this sect comparable to the Great Vehicle in Buddhism. Jainism has survived for over 2,000 years on the basis of these austere teachings alone.

Full salvation is not possible to the layman. In this Jainism differs from Buddhism and Hinduism, which concede it in exceptional cases. To attain Nirvāṇa a man must abandon all trammels, including his clothes. Only by a long course of fasting, self-mortification, study and meditation, can he rid himself of karma, and only by the most rigorous discipline can he prevent fresh karma from clinging to his soul. Hence a monastic life is essential for salvation. Very early, however, many Jaina monks gave up the rule of nudity, and today few if any monks, even of the Digambara sect, practise it regularly. Both sects of Jainas, however, would admit that it is necessary to full liberation. The universe is now rapidly declining, and no souls now reach Nirvāṇa or have any hope of reaching it in the foreseeable future, so in these degenerate days clothes are worn as a concession to human frailty.

The regimen of the Jaina monk was, and still is, strict in the extreme. At his initiation his hair was not shaved, but pulled out by the roots. He subjected himself to many hardships, such as meditating in the full sunlight of the Indian summer, or maintaining an uneasy posture for long periods on end, though Jainism did not permit the more spectacular penances of some Hindu ascetics. The monk's frugal meals were interrupted by numerous fasts, and many monks starved themselves to death, following the example of Mahāvīra himself.

The life of the monk was governed by five vows, abjuring killing, stealing, lying, sexual activity and the possession of property. These vows were interpreted quite strictly. Acts of violence and killing, whether intentional or not, were the most potent cause of the influx of karma, and were therefore particularly to be avoided. Meat-eating was quite forbidden to monk and layman alike. Even insect life was carefully protected. Like the Buddhist monks, the Jainas strained their drinking-water to save the lives of animalculas. Jaina monks usually carried feather dusters, to brush ants and other insects from their path and save them from being trampled underfoot, and they wore veils over their mouths, to prevent the minute living things in the air from being inhaled and killed. No lay Jaina could take up the profession of agriculture, since this involved not only the destruction of plant life, but also of many living beings in the soil itself. Kindling a light or fire was not permitted by the monk, since it destroyed lives both in the fuel and in the surrounding air, while putting a fire out was also forbidden, since it destroyed the life of the fire itself. Thus, in its insistence on ahiṃsā, or non-violence, Jainism went much further than any other Indian religion.

It has been suggested that Jainism survived in India, whereas Buddhism perished, because the former sect took better care of its layfolk. In Jainism the layman was a definite member of the Order, encouraged to undertake periodical retreats and to live as far as possible the life of the monk for specific periods. Like Buddhism, Jainism encouraged the commercial virtues of honesty and frugality, and at a very early period the Jaina lay community became predominantly mercantile. The splendid Jaina temples at such places as Mount Ābū and Śravaṇa Beḷgoḷā are testimonies of the great wealth and piety of medieval Jaina laymen.

Jainism had no special social doctrines. The domestic rites of the layman, such as birth, marriage and death, were those of the Hindus. At one time Jainism maintained a cult of stupas in the same way as Buddhism, but this has not survived, and early in the Christian era the Tīrthaṅkaras were adored in temples in the form of icons. By the Middle Ages this worship approximated to that of the Hindus, with offerings of flowers, incense, lamps and so on. As with Buddhism, the chief gods of the Hindus found their way into Jaina temples in subordinate positions, and though there was no real compromise with theism the sect easily fitted into the Hindu order, its members forming distinct castes.

Jaina religious literature is generally dull and pedantic, and its ethics, though they inculcate such virtues as honesty and mercy, tend to be negative and fundamentally selfish. The virtue of non-violence in Jainism often had little of love about it, but merely involved vegetarianism and precautions against the accidental killing of small animals. There are, however, passages in the Jaina scriptures which show warmth and human svmpathy. Thus, discussing the doctrine of non-violence, the early *Acārāṅga Sūtra* writes:

> "A wise man should be neither glad nor angry, for he should know and consider the happiness of all things. ... Life is dear to the many who own fields and houses, who get dyed and coloured clothes and jewels and earrings, and grow attached to them. ... Only those who are of controlled conduct do not desire these things; therefore, knowing birth and death, you should firmly walk the path.
>
> "For nothing is inaccessible to death, and all beings are fond of themselves, they love pleasure and hate pain, they shun destruction and cling to life. They long to live. To all things life is dear."[49]

More typical of Jaina moral teachings are the following verses, said to have been spoken by Mahāvīra to Gautama, one of his disciples (not, of course, to be confused with Gautama the Buddha).

"As the dead leaf when its time is up
falls from the tree to the ground,
so is the life of man.
Gautama, always be watchful!

"As the dewdrop that sways on a blade of grass
lasts but a moment,
so is the life of man.
Gautama, always be watchful!

"For the soul which suffers for its carelessness
is whirled about in the universe,
through good and evil karma.
Gautama, always be watchful!

"When the body grows old and the hair turns white,
and all the vital powers decrease …
despondency and disease befall, and the flesh wastes and decays.
Gautama, always be watchful!

"So cast away all attachments,
and be pure as a lotus, or as water in autumn.
Free from every attachment,
Gautama, always be watchful!"[50]

As an example of Digambara teaching we give a few verses, remarkable for their conciseness, by the 4th century monk Pūjyapāda.

"Body, house, wealth and wife,
sons and friends and enemies—
all are different from the soul.
Only the fool thinks them his own."

• • • •

"From all directions come the birds
and rest together in the trees;
but in the morning each goes his own way,
flying in all directions."

• • • •

"Death is not for me. Why then should I fear?
Disease is not for me. Why then should I despair?
I am not a child, nor a youth, nor an old man—
All these states are only of my body."

• • • •

"Time and again in my foolishness I have enjoyed
all kinds of body and have discarded them.
Now I am wise!
Why should I long for rubbish?"

• • • •

"The soul is one thing, matter another—
that is the quintessence of truth.
Whatever else may be said
is merely its elaboration."[51]

The Ājīvikas

A third unorthodox sect which emerged at the same time as Buddhism and Jainism was that of the Ājīvikas, a body of ascetics who were under a rigorous discipline similar to that of the Jainas, and who also practised complete nudity. The doctrines of the founder of the sect, Gośāla Maskarīputra, bear a generic likeness to those of his contemporary and former friend Mahāvīra. Like Mahāvīra, he looked back to earlier teachers and ascetic groups, whose doctrines he refurbished and developed. According to both Buddhist and Jaina tradition he was of humble birth; he died a year or so before the Buddha, about 487 B.C., after a fierce altercation with Mahāvīra in the city of Śrāvastī. His followers seem to have combined with those of other teachers, such as Pūraṇa Kāśyapa the antinomian and Pakudha Kātyāyana the atomist, to form the Ājīvika sect. After a period of prosperity in Mauryan times, when Aśoka and his successor Daśaratha presented caves to the Ājīvikas, the sect rapidly declined, and only retained some local importance in a small region of Eastern Mysore and the adjacent parts of Madras, where it survived until the 14th century, after which we hear no more of it.

No scriptures of the Ājīvikas have come down to us, and the little we know about them has to be reconstructed from the polemic literature of Buddhism and Jainism. The sect was certainly atheistic, and its main feature was strict determinism. The usual doctrine of karma taught that though a man's present condition was determined by his past actions he could influence his destiny, in this life and the future, by choosing the right course of conduct. This the Ājīvikas denied. The whole universe was conditioned and determined to the smallest detail by an impersonal cosmic principle, *Niyati*, or destiny. It was impossible to influence the course of transmigration in any way.

> "All that have breath, all that are born, all that have life, are without power, strength or virtue, but are developed by destiny, chance and nature, and experience joy and sorrow in the six classes [of existence]. There are ... 8,400,000 great æons (*mahākappa*), through which fool and wise alike must take their course and make an end of sorrow. There is no [question of] bringing unripe karma to fruition, nor of exhausting karma already ripened, by virtuous conduct, by vows, by penance, or by chastity. That cannot be done. Saṃsāra is measured as with a bushel, with its joy and sorrow and its appointed end. It can neither be lessened nor increased, nor is there any excess or deficiency of it. Just as a ball of string will, when thrown, unwind to its full length, so fool and wise alike will take their course, and make an end of sorrow."[52]

Though nothing that a man could do would in any way influence his future lot Ājīvika monks practised severe asceticism, because the force of destiny compelled them to do so, although their religious opponents accused them of licentiousness and immorality.

The Dravidian Ājīvikas developed their doctrines in a way resembling Buddhism of the Great Vehicle. Gośāla became an ineffable divinity, like the

Buddha in the Mahāyāna system, while the doctrine of destiny evolved into a Parmenidean view that all change and movement were illusory, and that the world was in reality eternally and immovably at rest. This view bears a certain resemblance to Nāgārjuna's doctrine of "the Void".

Scepticism and Materialism

Buddha, Mahāvīra, Godala, and many lesser teachers of their period ignored the gods, but they were not thoroughgoing atheists and materialists. All admitted the existence of supernatural beings of strictly limited powers, and all accepted the fundamental doctrine of transmigration, though they interpreted its mechanics individually. Some thinkers, however, rejected all immaterial categories completely, and their influence may have been wider than appears from the religious texts of the period. In the fairly early *Kaṭha Upaniṣad* the interlocutor Naciketas (p. 135) questions Yama, the god of death, in these terms: "There is doubt about the state of a man who is dead —some say he is, others, he is not." "On this point", Yama replies, "even the gods formerly had their doubts. It is not easy to understand." At this time unbelief must have been fairly widespread.

Ajita Keśakambalin ("Ajita of the Hair-blanket", no doubt so called from the garb of his order), a contemporary of the Buddha, was the earliest known teacher of complete materialism.

> "Man," he said, "is formed of the four elements. When he dies earth returns to the aggregate of earth, water to water, fire to fire, and air to air, while his senses vanish into space. Four men with the bier take up the corpse; they gossip [about the dead man] as far as the burning-ground, where his bones turn the colour of a dove's wing and his sacrifices end in ashes. They are fools who preach almsgiving, and those who maintain the existence [of immaterial categories] speak vain and lying nonsense. When the body dies both fool and wise alike are cut off and perish. They do not survive after death."[53]

If we are to believe the Buddhist scriptures, Ajita founded a sect of monks. The Buddha condemned them as having no good motive for their asceticism, the degree of which is nowhere made clear. It is possible that, like the Epicureans, they were not so much an ascetic order as a fraternity of men with common aims, cultivating together the simpler pleasures of life. In any case, an element of materialism is traceable in Indian thought from this time onwards. Religious and philosophical literature, whether Hindu, Buddhist or Jaina, devotes much space to attacking the evil tenets of the *Cārvākas* or *Lokāyatas*, as the materialist schools were called. Throughout the period which we treat these unbelievers are referred to with scorn and disapprobation which sometimes seems to contain an undertone of fear, as though the pious authors thought it really possible that the materialists might shake the foundations of the established order. Materialist and irreligious undercurrents are traceable in some secular literature, such as the *Arthaśāstra* and the *Kāmasūtra*.

The general attitude of the materialist schools, according to their adversaries, was that all religious observance and morality were futile. A man should make the most of life and get what happiness he could out of it. The frugal virtues of Buddhism and Jainism were rejected.

> "As long as he lives a man should live happily
> and drink ghee, though he run into debt,
> for when the body is turned to ashes
> how can there be any return to life?"[54]

A man must not turn back from pleasure for fear of concomitant sorrow. He must accept occasional sorrow gladly, for the sake of the joy which he finds in the world, as he accepts the bones with the fish or the husk with the corn. "Whoever turns in fear from the joy that he sees before him is a fool, no better than an animal."[55]

Their opponents ascribe only base ideals to the materialists, and there is no definite evidence that they had any ethical doctrines, but one verse attributed to them shows that they were not blind to the warm ties of family and friendship.

> "If a man really left his body,
> and passed on to the other world,
> would he not come back once more,
> drawn by his love for his kin?"[56]

Besides numerous quotations attributed to materialists in religious and philosophical works one anti-religious philosophical text has survived. This is the *Tattvopaplavasiṃha* (freely "The Lion Destroying all Religious Truth") written by a certain Jayarāśi in the 8th century A.D. The author was an out-and-out Pyrrhonist denying the possibility of any certain knowledge at all, and he demolished with able dialectic, to his own satisfaction at any rate, all the basic presuppositions of the chief religious systems of his day.

(IV) HINDUISM

Development and Literature

As well as the aristocratic religion of the brāhmaṇs, the Buddhist and Jaina scriptures mention popular cults, connected with earth-spirits (*yakṣas*), snake-spirits (*nāgas*), and other minor deities, centred round sacred spots or caityas (p. 230). Very early a god named Vāsudeva was widely worshipped, especially in Western India. It was to this god that the Besnagar column, to which we have more than once referred, was erected. The inscription on the column shows that by the end of the 2nd century B.C. the cult of Vāsudeva was receiving the support of the ruling classes, and even of the Western invaders. Soon after this Vāsudeva was identified with the Vedic god Viṣṇu, if indeed the identification had not already been made, and further syncretisms were taking place. Nārāyaṇa, a god of obscure origin mentioned in the Brāhmaṇa literature, was also identified with

Viṣṇu, whose name was by now closely connected with that of Kṛṣṇa, one of the heroes of the martial traditions which were brought together to form the great epic, the *Mahābhārata*.

The character of Viṣṇu, and those of the gods associated with him, developed through the centuries, as further popular divinities were in one way or another identified with him. Among some of the lower orders theriomorphic cults prevailed, especially in parts of Mālwā, where a divinity in the form of a boar was worshipped. By Gupta times the cult of the divine boar was assimilated to that of Viṣṇu. A pastoral flute-playing deity, popular among herdsmen and of uncertain origin, was identified with the hero Kṛṣṇa, by now recognized as an incarnation of Viṣṇu. The Brāhmaṇic hero Paraśurāma was similarly accounted for, while later Rāma, the hero of the second great Indian epic, was also brought into the Vaiṣṇavite pantheon.

Simultaneously a fertility deity, whose cult may have been kept alive in non-brāhmaṇic circles from the days of the Harappā culture, rose in prominence. This was Śiva, identified with the Vedic Rudra and usually worshipped in the form of the phallic emblem (*liṅga*). With Śiva were later associated certain other popular divinities, such as Skanda and the elephant-headed Gaṇeśa. At the end of the Gupta period goddesses rose to prominence, together with magical cults, religious sexuality, and a new form of animal sacrifice, which increased in importance throughout the early Middle Ages.

The final form of Hinduism was largely the result of influence from the Dravidian South. Here, on the basis of indigenous cults fertilized by Āryan influences, theistic schools had arisen, characterized by intense ecstatic piety. It was this devotional religion, propagated by many wandering preachers and hymn-singers in the medieval period, which had the greatest effect on Hinduism as it exists today.

During this period an enormous body of sacred literature was produced. The Vedas, Brāhmaṇas and Upaniṣads, theoretically still the most sacred of all India's religious literature, were studied only by those who had undergone the ceremony of initiation, and became more and more the preserve of the brāhmaṇs, who themselves often interpreted them figuratively in the light of the new doctrines. The real scriptures of Hinduism, as distinct from Brāhmaṇism, were available to all, even to men of low caste and to women. These were the Epics, the *Purāṇas*, the books of Sacred Law, which we have treated elsewhere (p. 96), and numerous hymns and religious poems. For the learned there was a voluminous literature of commentaries, and many treatises were written on various aspects of theology and philosophy.

The two great Epics were originally secular, and in their literary aspect will be treated later (p. 360ff). Very early, probably well before the Christian era, the *Mahābhārata* began to receive religious interpolations and to be looked on as a sacred text. The most important of these interpolations is the famous *Bhagavad Gītā*, itself a compilation of material from various sources, to which we shall often refer in the course of this chapter; and much literature on the Sacred Law, as well as religious legends of many kinds, has found its way into the Epic which, as it exists at present, forms an encyclopedia of early Hinduism. An important appendix to the *Mahābhārata* is the *Harivaṃśa*, giving the legend of the god Kṛṣṇa in a developed form. The second epic, the *Rāmāyaṇa*, was also at first secular, but at a comparatively late period, probably after the age of the Guptas, an introductory and a final canto were added, together with other interpolations, which raised the text to the status of a sacred scripture.

The Purāṇas ("Ancient Stories") are compendia of legends and religious instructions. There are eighteen chief Purāṇas, of which perhaps the most important are the *Vāyu*, *Viṣṇu*, *Agni*, *Bhaviṣya* and *Bhāgavata Purāṇas*. In their present form they are not very ancient, none going back earlier than the Gupta period and all containing interpolations, but most of their legendary material is very old indeed.

Much later religious poetry is of small literary value, and has little more sanctity than have "Hymns Ancient and Modern" in the Church of England. Certain poems, however, became very sacred in later Hinduism, notably the *Gītā Govinda*, a collection of interlinked religious songs by the 12th-century Bengali poet Jayadeva (p. 380f). Some medieval *stotras* or hymns of praise, such as those attributed to the theologian Śaṅkara, have considerable literary merit, and are looked on with great respect.

The Peninsula produced much vernacular sacred poetry during our period, some of which is of great value and is considered to be very holy. A beautiful collection of moral aphorisms in Tamil verse, the *Tirukkuraḷ* ("Sacred Couplets"), attributed to Tiruvaḷḷuvar, perhaps dates from the 4th or 5th centuries A.D., though some authorities would put it much earlier. Later, from the 7th to the l0th centuries, were composed the eleven sacred books (*Tirumurai*) of the Tamil Śaivites, anthologies of hymns by the sixty-three *Nāyanārs*, or Teachers. Chief of these eleven works are the *Tēvāram*, containing songs by the three poets Appar, Ñānasambandar, and Sundaramurti, and the *Tiruvāśagam* of Māṇikka Vāśagar. The Tamil Vaiṣṇavites at about the same period produced the *Nālāyiram* ("Four Thousand"), a collection of stanzas attributed to the twelve *Ālvārs* or saints of the sect. Similar collections of devotional poetry, still looked on locally as very holy, were composed at the end of our period in Canarese and Telugu. At a later time much devotional literature was written in the Aryan vernaculars, but none survives from the period before the Muslim invasions, except perhaps the works of some of the Marāthā Vaiṣṇavite hymn singers, Jñāneśvar, Nāmdev and a few others, who, according to tradition, lived at the end of the 13th century.

We cannot here catalogue the great mass of religio-philosophical literature of Hinduism, some of which will be mentioned in the following pages.

Viṣṇu

To the Vaiṣṇavite, the devotee of Viṣṇu, this god is the source of the universe and of all things. According to the most famous cosmic myth of Hinduism he sleeps in the primeval ocean, on the thousand-headed snake Śeṣa. In his sleep a lotus grows from his navel, and in the lotus is born the demiurge Brahmā* who creates the world. Once the world is created Viṣṇu awakes, to reign in the highest heaven, Vaikuṇṭha. He is usually depicted as a four-armed man of dark blue colour, crowned and seated on his throne, hearing in his hands his emblems, the conch, discus, mace and lotus, wearing the holy jewel called *Kaustubha* round his neck, and with a tuft of curly hair (*Śrīvatsa*) on his chest. He rides the great eagle Garuḍa, generally shown with a half-human face, who is perhaps the survival of an ancient theriomorphic cult and who was already associated with Vāsudeva, one of Viṣṇu's early forms, when Heliodorus erected his column at Besnagar. Viṣṇu's spouse, Lakṣmī, is an important goddess in her own right.

Viṣṇu's status as the Universal God, of whom all other gods are aspects or emanations, appears as early as the *Bhagavad Gītā*.

> "Now I will tell the chief of my holy powers....
> though there is no end to my fullness.
> I am the self in the inmost heart of all that are born....
> I am their beginning, their middle and their end....
> I am the beginning, the middle, the end, of all creation,
> the science of the soul among sciences,
> of speakers I am the speech,
> of letters I am A.†
>
> "I am unending time,
> I am the ordainer who faces all ways,
> I am destroying death,
> I am the source of all that is to be....
> I am the dice-play of the gamester,
> I am the glory of the glorious,
> I am victory, I am courage,
> I am the goodness of the virtuous....
> I am the force of those who govern,
> I am the statecraft of those who seek to conquer,
> I am the silence of what is secret,
> I am the knowledge of those who know,
> and I am the seed of all that is born....
>
> "There is nothing that can exist without me.
> There is no end to my holy powers....
> And whatever is mighty or fortunate or strong
> springs from a portion of my glory."[57]

* Not to be confused with the impersonal Brahman (p. 218) of the Upaniṣads.

† *A* is the first letter of the Sanskrit alphabet. It is also implicit in all the other letters, if they are not modified by special marks (p. 348).

Though his counterpart Śiva has a rather ferocious and dangerous side to his character, Viṣṇu is generally thought of as wholly benevolent. The god works continuously for the welfare of the world, and with this in view he has from time to time incarnated himself, either wholly or partially. The earliest version of this doctrine is contained in the *Bhagavad Gītā*, wherein Kṛṣṇa reveals himself as the ever active godhead incarnate.

"In essence I am never born, I never alter.
I am the lord of all beings
and the full master of my own nature,
yet of my own power I come to be.

"Whenever the Sacred Law fails, and evil raises its head,
I take embodied birth.
To guard the righteous, to root out sinners,
and to establish the Sacred Law,
I am born from age to age."[58]

The *Avatāras* ("Descents") or incarnations of Viṣṇu are, according to the most popular classification, ten. The divinities and heroes composing the list were adopted by Vaiṣṇavism at different times, but all were incorporated by the 11th century. It may be that the Vaiṣṇavite doctrine of incarnation owes something to the Buddhist and Jaina doctrines of former Buddhas and Tīrthankaras, which are certainly attested earlier. An incarnation might be total or partial— for "whatever is mighty or fortunate or strong springs from a portion of my glory"'. In this sense every good or great man was thought of as a partial incarnation of Viṣṇu. The ten chief incarnations, however, are of a more special type, for in them the full essence of the god is believed to have taken flesh to save the world from imminent danger of total destruction. They are as follows:

(1) The Fish (*Matsya*). When the earth was overwhelmed by a universal flood Viṣṇu took the form of a fish, who first warned Manu (the Hindu Adam) of the impending danger, and then carried him, his family, and the seven great sages (*ṛṣis*) in a ship fastened to a horn on his head. He also saved the Vedas from the flood. The fish legend first appears in the Brāhmaṇas, and the Noah's Ark theme suggests Semitic influence. The Fish incarnation was never widely worshipped.

(2) The Tortoise (*Kūrma*). Many divine treasures were lost in the flood, including the ambrosia (*amrta*),* with which the gods preserved their youth. Viṣṇu became a great tortoise, and dived to the bottom of the cosmic ocean. On his back the gods placed Mount Mandare, and, twining the divine snake Vāsuki

* The words ambrosia and *amṛta* are probably connected etymologically; but amṛta was a drink, and should therefore perhaps be translated "nectar".

around the mountain, churned the ocean in the manner in which an Indian dairyman churns butter, twirling the mountain by pulling the snake. From the churned ocean emerged the ambrosia and various other treasures, including the goddess Lakṣmī. The story is probably a piece of very early folklore, but the identification of the tortoise with Viṣṇu is comparatively late, and, though frequently mentioned in literature, this incarnation had little real importance.

(3) The Boar (*Varāha*). A demon, Hiraṇyākṣa, cast the earth once more into the depths of the cosmic ocean. Viṣṇu took the form of an enormous boar, killed the demon, and raised the earth on his tusk (pl. XXXVII*c*). The legend looks back to the Brāhmaṇas, but probably developed through a primitive non-Āryan cult of a sacred pig. The cult of the Boar incarnation was important in some parts of India in Gupta times.

(4) The Man-Lion (*Narasiṃha*). Another demon, Hiraṇyakaśipu, had obtained a boon from Brahmā ensuring that he could not be killed either by day or night by god, man or beast. Thus safeguarded he persecuted gods and men, including his own pious son Prahlāda. When Prahlāda called on Viṣṇu for help the god burst from a pillar of the demon's palace at sunset, when it was neither night nor day, in a form half man and half lion, and slew Hiraṇyakaśipu. Narasiṃha was worshipped as their special divinity (*iṣṭadevatā*) by a small sect, and was often depicted in sculpture.

(5) The Dwarf (*Vāmana*). A demon named Bali gained control of the world, and commenced a course of asceticism, by which his supernatural power so increased that he menaced even the gods. Viṣṇu appeared before him in the form of a dwarf, and asked as a boon as much space as he could cover in three strides. When the boon was granted the god became a giant, and in two strides covered earth, heaven and the middle air. Magnanimously he refrained from taking his third stride, and left the infernal regions to the demon. The three steps of Viṣṇu are as old as the *Ṛg Veda*, but other popular elements were incorporated into the story.

(6) Paraśurāma ("Rāma with the Axe"). Viṣṇu took human form as the son of a brāhmaṇ Jamadagni. When his father was robbed by the wicked King Kārtavīrya, Paraśurāma killed the latter. Jamadagni was in turn killed by the sons of Kārtavīrya, after which the enraged Paraśurāma destroyed all the males of the kṣatriya class twenty-one times in succession. Though Paraśurāma is frequently referred to in literature, he seems rarely to have been specially worshipped.

(7) Rāma, Prince of Ayodhya and hero of the *Rāmāyaṇa*. Viṣṇu incarnated himself in this form to save the world from the oppressions of the demon Rāvaṇa. To one who is not a Hindu his story is rather a matter of literature than of religion and it will be told in a later chapter (p. 365ff). Rāma may have been a chief who lived in the 8th or 7th century B.C., and in the earliest form of the story he has no divine attributes. Though he was believed to be an earlier incarnation than Kṛṣṇa, his cult developed later than Kṛṣṇa's, and does not appear to have become very important until towards the end of our period.

Rāma is usually depicted as of dark hue, often hearing a bow and arrow. He is attended by his faithful queen Sītā, the personification of wifely devotion, and often also by his three loyal brothers, Lakṣmaṇa, Bharata and Śatrughna, and by his friend and helper, the monkey-god Hanumant. To his devotees Rāma combines the ideals of the gentle, faithful husband, the leader brave in hardship, and the just and benevolent king. It is perhaps significant that his cult only became really popular after the Muslim invasion.

(8) Kṛṣṇa is undoubtedly the most important of the incarnations of Viṣṇu. His legend in its final form is very long and can only be outlined briefly here.

Kṛṣṇa was born at Mathurā, of the tribe of the Yādavas. His father was Vāsudeva, and his mother was Devakī, the cousin of the ruling King Kaṃsa.* It was prophesied that Kaṃsa would be killed by Devakī's eighth son, so he set out to destroy all her children. But Kṛṣṇa and his elder brother Baiarāma were saved, and were brought up as the sons of the cowherd Nanda and his wife Yaśodā. Kaṃsa, hearing that the boys had escaped his clutches, ordered the slaughter of all the male children in his kingdom, but Nanda smuggled the boys away, first to Vraja and then to Vṛndāvana, districts not far from Mathurā which are still very sacred to Kṛṣṇa.

In his childhood the incarnate god performed many miracles, killing demons, and sheltering the cowherds from a storm by holding Mount Govardhana over their heads with his finger; he also played numerous childish pranks, such as stealing Yaśoda's butter. In his adolescence he had many amours with the wives and daughters of the cowherds (*gopīs*), and accompanied their dances on his flute. His favourite was the beautiful Rādhā.

But his youthful days soon ended. Kaṃsa traced him and made further attempts on his life. Kṛṣṇa then gave up his idyllic pastoral ways, and turned on his wicked cousin. He slew Kaṃsa, and seized the kingdom of Mathurā, but, pressed between Kaṃsa's father-in-law, Jarāsandha king of Magadha, and an unnamed Yavana king of the North-West, he was forced to leave his kingdom, and with his followers founded a new capital at Dvārakā in Saurāshtra. Here he made Rukmiṇī, daughter of the king of Vidarbha (modern Berar), his chief queen, and amassed a total of over 16,000 wives and 180,000 sons. His adventures at this stage of his career include the destruction of wicked kings and demons all over India. Throughout the story of the *Mahābhārata* he appears as the constant friend and advisor of the five Pāṇḍavas, and he preached the great sermon of the *Bhagavad Gītā* to Arjuna before the battle which is the centre of the epic story.

After seeing the Pāṇḍavas safely installed in the Kuru land, Kṛṣṇa returned to Dvārakā. Here ominous portents beset the city, as the Yādava chiefs quarrelled among themselves. Kṛṣṇa banned strong drink, in the hope of staving off the evil day, but on the occasion of a festival he relaxed the ban.

* There is some ambiguity about the relationship of Kaṃsa and Kṛṣṇa, owing to the fact that Indian usage makes no sharp distinction between brothers or sisters and cousins. Hence Kaṃsa is often referred to as Kṛṣṇa's uncle, when according to strict English usage the two were second cousins.

The Yādava chiefs began to brawl, and the whole city was soon in uproar. For all his divinity, Kṛṣṇa could do nothing to quell the feud, which involved the whole people. His son Pradyumna was killed before his eyes, and his faithful brother Balarāma wounded to death; nearly all the chiefs of the Yādavas were slain. Kṛṣṇa dejectedly wandered in a forest near the city; there, as he sat musing on the loss of his friends and family, a hunter spied him through the undergrowth and mistook him for a deer. An arrow pierced his heel, which like that of Achilles was his one vulnerable spot, and he died. The city of Dvārakā was then swallowed by the sea.

Of the many elements which have gone to the making of this story that of Kṛṣṇa as hero was the earliest to have been given a place in orthodox tradition. A Kṛṣṇa son of Devakī is mentioned in one of the early Upaniṣads[59] as studying the new doctrines of the soul, and it seems certain that there is some historical basis for the legend of the hero-god; but evidently tales of many heroes from many ages and many parts of India have been fused together in the Kṛṣṇa myth, including a few which seem rather inconsistent with the general character of the conquering hero, such as that of his somewhat ignominious retreat from Mathurā. Other elements in the story, such as the destruction of the Yādavas and the death of the god, are quite un-Indian in their tragic character. The themes of the drunken brawl leading to general slaughter, of the hero slain by an arrow piercing his one vulnerable spot, and of the great city engulfed by the sea, are well known in European epic literature, but do not occur elsewhere in that of India, and are not hinted at in the Vedas. The concept of the dying god, so widespread in the ancient Near East, is found nowhere else in Indian mythology. Kaṃsa, the wicked cousin, seems to echo Herod, and perhaps also Acrisius, the cruel grandfather of Perseus. Some parts of the legend may be derived from very ancient stories, handed down and developed by Āryan warriors from the days before they entered India; others are of indigenous origin; and yet others are possibly inspired by garbled versions of tales from the West.

Kṛṣṇa in his pastoral and erotic aspect is evidently of different origin from Kṛṣṇa the hero. The name means "black", and the god is usually depicted as of that colour. Perhaps the oldest clear reference to the pastoral Kṛṣṇa is in the early Tamil anthologies, where "the Black One" (*Māyōn*) plays his flute and sports with milkmaids. He may have been originally a fertility god of the Peninsula, whose cult was carried to the North by nomadic tribes of herdsmen. A tribe which appeared in Mālwā and the Western Deccan early in the Christian era, the Ābhīras, is thought to have played a big part in the propagation of the worship of Kṛṣṇa Govinda ("Lord of Herdsman",* a very common epithet of the god in this aspect).

The young Kṛṣṇa's erotic exploits have been the source of much romantic

* *Govinda* is probably a Prākrit word, absorbed by Sanskrit in its original form. The correct Sanskrit equivalent would thus be *Gopendra*. On the orthodox assumption that the word is pure Sanskrit its translation would be "Cow-finder".

literature which, superficially, contains but a faint religious element. Invariably, however, the love of the god for the cowherds' wives is interpreted as symbolic of the love of God for the human soul. The notes of Kṛṣṇa's flute, calling the women to leave their husbands' beds and dance with him in the moonlight, represent the voice of God, calling man to leave earthly things and turn to the joys of divine love. So Jew and Christian alike have interpreted the Song of Songs, and so many mystical poets of all religions have depicted their spiritual experience. Despite its luxuriant eroticism the legend of the Divine Cowherd has produced great religious poetry (p. 380f), and inspired many pious souls.

The third element of the Kṛṣṇa legend is that of the child god. This is definitely the latest part to be assimilated, and its origin is quite unknown. Can it be partly inspired by tales brought by Christian merchants or Nestorian missionaries to the west coast of India in the early Middle Ages? Most authorities would deny this, but we do not reject the possibility out of hand. In any case, the story of the child Kṛṣṇa, often depicted in later sculpture as a plump infant crawling on all fours, gave the god a rare completeness. As hero he met the worshipper's need of a divine father and elder brother; as the young cowherd, he was a divine lover; and as infant, a son. The cult of the child Kṛṣṇa made a special appeal to the warm maternity of Indian womanhood; and even today the simpler women of India, while worshipping the divine child, so delightfully naughty despite his mighty power, refer to themselves as "the Mother of God".

Vāsudeva, the popular god of Western India in the early centuries B.C., was early identified with Kṛṣṇa, and it may be that the name, falsely interpreted as a patronymic, resulted in the tradition that Kṛṣṇa's father was called Vāsudeva (with short *a* in the first syllable). Other deities, originally independent, were associated with Kṛṣṇa in one way and another. Chief of these was his elder brother Balarāma, also called Halāyudha ("Armed with a Plough") and Saṅkarṣaṇa. Balarāma, hearing a wooden plough on his shoulder, was originally an agricultural deity. Traditionally he was a heavy drinker and had some of the characteristics of a Silenus. Temples to him existed at one time, but his importance waned in the Middle Ages, as that of Kṛṣṇa increased. Less important were the cults of Kṛṣṇa's son Pradyumna, of his grandson Aniruddha, and of his friend Arjuna, the Pāṇḍava hero. The chief feminine associate of Kṛṣṇa was Rādhā, the favourite mistress of his youth, who was often worshipped with him in the late Middle Ages. Rukmiṇī, his chief queen, also received some reverence.

(9) *Buddha*, the last historical incarnation of Viṣṇu. According to most theologians the god became Buddha in order to delude the wicked, lead them to deny the Vedas, and thus ensure their damnation. Jayadeva's *Gīta Govinda*, however, which contains one of the earliest lists of incarnations, states that Viṣṇu became Buddha out of compassion for animals,[60] in order to put an end to bloody sacrifice. This probably gives a due to the true background of the

Buddha avatāra. He was included in the list, as other deities were included, in order to assimilate heterodox elements into the Vaiṣṇavite fold: Until quite recently the temple of the Buddha at Gayā was in the hands of Hindus, and the teacher was there worshipped by Hindus as a Hindu god; but in general little attention was paid to the Buddha avatāra.

(10) *Kalkin*, the incarnation yet to come. At the end of this dark age Viṣṇu will appear in the form of a man mounted on a white horse, with a flaming sword in his hand. He will judge the wicked, reward the good, and restore the age of gold. This is a late addition to Vaiṣṇavite myth, and does not play a very important part in literature or iconography, though it is said that many simple Hindus take the Kalkin very seriously, and long for his arrival just as old-fashioned Christians look forward to the second coming of Christ. Christian parallels have been found, especially with the horseman of the Book of Revelation,[61] but the main inspiration of the Kalkin may have come from Buddhism, which taught the coming of Maitreya Buddha long before the Vaiṣṇavites devised the Kalkin. Zoroastrian ideas may also have helped in the formation of the myth.

Śiva

Almost as popular as the numerous forms of Viṣṇu was Śiva, who evolved from the fierce Vedic god Rudra (p. 208), with whom merged elements of a non-Āryan fertility deity. Though developed Śaivite sects often made of their chosen divinity a wholly moral and paternal father in heaven, Śiva's character, unlike that of Viṣṇu, is ambivalent. He lurks in horrible places, such as battlefields, burning-grounds and crossroads, which, in India as in Europe, were looked on as very inauspicious. He wears a garland of skulls and is surrounded by ghosts, evil spirits and demons. He is death and time (*Mahākāla*), which destroy all things.

But he is also a great ascetic, and the patron deity of ascetics generally. On the high slopes of the Himālayan Mount Kailāsa Śiva, the great yogī, sits on a tiger skin, deep in meditation, and through his meditation the world is maintained. He is depicted thus as wearing his long matted hair (*jaṭā*) in a topknot, in which the crescent moon is fixed, and from which flows the sacred river Gangā. In the middle of his forehead is a third eye, emblem of his superior wisdom and insight. His neck is black, scarred by a deadly poison which was the last of the objects churned from the cosmic ocean, and which he drank to save the other gods from destruction. Snakes, of which he is the lord, encircle his neck and arms. His body is covered with ashes, a favourite ascetic practice. Beside him is his weapon, the trident, while near him are his beautiful wife Pārvatī and his mount, the bull Nandi.

Though in this aspect Śiva is continually wrapped in meditation, he can, in his divine power, divide his personality. He is not only the god of mystical stillness, but also the Lord of the Dance (*Naṭarāja*) (pl. LXVI). This aspect of Śiva is specially popular in the Tamil country, where religious dancing was part of the earliest known tradition. In his heavenly palace on Mount Kailāsa, or in his southern home, the temple of Cidambaram or Tiḷḷai (near the sea-coast about fifty miles south of Pondicherry), mystically identified with Kailāsa, Śiva dances. He has invented no less than 108 different dances, some calm and gentle, others fierce, orgiastic and terrible. Of the latter the most famous is the *tāṇḍava*, in which the angry god, surrounded by his drunken attendants (*gaṇas*), beats out a wild rhythm which destroys the world at the end of the cosmic cycle.

A further form in which the god is worshipped is known as the "South-facing" (*Dakṣināmūrti*) (pl. LXVIII); in this aspect he is the universal teacher, depicted in an informal pose, with one foot on the ground and the other on the throne on which he sits, and with one hand raised in a gesture of explanation. This form of Śiva perhaps owes something to Buddhist inspiration.

But Śiva was and still is chiefly worshipped in the form of the *liṅga* (pl. XXVI*b*), usually a short cylindrical pillar with rounded top, which is the survival of a cult older than Indian civilization itself. Phalli have been found in the Harappā remains. Early Tamil literature refers to the setting up of ritual posts, which seem to have been phallic emblems. The cult of the liṅga, at all times followed by some of the non-Āryan peoples, was incorporated into Hinduism around the beginning of the Christian era, though at first it was not very important. As early as the *Ṛg Veda*, Rudra, the mountain god, was connected with plants and animals. The horned ithyphallic god of Mohenjo Daro, surrounded by animals, may well be the prototype of Śiva as the patron of reproduction in men, animals and plants. In this form he is known as *Paśupati* ("Lord of Beasts") and is often represented in South India as a four armed man, with one hand in an attitude of blessing, the second open, as though bestowing a boon, an axe in the third, and a small deer springing from the fingere of the fourth (pl. LXVII*b*).

Some Śaivite sects declare that Śiva has performed a series of avatāras, but these are pure imitations of those of Viṣṇu and have never played a big part in Śaivite thought. The god has, however, manifested himself from time to time in theophanies, or taken temporary incarnation to destroy demons or test the virtue of warriors or sages. Numerous legends are told of him, some of them quite uncomplimentary. The most famous of these legends is that of his marriage to Pārvatī, the daughter of Himālaya, the personified mountains.

The gods were troubled by the demon Tāraka, and it was prophesied that he could only be destroyed by the child of Śiva and the Daughter of the Mountains. But Śiva was continually wrapped in meditation, and the prospect of his producing offspring seemed to the other gods to be faint indeed. However Pārvatī, the beautiful daughter of Himālaya, was sent at their behest to wait upon Śiva, but though she made many attempts to win the god's attention he took no notice of her, and in the course of her efforts Kāma, the love-god, who had done his best to help her to win him, was burnt to ashes by the flames from Śiva's third eye. At last Pārvatī decided to follow the god in his asceticism. Laying aside her ornaments she became a hermitess on a nearby peak, and in this guise Śiva noticed her and fell in love with her. They were married at a great ceremony at which all the gods took part, and soon Pārvatī gave birth to the war-god Skanda, who, when he grew to manhood, destroyed the demon Tāraka.

In South India a rather similar story is told of the marriage of Śiva and Mīnākṣī, daughter of a Pāṇḍyan king of Madurai, and the event is commemorated by one of the most famous and splendid of South Indian temples.

The Relations of Viṣṇu and Śiva

From the beginning of the Christian era, if not before, most educated Hindus have been either Vaiṣṇavites or Śaivites—that is to say they have looked on either Viṣṇu or Śiva as the high god, or indeed as the only God, the others being merely secondary expressions of the divine, holding rather the same positions as the saints and angels in the mind of the Roman Catholic. Thus the Vaiṣṇavite does not deny the existence of Śiva, but believes that he is merely one god among many, the creation or emanation of Viṣṇu or of his demiurge Brahmā. In the same way the Śaivite looks on Viṣṇu as an emanation of Śiva. Occasionally this difference of viewpoint has led to friction and some degree of persecution, but generally the two great divisions of Hinduism have rubbed along happily together, in the conviction that on ultimate analysis both are equally right. Hinduism is essentially tolerant, and would rather assimilate than rigidly exclude. So the wiser Vaiṣṇavites and Śaivites recognized very early that the gods whom they worshipped were different aspects of the same divine being. The Divine is a diamond of innumerable facets; two very large and bright facets are Viṣṇu and Śiva, while the others represent all the gods that were ever worshipped. Some facets seem larger, brighter. and better polished than others, but in fact the devotee, whatever his sect, worships the whole diamond, which is in reality perfect. The more devout Hindus, even when illiterate and ignorant, have always been fundamentally monotheist. Thus in the *Bhagavad Gītā* Kṛṣṇa says:

> "If any worshipper do reverence with faith
> to any god whatever,
> I make his faith firm,
> and in that faith he reverences his god,
> and gains his desires,
> for it is I who bestow them."[62]

With this background of tolerance it is not surprising that attempts were made to harmonize Vaiṣṇavism and Śaivism. As early as Gupta times there was devised a holy trinity of Hinduism, the *Trimūrti* or Triple Form of Brahmā the creator, Viṣṇu the preserver, and Śiva the destroyer. The doctrine of the Trimūrti was popular in some circles, and is proclaimed in a fine hymn of Kālidāsa which inspired a once well-known poem of Emerson:

> "Praise to you, O Trinity,
> one before creation,
> afterwards divided
> in your three qualities! ...

"You, the one cause
of death and life and birth,
in your three forms
proclaim your own glory …

"In the cycle of your day and night
all things live and all things die.
When you wake we live,
when you sleep we perish….

"Hard and soft, large and small,
heavy and light, you are all things.
You are both substance and form,
ineffable in power….

"You are the knower and the known,
you are the eater and the food,
you are the priest and the oblation,
you are the worshipper and the prayer."[63]

Early western students of Hinduism were impressed by the parallel between the Hindu trinity and that of Christianity. In fact the parallel is not very close, and the Hindu trinity, unlike the Holy Trinity of Christianity, never really "caught on". All Hindu trinitarianism tended to favour one god of the three; thus, from the context it is clear that Kālidāsa's hymn to the Trimūrti is really addressed to Brahmā, here looked on as the high god. The Trimūrti was in fact an artificial growth, and had little real influence.

Another significant syncretism was the god Harihara (*Hari* being a title of Viṣṇu and *Hara* of Śiva), worshipped in the form of an icon which combined characteristics of both gods. The cult of Harihara developed in the middle ages, and had some success in the Deccan, where Harihara temples were patronized by Vijayanagara kings, and where the god is still worshipped.

The Mother Goddess

Mother Goddesses were worshipped at all times in India, but between the days of the Harappā Culture and the Gupta period the cults of goddesses attracted little attention from the learned and influential, and only emerged from obscurity to a position of real importance in the Middle Ages, when feminine divinities, theoretically connected with the gods as their spouses, were once more worshipped by the upper classes.

The goddess was the *śakti*, the strength or potency of her male counterpart. It was thought that the god was inactive and transcendent, while his female element was active and immanent, and by the Gupta period the wives of the gods, whose existence had always been recognized but who had been shadowy figures in earlier theology, began to be worshipped in special temples. In the early 5th century an inscription of Western India tells of a certain Mayūrākṣaka,

> "minister of the king, who established, to gain merit,
> this most awful temple,
> a temple filled with demonesses,...
> sacred to the Mothers, who shout
> most loudly in the thick darkness,
> where the lotuses are shaken
> by the fierce winds
> aroused by magic spells."[64]

From this time onwards the Mother Goddess increased in importance, until the wave of devotional Vaiṣṇavism swept Northern India early in the Muslim period, and stopped the progress of her cult, which is still strong in Bengal and Assam, and is known in other parts of India.

The chief form of the Mother Goddess was that of the wife of Śiva, called in her benevolent aspect *Pārvatī* ("Daughter of the Mountain"), *Mahādevī* ("the Great Goddess"), *Satī* ("the Virtuous"), *Gaurī* ("the Fair One"), *Annapūrṇā* ("Bestower of Much Food"), or simply "the Mother" (*Mātā*, Tamil *Ammai*). In her grim aspect she was known as *Durgā* ("Inaccessible"), *Kālī* ("the Black One"), and *Caṇḍī* ("the Fierce"). The terrible Tamil war-goddess *Korravai*, who danced among the slain on the battlefield and ate their flesh, though independent in origin, was early identified with her.

In her fierce aspect she is often depicted as a horrible hag (pl. LXX), frequently with many arms hearing different weapons, with fierce carnivorous tusks, a red tongue lolling from her mouth, and a garland of skulls. Her mount is a lion, and she is sometimes shown as a sternly beautiful woman, slaying a buffalo-headed demon in the manner of St. George and the dragon (pl. XLII*b*). The more gentle aspect of the goddess is that of a beautiful young woman, often portrayed with her lord Śiva. An interesting iconographical development is that of the *Ardhanārīśvara*, a figure half Śiva and half Pārvatī, representing the union of the god with his śakti. As Śiva is worshipped in the liṅga or phallic emblem, so Durgā is worshipped in the female emblem, or *yoni*. According to legend Pārvatī, in the incarnation before that in which she became the bride of Śiva, had been born as Satī, the daughter of the sage Dakṣa, and had then also become the wife of the great god. When her father quarrelled with her divine lord she flung herself into the flames of his sacrificial fire, and the ashes of her *yoni* fell in various spots in India, which became the *pīṭhas*, or sacred shrines of her cult.

Lesser Gods

As well as Viṣṇu, Śiva and Durgā, many other gods were worshipped. Unlike the gods of the Veda, the new gods of Hinduism were no longer closely tied to natural phenomena, but were thought of more anthropomorphically.

Brahmā, the Prajāpati of later Vedic times, had a history of slow decline. In the early Buddhist scriptures he and Indra were the greatest of the gods, and in the *Mahābhārata* he was still very important; but though depicted in medieval sculpture, sometimes with four faces, he was little worshipped after Gupta times. A single temple of Brahmā, by the sacred lake Puṣkara near the modern Ajmer, is the only one known.

The numerous solar deities of the Vedas were merged in Hinduism into a single god, usually known as *Sūrya* ("the Sun") (pl. XXXVI *la*). In Gupta and medieval times there existed numerous temples of the sun, especially in Western India, which was open to Zoroastrian influence, and some of his worshippers seem to have looked on him as the greatest god of all.

"He who is worshipped by the host of gods that they may live,
 and by the blessed for their welfare,
by ascetics, who suppress their senses, intent on meditation, for their
 salvation,
—may that shining one, cause of the world's rise and decline,
 protect you.

"The divine seers, wise in true knowledge, for all their efforts have
 not known him wholly,
 whose rays reach out to nourish the three worlds,
whom gods and demigods and men hymn together as he rises,
 who fulfils the desires of his worshippers—
 homage to the Sun!"[65]

In comparison with the sun, the Moon (*Candra* or *Soma*), masculine in gender, had but slight religious importance, being little more than an emblem of Śiva. He had no independent cult, but was worshipped as one of the nine planets (p. 442). The cult of the planets was popularized by the growth of astrology in medieval times, and representations of them are fairly numerous.

Indra, the Vedic war-god, lost much of his prestige but gained new attributes. Mounted on his elephant Airāvata, he was guardian of the eastern quarter of the universe, and ruler of one of the lower heavens, Amarāvatī. Under an alternative name, Śakra, perhaps originally a different god, he was among the chief divinities of early Buddhism, second only to Brahmā. By the Middle Ages he had few temples or worshippers.

Varuṇa, the all-seeing god of the Vedas (p. 206ff), descended from his heavenly palace to become a god of the waters, but he remained the guardian of the western quarter of the universe. The cult of Varuṇa disappeared early, though Tamil fishermen long worshipped a marine deity called Varuṇan, in the emblem of a "shark's horn". This god, however, is clearly an indigenous Tamil divinity who had acquired an Āryan name.

Yama, guardian of the southern quarter, the death-god of the Vedas, was still remembered, though rarely if ever specially worshipped. His role had somewhat altered, for he was no longer the cheerful lord of paradise, but the stern judge of the dead, ruling only over the purgatories where the wicked suffered until their rebirth. The idea of a divine judge, theoretically unnecessary according to the doctrine of karma, may have been imported from the West, where it was known in many cults. Sometimes Yama, aided by his clerk Citragupta, is described as weighing the deeds of the souls of the dead in a balance, rather like the Egyptian Thoth.

The northern quarter was ruled by the god *Kubera*, lord of precious metals, minerals, jewels, and wealth generally. This god, under the alternative name Vaiśravaṇa, first appears briefly and faintly in later Vedic literature, and is well known in Buddhism and Jainism. He dwells in the beautiful jewelled city of Alakā, near Mount Kailāsa, and commands hosts of gnomes (*guhyaka*) and fairies (*yakṣa*). He is usually depicted as a dwarfish figure with a large paunch. He was the object of a cult, though not of an important one.

These four gods, Yama, Indra, Varuṇa and Kubera, were known as *Lokapālas*, or Guardians of the Universe. In late texts four further guardians of the intermediate quarters were added—*Soma* in the North-East, *Vāyu* (the wind-god) in the North-West, *Agni* in the South-East, and *Sūrya* in the South-West. Of these Agni, the fire-god, was still important at the time of the Epics, but he too lost much of his hold on the imagination in later times, while Vāyu, the wind-god, was a vague and tenuous deity, except in the late school of Madhva (p. 293).

The war-god *Skanda*, also called *Kumāra* ("The Prince"), *Kārtikeya* and, in the South, *Subrahmaṇya*, was probably originally a non-Āryan divinity. He was the son of Śiva and Pārvatī and his sole function, according to orthodox tradition, was to slay the demon Tāraka, which scarcely accounts for his great popularity. From the beginning of the Christian era the cult of Skanda was widespread in North India, though it declined somewhat in medieval times. In the South it was even more important, for the name and attributes of the god were imposed on the chief deity of the ancient Tamils, Murugan, by which name Skanda is still sometimes known in the Tamil country. Murugan in his original form was a mountain god, worshipped in bacchanalian dances, at which he was impersonated by a medicine-man holding a spear (*vēlan*), whom the dancers identified with the god. He aroused passion and erotic frenzy in girls and women, and the dances of Murugan were evidently orgiastic. The Tamil Murugan was armed with a spear, and joined his fierce mother Korravai in her cannibal feasts on the battlefield; hence his identification with the Āryan Skanda is not surprising, though Murugan's original character as a fertility god is evident even today. Skanda is usually depicted as a handsome young man, often with six faces, mounted on a peacock.

Gaṇeśa or *Gaṇapati* (pl. LXIV*c*), "Chief of the *Gaṇas*" (a class of demigod attendant on Śiva), another son of Śiva and Pārvatī, is one of the best known Indian divinities in the West. He has an elephant's head with one broken tusk and a fat paunch, and he rides on a rat. Among the latest of the gods of the Hindu pantheon, he is not attested before the 5th century A.D., and he was of little importance before the Middle Ages. Evidently he is the survival of a primitive non-Āryan elephant god, but in Hinduism he has become mild and cultured. He is the "Lord of Obstacles" (*Vighneśvara*), and is worshipped at the beginning of all undertakings to remove snags and hindrances. He is particularly interested in literary and educational activities, and is the patron of grammarians; manuscripts and printed books often begin with the auspicious formula *Śrī-Gaṇeśāya namaḥ*, "Reverence to Lord Gaṇeśa". The cheerful and benevolent elephant-god was, and still is, revered by nearly every Hindu, whether Vaiṣṇavite or Śaivite. A small medieval sect looked on him as their chief god, but his status has generally been comparatively humble, though important.

Hanumant, the monkey god, the son of Vāyu and the friend and servant of Rāma, was no doubt a popular deity long before his incorporation in the pantheon. He is still an important village god, worshipped in many shrines in the form of a monkey with more or less human body. He is a beneficent guardian spirit, and in his honour monkeys are generally looked on as sacred.

Kāma ("Desire"), known by many other names and epithets, was the Indian love-god. Like his European counterpart he is depicted as a handsome youth, armed with a bow and arrow, but the Indian Eros has a bow of sugar-cane strung with a row of bees, and his arrows are flowers. He is attended by a troop of nymphs (*apsarases*), one of whom carries his standard, which bears a sea-monster. Kāma is referred to in the "Hymn of Creation" (p. 218f) and in certain other Vedic passages as being the firstborn of the primeval chaos, but this *kāma* is certainly not the Hindu love-god, but vaguely personified cosmic desire. On the strength of these early references it was generally believed by the theologians of Hinduism that Kāma had no parents, but emerged spontaneously at the beginning of time to act as a catalyst in the universal process. His flowery arrows affect gods and men alike, and have only once been known to fail in their purpose—when Kāma attempted to rouse the passion of the great god Śiva, and was burnt to ashes for his pains (p. 271), to be restored to life through the entreaties of his favourite wife, the goddess Rati ("Pleasure"). He is frequently referred to in literature and was evidently a popular deity among young people of both sexes, honoured at a great annual festival (p. 180). The Buddhist Māra ("the Smiter") was sometimes identified with Kāma, but had sinister attributes, and was a sort of Satan, the personification of the world, the flesh and the devil. His temptation of the Buddha is one of the most famous episodes of Buddhist legend.

All the gods have complementary goddesses, their wives, but most of these are pale reflexions of their lords, hearing the same names with feminine terminations (e.g. *Indrāṇī*, *Brahmāṇī*, etc.). They were often worshipped in a group, usually of seven, to which the gōds Kārtikeya and Ganesa were sometimes added, and portrayals of these goddesses (*Mātṛkā*, *Ambikā*, "the Little Mothers") are fairly common in medieval sculpture (pl. LXIV*c*). As well as Durgā, who must rank as one of the three chief deities of Hinduism, other goddesses were important, however.

Lakṣmī ("Fortune"), the wife of Viṣṇu, also often called *Śrī*, was the goddess of good luck and temporal blessing. In some legends she is said to be coexistent with Viṣṇu, but according to others she appeared in her full glory, like Aphrodite, at the churning of the primeval ocean (p. 265f). She is usually portrayed as a woman of mature beauty, seated on a lotus and often with a lotus in her hand, attended by two elephants, who sprinkle water on her from their trunks. Though never an object of a special cult, her icons are numerous, and she was much worshipped as a subsidiary deity. She was believed to incarnate herself as the wife of the incarnation of Viṣṇu, and thus she was worshipped as Sītā, the spouse of Rama, as Rukmiṇī, the chief queen of Kṛṣṇa, or as Rādhā, the favourite of his youth.

Sarasvatī (pl. L*b*), the wife of Brahmā, had an autonomous role as the patron of art, music and letters. In the *Ṛg Veda* she was a sacred river, but in later Vedic literature she was identified with a hypostatic goddess of temporary importance, Vāc ("Speech"). She was depicted as a beautiful fair young woman, often with a *vīṇā*, or Indian lute, and a book in her hand, and attended by a swan.* Traditionally she was the inventor of the Sanskrit language and the *Devanāgari* script. Sarasvatī has always been worshipped by students, writers and musicians, and her cult is still maintained.

Demigods and Spirits

As well as these greater gods there was an infinite number of lesser ones. Every village had its local god or goddess (*grāmadevatā*), often a rude image or fetish set up under a sacred tree. Some of these village fertility deities, through a process of assimilation, attained widespread popularity. Local goddesses were often vaguely identified with Durgā, but were rarely thoroughly incorporated into the mythological scheme, and they maintained an autonomous existence on the fringes of the orthodox pantheon. Chief of such goddesses was Śitalā ("the Cool"), called in the Tamil country Māriyammai ("Mother Death"), the goddess of smallpox, worshipped for prevention and cure, especially by mothers on behalf of their children. Similarly the snake-goddess Manasā protected from snakebite. Her worship is not certainly attested in our period, but in medieval Bengal she attained a respectable status in the orthodox pantheon, and she was almost certainly worshipped by the masses in the earlier period. A male deity of this type, widely popular in the Tamil countryside from ancient days, was Aiyanar, a beneficent guardian deity much revered by peasants, and sometimes thought of as a son of Śiva. The cities of ancient India, like those of the classical world, had their guardian deities, who might be important members of the pantheon but were often of only local significance. Besides these local gods the world was full of demigods and spirits, good and evil.

The snake-spirits (*Nāga*) (pl. XLI*b*), half-human but with serpents' tails, were very ancient objects of worship. They dwelt in the beautiful underground city of Bhogavatī, and guarded great treasures, some of which they occasionally bestowed on mortals whom they favoured. They could take wholly human form, and more

* *Haṃsa,* strictly a type of goose; but, owing to the connotation of the word "goose" in English, *haṃsa* is usually translated "swan" in this and other works on ancient India.

than one dynasty of ancient India claimed descent from the union of a human hero and a *nāginī*. Probably the prototypes of the nāgas were the dark primitive tribes, met by the Āryans in their expansion over India, for a primitive people called Nāgas exists in Assam to this day; the cult of serpents is so widespread in India that the nāgas must certainly owe much to aboriginal snake cults followed by many tribes all over India.

The *Yakṣas*, especially associated with the god Kubera, were a sort of gnome or fairy, reverenced by country people. Before the Christian era their cult was widespread, but they lost their significance as the great gods of Hinduism became more widely worshipped. They were generally looked on as friendly to men, but their women-folk might sometimes be malevolent, and ate little children.

The *Gandharvas* survived from Vedic times as servants of Indra and heavenly musicians. In the time of the Buddha they seem to have been specially connected with the procreation of children, and the presence of a Gandharva was thought necessary for conception. Associated with them, and sometimes referred to as a subdivision of their order, were the *Kinnaras*, also heavenly musicians, who had human heads and horses' bodies, and thus resembled the classical centaurs, with whom they may be connected.

The Gandharvas were all male. Their female counterparts were the *Apsarases*, in Vedic times connected with water, but later translated to heaven. They were beautiful and libidinous, and specially delighted in tempting ascetics in their meditations. Thus Menakā the apsaras seduced the great sage Viśvāmitra, and conceived Śakuntalā, the heroine of Kālidāsa's famous drama (p. 387ff). Another apsaras famous in story was Urvaśī, the heroine of another drama of Kāilidāsa, the story of whose love for the mortal king Purūravas (p. 358ff) is as old as the *Ṛg Veda*. Sometimes the apsarases appear in the role of valkyries, raising slain heroes from the battlefield and hearing them to heaven to be their lovers.

A further group of demigods was that of the *Vidyādharas* or heavenly magicians, mysterious beings who lived in magic cities in the high Himālayas. Like the Vedic munis (p. 213) they could fly through the air and transform themselves at will, and they were generally favourable to men.

The *Ṛṣis* ("sages" or more literally "seers"), were the composers of the Vedic hymns, and other legendary wise men of olden times who had been translated to heaven, where they enjoyed a status comparable to that of the gods. Chief of these were the "Seven Ṛṣis", identified with the stare of the Great Bear—Marīci, Atri, Aṅgiras, Pulastya, Pulaha, Kratu and Vasiṣṭha. Other important ṛṣis were Kaśyapa and Dakṣa, said in some stories to have been the progenitors of gods and men; Nārada, who īnvented the vīṇā and was a sort of patron saint of music; Viśvāmitra, a kṣatriya who by his piety and asceticism raised himself to brāhmaṇ status, and who is heard of in many legends; Bṛhaspati, the preceptor of gods and demons, who began his career in Vedic times as a god, but whose status fell to that of a ṛṣi, also identified with the planet Jupiter (pl. LIII*b*), and who is said to have founded the materialist system of philosophy and the science of statecraft; and Agastya, who taught the Southerners religion and culture. Less exalted than the rsis were the *Siddhas*, a large class of saints who had won a place in heaven by their piety.

Chief among evil spirits were the *Asuras*, or demons. The word *asura* was in Vedic times applied to certain gods (p. 207), but in Hinduism it was used for a group of supernatural beings continually at war with the gods, whose power they sometimes shook, but never conquered. More immediately dangerous to men were the various classes of goblin, such as the *Rākṣasas*, most famous of whom was Rāvaṇa the ten-headed demon king of Laṅkā (Ceylon), whom Rāma defeated and killed. Few rākṣasas had the same power as Rāvaṇa, but all were frightful and dangerous, taking terrible forms and lurking in dark places at night, to kill and eat men and otherwise distress them. Somewhat less terrible were the *Piśācas*, who, like the nāgas, may have had a material basis in a wild tribe, since a very base dialect of Prākrit was attributed to them. Both these classes of demon haunted battlefields, charnel grounds, and places of violent death, as did a special class of demon, the *Vetāla* or vampire, which took up its abode in corpses. Finally the night was haunted by ghosts (*preta*, *bhūta*), the naked spirits of those who had died violent deaths and for whom śrāddha had not been performed. These were very dangerous to men, particularly to their own surviving relatives.

Hindu worship was not confined to the propitiation of gods and demigods, for the whole of nature was in some sense divine. Great and holy men were reverenced, both during their lives and for long after their deaths, for they contained a portion of godhead. Thus the sixty-three Nāyanars of Tamil Śaivism and the twelve Ālvārs of Tamil Vaiṣṇavism still enjoy the status of demigods, as do other great religious teachers. Not only men, but animals and plants were and still are holy, notably the cow. According to legend the cow Surabhi, the mother of all cows, was one of the treasures churned from the cosmic ocean. The "five products of the cow" (*pañcagavya*)— milk, curd, butter, urine and dung—were all of great purifying potency, especially when combined in a single mixture. Despite her sanctity, there was no cow-goddess, and Surabhi and the various "wishing-cows" of legend, by milking which all desires were fulfilled, had no temples in their honour. The living beast was revered, not as representative of any deity, but in her own right. The bull, on the other hand, received honour as the mount of Śiva; the image of Nandi is found in most Śaivite temples and honoured with offerings.

After the cow the snake was perhaps the most revered animal of ancient India. Legendary serpents, such as Śeṣa (p. 263) and Vāsuki (p. 265), gave the snake prestige, but the cult no doubt sprang from very primitive levels, since the mysterious snake is revered all over the world by uncivilized peoples as an emblem of both death and fertility. An offering to snakes, made at the beginning of the rainy season, was part of the regular domestic ritual of Hinduism. Ant-hills were respected as the home of snakes. Other animals, though associated with various divinities, played little part in Hindu cults. The monkey, much revered by peasants and simple folk in many parts of India, is not referred to as specially sacred in early Hindu texts.

Tree cults, common the world over among ancient peoples, were widespread in India, where each village had its sacred tree or grove. Specially sacred were the *pippala* or *aivattha* (pīpal, *Ficus religiosa*), the sanctity of which spread to Buddhism, and the *vaṭa* or *nyagrodha*, the banyan (*Ficus indica*), the secondary roots of which, reaching down from its branches, formed the basis of much religious symbolism. Many other trees were more or less holy, notably the *aśoka* (p. 176), to which women prayed for children. There were also sacred plants, such as the *tulasī*, a type of basil, which was connected with Viṣṇu, and which is still grown in the courtyards of many Hindu homes and tended with great care. Two types of grass, *kuśa* and *darbha*, were also sacred from Vedic times onwards. The Vedic soma plant, however, was forgotten.

Every hill or mountain had some degree of sanctity, especially the Himālayas, which were the foothills of Mount Mera, the centre of the world. Around Meru, on mountains which reached to the heavens, dwelt the gods. Vaikuṇṭha, the home of Viṣṇu, was never satisfactorily identified, but Kailāsa, the mountain of Śiva, was recognized as a certain peak in the Central Himālayas which has long been a place of pilgrimage. Numerous other mountains and hills in many parts of India were famous for their sanctity. Even rocks often had a religious significance, especially if upright and vaguely resembling the lingaof Śiva. The ammonite (*śālagrāma*), a fossilized shellfish, was recognized as one of the symbols of Viṣṇu.

Rivers were also sacred, especially, of course, the Gangā, which sprang from the foot of the Viṣṇu, flowed over the sky in the form of the milky way (*Mandākinī*), and then fell to earth from the matted locks of Śiva. Gangā was often personified as a goddess in her own right, like her great tributary Yamunā. Other rivers held specially sacred were the Sarasvatī, which was believed to flow underground and join the Gangā at its confluence with the Yamunā at Prayāga (Allahābād), the Narmadā, the Godāvari, the Kṛṣṇā (modern Kistnā) and the Kāviri. Certain lakes, notably Mānasa in the high Himālayas near Mount Kailāsa, and Puṣkara, near Ajmer, were also sacred, and even cities were divine (p. 174, n).

Cosmogony

Hindu cosmology in its final form was perhaps later than the cosmologies of the Buddhists and Jainas. According to this system the cosmos passes through cycles within cycles for all eternity. The basic cycle is the *kalpa*, a "day of Brahmā", or 4,320 million earthly years. His night is of equal length. 360 such days and nights constitute a "year of Brahmā" and his life lasts for 100 such years.* The largest cycle is therefore 311,040,000 million years long, after which the whole universe returns to the ineffable world-spirit, until another creator god is evolved.†

In each cosmic day the god creates the universe and again absorbs it. During the cosmic night he sleeps, and the whole universe is gathered up into his body, where it remains as a potentiality. Within each kalpa are fourteen *manvantaras*,

---

* Brahmā is said to be now in his fifty-first year.

† Though the terms "day" and "year of Brahmā" are commonly used, the god whose life contains the universe is, as we have seen, thought of by Vaiṣṇavites as Viṣṇu and by Śaivites as Śiva, and Brahmā is a mere demiurge, the god in his creative aspect.

or secondary cycles, each lasting 306,720,000 years, with long intervals between them. In these periods the world is recreated, and a new Manu appears, as the progenitor of the human race. We are now in the seventh manvantara of the kalpa, of which the Manu is known as Manu Vaivasvata.

Each manvantara contains seventy-one *Mahāyugas*, or æons, of which a thousand form the kalpa. Each mahāyuga is in turn divided into four *yugas* or ages, called *Kṛta*, *Tretā*, *Dvāpara* and *Kali* (p. 180). Their lengths are respectively 4,800, 3,600, 2,400, and 1,200 "years of the gods", each of which equals 360 human years. Each yuga represents a progressive decline in piety, morality, strength, stature, longevity and happiness. We are at present in the Kali-yuga, which began, according to tradition, in 3102 B.C., believed to be the year of the Mahābhārata War.

The end of the Kali-yuga, according to many epic passages, is marked by confusion of classes, the overthrow of established standards, the cessation of all religious rites, and the rule of harsh and alien kings. Soon after this the world is destroyed by flood and fire. This view is propounded strongly in texts which date from about the beginning of the Christian era, when alien kings did in fact rule much of India, and when established practices were shaken by heresies such as Buddhism and Jainism. An earlier tradition would place the Mahābhārata War c. 900 B.C. (p. 34), according to which the 1,200 years of the Kali-yuga, if read as human years and not as "years of the gods", would at this time be nearing their end. Evidently some pious Hindus thought that the dissolution of the cosmos was imminent. Perhaps it is to the departure of this fear in later times that we must attribute the devising of the "years of the gods", which made the dissolution of the world comfortably distant. Most medieval texts state that the cosmic dissolution occurs only after the last cycle of the kalpa, and that the transition from one æon to the next takes place rapidly and comparatively calmly; the expectation of the Kalkin (p. 269), who will not destroy but will regenerate the world, could not otherwise be harmonized with the scheme of the yugas. In this, its final form, the Hindu system of world-cycles is clearly an imperfect synthesis of more than one independent doctrine; the manvantaras, especially, do not fit tidily into the scheme, and must surely be derived from a source different from that of the mahāyugas.

The system of the four yugas immediately brings to mind the four ages of ancient Greece—and indeed the Indian yugas are sometimes named after metals—gold, silver, copper and iron. A similar doctrine of four ages existed in ancient Persia, and the three schemes may have been borrowed from a common source.

The act of creation was thought of in more than one manner. The school called *Sāṅkhya* (p. 284f) and some lesser schools postulated the existence of primeval matter (*prakṛti*), of which the creator made use to form the world, but the *Vedānta* school, certainly the most influential in the Middle Ages, maintained that everything in the universe, souls and matter alike, was produced from God's own essence. The motive of creation was explained by the Vedānta school as the "sport" (*līlā*) of the World Soul, and the creation of the cosmos was thought of on the analogy of the production of a work of art from the mind of an artist.

The Soul, Karma and Saṃsāra

The doctrine of karma, elaborated in Upaniṣadic times and adopted by Buddhism and Jainism, was also part and parcel of Hinduism. According to the Hindu definition karma (literally "work," or "deed") was the unseen ripening of past actions, and though not in Hinduism a substantial category, as in Jainism, it was thought of as accumulating and dispersing. Through karma the body of the next life, divine, human, animal or hellish, was acquired; and on previous karma depended a man's character, fortune and social class, and his happiness and sorrow. Every good act sooner or later brought its result in happiness, and every evil act in sorrow.

The belief in karma does not necessarily involve fatalism. A fatalist strain often appeared in Hindu thought, but most teachers disapproved of it. Our present condition is inevitable, but only because of the karma accruing from our past deeds. We cannot escape the law of karma any more than we can escape the law of gravity or the passage of time, but by judgement and forethought we can utilize the law of karma to our own advantage.

The process of transmigration was interpreted somewhat variously, but all schools agreed that the soul does not transmigrate in a state of nudity, but with a sheath or series of sheaths of subtle matter; the condition of the sheaths depends on the balance of previous good and evil karma, and the new birth is determined by the nature of the sheaths which surround the soul. The subtle body of transmigration is deprived of sense-organs, including mind, the sixth sense, and therefore the soul cannot normally remember previous births or the passage from one body to another. Very advanced souls, however, can sometimes recapture memories of previous existences, and some sects evolved a special technique for doing so. Souls are liable to transmigration throughout the life of the god Brahmā, though at the end of each cosmic day or kalpa they return to his body as potentialities only. On the death of Brahmā, at the final dissolution of the universe at the end of a hundred Brahmā-years, they are absorbed into the World Spirit and their karma is annihilated.

Saṃsāra, the continual passage from body to body, often compared to an ever-rolling wheel, is infinitely tedious, and Hinduism inherited the desire for release from transmigration which was almost universal in Indian thought. Conceptions of the state of release or salvation (*mukti*) and the means of obtaining it differed widely.

The Six Systems of Salvation

Early in the Christian era, if not before, there was a theoretical classification of the various schools of thought looked on as orthodox, and the *Ṣaḍdarśana* or "Six Doctrines" became a regular feature of Hinduism. The Six Schools were actually of differing origin and purpose, but all were brought into the scheme by being treated as equally valid ways of salvation. They were divided into three groups of two, which were thought to be related and complementary. These were: *Nyāya* and *Vaiśeṣika*; *Sāṅkhya* and *Yoga*; and *Mimāṃsā* and *Vedānta*.

Nyāya ("Analysis") was rather a school of logie and epistemology than of theology. It looked back to the teacher Akṣapāda Gautama, the sūtras or aphorisms attributed to whom are probably no earlier than the Christian era. Logic was forced into the scheme as a means of salvation by the contention that clear thinking and logical argument were essential means to the highest bliss, and thus a religious basis was given to what was essentially a system of reasoning (p. 455f).

Vaiśeṣika ("the School of Individual Characteristics") was complementary to Nyāya, though perhaps older, and in medieval times the two merged into what was virtually a single school. While Nyāya specialized in logie, Vaiśeṣika was interested rather in physics than theology. The earliest text of the school is the sūtras of the legendary founder, Ulūka Kaṇāda, which had numerous exponents and commentators, the greatest of whom was Praśastapāda of the 5th century. The basic tenet of Vaiśeṣika, held in common with Jainism and some schools of Buddhism, was that nature is atomic. The atoms are distinct from the soul, of which they are the instrument. Each element has individual characteristics (*viśeṣas*), which distinguish it from the four non-atomic substances (*dravyas*) which the school recognizes—time, space, soul and mind. The atoms are eternal, but in the great dissolution at the end of the life of Brahmā they are separated one from another, and all things are destroyed. The new Brahmā utilizes the old atoms to create the world afresh. Vaiśeṣika thus postulated a dualism of matter and soul, and declared that salvation depends on fully recognizing the atomic nature of the universe, and its difference from the soul.*

Sāṅkhya ("the Count") is perhaps the oldest of the six systems, being mentioned in the *Bhagavad Gītā* and occurring in a primitive form in the Upaniṣads. Its legendary founder was the ancient sage Kapila, but the earliest surviving text of the system is the *Sāṅkhyakārikā* of Īśvarakṛṣṇa, perhaps of the 4th century A.D. Sāṅkhya resembles Jainism in its rigid dualism and fundamental atheism. It teaches the existence of twenty-five basic principles (*tattva*), of which the first is *prakṛti*—a term usually loosely translated "matter". Creation, or rather evolution, is not due to the operation of a divinity but to the inherent nature of prakṛti. From prakṛti develops (2) Intelligence (*buddhi*, also called *mahat* "the Great One"), and hence is produced (3) Self-consciousness (*ahaṅkāra*). Prakṛti has in fact evolved into an active divinity. Through self-consciousness emerge the five subtle elements (*tanmātra*), invisible matter in its most ethereal form; the five are (4) "ether" (*ākāśa*), (5) air, (6) light, (7) water and (8) earth. From the subtle elements the material elements (*mahābhūta*) emerge (9–13). Working on this material, Self-consciousness then produces the five organs of sense (*jñāendriya*): (14) hearing, (15) touch, (16) sight, (17) taste and (18) smell, and the five of action (*karmendriya*): (19) speech, (20) grasping, (21) walking, (22) evacuation and (23) procreation. Each of these organs corresponds to an element, in respective order.

* For further details on Vaiśeṣika atomism see p. 409.

Finally Self-consciousness produces the twenty-fourth of the basic components of the world, mind (*manas*), looked on as a sixth sense, which acts as intermediary between all the ten organs and the outside world. This remarkable and fantastic doctrine of cosmic evolution, interpreted in simple terms, implies that bodies, and indeed the whole cosmos, are products of the ego (*ahaṅkāra*), conceived as basically material.

But there is another tattva, the twenty-fifth. This is *Puruṣa*, literally "the Person", the soul. As in Jainism, there is an infinite number of souls in the universe, all equal, eternally inactive spectators of the evolution of prakṛti. Puruṣa is not dependent on prakṛti nor prakṛti on puruṣa—a universe is conceivable completely devoid of soul and yet evolving in the same way as the universe we know, for intelligence, personality and mind are not parts of the soul. Yet souls in some way become involved in matter, and their salvation lies in realizing their difference from it.

A very important feature of Sāṅkhya metaphysics is the doctrine of the three constituent qualities (*guṇa*), causing virtue (*sattva*), passion (*rajas*) and dullness (*tamas*). In its undeveloped state cosmic matter contains these three in equilibrium, but as the world evolves one or other of the three preponderates in different objects or beings, and the proportions account for the values of the universe. *Sattva guṇa*, the quality of virtue, is present in all things tending to truth, wisdom, beauty and goodness; the quality of passion inheres in all that is fierce, violent, energetic, forceful or active; while dullness is found in what is dark, stupid, gloomy, wretched or unhappy. This three-fold classification affected many aspects of Indian life and thought and its influence reached far beyond the Sāṅkhya school which made it its own.

The dualism of soul and matter and the fundamental atheism of Sāṅkhya were somewhat modified in the Middle Ages as a concession to the prevalent monism and theism. *Puruṣa* literally means "person" or "man", and *prakṛti* is of feminine gender. It is not surprising that the latter was personified as the wife of the former, especially by the tantric sects. The inactive purusa of the earlier system became a generative force, and the cold and rather pedantic Sāṅkhya, in a much modified form, became the common property of popular Indian religion of later times.

Yoga, the name of the fourth system, is a word well known in the West, and is connected etymologically with the English word "yoke". It may be freely translated "spiritual discipline" or "application". The term is loosely used to imply all the religious exercises and acts of self-mortification of Indian religion, the earnest follower of such practices being a *yogī*. In this broad sense yoga has been part of the teaching of every Indian sect, but it was also the name of a distinct school, which emphasized psychic training as the chief means of salvation. The basic text of this school is the *Yoga Sūtras* of Patañjali; this teacher was traditionally identified with a famous grammarian believed to have lived in the 2nd century B.C., but the sūtras in their present form are probably several centuries later.

The metaphysical ideas of the Yoga school were originally closely akin to those of Sāṅkhya, but they differed in that they brought a deity into the picture. The God (*Īśvara*) of Yoga was not a creator, but a specially exalted soul which had existed for all eternity without ever being enmeshed in matter. Thus the god of Yoga resembled the Buddha of the Lesser Vehicle, or the glorified Tīrthaṅkara of Jainsim, never coming in contact with his worshippers but invaluable as an example. He was specially symbolized in the sacred syllable *ŌM*, which in the Yoga school was much revered, as giving insight into the sublime purity of the soul and thus aiding meditation. A Yoga theism soon developed, however, and the God of later Yoga texts differs little from that of other schools.

The course of training of the yogī was divided into eight stages, reminding us of the eightfold path of Buddhism, but far less practical:

(1) Self-control (*yama*), the practice of the five moral rules: non-violence, truthfulness, not stealing, chastity, and the avoidance of greed.
(2) Observance (*niyama*), the regular and complete observance of five further moral rules, some of them rather overlapping with those in the category of self-control—purity, contentment, austerity, study of the Vedas, and devotion to God.
(3) Posture (*āsana*), sitting in certain postures, difficult without practice, which are thought to be essential to meditation. The most famous of these ispadmāsana, the "Lotus Posture", in which the feet are placed on the opposite thighs, and in which gods and sages are commonly depicted.
(4) Control of the Breath (*prāṇāyāma*), whereby the breath is held and controlled and the respiration forced into unusual rhythms, which are believed to be of great physical and spiritual value.
(5) Restraint (*pratyāhāra*), whereby the sense organs are trained to take no note of their perceptions.
(6) Steadying the Mind (*dhāraṇā*), by concentration on a single object, such as the tip of the nose, the navel, an icon, or a sacred symbol.
(7) Meditation (*dhyāna*), when the object of concentration fills the whole mind.
(8) Deep Meditation (*samādhi*), when the whole personality is temporarily dissolved.

Yoga was sometimes developed in special and rather dubious ways, especially by the tantric schools of the Middle Ages. The course of training outlined above was known as "Royal Yoga" (*rājayoga*), but other yoga systems developed, such as the "Yoga of Spells' (*mantrayoga*), which taught the continual repetition of magic syllables and phrases as a means of dissociating the consciousness; the "Yoga of Force" (*haṭhayoga*), which emphasized the importance of physical means such as special acrobatic exercises and very difficult postures, and sometimes advocated sexual union as a means of salvation; and the "Yoga of Dissolution"(layayoga), often identified with haṭha-yoga, based on certain ancient Indian physiological notions, which play a big part in the form of yoga sometimes taught by Western practitioners.

The chief vein of the body, known as *suṣumṇa*, runs through the spinal column.

Along it at different points are six "wheels" (*cakra*), or concentrations of psychic energy. At the top of the vein *suṣumṇa*, within the skull, is *sahasrāra*, a specially powerful psychic centre symbolically referred to as a lotus. In the lowest "wheel", behind the genitals, is the *kuṇḍalinī*, the "serpent power", generally in a quiescent state. By yogic practices the kuṇḍalinī is awakened, rises through the vein suṣumṇa, passes through all the six "wheels" of psychic force, and unites with the topmost sahasrāra. By awakening and raising his kuṇḍalinī the yogī gains spiritual strength, and by uniting it with sahasrāra he wins salvation.

The awakened kuṇḍalinī gives to the yogī superhuman power and knowledge, and many yogīs have practised yoga rather for this than for salvation. Some adepts of yoga have developed certain powers which cannot fully be accounted for by European medical science and which cannot be explained away as subjective, but the physiological basis of laya- and haṭha-yoga is certainly false; there is no *kuṇḍalinī, suṣumṇa* or *sahasrāra*. The ancient mystical physiology of India needs further study, not only by professional Indologists, but by open-minded biologists and psychologists, who may reveal the true secret of the yogī. For whatever we may think about his spiritual claims there is no doubt that the advanced yogī can hold his breath for very long periods without suffering injury, can control the rhythm of his own heart-beats, can withstand extremes of heat and cold, can remain healthy on a starvation diet, and, despite his austere and frugal life and his remarkable physical contortions, which would ruin the system of any ordinary man, can often survive to a very advanced age with full use of his faculties.

Mīmāṃsā ("Enquiry"), differed in origin from the other systems in that it was not so much a school of salvation as of exposition. Its original purpose was to explain the Vedas, and it was virtually a survival of brāhmaṇism. The earliest work of the school is the sūtras of Jaimini (perhaps of the 2nd century B.C.), which set out to show that the Vedas are eternal, self-existent, and wholly authoritative, and to defend their authenticity against all comers. This led to some development of logic, dialectics and semantics in the school. Śabarasvāmin (? 6th century) the greatest of Mīmāṃsā scholars, had much to say on law. It was only in the 7th and 8th centuries that the school developed a full philosophy of salvation, according to which respect for the Vedas and observance of their rules were essential first steps on the road. By the time of Kumārila (8th century) the Mīmāṃsā school was beginning to merge with the Vedānta.

Vedānta ("the End of the Vedas"), also called *Uttara Mimāṃsā* ("later Mīmāṃsā"), is the most important of the six systems, and in its many sub-schools ithas produced the characteristic features of modern intellectual Hinduism. The basic text of the system is the *Brahma Sūtras* of Bādarāyaṇa, written early in the Christian era, which have been commented on by many scholars of all ages, down to the present day. Vedānta is still a living school, and modern theologians and mystical teachers such as Vivekānanda and Aurobindo Ghose, and philosophers such as Rādhākrishnan, are all Vedantists. The doctrines of Vedānta were based on the Upaniṣads, and gave logical and organized form to their many mystical speculations. The classical Vedānta is that of the great philosopher Śaṅkara (? 788-820), a South Indian Śaivite brāhmaṇ who in a short lifetime composed extensive commentaries on the *Brahma Sūtras* and the chief Upaniṣads, travelled all over India preaching his doctrines, and founded an order of Hindu monks.

Śaṅkara was an orthodox brāhmaṇ, for whom all the Vedic literature was sacred and unquestionably true. To harmonize its many paradoxes he had recourse to an expedient already known in Buddhism (p. 245), that of a double standard of truth. On the everyday level of truth the world was produced by Brahmā, and went through an evolutionary process similar to that taught by the Sāṅkhya school from which Śaṅkara took over the doctrine of the three gunas. But on the highest level of truth the whole phenomenal universe, including the gods themselves, was unreal—the world was *Māyā*, an illusion, a dream, a mirage, a figment of the imagination. Ultimately the only reality was *Brahman*, the impersonal World Soul of the Upaniṣads, with which the individual soul was identical. As in the Upaniṣads, salvation was to be obtained by recognition of this identity through meditation. Śaṅkara's Brāhmaṇ is not really different from the "Void" or the Nirvāṇa of Mahāyāna Buddhism (p. 243), a fact well recognized by his opponents, who called him a crypto-Buddhist.

Śaṅkara's greatness lies in his brilliant dialectic. By able use of logical argument, and, we must admit, by interpreting some phrases very figuratively, he reduced all the apparently self-contradictory passages of the Upaniṣads to a consistent system which, though not unchallenged, has remained the standard philosophy of intellectual Hinduism to this day. The comparison of Śaṅkara in Hinduism with St. Thomas Aquinas in the Roman Catholic Church is a very fair one.

The doctrine of Śaṅkara is often known as *advaita* ("allowing no second", i.e. monism) or *kevalādvaita* (strict monism).

Theism and Devotion

The sect of the *Bhāgavatas*, worshippers of Vāsudeva, identified fled with Kṛṣṇa and Viṣṇu, was active at least a century before Christ. A little later arose a sect of *Pāśupatas*, devotees of Paśupati, or Śiva. We know little about the early history of these sects, but it is certain that they were theistic, and stressed the merits of worship rather than those of sacrifice. In the Middle Ages their doctrines were given a philosophy.

A widespread Vaisnavite school, known as the *Pāñcarātra* ("Of Five Nights", a term of uncertain significance), gave a cosmological basis to the myths of Vāsudeva-Kṛṣṇa by identifying him and his family with cosmic emanations, and thus building a system of evolution similar to those of the more orthodox six systems, of which we have described the Sāṅkhyan as a typical example. From Vāsudeva, identified with Viṣṇu the ultimate personal godhead, developed Saṅkarṣaṇa (another name of Kṛṣṇa's brother Balarāmā) at the beginning of time; this emanation was identified with *prakṛti*, or primal matter. The two produced

Pradyumna (Kṛṣṇa's son) identified with *manas* or mind; thence arose Aniruddha (Kṛṣṇa's grandson), who was self-consciousness (*ahaṅkāra*). Only then did the three gunas evolve, and with them Brahmā the demiurge.

In the Pāñcarātra system Saṅkarṣaṇa, Pradyumna and Aniruddha are not merely aspects of the divine character but gods in their own right, as they were with the early Bhāgavatas. The gods are thus simultaneously one and many. There is no question here of different levels of truth, as in Śaṅkara's system, but of an eternal paradox. The soul is one with God, but at the same time it is an individual. Even in the state of full salvation it retains enough individuality to realize the bliss of union with the godhead. The Pāñcarātra doctrine of emanations (*vyūha*) may have developed in Kashmīr, where it is believed that the earliest texts of the school were written; but it found a complementary development in the Tamil country, where a great growth of devotional religion was taking place at the same time.

The devotion (*bhakti*) of the early Bhāgavatas, as exemplified in the *Bhagavad Gītā*, had been somewhat restrained in its expression. By the less spiritually developed worshipper the god was probably not thought of as an ever-present and indwelling spirit, but as a mighty and rather distant king, to be adored from afar. This is the spirit of the Gupta hymn to the Sun quoted above (p. 275) and even in general of the *Bhagavad Gītā* itself. When Kṛṣṇa reveals himself as the supreme god and shows his transcendent form, Arjuna falls to the ground in terror, unable to bear the awful splendour of the theophany. The god admittedly states that he is in the heart of all beings, that he raises his worshippers from the sea of transmigration, and that they are very dear to him; but he is still rather God Transcendent than God Immanent. Arjuna compares Kṛṣṇa's relation to him to that of friend and friend, father and son, lover and beloved; but his chief feeling at the revelation of Kṛṣṇa's divinity is one of awe:

> "You are the father of the universe, of all that moves and all that moves not,
> its worshipful and worthy teacher.
> You have no equal—what in the three worlds could equal you,
> O power beyond compare?
>
> "So, reverently prostrating my body,
> I crave your grace, O blessed lord.
> As father to son, as friend to friend, as lover to beloved,
> bear with me, God.
>
> "I rejoice that I have seen what none has seen before,
> but my mind trembles with fear.
> Graciously show me again your earthly form,
> Lord of the Gods, Home of the World."[66]

Thus the early *bhakti* was inspired by feelings as much of respect as of love. Divine grace was the condescension of a mighty potentate, stern and functional.

His glory was the glory of an emperor, which the ordinary mortal could hardly contemplate.

Buddhism may have influenced the new form of piety which appeared in medieval times, for the concept of the Bodhisattva, looking down in love and pity and helping all creation, was probably earlier than any comparable idea in Hinduism. But the new form of devotion seems to have developed first in the Tamil country. One of its earliest expressions is a remarkable poem of the collection called the "Ten Odes", almost certainly earlier than the 7th century. This is the "Guide to the Lord Murugan", a description of the chief shrines of the old Tamil god, which the worshipper is advised to visit in turn. Throughout most of the poem the god retains his wild and primitive character, with the attributes of the northern Skanda added (p. 276f); but at last the worshipper meets him face to face.

> "When you see his face, praise him with joy,
> worship him with joined palms, bow before him,
> so that his feet touch your head. ...
>
> "Holy and mighty will be his form,
> rising to heaven, but his sterner face
> will be hidden, and he will show you
> the form of a young man, fragrant and beautiful;
> and his words will be loving and gracious—
> 'Don't be afraid—I knew you were coming!'"[67]

Here surely we find a new conception of godhead struggling to express itself, the idea of a god who feels an intense love for men and to whom the worshipper can return the same love. This found its first full expression in the hymns of the early Tamil devotees (*Nāyanārs* and *Āḷvārs*), which are among India's greatest contributions to the world's religious literature.

The devotion of the Tamil hymnodists is no longer reverence for a transcendent deity, but ecstatic love for an immanent one. The love of God, moreover, is reflected by the worshipper in love for his fellows. In the Tamil word *a<u>n</u>bu* we have something more closely approaching the Christian virtue of love than is to be found in any Sanskrit term. Moreover the Tamil devotees often worshipped their God with a deep sense of sin and inadequacy, which is rarely to be met in contemporary Āryan religious literature and recalls the Vedic hymns to Varuṇa.

> "You are father, you are mother,
> you are elder brother,
> you are all kinsmen,
> you are fair women, and abundant riches.
> You are family, friends and home,
> fount of pure wisdom, of wisdom to press onward.

You are gold, you are jewel, you are pearl—
    You are lord, Rider on the Bull,* you are bliss."[68]

"'O most desired, O king, O lord, eternal form,
    my fortune, supreme mystic!' Thus I sang each day.
My gold! My hill of coral! in love of you ...
    I have journeyed far to see the bright flower of your feet."[69]

"A sinner, I have left the way of love and service.
    Too well I have known the meaning of sickness and pain.
        I will go now and worship.
How foolish I have been! How long can I be parted
    from my pearl, my mighty jewel, my diamond, Lord of the shrine of
        Ārūr?"[70]

"He whom the King of Gods knows but in part, the God of Gods,
    The triple Lord, who makes, preserves and ends
the lovely universe, the Primal Form,
    the Ancient of Days, the Lord of Pārvatī, ...
came in his grace and took me for his own,
    so now I bow to none, and revere him alone.
I am among the servants of his servants,
    and I shall bathe in joy, and dance and sing."[71]

"Into my vile body of flesh
    you came, as though it were a temple of gold,
and soothed me wholly and saved me,
    O Lord of Grace, O Gem Most Pure.
Sorrow and birth and death and illusion
    you took from me, and set me free.
O Bliss! O Light! I have taken refuge in you,
    and never can I be parted from you."[72]

This impassioned devotionalism gradually affected the whole religious outlook of the Tamil country. The great Śaṅkara himself, though he maintained the rigid Upaniṣadic doctrine of salvation by knowledge, was the reputed author of some fine devotional poems in Sanskrit. It was only to be expected that the new forms of worship should receive formal shape and be harmonized with the Upaniṣads. This was done in different forms by a series of Dravidian theologians who succeeded Śaṅkara.

Chief of these was Rāmānuja, a brāhmaṇ who taught in the great temple of Śrīraṅgam. He is said to have lived from 1017 to 1137, but the first date is in all probability several decades too early. Like Śaṅkara he taught in many parts of India, and claimed to base his doctrines on earlier sources, writing lengthy commentaries

* An epithet of Śiva.

on the *Brahma Sūtras*, the *Bhagavad Gītā* and the Upaniṣads. Rāmānuja's system was founded on that of the Pāñcarātras, but his emphasis was rather different. He admitted the usefulness of ritual observances, but only in qualified measure, and he also admitted Śaṅkara's doctrine of salvation by knowledge, but declared that those so saved would find a state of bliss inferior to the highest. The best means of salvation was devotion, and the best yoga was *bhakti-yoga*, such intense devotion to Viṣṇu that the worshipper realized that he was but a fragment of God, and wholly dependent on him. Another means of salvation was *prapatti*, the abandonment of self, putting one's soul completely in the hands of God, trusting in his will, and waiting confidently for his grace.

Rāmānuja's God was a personal being, who was full of love for his creation. He could even override the power of karma to draw repentant sinners to him. Unlike the impersonal World Soul of Śaṅkara, which made the illusory universe in a sort of sport (*līlā*), Rāmānuja's God needed man as man needed God. By forcing the sense Rāmānuja interpreted the words of Kṛṣṇa, "the wise man I deem my very self"[73], to imply that just as man could not live without God, so God could not live without man. The individual soul, made by God out of his own essence, returned to its maker and lived forever in full communion with him, but was always distinct. It shared the divine nature of omniscience and bliss, and evil could not touch it, but it was always conscious of itself as an I, for it was eternal by virtue of its being a part of godhead, and if it lost self-consciousness it would cease to exist. It was one with God but yet separate, and for this reason the system of Rāmānuja was called *viśiṣṭādvaita*, or "qualified monism". Rāmānuja was not as brilliant a metaphysician as Śaṅkara, but Indian religion perhaps owes even more to him than to his predecessor. In the centuries immediately following his death his ideas spread all over India, and were the starting-point of most of the devotional sects of later times.

Many later theologians developed Rāmānuja's teaching, and in the Tamil country two main doctrinal divisions arose, analogous to the Arminians and Calvinists of early Protestantism. The Northern School taught that salvation could only be obtained "on the analogy of the monkey"; God saves souls as the monkey carries her young to safety, clinging to her body—some effort on the part of the believer was needed. The Southern School taught salvation "on the analogy of the cat"; just as a eat picks up her kittens in her teeth, so God saves whom he wills, with no effort on their part.

A teacher who developed Rāmānuja's doctrines in surprising directions was Madhva, who taught in the 13th century. This Canarese theologian broke completely with the Upaniṣadic doctrine of the unity of God and the human soul, and taught dualism (*dvaita*). He explained away as figurative all the passages of scripture which maintained monism, and declared that Viṣṇu, individual souls and matter were eternally and completely distinct. Viṣṇu has full power over both souls and matter, and saves the former entirely by his grace, which is only granted to those who live pure and moral lives. Evil souls are predestined to eternal damnation, which is conceived as infinite remoteness from God, while souls of mediocre quality will transmigrate eternally.

An interesting feature of Madhva's theology is the important part played by the wind-god Vāyu, the son of Viṣṇu, who is his agent in the world and has some of the features of the Holy Ghost of Christian theology.* The resemblances of Madhva's system to Christianity are so striking that influence, perhaps through the Syrian Christians of Malabār, is almost certain. The sharp distinction between God and the soul, the doctrine of eternal damnation, and the status of Vāyu are obvious points of similarity. In the legends about Madhva there are stories of miracles which must surely have been borrowed from the Gospels: as a boy he successfully disputed with learned brāhmaṇs in a temple; when he undertook asceticism a voice from heaven proclaimed his greatness; he fed multitudes with handfuls of food; he walked on water; and he stilled the raging ocean with a glance.

Śaivism too developed a theology adapted to the devotional literature of the hymnodists. The early literature of the Pāśupatas and other Śaivite sects, called *Āgamas* and written in Sanskrit, was supplemented and then virtually superseded by texts in Tamil repeating much of the older theology, but incorporating the devotional faith of the Nāyanārs. A series of fourteen such texts, all written by the 14th century, forms the bible of the *Śaivasiddhānta*, and is among the most influential religious literature of South India.

Tamil Śaivism teaches the reality of the three categories, God (*Pati*, "Lord"), souls (*pasu*, literally "animals") and matter (*pāśa*, "bond"). In salvation the soul is united, but not identified, with the deity. Tamil Śaivism thus goes further in the direction of dualism than the qualified monism of the Vaiṣṇavite Rāmānuja. Its most striking feature is the disappearance of all the harsh, capricious and amoral attributes of the old Śiva. In his character as bestower of karma he is pure justice, and his justice is but an aspect of his love for his creatures. He is ready at their call, and manifests himself to them in whatever form they worship him.

> "His form is love, his qualities, his knowledge are love,
> his deeds are love, his hands and feet are love, all his attributes are love.
> Unfathomable godhead assumes all these for the welfare of all things
> living."[74]

> "In his love the Lord punishes
> that the sinner may mend his ways
> and follow the right.
> All his acts flow from his love.
>
> "Goodness, love, grace and gentleness,
> courtesy, friendship and modesty,
> honesty, penance and chastity,
> charity, respect, reverence and truthfulness,

* In Hebrew and Syriac the word *rūḥ* means equally wind, breath or spirit.

purity and self-control,
wisdom and worship—
all these together are perfect virtue,
and are the word of the loving Lord."[75]

Tamil Śaivism perhaps approached nearer to thorough-going monotheism than did any other Hindu sect.

"Whatever god you accept, he is that god.
Other gods die and are born, and suffer and sin.
They cannot reward,
but he will see and reward your worship!"[76]

"We worship some god—our parents for instance—
but they do not reward us, even when they seem to show us their grace,
for all these gods are under the command of the Almighty,
and through them he fulfils our prayers.

"If Śiva alone rewards us, loving him is the highest virtue,
and the worship of other gods is of little use.
Dharma is his will; he has no desires
except to do good—so be firm in his worship."[77]

In Kashmīr another school of Śaivism arose, known as *Trika* or Triad, from the fact that the sect had three chief scriptures. This school, unlike the Tamil Śaivasiddhānta, was monistic, and shared Śaṅkara's doctrine of the unreality of the phenomenal world, which, it declared, only existed because the soul failed to recognize its true nature. For the school of the Trika salvation came with an act of recognition or sudden enlightenment, rather like the sudden conversion of old-fashioned Nonconformity. The greatest name in Kashmīr Śaivism is that of Abhinava Gupta (10th century), a brilliant theorist both in theology and poetics.

A third important Śaivite sect was that of the *Liṅgāyats* or *Vīraśaivas*, founded by Basava, a minister of King Bijjala Kalacuri who usurped the throne of the Cālukyas of Kalyāṇī in A.D. 1156. This sect is noteworthy rather for its cult and social doctrines than for its theology, which is a "qualified monism" with few striking features. Basava opposed image worship; in his sect the only sacred symbol is the linga of Śiva, a small specimen of which is constantly carried on the person of the believer. Basava completely rejected the Vedas and the authority of the brāhmaṇ class, and ordained a new priesthood— the *jaṅgamas*. He opposed pilgrimage and sacrifice and instituted complete equality among his followers, even to the equality of women, who were permitted to remarry on the death of their husbands. Among other Āryan practices which Basava condemned was cremation, and his followers are still usually buried. It is possible that he was influenced by what he had heard of Isiām. The Liṅgāyats still retain their individuality, though they have now compromised with orthodoxy in some respects, and they are an important sect in parts of Āndhra Pradesh and Mysore. Their sacred literature is mainly in Canarese and Telegu.

Hindu Rites and Ceremonies

Whereas the basic rite of the Vedic religion was sacrifice (*yajña*), that of Hinduism is worship (*pūjā*). In general a god is worshipped in the form of an icon (*arcā*) which has been sanctified by special rites, after which it is believed that the divinity has in some sense taken up his abode in it. Though devotees often ask for boons at the feet of the idol, pūjā is not so much an act of prayer as of homage and entertainment. The god is offered water for washing the feet, flowers and betel quids, like an honoured guest. In the morning he is ceremonially awakened with the sound of music, the ringing of bells, and the blowing of conches. He is washed, dried and dressed. He is honoured with flowers, garlands, incense and swinging lamps; he is fed, usually with rice and fruit, of which he eats the subtle part, leaving the gross material food for his worshippers, or to be given to the poor. In many temples he is taken to his bedroom at night, where he joins his wife or wives. In the larger shrines he is fanned by attendants and entertained by dancing girls like any ancient Indian king. On festival days he tours the city in a splendid car, often pulled by his devotees, followed by lesser gods in their care, musicians, bearers of yak's-tail flywhisks (*caurī*), parasols and fans, and dancers.

The temple originated as a small wooden hut enshrining a rough icon or fetish. Temples played no part in Vedic religion, and none has been traced in archaeological sites from before the Christian era. It is possible that they were introduced as a result of the wave of foreign influence following the Greek and Śaka invasions. In any case by Gupta times India was probably as much a land of temples as she is at present. The heart of the temple was the central shrine, the home of the chief divinity. Often a "tank" or a flight of steps leading down to a river adjoined the temple, for ritual ablution, important at all times, had by now become an essential part of religious observance. The temple might also contain a meeting hall, where the Epics, Purānas, and other non-Vedic sacred literature were recited for all who wished to listen, and a rest-house for pilgrims was also often provided, as well as many other offices and annexes, some of which served the social needs of the people.

Congregational worship of the Christian or Islāmic type was unknown in early Hinduism, though it developed in a few medieval sects. The worshipper went to the temple either alone or in a family group, made his offerings, and departed. In the greater temples the acts of worship by regular officiants might be watched by a large number of people, but they were rather an audience than a congregation.

Though the formal animal sacrifices of the Vedic period gradually disappeared, a new type of bloody sacrifice, almost certainly adopted from the non-Āryan aboriginals, became popular in the Middle Ages. Such rites rarely if ever took place in Vaiṣṇavite shrines, but some Śaivites and many devotees of Durgā adopted the new type of sacrifice. The animals were no longer killed with complicated ritual, but decapitated before the sacred icon, frequently in such a way that some of the blood fell on it. The ritual slaughter of animals was justified by the doctrine that the soul of the victim went straight to heaven, but it was not approved by the best minds of the times, and its survival in Bengal and elsewhere is a matter of shame to most modern Hindus.

Favourite animals for sacrifice were buffaloes, goats, sheep and cockerels. Human sacrifice was also practised. Theoretically the execution of every criminal was a sort of sacrifice, and his soul was thought to be purged of guilt thereby. The victims of human sacrifice were thus often criminals provided by the secular arm, but victims were also obtained by more dubious means. We read of girls being kidnapped to serve as human sacrifices in secret rites, and of a temple of Durgā at which a daily human sacrifice was offered. Voluntary human sacrifice, or religious suicide in various forms, became quite common in the Middle Ages, especially in the Deccan, where numerous inscriptions commemorate the many pious souls who, in fulfilment of vows or to ensure the success of their king, leapt from pillars and broke their necks, cut their own throats, or drowned themselves in sacred rivers. The last rite of the *satī* was, in one aspect, a human sacrifice.

Another form of religious ceremony was that practised by the sects which worshipped feminine divinities. These sects are generally known as tantric (from their scriptures, called tantras), śaktic (from their worship of the śakti, or personified energy of the god), or "left-hand" (from the fact that the goddess sits on the left of her lord). Their members believed that the usual Hindu rites and ceremonies, though not wholly ineffectual, were only suitable for ordinary worshippers; the adepts, who had undergone long rites of initiation, practised other ceremonies of much greater efficiency, similar to those of the Buddhists of the "Vehicle of the Thunderbolt" (p. 246f). The tantric rites involved the breaking of all the usual taboos of Hinduism. Small groups of initiates met at night, often in a temple or private house, but also frequently in a burning-ground, among the bones of the dead. The group formed a circle, seated around the circumference of a large circular magical diagram (*yantra*, *maṇḍala*) drawn on the ground. Though the members of the circle might include brāhmaṇs and outcastes, there was no class distinction at the ceremony—all were equal, and no ritual pollution occurred from their contact. After regular evening worship, the propitiation of ghosts, and other rites, the group would indulge in the five *Ms* (*pañca-makāra*): *madya* (alcoholic drink), *māṃsa* (meat), *matsya* (fish), *mudrā* (symbolical hand gestures, known in other branches of Indian religion and in dance and drama, also sometimes taken in this context as roasted grain), and *maithuna* (sexual intercourse). The rites concluded with the worship of the five elements, to which the five *Ms* mysteriously corresponded. Among some tantric groups the last of the five *Ms* involved promiscuous copulation, while the members of others brought their wives to the circle. With yet other groups those rites which were reprehensible to orthodoxy were performed only symbolically.

The remarkable "black mass" of the tantric sects, whether in Buddhism or Hinduism, became very popular in Eastern India in the late medieval period. It is still sometimes practised, but quite without publicity, and it is probable that with the growth of puritanism and rationalism the number of tantric groups in India is now comparatively small.

Hindu Ethics

At the bottom of most Hindu writing on ethics and morality lay the concept of the three ends of life (p. 147), and the full recognition that individuals of different classes and ages had different duties and standards of conduct. The ascetic should set his whole mind on unworldly things, but the layman was encouraged to blend the claims of religion, profession and material pleasure into a harmonious whole. This aspect of Hindu morality we have touched on already in other contexts and need not discuss further.

To the uninitiated Westerner the usual moral attitude of Hinduism, especially before the great changes of modern times, must seem a strange mixture of reason and taboo. The following passage, taken from the *Mānasollāsa*, a text on the duties and amusements of kings attributed to the 12th-century Deccan king Someśvara III Cālukya, illustrates perfectly this aspect of Hindu morals.

> "A king should avoid (1) untruth and (2) treachery, (3) illicit intercourse with
> women, and (4) eating what is forbidden.
> "He should shun (5) envy and (6) contact with outcastes, he should
> (7) revere all the gods, and satisfy (8) cows and (9) brāhmaṇs,
> "(10) reverence his ancestors, and (11) feed his guests, (12) obey his
> preceptors, (13) practise penance, and (14) bathe in sacred waters.
> "He should (15) nourish the poor, and (16) the orphan and widow,
> (17) the afflicted, and (18) his kin, and (19) his servants,
> "and (20) protect those who come to him for refuge.
> These are the twenty conditions of a successful reign."[78]

This passage shows that great emphasis was placed on such virtues as hospitality, charity and honesty, but piety, in the sense of the performance of such religious acts as worship, pilgrimage, and the feeding of cows and brāhmaṇs, was equally if not more important. The maintenance of taboos on contact with untouchables and eating forbidden food (not only meat, but food handled by low-caste persons or left over from a previous meal) was not clearly distinguished from honesty and self-control. At all times, however, the more intelligent teachers realized that mere outward observance was not as meritorious as inner goodness. Thus in the lawbook of Gautama, after a catalogue of the forty religious rites which the Āryan should practice, we read:

> "There are eight virtues of the soul—compassion for all beings, patience, contentedness, purity, earnest endeavour, good thoughts, freedom from greed, and freedom from envy. Whoever performs the sacred rites without possessing these eight virtues does not come to Brahmā or to his heaven; but if a man has performed only one rite and has all eight good qualities he comes to Brahmā."[79]

Many other sources give lists of virtues like this, all tending to encourage an earnest kindliness and tolerance in human relations. The doctrine of non-violence, qualified though it was, had a real effect on Hindu life, going far beyond mere restrictions on the killing of animals. All Hindu texts teach mercy, compassion and friendliness, but positive benevolence, except in the form of almsgiving, is less prominent, though often among lists of virtues we find "desire for the welfare of all beings". A positive ethic of love and forgiveness is a feature of much Tamil sacred literature. We quote from the maxims of the early *Tirukkuraḷ*.

> "Men without love think only of self,
> but the loving strip themselves to the bone for others."
>
> "For a kindness done without expecting reward
> heaven and earth are hardly sufficient recompense."
>
> "The joy of the avenger lasts but a day.
> The joy of the peacemaker lasts for ever."
>
> "They are great who fast and do penance,
> but they who forgive wrongs are even greater."
>
> "This, they say, is the highest wisdom—
> to return no harm to them that harm you."[80]

This exalted ethical tone is to be found in much Tamil literature, notably in the *Nālaḍiyār*, a collection of moral verses of somewhat later date than the *Tirukkuraḷ*, and in the devotional hymns which we have quoted elsewhere. But it is not only in Tamil literature that we find the call to love and kindness.

> "Viṣṇu is most pleased with him who does good to others,
> who never utters abuse, calumny or untruth,
> who never covets another's wife or wealth,
> and who bears ill will to none,
> who neither beats nor slays any living thing,
> who is ever diligent in the service of the gods
> and of brāhmaṇs and his teachers,
> who always desires the welfare of all creatures,
> as of his children and of his own soul."[81]

If the general ethical outlook of Hinduism favoured tolerance and kindliness, it was not equalitarian, and it recognized the needs of a society divided into many sections and classes with varied functions. A man's relation with his social inferiors should naturally differ from his relations with his betters. His standards of conduct depended on his social class. The virtues of the brāhmaṇ, such as the recitation of the Veda, were sins to the śūdrā, while the śūdrā might legitimately do things, such as drinking spirits, which were forbidden to the brāhmaṇ. Similarly the child, the student, the householder and the ascetic had their own codes and standards. Certain broad principles applied to all sections of the community, but beyond these no detailed code of morality was universally binding. Each group had its own rules of conduct, varying widely.

It is with this background in view that we must read the most famous ethical text of ancient India, the *Bhagavad Gītā*. Though this work contains much theology, its kernel is ethical and its teaching is set in the framework of an ethical problem. The hero Arjuna awaits in his chariot the beginning of battle. In the ranks of the enemy are his old friends, relatives and teachers, men whom he has known and loved all his life. Though convinced of the justice of his cause his spirits begin to sink, and he feels that he cannot fight against those who are so dear to him. He turns to Kṛṣṇa, who is acting as his charioteer, and asks his advice. Kṛṣṇa first explains that the death of the body does not involve the death of the soul and is comparatively unimportant:

"He who thinks this [soul] is the slayer
and he who thinks this is the slain
do not understand.
It neither slays nor is it slain.

"It is never born and never dies,
nor, once it exists, does it cease to be.
Unborn, eternal, abiding and ancient,
it is not slain when the body is slain …

"As a man puts off his worn out clothes
and puts on other new ones,
so the embodied [soul] puts off worn out bodies
and goes to others that are new.

"Weapons do not cleave it,
fire does not burn it,
waters do not wet it,
wind does not dry it.

"It cannot be cleft or burnt,
or wetted or dried.
It is everlasting, it dwells in all things,
firm, unmoving, eternal. …

"To be born is certain death,
to the dead, birth is certain.
It is not right that you should sorrow
for what cannot be avoided. …

"If you do not fight this just battle
you will fail in your own law
and in your honour,
and you will incur sin."[82]

Then Kṛṣṇa develops his teaching on the topic of human activity. The right course is not the inactivity of the meditating sage, for this attempt to put works on one side is impossible and futile. God himself is continually active, and man also should act; but, as far as possible, he should act without attachment, without personal desires or ambition. He must fulfil his function in the society of which he is a member, doing all things for the glory of God.

"There is nothing in the three worlds which I need,
nothing I do not own,
nothing which I must get—
and yet I labour forever.

"If I did not always work unwearying …
men would follow my ways.
The worlds would perish if I did not work—
I should bring back chaos, and all beings would suffer.

"So, as the unwise work with attachment,
the wise should work without attachment,
O son of Bharata,
and seek to establish order in the world…

"Cast all your acts upon me,
with your mind on the Highest Soul.
Have done with craving and selfhood.
Throw off your terror, and fight! …

"For there is more joy in doing one's own duty badly
than in doing another man's duty well.
It is joy to die in doing one's duty,
but doing another man's duty brings dread."[83]

The teaching of the *Bhagavad Gītā* is summed up in the maxim "your business is with the deed, and not with the result". In an organized society each individual has his special part to play, and in every circumstance there are actions which are intrinsically right— from the point of view of the poet who wrote the *Gītā* they are those laid down by the Sacred Law of the Āryans and the traditions of class and clan. The right course must be chosen according to the circumstances, without any considerations of personal interest or sentiment. Thus man serves God, and in so far as he lives up to this ideal he draws near to God.

The stern ethics of the *Gītā* are clearly intended as a defence of the old established order against the attacks of reformers and unbelievers. The virtue of the brāhmaṇ is wisdom, of the warrior, valour, of the vaiśya, industry, of the śūdrā, service; by fulfilling his class function to the best of his ability, with devotion to God and without personal ambition, a man will find salvation, whatever his class. It may be that the author of the *Gītā* sought merely to convey this message, rather barren and uninspiring when thus condensed. But behind his teaching was the fervour of a great religious poet, which transcended the narrow framework of contemporary social and religious law. Hence the inspiration of the *Bhagavad Gītā* has been widely felt in India from the time of the Guptas to the present day, and it has been commended by Christians and Muslims, as well as by the Hindus, whose most influential scripture it is. No one so ungrudgingly admitted his debt to its doctrine of tireless and unselfish service as Mahātma Gāndhī, who so strongly opposed the two features of ancient Indian society which the *Gītā* itself was in part written to defend—militarism and the class system.

(v) NON-INDIAN RELIGIONS

If we are to believe a very old tradition the first Christian converts in India were made by the Disciple Thomas himself, soon after the Crucifixion. The Indian king Gondophares sent to Syria for a skilful architect to build him a new city, and the envoy returned with St. Thomas, who told the king of a City not made with hands, and converted him and many members of his court. St. Thomas afterwards preached in other parts of India, and died a martyr's death at the hands of a king called in Christian tradition Misdeos, who cannot be identified. The historicity of Gondophares, however, is unquestioned (p. 52), and the story in its main outline is not impossible, for at the time contact between India and the West was close, and an enterprising missionary could easily have travelled from Palestine to India. Roman Catholics believe that the tomb of St. Thomas is to be found in the cathedral at Mailapur, a suburb of Madras, though the evidence for the Saint's martyrdom there is not sufficient to satisfy the historian.

Several rather unreliable references to other early missions exist in church tradition, but the first certain evidence of Christian activity in India is found in the *Christian Topography* of Cosmas Indicopleustes, an adventurous Alexandrian monk of the 6th century who left an account of his travels. He states that there were churches in Kerala and Ceylon, in the hands of Persian priests, and supervised by a Persian bishop at Kalliana (perhaps the modern Cochin). It is clear that the Indian Christians had embraced the Nestorian heresy, which was then widespread in Persia. The Nestorians were active missionaries, and their intrepid monks even crossed the wastes of Central Asia and founded successful churches in China. Whatever truth there may be in the legend of St. Thomas, it seems that these missionaries, no doubt following in the wake of Persian merchants, were chiefly responsible for establishing the Christian community in South India. When, at a later date, Islām stamped out both Zoroastrianism and Christianity in Persia, the Indian Christians turned for guidance to the patriarch of Antioch, and have maintained contact with Syria to this day.

When European travellers again visited India they noticed the Christian churches of the South. Marco Polo, at the end of the 13th century, saw the tomb of St. Thomas, and remarked on its popularity as a place of pilgrimage. But the Syrian church was corrupt. There is no evidence that Indian Christians ever accepted the doctrine of transmigration, but many Hindu customs had been adopted, and the Kerala Christians, like the Buddhists and Jainas before them, were in the process of becoming a rather heterodox Hindu sect. Jesuit missionaries of the 16th and 17th centuries succeeded in preventing further decadence. One section of the Syrian church in India accepted the authority of Rome, while the other, which remained true to its traditions, reformed and purified itself.

It is in this connexion that we find the first record of an Englishman visiting India. The *Anglo-Saxon Chronicle* states that in A.D. 884 King Alfred, to fulfil a vow, sent an envoy to India with rich gifts for the tomb of St. Thomas. Florence of Worcester, writing some 200 years later, adds that the name of the envoy was Swithelm, and that he returned safely. William of Malmesbury, on the other hand, gives his name as Bishop Sigelinus, and states that he brought back a rich present of jewels and spices from the local Indian king, who, if the story is true, must have been the Cōla King Āditya I or one of his chiefs. The *Anglo-Saxon Chronicle* is generally reliable, and it is reasonable to believe that Alfred sent the envoy, but "India" for 9th-century Europe was a very loose term, embracing many vaguely known parts of Asia and Africa, and we cannot be sure that the envoy actually visited the tomb of St. Thomas at Mailapur, or even that it was in existence at the time. The discrepancy in the names given to the envoy by the two later chroniclers shows that the tradition was not vividly remembered, and adds to our suspicion.

On the other hand we know that Christian pilgrims undertook very difficult journeys in order to visit holy places. At the time Islām was not violently anti-Christian, and the pilgrim might have found his way across Egypt without difficulty, and thence in an Arab merchant vessel to South India. It is pleasant to picture the brave English cleric, whatever his name, telling the Cola king through Arab and Tamil interpreters of King Alfred's battles with the Danes, and King Alfred, several years later, listening to the envoy's account of the wonders of India and sampling the rare spices of the Tamil land. Whatever our doubts, we cannot but hope that the story of Bishop Sigelinus is a true one.

As well as Christians small communities of Jews settled in Kerala. The earliest certain reference to this community is a 10th-century charter by which the king of the Cēras, Bhāskara Ravivarman, gave lands and privileges to a Jew named Joseph Rabbān; but the tradition of the Jews of Kerala tells of a large settlement at Cochin in the 1st century A.D. In any case a small Jewish community has existed in India for well over a millennium. One branch has mixed closely with the local Malayālī inhabitants and its members now have typical Indian complexions and features; the other branch retains its racial purity, and is still evidently Semitic.

A further ancient community of Indian Jews, the *Beni Israel*, has lived for many centuries on the west coast, and is now centred in Bombay.

Another non-Indian religious community was that of the Zoroastrians, now generally known as Pārsīs. Under Achasmenid and Sāsānian emperors Zoroastrianism was certainly practised in parts of N.-W. India, and had some influence on Hinduism and Buddhism, but no very clear traces of a Zoroastrian community have survived there. Though Zoroastrian merchants may have settled on the west coast of India very early, we have no record of them until after the Arab conquest of Persia, when Persian fugitives came to India in appreciable numbers. According to the Pārsīs' own traditions one band of refugees settled first at Diū in Saurāshtra, and then at Thānā near Bombay, in the early 8th century.

Yet another community was that of the Muslims. Arabs visited India long before the days of Muhammad, and there is evidence of small Muslim communities in many of the coastal towns of the Peninsula from the 8th century onwards. The Māppilā (Moplah) community of Kerala is undoubtedly descended from settlers and converts of long before the days of Muslim invasion of India. There is, however, no clear evidence of any influence of Islam on Hinduism until after the Muslim conquest.

Thus India, though always loyal to her indigenous cults, gave a welcome to those of the West. If we except the uncertain tradition of St. Thomas' martyrdom there is no good evidence of the persecution of any of these non-Indian sects. Their members quietly pursued their own cults, small but significant elements in the religious life of the coastal cities, while the great body of Hindus were scarcely aware of the alien faiths, and in no way antagonistic to them. This capacity for toleration contributed to the characteristic resiliency of Hinduism, and helped to assure its survival.

PLATE XLIX

Woman Writing. Khajurāho. 10th–11th century A.D.
(Now in the Indian Museum, Calcutta)

PLATE L

(a) Female Figure, Nokhās, U.P.
10th century

(b) Sarasvatī, Dhārā, M.P.
A.D. 1034

PLATE LI

British Museum

(a) Leogryph, Gujarāt. 11th–12th century

Dr H. Goetz, Baroda Museum

(b) Sculptured Panel from a Jaina Temple. Mehsānā, Barodā. 11th century

PLATE LII

Dr H. Goetz, Baroda Museum

(a) Musicians. Dabhoī, Barodā. 12th century

Dr H. Goetz, Baroda Museum

(b) Memorial to a Chieftain. Dumad, Barodā. A.D. 1298

PLATE LIII

British Museum

(a) Siva Dancing, Orissā. 12th Century

British Museum

b) Bṛhaspati, the God of the Planet Jupiter, Orissā. 12th century

PLATE LIV

Apsaras, Bhubanesar,
Orissā.12th century A.D.

PLATE LV

Dept. of Archaeology, Government of India

Lovers (*Maithuna*), Konārak, Orrissa. 13th century A.D.

A Girl Musician with Cymbals, Konārak. 13th century A.D.

PLATE LVII

Dept. of Archaeology, Government of India

Elephant, Konārak. 13th century A.D.

PLATE LVIII

Dept. of Archaeology, Government of India

Horse Trampling a Demon, Konārak. 13th century A.D.

A. Nawrath, "India and China", Cresset Press, London

Colossal Rock-cut Image of the Jaina Saint Gommateśvara, Śravaṇa Beḷgoḷā, Mysore. 10th century A.D.

Archaeological Survey of Ceylon

(a) Aged Man (probably King Parākramabāhu I) holding Palm-leaf Manuscript. Rock-sculpture, Polonnarava, Ceylon. 12th century A.D.

A. L. Basham

(b) The Buddha's *Parinirvāṇa*. Colossal Rock-scultpure, Polonnarava, Ceylon. 12th century

PLATE LXI

The Rt. Rev. the Bishop of Uganda

Christian Font, Kandurathy, Kerala. Medieval.

PLATE LXII
Terracottas

Messrs. Faber & Faber, Royal Academy Trustees and Patnā Museum

(a) Woman with Ornate Headdress, Patnā. *c.* 200 B.C.

(b) Dept. of Archaeology, Government of India

(c) *Dampatī* Couples. Ahicchatrā, U.P. c. 1st century B.C.

Dept. of Archaeology, Government of India

(d) Śiva. Ahicchatrā. Gupta Period

(e) Pārvati. Ahicchatrā

PLATE LXIII

Messrs. Faber & Faber, Royal Academy Trustees and Birmingham Museum and Art Gallery

Colossal Bronze Buddha, Sultānganj, Bihār. Gupta Period.

PLATE LXIV
Pāla Bronzes

Messrs. Faber & Faber, Royal Academy Trustees and Patnā Museum

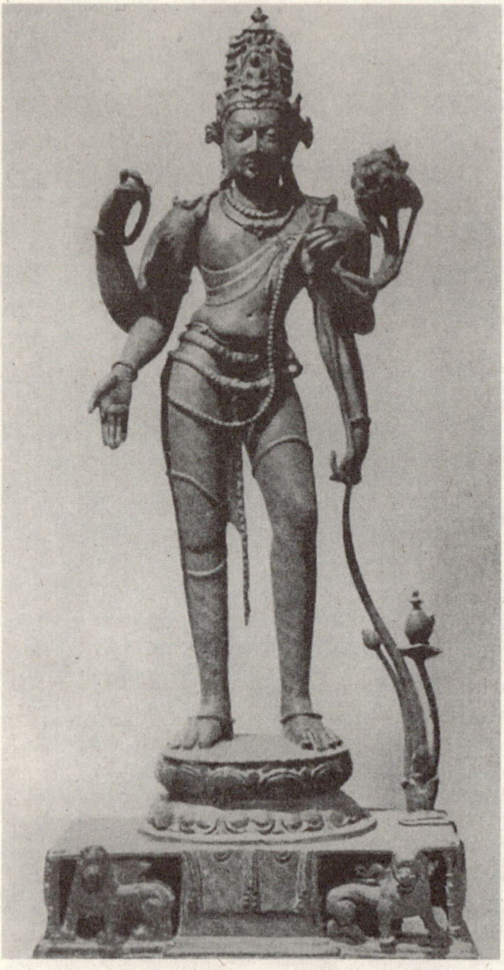

Dept. of Archaeology, Government of India

(b) Avalokiteśvara, Nālandā

(a) Avalokiteśvara-Padmapāṇi. Kurkihār, Bihār.

British Museum

(c) Gaṇeśa, Three Mother Goddesses and Kubera

VIII

THE ARTS: ARCHITECTURE, SCULPTURE, PAINTING, MUSIC AND THE DANCE

THE SPIRIT OF INDIAN ART

NEARLY all the artistic remains of ancient India are of a religious nature, or were at least made for religious purposes. Secular art certainly existed, for literature shows that kings dwelt in sumptuous palaces, decorated with lovely wall-paintings and sculpture, though all these have vanished. Much has been said and written about Indian art since, some sixty years ago, European taste began to doubt the established canons of the 19th century and looked to Asia and Africa for fresh aesthetic experience. From that time to this most authorities on the subject, Indian and European alike, have stressed the religious and mystical aspect of Indian art. While admitting the realism and earthiness of the earliest sculpture, they have read the truths of Vedānta or Buddhism into the artistic remains of our period, and have interpreted them as expressions of deep religious experience, sermons in stone on the oneness of all things in the Universal Spirit.[1]

One student at least disagrees with this interpretation. There are indeed a few remains which seem imbued with an intensity of religious feeling rare in the art of the world, but it is the full and active life of the times which is chiefly reflected in the art of ancient India, at first directly, as at Bhārhut, Sānchī and Amarāvatī, then with a gentle idealism, as at Ajantā, and finally in the multitude of figures, divine and human, carved on the many temples of the Middle Ages. In all these phases there is a *horror vacui* and an intense vitality which remind us rather of this world than the next, and suggest to us the warm bustle of the Indian city and the turbulent pullulation of the Indian forest.

Gothic architecture and sculpture are vertical. Spire and arch point upwards, and as the style develops the spire becomes taller and the arch more pointed. The Christs, saints and angels of the Middle Ages in Europe are often disproportionately tall, and their tallness is accentuated by long garments reaching to the ankles. Their poses are generally restful, and they rarely smile. Medieval European art was truly religious; its conventions seem to have been deliberately designed to lead the worshipper's thoughts away from the world of flesh to the things of the spirit. Much of it was the work of pious monks, or of men with deep religious vocations.

The tendency of Indian art is diametrically opposite to that of medieval Europe. The temple towers, though tall, are solidly based on earth. The ideal type is not abnormally tall, but rather short and stocky. Gods and demigods alike are young and handsome; their bodies are rounded and well-nourished, often by European standards rather effeminate. Occasionally they are depicted as grim or wrathful, but generally they smile, and sorrow is rarely portrayed. With the exception of the type of the dancing Śiva the sacred icon is firmly grounded, either seated or with both feet flat on the ground. We need hardly mention that all Indian temple sculpture, Hindu, Buddhist and Jaina alike, made full use of the female form as a decorative motif, always scantily dressed, and nearly always in accordance with Indian standards of beauty.

Asceticism and self-denial in various forms are praised in much Indian religious literature, but the ascetics who appear in sculpture are usually well fed and cheerful. As an example we may cite the colossal rock-cut medieval image of the Jaina saint Gommateśvara (pl. LIX) at Śravaṇa Beḷgoḷā in Mysore. He stands bolt upright in the posture of meditation known as *kāyotsarga*, with feet firm on the earth and arms held downwards but not touching the body, and he smiles faintly. The artist must have tried to express the soul almost set free from the trammels of matter, and about to leave for its final resting place of everlasting bliss at the top of the universe. Whatever the intentions of the artist, however, Gommateśvara is still an ordinary young man of his time, full of calm vitality. The saint is said to have stood for so long in meditation that creepers twined round his motionless legs, and these are shown in the sculpture; but, though intended to portray his sanctity, they do but emphasize that he is a creature of the earth whom the earth pulls back.

Ancient India's religious art differs strikingly from her religious literature. The latter is the work of men with vocations, brāhmaṇs, monks and ascetics. The former came chiefly from the hands of secular craftsmen, who, though they worked according to priestly instructions and increasingly rigid iconographical rules, loved the world they knew with an intensity which is usually to be seen behind the religious forms in which they expressed themselves. In our opinion the usual inspiration of Indian art is not so much a ceaseless quest for the Absolute as a delight in the world as the artist found it, a sensual vitality, and a feeling of growth and movement as regular and organic as the growth of living things upon earth.

THE EARLIEST ARCHITECTURE

Of the visual arts of ancient and medieval India much architecture and sculpture and a little painting have survived. As most of the existing sculpture was intended to be ancillary to architecture we deal with the latter first.

The utilitarian brick buildings of the Harappā Culture, strong and competent though they were, had apparently little aesthetic merit, and will not be mentioned here. With the exception of the walls of Rājagṛha (p. 173), which also have no artistic value, we have no significant architectural remains between the Harappā period and that of the Mauryas. This is due to the fact that few buildings were made of stone during this time.

Megasthenes mentions that the palace of Candragupta Maurya, though very large and luxurious, was built of carved and gilded wood, and the earliest stone buildings to have survived were evidently modelled on wooden originals. We must not assume from the almost complete lack of significant material remains that Indian building in the Mauryan period, or even before, was mean or primitive. The Mauryan monolithic columns prove that the craftsmen of those days had a thorough mastery of working in stone, and if the great cities of Mauryan times were mainly built of wood we must attribute this chiefly to the comparative scarceness of stone in the Gangetic Plain and to the abundance of timber where it is now scarce. There is no evidence of a cultural advance in the Middle Ages, when building in stone became common, but rather of a decline. The increasing adoption of stone as a building medium was due partly to foreign contacts, but also to the gradual disappearance of timber forests from the more populous and civilized regions of India.

The wonderful Mauryan columns with their finely carved capitals fall rather under the head of sculpture than of architecture, for most of those which survive had no architectural purpose. Fragments of similar columns, found at Patnā, supported the roof of a palace, which has been reasonably identified as that of Aśoka. The remains of the Patnā pillared hall are so fragmentary that the plan of the building cannot be accurately reconstructed, but it was evidently a large one. At this time, however, stone buildings must still have been quite rare. All the Mauryan pillars and other products of Mauryan stonemasons come from the same quarry, at Chunār, not far from Vārāṇasī, and all bear the stamp of the same school. They are the work of craftsmen who had learnt much from Persia, and perhaps a little from Greece, but had given their output distinctive Indian characteristics. Their workshops were probably maintained by the Mauryan kings, and vanished with the dynasty.

THE STŪPA

The stūpa began as an earthen burial mound, which was revered by the local population, and we have seen that the cult of stupas was taken up by Buddhism, and that Asoka raised stupas in the Buddha's honour all over India (p. 231). Only one stūpa, in Nepal, survives in the form in which the great emperor left it, but excavations of existing stūpas have shown the character of the earlier ones. They were large hemispherical domes, containing a small central chamber, in which the relics of the Buddha were placed in a casket, often beautifully carved in crystal. The core of the stūpa was of unburnt brick, and the outer face of burnt brick, covered with a thick layer of plaster. The stūpa was crowned by an umbrella of wood or stone, and was surrounded by a wooden fence enclosing a path for the ceremonial clockwise circumambulation (*pradakṣinā*), which was the chief form of reverence paid to the relics within it.*

In the period between the Mauryas and the Guptas much wealth and energy were spent on Buddhist architecture, and the older stupas were greatly enlarged and beautified. Of these three are specially noteworthy—those at Bhārhut and Sānchī in Madhya Pradesh, and at Amarāvatī in the lower Kistnā Valley. The Bhārhut stūpa, perhaps in its present form dating from the middle of the 2nd century B.C., is important chiefly for its sculpture, and the stūpa: itself has now vanished. That at Sānchī, on the other hand, is one of the most striking architectural remains of ancient India (pl. XI6).

In the 2nd century B.C. the old Sānchī stupa was enlarged to twice its original size, becoming a hemisphere of about 120 feet in diameter. It was then faced with well-cut masonry laid in regular courses, and, besides the lower path on ground level, an upper terraced path some 16 feet from the ground was added. The old wooden railings were replaced by stone ones 9 feet high, tenoned and mortised in imitation of carpentry. Finally, towards the end of the lst century B.C., four glorious gateways (*taraṇo*) were added at the four cardinal points. Lesser stupas and monastic buildings surrounded the great stupa (fig. xviii).

The Sānchī gateways (pl. XXVII) are perhaps more noteworthy for their carved ornamentation than their architecture. Each consists of two square columns, above which are three curved architraves supported by animals or dwarfs, the whole reaching some 34 feet above ground-level. The construction of these gateways, from the technical point of view, is primitive, and it has been suggested that their design is based on the log or bamboo portcullis of the ancient Indian village.[3] The finish, on the other hand, is remarkably good, and the carvings are among the most fresh and vigorous products of the Indian sculptor (pl. XXVIII).

In respect of size few Indian stūpas greatly exceeded that of Sānchī, but in Ceylon the stupa reached tremendous proportions. The Abhayagiri Dāgāba at Anurādhapura, the capital of the early kings of Ceylon, was 327 feet in diameter, and larger than some of the pyramids of Egypt. It reached its present size, after a succession of enlargements, in the 2nd century A.D.

In India stūpa architecture became more and more ornate. The Stūpa of Amarāvatī (fig. xix), which in its final form was completed c. A.D. 200, was larger than that of Sānchī, and it was adorned with carved panels (some of which can be seen in the British Museum) telling the story of the life of the Buddha. Meanwhile in Northern India stupas grew taller in proportion to their bases. They were often set on square platforms, which in Burma and Indonesia were developed into stepped pyramids, the largest of which is the enormous stūpa of Borobodūr, in

---

* It has been suggested that the stūpa, like the later Hindu temple, was thought of as a microcosm of the universe. There are Mesopotamian precedents for this belief, and the passion for cosmic symbolism, evident in India from Vedic times, certainly led to the making of the analogy at least in respect of the temple.[2] But, though many authorities would disagree with us, we do not believe that cosmic symbolism played any great part in the thought of the ancient Indian architect. Stūpas and temples were planned without thought of such symbolism, which was the work of pandits and not of architects.

Fig xviii.—Stūpas and Monasteries at Sānchī. (Reproduced from Percy Brown's "Indian Architecture (Buddhist and Hindu)", published by D. B. Taraporevala Sons & Co. Ltd., Bombay)

Jāva, built in the 8th century A.D. Pinnacles became higher, and developed towards the spiring forms of the present-day temples of Burma and Siam.

Of later Indian stūpas the two most famous are those of Sārnāth and Nālandā. Of the tali stūpa of Sārnāth (pl. XII*a*) near Vārāṇasī, the scene of the Buddha's first sermon, now little more than the inner core remains. It was once a most imposing structure of beautifully patterned brickwork with a high cylindrical upper dome rising from a lower hemispherical one, and with large images of the Buddha set in gable ends at the cardinal points. In its final form it dates from the Gupta period. The stūpa at Nālandā (pl. XII*b*), seven times successively enlarged, in its present ruined state gives the impression of a brick pyramid with steps leading up to its terraces. It was originally a tali stūpa raised on a high base, with a smaller stūpa at each corner, but the monument underwent so many alterations in Gupta and Pāla times that it is now difficult for the untrained eye to recognize its original form at any one stage of its development.

Around the great stūpas were lesser ones, often containing the ashes of monks famous for their piety and learning, and a whole complex of buildings—monasteries, shrine-rooms, preaching halls and resthouses for pilgrims (fig. xviii). At the greater Buddhist sites such as Nālandā the groups of monastic buildings were usually surrounded by fortress-like walls.

In their present partial dilapidation the heavy domes of the great stupas sometimes seem a little forbidding. Originally the lime-washed or plastered stūpa shone brilliantly white in the tropical sunlight, its pinnacle, now generally broken, rising like a golden spear from the ceremonial stone umbrella on top of the dome. Then it must have given a different impression. The great Ruvanvälī Dāgäba at

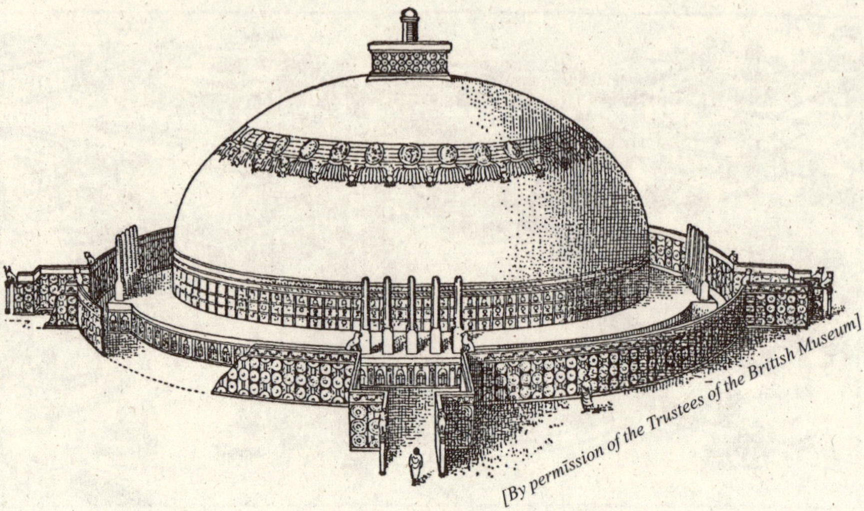

Fig. xix.—The Stūpa of Amarāvati. (Reproduced from Douglas Barrett's "Sculpture from Amarāvati in the British Museum", published by The British Museum, London).

Anurādhapura in Ceylon, which in recent years has been restored and is once more used in Buddhist worship, rising white in the distance out of the plain, shows the stūpa at its best, as a worthy emblem of a great religion.

CAVE TEMPLES

Of the centuries before the Gupta period the chief architectural remains, other than stupas and their surrounding gateways and railings, are artificial caves, excavated for religious purposes. Early specimens show a slavish imitation of carpentry which proves conclusively that the art of building in stone was still not fully developed. Thus two of the caves of Barābar Hill near Gayā, dedicated by Aśoka to Ājīvika monks, are in the form of a plain rectangular outer hall, at one end of which is an inner chamber with a curved wall and over-hanging eaves. The caves were evidently substituted for a standardized religious meeting place consisting of a round thatched hut standing in a courtyard, and their designer could not transcend the pattern to which he had been used. Similar dependence on wooden models is evident in many other features of design until the Gupta period.

The caves of the Barābar and Nāgārjunī Hills are quite unadorned, with the exception of one at Nāgārjunī, near Barābar, which has a comparatively simple carved entrance, added during or soon after the Mauryan period. The inner walls of all the caves are finely polished, no doubt by workmen of the school which was responsible for the polish of the Aśokan columns.

Later cave temples and monasteries are to be found in many parts of India, but it was in the Western Deccan, under the Sātavāhana Empire and its successors, that the largest and most famous artificial caves were excavated. The oldest Deccan cave, at Bhājā near Poona, consists of a deep apsidal hall cut in solid rock, with a row of plain octagonal pillars near the walls, which support curved ribs carved to represent the barrel vaulting of a wooden building. At the further end of the hall is a small stūpa, also cut from solid rock, and the outside of the cave has a facade carved like a gable, with smaller ornamental gables on either side. Beside this cave, which was a meeting hall for Buddhist monks and lay worshippers, is a second cave consisting of a broad cutting into the rock, leading to five cells, which were the dwellings of the monks.

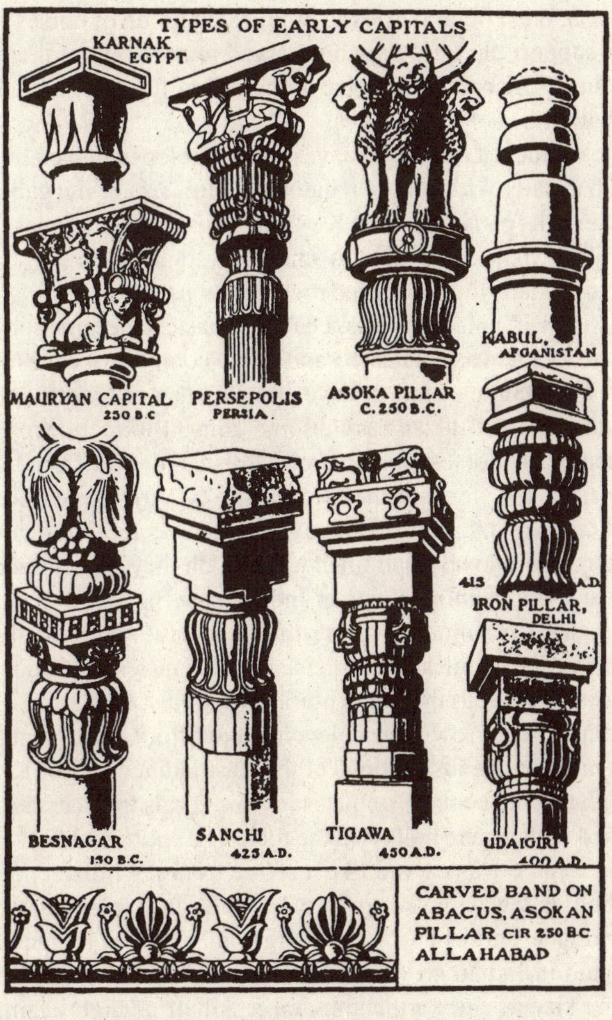

Fig. xx.—Early Capitals. (Reproduced from Percy Brown's "Indian Architecture (Buddhist and Hindu)", published by D. B. Taraporevala Sons & Co. Ltd., Bombay)

From these beginnings the cave temples developed in size and splendour. The finest single example is the great caitya hall at Kārlī (pl. XIII), probably made about the beginning of the Christian era. This is cut 124 feet deep into the rock, and is of the same general pattern as that at Bhājā and many other caves of the Western Deccan, but much developed in size and splendour. The columns are no longer plain and austere, but, by a process which can be traced through earlier stages, they have become heavy and ornate. Each is set on a square stepped plinth, and rises from a bulbous base, which is carved to represent a large pot with base and rim; this is another survival of wooden construction, for the octagonal wooden pillars of earlier days were bedded in large earthenware pots to protect them from ants and other insects. Each pillar carries a complicated group of horses and elephants with riders to support the roof, which is carved in imitation of the timber rafters of barrel vaulting. The caitya or shrine at the end of the hall is much enlarged in comparison with those of other caves.

The simple façades of the earlier caves were developed into elaborately carved verandas, each usually with a large window, the full size of the gable-end, which let light into the hall (pl. XIV*a*). The Kārlī cave has three entrances, and splendid relief panels of *dampatī* couples, with small carved gable-ends above.

With the caitya halls the associated rock-cut monasteries or *saṅghārāmas* also developed in size and splendour. As a cave monastery became too small for its inhabitants a new cave was cut nearby and so the complex of caves grew over the centuries. The most famous of these cave groups is that of Ajantā, in Mahārāshtra. Here no less than twenty-seven caves, some going 100 feet deep into the rock, were excavated in the horseshoe curve of a hillside, not far from the great trade route leading from the North to the Deccan (pl. XIV*b*). The earliest caves date from the 2nd century B.C., while others are as late as the 7th century A.D. The splendid sculpture and lovely paintings with which they are adorned make them one of the most glorious monuments of India's past (p. 331f).

Perhaps even more impressive are the later cave temples of Ellorā, near Aurangābād, some thirty miles from Ajantā. Here are no less than thirty-four caves, constructed from the 5th to the 8th centuries A.D., most of them Hindu but some Buddhist and Jaina. The crowning achievement of Ellorā is the great Kailāsanātha Temple, excavated on the instructions of the Rāṣṭrakūṭa emperor Kṛṣṇa I (c. A.D. 756–773). With this the concept of the cave temple was transcended, for the king was not satisfied with a mere hollow in the rock. The entire rock face was cut away and a splendid temple was carved like a statue from the hillside, complete with shrineroom, hall, gateway, votive pillars, lesser shrines and cloisters, the whole adorned with divine figures and scenes large and small of a grace and strength rarely seen again in Indian art (pl. XV). The ground plan of Kailāsanātha is of about the same size as the Parthenon, and it is half as high again. The labour necessary to construct it, however, was less than that which would be required to build a comparable temple of masonry, for transport created no problem, and the process of construction, beginning at the top of the cliff and working down to the base, avoided the need of scaffolding. But no considerations of this kind can disparage the glory of Kailāsanātha, "the most stupendous single work of art executed in India".[4]

Kailāsanātha is not the earliest temple hewn from solid rock. Others are to be found at Māmallapuram, on the sea-coast some fifty miles south of Madras, where seventeen temples, none very large in size, were carved from outcropping hillocks of granite under the patronage of 7th century Pallava kings. The most famous of these, the "Seven Pagodas", still show the influence of wood construction, and are of a distinctive style, possibly looking back to Dravidian prototypes.

The latest cave-temples of importance are those of Elephanta, a beautiful little island off Bombay. These, in the same style as those of Ellorā, are famous for their sculpture, especially for the great Trimūrti figure of Śiva (p. 327). After these no important caves were excavated. Indians had long known the art of building in stone. The Kailāsanātha Temple, carved in exact imitation of masonry, showed the dissatisfaction with the older cave form. The great period of medieval temple building had begun.

TEMPLES

The earliest free-standing religious building of which traces remain is a small round hall, probably originally containing a Buddhist stūpa, at Bairāt near Jaipur; this dates from the 3rd century B.C., and was made of brick and wood; little but the foundations now exist, and the form had no future.

The next landmark in temple architecture is the temple generally known, from the modern name of the site, as that of Jandiāl, excavated from one of the mounds which covered the city of Takṣaśilā. This, one of the important buildings of the Greek city, contained a square inner sanctuary, a meeting hall and a courtyard, and its outer and inner entrances were each flanked by two large pillars of orthodox Ionian pattern. The Jandiāl temple was probably Zoroastrian, and it had no direct successors, but the influence of Western architecture is clearly to be seen in Kashmīr, where columns of Hellenic type were used throughout the medieval period, in conjunction with distinctive pyramidal roofs and arches surmounted by pointed gables, which give the Kashmīr style an almost Gothic appearance. Most famous of Kashmīr's early temples is the Temple of the Sun at Mārtand, dating from the 8th century. There are no remains of free-standing Hindu temples erected before the Gupta period, though by this time they must long have been built in wood, day and brick. From the Gupta period, however, several examples survive, chiefly in Western India, all showing the same general pattern. Pillars were usually ornate, with heavy bell-shaped capitals surmounted by animal motifs, and the entrances were often carved with mythological scenes and figures. All the Gupta temples were small, and most had flat roofs. Their masonry was held together without mortar, and was far larger and thicker than was necessary for the comparatively small buildings. Evidently the builders had not yet fully mastered their technique, and were still thinking in terms of the cave. The finest Gupta temple, that of Deogarh near Jhānsī, probably of the 6th century, marks a great advance. Here iron dowels were used to hold the masonry together, and a small tower rose above the sanctum. The portal veranda was continued all round the building, making a covered walk.

The standard type of the Hindu temple, which has persisted from the 6th century to the present day, was not fundamentally different from that of the ancient Greeks. The heart of the temple was a small dark shrine-room (*garbhagṛha*), containing the chief icon. This opened on a hall for worshippers (*maṇḍapa*), originally a separate building, but usually joined to the shrine-room by a vestibule (*antarāla*). The hall was approached by a porch (*ardhamaṇḍapa*). The shrine-room was generally surmounted by a tower, while smaller towers rose from other parts of the building. The whole was set in a rectangular courtyard, which might contain lesser shrines and was often placed on a raised platform.

The medieval period in India was, like the Middle Ages in Europe, an age of faith. With better techniques of stone construction new temples sprang up everywhere to replace earlier wooden or brick buildings, and kings and chiefs vied with one another in their foundation. Strict canons of design in both architecture and sculpture were laid down in textbooks (*śilpaśāstra*), some of which survive.[5] The technique of architecture was not far advanced, despite the great achievements of the period. Though arches occur in the cave temples and in Kashmīr, the art of making a true arch, dome or vault, seems to have been ignored, although corbelling— the building up of an arch or dome by overlapping courses of brick or masonry—was widely practised, and produced work of great beauty. Mortar was known but rarely used, for the style of archless and domeless architecture employed made it virtually unnecessary.

The temple was ornately decorated, often even to the dark shrine-rooms lighted only by flickering oil-lamps. Despite this ornateness the apprenticeship of his tradition in rock architecture gave the architect a strong sense of mass. Heavy comices, strong pillars, wide in proportion to their height, and the broad base of the *śikhara*, or tower, give to Indian temple architecture a feeling of strength and solidity, only in part counteracted by the delicately ornate friezes, and the many figures in high or low relief which often fill the whole surface of the temple wall.

Considering the size of the land, Indian temple architecture is remarkably uniform, but authorities distinguish two chief styles and numerous schools. The Northern or Indo-Āryan style prefers a tower with rounded top and curvilinear outline, while the tower of the Southern or Dravidian style is usually in the shape of a rectangular truncated pyramid. The stages of stylistic development are clearer in the South than in the North, where many ancient temples were destroyed by the Muslim invaders. We therefore consider the styles of the Peninsula first.

Temple building gained much from the patronage of the Pallava and Cālukya kings in the 6th–8th centuries. Important early temples of the former dynasty are to be found at Māmallapuram, already referred to (p. 313), and Kāñcī, while the Cālukyas left temple remains at their capital Bādāmi and at the nearby site of Aihoḷe, both in Mysore. These styles show the gradual emancipation of the architect from the techniques of carpentry and cave architecture. The apogee of the Pallava style was reached in the Shore Temple at Māmallapuram (pl. XVI*a*) and the Kailāsanātha Temple of Kāñcī, built early in the 8th century. The latter has a pyramidal tower formed of two courses of small barrel vaults, surmounted by a solid cupola suggesting a Buddhist stūpa.

The style of the Pallavas was developed further under the Cōla dynasty (10–12th centuries); their finest products are the temple of Śiva at Tānjuvūr (Tanjore), built by Rājarāja the Great (985–1014), and the temple built by his successor, Rājendra I, at his new capital of Gaṅgaikoṇḍacōlapuram, near Kumbakonam. The former was probably the largest temple built in India up to that time; the comparatively modest tower of the Pallava style was replaced by a great pyramid, rising from a tall upright base and crowned with a domed finial, the whole being nearly 200 feet high. This set the style of the Dravidian śikhara, which has continued with some variation down to the present day. Both these temples contain elaborate pillared halls and beautiful decoration.

In the next phase of Dravidian architecture the emphasis shifted from the tower above the chief shrine to the entrance gateway of the surrounding wall. Though there are a few records of desecration by hostile sectarians or invaders, it is difficult to find a practical reason for the growing custom of protecting South Indian temples with strong and high walls, unless this was done in imitation of the palaces of kings, with which the temples had much in common. From the 12th century onwards it became usual to fortify the temple, often with three square concentric walls, with gates on the four sides. The gates were surmounted by watch-towers or gatehouses, and these developed into soaring towers (*gopuram*), generally much taller than the modest śikhara over the central shrine. The entrance tower was usually in the form of an oblong pyramid, with its broadest side parallel to the wall (pl. XIX*a*). The new style is often called Pāṇḍyan, from the name of the dynasty which supplanted the Cōlas in the Tamil country, the kings of which were responsible for building walls and gateway towers round many existing shrines. This style introduced more elaborate ornamentation, and the use of animal forms in pilasters and columns, including the rampant horses and leogryphs which give a distinctive character to late Dravidian architecture.

The culmination of the Pāṇḍyan style is to be seen in the mighty temple complexes of Madurai, Śrīraṅgam, and elsewhere, which are strictly outside our period, belonging in their present form to the 17th century. The great temple of Madurai is the most famous and beautiful of these (pl. XIX*b*), but the largest is the Vaiṣṇavite temple of Śrīraṅgam (fig. xv, p. 203), which is contained in an outer wall measuring 2,475 by 2,880 feet (758 x 878 m.), and has six inner walls, all with gopurams, surrounding a shrine of comparatively modest proportions. These later towers were covered with sculptured figures.

While these developments were taking place in the Tamil country, other styles developed in the Deccan, under the Cālukyas, Rāṣṭrakūṭas and Hoysaḷas. The earliest Cālukyan temples closely resemble the Guptan. By the 8th century they had developed individual features, including the wide overhanging eaves which became characteristic of the medieval temples of the Central Deccan. The later Cālukyas and Hoysalas (11th–14th centuries) developed a more elaborate style. Their temples were no longer constructed on a rectangular plan, but were polygonal or stellate, raised on tall solid platforms of the same shape as the buildings. These temples give a strong feeling of flatness, for platforms and walls alike are covered with rather narrow carved friezes of elephants, horsemen, geese, monster (*yāḷi*), and scenes of mythology and legend (pl. XVII). The grotesque mask (*kīrtimukha*)* became very common as a decorative feature, and turned columns, often ornately carved, were widely used. The largest and most famous temples of this style, at Halebīd (Dōrasamudra, the Hoysaḷa capital) and Bēlūr, have no towers, and it is thought that they were not completed. Some smaller buildings of the same period have towers, notably the charming temple of Somnāthpur (pl. XVI*b*), which has three low dome-like śikharas, their breadth emphasized by parallel mouldings. Its profusion of pillars and its abhorrence not only of blank spaces but even of plane surfaces and straight lines tend to give this style an impression of wedding-cake prettiness, despite the solid proportions of its masonry and the brilliance of its sculptured decoration.

The school which flourished under the Vijayanagara empire and reached its apogee in the 16th century shows both Pāṇḍyan and Hoysaḷa features. The florid carving of the Hoysalas was developed with even greater exuberance, and new elements appeared in the temple complex. As well as the main shrine, in every important temple in South India the *amman*, the god's chief wife, was provided with a shrine which was often nearly as large as the main shrine itself, and a marriage-hall (*kalyāṇamaṇḍapam*), wherein the icons of god and goddess were ceremonially united on festival days. Another feature of the Vijayanagara style is the profusion of strong yet delicate carving which adorns the pillared halls, the many columns of which are so decorated that they become sculptures in their own right. Prancing horses, vigorous and energetic, leap from the stone (pl. XVIII*c*), with leogryphs and other fantastic monsters. For brilliancy of decorative imagination the Vijayanagara style of architecture was never surpassed in Hindu India. Its finest production is undoubtedly the Viṭṭhala Temple at Hampī, the old Vijayanagara.

In the chief cities of Northern India almost all traces of the architecture of the Hindu period have vanished. Even in holy Vārāṇasī all the great and famous temples are comparatively recent. One important exception, however, is the Buddhist temple at Gayā (pl. XX*a*) the main tower of which is probably as early as the 6th century. This is a large pyramid of brickwork, set on a high plinth; it is adorned with parallel courses of "caitya window" pattern and is surmounted by a lofty pinnacle which was originally a small stūpa. Similar towers existed in other Buddhist monastic establishments, but have long since vanished. The Gayā

* The *kīrtimukha* is found in other South Indian schools as a decorative motif, especially in the *makara-toraṇa,* a gateway with above the lintel a large kīrtimukha mask connected by foliate designs to two *makaras* or sea-monsters at the base of the doorposts. These motifs were exported to South-East Asia and became regular features of Indonesian and Cambodian architecture.

tower suggests rather the Southern than the Northern style, but other temples of the period either have no towers or have small curvilinear ones which are evidently the prototypes of the later Northern śikhara.

Medieval North Indian architecture is best illustrated by three schools—those of Orissā, Bundelkhand, and Gujarāt and South Rājasthān. There were other local developments, as well as the distinctive style of Kashmīir which we have already noted, but these three are certainly the most important, and their products are the best preserved.

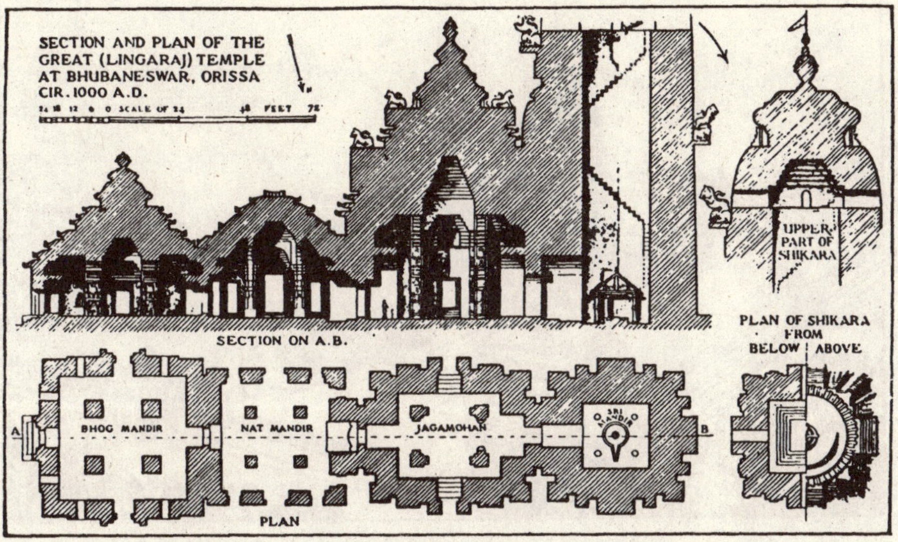

Fig. xxi.—Liṅgarāja Temple, Bhubanesar, Orissā. (Reproduced from Percy Brown's "Indian Architecture (Buddhist and Hindu)", published by D. B. Taraporevala Sons & Co. Ltd., Bombay)

The Orissan school flourished from the 8th to the 13th centuries, and its chief monuments lie in and around the towns of Bhubanesar and Purī. The finest Orissan temple is the Liṅgarāja at Bhubanesar (pl. XX*b*, fig. xxi), which shows the North Indian śikhara in its final form—a tower which begins to curve inwards at about one third of its height, with rounded top crowned by a flat stone disc (*āmalaka*) and a finial (*kalaśa*). The upward sweep of this graceful curving tower is emphasized by deep vertical inlets, but its solidity and firm basis on earth are very evident. The Liṅgarāja, like most Orissan temples, is built as a series of four halls—a hall of offerings, a dancing hall, an assembly hall and a sanctuary.* The sanctuary is crowned by the great tower, but the other three elements of the temple, leading one by one to the shrine, are also roofed with characteristic towers of smaller size, carrying the eye to the main śikhara. The

* Often referred to by the modern Hindi names, *bhog maṇḍir, nāṭ maṇḍir, jagmohan,* and *deul* respectively.

whole temple enclosure of the Liṅgarāja is filled with smaller shrines, built on the pattern of the great one.

The Orissan architects were lavish with their exterior decoration, and their sculptors produced works of great merit, but the interiors of their temples are unadorned. In the larger temples the corbelled roofs of the halls rested on four large pilasters, but pillars were not generally used, and roofs were often partly supported by iron girders, a striking technical innovation.[6]

Fig. xxii.—Temple of the Sun, Konārak, Orissā. (Reproduced from Percy Brown's "Indian Architecture (Buddhist and Hindu)", published by D. B. Taraporevala Sons & Co. Ltd., Bombay)

Among the most important Orissan temples are the Temple of Viṣṇu-Jagannātha at Purī, still one of the most famous shrines of India, and the "Black Pagoda" of Konārak, built in the 13th century. The latter, a temple of Sūrya, the sun-god, was formerly one of the largest and most splendid temples of India, much larger than those of Bhubanesar (fig. xxii). The tower, over 200 feet high, has long since fallen, but the great assembly-hall remains. Unlike the other temples of this region that of Konārak had the two smaller outer halls completely separate from the main structure, and the assembly-hall and tower were built on an imposing platform, round which were carved twelve decorated wheels, 10 feet in diameter (pl. XXI*a*). The entrance is reached by a broad flight of steps, flanked on either side by prancing horses, the whole representing the chariot in which the Sun-god rides across the heavens. The court of the temple was decorated with free-standing sculptures of great strength and beauty (pls. LVII–III). The exceptionally frank eroticism of many of the Konārak sculptures has given the "Black Pagoda" a rather infamous reputation. *Maithuna* figures, of couples closely embracing or actually *in coitu*, are common enough as decorative features of many Indian temples, but those of Konārak are exceptionally vivid. Many suggestions have been made as to the true significance of these figures; it has been suggested that they merely served the mundane purpose of advertising the charms of the devadāsis, or temple prostitutes,[7] or that they were intended to represent the world of the flesh, in contrast to the bare and austere interior, which symbolized the things of the spirit; possibly they were connected, in the minds of their designers, with the sexual mysticism which played so great a part in medieval Indian religious thought,[8] or it may be that they represent the delights of heaven, on its lower planes. Possibly the temple of Konārak was a centre of a tantric cult though the erotic sculpture does not suggest the solemn ritual of the Śāktas, but something much less inhibited.[9]

Under the Candella kings of Bundelkhand a great school of architecture flourished in the 10th and 11th centuries, the chief work of which is a beautiful group of temples at Khajurāho, about 100 miles south-east of Jhānsī. These temples are built on a rather different plan from those of Orissā, and are not very large; the finest, a Śaivite temple known as Kandāriya-Mahādeo, was built about A.D. 1000, and is not more than 100 feet high. The standard type of Khajurāho temple contains a shrine-room or sanctuary, an assembly-hall, and an entrance portico. Whereas in the Orissan temple these elements were conceived rather as separate entities joined together by vestibules, the Khajurāho architects treated them as a whole, and though each part has its own roof they are not structurally separate. The Khajurāho śikhara, like those of most Northern temples, is curvilinear (pl. XX*c*), but differs from the type of Orissā. It is curved for its whole length, and its upward thrust is accentuated by miniature śikharas emerging from the central tower. The crowning discs of these projections break the upward movement, and remind the observer that the divine is to be found on earth as well as in heaven. The effect of the whole, despite its symmetry, is one of organic and natural growth. The tower, and indeed the whole temple, seems intimately at one with the earth, suggesting an enormous ant-hill, or a high peak surrounded by lesser mountains. Though expressed in the most baroque of styles, the Kandāriya-Mahādeo is a striking instance of a feature common in much Indian art, a feeling of unity with nature.

The halls and porticoes of the Khajurāho temples are also crowned with smaller towers, which rise progressively to lead the eye up to the main tower, and thus intensify the impression of a mountain range. While the Orissan roof is pyramidal in pattern, the Khajurāho builders employed corbelling to produce the effect of a flattish dome. The mass of the buildings is broken by pillared window openings, which relieve the monotony of the ornately carved stone. A further distinctive feature of the style was the introduction of small transepts to the assembly hall, giving the whole a ground-plan not unlike that of a Gothic cathedral.

Like all other schools of architecture, that of Khajurāho made much use of carving. Here, in contrast to Orissā, the temples were adorned with sculpture both outside and in, and the halls have beautifully carved domed ceilings. The style of Khajurāho sculpture lacks the solidity and vigour of the best of Orissā, but the wonderful friezes of statuary contain figures of a graceful vitality, warmer and more immediately attractive than those of the Orissan temples (pls. XLVI–VIII).

In Rājasthān and Gujarāt are many medieval temples, some of much architectural merit. Here we can only mention the greatest of these Western schools, that which rose under the patronage of the Caulukya or Solāṅki kings of Gujarāt, and flourished from the 11th to the 13th centuries. This kingdom was wealthy from the sea-borne trade with the Arabs and Persians, and much of the treasure of kings, ministers and merchants alike was expended on beautiful Jaina and Hindu temples.

The most famous buildings of this school are the lovely Jaina shrines of Mount Ābū, the style of which is fundamentally not very different from that of Khajurāho. The temples were built on high platforms and usually consisted of a shrine and hall only, without an entrance portico. The śikhara over the shrine, like those of Khajurāho, was adorned with a large number of miniature towers, and the ceilings were in the form of corbelled domes. Perhaps through the influence of Muslim architectural styles, these ceilings were carved so as to give the impression of a true dome, the steps of the corbelling being skilfully concealed by the sculptor, and the flat crossbeams, supported on pillars, often being adorned with large brackets meeting at the centre, which gave an arch-like effect, though the true arch was never employed. The most outstanding feature of this style is its minute and lovely decorativeness (pls. XXI*c*, XXII). The shrines of Mount Ābū, made of cool white marble, are covered with the most delicate and ornate carving, especially in the interiore: it is, however, rather flaccid and repetitive. In comparison with Bhubanesar, Konārak and Khajurāho the rich decoration of Mount Ābū has a flavour of cold lifelessness.

Remains of pre-Muslim secular buildings are few. In the Middle Ages kings and chiefs certainly built stone palaces, but of these only the base of the Vijayanagara throne-room, and some remains in Ceylon, have survived. Several cities of Rājasthān and Gujarāt have finely carved gateways from the medieval period (pl. XXI*b*). But, though secular architecture was no doubt highly developed, it is clear that India's architects and masons devoted their greatest energies to temple building. Working according to strict traditions, but showing much ingenuity and originality within the main standardized pattern, they erected monuments of fantastic beauty with the simplest technical equipment. Many patient hands reared the śikharas above the plain, and, capped them with great slabs of stone, raised on enormous ramps of earth, like the higher courses of the pyramids of Egypt. Whether or not the architects and craftsmen were conscious of the symbolism, the temple was looked on by some as a microcosm of the world, as the open air sacrifice had been in earlier days. In sculpture, and often in painting also, all the gods were depicted on its walls, every aspect of divine and human existence symbolized. Like Hindu civilization itself, the temple was at once voluptuous and austere, rooted in earth, but aspiring to heaven.

SCULPTURE

In architecture there is no real trace of relationship between the brick houses of Harappā and the stone temples of Hindu India. The earliest sculpture of historical times, on the other hand, shows a generic likeness to that of Harappā, which we have already described (p. 17f). From the end of the Indus cities to the rise of the Mauryas over a millennium elapsed, with no surviving work of art to fill it. Somewhere in North India the art of sculpture, no doubt in perishable materials, was certainly kept alive. The patronage of the Mauryan emperors, the influx of western influence, and growing material prosperity led to its revival, and to the making of stone figures and reliefs which are preserved to this day.

The capitals of Aśoka's columns, some of which were perhaps made before his reign, are the earliest important sculptures after those of the Indus cities. They are not characteristic of Indian sculpture, though they contain many native features. The famous lions of the Sārnāth column and the less famous but more beautiful bull of the column of Rāmpūrvā (pl. XXIII*b*) are the work of realistic sculptore, owing something to Iranian and Hellenist tradition. Yet, if we did not know that the possibility of Western influence existed, we might suggest that the animal sculptures of the columns were those of a school directly descended from the engravers of the Indus seals, which also show a realistic treatment very unusual for so early a civilization. The abaci of the capitals perhaps show native influence more clearly than the crowning figures, and bear animals in lively postures, wheels, representing both the Buddha and the Mauryan World-emperor, and fioral and foliate designs in which typical Indian motifs appear side by side with some borrowed from the West. Other than the pillars there are few remains of the Mauryan school, with its high polish and fine finish. One beautiful figure, the "Dīdārganj Yakṣī" (pl. XXVI*a*), bears the distinctive brilliant polish of the school, but the treatment suggests that it is post-Mauryan. The yakṣī bears a *caurī*, or ceremonial yak's tail fly-whisk with which kings and gods were fanned; this shows that she was made as the attendant on another figure or a sacred object, which has now vanished.

A number of images of yaksas, somewhat larger than life-size, are the only other important free sculptures of the centuries immediately before Christ. They are strong, bull-necked and heavy, and, though not technically perfect, have an elemental solidity rarely found in later sculpture. The treatment of the ample abdomens of these figures has been compared with that of the abdomen of the Harappā torso and gives further evidence of the survival of tradition over the long intervening period.

The most important sculptural remains of the post-Mauryan period are the carvings on the rails and gateways of the great Buddhist sites at Bhārhut, Gayā and Sānchī. There is no absolute certainty about the dating of these remains, but the sculpture of Bhārhut is in a less highly developed style than that of Gayā and Sānchī and is probably the earliest, while the gateways of Sānchī, carved with great sureness and skill, are probably the latest of the three. The series Bhārhut-Gayā-Sānchī is to some extent confirmed by epigraphic evidence, and we may date Bhārhut c. 150 B.C. and Sānchī about the end of the lst century B.C., with Gayā somewhere between the two. The criteria are not, however, absolutely certain, and it is possible that the backward and advanced schools were approximately contemporary.

At Bhārhut (pls. XXIII-V) the upright posts of the stūpa railings are carved with yakṣas and yakṣīs, beautifully finished and very decorative, like all the best Indian sculpture, but archaic and uncertain in treatment. Their flatness suggests that the artists were trained in the working of ivory, and were laboriously learning to translate their skill into a different medium. The medallions of the crosspieces (pl. XXIII*c-e*), mostly depicting scenes from Jātaka stories, have a similar archaic flavour.

The Gayā railing, enclosing not a stūpa but the sacred path where the Buddha was believed to have walked in meditation after he had obtained enlightenment, shows an advance on Bhārhut. The figures are deeper, more vital, and more rounded, and the sculptors had by this time evidently gained greater mastery of their technique. Figures are no longer always carved flat on the stone, but begin to appear in three-quarter poses. Notable at Gayā are the medallions containing human heads, which have such realism that they may well be portraits.

The crowning achievement of early North Indian sculpture is undoubtedly Sānchī. Here a smaller stūpa (Stūpa II) is adorned with carvings of very archaic character, according to some authorities older than those of Bhārhut. The railings of the main stūpa are quite unadorned, but, in sharp contrast, the great gateways are carved with a multitude of figures and reliefs. From top to bottom and on all sides the massive square uprights and triple architraves are alive with the life of the times. Yakṣīs smile as they lean in easy graceful poses,* or serve as brackets to the architraves (pl. XXVII*b*), which are supported by massive elephants or cheerfully grinning dwarfs. The flat surfaces of the uprights and architraves are covered with panels depicting scenes from the life of the Buddha or from Jātaka stories (pl. XXVIII). Cities are besieged, riders on elephants and horses pass in procession, men and women worship sacred shrines, elephants roam the jungle; lions, peacocks, yakṣīs, nāgas, mythical animals and ornate floral designs fill the whole. Some of the motifs are evidently of Mesopotamian or Persian inspiration, but the overall impression is typically Indian in its complexity of pattern, its cheerful busy realism, and its exuberance.

The carvings of the Sānchī gateways were not carried out according to any preconceived scheme. The sculptors were not commissioned by the monastery, but by private patrons, who wished to gain merit by beautifying the stūpa, and they carved what their patrons told them in the way they thought best. Superficially the result is lacking in formal unity, but is endowed with a unity transcending

---

* The *tribhaṅga,* a pose in dancing and dramatics with one leg bent and the body slightly turned at the hips, was a favourite with the sculptor from the earliest times. It contrasts sharply with the rather rigid poses of most ancient art other than that of the Greeks, and gives an impression of life and vitality.

rule and pattern, the unity of a prosperous culture, pious in devotion to its shrines, and delighting in the world it lived in and knew. The visitor, standing on the hill of Sānchī on a sunny winter day, when the wild peacocks walk among the ruins and the great plain shimmers in the hazy distance, gets the overriding impression that this is the work of a contented people at one with itself.

Technically the carvings are of high excellence. The sculptors have now fully mastered their material. Their treatment, while not, of course, realistic in the nineteenth-century sense, has transcended the rather stiff formalism of Bhārhut, and is free and alive. The sculpture of Sānchī everywhere gives a sense of certainty; the artists knew what they had to depict, and clearly saw in their mind's eye how to do so.

At Bhārhut, Gayā and Sānchī, and indeed in all the Buddhist sculpture of this period, the Buddha himself is never shown, but symbolized by such emblems as a wheel, an empty throne, a pair of footprints or a pīpal tree (pl. XXVIII). The obvious reason for this iconographical peculiarity is that he was so venerated that it seemed sacrilegious to portray him, but we have no literary or other evidence to confirm this. The aversion to depicting the Buddha may have been due to the fact that, since he had passed quite out of the universe, it was thought misleading to show him in human form. In any case the familiar Buddha image of later times is not to be found at these three early Buddhist sites. The schools of Gandhāra (the lower Kābul Valley and the upper Indus, around Peshāwar) and Mathurā, both of which flourished under the Kuṣāṇa kings, vie for the honour of having produced the first images of the Buddha. Most Indian authorities now believe that the Buddha image originated at Mathurā; most earlier Europeans supported Gandhāra, but some recent experts are less certain.

The school of Mathurā probably began at the end of the 1st century B.C., though some authorities would date it later. Working for centuries in the white-spotted red sandstone of the locality, it produced works which were carried far and wide, and had much influence on later sculpture. Some of the school's inspiration was Jaina, and at an early period the Mathurā craftsmen were making votive plaques depicting the cross-legged naked figure of a Tirthankara in meditation, which may have inspired the Buddhists to depict their own teacher. Perhaps the most striking remains of the Mathurā school are the yakṣīs from the railings of a stūpa, which was probably Jaina. (pl. XXIX*a*). These richly jewelled ladies, their figures exaggeratedly broad of hip and slender of waist, stand in pert attitudes reminiscent of the Indus dancing-girl (pl. VIII*b*), and their gay and frank sensuality in a context of piety and renunciation gives another example of the remarkable antinomy of the ancient Indian outlook on life, which found nothing incongruous in such a juxtaposition.

Rather outside the main range of Mathurā art are the Kuṣāṇa royal statues, most of which were found at the nearby village of Māt, where the kings no doubt had a winter residence, with a chapel in which the memory of former monarchs and princes was revered. The figures have nearly all been broken by succeeding rulers, and that of the great Kaniṣka, the most striking of the statues, unfortunately lacks its head (pl. XXX*a*). Wearing the dress of Central Asia, a long coat and quilted boots, and grasping in one hand a sword and in the other its sheath, the king stands with legs apart, in an attitude of authority. This statue may be criticized technically as showing no sense of depth, being virtually in two dimensions. The sculptor was evidently working on a theme to which he was not used, but he succeeded in producing a work of much power, suggesting the hieratic royal statues of Egypt.

The early Buddhas and Bodhisattvas of the Mathurā school are happy fleshy figures with little spirituality about them, but later they developed in grace and religious feeling (pl. XXXVI*b*). Though the Mathurā school owed much to earlier Indian tradition, it also borrowed from the North-West, and adopted more than one Greco-Roman motif. Through Mathurā the style generally known as Gupta developed, and produced some of the greatest Indian religious sculpture.

The school of Gandhāra was evidently influenced by the art of the Roman Empire, and some of its craftsmen may have been Westerners. Though often called Greco-Buddhist, the Greek kingdoms of Bactria and N.-W. India had vanished when this school emerged. It is not to the Greco-Bactrian heirs of Alexander, but to the trade with the West, encouraged by the rising prosperity of Rome and the eastward march of her legions, that we must attribute this syncretistic school. The Greeks left only a few lovely silver articles, beautiful coins, and one or two other objects, perhaps imported from the West. It was Kaniṣka and his successors and their wealthy subjects who gave to the school of Gandhāra the encouragement and support through which it flourished. The new devotional Buddhism demanded images for worship, and figures of the Buddha and Bodhisattvas were produced in large numbers, as well as small votive plaques depicting scenes from the Buddha's life or Jātaka stories (pl. XXXIII).

The Mathurā sculptors drew inspiration for their Buddha images from the burly yakṣa figures of the earlier centuries on the one hand and from the meditating Jaina Tirthaṅkaras on the other. The Gandhāra sculptors had other models in the gods of the Greco-Roman World. Often their inspiration seems almost wholly Western (pl. XXXI), and it is hard not to believe that some of the Gandhāra masters were foreigners from Syria or Alexandria. The school has depreciated in recent years. When all art was judged by classical norms it was thought to be the finest school of Indian art, which once and once only produced work of grace and realism. Now the sculpture of Gandhāra is sometimes described as a mere imitation of an imitation, the weak copy of a great art in decline. Neither judgement is fair. In an Indian context the style of Gandhāra has a rather insipid flavour, but it is not without originality. The Buddhas of Gandhāra, though perhaps lacking in the spirituality of those of the Gupta period, are gentle, graceful and compassionate, while some of the plaques are vivid and energetic. The school continued after the great Kuṣāṇas, though with less prosperous times it produced few works in stone, but many in plaster or stucco. Its influence was felt far beyond the bounds of India, and can be traced even in China.

While these schools were developing in the North others appeared in the Peninsula. Here, in the Bhājā cave (p. 310f) and at Udayagiri in Orissā, very ancient sculpture is to be found, possibly no later than that of Bhārhut. The great Buddhist cave temples of the Western Deccan contain much sculpture of great merit, perhaps the finest of which are the numerous figures of donors, often carved in high relief on the cave walls. These are frequently in couples, their arms on one another's shoulders, and seem to be idealized portraits of the wealthy patrons of the Buddhist caves (pl. XXXIV). Such couples are also to be found in early terracottas (pl. LXII*b*), and no doubt their originals believed that by placing their effigies in shrines they would obtain both material and spiritual benefits. It may be that these are the forerunners of the *maithuna* couples of the medieval temples (p. 319), but the spirit behind the early *dampatī* pairs seems very different, for these figures have no overt sexual significance. The man usually looks not at his wife but outwards into the hall, while the woman glances downwards, and, quite unlike the bold yaksis of the North, holds her body diffidently, almost timidly, as if rather embarrassed at being stared at in public. We believe that these figures represent the ideals of ancient Indian married life, and are no more esoteric than the family memorial brasses in many English churches.

The region between the lower valleys of the Kistnā and Godāvarī became an important centre of Buddhism at least as early as the 2nd century B.C., and some very ancient sculpture in low relief, intended to adorn the sides of stūpas, is to be found there. This already shows the characteristic elongation of the mature style of Amarāvatī. In the late Sātavāhana period (2nd–3rd century A.D.) the great stūpa of Amarāvatī was adorned with limestone reliefs depicting scenes of the Buddha's life and surrounded with free-standing Buddha figures. The relief medallions are certainly among the greatest works of Indian art (pl. XXXV). Beautifully balanced in composition to fit the circular frames, they convey an intense vitality and sense of rapid movement, quite unexpected in the context of the grave and calm religion they illustrate. The slender, long-legged figures are portrayed in vigorous action, often rising almost to frenzy, as in the famous medallion showing a host of ecstatic demigods carrying the Buddha's begging-bowl to heaven. The Amarāvatī school had great influence. Its products were carried to Ceylon and South-East Asia and had a marked effect on local styles, while its influence on later South Indian sculpture is also very evident.

Meanwhile in the North the Śaka and Kuṣāṇa invaders had in part retreated and in part merged with the indigenous population, to make way for the great Gupta empire. From the point of view of art the Gupta Period is generally taken to include at least the 4th-6th centuries and the first half of the 7th. The plastic remains of this age are comparatively few, but enough survive to show the achievement of the time. If the schools of Bhārhut, Sānchī and Mathurā are marked by a sensual earthiness, and that of Amarāvatī by vital, excited movement, the Guptan sculpture suggests serenity, security and certainty. It was at this time that India produced some of her most truly religious art, especially in the lovely Buddhas of Sārnāth. Most famous of these is the icon of the Buddha "turning the Wheel of the Law", or preaching his first sermon (pl. XXXVI*a*), which, more than any other Indian sculpture, seems to convey the true message of Buddhism. Surrounded by a large and ornate halo, flanked by two small demigods, the Master sits majestically, his body slender and rounded, plastically so simplified that no trace of muscular contour can be seen, his delicate fingers forming the *dharmacakra mudrā*, which indicates that he is preaching. His face is, as usual, that of a young man, with full, smoothly modelled lips; his half-closed eyes and slight smile tell more graphically and vividly than any of the rather dry Buddhist scriptures his fundamental message, and emphasize not its first part, that the world is full of sorrow, death and decay, but that it is possible to transcend these evīls, and reach a state where age and grief no longer affect the mind, and where earthly pleasure is transmuted into serene inner joy.

This great masterpiece, however, illustrates only one aspect of Gupta art. In the region of Gwālior and Jhānsi an excellent school of Hindu sculptors existed, and the carvings of the temple of Deogarh, depicting Hindu gods and mythological scenes, show the beginnings of the early medieval style. The splendid figure of the sun-god Sūrya from Gwālior (pl. XXXVII*a*) illustrates another aspect of the outlook of the times. Broad and sturdy, cheerfully smiling, the god looks straight ahead at his worshippers, his right hand raised in blessing—the god of a good-natured, happy people. Equally significant of the spirit of the Gupta Period, if less perfect in execution, is the charming relief of a dancer accompanied by girl-musicians, found at Pāwayā, near Gwālior (pl. XXXVII*b*). Probably of the 9th century, but continuing the Guptan tradition, is the "Sanchi Torso",* the delicately but vigorously modelled body of a Bodhisattva, its smooth contours emphasized by the minutely carved jewelled collar and belt and the scarf of antelope skin hanging over the left shoulder (pl. XXXVIII).

Perhaps the most immediately impressive of all Guptan sculpture is the Great Boar, carved in relief near the entrance of a cave at Udayagiri, near Bhīlsā (pl. XXXVII*c*). The body of the god Viṣṇu, who became a mighty boar to rescue the earth from the cosmic ocean (p. 266), conveys the impression of a great primeval power working for good against the forces of chaos and destruction, and beare a message of hope, strength and assurance. The greatness of the god in comparison with his creation is brought out by the tiny female figure of the personified earth, clinging to his tusk. The deep feeling which inspired the carving of this figure makes it perhaps the only theriomorphic image in the world's art which conveys a truly religious message to modern man.

Sculptures of the medieval period are so numerous that they cannot be discussed here in detail. By this time iconographical canons were fixed. Every god had his special attributes, which were regularly portrayed in his image; the proportions of body, limbs and features were laid down, and were adhered to with increasing rigidity; but the Indian sculptor succeeded in producing remarkable variety in his now almost hieratic art.

Under the Pāla and Sena kings of Bihār and Bengal (8th–12th centuries) both Buddhists and Hindus made fine icons, many in the local black basalt. The special

---

* Said by some to be an exceptional Pāla production.[10]

characteristic of Pāla art is its fine finish; its figures are much decorated and well polished, and often seem rather made of metal than of stone (pl. XLV).

The sculpture of Orissā was greater than that of the Pālas. The carvings of the temples of Bhubanesar and Konārak (pls. LIV–VIII) show a deep sensuous appreciation of the human form and an expressiveness which gives them a characteristic beauty of their own. The finest Orissan sculptures are those in the courtyard of the Temple of the Sun at Konārak, where the forceful horses (pl. LVIII) and the mighty elephant crushing a malefactor in his trunk (pl. LVII) show a strength of treatment and a feeling for animal form rare in the world's art, and reminiscent of the animal sculpture and ceramics of the T'ang dynasty of China.

The Khajurāho temples are covered with figures of divinities and pairs of lovers of wonderful delicacy and grace (pls. XLVI-VIII), and in many other parts of North India works of beauty survive, although few can vie with those of Orissā.

In the Deccan individual schools of sculpture appeared. The temples of Aihoḷe and Badami contain fine work of the 6th century onwards (pl. XL), which shows the influence of the Guptan style, with a tendency to elongation perhaps inherited from Amarāvatī. More important are the sculptures of Māmallapuram, adorning the wonderful complex of rock-temples made by the Pallava kings of Kāñcī. Most striking of these is the relief of the descent of the Ganga (pl. XLI), covering a rock face over 80 feet long and nearly 30 feet high (24.4 x 9.1 m.). A natural cleft in the rock has been utilized to represent the Sacred River, who is watched on either side by gods, demigods, ascetics and elephants as she descends from the head of Śiva, and who has sinuous snake-spirits (*nāgas*) swimming in her waters. The artists who designed this splendid relief had a sardonic sense of humour, for among the worshipping ascetics they carved the crafty cat, who performed penance in order to lure the mice to their doom. Māmallapuram contains other fine relief sculpture, including an idealized portrait of the versatile king Mahendravikramavarman and his queens (pl. XLII), and a number of free-standing animal figures, which are remarkable for their simple strength.

The influence of the Pallava school of sculpture was felt in Ceylon (pl. XLIII*a*), and also in the Western Deccan. Here the Buddhist carvings of the Ajantā caves, though important, are dwarfed in significance by the wonderful mural paintings. The carvings of the later Ellorā caves, on the other hand, especially those of the Kailāsanātha Temple (p. 312), are among the finest sculptures of India. They are chiefly in the form of deep reliefs giving the effect of free-standing sculpture, and illustrate scenes of mythology (pl. XLIII*b*). The whole series of carvings is characterized by balanced design and a graceful energy akin to that of Amarāvatī. Of the same school, but about a century later, are the cave sculptures of Elephanta. The rock temple of Śiva contains a fine series of deep reliefs, all of which are dwarfed in significance by the colossal *Trimūrti*, which is perhaps the best known of all Ancient Indian sculptures (pl. XLIII*c*). The three-headed bust of Śiva, calm with the calmness of eternity, is so impressive and so religiously inspired that it needs little comment. The serene god is perhaps the highest plastic expression of the Hindu concept of divinity.

After Māmallapuram, Ellorā and Elephanta much stone sculpture was produced in the Peninsula, but though often of great merit it lacked the depth and beauty of the work of the earlier schools. The splendid bronzes of the Cōlas and their successore are the most outstanding products of the Dravidian artists of the later Middle Ages.

TERRACOTTAS

While the rich delighted in figures of stone, metal or ivory, poorer people contented themselves with small images and plaques of baked clay, no doubt originally painted in bright colours. They were evidently mass-produced, and most of the finer specimens were made in moulds.

Nearly every archaeological site, from Harappā onwards, has produced many of these terracotta objects. Most are religious. Crude day figures of goddesses—apparently early forms of Durgā, worshipped by the lower classes before her inclusion in the orthodox pantheon—are common, and recall the similar but even cruder mother-goddess figurines of Harappā (fig. ii, p. 13). Other objects have little if any religious significance, though they may have been charms or votive offerings; figures of mother and child, a type rare in sculpture, suggest offerings made by childless women, while the numerous figures of a man and a woman (pl. LXII*b*), standing in modest poses reminiscent of the donors of the cave temple sculpture, may have been charms for a happy marriage. While many terracottas are crude, others are of fine workmanship and real beauty. Some faces are well characterized and divine heads are sometimes beautifully modelled (pl. LXII*d–e*). The terracotta plaques often have much charm.

Most of the terracottas so far found date from the Mauryan to the Gupta period, but the art of modelling in terracotta must have existed earlier, and certainly continued later, for the Buddhist sites of Bihār have yielded many medieval votive plaques of no great artistic interest.

METAL SCULPTURE AND ENGRAVING

Several works of art in metal, very Hellenistic in style, have been found in the North-West, dating from the early centuries of the Christian era. Some of these are quite un-Indian, and may have been imported, or produced by foreign craftsmen, for instance the lovely little golden and jewelled reliquary casket from Bimārān (pl. LXXXV*a*). Further afield, in Soviet Central Asia and Northern Afghānistān, have been found beautiful silver cups and other objects, omamented with motifs usually Hellenistic in inspiration and technique, but showing clear evidence of Indian contacts (pls. LXXXV–VI). Soviet archaeologists believe that these are the products of the Greek kingdom of Bactria, and date from the 3rd and 2nd centuries B.C. Thus they are in no way connected with the Gandhāra sculpture of the early centuries of the Christian era. Wholly Indian in style, and dating from pre-Gupta times, is the copper vase from Kulū, on the borders of Kashmīr, engraved with a gay procession (fig. xxiii).

Fig. xxiii.—Copper Vase from Kulū, *c.* 1st–2nd century, A.D. (By permission, Victoria and Albert Museum)

From the Gupta period a number of bronze and copper figures have survived, mostly Buddhist. The most impressive of these is the "Sultānganj Buddha" (pl. LXIII), some 7½\ feet high, now in Birmingham Museum—a graceful figure, dressed in a diaphanous cloak. Like most of the work of the period it conveys a feeling of aliveness, not by attention to realistic detail and proportion, but by the sense of movement in the slightly tilted body, the delicate fingers, lightly clasping the corners of the robe, and the face, impassively symmetrical yet with a vitality imparted by the delicate moulding of its features.* The Sultānganj Buddha was found in Bihār, the most important centre of Buddhism, where one of the two great medieval schools of metal sculpture arose, under the patronage of the Pāla kings. Pāla bronzes are so numerous that there is no doubt that they were mass-produced. They were exported to South-East Asia, where they are still found, and to Nepāl and Tibet, where they provided prototypes for indigenous schools. These images are characterized chiefly by delicacy of design and ornamental detail, and deep religious inspiration is usually lacking (pl. LXIV). The earliest Nepāl bronzes, which go back to our period, are less ornate in design, but are gilded and set with semi-precious stones, and give an impression of great brilliance and smoothness.

Other parts of India also produced metal icons, but many of those which have survived have no great artistic value. The Tamils still prefer metal to

* Very recently doubts have been cast on the date generally attributed to the Sultānganj Buddha. It may be a work of the 9th century.

stone for the images used in temple and domestic worship, and it was in South India, especially in the kingdom of the Cōlas, that the greatest Indian works of art in metal were made, by a school of bronze-casters which has not been excelled in the world. South Indian bronzes vary in size, but many of the finest specimens are very large and heavy, their pedestals fitted with lugs for carrying in processions. The best specimens of South Indian metal work are of great grace and simplicity, for though the statues have much ornamentation this, as in most of the best Indian sculpture, is relieved by areas of bare smooth flesh. Physical features and the contours of face and limb are simplified and idealized, the proportions are rigidly fixed by canons laid down in iconographical textbooks, and every attribute of the deity portrayed is determined by convention. It is surprising that, bound as they were by these rigid rules, the Tamil craftsmen succeeded in producing works of such great beauty and often of considerable individuality. As well as images of the gods and goddesses the Tamil school produced many figures representing the saints of devotional theism, and portrait figures of kings and queens, who, in theory, were themselves divine, and whose images were often placed in temples among the lesser divinities surrounding the chief god.

Of the latter class the finest figures are the life-size 16th century statues of King Kṛṣṇa Deva Rāya and two of his chief queens (pl. LXXI), which still stand in a temple at Tirumalai. The faces of the queens seem quite conventional, though very beautiful, but that of the great king himself is almost certainly intended to give some idea of his actual appearance. Their hands pressed together in the gesture called *añjali*, to mark their homage and respect to the gods, their large eyes half closed, these three dignified figures seem to represent all that was good and noble in the old Hindu ideals of kingship, and, looking at them, we can understand why the king made so deep an impression on the Portuguese envoys (p. 67).

The greatest and most triumphant achievements of Tamil bronze casting are undoubtedly the dancing Śivas, of which there are many examples dating from the 11th century onwards (pl. LXVI). It was as "Lord of the Dance" (*Naṭarāja*, p. 270) that the Tamil masters specially delighted in portraying the god—a graceful young man, his four arms delicately posed, often with a flame in the open palm of one hand and a halo of flames encircling him, one foot firm on the back of a demon, and the other raised in a posture well known in the Indian dance. Thus the god appears as the very essence of vital, ordered movement, eternal youth, and ethereal light. This is not the Western conception of the highest godhead, but, once the religious background is understood, even the Westerner can recognize in the finest specimens of the dancing Śiva a genuine religious inspiration, a wholly successful effort at depicting in plastic terms divine truth, beauty and joy.

An important school of bronze casting existed in Ceylon, and produced works similar in style to those of South India. The finest metal product of Ceylon is undoubtedly the lovely large figure of a goddess, generally believed to be that of a Buddhist Tārā, but perhaps Pārvatī, the wife of Śiva (pl. LXV)*. This lovely and delicate casting, now in the British Museum, can hold its own with the greatest products of the South Indian bronzesmith.

Nearly all Indian bronzes were made by the "cire perdue" process. The figure was first designed over a core in wax, which was covered with a coating of day. The whole was then heated, so that the wax melted away, leaving a mould to be filled with molten metal. Larger standing figures, such as the Sultānganj Buddha which weighs nearly a ton, were often made in parts which were welded together.

PAINTING

Literary references alone would prove that painting was a very highly developed art in ancient India. Palaces and the homes of the rich were adorned with beautiful murals, and smaller paintings were made on prepared boards. Not only were there professional artists, but also many men and women of the educated classes could ably handle a brush.

Though now all in very bad condition, the surviving remains of ancient Indian painting are sufficient to show its achievement. They consist almost entirely of murals in certain of the cave temples. No doubt most temples were painted in some way, and the statuary was brightly coloured, as it often is in Hindu temples today, and here and there more elaborate schemes of mural decoration were carried out. A few caves in outlying places contain rough painted sketches of no special merit, mostly primitive in style, and believed by many authorities to be prehistoric. Some of the artificial caves dedicated to religious purposes, however, give us samples of the work of highly developed schools, and few would dispute that these are among the greatest surviving paintings of any ancient civilization.

The cave paintings of Ajantā (pls. LXXII–IX) are often referred to as frescos, but this term is incorrect, for a true fresco is painted while the plaster is still damp, and the murals of Ajantā were made after it had set. The walls were first covered with a coating of day or cow-dung bound together with straw or hair, and then finished with white gypsum. Considering the climate the surface has stood well, but in many places it has flaked away, and even since they were first copied in the last century the condition of the paintings has deteriorated. The tempera pigments, on the other hand, are still remarkably fresh; in their original state the paintings must have been of great brilliance, and their colours are even now clear and well contrasted. The artists probably worked in the dim caves by light reflected from outside by metal mirrors.

The paintings in Cave X have been shown with fair certainty to date from before the beginning of the Christian era, while those of Caves I and XVI are from perhaps as much as six centuries later. The earlier paintings are more sharply outlined and the later show more careful modelling, but there is no clear evidence of

* In Ceylon this figure was worshipped as the goddess Paṭṭini, the divinized form of the faithful Kaṇṇagi of Tamil legend (pp. 472–77), the ideal of wifely devotion.

a progressively developing style, as in contemporary sculpture, and the differences may be accounted for by the personal tastes of the craftsmen who supervised the work in the respective caves. The murals chiefly depict scenes from the life of the Buddha and from the Jātakas. No frame divides a scene from the next, but one blends into the other, the minor figures and the pattern skilfully leading the eye to the central figures of each scene. There is no perspective, but an illusion of depth is given by placing the background figures somewhat above those in the foreground. The effect of this convention is rather like that of a photograph taken with a telescopic camera, and makes the figures stand out from the flat wall as though coming to meet the observer.

Though painted for religious purposes the murals of Ajantā bear rather a secular than a religious message. Here, even more vividly than at Sānchī, we see the whole life of ancient India in panorama. Here are princes in their palaces, ladies in their harems, coolies with loads slung over their shoulders, beggars, peasants and ascetics, together with all the many beasts and birds and flowers of India, in fact the whole life of the times, perpetuated on the dim walls of the caves by the loving hands of many craftsmen. Everything is gracefully and masterfully drawn and delicately modelled.

Among the many masterpieces of Ajantā we must mention the figure of a handsome young man, his body bent slightly in the pose called *tribhaṅga* (p. 32, n.), loved by Indian sculptors andartists,with jewelled crown on his head and a white lotus in his right hand. His smooth features betray gentle sorrow, and his eyes look downwards compassionately, as if at something far below him (pls. LXXII–III). Around him are *apsarases*, or heavenly damsels, and divine minstrels, all much smaller than the central figure, who is the Bodhisattva Avalokiteśvara Padmapāṇi, the Lord who Looks Down in Compassion (p. 242). Here, once more, a work of deep religious feeling appears among the cheerfully sensuous scenes of everyday life. The Bodhisattva, for all his jewels and his smooth youthfulness, has shared the sorrows of the world; his gentle eyes have seen countless ages of pain, and his delicately formed lips have spoken words of consolation to countless sufferers. The artist of the Bodhisattva has well conveyed his message—the universe is not indifferent to the sorrows and strivings of its creatures.

Religious feeling of a different type is found in the painting of the glorified Buddha, begging his daily bread from a woman and child believed to represent his wife Yaśodharā and his son Rāhula. The lovely portrayal of the two minor figures is scarcely noticed against the majesty of the Master, whose calm features and robed body convey, like the Sārnāth Buddha, the serenity of self-transcendence (pl. LXXV).

A few other paintings are to be found elsewhere. Those on the walls of the veranda of a cave at Bāgh, some hundred miles to the North of Ajantā, depict a procession of elephants, perhaps more impressive in composition than anything Ajantā has to offer (pl. LXXX), and a lovely scene of a dancer and women musicians (frontispiece). Traces of paintings in the Ajantā style are to be found in other Deccan caves, notably at Bādāmi and Ellorā. Further south, in the Tamil country, a Jaina cave at a place called Śītannavasal has yielded fine, though much decayed, murals, and recently some splendid paintings of the Cola period have been revealed under layers of plaster in the Rājarājeśvara Temple at Tānjuvūr.

Some of the best preserved paintings of these schools are to be found in Ceylon. In the centre of the island a great rock, Sīgiriya, the "Lion Mountain", rises sharply for 600 feet above the surrounding plain. Here, at the end of the 5th century, the parricide king Kāśyapa I built a palace and a fortress. Kāśyapa, evidently a megalomaniac, was so convinced of his own divinity that he tried to identify his rock-fortress with heaven, and had demigods and heavenly beings painted on the bare walls of the rock, to show his subjects that he transcended them all. Nearly all these paintings have vanished under the hot sun and driving monsoon rain, but half way up the rock face, preserved by an overhanging ledge, are the figures of twenty-one apsarases immersed from their hips downwards in banks of cloud.* These charming ladies, toying with flowers in languid poses (pl. LXXXII), are so freshly preserved that one can hardly believe that they were painted 1,500 years ago.

Most of the surviving traces of medieval Hindu painting, at Vijayanagara, Polonnaruva in Ceylon, and elsewhere, indicate that there was some technical decline after the 8th century. Outlines become sharper, and the delicate modelling of the earlier period is lacking, but the achievement is still considerable, and the tradition of mural painting continued down to the Muslim invasion.

After the spread of Islāmic influence the Indian painter turned his attention mainly to miniatures and book illustration, deriving much inspiration from Persian models. Literary evidence shows that miniature painting existed long before the coming of the Muslims, however, and a few examples have survived from the 11th and 12th centuries from Bihār, Bengal and Nepāl (pl. LXXXI*a*). These little pictures show great delicacy and skill, but they lack the comparative realism of Ajantā, and the figures are almost unmodelled. They are the products of a formalized Buddhism, the religious inspiration of which was languishing, and which was largely detached from contact with everyday life. Unlike the Ajantā murals, they are probably the work of monks, and not of secular craftsmen.

The dry sands of Central Asia have preserved paintings which, though not strictly Indian, owe much to Indian inspiration. The earliest of these surround a colossal rock-cut Buddha at Bāmiyān in Afghānistān (pl. LXXX) and are older than most of the paintings at Ajantā. The many murals and paintings on boards found at sites in Chinese Turkistān and other parts of Central Asia are mostly somewhat later, and show greater deviation from Indian models, though their debt to India is still quite evident. They date from a period when the trade route to China was wide open, and give proof of the debt which Chinese art, despite its very individual character, owes to India.

---

*At one time these figures were thought to be portraits of Kāśyapa's queens and concubines, and some of the faces seem to show individual character. A few authorities might still support the older theory, but the context of the paintings leaves little doubt that this interpretation, first put forward by Dr. S. Paranavitāna, is correct.

MINOR ARTS

The excavations at Takṣaśilā and other sites of the North-West have revealed fine jewellery (pl. LXXXI*b*), with semi-precious stones set in gold filigree, much in the manner of the Indian jewellery of the present day. The Bīmarān Casket (pl. LXXXV*a*), and a few other objects in gold and silver, are delicately worked, as are the crystal relic caskets found in Buddhist sites in many parts of India. Engraved intaglio gems from the North-Western sites are usually of no great artistic merit, and nearly all these small objects of art show the influence of western models, while some may well have been imported.

Though little survives, much beautiful work was done in ivory. Guilds of ivory carvers are mentioned in inscriptions and their profession was evidently a well-patronized and honourable one. Of surviving ivory work the most interesting if not the most beautiful specimen is a small statuette of a goddess, found at Herculaneum (pl. LXXXV*b*) and no doubt imported with spices and fine textiles via Egypt. More beautiful are the ivory plaques, originally fastened to the lids and sides of furniture and boxes, found at the Kuṣāṇa site of Begrām, some fifty miles west of Kābul. Though discovered in the region most open to Western influence, the designs of these plaques are purely Indian in inspiration and they were either imported from India proper or made by craftsmen who had learnt their trade from Indian masters (pl. LXXXV*c*). The figures are outlined with deep-cut lines, and, although only lightly modelled, give a wonderful impression of depth. Their delicacy and grace are unexcelled in any work of art of ancient India. The art of ivory carving has continued down to the present day both in India and Ceylon (pl. LXXXVI), but it has never again produced works as lovely as these.

Since they delighted in minute detail and gave great care to the finish of their productions it is surprising that the Indians did not develop their coinage artistically. Ancient Indian coins are generally crude and ugly. Only under the Gupta emperors did they approach the status of works of art, and even the Gupta gold coins are but works of art of the second order. They have originality and charm, however. Thus Candra Gupta I lovingly gazes at his chief queen, Kumāradevī; Samudra Gupta, enthroned, performs on the harp; Candra Gupta II slays a rhinoceros; and Kumāra Gupta I rides on a splendid elephant (fig. xxiv). After this, however, the standard of coin production deteriorated rapidly, and medieval kings who patronized great artists and craftsmen were satisfied with coins of the crudest type.

Exceptional are the large silver coins minted by the Greek kings of Bactria, which bear some of the finest numismatic portraits in the world (pl. LXXXIII*a-c*); but the inspiration of these coins is purely Hellenistic, and they were no doubt designed by Greek craftsmen. It is unlikely that they circulated widely in India, where the Greek kings issued cruder bilingual coins (pl. LXXXIII*d*), in a style followed by the later Śakas and Kuṣāṇas (pl. LXXXIII*e*).

Fig. xxiv.—Gupta Gold Coins.
a. Candra Gupta I and his queen Kumāradevī. *b*. Samudra Gupta playing the harp. *c*. Candra Gupta II as lion-slayer. *d*. Kumāra Gupta I slaying a rhinoceros. *c*. Kumāra Gupta I riding an elephant. *f*. Coin commemorating Kumāra Gupta I's horse sacrifice. (By permission of Prof. A. S. Altekar and the Numismatic Society of India.)

MUSIC

There is some evidence to show that the Āryans knew a heptatonic scale, and the instructions for intoning the hymns of the *Sāma Veda* show that the style of liturgical singing in Vedic times was rather like that of medieval plain chant, and has been preserved fairly accurately by the brāhmaṇs down to the present day. Between this and the early centuries of the Christian era we have little knowledge of the progress of Indian music, but in the latter period an anonymous writer composed a textbook on drama, music and dancing, which, in accordance with the custom of the time, he attributed to the ancient sage Bharata, and which has survived to this day. This *Bhārata Nāṭyaśāstra* is our earliest Indian authority on these three arts, and shows that by this time India had a fully developed system of music, out of which later Indian "classical" music developed. Because of the highly technical nature of the subject, which for its full understanding demands special training, we treat ancient Indian music briefly.

The basic scale of modern North Indian music is heptatonic and its seven notes (called *saḍja*, *ṛṣabha*, *gāndhāra*, *madhyama*, *pañcama*, *dhaivata* and *nisāda*, abbreviated to *sa*, *ri*, *ga*, *ma*, *pa*, *dha* and *ni*) correspond approximately to those of the European major scale. They may be elaborated with half-tones of varying intervals classified according to the number of *śrutis* they contain. The śruti is a theoretical interval of which the scale contains 22. According to modern Indian theory the 22 srutis are divided as follows:

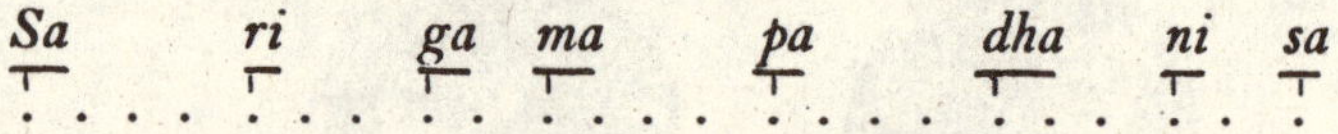

But from the time of Bharata down to the 18th century a scale corresponding to the Ecclesiastical Dorian mode (approximately equivalent to the white notes of the piano from D to D) was looked on as fundamental:

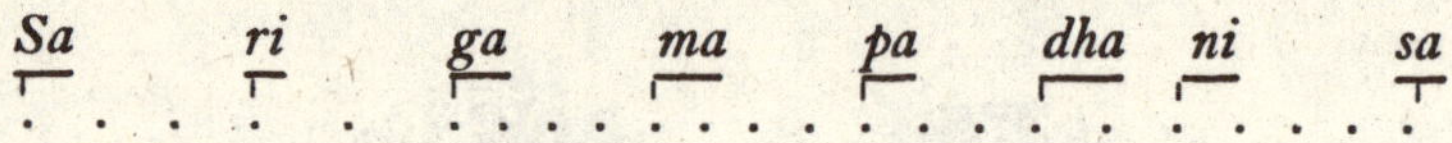

This strange alteration in the terminology of the Indian scale has led to considerable confusion in interpreting earlier Indian musical texts. As well as the above scale, known as *sa-grāma*, Bharata recognized another as of special importance, the *ma-grāma* which approximately corresponds to the white notes of the piano from G. to G. Besides these any other of the seven notes might be used as the home-note of a scale, and the system thus corresponded to the modes of medieval Western ecclesiastical music.

From the diagrams it will be seen that some notes may have as many as three degrees of sharpness. The quarter-tones of Indian music are chiefly noticeable in ornamentation, but they also occur to some extent in melody.

Besides the *grāma*, which we have translated "scale", there are other basic classifications of tune-types, chief of which is the *rāga*. A rāga is a series of five or more notes, upon which a melody is based. Rāga as a technical term only appears in musical texts later than that of Bharata, but by the 10th century the rāgas were firmly established. According to orthodox medieval theory there are six basic rāgas, the others being *rāgiṇīs*, personified as the wives of the masculine rāgas. The six original rāgas are variously given, and the following is one of the oldest classifications, with the notes according to modern theory:

Bhairava:	C, *DI*^{b} E, F, G, A^{b}, B, C.
Kauśika:	C, E^{b}, F, A^{b}, B^{b}, C.
Hindola:	C, E, F^{b}, A, B, C.
Dīpaka:	C, D^{b}, E, F^{b}, A, B, C.
Śrirāga:	C, *D*^{b} E, F^{b} G, *A*^{b}, B, C.
Megha:	C, D, F, G, A, C.

The rāgas are classified according to the time of day or night for which they are most appropriate. Thus, of the examples above, Bhairava is suitable for performance at dawn, Megha in the morning, Dīpaka and Śrīrāga in the afternoon, and Kauśika and Hindola at night. Bhairava is associated with awe and fear, Kauśika with joy and laughter, Hindola, Dīpaka and Śrīrāga with love, and Megha with peace and calm. It is interesting that the rāga most closely corresponding to the European major scale, *Pañcama*, is associated with the night and love in the Indian system.

There is no developed harmony in Indian music and the melody, which usually proceeds by conjunct intervals (i.e. adjacent notes on the keyboard), never suggests a harmonic basis, as do many European melodies. The tune is sustained by one or more drone notes and by drumming. The melodic line and the subtle and complex cross rhythms of Indian music take the place of harmony and counterpoint in the ear of the trained listener. Like the ancient Greeks the Indians delighted and still delight in unusual times, such as 5/4 and 7/4. The *tāla* or system of musical time is, after the rāga, the most important element of Indian music. Bharata recognized tālas, and since his day many more have been introduced. Tālas range in complexity from simple 2/4 time (*āditāla*)* and 3/4 (*rūpaka*[§] stressed as | ♪♪ ⁝ ♪♪♪♪ |) to such remarkable rhythms as *jhampā*,[§] a 10/8 rhythm stressed: | ♪♪ ⁝ ♪♪♪ ⁝ ♪♪ ⁝ ♪ ⁝ ♪♪ or *āṭā*[§] which has fourteen units, thus: | ♪♪ ⁝ ♪♪♪ ⁝ ♪♪ ⁝ ♪♪♪ ⁝ ♪♪ ⁝ ♪♪ \. These complex rhythms, ornamented with grace notes and varied by syncopation, result often in a rhythmic texture nearly as difficult for a Westerner to disentangle as a four-part fugue would be to an Indian.

The Indian musician was, and still is, an improviser. While a simple melody could be recorded in alphabetic notation India never devised a finished system of writing music and the music of her ancient masters has vanished for ever. As at the present day, every performance was virtually a new work. The musician would choose his rāga and tāla and, often starting from a well-known melody, would elaborate his theme in the form of free variations, working up to a climax of complex and rapid ornamentation.

The chief musical instrument was the *vīṇā*, usually loosely translated "lute". The term was originally applied to the bow-harp, often with ten strings, of a type very similar to the small harp used in ancient Egypt and the early civilizations of the Middle East (pl. XXXVII*b*). By the end of the Gupta period this instrument

---

* These definitions are according to the South Indian system. In the theory of North Indian Classical music there is no systematic enumeration of rhythms.

had begun to go out of fashion, and its place was largely taken by a lute with a pear-shaped body, played either with the fingers or with a plectrum. Archaeological evidence shows that this instrument had been played long before, and it is not clear why it ousted the older harp-type vīṇā. This is still played in South-East Asia, but in later Indian music it has no place. The pear-shaped lute was in turn superseded in the 8th century by the early form of the modern vīṇā, with long finger-board and small round body, often made of a dried gourd. Bowed instruments may have been known, but seem to have been little used in polite circles until the coming of the Muslims. Flutes and reed-instruments of various kinds were widely played, but instruments of the trumpet type were rarely used except as signals. Of these the most mentioned was the conch, the shell of a large mollusc, blown through its sawn-off point before battle, as an invocation to a deity, and on important occasions generally; its sound was very auspicious. Percussion instruments were numerous and varied. The smaller drums, played with the fingers as at present, were looked on as almost essential for any musical performance. Larger drums were used for state occasions, and there was a wide range of cymbals, gongs and bells.

The evidence of Bharata shows that, as at the present day, the Indian of two thousand years ago preferred the throaty type of singing, which comes more naturally than that which the West has learnt to appreciate. The singing voice was often treated as a musical instrument, the vocalist performing long impromptu variations on a simple melody, sung to a single phrase, often an invocation to a deity.

In the late medieval period music became largely the preserve of professionals, who, though much in demand by the well-to-do people who employed them, were mostly either Muslims or of low caste. This was not the case in India's greatest days, when a knowledge of music was looked on as an essential attribute of a gentleman. "The man who knows nothing of literature, music or art," runs an ancient Indian proverb, "is nothing but a beast without the beast's tail and horns".

THE DANCE

Like music, Indian dancing has changed little with the centuries, and the best modern Indian dancers, such as Uday Shankar and Rām Gopāl, still dance according to the rules of the *Bhārata Nāṭyaśāstra*. Dancing (*nṛtya*) was closely connected with acting (*nāṭya*); in fact both are forms of the same word, the latter being a Prākritism, and both are aspects of a single art, *abhinaya*, the portrayal of the eight emotions (p. 370). The drama employed chiefly word and gesture, the dance chiefly music and gesture. As in most other civilizations there is little doubt that in India the drama, which we consider in the following chapter, developed from ritual miming, song and dance.

Indian dancing is not a thing of legs and arms alone, but of the whole body. Every movement of the little finger or the eye-brow is significant, and must be fully controlled. The poses and gestures are classified in detail, even as early as the *Bhārata Nāṭyaśāstra*, which mentions thirteen postures of the head, thirty-six of the eyes, nine of the neck, thirty-seven of the hand, and ten of the body. Later texts classify many more poses and gestures, every one of which depicts a specific emotion or object. With so many possible combinations the dancer can tell a whole story, easily comprehensible to the observer who knows the convention.

The most striking feature of the Indian dance is undoubtedly the hand-gesture (*mudrā*). By a beautiful and complicated code, the hand alone is capable of portraying not only a wide range of emotions, but gods, animals, men, natural scenery, actions and so on. Some hundreds of mudrās are classified in later textbooks, and they are used not only in the dance, but, as we have seen, in religious worship and iconography.

This highly developed dance style demanded years of training, and was probably always chiefly performed by professionals, though there are references in literature to princes and their ladies dancing in their palaces. Ancient India was rich in folk-dances, which were performed at festivals. In later years only low caste people would think of dancing in public, but there seems to have been no social taboo on the art in ancient times, except perhaps for practising brāhmaṇs.

PLATE LXV

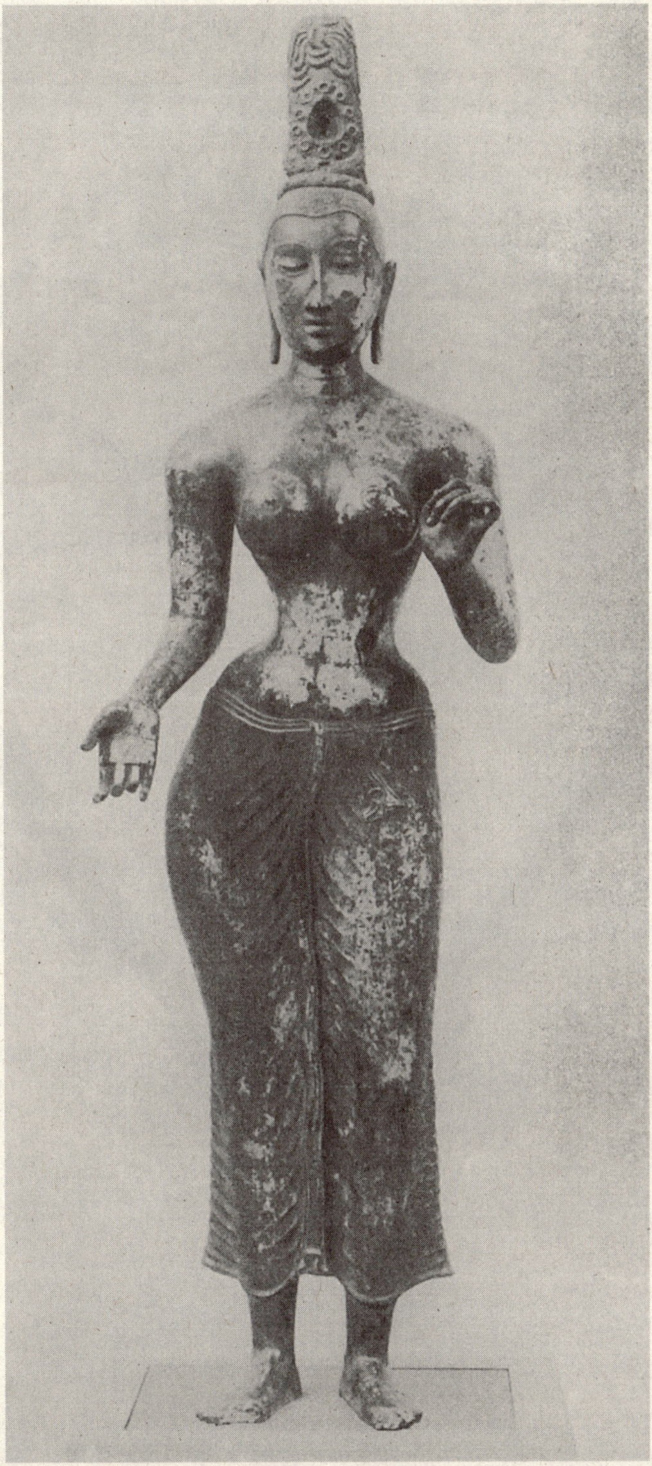

British Museum

Goddess (? Tārā). Large Bronze, Ceylon. 10th– 12th Century A. D.

PLATE LXVI

Dancing Śiva (*Naṭarāja*). Bronze, Cōla. *c.* 11th century

PLATE LXVII

a) Head of Dancing Śiva. Bronze, Cōla

b) Śiva as Lord of Beasts (Paśupati). Bronze, Cōla
British Museum. 14–15th century

PLATE LXVIII

Śiva as Teacher (*Daksināmurli*). Bronze, Cōla

PLATE LXIX

(a) Pārvatī or Umā, the Wife of Siva, Bronze, Cōla
(Part of the same piece as plate LXVIII)

(b) Kālī, the sterner form of Pārvatī, Bronze, Cōla

PLATE LXX

Kālī as Demoness playing Cymbals. Bronze, Cōla

PLATE LXXI

Dept. of Archaeology, Government of India

King Kṣṇa Deva Rāya and two Queens. Bronze, life-size.
S. India. 16th century A.D.

PLATE LXXII

Fogg Museum of Art, Harvard University

Avalokiteśvara-Padmapāṇi. Mural painting, Ajantā
Gupta period

Musée Guimet, Paris

Head of Avalokiteśvara, Ajantā (plate LXXII)

PLATE LXXIV

Copy by J. Griffiths. Commonwealth Relations Office

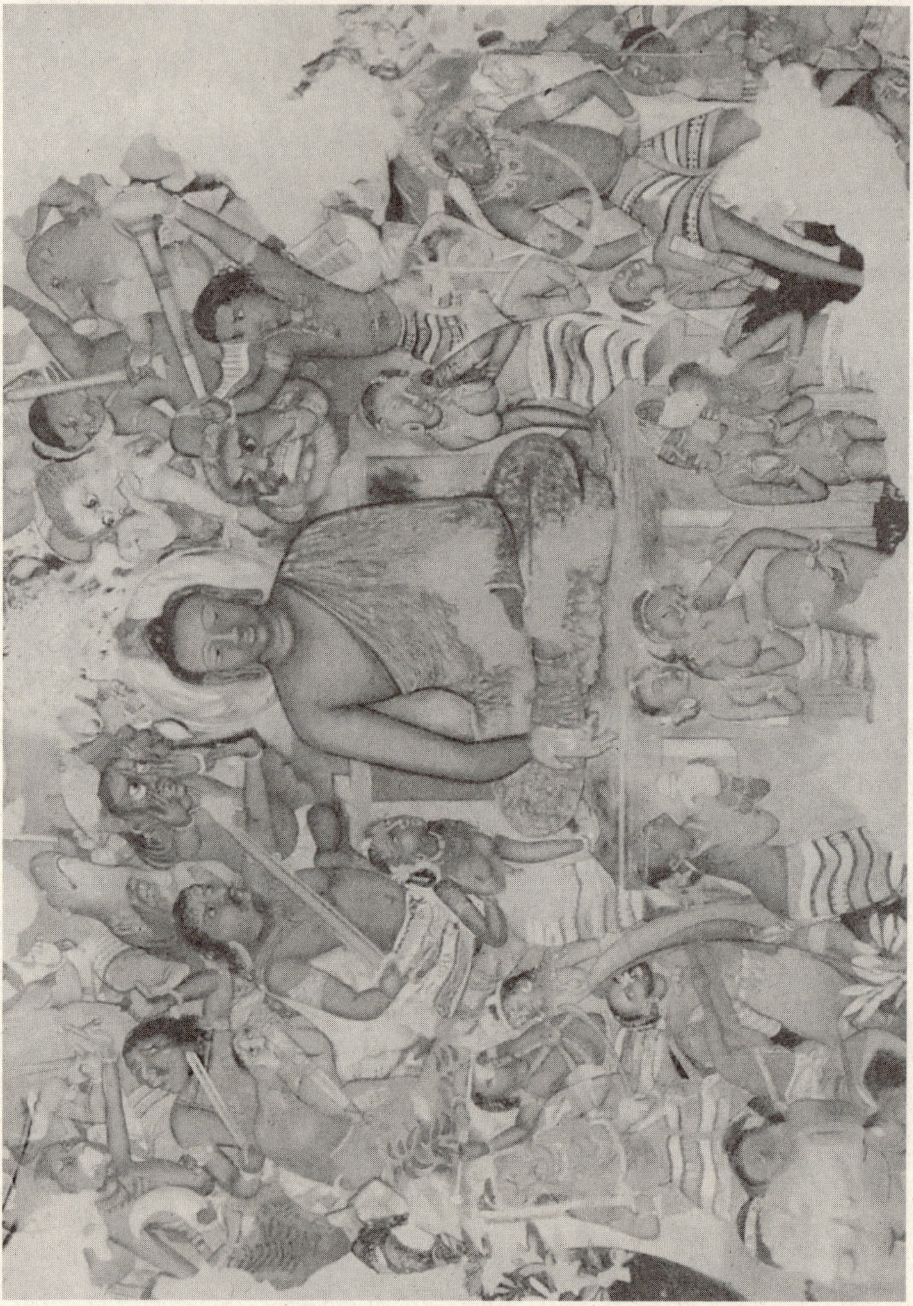

The Temptation of the Buddha, Ajantā

PLATE LXXV

British Museum

The Buddha receiving Alms from a Woman and Child. Ajantā

PLATE LXXVI

Country Scene, Mural Painting, Ajantā. Gupta Period.

PLATE LXXVII

Copy by J. Griffiths. Commonwealth Relations Office

PLATE LXXVIII (a)

Copy by J. Griffiths. Commonwealth Relations Office

A Persian Prince and Princess, Ajantā

PLATE LXXVIII (b)

Fighting Bulls, Ajantā

PLATE LXXIX

Musée Guimet, Paris

Seated Girl. Mural Painting, Ajantā. Gupta Period

IX

LANGUAGE AND LITERATURE

I. LANGUAGE

Sanskrit

It has long been universally accepted that Sanskrit is a remote cousin of all the languages of Europe, with the exception of Finnish, Estonian, Hungarian, Turkish and Basque. The other European tongues look back to a common ancestor in a group of dialects spoken by tribesmen in the steppelands of South Russia some 2,000 years B.C. The relationship of Sanskrit to the languages of the West is indicated by several obvious resemblances, such as *piṭr*, "father", and *māṭr*, "mother", and many others which are less obvious. For instance the Sanskrit *śvan*, "dog", is cognate with the Greek kucov, the Latin *canis*, the German *Hund*, and the English *hound*, the Germanie *h* representing an original *k*. The Sanskrit *cakra* is related to the word with the same meaning in English, *wheel*, both of which originated from a word pronounced something like *kwekulo*, which was also the ancestor of the Greek κυκλος, the Latin *circus*, and the Old English *hweogol*, from which our word "wheel" is derived. Many hundreds of relationships of this kind, at first not obvious, have been established with virtual certainty.

The reader with a slight knowledge of Latin or Greek will immediately recognize the relationship between their verbal systems and that of Sanskrit. Thus the present tense of the Sanskrit verb *as* "to be", is declined in singular and plural as follows:

asmi, "I am";	*smas*, "we are";
asi, "thou art";	*stha*, "you are";
asti, "he is";	*santi*, "they are".

Vedic Sanskrit is in many respeets closer than any other Indo-European language to the parent tongue or tongues, and it was the discovery of Sanskrit which enabled Bopp, Rask, and other scholars of the first half of the last century to establish a clear relationship between the languages of the Indo-European group and to develop the science of comparative philology.

The earliest surviving form of Sanskrit, that of the *Ṛg Veda*, bears about the same relation to the classical tongue as does Homeric to classical Greek. At all its stages Sanskrit is a language of many inflexions, but the Vedas contain numerous forms which later went out of use. The verb is of a complexity rivalling the

Greek, with a bewildering array of voices and moods, later much simplified. The Vedic noun, as in later Sanskrit, has eight cases, and both verb and noun have dual numbers.

A striking feature of Vedic Sanskrit is the tonic accent. Every important word had an accented syllable, which was not necessarily stressed, but on which the voice rose in pitch, as in classical Greek. The tonic accent of a Sanskrit word is, with exceptions due to the special rules of the languages, the same as in the cognate Greek word.

Sanskrit and most of the languages derived from it are characterized by the presence of aspirated consonants. Thus *k*, pronounced without appreciable emission of breath, is to the Indian quite a different sound from the aspirated *kh*, which is pronounced with a strong breathing, rather like the first sound of the English word *come*. To the average European, the difference is hardly noticeable. The distinction goes back to the Indo-Europeans, and was made in classical Greek, though in Greek the aspirate letters θ, φ and χ had lost their original pronunciation before the beginning of the Christian era. Another phonetic characteristic of Vedic Sanskrit, also surviving to modern times, is the series of "retroflex" or "cerebral" consonants. *ṭ*, *ṭh*, *ḍ*, *ḍh*, and *ṇ*. These to the Indian are quite different from the "dentals", *t*, *th*, etc, though the European finds them hard to distinguish without practice. The retroflex sounds are not Indo-European, and were borrowed very early from the indigenous inhabitants of India, either proto-Australoid or Dravidian. A further feature of the phonetics of Sanskrit is the predominance of the vowels *a* and *ā*. Vedic is a fine language, capable of vigorous and noble expression. On p. 511 we quote two verses of the Vedic hymns in the original, which will give the reader some idea of its sound.

After the composition of the *Ṛg Veda* Sanskrit developed considerably. In the early centuries of the lst millennium B.C. old inflexions disappeared, and the grammar was somewhat simplified, though still remaining very complex. New words, mostly borrowed from non-Āryan sources, were introduced, while old words were forgotten, or lost their original meanings. In these circumstances doubts arose as to the true pronunciation and meaning of the older Vedic texts, though it was generally thought that unless they were recited with complete accuracy they would have no magical effectiveness, but would bring ruin on the reciter. Out of the need to preserve the purity of the Vedas India developed the sciences of phonetics and grammar. The oldest Indian linguistic text, Yāska's *Nirukta*, explaining obsolete Vedic words, dates from the 5th century B.C., and followed much earlier work in the linguistic field. Pāṇini's great grammar, the *Aṣṭādhyayī* ("Eight Chapters"), was probably composed towards the end of the 4th century B.C. With Pāṇini the language had virtually reached its classical form, and it developed little thenceforward, except in its vocabulary.

By this time the sounds of Sanskrit had been analysed with an accuracy never again reached in linguistic study until the 19th century. One of ancient India's greatest achievements is her remarkable alphabet, commencing with the vowels and followed by the consonants, all classified very scientifically according to their mode of production, in sharp contrast to the haphazard and inadequate Roman alphabet, which has developed organically for three millennia. It was only on the discovery of Sanskrit by the West that a science of phonetics arose in Europe.

The great grammar of Pāṇini, which effectively stabilized the Sanskrit language, presupposes the work of many. earlier grammarians. These had succeeded in recognīzing the root as the basic element of a word, and had classified some 2,000 monosyllabic roots which, with the addition of prefixes, suffixes and inflexions, were thought to provide all the words of the language. Though the early etymologists were correct in principle, they made many errors and false derivations, and started a precedent which produced interesting results in many branches of Indian thought (p. 71).

Though its fame is much restricted by its specialized nature, there is no doubt that Pāṇini's grammar is one of the greatest intellectual achievements of any ancient civilization, and the most detailed and scientific grammar composed before the 19th century in any part of the world. The work consists of over 4,000 grammatical rules, couched in a sort of shorthand, which employs single letters or syllables for the names of the cases, moods, persons, tenses, etc. in which linguistic phenomena are classified. The great terseness of Pāṇini's system makes his work very difficult to follow without preliminary study and a suitable commentary. Later Indian grammars are mostly commentaries on Pāṇini, the chief being the "Great Commentary" (*Mahābhāṣya*) of Patañjali (2nd century B.C.) and the "Banāras Commentary" (*Kāiśkā Vṛtti*) of Jayāditya and Vāmana (7th century A.D.).

Some later grammarians disagreed with Pāṇini on minor points, but his grammar was so widely accepted that no writer or speaker of Sanskrit in courtly or brāhmaṇic circles dared seriously infringe it. With Pāṇini the language was fixed, and could only develop within the framework of his rules. It was from the time of Pāṇini onwards that the language began to be called *Saṃskṛta*, "perfected" or "refined", as opposed to the *Prākṛtas* ("natural"), the popular dialects which had developed naturally.

Pāṇinian Sanskrit, though simpler than Vedic, is still a very complicated language. Every beginner finds great difficulty in surmounting Pāṇini's rules of euphonic combination (*sandhi*), the elaboration of tendencies present in the language even in Vedic times. Every word of a sentence is affected by its neighbours. Thus *na-avadat* ("he did not say") becomes *nāvadat*, but *na-uvāca* (with the same meaning) becomes *novāca*; *Rāmas-uvāca* ("Rāma said") becomes *Rāma uvāca*, and *Rāmas-avadat* becomes *Rāmo 'vadat*, but *Harisavadat* ("Hari said ") becomes *Harir avadat*. There are many rules of this kind, which were even artificially imposed on the *Ṛg Veda*, so that the reader must often disentangle the original words to find the correct metre.

Pāṇini, in standardizing Sanskrit, probably based his work on the language as it was spoken in the North-West. Already the lingua franca of the priestly class, it gradually became that of the governing class also. The Mauryas, and most Indian dynasties until the Guptas, used Prākrit for their official pronouncements. The first important dynasty to use Sanskrit was that of the Sakas of Ujjain, and the inscription of Rudradāman at Girnar (p. 54) is the earliest written Sanskrit document we possess, with the exception of a few inscriptions which are brief and unimportant.

As long as it is spoken and written a language tends to develop, and its development is generally in the direction of simplicity. Owing to the authority of Pāṇini, Sanskrit could not develop freely in this way. Some of his minor rules, such as those relating to the use of tenses indicating past time, were quietly ignored, and writers took to using imperfect, perfect and aorist indiscriminately; but Pāṇini's rules of inflexion had to be maintained. The only way in which Sanskrit could develop away from inflexion was by building up compound nouns to take the place of the clauses of the sentence.

In the Vedic and Epic literature compound nouns are common enough, but they are usually of only two or three members, like the English "houseboat", or "blackbird". In classical Sanskrit, on the other hand, they may have as many as twenty or thirty components. Earlier classical poets such as Kālidāsa are comparatively restrained in their use of compound words, though even in poetry compounds of six elements are not uncommon; the earliest royal panegyrics in Sanskrit employ long compounds. For instance the emperor Samudra Gupta is referred to as "binding together the whole world by displaying the valour of his arm and by [accepting] acts of service [from other kings], such as paying personal homage, the presentation of gifts of maidens, and soliciting his charter, sealed with the Garuḍaseal, to confirm them in possession of their territories" in a single word of twenty components.* This remarkable use of long compounds may be due to the influence of Dravidian speech on the language, for early Tamil has few inflexions, and its words are put together in concatenations without definite indication of their relationship. If the elements of a Sanskrit compound word are thought of as separate words, as in such an English phrase as "my top right-hand waistcoat pocket" which in Sanskrit would be treated as a single compound, the new constructions of the classical period become intelligible.

With the growth of long compounds Sanskrit also developed a taste for long sentences. The prose works of Bāṇa and Subandhu, written in the 7th century, and the writings of many of their successors, contain single sentences covering two or three pages of type. To add to these difficulties writers adopted every conceivable verbal trick, until Sanskrit literature became one of the most ornate and artificial in the world.

The interest in language which India had shown from the earliest times continued in the medieval period. A number of valuable "dictionaries" survive from this time; these are not comparable to the alphabetically arranged dictionaries of the West, but rather to such works as *Roget's Thesaurus*. They contain lists of words of approximately the same meaning or used in similar contexts, sometimes with brief definitions, the whole arranged in simple verse. The most famous

---

* *Ātma-nivedana-kany'-opāyana-dāna-garutmad-anka-sva-viṣaya-bhukti-iāsana-yācan'-ādy-upāya-sevā-kṛta-bāhu-virya-prasara-dharaṇi-bandhasya.*[1]

lexicographer, and the earliest whose work has survived, was Amarasiṃha, by tradition a contemporary of Kālidāsa. Another form of dictionary, more akin to our own, was the list of homonyms, classifying words with more than one meaning.

Indian interest in language spread to philosophy, and there was considerable speculation about the relations of a word and the thing it represented. The Mīmāṃsā school (p. 286f), perpetuating the verbal mysticism of the later Vedic period, maintained that every word was the reflexion of an ideal prototype, and that its meaning was eternal and inherent in it. Its opponents, especially the logical school of Nyāya (p. 245), supported the view that the relation of word and meaning was purely conventional. Thus the controversy was similar to that between the Realists and Nominalists in medieval Europe.

Classical Sanskrit was probably never spoken by the masses, but on the other hand it was never wholly a dead language. As the official tongue of church and state it was read and spoken by the upper classes, and was understood to some extent by many of the lower orders. It served as a lingua franca for the whole of India and even today learned brāhmaṇs from the opposite ends of the land, meeting at a place of pilgrimage, will converse in Sanskrit and understand one another perfectly, though there are local differences in pronunciation.

Prākrits and Pāli

The language of the *Ṛg Veda* was already rather archaic when the hymns were composed, and the ordinary Āryan tribesman spoke a simpler tongue, more closely akin to classical Sanskrit. In the Veda itself there is evidence of dialectal differences. By the time of the Buddha the masses were speaking languages which were much simpler than Sanskrit. These were the Prākrits, of which several dialects have been attested.

The everyday speech of ancient India has been preserved for us largely through the unorthodox religions, whose earliest scriptures were composed in languages approximating to those spoken by the people. Most inscriptions of pre-Guptan times, notably the great series of Aśokan edicts, are in Prākrit, and the women and humbler characters of the Sanskrit drama are made to speak in formalized Prākrit of various dialects. A few works of secular literature were composed in Prākrit. Thus there is much material for reconstructing the popular languages.

Prākrits were much simpler than Sanskrit both in sound and grammar. Except for certain combinations which were easy to pronounce, such as doubled consonants, or compounds of which a nasal letter was the first member, groups of consonants were drastically simplified. Those at the ends of words disappeared, and in some dialects even single consonants in the middle of words were omitted. The diphthongs *ai* and *au* of Sanskrit vanished, as did the old vowels *ṛ* and *ḷ*, the correct pronunciation of which was almost forgotten very early. In one dialect, Māgadhī, *r* regularly became *l*, giving *lājā* for *rājā*. The rules of euphonic combination were practically ignored, and the dual number disappeared, while the inflexions of the noun and verb were much reduced.

One very important early Prākrit was Pāli, which became the language of the Sthaviravādin Buddhists. Buddha probably taught in Māgadhī, but as his doctrines spread over India they were adapted to the local dialects. The language chosen by the Sthaviravādins was a Western one, probably spoken in the region of Sānchī and Ujjayinī. Pāli, which is still the religious language of the Buddhists of Ceylon, Burma and South-East Asia, seems to look back rather to Vedic than to classical Sanskrit.

Māgadhī was the official language of the Mauryan court, and the edicts of Aśoka were composed in it, though the language in which they are inscribed in different parts of India is evidently affected by local vernaculars. A later hybrid Māgadhī, somewhat influenced by the Western Prākrits and usually known as *Ardha-māgadhī* ("Half Māgadhī"), became the sacred language of the Jainas, and a large literature was written in it.

Other important Prākrits were Śaurasenī, spoken originally in the western part of modern Uttar Pradesh, and Māhārāṣṭī, spoken in the north-western Deccan. Śaurasenī was particularly used in drama, for the speech of women and respectable people of the lower orders. Māhārāṣṭrī was a literary language, especially popular for lyric song. There were several other Prākrits of lesser importance. By the time of the Guptas the Prākrits were standardized and had lost their local character. The vernaculars had already developed beyond them. What Pāṇini did for Sanskrit others did for the Prākrits, and they began to bear little resemblance to the languages actually spoken. Dramatists, employing various Prākrits by convention, thought first in Sanskrit, and produced their Prākrit passages by following mechanically the rules for conversion from one language to another as laid down by the grammarians.

Another stage in the development of the Indo-Āryan languages was *Apabhraṃśa* ("falling away"), a vernacular of Western India which achieved literary form in the Middle Ages and was used by Jaina writers in Gujarāt and Rājasthān for the composition of poetry. Its chief characteristic is the further reduction of inflexions, which are in part replaced by postpositions, as in modern Indian vernaculars. A similar degenerate Prākrit was used in Bengal by a few late Buddhist poets, and is the ancestor of modern Bengālī.

The next stage saw the development of the modern vernaculars of North India and is outside the scope of this work, although the earliest vernacular literature is little later than the end of our period. One Indo-Āryan vernacular, however, had a long history behind it by this time—this was Sinhalese, the development of which can be traced in inscriptions and literature from the 2nd century B.C. down to the present day. The prākritic dialect spoken by the early settlers of Ceylon was already far removed from the original Sanskrit. Influenced by the local speech, and also by Tamil, Sinhalese developed rapidly and independently. Very early the aspirated letters, characteristic of most Indo-Āryan languages, were forgotten. Vowels were shortened, and the short vowels *ĕ* and *ŏ*, absent in most Indo-Āryan languages, appeared, as well as a wholly new vowel, *ä*, rather like that in the English *hat*. Many words were borrowed from the aboriginals and the Tamils. By the beginning of the Christian era Sinhalese was no longer a Prākrit, but a distinct language. Surviving Sinhalese literature dates from the 9th century A.D., but it is certain that there was much earlier work which is now lost.

Dravidian Languages

While the modern Indo-Āryan languages, with the exception of Sinhalese, had not found literary expression at the time of the Muslim invasion, the Dravidian languages had been flourishing for centuries.

Four of these tongues—Tamil, Canarese, Telegu and Malayālam— have distinctive scripts and written literatures. Of these Tamil is spoken in the south, from Cape Comorin to Madras, Canarese in Mysore and parts of Andhra Pradesh, Telegu from Madras northwards to the borders of Orissā and Malayālam in Kerala. Tamil is certainly the oldest of these languages, with a literature going back to the early centuries A.D.

Some authorities believe that the Dravidian languages are remotely affiliated to the Finno-Ugrian group, which includes Finnish and Hungarian.[2] If this is the case it involves interesting corollaries concerning prehistoric race movements, but the hypothesis is not certain. Dravidian is virtually an independent group of languages with a distinctive character. Its sound system is rich in retroflex consonants, which give it a crisp character, and its varied vowels (including *ĕ* and *ŏ*, not present in Sanskrit) distinguish it from the northern languages, where the vowels *a* and *ā* predominate. Like Sanskrit it has a complicated system of euphonic combination. It does not recognize the aspirated consonants of Indo-Āryan languages—by the peculiar phonetic laws of Tamil, Sanskrit *bhūta* ("ghost") becomes in Tamil *pūda*.

Tamil is not inflected, in the sense that Sanskrit is, but the relations of one word with another, and the number, person and tense of verbs, are shown by suffixes, which may be piled up one upon another indefinitely. Sanskrit began to affect the language very early, and by the Middle Ages the learned looked on their suffixes as nominal and verbal endings, on the analogy of Sanskrit. In the oldest texts, however, these suffixes are sparingly used, and related words are juxtaposed in clusters, with few if any indications of their relationship one to another—a system similar to the great compound words of Sanskrit, and giving much difficulty to all but the expert.

The earliest Tamil literature contains comparatively few Sanskrit loan-words, and those that it does contain are generally adapted to the Tamil phonetic system. The gradual growth of Āryan influence resulted in the borrowing of many more words in the Middle Ages, often in their correct Sanskrit form. Telegu and Canarese, which are spoken further north, are naturally even more strongly influenced by Sanskrit. Canarese first appears in inscriptions at the end of the 6th century, and its earliest surviving literature goes back to the 9th. Telegu did not become a literary language until the 12th century and only became really important under the Vijayanagara Empire, of which it was the court language. Malayālam, very closely akin to Tamil, was a separate language by the 11th century.

Writing

We have seen that the people of the Harappā Culture had a script, which cannot be deciphered. From the time of the fall of Harappā, that is before 1550 B.C., to the middle of the 3rd century B.C. no Indian written material has survived. References to writing occur in the Pāli scriptures of the Buddhists and in the Sūtra literature, but there is no clear mention of it in the Vedas, Brāhmaṇas or Upaniṣads. This negative evidence, however, is not wholly conclusive, and in the later Vedic period some form of script may have been used by merchants. The Aśokan inscriptions, which are the earliest important written documents of India, are engraved in two scripts almost perfectly adapted to the expression of Indian sounds. It is generally thought that these scripts had many years, perhaps many centuries, of development before the days of Aśoka.

The most important of the Aśokan scripts, used everywhere in India except the North-West, was *Brāhmī*, about the origin of which two theories exist. Most Indian authorities would now maintain that the script was derived from that of Harappā. Many Europeans and some Indians believe that it was derived from a Semitic script. The first theory, tentatively put forward by Sir Alexander Cunningham and elaborated by the Assyriologist Professor S. Langdon,[3] has many difficulties. Until we know the pronunciation of the 270 Harappā signs we cannot be sure that the dozen or so letters of the Brāhmī script which somewhat resemble them are derived from them, and with so many Harappā signs it is unlikely that there should be no resemblances at all. Similarities between Brāhmī and some early North Semitic scripts are perhaps more striking, especially as the latter offer only twenty-two letters to choose from,[4] but the resemblances are still not strong enough to be altogether convincing, and the whole problem needs reopening.

Brāhmī (fig. xxv) is normally read from left to right, as are European scripts, while the Semitic scripts are read from right to left. There is a very defective series of Aśokan inscriptions at Yeṛṛaguḍi in Āndhra Pradesh, of which some parts are *boustrophedon* (reading alternately left to right and right to left). Moreover a very early Sinhalese inscription and an early coin from Eran in Madhya Pradesh are read from right to left.[5] These facts would suggest that this was the original direction of Brāhmī, though the data are insufficient to prove the case conclusively. But this is no evidence of its origin, since it is believed that the Harappā script was also read from right to left.

Whatever its ultimate origin Brāhmī is so skilfully adapted to the sounds of Indian languages that its development must have been at least in part deliberate. In the form in which we have it it is the work not of merchants but of brāhmaṇs or other learned men who knew something of the Vedic science of phonetics. It may have begun as a mercantile alphabet, suggested by the shapes of Semitic letters or by vague memories of the Harappā script, but by the time of Aśoka, though still not completely perfect, it was the most scientific script of the world.

The words of Semitic languages, based largely on roots of three consonants modified by internal vowel changes, need few indications of vowels to prevent ambiguity, and until comparatively late times vowels were marked only at the

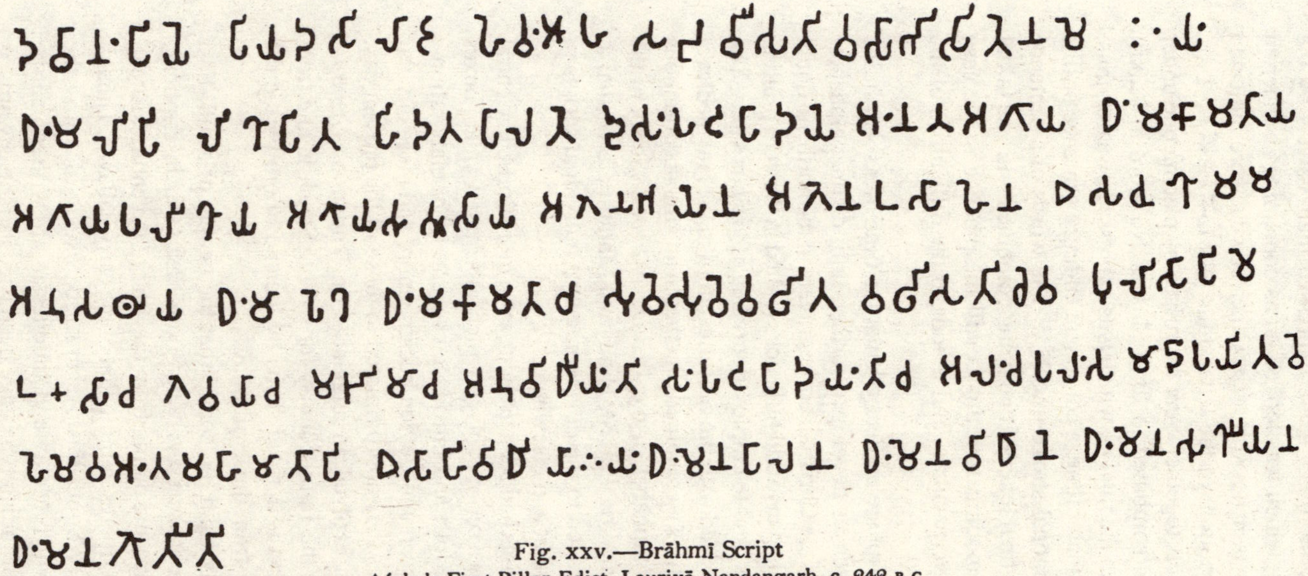

Fig. xxv.—Brāhmī Script

Aśoka's First Pillar Edict, Lauriyā Nandangarh, c. 242 B.C.

Transcript

(Line 1) De-vā-naṃ-pi-ye Pi-ya-da-si lā-ja he-vaṃ ā-ha sa-ḍu-vī-sa-ti-va-sā-bhi-si-te-na me i-yaṃ
(2) dhaṃ-ma-li-pi li-khā-pi-ta. Hi-da-ta-pā-la-te du-saṃ-pa-ṭi-pā-da-ye aṃ-na-ta a-gā-ya dhaṃ-ma-kā-ma-tā-ya
(3) a-gā-ya pa-lī-khā-ya a-gā-ya su-sū-sā-ya a-ge-na bha-ye-na a-ge-na u-sā-he-na. E-sa cu kho ma-ma
(4) a-nu-sa-thi-ya dhaṃ-mā-pe-kha dhaṃ-ma-kā-ma-tā ca su-ve su-ve va-ḍhi-ta va-ḍhi-sa-ti ce-va. Pu-li-sā pi me
(5) u-ka-sā ca ge-va-yā ca ma-jhi-mā ca a-nu-vi-dhī-yaṃ-ti saṃ-pa-ṭi-pā-da-yaṃ-ti ca a-laṃ ca-pa-laṃ sa-mā-dā-pa-yi-ta-ve,
(6) he-me-va aṃ-ta-ma-hā-mā-tā pi. E-sā hi vi-dhi yā i-yaṃ dhaṃ-me-na pā-la-na dhaṃ-me-na vi-dhā-ne dhaṃ-me-na su-khī-ya-na
(7) dhaṃ-me-na go-tī ti.

Translation.

Thus speaks the King, Dear to the Gods, Priyadarśī. When I had been consecrated twenty-six years I ordered this inscription of Righteousness (*Dharma*) to be engraved. Both this world and the other are hard to reach, except by great Love of Righteousness, great self-examination, great obedience (to Righteousness), great respect (for Righteousness), great energy. But through my leadership respect for Righteousness and love of Righteousness have grown and will grow from day to day. Moreover my officers, of high, low and medium grades, follow it and apply it, sufficiently to make the waverer accept it; the officers on the frontiers do likewise. For this is (my) rule: government by Righteousness, administration according to Righteousness, gratification (of my subjects) by Righteousness, protection by Righteousness.

beginning of words, and then not perfectly. The Greeks, when they borrowed the Phoenician alphabet, adapted it to express vowels other than *a* by the introduction of new signs. The Indians, on the other hand, expressed their vowels by the modification of the basic letter, which was looked on as containing an inherent short *a*. Thus the Brāhmī letter is 𑀓 not *k*, but *ka*. Other vowels were indicated by ticks attached to the top or bottom of the letter, thus: 𑀓𑀸 *kā*, 𑀓𑀺 *ki*, 𑀓𑀻 *kī*, 𑀓𑀼 *ku*, 𑀓𑀽 *kū*, 𑀓𑁂 *ke*, 𑀓𑁄 *ko*. Two consonants together were expressed by placing one under the other; thus 𑀓 *ka* and 𑀬 *ya* combined to form 𑀓𑁆𑀬 *kya*. No word in Prākrit ends with a consonant other than the final *ṃ*, which was expressed by a dot, thus: 𑀓𑀁 *kaṃ*. In writing Sanskrit, at a later time, a consonant ending a sentence or line of poetry was marked by a diagonal stroke thus क् *k*. The words of a sentence were not generally divided, the final letter of one being combined with the initial letter of the other; with some modification this is still the practice in the case of Sanskrit, though not of the vernaculars, and it adds to the difficulties of the language for the beginner.

Variations of the Brāhmī script are evident even at the time of Aśoka. In the following centuries these differences developed further, until distinct alphabets evolved. Before the beginning of the Christian era engravers in the north, no doubt following the custom of scribes, began to add little ticks (called in Western printing terminology serifs) to the letters, and to employ flourishes of various kinds. The tendency to ornamentation increased with the centuries, until in the late medieval period the serifs at the tops of letters were joined together in an almost continuous line, to form the *Nāgari* ("City" alphabet, also called *Devanāgari*, "Script of the City of the Gods"), in which Sanskrit, Prākrit, Hindi and Marāthi are written at the present day. Local variations led to the development of individual scripts in the Panjāb, Bengal, Orissā, Gujarāt and elsewhere.

Meanwhile in the Deccan scripts had been growing even more florid. In Central India in the 5th and 6th centuries a script evolved which substituted square boxes for the serifs of the northern scripts, and introduced several other elaborations. The scripts of the Southern Deccan and Ceylon became more and more circular in form, until in the Middle Ages they approximated to those of the present day. The Tamils, on the other hand, evolved an angular script known as *Grantha*, which is still sometimes used in the Tamil country for writing Sanskrit, and from which the modern Tamil alphabet is derived. Thus by the end of our period the alphabets of India differed little from those of today.

It was from India, especially from the south, that the people of South-East Asia learnt the art of writing. The earliest surviving South-East Asian inscriptions, found in Borneo, Java and Malaya and dating from the 4th or 5th centuries, are in fairly correct Sanskrit, and in a script resembling that of the early Pallavas. Though superficially very different, every South-East Asian script, except of course the Arabic and Roman scripts in which Malay and Indonesian are written, can be traced back to Brāhmī. Scripts of Indian type have been used as far eastwards as the Philippine Islands.

The origin of the other Aśokan script, called *Kharoṣṭhī* (a strange term, meaning

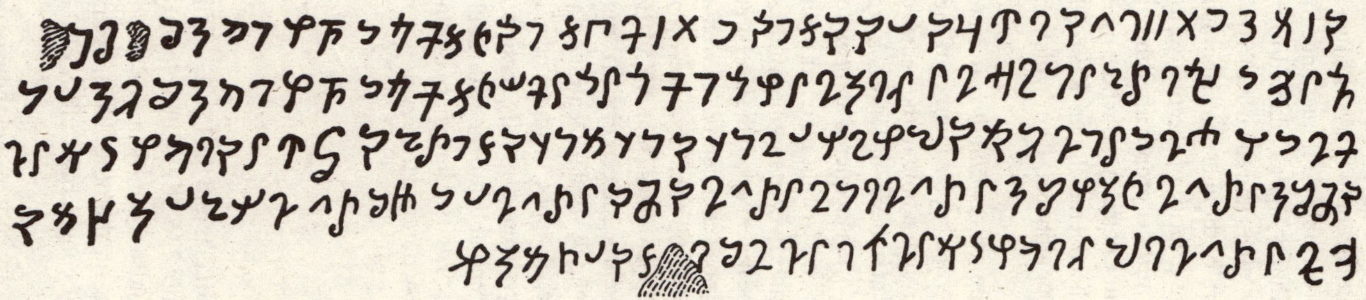

Fig. xxvi.—Kharoṣṭhī Script

From an inscribed silver leaf, Takṣaśilā. 1st c. A.D.

Transcript (Reading the script from right to left)

(Line 1) Sa 1 100 20 10 4 1 1 A-ya-sa A-ṣa-ḍa-sa ma-sa-sa di-va-se 10 4 1. I-śa di-va-se pra-di-sta-vi-ta Bha-ga-va-to dha-tu-(o) U-ra-(sa)-

(2) ke-ṇa Iṃ-ta-vhri-a-pu-tre-ṇa Ba-ha-li-e-ṇa Ṇo-a-ca-e ṇa-ga-re va-sta-ve-na. Te-na i-me pra-di-sta-vi-ta Bha-ga-va-to dha-tu-o Dha-ma-ra-

(3) i-e Ta-kṣa-śi-e ta-ṇu-va-e Bo-si-sa-tva-ga-ha-mi ma-ha-ra-ja-sa ra-ja-ti-ra-ja-sa de-va-pu-tra-sa Khu-ṣa-ṇa-sa a-ro-ga-da-kṣi-ṇa-e

(4) sa-rva-bu-dha-ṇa pu-ya-e pra-tya-ga-bu-dha-ṇa pu-ya-e a-ra-ha-ṇa pu-ya-e sa-rva-sa-ṇa pu-ya-e ma-ta-pi-tu pu-ya-e mi-tra-ma-ca-ña-ti-sa-

(5) lo-hi-ṇa pu-ya-e a-tva-ṇo a-ro-ga-da-kṣi-ṇa-e Ṇi-a-ṇa-e. Ho-tu a-(ya)-de sa-ma-pa-ri-ca-go.

Translation

In the year Aya 136 in the month Āṣāḍha[1] on the 15th day. On the day the relics of the Lord (Buddha) were deposited by the Urasaka the Bactrian, the son of Iṃtavhria, a citizen of the town of Noaca. These relics of the Lord were deposited by him in his own Bodhisattva chapel of the Dharmarājika (Stūpa) of Takṣaśilā, for the blessing of health for the great King, the King over Kings, the Son of the Gods, the Kuṣāṇas, and in reverence to all the Buddhas, in reverence to all the Pratyeka Buddhas[2], in reverence to the Arhants[3], in reverence to all beings, in reverence to all mother and father, in reverence to his friends, his advisers, his kinsmen, and those of common blood, and for the boon of health and Nirvāna for himself. May right renunciation be spread.

[1] The correct interpretation of this word is much disputed; [2] See p. 241; [3] See p. 241–42.

"Ass-lip") (fig. xxvi), is not in doubt. It was certainly derived from the Aramaic alphabet, which was widely used in Achaemenid Persia, and was also known in North-West India. Many Kharoṣṭhī letters closely resemble Aramaic, and, like Aramaic, the alphabet is read from right to left. Kharoṣṭhī was adapted to the sounds of Indian languages by the invention of new letters and the use of vowel marks, which were lacking in Aramaic. It is generally thought that Kharoṣṭhī was adapted under the influence of Brāhmī, but the priority of the two scripts is not absolutely certain. Kharoṣṭhī was little used in India proper after the 3rd century A.D., but it survived some centuries longer in Central Asia, where many Prākrit documents in Kharoṣṭhī script have been discovered. Later, Kharoṣṭhī was replaced in Central Asia by a form of the Gupta alphabet, from which the present-day script of Tibet is derived.

The usual writing material was the leaf of the talipot palm (*tālapatra*, in Tamil *ālai*), dried, smoothed, sized and cut into strips. To form a book a number of such strips was held loosely together by a cord passed through a hole in the centre of the leaf, or, in the case of large books, by two cords at either end. The book was usually strengthened by wooden covers, which were often lacquered and painted (pl. LXXXI*a*). Palm leaves are still sometimes used as writing material in the outlying parts of South India. In the Himālayan districts, where supplies of dried palm leaf were difficult to obtain, it was replaced by the inner bark of the birch tree, which, carefully pared and smoothed, served the purpose excellently. As well as these materials, sized cotton and silk, and thin slips of wood or bamboo were also used, and important documents were engraved on copper plates (pl. LXXXVII). Paper, believed to have been invented in China in the early 2nd century A.D., may have been known in North India and it was certainly widely used in Central Asia.[6]

In most of India ink made from lampblack or charcoal, applied with a reed pen, was the usual writing medium. In the South, the letters were generally scratched on the palm-leaf with a stylus, and the leaf was then rubbed over with finely powdered lampblack. This system of writing gave the letters a fine sharp outline and allowed the use of very small script; it probably encouraged the development of the angular forms of the Tamil alphabet.*

II. LITERATURE

Vedic Literature

We have already referred to the Four Vedas, the Brāhmaṇas and the Upaniṣads in many contexts, and have given extracts from them (pp. 236-58). In their literary aspect much of this literature is of high merit, especially some hymns of the *Ṛg Veda* and some parts of the early Upaniṣads; much, on the other hand, is dry and monotonous, or can only be appreciated after a considerable effort of the imagination.

The 1028 hymns of the *Ṛg Veda* are the work of many authors and show great

* For further information on the Indian alphabet see Appendix, p. 508ff.

variation of style and merit. Though their composition may have covered several centuries, even the earliest of these poems is the product of a long tradition, composed according to a strict metrical scheme* and a settled literary convention.

The collection is divided into ten "circles" (*maṇḍala*) or books. Of these, books ii to vii are ascribed to individual families of seers, and contain the earliest hymns; books i, viii, and x are later, especially parts of x, while the ninth book was compiled by extracting the hymns to the god Soma from the other parts of the *Ṛg Veda*. The hymns contain many repetitions and the majority have a general sameness of outlook. Owing to their archaic language and the obscurity of their allusions many passages are not fully understood. The reader will already have obtained some idea of the style of the *Ṛg Veda*, as far as it can be conveyed in fairly literal translation, from the passages we have quoted. We add here a few further translations of hymns of special literary merit.

Our first translation describes Indra's fight with the cloud-dragon Vṛtra. The hymn evidently refers to a well-known legend, which has since been forgotten, but which was probably a variant of the creation myth of Mesopotamia, in which the god Marduk slays the demon of chaos, Tiamat, and creates the universe. Here Indra's function as a rain-maker is also in evidence, and if the story was originally borrowed from Mesopotamia it had evidently developed far from its prototype. Interesting is the fleeting reference to Indra's fear, from which it would seem that his battle with the dragon did not go all his own way. The last verse is evidently an addition by another hand.

"Let me proclaim the valiant deeds of Indra,
the first he did, the wielder of the thunder,
when he slew the dragon and let loose the waters,
and pierced the bellies of the mountains.

"He slew the dragon lying on the mountain,
for Tvaṣṭṛ† made him a heavenly thunderbolt.
The waters suddenly, like bellowing cattle,
descended and flowed on, down to the ocean.

"In his strength he chose the soma—
from three cups he drank the essence.
The Generous seized his thunderbolt,
and smote the firstborn of dragons.

"When, Indra, you slew the firstborn of dragons,
and frustrated the arts of the sorcerers,
creating sun and heaven and dawn,
you found no enemy to withstand you.

---

* For notes on the prosody of ancient Indian poetry see Appendix, p. 510ff.

† The Vedic Vulcan.

"Indra slew Vṛtra, and Vyaṃsa, stronger than Vṛtra,
with his thunderbolt, with his mighty weapon.
Like the branches of a tree felled by the axe
the dragon lay strewn over the earth.

"Like an enraged coward he called a challenge
to the great hero, the strong's oppressor, charging.
But he did not escape the force of his blows—
the foe of Indra crushed the clouds together [in falling].

"Footless and handless, he still gave Indra battle,
until the thunderbolt struck him hard on his back.
The bullock sought to be match for the bull,
but Vṛtra lay, his members scattered afar.

"The waters, flowing for man's good, pass over him,
as he lies thus, broken like a reed.
Beneath the waters which he had encompassed
in his great might, Vṛtra the serpent lay.

"The strength of the mother of Vṛtra was exhausted,
and Indra bore away her weapon.
The mother lay above, the son below.
Dānu lay like a cow beside her calf.

"Fallen in the midst of water-courses,
never pausing, never resting,
floods overwhelm the hidden corpse of Vṛtra.
In a long darkness lay the foe of Indra.

"Lorded by Dāsas and guarded by the dragon
the waters lay, penned in as cows by a Paṇi.
When the opening of the waters was closed up
the slayer of Vṛtra threw it open.

"O Indra, you became a wreath of vapour*
when he impaled you on his lance. Alone
you won the cows, hero, you won the soma,
and you let loose the Seven Streams to flow.

"Thunder and lightning availed him nothing,
nor the mist he scattered abroad, nor hail.
When Indra and the dragon fought he conquered,
as he, the Generous, will in future conquer.

---

* Literally "a horse's tail", probably implying a wisp of cloud.

"And what avenger of the dragon did you see,
Indra, as fear entered your heart when you had killed him,
when you crossed over nine and ninety streams,
as a frightened hawk crosses the skies?

"Indra is king of all that moves or rests,
of tame and fierce, the wielder of the thunder.
He is the king of mortals, whom he rules,
encircling them as a wheel's rim the spokes."[7]

A number of hymns show deep feeling for nature, the most famous of these being the hymns to Uṣas, the goddess of dawn; but the hymns to Uṣas are perhaps less beautiful than the single hymn to Rātri, the personified night.

"The goddess Night has looked abroad
with her eyes, everywhere drawing near.
She has put all her glories on.

"The immortal goddess now has filled
wide space, its depths and heights.
Her radiance drives out the dark.

"Approaching, the goddess has expelled
her sister Dawn.
Now darkness also disappears.

"And so you have drawn near to us,
who at your coming have come home,
as birds to their nest upon the tree.

"The clans have now gone home to rest,
home the beasts, and home the birds,
home even the hawks who lust for prey.

"Guard us from the she-wolf and the wolf,
and guard us from the thief, O Night,
and so be good for us to pass.

"For darkness, blotting out, has come
near me, black and palpable.
O Dawn, dispel it like my debts.

"I have offered my hymn as a cow
is offered, Daughter of Heaven. O Night,
accept it, as a victor praise."[8]

Similarly sensitive to the moods of nature is the little hymn to Araṇyānī, the elusive spirit of the forest*

"Lady of the Forest! Lady of the Forest!
who seem to vanish from sight in the distance,
why do you never come to the village?
Surely you are not afraid of men!

"When the grasshopper replies
to the distant lowing of cattle,
as though to the sound of tinkling bells
the Lady of the Forest makes merry.

"Sometimes you catch a glimpse of her, and think it is cattle grazing,
or a house, far away,
and at evening you hear the Lady of the Forest
like the distant sound of moving wagons.

"Her voice is as the sound of a man calling his cattle,
or as the crash of a felled tree.
If you stay in the forest in the evening,
you will hear her like a far voice crying.

"But the Lady of the Forest will not slay
unless an enemy draws near.
She eats the sweet wild fruits,
and then she rests wherever she will.

"Now I have praised the Lady of the Forest,
who is perfumed with balm and fragrant,
who is well fed although she tills not,
the mother of all things of the wild."[9]

A few Vedic hymns are by our standards primarily secular. Of these the "Gamester's Lament" is the most famous. Probably the poem was originally a spell to ensure success in gaming, addressed to the *vibhīdaka* nuts themselves. This was converted by an anonymous poet into a cautionary poem, which obtained a place in the *Ṛg Veda* on account of its reference to the god Savitṛ as attempting to reform the gamester.

"The dangling nuts, born where the wind blows the lofty tree,
delight me with their rolling on the board.

* The exact meanings of several words and phrases of this hymn are quite uncertain. In translating I have given the sense which seems to me most probable, and filled out the elliptical Sanskrit to make the meaning clearer.

The cheering *vibhīdaka* has brought me joy,
    like a draught of soma from Mount Mūjavant.

"She did not scold me, or lose her temper.
    She was kind to my friends and me.
But because of a throw too high by one
    I have rejected my loving wife.

"Her mother hates me; my wife repels me—
    a man in trouble finds no one to pity him.
They say, 'I've no more use for a gambler
    than for a worn-out horse put up for sale.'

"When the conquering die has got his possessions
    others embrace the gamester's wife.
His father, his mother, his brothers say of him:
    'We don't know him! Take him as a bondman!'

"I think to myself: 'I won't go with the others!
    I'll stop behind when my friends go to play!'
But then the brown ones* raise their voices,
    and off I go, like a mistress to her lover.

"The gambler goes to the hall of assembly.
    'Shall I win?' he wonders. His body trembles.
The dice run counter to his hopes,
    and give his opponent the lucky throws.

"The dice are armed with hooks and piercing,
    they are deceptive, hot and burning.
Like children they give and take again, they strike back at their
    conquerors.
They are sweetened with honey through the magic they work on
    the gambler.

"They play in a troop of three times fifty.
    Like the god Savitṛ, they are true to their laws.
They will not bend to the wrath of the mighty,
    and even a king bows low before them.

"The dice roll down, the dice leap upwards,
    unarmed they withstand the man with arms.
They are heavenly coals, strewn over the board,
    and though they are cool they burn up the heart.

* I.e. the vibhīdaka nuts, loosely translated "dice". See p. 209f.

"The forsaken wife of the gambler sorrows,
  and the mother of the son who wanders afar.
In debt, in fear, in need of money,*
  he goes by night to the house of others.

"The gambler grieves when he sees a woman,
  another man's wife, in their pleasant home.
In the morning he yokes the chestnut horses.†
  In the evening he falls by the hearth, a beggar.

"So to the general of your great army,
  to him who is king, the chief of your host,
I say, stretching out to him my ten fingers:
  'I risk my all! I am speaking the truth!'

"'Don't play with dice, but plough your furrow!
  Delight in your property, prize it highly!
Look to your cattle and look to your wife,
  you gambler!' Thus noble Savitṛ tells me.

"So make friends with us, be kind to us!
  Do not force us with your fierce magic!
May your wrath and hatred now come to rest!
  May no man fall into the snares of the brown ones!"[10]

We need say little here of later Vedic literature. The *Atharva Veda*, in the main a monotonous collection of spells, contains a few poems of great merit. The prose Brāhmaṇas and the various recensions of the *Yajur Veda* are in general without any pretensions to literary qualities, though written in simple straightforward language, very different in style from Classical Sanskrit. Here and there legends are told in terse nervous prose, which gains in effectiveness from its austere economy. We give the story of Purūravas and Urvaśī, which is told in the *Śatapatha Brāhmaṇa* as part of the instructions for becoming a Gāndharva (p. 208) by means of a magical sacrifice. The story is as old as the *Ṛg Veda*, for one hymn[11] consists of a dialogue between the earthly lover and his heavenly mistress, and the verses quoted in the Brāhmaṇa version are taken from it. The story was very popular in later times, and was the subject of one of Kālidāsa's plays.

"The nymph Urvaśī loved Purūravas the son of Iḍā. When she married him she said: 'You must embrace me three times a day, but never lie with me against my will. Moreover I must never see you naked, for this is the proper way to behave to us women!'

* Literally "wealth". It is almost certain that there was no coined money in India at the time of this poem's composition (p. 191).

† I.e. gambles with the brown nuts.

"She lived with him long, and she was with child by him, so long did she live with him. Then the Gandharvas said to one another: 'This Urvaśī has been living too long among men! We must find a way to get her back!'

"She kept a ewe with two lambs tied to her bed, and the Gandharvas carried off one of the lambs. 'They're taking away my baby,' she cried, 'as though there were no warrior and no man in the place!' Then they took away the second, and she cried out in the same way.

"Then he thought to himself: 'How can the place where I am be without a warrior and a man?' And, naked as he was, he leapt up after them, for he thought it would take too long to put on a garment.

"Then the Gandharvas produced a flash of lightning, and she saw him as clearly as if it were day—and she vanished....

"Bitterly weeping, he wandered all over Kurukṣetra. There is a lake of lotuses there, called Anyataḥplakṣā. He walked on its banks, and there were nymphs swimming in it in the form of swans.

"And she noticed him, and said: 'That's the man with whom I lived!'

'Let us show ourselves to him,' they said. 'Very well' she replied, and they appeared to him [in their true forms].

"Then he recognized her and entreated her:
'O my wife, with mind so cruel,
stay, let us talk together,
for if our secrets are untold
we shall have no joy in days to come!'...

"Then she replied:
'What use is there in my talking to you!
I have passed like the first of dawns.
Purūravas, go home again!
I am like the wind, that cannot be caught."...

"Mournfully Purūravas said:
'Today your lover will perish,
he will go to the furthest distance and never come back.
He will lie in the lap of disaster,
and fierce wolves will devour him.

"She replied:
'Purūravas do not die! do not go away!
do not let the fierce wolves devour you!
Friendship is not to be found in women,
For they have hearts like half-tamed jackals!'

"And then she said to him:
'When I dwelt in disguise in the land of mortals
and passed the nights of four autumns,

I ate a little ghee once a day,
and now I have had quite enough!'...

"But her heart pitied him, and she said: 'Come on the last evening of the year, then, when your son is born, you shall lie one night with me.'

"He came on the last night of the year, and there stood a golden palace. They told him to enter, and brought her to him.

"She said: 'Tomorrow the Gandharvas will grant you a boon and you must make your choice'. He said: 'You choose for me!' She answered: 'Say, "Let me become one of you!"'

"In the morning the Gandharvas gave him a boon, and he asked: 'Let me become one of you'.

"'There is no fire among men,' they said, 'which is so holy that a man may become one of us by sacrificing with it.' So they put fire in a pan, and said: 'By sacrificing with this you will become one of us.'

"He took it and his son, and went homeward. On the way he left the fire in the forest and went to a village with the boy. When he came back the fire had vanished. In place of the fire was a pipal tree and in place of the pan a mimosa. So he went back to the Gandharvas.

"They said: 'For a year you must cook rice enough for four [every day]. Each time [you cook] you must put on the fire three logs of the pipal anointed with ghee ... and the fire which is produced [at the end of the year] will be the fire [which will make you one of us]. But that is rather difficult,' they added, 'so you should make an upper firestick of pipal wood and a lower one of mimosa wood, and the fire you get from them will be the fire [which will make you one of us]. But that too is rather difficult,' they added, 'so you must make both the upper and lower firestick of pipal wood, and the fire you get from them will be the fire.'

"So he made an upper and a lower firestick of pipal wood, and the fire he got from them was the fire [which would make him one of them]. He sacrificed with it and became a Gandharva."[12]

The Upaniṣads rank high as literature, but their chief importance is religious and they have been sufficiently treated and quoted in that setting.

Epic Literature

The earliest Indian literature of a fundamentally secular character is found in the two great epics, the *Mahābhārata* and the *Rāmāyaṇa*, which, though worked over by a succession of priestly editors, give clear evidence of their origin as martial legends. Their religious importance lay at first in the royal sacrificial ritual, part of which involved telling stories of the heroes of the past. This put the martial ballads into the hands of the priesthood, who, in transmitting them, often altered their superficial character, and interpolated many long passages on theology, morals and statecraft.

Of the two epics the *Mahābhārata* is the more important. It contains over 90,000 stanzas, most of them of thirty-two syllables, and is therefore probably the longest single poem in the world's literature. Traditionally the author of the poem was the sage Vyāsa, who is said to have taught it to his pupil Vaiśampāyana. The latter, according to tradition, recited it in public for the first time at a great sacrifice held by King Janamejaya, the great grandson of Arjuna, one of the heroes of the story. Stripped of its episodes and interpolations the poem tells of the great civil war in the kingdom of the Kurus, in the region about the modern Delhi, then known as Kurukṣetra.

> The throne of the Kurus, whose capital was Hastināpura, fell to Dhṛtarāṣṭra. But he was blind and therefore, according to custom, was not eligible to rule, so his younger brother Pāṇḍu became king. Soon Pāṇḍu, as a result of a curse, gave up the kingdom and retired to the Himālayas as a hermit with his two wives, leaving Dhṛtarāṣṭra on the throne. When Pāndu died his five sons, Yudhiṣṭhira, Bhīma, Arjuna, Nakula and Sahadeva, were still children, and were taken back to Hastināpura to be educated with the hundred sons of Dhṛtarāṣṭra. When he came of age Yudhiṣṭhira was consecrated heir-apparent. But the sons of Dhṛtarāṣṭra, led by the eldest, Duryodhana, resented the Pāṇḍavas, and plotted against them, though Duryodhana was not legally heir to the throne, owing to his father's blindness and the stop-gap nature of his rule. After foiling a number of plots against their lives the five brothers decided to leave the country, and travelled from one court to another as soldiers of fortune. At the court of the king of the Pañcālas Arjuna won the Princess Draupadī in a *svayaṃvara*, and, to avoid strife, she became the joint wife of all five brothers. Here they met their great friend and helper, Kṛṣṇa, the chief of the Yādavas. Soon after this the blind Dhṛtarāṣṭra recalled them, renounced the throne, and divided the kingdom between them and his own sons. The five brothers built a new capital at Indraprastha, not far from the modern Delhi.
>
> But the sons of Dhṛtarāṣṭra were not content with this settlement. Duryodhana invited Yudhiṣṭhira to a great gambling match. With the aid of his uncle Śakuni, who knew all the secrets of the dice, he won from Yudhiṣṭhira his whole kingdom, including his brothers and their joint wife. A compromise was arranged, whereby the five brothers and Draupadī agreed to go into banishment for thirteen years, spending the last year incognito, after which they were to receive back their kingdom.
>
> At the end of the thirteenth year they declared themselves, and sent to Duryodhana demanding their kingdom according to his promise; but he returned no reply. So the brothers prepared for war. They had many friends among the kings of India, and were able to gather a great army together. Meanwhile the Kauravas (Duryodhana and his brothers) marshalled their own forces. The kings of all India, and even the Greeks, Bactrians and Chinese, took sides with one or other faction, and two enormous armies assembled on the plain of Kuruksetra.

For eighteen days the battle raged, until at last no important chief was left alive but the five brothers and Kṛṣṇa. Yudhiṣṭhira was crowned king and for many years he and his brothers ruled peacefully and gloriously. At last Yudhiṣṭhira renounced the throne and installed Parikṣit, the grandson of Arjuna, in his place. With their joint wife the five brothers set out on foot for the Himālayas, where they climbed Mount Mera, and entered the City of the Gods.

If we ignore interpolations the style of the *Mahābhārata* is direct and vivid, though it contains many often repeated clichés and stock epithets, which are typical of traditional epic literature everywhere. The chief characters are delineated in very simple outline, but with an individuality which makes them real persons. The blind Dhṛtarāṣṭra is a weakling, anxious to do the right thing, but easily persuaded to evil. Of the five brothers the eldest, Yudhiṣṭhira, is pious, righteous and gentle, but a little negative in character; Arjuna is the ideal knight, noble, generous and brave; while Bhīma is a rougher character, gluttonous and immensely strong, but not very intelligent, and completely lacking in guile. Draupadī, their wife, is a woman of spirit, who is not afraid to upbraid her five husbands on occasion. The villain Duryodhana and his associates are not painted in the blackest of colours, but have elements of nobility and courage in their characters.

Some of the interpolated episodes are of much merit, while others are of no literary value. The longest is the *Śānti Parvan*, a dissertation on statecraft and ethics, recited by Bhīṣma, the elder statesman of the Kurus, as he lies dying on a pile of arrows after the great battle (p. 70). This has been treated elsewhere and has little merit as literature. The *Bhagavad Gītā*, the sermon of Kṛṣṇa to Arjuna before the great battle, has already been quoted (pp. 264f, 264f). There are many other theological and ethical passages, as well as many narrative episodes. Some of the latter tell legends of the gods, but others are more or less secular, including the famous stories of Rāma and Sītā (p. 364f), Śakuntalā (p. 387ff), and Sāvitrī (p. 156). The longest narrative episode is the story of Nala and Damayantī, told to Yudhiṣṭhira during his exile to convince him of the evils of gambling. It tells how King Nala won Princess Damayantī at a svayaṃvara, at which she chose him in preference to the gods themselves, and then lost his queen and his kingdom at a gambling tournament, to regain them both after many exciting adventures. This long story is probably as ancient as the main part of the epic, and is told in very simple verse. As a brief example of the *Mahābhārata's* narrative style we give the description of Damayantī's choice. Among the suitors at the svayaṃvara are four great gods, who, knowing that she is determined to choose Nala, have all taken his appearance, in the hope that she will choose one of them by mistake.

"Then, when the right time had come,
  at the auspicious day and hour,
King Bhīma invited
  the lords of earth to the bride-choice.

"When they heard, the lords of earth,
all sick at heart with love,
in haste assembled,
desiring Damayantī.

"Like great lions the kings entered
the hall, firmly founded,
with its splendid porch
and shining golden columns.

"There on their several thrones
the lords of earth sat down
all decked in fragrant garlands,
with bright gems in their ears.

"Their arms were thick
as iron bars,
shapely and smooth
as five-headed snakes.

"With lovely shining locks,
and well-formed noses, eyes and brows,
the faces of the kings were bright
as the stars in heaven.

"Then fair-faced Damayantī
entered the hall,
stealing with her splendour
the eyes and thoughts of the kings.

"When the glance of the noble
spectators fell on her limbs
there it was fixed,
and never wavered.

"Then, while the names of the kings
were being proclaimed,
the daughter of Bhīma saw
five men of the same form.

. . . .

"Whichever of them she looked at
she recognized as Nala.
Wondering in her mind,
the fair one was filled with doubt.

"'Of all the signs of godhead
that I learned from the elders

I see not even one
in those who are standing here.'

"Thus thinking over and over,
and pondering again and again,
she resolved that the time had come
to take refuge in the gods.

"'I heard from the mouth of the swans
that Nala had chosen me as his bride,
and so, if that be true,
may the gods show him to me!

"'Never in word or deed
have I committed sin,
and so, if that be true,
may the gods show him to me!

"'The gods have ordained
the king of Niṣadha to be my lord,
and so, if that be trae,
may the gods show him to me!'

. . . .

"'May the great gods, the world-protectors
take on their own true form,
that I may recognize
the king of men, of good fame!'

"When they heard Damayantī,
mournful and piteous
they did as she had asked,
and put on their true forms.

"She saw the four gods
sweatless, not blinking their eyelids,
their garlands fresh and free from dust,
not touching the ground with their feet.

"But the king of Niṣadha had a shadow,
his garlands were faded,
his body bore dust and sweat,
and he blinked his eyelids.

"The modest long-eyed girl
seized the hem of his garment,
and on his shoulder she placed
the loveliest of garlands.

"She chose him for her lord,
she of the fair complexion,
and suddenly all the kings
together shouted and cheered.

"And all the gods and sages
thereupon cried bravo,
and shouted at the wonder,
praising Nala the king."[13]

The second epic, the *Rāmāyaṇa*, is rather different from the *Mahābhārata* in style and content. It is little more than a quarter of the size of the other epic, and of its seven books the first and the last are certainly later additions. The poem, like the *Mahābhārata*, contains interpolations, but they are much briefer and are mostly didactic. The main body of the poem gives the impression of being the work of a single hand, that of a poet whose style was based on that of the other epic, but showed some kinship to that of classical Sanskrit poetry.

Though the *Rāmāyaṇa* does not contain so many archaic features as the *Mahābhārata*, and gives the general impression of being the later of the two, the *Mahābhārata* contains as an episode the story of Rāma, in a form which suggests that the editor of the final version of the *Mahābhārata* knew the *Rāmāyaṇa*. The *Mahābhārata* as it is at present is probably later than the *Rāmāyaṇa*, but its main narrative portions are appreciably earlier.

The traditional author of the *Rāmāyaṇa* was the sage Vālmīki, a contemporary of its hero. In fact the legend was perhaps committed to verse in the form in which we have it, but excluding the first and last books, a little before the commencement of the Christian era. The central scene of the poem is Ayodhyā, the capital of the old kingdom of Kosala, and it evidently grew up in a milieu to the east of that of the *Mahābhārata*.

Daśaratha king of Kosala had by his three wives four sons named Rāma, Bharata, Lakṣmaṇa and Śatrughna. The four attended the court of King Janaka of Videha, where Rāma won the hand of Janaka's daughter, Sītā, at a great archery contest. Rāma and Sītā were married and for a time lived happily at the court of Daśaratha. (In this part of the story, contained in the first book of the epic, Rāma is explicitly described as an incarnation of the god Viṣṇu, and the original text has evidently been much added to and altered at a late period.)

When Daśaratha grew old he named Rāma as his heir; but his second queen, Kaikeyī, reminded her lord of a boon which he had promised her long ago, and demanded its fulfilment in the banishment of Rama and the installation of her own son, Bharata, as heir apparent. Daśaratha and Bharata both demurred, but Rāma insisted on his father fulfilling his promise, and went into voluntary exile with Sita and his brother Lakṣmaṇa. When Daśaratha died Bharata took over the kingdom, but only as regent for the exiled Rāma.

Meanwhile Rāma, Sītā and Lakṣmaṇa dwelt as hermits in the forest of Daṇḍaka, where Rāma destroyed many demons who were harassing ascetics and villagers. Rāvaṇa, the demon king of Laṅkā (Ceylon), decided to avenge his fallen kinsmen, and, while Rāma and Lakṣmaṇa were on a hunting expedition, came to their hermitage in the guise of an ascetic, seized Sītā, and carried her off to Laṅkā in his aerial car (*vimāna*). The brothers sought far and wide for Sītā, and enlisted the help of Sugrīva, the king of the monkeys, and his general, the brave and loyal Hanumant. Hanumant went in search of Sītā, and, leaping over the straits, at last found her in Rāvaṇa's palace. With the aid of a great army of monkeys Rāma built a causeway of stones across the sea to Laṅkā. After a fierce battle Rāma, Lakṣmaṇa and their allies slew Rāvaṇa and his hosts, and rescued Sītā.

Sītā had been treated with respect by her captor, and had in no way yielded to his blandishments. But she had dwelt under the roof of another man, and Rāma, in accordance with the Sacred Law, could do nothing but repudiate her. She threw herself on a funeral pyre, but the fire-god Agni refused to accept her. After this proof of her innocence she was reunited with Rāma, and the two returned to Ayodhyā, where Bharata renounced the throne and Rāma was crowned, to rule long and righteously.

The last book, certainly later in composition, gives an unnecessary sequel to the story, which was probably added on account of growing prejudice on the part of the orthodox, and misgivings about Sītā's lawful status after her unwilling residence in her captor's house. The people murmured because their queen had been forced to break her marriage vows, and suspicions as to her purity were not allayed, even by her ordeal by fire. Though he was quite convinced of her innocence Rāma, whose first duty was to "please the people", was regretfully forced to banish her, and she took refuge in Vālmīki's hermitage, where she gave birth to twins, Kuśa and Lava. Years later Rāma found Sītā again, and acknowledged her sons. As final proof of her innocence she called on her mother, the Earth,* to swallow her up. The earth opened, and she disappeared. Soon after this Rāma returned to heaven, and resumed the form of the god Viṣṇu.†

The fact that the Theravāda Buddhists preserved in the Jātakas a version of the tale in which there is no mention of the abduction of Sītā and the war with the demons, the most exciting part of Vālmīki's story, suggests that the author conflated two separate traditions, the first that of the righteous prince who was wrongly banished and the second of the conquest of Ceylon. The story of Rāma's

* *Sītā* means "furrow", and the heroine of the epic has some of the attributes of an agricultural goddess. According to the story she was not the natural daughter of King Janaka, but sprang from his plough while he was working in the fields. This story evidently looks back to a time when the tribal chieftain was ready to lend a hand with the work of the tribe.

† This rather grim ending to the story did not satisfy some gentler spirits. Bhavabhūti's *Uttararāmacarita,* a drama of the 8th century, concludes with the full reconciliation of Rāma and Sītā.

adventures in exile has thus no historical basis whatever, even if we rationalize his monkey allies into aboriginal tribesmen with a monkey totem.

The style of the *Rāmāyaṇa* is less rugged than that of the *Mahābhārata*. The latter contains occasional grammatical and prosodical errors, the former few if any. It is a work of greater art, but less vigour, though it contains many dramatic passages, and beautiful descriptive writing, which the *Mahābhārata* lacks. We give a much abridged translation of the description of the death of Rāvaṇa, which is typical of the treatment of battle in both epics.

"Then Rāma, reminded
by the words of Mātali,
took his flaming arrow
like a hissing snake. ...

"He spoke a mantra upon it
as the Vedas ordain.
The strong one placed in his bow
that great and mighty arrow....

"Enraged he fiercely bent
his bow against Rāvaṇa,
and, intent on his mark, he shot
the entrail-tearing arrow. ...

"Bearing the death of the body
the arrow flew with great speed,
and tore through the heart
of the evil-working Rāvaṇa.

"Then, red with his blood and rapid,
that arrow, destroyer of bodies,
robbing the life-breath of Rāvaṇa,
drove into the face of the earth. ...

"Swiftly struck from his hand,
his bow and his arrow
dropped, with his life-breath,
upon the ground.

"Unbreathing, with awful speed,
the glorious lord of die demons
fell from his chariot to earth,
like Vṛtra struck by the thunderbolt*

"When they saw him fallen to earth
the remaining demons of night
in terror, their lord destroyed,
fled in every direction. ...

* See p. 402f above.

'Falling, struck down by the monkeys,
they fled to Laṅkā in terror,
their faces swimming in tears,
piteous at the loss of their refuge.

"And in joy the monkeys
roared a cheer of triumph
and proclaimed the victory of Rāma,
and his slaying of Rāvaṇa.

"In the sky there sounded
the lovely drums of the gods,
and there blew a pleasant wind
hearing a heavenly fragrance.

"A rain of flowers fell
from heaven upon earth,
flowers rare and lovely
bestrewing Rāma's chariot."[14]

The epic style and metre became usual for didactic literature of all kinds. Much of this, the Purāṇas, Dharma Śāstras, and other texts, has been referred to elsewhere. It contains passages of literary merit, but we must pass them over for the great body of courtly literature.

Classical Sanskrit Poetry

The earliest surviving Sanskrit poetry of the classical type is that of the Buddhist writer Aśvaghoṣa, who is believed to have lived at the end of the lst century A.D., and who composed a metrical life of the Buddha (*Buddhacarita*) in a comparatively simple classical style. The Girnar Inscription of Rudradāman, dated A.D. 150, is the earliest surviving example of courtly Sanskrit prose. Thus the courtly style is a comparatively late development in Indian literature, although it must have had a long period of evolution before the dates which we have mentioned.

On the whole classical Sanskrit literature has not been well received in the West. Though the works of Kālidāsa delighted Goethe, the literature taken as a whole has been called artificial, over-ornate, lacking in true feeling, or even an example of wasted and perverted ingenuity. Indians themselves are not always satisfied with it. Thus a modern authority writes: "As a result of the particular demand in the court atmosphere the natural spontaneity of the poet was at a discount. … Learning and adaptation to circumstances were given more importance than the pure flow of genius. … As a result Sanskrit poetry not only became artificial but followed a traditional scheme of description. … The magic of the Sanskrit language … also led the poets astray and led them to find their amusement in verbal sonorousness."[15]

This judgement, which the author later qualifies, is in part correct. It is, moreover, an indication of how deeply modern India has been affected by European aesthetic standards, judged by which much Indian classical literature is indeed artificial. It was written mainly for recitation or performance at court, or for comparatively small circles of litterati, all well versed in the rigid canons of the literary convention and highly appreciative of verbal ingenuity. In such circumstances it would be futile to expect the native wood-notes of a Clare or the natural mysticism of a Wordsworth. The poets lived in a comparatively static society, and their lives were controlled in detail by a body of social custom which was already ancient and which had the sanction of religion behind it. They were never in revolt against the social system, and Indian Shelleys and Swinburnes are lacking. Most of this literature was written by men well integrated in their society and with few of the complex psychological difficulties of the modern writer; hence the spiritual anguish of a Cowper, the heart-searchings of a Donne, and the social pessimism of an early T. S. Eliot, are almost entirely absent. Despite their reputation for pessimism in the West, Hindu thought and literature are fundamentally optimistic, and the tragic drama, or the story with an unhappy ending, was not looked on with favour.

The chief raw materials of the Indian poet were love, nature, panegyric, moralizing and story telling. Religious subjects, in the sense of legends of the gods, are common enough, but deep religious feeling is comparatively rare in courtly literature. A few poets, such as Bhaṛtrhari, wrote occasionally on religious themes with the intensity of deep faith, but for all its mythological trappings and polite invocations to deities classical Sanskrit poetry is predominantly secular. The gods, when they appear, usually have the character of enlarged human beings.

Love was passionately physical, and we have said something of the approach of the Indian poet to the subject in another chapter (p. 147ff). As in most European literature of ancient and medieval times, nature was usually treated in its relation to man, and rarely described for its own sake. The phenomena of the seasons, day and night, birds and beasts and flowers, were used to frame human emotions, or were personified as counterparts of the human subjects of the poet. But throughout the literature a deep love of nature is implicit, especially in Kālidāsa who, for this reason among others, has a higher reputation in the West than any other ancient Indian poet. Panegyrics, in praise of a king and his ancestors, are very numerous and form one of the chief sources of our historical knowledge. The element of moralizing is prominent in the writing of most poets. Kālidāsa was particularly fond of including generalizations of a sententious or moral nature in his verses, and this practice was recognized as one of the legitimate *alaṃkāras* ("adomments") of Sanskrit poetry. Gnomic verses, often of a dry worldly-wise humour, were very popular.

The technique of poetry was thoroughly studied and rules were laid down in numerous textbooks. The purpose of poetry is usually described as emotive; the emotion aroused, however, is not the pity and terror of Aristotle, but a calmer experience, an aesthetic sensation based on feeling lifted to such a plane that grief is no longer felt as grief, and love no longer as love—according to one definition "impersonalized and ineffable aesthetic enjoyment from which every trace of its component ... material is obliterated".[16] The basic *rasas* or "flavours" from which this aesthetic experience should arise are usually classified as eight—love, courage, loathing, anger, mirth, terror, pity and surprise. Theoretically every poem should contain one or more of these flavours.

An important element in Sanskrit poetic theory was *dhvani* ("reverberation"), the suggestion or incantation of words and phrases. Words have their denotations and their connotations, their primary meanings and their undertones, and it is with these latter that the poet has to do. By carefully choosing his words he can make them say far more than their bare meanings and induce a whole series of emotions by a single brief verse. Indian literary philosophers advanced far in this direction and produced theories on the psychology of poetic appreciation which, in broad outline, would not be inacceptable to many modern poets of the West.*

Perhaps the most important tool of the poet was *alaṃkāra*, or ornamentation, which included simile and metaphor, generalization, punning, alliteration of various kinds, and so on. This branch of poetic technique was also worked out in great detail by the theorists, and the free use of ornamentation resulted in poetry of great floridity. This was encouraged by the enormous number of synonyms and homonyms in Sanskrit, and by the very numerous and universally accepted stock epithets, such as "the mine of jewels" (*ratnākara*) for "the sea", "the unmoving" (*acala*) for "mountain", "sky-goer" (*khaga*) for "bird", and "the frail" (*abalā*) for "woman". The ancient Indian poet would have been quite at home with Pope's "denizens of air" and "finny tribes".

The unit of poetry is the stanza, usually grammatically complete in itself. The *mahākāvya*, loosely translated "epic", often degenerates into a string of verses or groups of verses, linked only by a very slender thread of narrative. In the more ornate courtly literature plot and construction are in general weak, and there is little sense of balance. This is not the case with purely narrative poetry, as in such works as the "Ocean of Story", the author of which tells his tales with economy and restraint (p. 382ff). And often, even in the most ornate *kāvya*, the poet will from time to time rise to the occasion with vivid and dramatic description, though it must be admitted that the longer Sanskrit poem is usually prolix and shapeless.

On the other hand the individual verse is balanced and succinct. Single-verse poems, reminiscent of the Persian *rubā'ī* or the Japanese *tanka*, were very popular, either standing alone or included in dramas and prose works. Many of these are very beautiful, and make an immediate appeal to the Western reader, even in translation. They were collected in anthologies, of which a number survive, preserving thousands of lovely verses which would otherwise have been lost.

Metrically Sanskrit poetry was quantitative and rigidly regulated. The normal stanza was one of four quarters, each of equal length varying from eight to twenty-one syllables, and generally unrhymed. The Epics usually employed the metre

---

* The most important and original literary theorists were Daṇḍin (p. 394ff) (*Kāvyādarśa,* 6th–7th century), Bhāmaha (*Kāvyālaṃkāra,* 7th century), Ānandavardhana (*Dhvanyāloka,* 9th century), Mammata (*Kāvyaprakāśa,* early 12th century), and Viśvanātha (*Sāhityadarpaṇa,* 14th century).

called *śloka*, of eight syllables to the quarter, and this allowed some scope for variation; but classical poets preferred more complex and rigid metres, of which many are listed in textbooks on poetics, though only a dozen or so were popular. These metres allowed little or no scope for variation and their syllables were arranged in complicated pattems, usually of great beauty.*

Owing to the structure of Sanskrit, literal translation of classical Indian poetry into English is quite impossible, and we cannot convey the aesthetic effect of a Sanskrit verse. The brief extracts here translated in rhythmic prose give but a faint impression of the rich and closely knit texture of the originals or of the wonderful sonority of the language, which, when well handled, with all the arts of prosody and ornamentation, surely has a splendour unsurpassed by any other language in the world. Classical Indian poetry, like Indian music and art, developed along lines of its own and its canons are not those of the West, but it has its own special merits and beauties.

Indian and European judges alike agree that Kālidāsa was the greatest Sanskrit poet. He probably flourished in the reigns of the emperors Candra Gupta II and Kumāra Gupta I (376-454), and thus saw ancient Indian courtly culture at its zenith. Like the murals of Ajantā, his work seems to reflect that culture completely and convincingly. Though deeply imbued in tradition, he carried tradition lightly, and in all his work his personality breaks through. A few legends are told of him in late sources, but we have no reliable information about his life and character. From his work he seems to have been a happy and gentle man, sympathetic to sorrow, deeply understanding the moods of women and children, and loving flowers and trees, beasts and birds, and the pomp of court ceremonial. He was the author of three dramas (p. 387), two long poems, "The Birth of the War-god "(*Kumārasambhava*) and the "Dynasty of Raghu" (*Raghuvaṃśa*), and two shorter, the "Cloud-messenger"(*Meghadūta*) and the "Garland of the Seasons" (*Ṛtusamhāra*), as well as of several other works which have not survived.

The "Cloud Messenger" is a work of little over 100 verses, which has always been one of the most popular of Sanskrit poems. Its theme has been imitated in one form or another by several later poets in both Sanskrit and the vernaculars. More than most Indian poems this work has unity and balance, and gives a sense of wholeness rarely found elsewhere. In its small compass Kālidāsa has crowded so many lovely images and word-pictures that the poem seems to contain the quintessence of a whole culture. It describes a yakṣa who dwells in the divine city of Alakā, in the Himālayas. He has offended his master Kubera (p. 276), and has been banished for a year to the hill of Rāmagiri, in the modern Madhya Pradesh. The worst aspect of his exile is his separation from his beautiful wife, whom he has left behind in the mountain city. So, at the beginning of the rainy season, he sees a large cloud passing northward to the mountains and pours out his heart to it. After a verse or two of introduction the rest of the poem consists of the yakṣa's address to the cloud.

* For further notes on Sanskrit prosody see Appendix, p. 510 ff.

First he tells it the route which it should take to reach the mountains; here Kāḷidāsa describes the lands, rivers and cities over which it must pass in very beautiful verses. We quote two describing the river Narmadā and the forests on its banks. Notable in the first verse is the bird's-eye-view implied in the simile.

"Stay for a while over the thickets, haunted by the girls of the hill-folk,
then press on with faster pace, having shed your load of water,
and you'll see the Narmadā river, scattered in torrents, by the rugged
rocks at the foot of the Vindhyas,
looking like the plastered pattern of stripes on the flank of an elephant.*

"Note by the banks the flowers of the *nīpa* trees, greenish brown, with
their stamens half developed,
and the plantains, displaying their new buds.
Smell the most fragrant earth of the burnt out woodlands,
and as you release your raindrops the deer will show you the way."[17]

Then the cloud is told to turn westwards and visit the splendid city of Ujjayinī. Kālidāsa cannot long resist the *śṛṅgāra rasa*, the erotic sentiment, and this is evoked by his description of the city,

"where the wind from the Śiprā river prolongs the shrill melodious cry of
the cranes,
fragrant at early dawn from the scent of the opening lotus,
and, like a lover, with flattering requests,
dispels the morning languor of women, and refreshes their limbs.

"Your body will grow fat with the smoke of incense from open windows
where women dress their hair.
You will be greeted by palace peacocks, dancing to welcome you,
their friend.
If your heart is weary from travel you may pass the night above mansions
fragrant with flowers,
whose pavements are marked with red dye from the feet of beautiful
girls."[18]

Then, as the cloud nears the Himālayas, it will see the magic city

---

* The second line of the original of this verse ("press on with faster pace, having shed your load of water") is skilfully alliterated on the consonant *t,* giving an impression of haste to the slow metre and suggesting the patter of raindrops:

Sthitvā tasmin vanacara-vadhū-bhukta-kuñje muhūrtaṃ,
toyotsarga-drutatara-gatis tatparaṃ vartma tīrṇaḥ,
Revāṃ drakṣyaṣy upala-viṣame Vindhya-pāde viśirṇāṃ,
bhakti-cchedair iva viracitāṃ bhūtim aṅge gajasya.

"where yakṣas dwell with lovely women in white mansions,
whose crystal terraces reflect the stars like flowers.
They drink the wine of love distilled from magic trees,
while drums beat softly, deeper than your thunder."[19]

Then the yakṣa describes his home and his beautiful wife, weak from sorrow and longing. He gives the cloud a message to her, that his love is still constant and that the time of reunion is approaching.

"I see your body in the sinuous creeper, your gaze in the startled eyes of deer,
your cheek in the moon, your hair in the plumage of peacocks,
and in the tiny ripples of the river I see your sidelong glances,
but alas, my dearest, nowhere do I find your whole likeness!"[20]

"The Birth of the War...god" may be described as a religious poem, but though all its characters are supematural, and include Śiva himself, the atmosphere of the poem is essentially secular. It begins with a fine description of the Himālayas, from which we quote a few verses. The daring comparison of the chain of mountains with a surveyor's measuring rod is worthy of John Donne, and gives another example of Kālidāsa's bird's-eye-view approach.

"In the northern quarter is divine Himālaya,
the lord of mountains,
reaching from Eastern to Western Ocean,
firm as a rod to measure the earth. ...

"There demigods rest in the shade of the clouds
which spread like a girdle below the peaks,
but when the rains disturb them
they fly to the sunlit summits. ...

"The hollow canes are filled with the wind
that bursts from the chasms,
as though to provide an ostinato
to the songs of heavenly minstrels. ...

"All through the night the phosphorescent herbs
shine in the caverns with their glimmering radiance,
and light the loves
of hill-women and their paramours. ...

"And the wind forever shaking the pines
carries the spray from the torrents of the young Gangā
and refreshes the hunting hillman,
blowing among his peacock plumes."[21]

The poem, which is a long one, describes the courtship and marriage of Śiva and Pārvatī (p. 271), and the birth of their son, Kumāra or Skanda, the war-god. As he grows to manhood Kumāra is appointed general of the gods, and he leads them forth to battle with the terrible demon Tāraka, who has long been afflicting the whole universe. Tāraka hears of their approach, musters his forces, and goes out to meet them; but terrible omens greet the army of demons. Here Kālidāsa embarks on a remarkable description, which reminds us of the more macabre work of Gustave Doré.

"A fearful flock of evil birds,
ready for the joy of eating the army of demons,
flew over the host of the gods,
and clouded the sun.

"A wind continually fluttered their umbrellas and banners,
and troubled their eyes with clouds of whirling dust,
so that the trembling horses and elephants
and the great chariots could not be seen.

"Suddenly monstrous serpents, as black as powdered soot,
scattering poison from their upraised heads,
frightful in form,
appeared in the army's path.

"The sun put on a ghastly robe
of great and terrible snakes, curling together,
as if to mark his joy
at the death of the enemy demon.

"And before the very disc of the sun
jackals bayed harshly together,
as though eager fiercely to lap the blood
of the king of the foes of the gods, fallen in battle.

"Lighting heaven from end to end,
with flames flashing all around,
with an awful crash, rending the heart with terror,
a thunderbolt fell from a cloudless sky.

"The sky poured down torrents of red-hot ashes,
with which were mixed blood and human bones,
till the flaming ends of heaven were filled with smoke
and bore the dull hue of the neck of an ass.

"Like the thundered threat of the angry death-god
a great crash broke the walls of the ears,
a shattering sound, tearing the tops of the mountains,
and wholly filling the belly of heaven.

"The host of the foe was jostled together.
The great elephants stumbled, the horses fell,
and all the footmen clung together in fear,
as the earth trembled and the ocean rose to shake the mountains.

"And before the host of the foes of the gods
dogs lifted their muzzles to gaze on the sun,
then, howling together with cries that rent the eardrums,
they wretchedly slunk away."[22]*

The poem ends with the death of Tāraka in single combat with Kumāra.

We have no space to discuss the rest of Kālidāsa's poetry, all of which is of fine quality. "The Dynasty of Raghu" especially contains many passages of great beauty, including a concise version of the story of Rāma, but the work is apparently incomplete. "The Garland of the Seasons" describes the six seasons of the Hindu year in relation to *śṛṅgāra*, the erotic sentiment, but though charming it is slighter and less impressive than the rest of Kālidāsa's work.

Many other poets after Kālidāsa wrote mahākāvyas, or long courtly "epics", but none so ably as he. Kumāradāsa's "Rape of Sītā" (*Jānakī-haraṇa*) continues his tradition, while Bhāravi's "Arjuna and the Kirāta" (*Kirātārjuniya*), describing an encounter of the hero Arjuna and the god Śiva, in the guise of a Kirāta or wild mountaineer, is somewhat more florid. Bhaṭṭi, of the 7th century, wrote a remarkable poem on the story of Rāma, usually known as "Bhaṭṭi's Poem" (*Bhaṭṭikāvya*), containing passages of real beauty, as an exercise to illustrate rules of grammar. Even more ingenious was the 7th-century poet Māgha, who wrote a long poem on an incident in the life of Kṛṣṇa, the "Slaying of Śiśupāla" (*Śiśupāla-vadha*). Though the work contains many fine stanzas the story is so badly told that the poem as a whole has no semblance of unity. In the nineteenth canto, which describes the battle between Kṛṣṇa and his enemy, Māgha thought fit to display his mastery of language by inserting many stanzas of amazing ingenuity. We give an example of an *ekākṣara* stanza, employing only one consonant throughout:

---

*The mastery of language in the last three stanzas quoted is so remarkable that it must impress even the reader who knows no Sanskrit. With brilliant use of assonance and alliteration Kālidāsa has wedded sound to sense in a way rarely achieved in the literature of the world.

Nirghāta-ghoṣo giri-śṛṅga-śātano
ghano 'mbarāśā-kuharodarambhariḥ
babhūva bhūmnā śruti-bhitti-bhedanaḥ,
prakopi-Kāl'-ārjita-garji-tarjanaḥ.

Skhalan-mahebhaṃ prapatat-turaṅgamam
parasparāśliṣṭa-janaṃ samantataḥ,
prakṣubhyad-ambhodhi-vibhinna-bhūdharād
balaṃ dviṣo 'bhūd avani-prakampāt.

Ūrdhvikṛtāsyā ravi-datta-dṛṣṭayaḥ
sametya sarve sura-vidviṣaḥ puraḥ,
śvānaḥ svareṇa śravaṇānta-śātinā
mitho rudantaḥ karuṇena niryayuḥ.

Dādado dudda-dud-dādī
dādādo duda-dī-da-doḥ
dud-dādam dadade dudde
*dad'-ādada-dado 'da-daḥ.**

This stanza, using very rare and obscure words and exceedingly elliptical, may be translated as follows:

"The giver of gifts, the giver of grief to his foes,
the bestower of purity, whose arm destroys the givers of grief,
the destroyer of demons, bestower of bounty on generous and miser alike,
raised his weapon against the foe."[23]

The following is a *dvyakṣara*, containing only two consonants:

Krūrāri-kārī kor eka-
kārakaḥ kārikā-karaḥ
korakākāra-karakaḥ
*karīraḥ karkaro 'rka-ruk.**

"The destroyer of cruel foes, the only creator of the world,
bestower of woes on the wicked, with hands like the buds of lotuses,
the overthrower of elephants,
fierce in battle, shone like the sun."[24]

The next stanza is called *sarvatobhadra* ("valid all ways"), and is a complicated mixture of syllabic palindrome and acrostic. Each quarter-stanza is a palindrome; the first four syllables of the first quarter are the same as the first syllables of each quarter, and in the same order; the first four syllables of the second quarter are the same as the second syllables of each quarter, and so on. This verse is positively startling in its ingenuity, and when read in the original produces an impression resembling that of complex polyphony.

Sakāra-nān'-āra-kāsa-
kāya-sāda-da-sāyakā
ras' -āhavā vāha-sāra-
nādavāda-da-vādanā.

"His army was eager for battle,
whose arrows destroyed the bodies of the varied hosts of his brave enemies.
Its trumpets vied with the cries
of the splendid horses and elephants."[25]

* In these verses the breathing at the end of a word, known as visarga and indicated by ḥ, is not counted as a full consonant

Finally a stanza called *gatapratyāgatam* ("gone and come back") It is a perfect syllabic palindrome.

Taṃ Śriyā ghanayā 'nasta-
rucā sāratayā tayā
yātayā tarasā cāru-
stanayā 'naghay' āśritam.

"He who was eagerly and close embraced
by the fair-bosomed Śrī, the sinless goddess,
of never-failing beauty, and endowed
with every excellence."[26]

After Māgha longer poems were often mere displays of verbal ingenuity. The narrative became progressively less important, and the style progressively more ornate, though there were important exceptions. The climax of the tendency came with the *dvyāirayakāvya*, telling two stories simultaneously by deliberately utilizing the ambiguity of words and phrases. A well-known example of this genre is the *Rāmacarita* ("Deeds of Rāma") of the 12th-century poet Sandhyākara, which may be read as applying either to the legendary Rāma of Ayodhyā or to the historical king Rāmapāla of Bengal, who was the poet's contemporary and patron. Achievements like this are not to be disparaged, but they make little appeal to the modern reader and are quite untranslatable.

The best things in medieval poetry are to be found in the single-stanza poems, of which there are many collections, either by one or many hands. The finest poet in this genre was Bhartṛhari, thought to have lived in the 7th century, who left no long poems, but only three centuries of separate stanzas on the subjects of worldly wisdom, love and renunciation respectively. These are masterpieces of concise expression, and, unlike most Sanskrit poems, tell us much about the personality of the author. We quote first two stanzas in an amusingly sententious vein.

"You may boldly take a gem from the jaws of a crocodile,
you may swim the ocean with its tossing wreath of waves,
you may wear an angry serpent like a flower in your hair,
but you'll never satisfy a fool who's set in his opinions!

"You *may*, if you squeeze hard enough, even get oil from sand,
thirsty, you *may* succeed in drinking the waters of the mirage,
perhaps, if you go far enough, you'll find a rabbit's horn,
but you'll never satisfy a fool who's set in his opinions!"[27]

In his erotic verses Bhartṛhari often shows an undercurrent of dissatisfaction, as though trying to convince himself that love is not a futile waste of time after all. In the midst of his amours he feels the call of the religious life, and in one remarkable stanza he indulges in striking punning to this effect. The obvious meaning is:

> "Your hair well combed, your eyes reaching to your ears,*
> your mouth filled with ranks of teeth that are white by nature,
> your breasts charmingly adorned with a necklace of pearls,
> slim girl, your body, though at rest, disturbs me."

But this might also be fancifully translated as:

> "Your hair self-denying, your eyes understanding the whole of scripture
> your mouth full of groups of naturally-pure brāhmaṇs,
> your breasts lovely from the presence of emancipated souls,
> slim girl, your body, though free from passion, disturbs me."[28]

This is the sort of thing which most critics of Sanskrit poetry object to; but Bhartṛhari might justify his punning here, for by employing words with religious connotations he has given expression to his own divided mind. This is very forcibly expressed in another stanza, which we quote. "The forest" implies the life of the hermit.

> "What is the use of many idle speeches!
> Only two things are worth a man's attention—
> the youth of full-breasted women, prone to fresh pleasures,
> and the forest."[29]

It would seem that in the end Bhartṛhari gave up the love of women for the love of God, though the word which we here translate "God" is the impersonal Brāhmaṇ (p. 219).

> "When I was ignorant in the dark night of passion
> I thought the world completely made of women,
> but now my eyes are cleansed with the salve of wisdom,
> and my clear vision sees only God in everything."[30]

Bhartṛhari's religious experience was intense enough to produce the following splendid pæan, in which he addresses the five elements of Hindu physics.

> "Oh Earth, my mother, Air, my father, Oh Fire, my friend,
> Water, my kinsman, Space, my brother,
> here do I bow before you with folded hands!
> With your aid I have done good deeds and found clear knowledge,
> and, glorious, with all delusion past, I merge in highest godhead."[31]

* This is one of the conventions of poetry. The eyes of a pretty girl are so long that their corners almost touch her ears.

An erotic poet with none of Bhartṛhari's doubts was Amaru, also probably of the 7th century. His stanzas on love are often voluptuous, but they can be humorously tender, and always show a sound understanding of feminine psychology. Amaru loved to describe a poignant moment in a human relationship in a single verse, in which the reader is given only the climax of the story, the reconstruction of the rest being left to his imagination.

"I'll see what comes of it, 'I thought, and hardened my heart against her.
'What, won't the villain speak to me?' she thought, flying into a rage.
And there we stood, sedulously refusing to look one another in the face,
until at last I managed an unconvincing laugh, and her tears robbed
me of my resolution."

. . . .

"'Why are your limbs so weak, and why do you tremble?
And why, my dear,' asked her lord, 'is your cheek so pale?'
The slender girl replied, 'It's just my nature!'
and turned away and sighed, and let loose the tears that burdened
her eyelids."

. . . .

"'Fool that I was, why didn't I clasp the lord of my life to my neck?
Why did I turn my face away when he wanted to kiss me?
Why did I not see? Why did I not speak?' So, when love is first
awakened,
a girl is filled with remorse as she thinks of her childish shyness."[32]

We cannot devote much more space to the many brief poems of the Middle Ages, which are so full of charm and skill, and which need a competent translator to introduce them to the West. In passing, however, we would quote two stanzas contained in the prose work called "The Deeds of Harṣa", by the 7th-century writer Bāṇa (p. 397ff), which are sung by a bard at dawn to rouse his companions. In our opinion these neglected verses are among the finest in Indian literature. Ostensibly they describe a great stallion waking from sleep, but it may be that the poet remembered the cosmic symbolism of the horse in Vedic times (p. 217), and intended to speak of the universal in terms of the particular. Baṇa has evidently carefully studied his subject, which he describes almost anatomically, in words which have few overtones of meaning; but he succeeds in conveying his own deep delight in the horse by subtle alliterative effects, by the heavy metre, which he handles with masterly skill, and by the implicit contrast of the tiny piece of chaff in the last line.

"He stretches his hind-leg, and, bending his spine, extends his body upwards.
Curving his neck, he rests his muzzle on his chest, and tosses his dust-grey mane.
The steed, his nostrils ceaselessly quivering with desire of fodder,
rises from his bed, gently whinnies, and paws the earth with his hoof.

"He bends his back and turns his neck sideways, till his face touches his buttock,
and then the horse, the curls matted about his ears,
rubs with his hoof the red corner of his eye, itching from sleep,
his eye, struck by his dewdrop-scattering mane, waving and tossing,
his eye, to the point of whose quivering eyelash there clings a tiny fragment of chaff."[33]*

Before leaving this style of poetry we should mention the Kashmīrī Bilhaṇa, of the 11th and 12th centuries, whose "Fifty Stanzas of the Thief" (*Caurapañcāśikā*), purporting to describe the secret love of a bold housebreaker and a princess, are full of intense emotion recollected without tranquillity. Each begins with the words "Even today".

"Even today I can see her, her slender arms encircling my neck,
my breast held tight against her two breasts,
her playful eyes half-closed in ecstasy,
her dear face drinking mine in a kiss.

"Even today, if this evening
I might see my beloved, with eyes like the eyes of a fawn,
with the bowls of her breasts the colour of milk,
I'd leave the joys of kingship and heaven and final bliss."[34]

In a class of its own is Jayadeva's "Songs of the Cowherd" (*Gīta Govinda*), written in Bengal in the 12th century. This is a series of dramatic lyrics intended for singing, and describes the love of Kṛṣṇa for Rādhā and the milkmaids (p. 267).

---

* We quote the Sanskrit, in the hope that some of Bāṇa's wonderful sound effects, which seem so well to fit the sense of his verses, may be recognized.

Paścād aṅghrim prasārya, trika-nati-vitataṃ, drāghayitvāṅgam uccair,
āsajyābhugna-kaṇṭho mukham urasi, saṭā dhūli-dhūmrā vidhūya,
ghāsa-grāsābhilāṣād anavarata-calat-protha-tuṇḍas turaṅgo.
mandaṃ śabdāyamāno, vilikhati, śayanād utthilaḥ, kṣmāṃ khurena.

Kurvann ābhugna-pṛṣṭho mukha-nikaṭa-kaṭiḥ kandharām ā tiraścim
lolenāhanyamānaṃ tuhiṇa-kana-mucā cañcata kesareṇa
nidrā-kaṇḍū-kaṣāyaṃ kaṣati, niviḍita-śrotra-śuktis, turaṅgas
tvaṅgat-pakṣmāgra-lagna-pratanu-busa-kaṇam koṇaṃ akṣṇaḥ khureṇa.

The poem is still sung at the festivals of the Bengali Vaiṣṇavite sects, but though it begins with a beautiful invocation to the ten incarnations of Viṣṇu its inspiration to the Western mind seems rather erotic than religious. Unlike almost all other classical Sanskrit poetry Jayadeva's lyrics are rhymed, and look forward to the verse forms of vernacular literature. Each commences with an introductory stanza in one of the more usual Sanskrit metres, and the final stanza of each introduces the poet's name. The verses which we translate describe Kṛṣṇa's longings when separated from his beloved Rādhā. "The foe of Madhu" (a demon killed by Kṛṣṇa) and "Hari" are epithets of the god.

"'Here I am dwelling. Go now to Rādhā,
  console her with my message, and bring her to me.'
Thus the foe of Madhu commissioned her friend,
  who went in person, and spoke to Rādhā thus:

"'When the breeze blows from the Southern Mountains,
  and brings the Love-god with it,
when masses of flowers burst forth
  to rend the hearts of parted lovers,
he is grieved at separation from you, decked with his forest garland.

"'Even the cool-rayed moon inflames him,
  he is as if dead.
Struck by the arrows of love
  he complains most wretchedly
He is grieved …

"'When the swarming bees are murmuring
  he closes fast his ears.
His heart is clenched by parting,
  he spends his nights in fever.
He is grieved.…

"'He dwells in the depths of the forest,
  he has left his lovely home.
He tosses in sleep on the earth
  and much he murmurs your name.
He is grieved.…'

"When the poet Jayadeva sings,
  through this pious description
of the deeds of the parted lover,
  may Hari arise in hearts full of zeal.

He is grieved at separation from you, decked with his forest
garland."[35]*

Narrative Poetry

As well as various smaller collections there exists in various recensions a large series of popular stories, the *Bṛhatkathā* ("Great Story"), boxed one within the other in the manner of "The Thousand and One Nights". The most famous of these versions is Somadeva's "Ocean of Story" (*Kathā-sarit-sāgara*), written in the 11th century in easy but polished verse. The stories are told with comparative simplicity and directness, and with many touches of humour and pathos. We quote from the tale of the thief and the merchant's daughter. A wealthy merchant, Ratnadatta, has no sons, and his only daughter Ratnāvatī, much loved and pampered by her father, refuses to marry despite the pleading of her parents. Meanwhile a desperate thief has been captured by the king, and is led through the streets to execution by impalement.

"To the beat of the drum the thief was led
to the place of execution,
and the merchant's daughter Ratnāvatī
sat on the terrace and watched him.
He was gravely wounded and covered with dust,
but as soon as she saw him she was smitten with love.
"Then she went to her father Ratnadatta, and said:
'This man they are leading to his death
I have chosen for my lord!
Father, you must save him from the king,
or I will die with him!'
And when he heard, her father said:
'What is this you say, my child?
You've refused the finest suitors,
the images of the Love-god!
How can you now desire
a wretched master-thief? '
"But though he reproached her thus
she was firm in her resolve,

* The rhyme scheme varies from lyric to lyric. Here the second and fourth quarters end with a rhyme of two syllables, while the first and third quarters of each stanza end with the same syllable. The first and third quarters end in *e* throughout the poem. The refrain applies equally to the love of Kṛṣṇa for Rādhā and the love of God for the soul. We quote the last verse so that the reader may have some idea of the mellifluousness of the original:

Bhaṇati kavi-Jayadeve
virahi-vilasitena
manosi rabhasa-vibhave
Harir udayatu sukṛtena.
Yava virahe vanamālī sakhi sīdati.

so he sped to the king and begged
    that the thief might be saved from the stake.
In return he offered
    the whole of his great fortune,
but the king would not yield the thief
    for ten million pieces of gold,
for he had robbed the whole city,
    and was brought to the stake to repay with his life.
"Her father came home in despair,
    and the merchant's daughter
determined to follow
    the thief in his death.
Though her family tried to restrain her
    she bathed,
and mounted a litter, and went
    to the place of impalement,
while her father, her mother and her people
    followed her weeping.
"The executioners placed
    the thief on the stake,
and, as his life ebbed away,
    he saw her come with her people.
He heard the onlookers speaking
    of all that had happened,
For a moment he wept, and then,
    smiling a little, he died.
At her order they lifted the corpse
    from the stake, and took it away,
and with it the worthy merchant's daughter
    mounted the pyre."[36]*

The modern European reader would find this a conclusive ending to a tale of old, unhappy far-off things; but to the Indian of medieval times such an ending would have been quite unsatisfactory, so a *deus ex machina* was brought in in the form of the god Śiva, who was so impressed by the girl's love and faithfulness that he restored the corpse of the dead thief to life. He reformed his ways and became the king's general, and the two were married and lived happily ever after.

In the category of narrative poems we must include Kalhaṇa's great chronicle of Kashmīr "The River of Kings" (p. 39), and several other medieval works of comparatively small literary value. Midway between the purely narrative poem

* Stories such as this puzzle the social historian. If the texts on the Sacred Law have any relation to real life it is quite incredible that a girl of good class in the 11th century should have been given such freedom by her parents, or should even have thought of legally marrying a despised outcaste. The story probably looks back to a far earlier time, when social relations were very much freer.

and the courtly "epic" are a number of historical works partly descriptive, partly panegyric, and partly sober history. The most famous of these is "The Deeds of Harsa", by Bāṇa, written in ornate poetic prose, which is discussed below (p. 398ff). Of some literary merit is "The Deeds of Vikramāṅka" (*Vikramāṅkadevacarita*) of Bilhaṇa (p. 380), dealing with the life and adventures of the great Cālukya emperor Vikramāditya VI (c. 1075–1125). Another example of this type is the *Rāmacarita*, already mentioned. Yet another is the work of a Jaina monk, Nayacandra Suri, the *Hammīra-mahākāvya*, which is among the latest important works of Sanskrit literature. This beautiful but little known poem deals with the life of Hammīra, the last of the dynasty of the Cāhamānas, who was defeated and killed by the Delhi sultan 'Alā-ud-dīn Khaljī in 1301, after a long siege of his capital Raṇasthambhapura (now known as Ranthambhor). As Hammīra was slain with all his followers the poet was forced by his theme somewhat to flout convention, but he managed to retain a semblance of the happy ending demanded by tradition by concluding his work with a description of the entry of Hammīra and his followers into heaven. Much of the poem, though not without beauty, is irrelevant to the main theme, but the description of the king's last days is direct and forceful.

Towards the end of the poem Nayacandra introduces a remarkable episode. We cannot say whether he consciously intended the beautiful dancer, who died so tragically, as a symbol of the courtly culture which fell to the invader, but it is thus that the passage, occurring so portentously just before Hammīra's death, strikes the reader. In the course of the siege a temporary truce has been arranged, and the Rājputs are making the most of it. On the battlements a musical entertainment is taking place, and Hammīra's favourite dancer, Rādhādevī, is performing for the king and his courtiers. A long bowshot away, on the other side of the moat, sits the sultan, also watching the dance with interest. He is referred to in the poem as the Lord of the Śakas, a term by now applied to all the invaders of the North-West. The first part of our extract is exceedingly florid, and full of untranslatable puns, but the style suddenly becomes simple and terse when the episode moves to its climax.

> "In time the drummers beat their drums, the lutanists plucked their lutes,
> the flautists blew their flutes.
> Their voices in tune with the shrill flutes, the singers
> sang the glory and fame of the brave Hammīra. ...
> Then, the vine of her body entrancing her lovers,
> awakening passion with the glance of her half-closed eyes,
> to delight the hearts of the courtiers,
> came Rādhādevī the dancer, arrayed for the dance.
>
> "The quivering buds of her fingers moved in the dance
> like tendrils of a vine, thrilling with passion. ...
> As the tips of her fingers bent, as though in a circle,

with her grace and delicate beauty all other girls seemed her slaves.
The moon, in the guise of the ring that trembled from the tip of her ear,
said: 'Your face is my likeness, the delusion even of sages!'
And as she danced she stirred the hearts of the young men watching—
the hearts which lay like motes of camphor under her feet. ...
With her gestures the necklace trembled on the tips of her breasts
like a lotus twined in the beak of a swan.
When her body bent back like a bow in the dance
like a bowstring the braid of her hair stretched down to her heel. ...

"And as she danced, at every beat of the rhythm,
she turned her back on the Śaka king below.

"Then in fury of soul the Lord of the Śakas spoke to his chamberlain:
'Is there any bowman who can make her his mark?'
His brother said: 'Sire, there is he whom you formerly threw into prison,
Uḍḍānasiṃha—he is the only man who can do it!'
At once the Śaka king had him brought, and struck off his fetters,
and arrayed the traitor finely, with double gift of affection.
And thus apparelled he took the bow which none but he could draw,
and the sinner shot her, as a hunter shoots a doe.

"At the stroke of the arrow she fainted and fell in the moat,
as lightning falls from heaven."[37]*

The Drama

The origin of the Indian theatre is still obscure. It is certain, however, that even in the Vedic period dramatic performances of some kind were given, and passing references in early sources point to the enaction at festivals of religious legends, perhaps only in dance and mime. Some writers have found elements in common between the Indian and the classical Greek theatre. The curtain at the back of the stage was called *yavanikā*, a diminutive form of the name by which the Greeks were generally known in India. One play at least, "The Little Clay Cart" (p. 393), has a superficial resemblance to the late Greek comedy of the school of Menander. We cannot wholly reject the possibility that Greek comedies, acted at the courts of the Greco-Bactrian kings of N.-W. India, inspired unknown Indian poets to develop their own popular stage into a courtly art form.

The surviving Sanskrit dramas are numerous and varied, ranging from short one-act playlets to very long plays in ten acts. They were normally performed by troupes of professionals of both sexes, but amateur dramatics were not wholly unknown, since we have occasional references to kings and the ladies of the harem performing dramas in the palace. There was no regular theatre, though

* The simile is not unduly exaggerated, as the dancer was covered with jewellery which glittered in the sunlight.

it has been suggested that one of the caves of Rāmgarh (p. 160) was specially adapted for theatrical performances. Normally dramas were performed privately or semi-privately in palaces or the homes of the rich, or were given public showing in temple courts on days of festival.

A curtain (*yavanikā*) divided the stage (*raṅga*) from the backstage (*nepathya*), and through this the actors made their entrances. There was no curtain between stage and auditorium. The drama was performed without scenery and with a minimum of properties; the absence of both was made up for by the highly developed gesture language of the dance, which we have discussed elsewhere (p. 338). Every part of the body was used to help tell the story, and the well-trained audience recognized from conventional movements of hands, limbs and features that the king was riding in his chariot, or that the heroine was caressing her pet fawn. The splendid attire of the actors was regulated by convention, so that heroes, heroines, gods, demons and villains were immediately recognizable.

The drama regularly began with an invocation to one or more of the gods, and a prologue, in which the chief actor and stage manager (*sūtradhāra*) humorously discussed with his wife, the chief actress, the occasion of the performance and the nature of the play to be performed.* The main dialogue of the play was in prose, but this was freely interspersed with verses, which were usually declaimed or intoned, but not sung. In this ancient Indian taste differed from that of present-day India, which demands many songs in plays and films. The classical unities were not observed; years in time and a thousand miles in space might divide one scene from the next; but within the act unity of time and place was demanded. If in this respect the Indian dramatic convention differed from that of classical Europe, it agreed in forbidding the portrayal of violence, though this and other rules were sometimes ignored. The act was often preceded by a prelude (*praveśaka*), in which one or two characters set the scene and described what had gone before.

As in literature generally, so in the theatre Indian convention allowed no tragedy. Tragic and pathetic scenes were common enough, but endings were almost invariably happy. From the European point of view the insistence on the happy ending often led to the unnatural forcing of the plot. But if he rejected tragedy the ancient Indian playgoer delighted in melodrama and pathos. Though the emotion which the Indian writer sought to arouse was theoretically a sublimated one (p. 350), in fact the Sanskrit drama contains so many melodramatic scenes that the emotional Indian audience must often have been moved to tears. Noble heroes are led to execution for crimes they did not commit, declaiming their innocence to their sorrowing wives and children, only to be saved from the stake at the last moment. Unhappy wives are unjustly expelled from their homes by their husbands. Long-lost children are reunited with their parents in the final act. Whatever the theorists, beginning with Bharata (p. 336), may have said, the sentiment of the

---

*This convention of the Indian stage was known to Goethe from Sir William Jones' translation of *Śakuntalā,* and was adapted by him for the prologue of *Faust.*

Indian drama was warm and living, sometimes a little reminiscent of that of more popular English authors of the last century.

Like Greek and Elizabethan dramatists Indian writers usually borrowed their plots from earlier sources, often adapting them freely in the process. Legends of the gods and ancient heroes formed an inexhaustible mine of dramatic material. Other plays were written around popular tales of a secular type. There are dramas of statecraft, based very freely on stories of historical kings of the past, and light comedies of harem intrigue, wherein the hero, a king, succeeds in pacifying the chief queen, who has set her heart against the promotion of the heroine, a servant girl (usually a princess in disguise), to queenly status and her husband's bed. There are also allegorical dramas, in which the characters are personified virtues and vices, and there are a few surviving examples of farces. Plays were classified by the theorists according to style and length into over a dozen categories.

The hero (*nāyaka*) and heroine (*nāyikā*) are inevitable characters in most types of drama, as is the villain (*pratināyaka*). An interesting stock character is the *vidūṣaka*, who provides comic relief; he is an ugly and misshapen brāhmaṇ, the loyal friend of the hero, but invariably a figure of fun. Another stock character, occurring in one or two extant dramas and noted by the theorists, is the *viṭa*, the cultured but rather shallow man of the world who befriends the hero, and somewhat resembles the parasite of classical Greek comedy.

The earliest known dramas to have survived are fragments of plays by Aśvaghoṣa (p. 368), preserved in manuscripts found in the desert sands of Central Asia. The oldest complete plays are probably those attributed to Bhāsa, which seem to be earlier than those of Kālidāsa, though there is no complete unanimity of experts on this point. Bhāsa's thirteen surviving plays include several works of great merit, notably "The Dream of Vāsavadattā" (*Svapnavāsavadatta*) and "Yaugandharāyaṇa's Vows "(*Pratijñāyaugandharāyaṇa*). Bhāsa also wrote a number of short dramas based on epic stories in simple and vigorous style. Nowadays his plays are often the first introduction of the student of Sanskrit to dramatic literature. He excelled in portraying the heroic sentiment, and ably individualized his characters. More than once he broke the rules of later dramatic theory by permitting acts of violence on the stage.

As in English literature so in Sanskrit, the greatest poet was also the greatest dramatist. Three plays of Kālidāsa have survived: "Mālavikā and Agnimitra", a comedy of harem intrigue, its scene set in the Sunga period; "Urvaśī Won by Valour" (*Vikramorvaśī*), telling the ancient story of the love of Purūravas and Urvaśī (p. 407ff); and "The Recognition of Śakuntalā" (*Abhījñānaśakuntala*). At all times the last has been reckoned Kālidāsa's masterpiece, and merits special consideration. The plot is set in the days of legend, when gods and men were not so far apart as they later became. We give an almost complete translation of the fifth act, with a summary of the rest of the play.

The play opens with King Duṣyanta chasing the deer in the neighbourhood of a forest hermitage. He alights from his chariot to pay homage to the chief of the hermits, the sage Kaṇva. Kaṇva is not at home, but the king meets his foster-daughter, Śakuntalā, the illegitimate child of the nymph Menakā (p. 279). The girl runs on to the stage harassed by a bee, and is freed from its attentions by the gallant King. Naturally he falls in love with her, and with due modesty she shows that she returns his affection. The second act shows Duṣyanta in the throes of love. He cannot press his suit in the absence of Śakuntalā's foster-father, so he remains in the neighbourhood of the hermitage, ostensibly to defend it from wild elephants and demons. In the third act Śakuntalā is languid and sick with love. She confesses her feelings to her two friends, Anasuyā and Priyaṃvadā, who persuade her to write a letter to the King. As she is writing, the King, who has heard everything from a nearby thicket, comes; on the scene, and the two friends withdraw. He gives Śakuntalā a ring, and, by plighting their troth, they are married by the *gāndharva* rite (p. 145).

In the fourth act Duṣyanta has been recalled to his capital by affairs of state, leaving Śakuntalā behind. Kaṇva is still away. Meanwhile a great and irascible hermit, Durvāsas, visits the hermitage, and, as a result of a fancied slight, he curses Śakuntalā, saying that she will be forgotten by her husband until he sees the ring he gave her. Meanwhile Kaṇva returns. He knows already of what has happened, and decides to send the now pregnant Śakuntalā to the King. In a scene of great pathos she takes leave of her foster-father and her friends, and sets out for the capital in the care of two young hermits and an elderly hermit-woman, Gautamī. The fifth act shows us the court of Duṣyanta. Śakuntalā, veiled, is ushered in with her attendants. She reminds the King of their love, and the attendants testify to her words; but the curse of Durvāsas has effaced all memory of her from the King's mind, and he does not recognize her.

GAUTAMĪ. Child! Put your modesty on one side a minute and take off your veil. Then His Majesty will recognize you. (*She does so.*)

THE KING (*looking at Śakuntalā, aside*).

> This shape of untarnished beauty is offered me.
> I wonder whether or not I really wed her.
> I am like a bee in a jasmine wet with the dawn dew—
> I cannot now enjoy her, nor can I leave her.

(*He remains deep in thought.*)

THE DOORKEEPER (*aside*). How His Majesty respects the Sacred Law! Who else would think twice about a beauty so easily come by?

ŚĀRṄGARAVA (one of the hermits). Your Majesty, why are you so silent?

THE KING. Hermits, I've been racking my brains, but I've no recollection whatever of marrying this lady. How can I accept her, ... especially when she shows such obvious signs of pregnancy?

ŚAKUNTALĀ (*aside*). His Majesty doubts that we were ever married! What has become of my high-soaring hopes?

ŚĀRṄGARAVA. So you won't take her!

The sage indeed deserves your scorn,
 for he respects his outraged daughter,
he gives to you the wealth you stole from him,
 and treats a robber as an honest man!

ŚĀRADVATA (the other hermit). That's enough, Śārṅgarava! Śakuntalā, we've said all we can say, and His Majesty has spoken! Now it's up to you! You must say something that will convince him.

ŚAKUNTALĀ (*aside*). When his passion has sunk to such depths what's the good of reminding him of it! The only thing I'm sure of is that I'm to be pitied! (*Aloud.*) Your Majesty! (*Her voice drops to an undertone*). Even though you doubt your marriage to me, this isn't the way you ought to receive me. I'm a girl who is naturally open-hearted. Is it right that you should make promises to me at the hermitage and then deceive me, and now use such harsh words to throw me aside?

THE KING (*putting his hands to his ears*). Heaven forbid!

Why do you try to sully your kin
 and bring me to ruin,
as a river dashing against its banks
 sullies its water and fells the tree on the shore?

ŚAKUNTALĀ. All right! If you really think I'm another man's wife I'll clear up your doubts by this token!

THE KING. That's a good idea!

ŚAKUNTALĀ (*feeling her ring-finger*). Oh dear! Oh dear!! The ring isn't on my finger! (*She looks at Gautamī in distress.*)

GAUTAMĪ. The ring must have slipped off your finger while you were bathing.

THE KING (*smiling*). There's a well-known saying—"A woman always has her wits about her"!

ŚAKUNTALĀ. Fate's against me again! One thing more I want to say.

THE KING. Very well! I'll listen!

ŚAKUNTALĀ. One day when we were in the bower of creepers you had a lotus leaf filled with water in your hand.

THE KING. I'm listening.

ŚAKUNTALĀ. Then my pet fawn Dīrghāpāṅga came up, and you held out the water and tried to get him to come to you, and said tenderly that he should have the first drink, but he wouldn't come near your hand because he didn't know you. So I held him, and he took the water from me, and you laughed and said, "Everyone trusts his own kind—after all, you're both children of the forest!"

THE KING. Those are the sort of sweet and lying phrases with which scheming women fool men of the world!

GAUTAMĪ. Good sir, you shouldn't say such things. This girl was brought up in a hermitage, and she knows nothing of deceit.

THE KING. Old woman!

Even in birds and beasts the female needs no lessons in deceit!
How much less she who has the power of reason!
Cuckoos, before they take to flight,
make sure that other birds will rear their chicks!

ŚAKUNTALĀ (*angrily*). You wretch! You judge me by the measure of your own heart! Was there ever a bigger hypocrite? You, in your cloak of righteousness—you're like a well covered over with grass!

THE KING (*aside*). Her anger seems quite genuine and makes me have second thoughts.

She must think my soul is vile in its forgetfulness,
and in not acknowledging our secret love.
At the knitting of the brows of her eyes red with anger
the bow of the Love-god is snapped in two.

(*Aloud*). Good woman. The movements of King Duṣyanta are common knowledge, and nobody knows anything about this.

ŚAKUNTALĀ. So be it! Here am I, turned into a wanton, and all because I trusted the race of Pūru, and fell into the clutches of a man who had honey on his tongue and poison in his heart. (*She covers her face with the end of her robe and weeps.*)

ŚĀRṄGARAVA. So you have to suffer for your own folly, when you don't keep a check on your impulses.

One should think hard before making love,
especially in secret.
Friendship to those whose hearts we know not
soon turns to hatred.

THE KING. What, do you trust this lady enough to attack me with your censorious words?

ŚĀRṄGARAVA (*scornfully*). You hear things upside down!

The word of one who from her birth
has learnt no guile carries no weight at all,
but they who have mastered the science of deceit
have power to speak words of authority.

THE KING. Honest sir, if for the sake of the argument I admit your accusation, tell me what good it would do me to deceive her.

ŚĀRṄGARAVA. You'd reap your own ruin.

THE KING. And surely it's unbelievable that a king of the line of Pura should seek his own ruin?

ŚĀRADVATA. Śārṅgarava, what's the use of arguing with him? We've carried out the Teacher's command, now let's go home. (*To the King*.)

Here is Your Lordship's wife—
leave her or accept her.
It is said that the husband's power
over the wife is all-embracing.

Gautamī, let's go! (*They make for the door*.)

ŚAKUNTALĀ. Oh, how I've been cheated by this deceiver! You mustn't leave me! (*She follows them*.)

GAUTAMĪ. (*pausing*.) Look, Śārṅgarava, my child Śakuntalā is following us and crying pitifully. Oh, what will my little girl do, now that her husband has cast her off so cruelly?

ŚĀRṄGARAVA (*turning sternly*). Wanton, you are too independent!

(*Śakuntalā trembles with fear*.)

ŚĀRṄGARAVA. Śakuntalā!

If you are what the king says you are
you are cast off by your family, and your father is nothing to you;
but if you know your vow to be true
even bondage in your husband's home is good.

You must stay behind, and we must go!

THE KING. Hermit, why do you delude this lady?

The moon awakens the night-flowering lotuses,
and the sun those that flower by day.
The way of the man of self-control
is to have no dealings with the wife of another.

ŚĀRṄGARAVA. When Your Majesty has such a short memory for his past deeds he does well to be so fearful of sin!

THE KING (*to the Chief Priest*).* I ask you the rights and wrongs of the matter.

I wonder, am I forgetful,
or has she told me lies?
Shall I abandon my own wife
or sin by touching another's?

* This stage direction is inserted by us. All the others are Kālidāsa's. In their comparatively full stage directions Sanskrit plays contrast strikingly with those of ancient Greece.

THE CHIEF PRIEST (*thoughtfully*). If you ask me, this is what I think should be done.

THE KING. Command me, Your Honour!

THE CHIEF PRIEST. Let the lady stay in my home until the child is born. If you ask why, this is my reason—Long ago the wise men told you that your first son would become a universal emperor. If the son of the hermit's daughter bears the tokens of such kingship you should congratulate her and take her into your harem—otherwise send her back to her father.

THE KING. It shall be as my master pleases.

THE CHIEF PRIEST. Child, follow me!

ŚAKUNTALĀ. O holy Earth, open for me! (*She starts to go, and leaves with the Chief Priest. The hermits depart. The King, his memory clouded by the curse, thinks about Śakuntalā.*)[38]

Soon the Chief Priest returns. As he was leading Śakuntalā to his home a heavenly shape appeared and carried her up to heaven. It was her mother, the nymph Menakā, who had come to take her to her true parents' home for her confinement.

Act six introduces two policemen and a fishermen. He has found a precious ring in the maw of a fish, and is hauled before the king under the suspicion of having stolen it. As soon as Duṣyanta sees the ring he recognizes it as the one he gave Śakuntalā, and his memory returns. But Śakuntalā has vanished. For a while the King gives himself up to grief, for he has lost his wife and he has no heir. Soon he assuages his sorrow in action, for Mātali, the charioteer of Indra, brings him word that his help is needed in the long war between gods and demons.

The final act takes place several years later on the lower slopes of heaven, at the hermitage of the divine sage Mārīca. Duṣyanta is returning victorious from battle, when he sees a small boy, nobly wrestling with a tame lion cub. He stops his chariot to admire the child's courage and strength, and is told that he is Bharata, the son of Śakuntalā. The lovers are reunited, and all ends happily.

In many respects "Śakuntalā" is comparable to the more idyllic comedies of Shakespeare, and Kaṇva's hermitage is surely not far from the Forest of Arden. The plot of the play, like many of Shakespeare's plots, depends much on fortunate chances and on the supernatural, which, of course, was quite acceptable to the audience for which Kālidāsa wrote. Its characters, even to the minor ones, are happily delineated individuals. In the passage we have quoted the two hermits, who play no further part in the action, are sharply differentiated. Śārṅgarava is a brave and upright man, fearless in his denunciation of wickedness in high places, but rather stem and hard in his righteousness. Śāradvata, on the other hand, betrays himself in two lines as a moral weakling, anxious to escape from an unpleasant situation as quickly as possible. Kālidāsa makes no pretence to realism, but his dialogue is fresh and vigorous. In fact the dialogue of the better Sanskrit plays generally seems based on vernacular, and is full of idiomatic expressions. Indian playgoers did not demand the conflict of feelings and emotions which is the chief substance of serious European drama, but Kālidāsa was quite capable of portraying such conflict effectively. His beauties and merits are tarnished by any translation, but few who can read him in the original would doubt that, both as poet and as dramatist, he was one of the great men of the world.

There were many other dramatists, of whom we can only mention a few. Śūdraka, probably Kālidāsa's approximate contemporary, has left only one play "The Little Clay Cart" (*Mṛcchakaṭika*). This is the most realistic of Indian dramas, unravelling a complicated story, rich in humour and pathos and crowded with action, of the love of a poor brāhmaṇ Cārudatta for the virtuous courtezan Vasantasenā; this story is interwoven with one of political intrigue, leading up to the overthrow of the wicked king Pālaka, and the play contains a vivid trial scene, after which the hero is saved from execution at the last moment. It is notable for its realistic depiction of city life and for its host of minor characters, all of whom are drawn with skill and individuality. It has more than once been performed in translation on the European stage, and, to a Western audience, it is certainly the most easily appreciated of Indian plays.

Viśākhadatta (?6th century) was the dramatist of politics. His only complete surviving play, "The Minister's Signet Ring" (*Mudrārākṣasa*), deals with the schemes of the wily Cāṇakya (p. 44) to foil the plots of Rākṣasa, the minister of the last of the Nandas, and to place Candragupta Maurya firmly on the throne. The plot is exceedingly complicated, but is worked out with great skill, and the play is beautifully constructed to lead up, like "The Little Clay Cart", to a pathetic scene where one of the chief characters is saved from death by impalement at the last moment. Another play by Viśākhadatta, "The Queen and Candra Gupta" (*Devīcandragupta*), purporting to tell the story of the rise to power of Candra Gupta II (p. *57*), exists only in fragments.

Three plays are ascribed to the great king Harsa (p. 57f), though they may be the work of a "ghost writer". They are "Ratnāvall", "Priyadarśikā", and "The Joy of the Serpents" (*Nāgānanda*). The first two, named after their heroines, are charming harem comedies, while the last is a play of religious purport, telling of prince Jīmūtavāhana, who gives his own body to put a stop to the sacrifice of snakes to the divine Garuda (p. 264).

With Harṣa we may link his royal contemporary, the Pallava king Mahendravikramavarman, who has left a one-act play "The Sport of the Drunkards" (*Mattavilāsa*). It treats of a drunken Śaivite ascetīc, who loses the skull which he uses as a begging bowl and accuses a Buddhist monk of stealing it. After much satirical dialogue, in which other dissolute ascetics of various persuasions and both sexes are involved, it is found that the skull has been stolen by a dog. This little farce, though slight, throws a flood of light on the life of the times and is full of Rabelaisian humour.

Second only to Kālidāsa in the esteem of the critics was Bhavabhūti, who lived at Kānyakubja in the early 8th century. Three of his plays survive—"Mālatī and Mādhava", "The Deeds of the Great Hero" (*Mahāvīracarita*), and "The Later Deeds of Rama" (*Uttararāmacarita*). The first is a love story with a pseudo-realistic background, full of incident of an exciting or horrific type, in which the heroine is more than once rescued from death, while the two latter plays tell the story of Rāma. By Western standards as a dramatist Bhavabhūti falls short of those we have mentioned earlier. His plots are weakly constructed and his characters lack individuality. His greatness rests on his deep understanding of sorrow; in his treatment of the pathetic and the terrible he perhaps excels Kālidāsa.

After Bhavabhūti the quality of Sanskrit drama declined. Playwrights of some merit, such as Bhaṭṭa Nārāyaṇa (? 8th century), Murāri (early 9th century), Rājaśekhara (9th–10th centuries), and Kṛṣṇamiśva (11th century), continued to write dramas, but their work grew more and more literary, and was evidently often intended rather for reading than for performance. We have records of the occasional production of Sanskrit plays after the Muslim invasion, but the Sanskrit theatrical tradition, though not forgotten, had by now become a thing of the past.

Sanskrit Prose Literature

The earliest surviving prose stories are a few narrative episodes in the Brāhmaṇas (p. 358ff), followed by the Pāli Jātakas (p. 405f). In the Gupta period, however, there developed a style of ornate prose narrative, which was very different from the simple Pāli stories and was classed as *kāvya*. The chief writers in this genre were Daṇḍin, Subandhu and Bāṇa, all of whom lived in the late 6th and early 7th centuries.

Daṇḍin's "Tales of the Ten Princes" (*Daśakumāracarita*) is a collection of exciting and ingenious stories, held together by a framing narrative and all interwoven with great skill. The prose is comparatively simple. Long compounds are numerous, but the inordinately lengthy sentences of Bāṇa are not to be found. The stories are secular, often humorous, and sometimes amoral, while the characters are well delineated. Some of the interest of the "Ten Princes" lies in its comparative realism, for in their adventures the ten heroes come in contact with merchants and thieves, princesses and prostitutes, peasants and wild hillmen. Few works of Indian literature tell us so much about low life.

As examples of Daṇḍin's style we give two little stories which are contained within the larger tales, and are intended to show contrasting aspects of the character of the fair sex. The styles are sharply differentiated to fit the themes; the grisly story of Dhūminī is told in crisp short sentences with great economy of detail, while in the domestic idyll of Gominī Daṇḍin lingers lovingly on his words, and describes the charming scene in leisurely periods.

"There is a country called Trigarta, where there lived three householders, who had accumulated a great fortune. They were brothers, called Dhanaka, Dhānyaka and Dhanyaka. In those days Indra gave no rain for twelve years. The corn withered, plants were barren, trees bore no fruit, and the clouds were impotenti water courses dried up, ponds became mere mudholes, and the springs ceased to flow. Bulbs, roots and fruit became scarce, folk-tales were forgotten, and all festive merrymaking ceased. Robber bands multiplied, and people ate one another's flesh. Human skulls, white as cranes, rolled on the ground. Flocks of thirsty crows flew hither and thither. Villages, cities, whole districts, were deserted.

"The three householders first ate their store of grain and then one by one their goats, their sheep, their buffaloes, their cows, their maidservants, their menservants, their children, and the wives of the eldest and the middle brother. Finally they decided that next day they would eat Dhūminī, the wife of the youngest; but the youngest brother, Dhanyaka, could not bring himself to eat his darling, so that night he stole away with her.

"When she grew weary he carried her, until they came to a forest... and they walked on through it until at last they came upon a man who was writhing on the ground, with his hands, feet, ears and nose cut off. He compassionately supported this man too on his shoulder, and for a long time the three dwelt in a hut which he painstakingly built of leaves in a corner of the forest, which abounded in edible bulbs, roots and game. He healed the man's wounds with almond and sesamum oil, and fed him with a full share of his own meat and vegetables.

"One day when the man had quite recovered and was restored to health, while Dhanyaka was hunting, Dhūminī approached the man with desire for pleasure, and though he upbraided her she compelled him to satisfy her. When her husband came back and asked for water she said, 'Draw it from the well yourself, I've got a splitting headache', and tossed him the bucket and rope. As he was drawing water from the well she crept up suddenly behind him and pushed him in.

"Supporting the cripple on her shoulder she wandered from land to land, and gained the reputation of a devoted wife, and was much honoured. Finally she settled in Avanti, and lived in great affiuence, thanks to the generosity of the king. One day she heard that her husband had been rescued from the well by a band of thirsty merchants, and was now roaming about the land of Avanti, begging his food. So Dhūminī declared to the unwitting king that he was the villain who had crippled her husband, and he condemned the good man to death by torture.

"As Dhanyaka was being led to execution, knowing that his appointed time had not yet come, he boldly said to the officer in charge, 'If the beggar I'm supposed to have crippled is ready to condemn me I deserve my punishment!' The officer thought that no harm could come of testing [his words, so he sent for the cripple]. As soon as the cripple was brought and saw Dhanyaka his eyes filled with tears. He fell at the good man's feet, and, being a man of noble mind, he told of Dhanyaka's kindness and the false Dhūminī's wickedness. The enraged king had the wicked woman's face disfigured, and made her serve as a cook in his kennels, while he bestowed great favour on Dhanyaka. And that is why I say that women are hardhearted."

"In the land of the Dravidians is a city called Kāñcī. Therein dwelt the very wealthy son of a merchant, by name Śaktikumāra. When he was nearly eighteen he thought: 'There's no pleasure in living without a wife or with one of bad character. Now how can I find a really good one?' So, dubious of his chance of finding wedded bliss with a woman taken at the word of others, he became a fortune-teller, and roamed the land with a measure of unhusked rice tied in the skirts of his robe; and parents, taking him for an interpreter of birthmarks, showed their daughters to him. Whenever he saw a girl of his own class, whatever her birthmarks, he would say to her: 'My dear girl, can you cook me a good meal from this measure of rice?' And so, ridiculed and rejected, he wandered from house to house.

"One day in the land of the Śibis, in a city on the banks of the Kāverī, he examined a girl who was shown to him by her nurse. She wore little jewellery, for her parents had spent their fortune, and had nothing left but their dilapidated mansion. As soon as he set eyes on her he thought: 'This girl is shapely and smooth in all her members. Not one limb is too fat or too thin, too short or too long. Her fingers are pink; her hands are marked with auspicious lines—the barleycorn, the fish, the lotus and the vase; her ankles are shapely; her feet are plump and the veins are not prominent; her thighs curve smoothly; her knees can barely be seen, for they merge into her rounded thighs; her buttocks are dimpled and round as chariot wheels; her navel is small, flat and deep; her stomach is adorned with three lines; the nipples stand out from her large breasts, which cover her whole chest; her palms are marked with signs which promise corn, wealth and sons; her nails are smooth and polished like jewels; her fingers are straight and tapering and pink; her arms curve sweetly from the shoulder, and are smoothly jointed; her slender neck is curved like a conch-shell; her lips are rounded and of even red; her pretty chin does not recede; her cheeks are round, full and firm; her eyebrows do not join above her nose, and are curved, dark and even; her nose is like a half-blown sesamum flower; her wide eyes are large and gentle and flash with three colours, black, white and brown; her brow is fair as the new moon; her curls are lovely as a mine of sapphires; her long ears are adorned doubly, with earrings and charming lotuses, hanging limply; her abundant hair is not brown, even at the tips,* but long, smooth, glossy and fragrant. The character of such a girl cannot but correspond to her appearance, and my heart is fixed upon her, so I'll test her and marry her. For one regret after another is sure to fall on the heads of people who don't take precautions!' So, looking at her affectionately, he said, 'Dear girl, can you cook a good meal for me with this measure of rice?'

"Then the girl glanced at her old servant, who took the measure of rice from his hand and seated him on the veranda, which had been well sprinkled and swept,

* Though a fair complexion was much prized in ancient India a trace of brownness in the hair, fairly common in the North, was thought very unbeautiful and inauspicious.

giving him water to cool his feet. Meanwhile the girl bruised the fragrant rice, dried it a little at a time in the sun, turned it repeatedly, and beat it with a hollow cane on a firm fiat spot, very gently, so as to separate the grain without crushing the husk. Then she said to the nurse, 'Mother, goldsmiths can make good use of these husks for polishing jewellery. Take them, and, with the coppers you get for them, buy some fire-wood, not too green and not too dry, a small cooking pot, and two earthen dishes.'*

"When this was done she put the grains of rice in a shallow wide-mouthed, round-bellied mortar, and took a long and heavy pestle of acacia wood, its head shod with a plate of iron. ... With skill and grace she exerted her arms, as the grains jumped up and down in the mortar. Repeatedly she stirred them and pressed them down with her fingers; then she shook the grains in a winnowing basket to remove the beard, rinsed them several times, worshipped the hearth, and placed them in water which had been five times brought to the boil. When the rice softened, bubbled and swelled, she drew the embers of the fire together, put a lid on the cooking pot, and strained off the gruel. Then she patted the rice with a ladle and scooped it out a little at a time; and when she found that it was thoroughly cooked she put the cooking pot on one side, mouth downwards. Next she damped down those sticks which were not burnt through, and when the fire was quite out she sent them to the dealers to be sold as charcoal, saying, 'With the coppers that you get for them, buy as much as you can of green vegetables, ghee, curds, sesamum oil, myrobalans and tamarind.'

"When this was done she offered him a few savouries. Next she put the rice-gruel in a new dish immersed in damp sand, and cooled it with the soft breeze of a palm-leaf fan. She added a little salt, and flavoured it with the scent of the embers; she ground the myrobalans to a smooth powder, until they smelt like a lotus; and then, by the lips of the nurse, she invited him to take a bath. This he did, and when she too had bathed she gave him oil and myrobalans [as an unguent].

"After he had bathed he sat on a bench in the paved courtyard, which had been thoroughly sprinkled and swept. She stirred the gruel in the two dishes, which she set before him on a piece of pale green plantain leaf, cut from a tree in the courtyard. He drank it and felt rested and happy, relaxed in every limb. Next she gave him two ladlefuls of the boiled rice, served with a little ghee and condiments. She served the rest of the rice with curds, three spices [mace, cardamom and cinnamon], and fragrant and refreshing buttermilk and gruel. He enjoyed the meal to the last mouthful.

"When he asked for a drink she poured him water in a steady stream from the spout of a new pitcher—it was fragrant with incense, and smelt of fresh trumpet-flowers and the perfume of full-blown lotuses. He put the bowl to his lips, and his eyelashes sparkled with rosy drops as cool as snow; his ears delighted in the

---

* The economics of this and the other transaction referred to are very hard to explain. No doubt the rice husks, so carefully threshed, had some commercial value, but it is hardly likely that they would have bought the wares mentioned. If this passage has any historical significance it confirms the evidence of other sources that in ordinary times the means of subsistence were plentiful and cheap.

sound of the trickling water; his rough cheeks thrilled and tingled at its pleasant contact; his nostrils opened wide at its sweet fragrance; and his tongue delighted in its lovely flavour, as he drank the pure water in great gulps. Then, at his nod, the girl gave him a mouthwash in another bowl. The old woman took away the remains of his meal, and he slept awhile in his ragged cloak, on the pavement plastered with fresh cowdung.

"Wholly pleased with the girl, he married her with due rites, and took her home. Later he neglected her awhile and took a mistress, but the wife treated her as a dear friend. She served her husband indefatigably, as she would a god, and never neglected her household duties; and she won the loyalty of her servants by her great kindness. In the end her husband was so enslaved by her goodness that he put the whole household in her charge, made her sole mistress of his life and person, and enjoyed the three aims of life—virtue, wealth and love. So I maintain that virtuous wives make their lords happy and virtuous."[39]

Subandhu, the next of the three great prose writers, is known only from one work, called after its heroine *Vāsavadattā*, which tells of the vicissitudes of her love for the prince Kandarpaketu. Unlike Daṇḍin, Subandhu was quite unable to tell a story and had no sense of character. His merits lie in his ornate descriptions and his mastery of language, and his work consists of a series of descriptive tableaux, linked by a thin thread of narrative, each long description told in a single sentence which covers two or more pages of type. The work abounds in flowers of speech of all kinds—puns, *doubles entendres*, alliterations and assonances, and is a typical example of the *Gauda* (Bengālī) style of literary composition, as distinguished from the simpler *Vaidarbha* (Berār) style, with shorter, less involved sentences, employed by Kālidāsa and Daṇḍin. It cannot be enjoyed in translation and its merits are only apparent in the framework of its own standards. Of European literature perhaps Lily's *Euphues* and similar late Renaissance prose works most closely approach it in style and spirit.

Bāṇa's style is similar to that of Subandhu, but his work is much more vital and congenial to Western taste. Not only do his elaborate descriptions show accurate and close observation, but throughout his two works, the "Deeds of Harsa" (*Harṣacarita*) and *Kādambari*, the personality of the author breaks through. In the former work, moreover, he gives us a fragment of autobiography unparalleled in Sanskrit literature. Bāṇa was born of a well-to-do brāhmaṇ family, and his mother died in his early childhood. At the age of fourteen he lost his father also, and, after a period of mourning, he began to sow his wild oats. He names with evident affection the bosom friends of his dissolute youth, which was spent in wandering from city to city among the intellectual bohemians of the time. His circle was remarkably wide, including ascetics of various types, both orthodox and otherwise, literary men, actors, musicians, entertainers, doctors, and even humble people of low caste. The list of Bāṇa's friends, mentioned in no special order, is in itself sufficient to show how lightly the rules of caste weighed on the educated man. The author gives us no details of his adventures, but it would seem that in the course of them he was received at the court of Harṣa, whom he offended in some way. Later he returned for a while to his home, and resumed the peaceful life of a country brāhmaṇ; but soon a message came from Harṣa, demanding his attendance at court. He was at first received coldly, but afterwards was restored to favour.

Though religiously minded, Bāṇa seems throughout his life to have transcended the bounds of orthodoxy and to have retained some of the unconventionality of his wild youth. He was not afraid to put forward opinions which might have made him unpopular with his royal patron —for instance he condemned the doctrine of royal divinity as gross sycophancy, and attacked the Machiavellian system of statecraft associated with the name of Kauṭilya as immoral and inhuman. Here and there in his work occur passages which show implicit sympathy with the poor and humble—a sentiment rarely found in ancient Indian literature—and he is a master of exact observation. For all the floweriness of his style Bāṇa's outlook has more in common with the 20th century than has that of any other early Indian writer.

Of his two works the "Deeds of Harṣa" tells of the events leading up to Harṣa's rise to power with general authenticity, but with some evident exaggeration and with a lack of circumstantial detail which the historian finds irritating. *Kādambarī* is perhaps a conscious and successful attempt to improve on Subandhu's *Vāsavadattā*. The story is a romance, told in a series of narrated episodes which link together to build up a complicated plot. This work was unfinished, and was completed by the author's son, whose prentice hand is quite evident.

As an example of Bāṇa's style we give a somewhat abridged and adapted version of his description of Harṣa's army striking camp to march against his enemies. In the original the whole consists of a single sentence, the basis of which is the phrase "the royal court was filled with chieftains" near the end of the passage. The separate sentences or clauses of our translation are single compound words in the original.

> "Then it was time to go. The drums rattled, the kettledrums beat joyfully, the trumpets blared, the horns blew, the conches sounded. By degrees the hubbub of the camp grew louder. Officers busily roused the King's courtiers. The sky shook with the din of fast-hammering mallets and drumsticks. The generals assembled the ranks of the subordinate officers. The darkness of the night was broken by the glare of a thousand torches which the people lighted. Lovers were aroused by the tramping feet of the women who kept watch. The harsh shouts of the elephant-marshals dispelled the slumber of their drowsy riders as awakened elephants left their stables.
>
> "Squadrons of horses woke from sleep and shook their manes. The camp resounded loudly as spades dug up the tent-pegs, and the tethering chains of elephants clinked as their stakes were pulled up. ... As the foragers released the elephants all space was filled with the clanking of their fetters. Leather bags full to bursting were placed on their dusty backs, which had been rubbed down with tufts of hay. Servants rolled up the canvasses and awnings of tents

and pavilions, and the bundles of tent-pegs were stored away in bulging leather sacks. Store-keepers assembled their stores, and many elephant-drivers loaded them. The dwellings of the vassals were cluttered with cups and cooking utensils, which were lifted on to the backs of elephants, steadied by their riders. The soldiers laughed as the fat strumpets were dragged away by force, resisting vigorously with feet and hands. The many mighty and savage elephants trumpeted, as the girthbands of their bright harness were tightened, and restricted the freedom of their limbs. ... Camels neighed in annoyance as sacks were loaded on their backs.

"The wives of highborn gentlemen were visited in their carriages by go-betweens sent by princes. Elephant-captains, who had forgotten that it was time to go, looked for their servants. The splendid horses of the King's favourites were led by footmen wealthy with their masters' gifts. Troops of handsome warriors adorned their bodies with circles of unguent, scented with camphor. The harness of the marshals' horses was hung with bags of salted peas, little bells, and whistles.* Monkeys sat among the troops of horses, as the grooms straightened their tangled reins. Stablemen dragged sacks of musty fodder for the horses' morning meal. The calls of the grass-cutters grew louder and louder. There was uproar in the stables as young horses strained and reared and swerved at the confusion of starting. Girls hurried at the call of the riders of the harnessed horses with unguents for their faces. As the elephants and horses set out the poor folk of the neighbourhood ran up to loot the remains of the heaped grain. Donkeys plodded on together, loaded with piles of clothing. The trampled roads were filled with carts with creaking wheels. Oxen were loaded with equipment which would suddenly fall off. The strong oxen, first to be driven away, lagged behind, drawn by the grass which grew by the roadside.

"In front went the field-kitchens of the chief vassals. Standard bearers led the ranks. As the troops left their small huts hundreds of their friends came out to meet them. The feet of the elephants trampled the hovels by the roadside, and the people came out and threw clods at their keepers, who called on the bystanders to witness their assaults. Poor families ran from their wrecked and ruined huts. Oxen, hearing the wealth of unfortunate merchants, fled from the hubbub. Clearing a path through the crowd with the giare of their torches, runners led the way for the elephants hearing the women of the harem., Horsemen shouted to the dogs running behind them. The veterans praised the tall Tangana horses, which trotted so smoothly and quickly that they made travelling a pleasure. Unhappy Southerners upbraided their fallen mules. The whole world was swallowed in dust.

* Cowell and Thomas (*The Harṣacarita of Bāṇa,* p. 200) take *lavaṇakalāyī* as "wooden figures of deer" on the basis of a late commentary. *Lavaṇa* means salt, and *kalāya* a type of pea, and we believe the compound to mean a bag of salted peas, the horse's iron rations. The translation of *kiṅkini-nālī-sanātha* as "bells with reeds attached" is equally improbable. The horse's harness would be hung with bells, but *nālī,* "reed" or "tube", may well mean a whistle attached to the harness by a cord, and used for signalling.

> "The royal court was filled with chieftains who had come from every quarter, riding on cow-elephants, whose drivers bore bows adorned with stripes of gold-leaf. Seated within [the howdahs] their batmen carried their swords. Their betel-bearers fanned them with flywhisks. The soldiers seated in the rear bore bundles of javelins in cases. The trappings [of the elephants] bristled with curved sabres and gilded arrows. ... The thighs [of the chieftains] were clothed in fine-patterned silk, but their legs were covered with mud-stained trousers. ... Their tunics were decked with dark jewels, which glistened against their bodies. They wore Chinese cuirasses, doublets adorned with bright clusters of pearls, ... and scarves as bright as a parrot's wing. All the ends of the earth were filled with knights and warriors, who hurried on with tossing shields and plumes. The ends of heaven were loud with the jingling golden ornaments on the harness of the prancing Kamboja steeds in their hundreds. The ear was deafened by the harsh booming of hundreds of large kettledrums, mercilessly beaten. The roll was called. With upturned faces the footmen awaited the order to march."[40]

After Bāṇa similar prose romances were often written, as well as stories in mixed prose and verse (*campū*), but none is of much literary importance, and most are derivative, pedantic and dull.

Another branch of prose narrative literature was the fable, which we meet first in the Pāli Jātakas. These cheerful little stories, whose characters are often talking animals, have much in common with the fables popular in ancient Greece, and there has been some discussion on the question of influence. Direct borrowing is unlikely, though it may be that some of the tales were derived from a common source in the ancient Middle East. Whatever the origin of these stories Indian folklore did influence the literature of the West, for one of the most famous Indian collections of fables, the *Pañcatantra*, was translated into Pahlavī, or Middle Persian, in the 6th century. Thence it was translated into Syriac, and thence again, in the 8th century, into Arabic. In various versions it appeared in Hebrew, Greek and Latin, and found its way all over Europe. The earliest English version is that of Sir Thomas North, called "The Morall Philosophie of Doni" after the name of the translator of the Italian version, which North used. This appeared in 1570, and was the earliest work of Indian literature (much garbled by successive translations) to be published in English. The fables of La Fontaine are admittedly based on "Pilpay", the form in which Vidyāpati, the title of the Indian sage who is said to have narrated the stories, reached Europe. As well as the fables of La Fontaine the stories of Reynard the Fox, popular in the folk literature of many parts of Europe and given finished form by Goethe, owe much to this source. Other Indian tales, including several from the *Bṛhatkathā* (p. 382), found their way westwards, and the "Arabian Nights" owes several of its stories and themes to India, including some of the marvels met by Sindbad the Sailor.

The *Pañcatantra* ("Five Treatises") is in theory a book of instruction in *nīti*, or the conduct of one's affairs, especially intended for kings and statesmen. The little stories are contained in a framing narrative which tells how a king was distressed at the evil and stupidity of his sons, and entrusted them to a sage who reformed them in six months by telling them a series of fables. The book exists in several versions of varying length and merit, mostly in prose, but containing many verses of a gnomic type. The most famous of these versions is Nārāyaṇa's *Hitopadeśa* ("Salutary Instruction"), composed in Bengal in the 12th century. The work was intended as a "reader" for students of Sanskrit, and serves that purpose well down to the present day. Never was a school textbook better written. The author was compelled by his purpose to avoid the euphuisms and pedantries which affected most of the literature of his time, and he wrote lucidly and wittily, liberally including memorably terse gnomic stanzas. Ethically many of the stories are dubious, for they encourage caution and self-interest rather than altruism. The two stories we quote are boxed within others.

"'It is said:

He who takes a well-spoken knave
  to be a man of his own stamp
is fooled by rogues, like the brāhmaṇ
  who was robbed of his goat.'

"'How did that happen?' asked the King.

"'In the forest of Gautama,' said Meghavarna, 'there lived a brāhmaṇ famous for his sacrifices. Once he went to a village and bought a goat for sacrifice, and as he was carrying it home on his shoulder he was seen by three rogues. "If we could find a way to get that goat," they said to themselves, "it would be a fine trick!" So they stationed themselves each under a tree about a *krośa* apart. As the brāhmaṇ passed by, the first rogue said, "Why, brāhmaṇ, that's a dog you're carrying on your back!" "It's not a dog," replied the brāhmaṇ, "it's a goat for sacrifice!"

"'Then the next rogue addressed him with the same words. This time the brāhmaṇ put the goat on the ground and looked at it hard, and again slung it over his shoulder and went on, his mind wavering like a swing; for

The words of rogues make even the mind of a good man waver.
If he trusts them he dies as Pretty-ears died.'

"'How did that happen?' asked the King.

"'In a forest land,' he said, 'there lived a lion named Madotkaṭa, who had three servants, a crow, a tiger and a jackal. Once as the three were out walking they met a camel, and they asked him whence he came, and whether he had fallen out of a caravan. He told them his story, and they took him back and handed him over to the lion, who gave him his freedom and security; and he took the name of Pretty-ears.

"'Later the lion was taken ill, and there was heavy rain and they were very distressed for want of food. So they agreed to arrange matters in such a way that their lord should kill Pretty-ears. "Of what other use to us," they said to themselves, "is that eater of thorns?" "But how can we manage it," said the tiger, "when our master has given him a pledge of security and has him in his favour?" "At a time like this," said the crow, "when the master is reduced to skin and bone, he won't scruple at a sin; for

A woman torn by hunger will abandon her child.
 A snake torn by hunger will eat its own eggs.
What evil will a hungry man not do?
 Lean men are always pitiless!

And, what is more,

A drunkard, an imbecile, a lunatic,
 a man tired out, an angry man, a hungry man,
a greedy man, a frightened man, a hasty man,
 and a man in love never do the right thing."

"'After thus deliberating they all went to the lion. "Have you found anything to eat?" the lion asked. "We've done our best," they replied, "but we haven't found a thing!" "Well," said the lion, "how are we to keep alive now?" "Sire," said the crow, "if we don't get our natural food we'll all surely die." "And what," asked the lion, "is our natural food?" "Pretty-ears!" whispered the crow in the lion's ear.

"'The lion touched the earth and covered his ears in horror. "We've given him a pledge of security," he said, "and we must stand by it. How can we eat him? For

Not gifts of land nor gifts of gold,
 nor gifts of cattle nor gifts of food
are said to be the greatest gift.
 Of all gifts greatest is the gift of safety.

"'"Moreover

The merit of the horse-sacrifice
 and the fulfilment of all desires
come to the man who protects
 those who take refuge with him."

"'"True!" said the crow. "Our lord must not kill him. But there's no reason why we shouldn't so arrange things that he offers his body voluntarily." At this the lion kept silence. So when a suitable occasion offered the crow found a pretext to bring them all into the lion's presence. "Sire," he said, "however hard we try we can find no food. Your Majesty is weak from days of fasting. So now make a meal of my flesh, for

All subjects are dependent on their lord.
 Only well-rooted trees bear fruit,
and only when the king is strong
 do men's works prosper."

"'"I'd rather die myself than do such a thing!" said the lion.

"'Then the jackal made the same offer. "Never!" the lion replied.

"'The tiger next spoke up. "Let my lord live on my own body!" he said. "Such a thing can never be right!" the lion replied.

"'Finally Pretty-ears, full of confidence, offered himself in the same way. And, in accordance with his offer, the lion ripped his belly open and they all ate him up.

"'And that is why I say:

> The words of rogues make even the mind of a good man waver.
> If he trauts them he dies as Pretty-ears died.

"'Meanwhile the brāhmaṇ met the third rogue, who spoke to him in the same way. This time he decided that his senses were defective. So he abandoned the goat, performed a ritual ablution, and went home, while the rogues took the goat away and ate it And so I say:

> He who takes a well-spoken knave
> to be a man of his own stamp
> is fooled by rogues like the brāhmaṇ
> who was robbed of his goat.'"[41]

Pāli Literature

The Pāli language was closer to the speech of the ordinary man than was Sanskrit, and its style was in general simpler; but though they contain many fine passages the Pāli scriptures are largely prosaic and repetitive. The same stock phrases and descriptions, often quite lengthy, occur again and again with a dull monotony which can only be circumvented by drastic abridgement. Yet the narrative portions of the Pāli canon are frequently of much merit. Here for instance, somewhat abridged, is an account of the Buddha's "Great Going Forth", a passage of intense dramatic force.

> "Then lovely women, decked like the damsels of the gods with every kind of ornament and well trained in dance and song, began to perform. But the Bodhisattva had no taste for dancing, and for a while sleep overcame him. The women thought: 'He for whose sake we danced and sang has fallen asleep—why should we trouble ourselves further?' And they put up their instruments and lay down. The lamps of scented oil burned on.
>
> "The Bodhisattva awoke and sat cross-legged on his couch. He saw the women with their instruments laid aside, fast asleep. Saliva trickled from the mouths of some; some were covered in sweat; some ground their teeth in sleep; some snored; the garments of some were in disarray, so that they repulsively showed their private parts. When he saw them thus in their dishevelment he was more than ever disgusted with the life of passion. The great hall, decked like the heavenly palace of Indra, seemed to him like a charnel ground full of scattered corpses. Life seemed as fleeting as a house on fire. 'How wretched it all is! How afflicted it all is!!' he cried, and his mind was set even more

strongly on asceticism. 'Today I must leave on the Great Going Forth,' he thought, and he rose from his bed and went to the door.

"There lay Channa, his head on the threshold. 'Today I must go forth on the Great Going Forth,' he said, 'get ready my horse'. ... When he had thus sent Channa he thought 'I will see my son', and he went to the apartments of the Mother of Rāhula, and opened the bedroom door. A little lamp of scented oil burned in the inner room. The Mother of Rāhula was sleeping on a bed thickly strewn with flowers, with her son's head on her arm. The Bodhisattva set one foot on the threshold and stood gazing at them. 'If I move her hand and take up my son I shall waken the queen,' he thought, 'and then I shall not be able to go. When I am a Buddha I will come back and see my son.' And he left the palace."[42]

As a further example of Pāli prose we give a Jātaka tale. This story, inculcating the fickleness of women, has of course no religious value and its origin is certainly secular, but we give its framework, in order that the reader may see how the most unpromising material was pressed into service for religious purposes. This story is typical of the terse dry style of the collection, and of the tales of marvels which were very popular in India then as now. The reader will recall that the verses are the original, round which the story itself is built as a sort of commentary.

"The Master, who was living at Jeta's Grove at the time, told this story in connexion with a backsliding brother. The Master asked him if he wanted to return to the world and regretted taking orders. 'It's all because of the wiles of women,' the monk answered. 'Brother,' said the Master, 'it's impossible to keep on your guard against women! Wise men of old couldn't guard against them, even when they dwelt in the realms of the *suparnas*.'* And when the brother pressed him the Master told an old story.

"'In former times King Tamba ruled the kingdom of Vārāṇasī. He had a chief queen named Sussondī, a woman of the utmost beauty. The Bodhisattva was born then as a suparṇa. At that time there was an island of serpents called the Island of Seruma. In that island the Bodhisattva dwelt in a palace of suparnas.

"'One day he went to Vārāṇasī in human guise, and gambled with King Tamba. The attendants saw how fair he was, and told Sussondī that a handsome man was gambling with the King. She wanted to see him, so one day she put on all her ornaments and came to the gambling-hall, where, standing among her maids, she watched him. And then he saw the Queen. The two fell in love with one another. The King of the Suparnas stirred up a magic wind in the city, and everyone rushed from the royal palace, fearing that it might fall. With his magic power he created darkness, seized the Queen, and flew to his palace in the Isle of Serpents.

"'Nobody knew where Sussondī had gone, but the Suparṇa took his pleasure of her and went back to play with the King. Now the King had a minstrel named

*A class of large mythical bird, of whom Garuḍa (p. 265) is the chief.

Sagga. Not knowing what had happened to the Queen he said to the minstrel, "Go and seek over land and sea, and find out where the Queen has gone." So he took money for his journey and, starting in the suburbs, he sought everywhere until he came to Bhṛgukaccha. Just then some merchants of Bhrgukaccha were setting out by ship for the Land of Gold (? Burma). He went up to them and said, "I'm a minstrel. If you'll remit my fare and take me with you I'll make music for you." They agreed, took him aboard, and set sail.

"'When the ship was well under way they called him to make music for them. "I'd willingly make music for you," he said, "but if I did the fish would leap out of the water and smash your ship". "When a mere man makes music the fish don't get excited," they said, "so tune up!" "Then don't blame me for anything that may happen," he said, and he tuned his lute and made music, with strings and voice in perfect unison. The fish heard the sound, and leapt with excitement. Then a sea-monster (*makara*) leapt from the sea, fell on the ship, and smashed it to pieces. Sagga lay on a plank and drifted with the wind to the Isle of Serpents, and landed by a banyan tree near the palace of the King of the Suparnas.

"'Now the King of the Suparṇas had gone away to play dice, and so Queen Sussondī had come down from the palace and was walking on the shore; and she saw and recognized Sagga the minstrel, and asked him how he came. He told her all his story. She told him not to be afraid, and comforted him, and clasped him in her arms, and had him taken to the palace, where she laid him on a couch. When he was revived she gave him fine food, bathed him in sweetly scented water, dressed him in fine clothes, adorned him with beautiful fragrant flowers, and again made him rest on the fine couch. So she cared for him, and whenever the King of the Suparṇas returned she hid him; then, as soon as he went again, she took passionate pleasure with him.

"'When a month and half a month had passed, merchants from Vārāṇasī landed on that island at the foot of the banyan tree in search of fuel and water. He boarded their ship, went back to Vārāṇasī, and saw the King while he was gambling. Then he took his lute, and, making music, sang the first stanza:

"There blows the scent of timīra trees
with the sounding of the evil sea,
but Sussondī is far away.
Tamba, desires torment me!"

"When he heard this, the Suparṇa sang the second stanza:

"How did you cross the ocean?
How came you to see Serama?
How was it, Sagga,
that she and you did meet?"

'Then Sagga sang three stanzas:

"From Bhṛgukaccha there sailed
traders in search of wealth.
A monster broke their ship.
I floated on a plank.

"In her soft and tender lap
ever fragrant with sandal
the gentle lady pillowed me,
as a mother her own son.

"This you should know, King Tamba,
the fair-eyed lady gave me
food with her own hands,
and drink, and raiment, and a bed."

"'Even as the minstrel sang the Suparṇa was filled with regret. "Though I dwelt in the Palace of the Suparṇas," he thought, "I could not keep her! What is the wanton to me?" So he brought her back, gave her to the King, and went away. And he never came again.'

"When the story was over the Master declared the Four Noble Truths (p. 237), and identified the births.... 'Ānanda (p. 229) was the King of Vārāṇasī, and I was the King of the Suparṇas.'"[43]

As examples of Pāli poetry we give a few verses from the "Songs of the Elder Monks and Nuns" (*Theragāthā* and *Therīgāthā*), a collection of poems ascribed, falsely no doubt, to the great disciples of the Buddha in the early days of the Order. The style of these poems is simpler than that of courtly Sanskrit literature, and suggests the influence of popular song. The first is attributed to Ambapāli, the beautiful courtezan of Vaisāli who became a Buddhist nun.

"Black and glossy as a bee and curled was my hair;
now in old age it is just like hemp or bark-cloth.
Not otherwise is the word of the truthful. ...

"My hair clustered with flowers was like a box of sweet perfume;
now in old age it stinks like a rabbit's pelt.
Not otherwise is the word of the truthful ...

"Once my eyebrows were lovely, as though drawn by an artist;
now in old age they are overhung with wrinkles.
Not otherwise is the word of the truthful. ...

"Dark and long-lidded, my eyes were bright and flashing as jewels;
now in old age they are dulled and dim.
Not otherwise is the word of the truthful. ...

"My voice was as sweet as the cuckoo's, who flies in the woodland thickets;
now in old age it is broken and stammering.
Not otherwise is the word of the truthful. …

"Once my hands were smooth and soft, and bright with jewels and gold;
now in old age they twist like roots.
Not otherwise is the word of the truthful. …

"Once my body was lovely as polished gold;
now in old age it is covered all over with tiny wrinkles.
Not otherwise is the word of the truthful. …

"Once my two feet were soft, as though filled with down;
now in old age they are cracked and wizened.
Not otherwise is the word of the truthful. …

"Such was my body once. Now it is weary and tottering,
the home of many ills, an old house with flaking plaster.
Not otherwise is the word of the truthful."[44]

Few ancient Indian poems show such a deep love of nature as some of these verses, ascribed to pious monks of the 5th century B.C.

"When the dram of the clouds thunders in heaven,
    and all the ways of the birds are thick with rain,
the monk sits in the hills in ecstasy
    and finds no joy greater than this.

"When by rivers covered with flowers,
    and gaily adorned with reeds of varied hue,
the goodly monk sits on the bank in ecstasy
    he finds no joy greater than this.

"When the rain pours down at night,
    and elephants trumpet in die distant thickets,
the monk sits in the hills in ecstasy,
    and finds no joy greater than this."[45]

"When the crane with clear pale wing
    flies in fear from the black cloud,
seeking shelter and finding none,
    The river Ajakaraṇī gives me joy.

"Who would not love
    the rose-apple trees
fair on either bank
    beside the great cavern?

"Freed from the fear of flocks of cranes
 the frogs croak softly now.
This is no time to leave the hills and streams!
 Safe, good and pleasant is Ajakarani."[46]

As an example of Pāli descriptive poetry we give a stirring passage from the Ceylon Chronicle, the *Mahāvaṃsa*, describing the capture of Vijitanagara, the capital of the Tamil invader Eḷāra, by the Sinhalese national hero, King Duṭṭhagāmaṇī (161-137 B.C.), with the aid of his favourite elephant, Kaṇḍula.

"The city had three moats,
 and was guarded by a high wall.
Its gate was covered with iron
 hard for foes to shatter.

"The elephant knelt on his knees
 and, battering with his tusks
stone and mortar and brick,
 he attacked the iron gate.

"The Tamils from the watch-tower
 threw missiles of every kind,
balls of red-hot iron
 and [Vessels of] molten pitch.

"Down fell the smoking pitch
 upon Kaṇḍula's back.
In anguish of pain he fled
 and plunged in a pool of water.

"'This is no drinking bout!'
 cried Goṭhaīmbara.
'Go, batter the iron gate!
 Batter down the gate!!'

"In his pride the best of tuskers
 took heart and trumpeted loud.
He reared up out of the water
 and stood on the bank defiant.

"The elephant-doctor washed away
 the pitch, and put on balm.
The King mounted the elephant
 and rubbed his brow with his hand.

"'Dear Kaṇḍula, I'll make you
 the lord of all Ceylon!'
he said, and the beast was cheered,
 and was fed with the best of fodder.

"He was covered with a cloth,
and he was armoured well
with armour for his back
of seven-fold buffalo hide.

"On the armour was placed
a skin soaked in oil.
Then, trampeting like thunder,
he came on, fearless of danger.

"He pierced the door with his tusks.
With his feet he trampled the threshold.
And the gate and the lintel
crashed loudly to the earth."[47]

Prākrit Literature

Space will not permit more than a brief reference to the Prākrit scriptures of the Jainas, examples of which we have already quoted (p. 256f). In general they have little literary value. Like Jainism itself they tend to be arid, and, like the Pāli scriptures but in even greater measure, they repeat lengthy stock phrases and descriptions, which may have had some mnemonic value but which to the modern reader are very irritating. Lengthy descriptions of the Tirthaṅkaras, of pious monks, mighty kings, wealthy merchants, prosperous cities etc. occur over and over again, in exactly the same words throughout the canon, and give it a flavour of uninspired dryness. The style is somewhat more ornate than that of the Pāli scriptures, and closer to courtly Sanskrit.

The poetry of the Jainas is better than their prose. In this connexion we cannot refrain from quoting a remarkable poem, which is one of the most humorous things in ancient Indian literature, and which, by some lucky chance, has found its way into the Jaina canon among the austere pages of the *Sūtrakṛtāṅga*. It is intended as a waming of the grim fate in store for the backsliding monk, and throws a most unexpected light on one aspect of Indian marriage. Our translation is rather free, but we have tried to keep some of the lively vernacular style of the original.

"A celibate monk shouldn't fall in love,
and though he hankers after pleasure he should hold himself in check.
for these are the pleasures
which some monks enjoy.

"If a monk breaks his vows,
and falls for a woman,
she upbraids him and raises her foot to him,
and kicks him on the head.

"'Monk, if you won't live with me
as husband and wife,

I'll pull out my hair and become a nun,
for you shall not live without me!'

"But when she has him in her clutches
it's all housework and errands!
'Fetch a knife to cut this gourd!'
'Get me some fresh fruit!'

"'We want wood to boil the greens,
and for a fire in the evening!'
'Now paint my feet!'
'Come and massage my back!'

"'Get me my lip-salve!'
'Find my sunshade and slippers!'
'I want a knife to cut these leaves!'
'Take my robe and have it dyed blue!' …

"'Fetch me my tweezers and my comb!'
'Get me a ribbon to tie my hair!'
'Now pass me my looking-glass!'
Go and fetch me my toothbrush!' …

"'Fetch the pot and the drum and the rag-ball,
for our little boy to play with!'
'Monk, the rains are on the way,
patch the roof of the house and look to the stores!'

"'See to getting that chair re-upholstered!
Fetch my wooden-soled slippers to go out walking!'
So pregnant women boss their husbands,
just as though they were household slaves.

"When a child is born, the reward of their labours,
she makes the father hold the baby.
And sometimes the fathers of sons
stagger under their burdens like camels.

"They get up at night, as though they were nurses,
to lull the howling child to sleep,
and, though they are shamefaced about it,
scrub dirty garments, just like washermen. …

"So, monks, resist the wiles of women,
avoid their friendship and company.
The little pleasure you get from them
will only lead you into trouble"[48]

A number of medieval works of a secular nature were written in Prākrit, chief of which are the poems "The Building of the Causeway" (*Setubandha*), describing Rāma's invasion of Ceylon and falsely ascribed to Kālidāsa; "The Slaying of the King of Bengal" (*Gaudavadha*), a long panegyric by the 8th-century poet Vākpati, describing the exploits of Yaśovarman, king of Kānyakubja (p. 60); and a drama named after its heroine, Karpūramañjarī, by the 10th-century dramatist Rājaśekhara. These works, though not without merit, are indistinguishable in style and content from comparable Sanskrit production, and need not detain us.

The most important literary work in Prākrit is the "Seven Hundred" (*Saptaśataka*) of Hāla. This is a large collection of self-contained stanzas of great charm and beauty, in the *Āryā* metre (p. 468f). Their traditional author was the shadowy Sātavāhana king Hāla, who ruled in the Deccan in the 1st century A.D., but in fact many of these verses seem considerably later, and they must be looked on as anonymous. They are notable for their conciseness; like Amaru, their authors were able to suggest a whole story in four short lines. This great economy of words and masterly use of suggestion would indicate that the verses were written for a highly educated literary audience; but they contain simple and natural descriptions and references to the lives of peasants and the lower classes, which point to popular influence. The treatment of the love affairs of country folk reminds us of early Tamil poetry, and suggests that "Hāla" may have tapped a widely diffused source in South Indian folksong.

"Last night with scorn the lady gave the wanderer
    Straw for his bed.
This morning she gathers it together,
    weeping."

"'This morning, my friend, I heard a man singing,
    and his song reminded me of my lover,
and opened all the wounds
    that the shafts of the Love-god had made in my heart.'"

. . . .

"'Waiting for you, the first half of the night
    passed like a moment.
The rest was like a year,
    for I was sunk in grief.'"

. . . .

"When the season of rains, with its high clouds,*
    has passed like youth,
the earliest single *kāsa* flower
    comes, like a grey hair on the earth."

. . . .

* There is a pun here on *paohare,* which may mean either "clouds" or "breasts".

"'Ungrateful lover, still I see the mud
in the village Street,
which, on a rainy night,
I trod for your sake, shameless one!'"[49]

Tamil Literature

The oldest Tamil literature goes back to the early centuries of the Christian era. Its dating is still a matter of some dispute but it seems almost certain that the most ancient stratum was composed before the great Pallava dynasty of Kāñcī became dominant in the Tamil Land in the 6th century, and it is probably some centuries older than this.

Tamil tradition tells of three literary academies (*śaṅgam*) which met at Madurai. The first of these was attended by gods and legendary sages, and all its works have perished. Of the second, there survives only the early Tamil grammar, *Tolkāppiyam*. The poets of the Third Śaṅgam, on the other hand, wrote the "Eight Anthologies" (*Ettutogai*), which are the greatest monument of ancient Tamil literature, as well as a number of later works. Some authorities have doubted the tradition of the Śaṅgams, and it is almost certain that the grammar *Tolkāppiyam*, attributed to the Second Śaṅgam, is later than many of the poems of the Third. But the tradition of the Śaṅgams, which is a strongly held one, has no parallel in Northern legend, and we may believe that the bards of the Tamil Land, who wandered over the country enjoying the patronage of chieftains and villagers alike, would meet from time to time in the city of Madurai for great festivals of poetry and music, and that many of the verses of the Anthologies were recited there.

The poetry of the "Eight Anthologies" is little known outside the land of its origin, and its language is so archaic that the modern educated Tamil cannot read it without special study. The relation of the language of the Śaṅgam literature to Tamil as it is now written is perhaps similar to that of *Piers Plowman* to modern English. The tradition of Tamil poetry at the time of the composition of these works must already have been a long one, for the poetic conventions finally fixed in the *Tolkāppiyam* had almost reached their finished form even in the earliest poems of the Anthologies. But their style is much nearer that of folk literature than is the style of courtly Sanskrit. The life of the peasant and the scenes of the countryside, the bustle of the towns and the ruthlessness of war, are here depicted as though from direct experience, and with no formal unrealistic īdealization.

Together the "Eight Anthologies"* make up a very large body of poetic literature, and contain well over 2,000 poems, ascribed to more than 200 authors. To them must be added "The Ten Songs" (*Pattuppāṭṭu*), containing ten longer poems of similar style but somewhat later date. Until the end of the last century

---

* *Naṟṟiṇai:* 400 short poems on love, each of from nine to twelve lines; *Kuṛuntogai,* 400 love poems of from tour to eight lines each; *Ainguṛunūṛu,* 500 short erotic poems; *Padiṟṟuppaṭṭu,* a short collection of eight (originally ten) poems, each of ten verses, in praise or the king of the Cāra country (Kerala); *Paripādal,* twenty-four (originally seventy) poems in praise of gods; *Kalittogai,* 150 love poems; *Aganānūṛu,* 400 love-lyrics of varying length; and *Puṛanāṃiṛu,* 400 poems in praise of kings.

this great collection was almost forgotten, even by the Tamils themselves; only within the last fifty years have the rare manuscripts containing it been edited and given to the world. Much is still untranslated, and a full and thorough study of the Śaṅgam literature from the critical and historical point of view has yet to be made.

Very early the Tamils developed the passion for classification which is noticeable in many aspects of ancient Indian learning. Poetry was divided into two main groups: "internal" (*agam*), dealing with love, and "external "(*puram*), dealing with the praise of kings. A further division was made according to the region of the Tamil Land to which the poem referred or was most appropriate. Conventionally there were five regions (*tiṇai*): the hills (*kuriñji*), the dry lands (*pālai*), the jungle and woodland (*mullai*), the cultivated plains (*marudam*), and the coast (*neydal*). Each was connected with some special aspect of love or war; thus the hills were the scene of poems on pre-nuptial love and on cattle-raiding; the dry lands, of those on the long separation of lovers and on the laying waste of the countryside; the jungle, on the brief parting of lovers and on raiding expeditions; the valleys, on post-nuptial love or the wiles of courtezans and on siege; and the seacoast, on the parting of fishermen's wives from their lords and on pitched battle. To each region were attributed its own appropriate flowers, animals and people. Every poem of the "Eight Anthologies" was classified in one of the five sections, but much of the poetry was written with little regard to this formal classification.

A unique feature of Tamil poetry is the initial rhyme or assonance. This does not appear in the earliest Tamil literature, but by the end of the Śaṅgam period it was quite regular. The first syllable or syllables of each couplet must rhyme. Thus:

IŚAIYĀD' eninum iyarrior ārrāl
AŚAITĀDu nirpadām āṇmai; iśaiyuṅgaḷ
KAṆḌARirai alaikkuṅ kānal an tan śērppa
PEṆḌIRum vālārō marru."

"Though you fail, to work and struggle,
unwaveringly steadfast—this is manliness.
Lord of the cool and lovely shore, where the waves shake the thorny groves!
Will not even women flourish in prosperity?"[50]

This initial assonance, in some poems continued through four or more lines, is never to be found in the poetry of Sanskritic languages, or, as far as we know, in that of any other language. Its effect, a little strange at first, rapidly becomes pleasant to the reader, and to the Tamil it is as enjoyable as the end rhyme of Western poetry.

We give a brief anthology of short poems and extracts from this wonderful literature.*

---

* The first ten extracts are the work of Dr J. R. Marr, to whom I am much indebted for permission to use them. The other versions are my own, some made with the help of the many literal translations of Prof. P. T. S. Iyengar.[51]

Here a mother tells of her son, who has gone to war.

"If you lean against the pillar of my little home
and ask the whereabouts of my son,
I reply, 'I cannot tell you'.
Behold, like a tiger's cavern of rock,
the womb that bore him!
You will find him on the field of war."[52]

The three following poems are attributed to the poetess Avvaiyār.

"It charms not like the harp,
it accords not with the time-beat,
it conveys no meaning,
but the prattling of a son
brings bliss to his father.
So, O King Nedumān Añji,
through the grace of your favour
my empty words are imbued with meaning.
O King, you have overcome the enemy's forts,
though unscaleable were their walls."[53]

. . . .

"To allow the little children of the village
to wash clean its white tusks,
the huge elephant will lie on the river bank.
O great. King, you favour me like that!
But to approach an elephant in rat is death,
and you are death to your foes, O King!"[54]

Here Avvaiyār compares the wealth of the luxurious king of Toṇḍai (Kāñcī) with that of her own warlike chief.

"Bedecked with peacock-feathers, garlanded with flowers,
fine are the Toṇḍai spears in the spacious armoury,
with their strong shafts, and sharp points bright with ghee.
The weapons of my king are blunt with fighting,
broken their points through parrying the thrusts of the foe.
The swordsmith's forge is busy with repairs.
My king, when rich, freely gives food away,
when poor he messes with his men.
He is the head of the family of the poor,
yet great is he, with his sharp-pointed spear."[55]

"O bee, fair of wing, ever in search of flower-garlands,
tell me not what I fain would hear, but what you really saw!
Among all the flowers you know is any more fragrant
than the tresses of my lady of the close-set teeth?
Graceful as the peacock she dwells, rich in love, with me!"[56]

"Ever anew aches my heart!
Again and again I brush off the burning tears.
My love, once peaceful at my side, grows restless.
My heart aches!"[57]

"In the gathering night
hushed of speech all men sweetly sleep.
Devoid of wrath,
countless people in the world are resting.
I alone sleep not!"[58]

Here a mother asks an ascetic the whereabouts of her daughter, who has eloped with her lover. The sage offers her this consolation:

"Save to the wearer of its scent,
of what use is the sandalwood tree,
even to the mountains amid which it was born?
If you ponder the matter, it is so with your daughter.

"Except to the wearer of it
of what avail is the highly prized white pearl,
even to the sea in which it was reared?
If you ponder the matter, it is so with your daughter."[59]

Here a girl speaks to her playmate:

"What bright bracelets you have! Do listen!
As I was playing in the road
he kicked over my mud castle with his foot,
and snatched the garland from my head,
and ran away with my striped ball.
How he teased me, the naughty boy!

"Another day my mother and I
were together, when a voice called out:
'Whoever's at home, please give me some water!'
Mother said to me: 'My dear,
fill the gilded vessel, and give him water to drink!'
I went out, not knowing who it was.
He caught my wrist, with the bangles on, and squeezed it,
and I was frightened, and cried out:

'Mother, just look what he's done!'
She was very upset, and hurried down,
but I told her he'd hiccups because of the water.
He looked at me as if he could kill me,
but then the rogue made friends with a smile."[60]

Here a newly married girl makes her first attempts at cooking:

"Her fingers, slender as the *kāndaḷ* blossom, had been squeezing the new curds.
Her clothes had not been washed since she wiped her fingers on them.
The appetizing steam had got into her lily-like eyes.
Yet, as she rubbed them, he just said, 'The curry you've cooked is delieious.'
He of the bright brow was most pleased with what he was eating."[61]

Striking touches of natural description often illumine the rather monotonous panegyrics:

"Though milk turn sour [in the udder], though day turn to night,
though the path of the Vedas lead men astray,
may you stand unshaken, long famed, with loyal
supporters, that, in the foothills of the mountains,
the large-eyed mother doe with her small-headed fawn
may sleep secure at evening by the flame of the three fires
of hermits who perform hard penances."[62]

. . . .

"Unfailing in the hard tasks of war,
O king, like death, for whom there is no cure,
though the earth be moved from her place, your name is eternal—
you, whose legs wear golden anklets, whose broad breast
is spread with drying sandal-paste!
In an uninhabited land, a land of bitter hardship,
a land without water, a land of long tracks,
your valiant warriors fight, unerring in their archery,
gazing afar, with their hands hung over their eyes.
There, in the silk-cotton tree, where roads diverge,
the eagle, with trim feathers and crooked beak,
wails over the new cairns of those who have shot their arrows."68

Here a girl consoles her lovelorn friend:

"'The toiling fishermen catch the shoals
in their close-meshed nets, and the soft-headed prawn,
thin as the cassia bud in the forest.

"'Like hunters who chase the deer in the woods
young fishermen chase in the waste of the waters
the saw-toothed shark, and return with meat

"'They return to the shore and unload on the sanri,
where the wind plays wild across the saltpans,
and soon the street of the fishing village
will ring with the wheels of your lover's chariot.'"[64]

A young man praises his sweetheart's cooking:

"'At every post before the house
is tied the gentle calf of a crooked-horned buffalo.
There dwells my sweetheart, curving and lovely,
languid of gaze, with big round earrings,
and little rings on her tiny fingers.

"'She has cut the leaves of the garden plantain
and split them in pieces down the stalk
to serve as platters for the meal.
Her eyes are filled with the smoke of cooking.
Her brow, as fair as the crescent moon,
is covered now with drops of sweat.
She wipes it away with the hem of her garment
and stands in the kitchen, and thinks of me.

"'Come in then, if you want a good meal!
You'll see her smile and show her tiny
sharp teeth, whom I long to kiss.'"[65]

A village festival:

"The farmers who harvest rice in the hot sun
now leap into the waves of the clear sea.
The sailors, captains of stout craft,
drink strong liquor and dance for joy,
as they clasp the bright-bangled hands of women
who wear garlands of clustering *punnai*. ...

"In the cool woods, where the bees seek flowers,
women, bright-bangled and garlanded, drink
the sap of the palm and the pale sugar-cane,
and the juice of the coconut which grows in the sand,
then running they plunge into the sea."[66]

A poignant description of famine:

"The hearth has forgotten cooking:
It is overgrown with moss and mould.
The woman, thin with hunger,
has breasts like wrinkled bladders.
Their nipples are quite dry,
but the child chews them, weeping.
She looks down at his face
and tears hang on her lashes."[67]

Our final quotation from the "Eight Anthologies" is the plaint of a neglected wife:

"My garment smells of ghee and frying curry,
and is stained with dirt and lampblack.

"My shoulders stink with the sweat of the child
whom I carry upon them and feed at my breast.

"I cannot face my lord, who, in gay attire,
rides in his car to the street of the harlots."[68]

The next stratum of Tamil literature shows much greater Āryan influence. Āryan religious ideas and practices, not unknown even in the Eight Anthologies, had by now been thoroughly grafted on to the original Tamil heritage, and Jaina influence is prominent. "The Eighteen Minor Works" (*Padineṇkīlkaṇakku*) are largely gnomic and moralizing in character, the two most famous being the *Tirukkuraḷ*, and the *Nālaḍiyār*. The former, sometimes called the "Bible of the Tamil Land" is a series of brief metrical proverbs on many aspects of life and religion, and we have already quoted some of its aphorisms (p. 297f). We add a few others of a more secular type.

"Vain is the kingdom where are all good things
but no love between ruler and ruled."

. . . .

"Even the hermit ceases his penance
if the husbandman folds his arms."

. . . .

"Earth laughs in scorn
at those who plead poverty."

. . . .

"No food is sweeter than rice-gruel,
when you have worked for it."

. . . .

"Wide as the sea is the joy of love,
but wider still the sorrow of parting."

. . . .

"Love is stronger than wine,
for the very thought of it intoxicates."

. . . .

"Sweethearts delight in a lover's quarrel
for the greater delight of making it up."[69]

Nālaḍiyār is more formal and literary in style, and contains verses of much merit and high ethical content.

"Better hatred than the friendship of fools.
Better death than chronic illness.
Better to be killed than soul-destroying contempt.
Better abuse than praise undeserved."

. . . .

"True housekeeping is to eat a meal
sharing, as far as may be, with friend and foe alike.
The useless men who eat their food alone
will never pass the gate of heaven."

. . . .

"Though you feed him with care from a golden dish
a dog will always prefer carrion.
Though you deal with the base as you would with the good
their deeds will always show them up."

. . . .

"Hillmen remember their lovely hills.
Farmers remember their fertile fields.
The good remember another's kindness.
The base recall only fancied slights."

. . . .

"As a scroll read by one who well understands it,
as wealth to the man of generous spirit,
as a sharp sword in a warrior's hand,
is the beauty of a faithful wife."

. . . .

"To those who once embraced their lovers
whose broad chests were hung with garlands,
when their loved ones are far away
the thunder sounds like a funeral dram."[70]

By the 6th century Āryan influence had penetrated the whole of the Tamil land, and her kings and chiefs worshipped and supported the gods of Hinduism, Jainism and Buddhism. The indigenous style of poetry was rapidly altering under the influence of Sanskrit, and Tamil poets took to writing long poems which they called by the Sanskrit name *kāvya*. The earliest and greatest of these is "The Jewelled Anklet" (*Śilappadigāram*), which is still very different from Sanskrit poetry. Though written for an educated audience and in faultless literary style it is near to the life of the people; by comparison realistic, it deals with the lives of two ordinary folk enmeshed in unhappy circumstance, and, unlike the Sanskrit courtly "epic", it sounds a note of true tragedy.

The traditional author of the poem was Ilangōvadigal, a grandson of the great Cōla king Karikālan, who lived in the lst or 2nd century A.D. The tradition is certainly false, and the poem is several centuries later. Its author, whoever he was, though a great poet, was not a great storyteller. His tale was well known to his hearers, and he could afford to be irritatingly allusive and terse in important narrative passages, and linger lovingly over interesting description. He successfully drew together all the themes of earlier Tamil poets and welded them into a whole, in the framework of the story of the luckless Kōvalan and Kaṇṇagi. Rightly this poem and Kamban's *Rāmāyaṇam* are looked on as the national epics of the Tamil people. We give an outline of the story, with a translation, considerably abridged, of its climax, which has a grim force and splendour unparalleled elsewhere in Indian literature. It is imbued with both the ferocity of the early Tamils and their stern respect for justice, and, incidentally, it throws much light on early Tamil political ideas.

Kōvalan, the son of a wealthy merchant of the city of Pugār or Kāvirippaṭṭinam, married Kaṇṇagi, the lovely daughter of another merchant. For some time they lived together happily, until, at a festival at the royal court, Kōvalan met the dancer Mādavi and fell in love with her. He bought her favours and in his infatuation forgot Kaṇṇagi and his home. Gradually he spent all his wealth on the dancer, even to Kaṇṇagi's jewels. At last he was penniless, and returned repentantly to his uncomplaining wife. Their only fortune was a precious pair of anklets, which she gave to him willingly. With these as their capital they decided to go to the great city of Madurai, where Kōvalan hoped to recoup his fortunes by trade.

On their arrival at Madurai they found shelter in a cottage, and Kōvalan went to the market to sell one of Kaṇṇagi's anklets. But the queen of Neduñjeliyan, king of the Pāṇḍyas, had just been robbed of a similar anklet by a wicked court jeweller. The jeweller happened to see Kōvalan with Kaṇṇagi's anklet, and immediately seized it and informed the King. Guards were sent to apprehend Kōvalan, who was cut down immediately, without trial. When the news was brought to Kaṇṇagi she fainted away; but she quickly recovered and, with her eyes ablaze with anger, she went out into the town, carrying the remaining anklet in her hand as proof of her husband's innocence.

"'Chaste women of Madurai, listen to me!
Today my sorrows cannot be matched.
Things which should never have happened have befallen me.
How can I bear this injustice?'…

"All the folk of the rich city of Madurai
saw her, and were moved by her grief and affiiction.
In wonder and sorrow they cried:
'Wrong that cannot be undone has been done to this lady!

"'Our King's straight sceptre is bent!
What can this mean?
Lost is the glory of the King Over Kings,
the Lord of the Umbrella and Spear! …

"'A new and a mighty goddess
has come before us,
in her hand a golden anklet!
What can this mean?

"This woman afflicted and weeping
from her lovely dark-stained eyes
is as though filled with godhead!
What can this mean?'

"Thus, raising loud accusing voices,
the people of Madurai befriended and comforted her,
and among the tumultuous throng
some showed her her husband's body.

"She, the golden vine, beheld him,
but her he could not see. …

"Then the red-rayed sun folded his fiery arms
and hid behind the great mountain,
and the wide world
was veiled in darkness.

'In the brief twilight
Kaṇṇagi cried aloud
and the whole city
echoed her wailing.

"In the morning she had taken the wreath from his neck
and decked her hair with its flowers;
in the evening she saw him lying
in a pool of his own blood.

"But he saw not the agony of her grief
  as she mourned in sorrow and wrath. …

"'Are there women here? Are there women
  who could bear such wrong
done to their wedded lords?
  Are there women here? Are there such women?

"'Are there good men here? Are there good men
  who cherish their children
and guard them with care?
  Are there men here? Are there such men?

"'Is there a god here? Is there a god
  in this city of Madurai, where the sword of a king
has slain an innocent man?
  Is there a god here? Is there a god?'

"Lamenting thus she clasped her husband's breast,
  and it seemed that he rose to his feet and said,
'The full-moon of your face has faded,'
  and he stroked her face with his hands.

"She fell to the ground, sobbing and crying,
  and clasped her lord's feet with her bangled hands;
and he left behind his human form
  and went, surrounded by the gods.

"And, as he went, he said,
  'My darling, you must stay!'
'Surely this
  was a vision,' she cried.

"'I will not join my lord
  till my great wrath is appeased 1
I will see the cruel King,
  and ask for his explanation!'

"And she stood on her feet,
  her large eyes full of tears,
and, wiping her eyes,
  she went to the gate of the palace.

"'I saw, alas, I saw in a dream
  the sceptre fall and the royal umbrella.
The beli at the palace gate rang of itself,
  while the whole heaven shook in confusion!

"'A darkness swallowed the sun,
a rainbow glowed in the night,
and a burning meteor
crashed to the earth by day.'

"Thus spoke the Queen,
and took her maids and her bodyguard,
and went to the King on the lion-throne,
and told him her evil dream.

'Then came a cry from the gate:
'Ho, Gatekeeper! Ho, Gatekeeper!!
Ho, Gatekeeper of the King who has lost wisdom,
whose evil heart has swerved from justice!!

"Tell the King that a woman with an anklet,
an anklet from a pair of tinkling anklets,
a woman who has lost her husband,
is waiting at the gate.'

"And the gatekeeper went to the King and said:
'A woman waits at the gate.
She is not Korravai, goddess of victory,
with triumphant spear in her hand. …

"'Filled with anger, boiling with rage,
a woman who has lost her husband,
an anklet of gold in her hand,
is waiting at the gate.'"

Kaṇṇagi was then admitted to the King's presence.

"'Cruel King, this I must say. …

"'My lord Kōvalan came
to Madurai to earn wealth,
and today you have slain him
as he sold my anklet.'

"'Lady,' said the King,
'it is kingly justice
to put to death
an arrant thief.'"

Then Kaṇṇagi showed her anklet to the King. On comparing it very carefully with the remaining anklet of the pair belonging to the Queen, he realized that Kōvalan had been innocent.

"When he saw it the parasol fell from his head
  and the sceptre trembled in his hand.
"'I am no king,' he said,
  'who have heeded the words of the goldsmith.

"'I am the thief. For the first time
  I have failed to protect my people.
Now may I die!'
  [And he fell to the ground, dead.]

Then Kaṇṇagi said to the Queen:

"'If I have always been true to my husband
  I will not suffer this city to flourish,
but I will destroy it as the King is destroyed!
  Soon you will see that my words are true!'

"And with these words she left the palace,
  and cried out through the city, 'Men and women
of great Madurai of the four temples,
  listen! Listen you gods in heaven!

"'Listen to me, you holy sages!
  I curse the capital of the King
who so cruelly wronged
  my beloved lord!'

"With her own hand she tore the left breast from her body.
  Thrice she surveyed the city of Madurai,
calling her curse in bitter agony.
  Then she flung her fair breast on the scented street. …

"And the burning mouth of the Fire-god opened
  as the gods who guarded the city closed their doors. …

"The high priest, the astrologer and the judges,
  the treasurer and the learned councillors,
the palace servants and the maids,
  stood silent and still as painted pictures.

"The elephant-riders and horsemen,
  the charioteers and the foot-soldiers
with their terrible swords, all fled from the fire
  which raged at the gate of the royal palace. …

"And the street of the sellers of grain,
  the street of the chariots, with its bright-coloured garlands,
and the four quarters of the four classes
  were filled with confusion and flamed like a forest on fire. …

"In the Street of the singing girls
where so often the tabor had sounded
with the sweet gentle flute and the tremulous harp ...
the dancers, whose halls were destroyed, cried out:

"'Whence comes this woman? Whose daughter is she?
A single woman, who has lost her husband,
has conquered the evil King with her anklet,
and has destroyed our city with fire!'"[71]

At last the patron goddess of the city interceded with Kaṇṇagi, and she agreed to withdraw her curse, and the fire abated. Weak with loss of blood from her self-amputated breast, Kaṇṇagi struggled to a hill outside the city, where after a few days she died, and was reunited with Kōvalan in heaven. Meanwhile the news of her death spread throughout the Tamil Land. She was deified, temples were raised and festivals held in her honour, and she became the patron goddess of wifely loyalty and chastity.

A little later than "The Jewelled Anklet" was composed its sequel *Maṇimēgalai*, attributed to the poet Śāttan of Madurai. Though by tradition it is the earlier of the two all other evidence suggests the opposite, for it assumes the reader's knowledge of "The Jewelled Anklet", to which it is a sort of Buddhist supplement. "The Jewelled Anklet", though containing many religious and moral lessons, was primarily written to tell a story, while in *Maṇimēgalai* the story is a mere framework for philosophical polemic, and the atmosphere of the narrative passages has some of the otherworldly formality of the courtly Sanskrit kāvya. The heroine, Maṇimēgalai, is the daughter of Kōvalan, the hero of "The Jewelled Anklet", by the dancer Mādavi, who became a Buddhist min on hearing of her former lover's death. The story tells of the love of Prince Udayakumāran for Maṇimēgalai, and the miraculous preservation of her chastity. In the end she becomes a Buddhist nun like her mother, and most of the poem is taken up with her discussions with members of various sects, both Hindu and heterodox, and her triumphant refutation of their doctrines.

A third Tamil "epic", *Śīvaga-Śīndāmaṇi*, describes the exploits of the hero Śīvaga or Jīvaka, a superman who excels in every art from archery to the curing of snake-bite, and who wins a new bride for his harem with every feat, only to become a Jaina monk after his many triumphs. The author was a Jaina, Tiruttakkadēvar. His work is fantastic and lacking in any contact with real life; its style is elegant and ornate, and much influenced by courtly Sanskrit. It is definitely later than the other two "epics".

By now Tamil poets were not satisfied with their own traditions, translations and adaptations of various Northern works were made, the most notable of which is Kamban's *Rāmāyaṇam*, composed in the 9th century. This great poem is still known and loved in the Tamil Land, and is by no means a mere translation of the original, for Kamban adapts themes as he thinks fit, and here and there adds episodes of his own. It is noteworthy that in Kamban's hands the demon Rāvaṇa frequently takes on the proportions of a heroic figure, and contrasts favourably with the rather weak and unimpressive Rāma. Like Milton, Kamban was of the devil's party without knowing it. The greatest glory of medieval Tamil literature, however, is undoubtedly the hymns of the Śaivite and Vaiṣṇavite devotional teachers, which are among the great religious literature of the world, and which we have discussed and quoted in another connexion (p. 289ff). Other than these, later Tamil literature produced little of the first order. The canon of the Tamil Śaivites contains work of merit (p. 293), but the adaptations of the Purāṇas and the lengthy commentaries on earlier literature, though not unimportant, need not be discussed here.*

The early literatures of Canarese, Telegu and Malayālam, which had begun to be written before the end of our period, are less important than that of Tamil, and need not detain us. They originated at a time when Āryan influence was already thoroughly entrenched, and, though containing many beauties, lack the originality of early Tamil poetry. Thus they cannot aspire to the importance of Tamil, which can claim one of the longest unbroken literary traditions of any of the world's living languages.

Folk Poetry†

The literatures which we have been discussing were all the work of schools with formal conventions and long traditions. Some poetry, obviously, is less formalized than that of classical Sanskrit, and here and there, notably in the verses of the Tamil anthologies and the Prākrit *Saptaśataka*, we seem to catch echoes of folk-song and popular oral literature. No Indian writer however, as far as we know, thought fit to record the folk-song of ancient India, which, if we are to judge by modern analogy, must have been plentiful and of high quality. But a few verses have been preserved in Chinese translation, which may well be the words of genuine folk-songs of pre-Gupta times.

That part of the Buddhist canon called *Saṃyutta Nikāya* (p. 235) was first translated into Chinese about A.D. 440, from a manuscript acquired in Ceylon by Fa-hsien in 411. At the end of the book occurs a section which is not to be found in the Pāli version as it exists at present, but which must have been included in Fa-hsien's manuscript. Probably the verses here quoted were sung in India between

---

* Perhaps the greatest literary figure in later Tamil was Vīramāmuṇivar (1680-1747), a pseudonym of Father Costanzio Beschi, an Italian Jesuit who taught for thirty-six years in the Tamil country. Like many early Christian missionaries, he lived in wholly Indian fashion and attained a complete mastery of the Tamil language and literary conventions. It is doubtful if any European before or since has gained so profound a knowledge of an Indian language. Beschi's long poem *Tēmbāvani* tells stories from the Old and New Testaments in ornately beautiful Tamil. His style and the treatment of his themes were altogether in keeping with tradition, but the influence of Tasso has been tracced in his work.

† The material for this section, together with the translations of the Chinese verses, has been provided by Dr Arthur Waley. We are much indebted to him for the honour of being permitted to publish them here for the first time.

the time of the codification of the Pāli canon in the lst century B.C. (p. 233) and the beginning of the 5th century A.D.

The passage in question describes a monk, who hears the singing of various secular songs and converts them to Buddhist purposes by comparatively slight alterations. Thus the first verse quoted is capped by the monk with a pious wish that he may gently flow to Nirvāṇa, and so on.

The song of a lady who got on badly with her "in-laws":

"O river Ganges, all I now want
is to go with your waters that flow gently to the sea;
that never again by my father- and mother-in-law
I may at every turn be scolded and abused."

The song of a melon-thief:

"Bright moon, I beg you not to come out.
Wait where you are till I have cut these melons.
But when I have got my melons safely away,
then come out or not, just as you please."

The song of a poor man:

"So long as I own just one pig,
and a single jar full of good wine,
one cup to pour the wine into,
and someone to fill my cup again and again—
so long as I own just as much as that,
there is nothing else that bothers me at all."

The song of a girl who, going to a tryst with her lover on a rainy night, slips and falls in the mud:

"The hair of my head is all loose and astray;
my lovely necklace has fallen in the deep mud.
My rings and bracelets are all broken and spoiled;
when I come to my lover, what shall I give him to wear?"

The song of a lover, picnicking with his mistress:

"With thoughts of love, all for our ease and pleasure,
we loiter under the shade of the green trees.
The running stream flows swift and clear,
the sound of my zither is very tuneful and sweet.
The spring weather is just right for our jaunt;
what happiness could there be greater than ours?"

Advice to a dove:

> "Dove, my bird, you must lay up your stores—
> sesamum-seed, rice, millet and the rest—
> and take them to a tree on the very top of the hill,
> and make yourself a nest-cavern high and bright.
> Then when Heaven sends the rainy season
> you will be sure of lodging, food and drink."

PLATE LXXX

British Museum

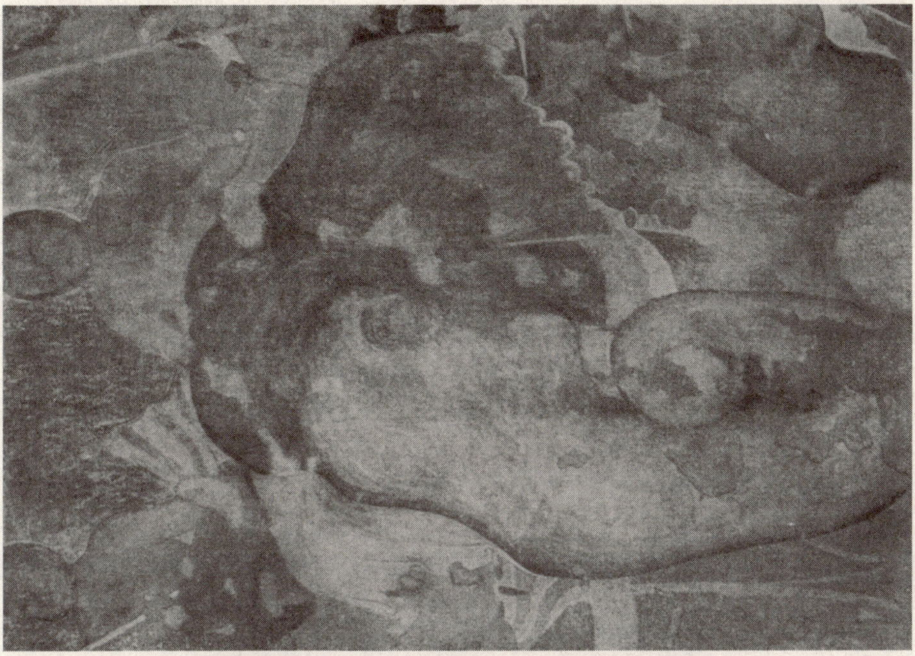

Elephant and Rider in Procession. Bāgh. 7th century

Musée Guimet, Paris

Flying Demigods. Bāmiyān, Afghanistan. 5th century A.D.

PLATE LXXXI

Messrs. Johnston & Hoffman, Calcutta

(a) Painted Cover of Palm-leaf Manuscript, Nepāl. 13th century

Messrs. Faber & Faber, Royal Academy Trustees and Museum of Central Asian Antiquities, New Delhi

(b) Necklace of Gold, Garnets, and Falence. Sirkap (Taksasilā).
c. 1st century A.D.

PLATE LXXXII

Archaeological Survey of Ceylon

Apsaras, with Attendant, drops Flowers upon the Earth. Mural painting on the rock-face of the fortress of Sīgiriya, Ceylon. 5th century A.D.

PLATE LXXXIII
Coins of Bactria and N.W. India

(a) Euthydemus. Silver. End of 3rd century, B.C.

(b) Demetrius, wearing elephant headdress. Silver. Early 2nd century B.C.

(c) Antimachus, wearing Macedonian headdress (*kansia*). Silver. Early 2nd century B.C.

(d) Menander. Silver, bilingual. 2nd century B.C.

(e) Kaniska. Gold. On the reverse a standing Buddha with Greek inscription BOAAO. End of 1st century A.D.

PLATE LXXXIV

Greco-Bactrian Silver Discs. 3rd–2nd century B.C

(a) Fighting Elephant

(b) Iranian Goddess

Greco-Bactrian Silver Cups. 3rd–2nd century B.C

(a) Marriage Feast, with Monkey-musicians

(b) Cup with Floral design

PLATE LXXXV

British Museum

(a) Buddhist Relic-casket. Gold Repousse, set with Rubies.
Bīmarān, Afghānistān. *c.* 2nd century A.D.

Museum of Pompeii & Herculaneum

(b) Indian Ivory Statuette, found at Herculaneum. 1st century A.D.

Musée Guimet, Paris

(c) Ivory Plaque, Begrām, Afghānistān. 2nd century A.D.

PLATE LXXXVI

Greco-Bactrian Silver Cups

British Museum

Ivory Combs, Ceylon and S. India. *c*. 17th century

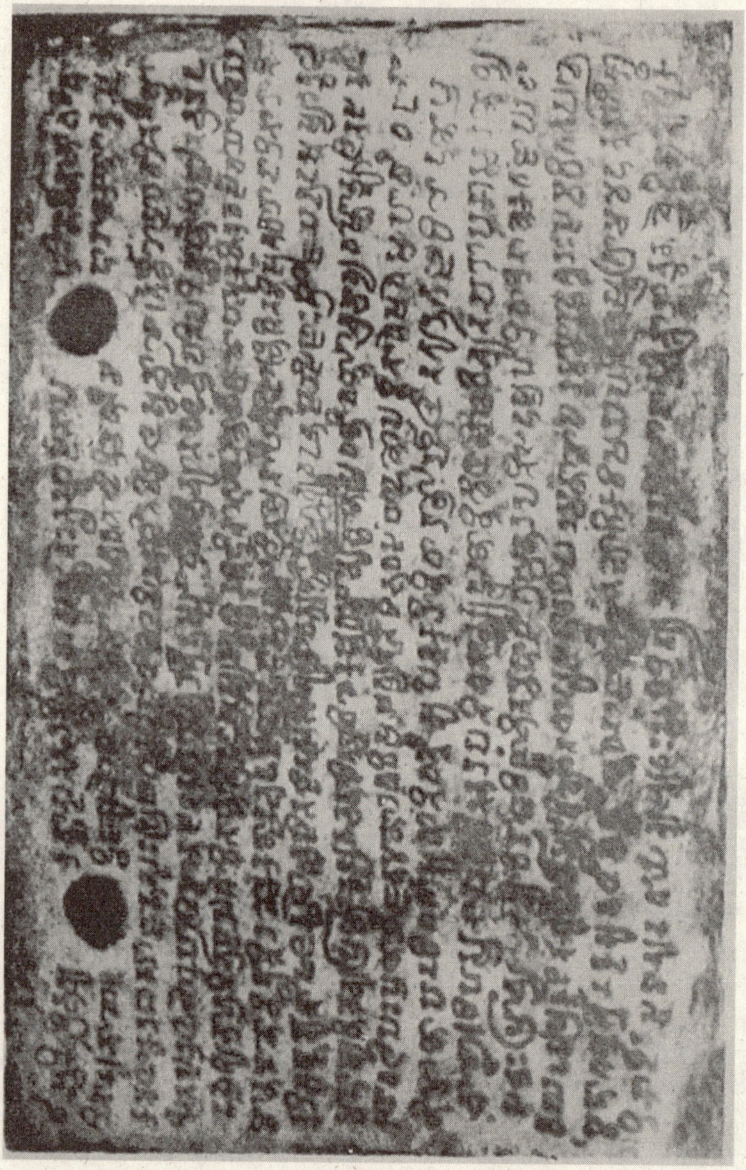

Dept. of Archaeology, Government of India

Copper-plate Charter of King Dadda III of Broach. Dated A.D. 675

X

EPILOGUE: THE HERITAGE OF INDIA

THE IMPACT OF THE WEST

INDIA'S ancient culture did not perish before the onslaughts of the Muslims, as did that of Persia. Under the rule of some of the Delhī sultans of the Middle Ages there was persecution, and we read of temples being razed to the ground and brāhmaṇs put to death for practising their devotions in public; but in general the Muslims were reasonably tolerant, and at all times Hindu chiefs continued to rule in outlying parts of India, paying tribute to their Muslim overlords. Conversions to Islām were numerous, though only in a few regions were the majority of Indians persuaded to embrace the alien faith. Hindu and Muslim lived side by side and, after a few centuries, the Hindus in those parts of India dominated by Muslims often accepted the situation as normal. In such conditions mutual influence was inevitable. Hindus began to learn Persian, the official language of their Muslim rulers, and Persian words found their way into the vernaculars. Well-to-do Hindu families often adopted the system of "strict parda" from the Muslims, and made their womenfolk veil their faces in public. The surviving Hindu kings borrowed new military techniques from the Muslims, learnt to employ cavalry with greater effect, and to use heavier armour and new types of weapon. One great religious teacher of medieval India, Kabīr (1440–1518), a poor weaver of Vārāṇasī, taught the brotherhood of Hindu and Muslim alike in the fatherhood of God, and opposed idolatry and caste practices, declaring that God was equally to be found in temple and mosque. Later, Nānak (1469–1533), a teacher of the Panjāb, taught the same doctrine with even greater force, and founded a new faith, that of the Sikhs, designed to incorporate all that was best of both Hinduism and Islām.

Nevertheless the Muslim invasions, and the enforced contact with new ideas, did not have the fertilizing effect upon Hindu culture which might have been expected. Hinduism was already very conservative when the lieutenants of Muhammad of Ghor conquered the Gangā Valley. In the Middle Ages for every tolerant and progressive teacher there must have been hundreds of orthodox brāhmaṇs, who looked upon themselves as the preservers of the immemorial Āryan Dharma against the barbarians who overran the holy land of Bhāratavarṣa. Under their influence the complex rules of the Hindu way of life became if anything stricter and more rigidly applied.

In the 16th and 17th centuries the Mughal emperors unified practically the whole of North India and much of the Deccan, and built up an empire such as had not been seen since the days of the Guptas. The Mughal period was one of great splendour, and has left its mark on India in the form of many lovely buildings, wherein Islāmic and Hindu motifs often blended in a perfect unity. The Tāj Mahal at Āgrā, one of the Mughal capitals, is of course the most famous memorial of the times. Akbar (1555–1606), the contemporary of Queen Elizabeth I and the first of the four great Mughal emperors, fully realized that the Empire could only stand on a basis of complete toleration. All religious tests and disabilities were abolished, including the hated poll-tax on unbelievers. Rājput princes and other Hindus were given high offices of state, without conversion to Islām, and inter-communal marriages were encouraged by the example of the Emperor himself. If the policy of the greatest of India's Muslim rulers had been continued by his successors, her history might have been very different.

The great-grandson of Akbar, Aurangzeb (1659–1707), reversed the policy of toleration. Restrictions were placed on the free practice of Hindu rites and preferment at court was confined to orthodox Muslims; later the tax on non-Muslims was reimposed. After nearly a century of equality this was bitterly resented by the Hindus, especially by the chiefs, many of whom had loyally served the earlier Mughals. The main resistance came from the Western Deccan where, around Poona, the Marāthā chief Śivājī (1627–1680) laid the foundations of a new Hindu empire. At about the same time the Sikhs of the Panjāb, incensed at the new policy and the persecution of their leaders, reformed their faith, and were welded into a closely-knit martial brotherhood. When the aged Aurangzeb died the Mughal empire was virtually at an end.

Politically the 18th century was one of Hindu revival. Though the Marāthā successors of Śivājī could not build up a large, unified empire their horsemen ranged far and wide over India, levying tribute from local chiefs, Hindu and Muslim alike. In the Panjāb towards the end of the century the Sikhs built an important kingdom, and almost everywhere Islām was on the defensive. But there was still no real cultural revival in Hinduism. Śivājī, a brilliant leader, a just ruler, and a statesman of consummate craft, was conservative in his outlook, and appeared to his contemporaries rather as a restorer of the old than as a builder of the new. Unlike Akbar, he had no fresh vision of a state transcending religious differences, though he leamt much from the Mughals in statecraft and military science and respected the faith of his adversaries. The Marāthās did not encourage reforms in Hindu society, and the India of the 18th century was if anything more conservative than it had been in the days of the first Muslim invasions.

It was through the influence of Europe that revival came. Early in the 16th century the Portuguese founded the first European trading stations and settlements. They were followed by Dutch, British, Danes and French, and throughout the 17th century the number of European "factories" increased. In the 18th century, with the break-up of the Mughal empire, the Europeans began to take greater interest in local politics, and by the early 19th century the British East India Company had virtually pushed out its rivals and dominated most of the sub-continent. The comparative ease with which the British established their supremacy is a measure of the political decadence of India at the time. By the middle of the 19th century the whole of India was either directly ruled by Britain or governed indirectly through petty princes with local autonomy. A new conqueror had come, a conqueror far more alien to the Hindu than the Muslims had been, with an aggressive culture and immense technical superiority.

Hindu society reacted at first to the British rulers as it had done to the Muslims, tending to withdraw itself even more into the closed circle of its ancient traditions, and there was no realization of a fundamental break with the past. From the orthodox point of view the British rulers of India constituted a caste, low in the social scale, which had succeeded in gaining political power. This caste had its own rules and customs which were not those of the Āryan, and should therefore not be imitated. The British readily accepted this position, and after the 18th century made few attempts at close social contact. Any real friendship between Englishman and Indian became more and more difficult as the century progressed—in fact the Englishman in India unconsciously tended to adopt the ideas of social stratification of the Indians whom he ruled, and to look upon his own people as members of a class so exalted above the Indians that friendly association with them was taboo. This attitude was strengthened by the Sepoy Revolt of 1857.

Nevertheless the presence of Europeans could not but have its effect. Except in certain parts of South India missionary activity in the 18th century was insignificant; but early in the 19th century the British evangelical conscience awakened to India, and missions and mission schools sprang up in all the larger towns. Meanwhile the Company felt a growing need of subordinate officers and clerks trained in English. Just as in Muslim times the Hindu desirous of government employment was compelled to learn Persian, so now he had to learn English. Middle class Hindu fathers began to send their sons to European schools, despite the dangers of ritual impurity, and Western ideas began to affect the well-to-do educated Indian.

The Portuguese had succeeded in "westernizing" many of their Indian and Sinhalese subjects, and to this day Indian blood flows in the veins of some old Portuguese families; a few Indians in the service of France came to understand and admire the culture of their conquerors; but perhaps the first Indian to learn enough from the West to be able to hold his own with the best minds of Europe, and yet still to love and respect his own culture, was the Bengālī Rām Mohan Roy, the friend of Jeremy Bentham. Rām Mohan Roy, who was born in 1772 and died in England in 1833, advocated the frank acceptance of all of value that Europe had to teach, and the sect which looked to him for inspiration, the Brāhma Samāj, was in many ways closer to Christianity than to Hinduism. Never large in numbers, its influence was widespread.

From the days of Rām Mohan Roy young Indians, at first very few but soon in greater numbers, began to come to England for education. The little band of Hindus educated on western lines, first in Bengal and then in other parts of India, tended to go further in the rejection of their own culture than did their descendants; they were fully conscious of the degeneracy which beset their land, and many seem to have been rather ashamed of their Hindu background. The Sepoy Revolt, which was fundamentally reactionary, found no support among this tiny Westernized intelligentsia. The Universities of Calcutta, Bombay and Madras, founded in 1857, the year of the Revolt, at first paid scant attention to the ancient culture of India, but taught a predominantly Western curriculum through Western staff.

By the end of the 19th century, however, the situation had changed. A new generation began to realize that Hindu culture had much of permanent value, and that the slavish imitation of the West could not solve India's problems. New organizations gave expression to this outlook. The Ārya Samāj claimed to reform Hinduism by purging it of all later degenerate features and by a return to the Vedas, very liberally interpreted, and had considerable success. The Indian National Congress, founded in 1885, became the mouthpiece of Indian public opinion. Newspapers in English and the vernaculars multiplied.

Not only was Hindu culture largely rehabilitated in the eyes of intelligent Hindus, but it even began to make counter-propaganda. A few learned Europeans and Americans had long recognized the nobility of much ancient Indian religious thought. Now, through the Theosophical Society (which, despite its claim to represent the quintessence of all religions, propagates a modernized Hinduism) and the Rāmakrishna Mission, the voice of Hinduism was heard in the West. Swāmī Vivekānanda (1862–1902), a splendid speaker of great spiritual power and personal magnetism, preached Hinduism to large audiences in Europe and America and found willing hearers. Here and there Indians abjured the West root and branch, and fanatically defended even those aspects of Hinduism which had completely outlived their usefulness; but, despite these reactionaries, the new Hinduism was very different from the old.

Rām Mohan Roy had sounded the theme with his passionate advocacy of social reform; Vivekānanda repeated it with a more nationalist timbre, when he declared that the highest form of service of the Great Mother was social service. Other great Indians, chief of whom was Mahātmā Gāndhī, developed the theme of social service as a religious duty, and the development continues under Gāndhī's successors.

Mahātmā Gāndhī was looked on by many, both Indian and European, as the epitome of Hindu tradition, but this is a false judgement for he was much influenced by Western ideas. Gāndhī believed in the fundamentals of his ancient culture, but his passionate love of the underdog and his antipathy to caste, though not unprecedented in ancient India, were unorthodox in the extreme, and owed more to European 19th-century liberalism than to anything Indian. His faith in non-violence was, as we have seen, by no means typical of Hinduism—his predecessor in revolt, the able Marāthā brāhmaṇ B. G. Tilak, and Gāndhī's impatient lieutenant Subhās Chandra Bose were far more orthodox in this respect. For Gāndhī's pacifism we must look mainly to the Sermon on the Mount and to Tolstoy. His championing of women's rights is also the result of Western influence. In his social context he was always rather an innovator than a conservative. Though some of his colleagues thought his programme of social reform too slow, he succeeded in shifting the whole emphasis of Hindu thought towards a popular and equalitarian social order, in place of the hierarchy of class and caste. Following up the work of many less well-known 19th-century reformers Gāndhī and his followers gave a new orientation and new life to Hindu culture, after centuries of stagnation.

Today there are few Indians, whatever their creed, who do not look back with pride on their ancient culture, and there are few intelligent Indians who are not willing to sacrifice some of its effete elements that India may develop and progress. Politically and economically India faces many problems of great difficulty, and no one can forecast her future with any certainty. But it is to be hoped that, whatever that future may be, the Indians of coming generations will not be unconvincing and self-conscious copies of Europeans, but will be men rooted in their own traditions, and aware of the continuity of their culture. Already the extremes of national self-denigration and fanatical cultural chauvinism are disappearing. In the past Hindu civilization has received, adapted and digested elements of many different cultures—Indo-European, Mesopotamian, Iranian, Greek, Roman, Scythian, Turkish, Persian and Arab. With each new influence it has somewhat changed. Now it is well on the way to assimilating the culture of the West.

Hindu civilization will, we believe, retain its continuity. The *Bhagavad Gītā* will not cease to inspire men of action, and the Upaniṣads men of thought. The charm and graciousness of the Indian way of life will continue, however much affected it may be by the labour-saving devices of the West. People will still love the tales of the heroes of the *Mahābhārata* and the *Rāmāyaṇa*, and of the loves of Duṣyanta and Śakuntalā and Purūravas and Urvaśī. The quiet and gentle happiness which has at all times pervaded Indian life where oppression, disease and poverty have not overclouded it will surely not vanish before the more hectic ways of the West.

Much that was useless in ancient Indian culture has already perished. The extravagant and barbarous hecatombs of the Vedic age have long since been forgotten, though animal sacrifice continues in some sects. Widows have long ceased to be burnt on their husbands' pyres. Girls may not by law be married in childhood. In buses and trains all over India brāhmaṇs rub shoulders with the lower castes without consciousness of grave pollution, and the temples are open to all by law. Caste is vanishing; the process began long ago, but its pace is now so rapid that the more objectionable features of caste may have disappeared within a generation or so. The old family system is adapting itself to present-day conditions. In fact the whole face of India is altering, but the cultural tradition continues, and it will never be lost.

THE WORLD'S DEBT TO INDIA

We have said much about India's debt to other cultures, but we must make it clear that she has given as much as or more than she has taken. Let us summarize the world's debt to India.

The whole of South-East Asia received most of its culture from India. Early in the 5th century B.C. colonists from Western India settled in Ceylon, which was finally converted to Buddhism in the reign of Aśoka. By this time a few Indian merchants had probably found their way to Malaya, Sumātra, and other parts of South-East Asia. Gradually they established permanent settlements, often, no doubt, marrying native women. They were followed by brāhmaṇs and Buddhist monks, and Indian influence gradually leavened the indigenous culture, until by the 4th century A.D. Sanskrit was the official language of the region, and there arose great civilizations, capable of organizing large maritime empires, and of building such wonderful memorials as the Buddhist stūpa of Borobodūr in Java, or the Śaivite temples of Angkor in Cambodia. Other cultural influences, from China and the Islāmic world, were felt in South-East Asia, but the primary impetus to civilization came from India.

Indian historians, proud of their country's past, often refer to this region as "Greater India", and speak of Indian "colonies". In its usual modern sense the term "colony" is hardly accurate, however. Vijaya, the legendary Āryan conqueror of Ceylon, is said to have gained the island by the sword, but beyond this we have no real evidence of any permanent Indian conquest outside the bounds of India. The Indian "colonies" were peaceful ones, and the Indianized kings of the region were indigenous chieftains who had learnt what India had to teach them.

Northwards Indian cultural influence spread through Central Asia to China. Faint and weak contact between China and India was probably made in Mauryan times, if not before, but only when, some 2,000 years ago, the Han Empire began to drive its frontiers towards the Caspian did India and China really meet. Unlike South-East Asia, China did not assimilate Indian ideas in every aspect of her culture, but the whole of the Far East is in India's debt for Buddhism, which helped to mould the distinctive civilizations of China, Korea, Japan and Tibet.

As well as her special gifts to Asia, India has conferred many practical blessings on the world at large; notably rice, cotton, the sugar cane, many spices, the domestic fowl, the game of chess (p. 181), and, most important of all, the decimal system of numeral notation, the invention of an unknown Indian mathematician early in the Christian era (p. 448f). The extent of the spiritual influence of India on the ancient West is much disputed. The heterodox Jewish sect of the Essenes, which probably influenced early Christianity, followed monastic practices in some respects similar to those of Buddhism. Parallels may be traced between a few passages in the New Testament and the Pāli scriptures.[1] Similarities between the teachings of western philosophers and mystics from Pythagoras to Plotinus and those of the Upaniṣads have frequently been noticed. None of these similarities, however, is close enough to give certainty, especially as we have no evidence that any classical writer had a deep knowledge of Indian religion. We can only say that there was always some contact between the Hellenic world and India, mediated first by the Achaemenid Empire, then by that of the Seleucids, and finally, under the Romans, by the traders of the Indian ocean. Christianity began to spread at the time when this contact was closest. We know that Indian ascetics occasionally visited the West, and that there was a colony of Indian merchants at Alexandria. The possibility of Indian influence on Neo-platonism and early Christianity cannot be ruled out.

Many authorities may doubt that Indian thought had any effect on that of the ancient West, but there can be no doubt of its direct and indirect influence on the thought of Europe and America in the last century and a half, though this has not received adequate recognition. This influence has not come by way of organized neo-Hindu missions. The last eighty years have seen the foundation of the Theosophical Society, of various Buddhist societies, and of societies in Europe and America looking for inspiration to the saintly 19th-century Bengālī mystic, Paramahaṃsa Rāmakrishna, and to his equally saintly disciple, Swāmī Vivekānanda. Lesser organizations and groups have been founded in the West by other Indian mystics and their disciples, some of them noble, earnest and spiritual, others of more dubious character. Here and there Westerners themselves, sometimes armed with a working knowledge of Sanskrit and first-hand Indian experience, have tried to convert the West to a streamlined Yoga or Vedānta. We would in no way disparage these teachers or their followers, many of whom are of great intellectual and spiritual calibre; but whatever we may think of the Western propagators of Indian mysticism, we cannot claim that they have had any great effect on our civilization. More subtle, but more powerful, has been the influence of Mahātmā Gāndhī, through the many friends of India in the West who were impressed by his burning sincerity and energy, and by the ultimate success of his policy of non-violence in achieving India's independence. Greater than any of these influences, however, has been the influence of ancient Indian religious literature through philosophy.

The pioneers of the Asiatic Society of Bengal quickly gained a small but enthusiastic following in Europe, and Goethe and many other writers of the early 19th century read all they could of ancient Indian literature in translation. We know that Goethe borrowed a device of Indian dramaturgy for the prologue to "Faust" (p. 386n), and who can say that the triumphant final chorus of the second part of that work was not in part inspired by the monism of Indian thought as he understood it? From Goethe onwards most of the great German philosophers knew something of Indian philosophy. Schopenhauer, whose influence on literature and psychology has been so considerable, indeed openly admitted his debt, and his outlook was virtually that of Buddhism. The monisms of Fichte and Hegel might never have taken the forms they did if it had not been for Anquetil-Duperron's translation of the Upaniṣads and the work of other pioneer Indologists. In the English-speaking world the strongest Indian influence was felt in America, where Emerson, Thoreau and other New England writers avidly studied much Indian religious literature in translation, and exerted immense influence on their contemporaries and successors, notably Walt Whitman. Through Carlyle and others the German philosophers in their turn made their mark on England, as did the Americans through many late 19th-century writers such as Richard Jeffries and Edward Carpenter.

Though in the contemporary philosophical schools of Europe and America the monistic and idealist philosophies of the last century carry little weight, their influence has been considerable, and all of them owe something at least to ancient India. The sages who meditated in the jungles of the Gangā Valley six hundred years or more before Christ are still forces in the world.

It is today something of an anachronism to speak of Western civilization or Indian civilization. Until very recently cultures were sharply divided, but now, when India is less than a day's journey from London, cultural divisions are beginning to disappear. If a *modus vivendi* is reached between liberal democracy and communism, and civilization survives, the world of the future will have a single culture with, it is to be hoped, many local differences and variations. India's contribution to the world's cultural stock has already been very large, and it will continue and grow as her prestige and influence increases. For this reason if for no other we must take account of her ancient heritage in its successes and its failures, for it is no longer the heritage of India alone, but of all mankind.

APPENDIX I

COSMOLOGY AND GEOGRAPHY

THE universe of the Vedas was a simple affair—a flat circular earth below, a heaven above, through which sun, moon and stars moved, and between them the middle air (*antarīkṣa*), the abode of birds, clouds and demigods. This picture of the world was much complicated by later religious thought.

Indian ideas on the origin and evolution of the universe are rather a matter of religion than of science and are considered elsewhere (p. 282ff). All Indian religions, however, maintained certain cosmological doctrines which were fundamental presuppositions of Indian thought, and were strikingly at variance with the Semitic ideas which long influenced the thinking of the West—the universe is very old; its evolution and decline are cyclic, repeated ad infinitum; it is immensely large; and there are other universes beyond our own.

The Hindus believed that the universe was shaped like an egg—the *Brahmāṇḍa*, or Egg of Brahmā—divided into twenty-one zones or regions, of which the earth was seventh from the top. Above the earth were six heavens (not, as with the Greeks, associated with the planets), of increasing beatitude. Below earth were the seven stages of *Pātāla*, the nether world, which were the abode of nāgas and other mythical beings and were not thought of as in any way unpleasant. Below Pātāla lay *Naraka*, or purgatory, also divided into seven zones, which were of increasing misery, and were inhabited by souls in torment. The universe hung in empty space, and was virtually isolated from other universes.

The cosmic schemes of the Buddhists and Jainas differed from this in many details, but in fundamentals they were the same. All originally postulated a flat earth, but this was recognized by Indian astronomers to be incorrect early in the Christian era, and, though the idea of a flat earth remained for religious purposes, the learned realized, perhaps through the influence of Greek astronomy, that it was in fact spherical. Various estimates of its size were made, the most popular being that of Brahmagupta (7th century A.D.), who gave its circumference as 5,000 yojanas. Assuming Brahmagupta's yojana to be the short league of about 4 1/2 miles (7.2 km.), this figure is not far out, and is as accurate as any given by ancient astronomers.

The modest spherical earth of the astronomers did not satisfy the theologians, however, and even later religious literature described the earth as a flat disc of enormous size. In its centre was Mount Meru, round which sun, moon and stars revolved. Around Meru were four continents (*dvīpa*), separated from the central peak by oceans, and named according to the great trees which stood on their shores opposite Meru. The southern continent, on which human beings dwell, had a *jambu* (rose-apple) as its distinctive tree, and it was therefore called *Jambudvīpa*. The southern zone of this continent, separated from the rest by the Himālayas, was "the Land of the Sons of Bharata" (*Bhāratavarṣa*), or India. Bharatavarsa alone was 9,000 yojanas across, and the whole of Jambudvīpa 33,000, or, according to some sources, 100,000 yojanas.

This fantastic geographical scheme was not the only one. In the Purāṇas Jambudvīpa is described as a ring around Meru, separated from the next continent, *Plakṣadvīpa*, by an ocean of salt. Plakṣadvīpa in turn forms a concentric circle round Jambudvīpa, and so on to make a total of seven continents, each circular and divided from its neighbour by an ocean of different composition—starting with Jambudvīpa's salt ocean and moving outwards, of treacle, wine, ghee, milk, curds and fresh water respectively. This brilliantly imaginative picture of the world, which aroused the scorn of Lord Macaulay, seems to have been implicitly believed in by later Hindu theologians, and even the astronomers could not emancipate themselves from it, but adapted it to their spherical earth by making Meru the earth's axis, and the continents zones on the earth's surface.

The oceans of butter and seas of treacle formed an effective barrier to the growth of a true science of geography. The seven continents cannot in any way have been related to actual portions of the earth's surface (though some modern students have tried to identify them with parts of Asia) and, as far as is known, no attempt was made to collate the experience of travellers as practical geography. The astronomers gave fairly accurate longitudes of important places in India. In the early centuries of the Christian era Alexandria was known, and there are vague references to the city of the *Romakas* in astronomical works; but the geographical knowledge of the learned was of the vaguest description. Even within India distances and directions, as given in texts, are usually very inaccurate and vague. The conquerors who led armies thousands of miles on their campaigns, the merchants who carried their wares from one end of India to the other, and the pilgrims who visited sacred places from the Himālayas to Cape Comorin must have had a sound practical knowledge of Indian geography, while that of the seamen who sailed the ocean from Socotra to Canton must have been even wider; but there are few echoes of this knowledge in the literature of the time.

APPENDIX II

ASTRONOMY

ONE of the subsidiary studies (*vedāṅga*) of Vedic lore *jyotiṣa*, a primitive astronomy designed mainly for the purpose of settling the dates and times at which periodical sacrifices were to be performed. The existing literature on this topic is comparatively late, and gives no true indication of India's astronomical knowledge in the Vedic period, though it is quite clear from passages in the Vedic texts themselves that it was adequate for the practical purposes of the time. It is probable that even at this early period there was some Mesopotamian influence on Indian astronomical ideas, but this cannot be established with certainty. Virtually certain, however, is the influence of classical European astronomy, which was felt in the early centuries of the Christian era, if not before.

Several Greek words have become common in Sanskrit and in later Indian languages through astronomy (p. 201), and other technical terms, not so widely known, are indisputably of Greek origin. Of the five astronomical systems (*siddhānta*) known to the 6th-century astronomer Varāhamihira one is called the *Romaka Siddhānta* and another the *Pauliśa Siddhānta*, a title which can only be reasonably explained as a recollection of the name of the classical astronomer Paul of Alexandria.

The new astronomy was adopted chiefly for purposes of prognostication; for the establishment of dates the old luni-solar calendar, based on simpler observations, was quite adequate. In earlier times Indians, though no less interested than other ancient peoples in foretelling the future, preferred to do so by the interpretation of dreams and omens (*utpāta*), and by physiognomy, birthmarks, the shape and size of the features, and other signs which were believed to give tokens of an individual's fate. The older systems of prognostication were not forgotten, but from Gupta times onwards they gave pride of place to astrology, which from that day to this has been implicitly believed in by nearly all Indians.

Before this great development of astronomical knowledge the heavens had been charted by means of the lunar mansions or *nakṣatras*, which were apparently known even in the time of the *Ṛg Veda*. The moon's relation to the fixed stars changes through a cycle of approximately 27 solar days and 7¾ hours, and thus the heavens were divided into 27 portions, named according to the group of stars on the ecliptic (the apparent orbit of the sun) near which the moon passes on each day of its cycle. As the sidereal month is in fact nearly eight hours more than

27 days a twenty-eighth intercalary naksatra was added by later astronomers to correct the error.*

Western astronomy brought to India the signs of the zodiac, the seven-day week, the hour, and several other ideas. Thanks to their achievements in mathematics Indian astronomers made some advances on the knowledge of the Greeks, and passed their lore, with that of mathematics, back to Europe by way of the Arabs. As early as the 7th century the Syrian astronomer Severus Sebokht knew of the greatness of Indian astronomy and mathematics (p. vi), and the caliphs of Bāghdād employed Indian astronomers. One word of the terminology of medieval European astronomy, *aux*, the highest point of a planet's orbit, is certainly borrowed from the Sanskrit *ucca* through Arabic.

Like all ancient astronomy, that of India was restricted owing to ignorance of the telescope; but methods of observation were perfected which allowed very accurate measurement, and calculations were aided by the decimal system of numerals. We know of no remains of observatories of the Hindu period, but those of the 17th and 18th centuries, at Jaipur, Delhī and elsewhere, with their wonderfully accurate instruments constructed on an enormous scale to minimize error, may well have had their ancient counterparts.

With the naked eye as their sole means of observation the Indians knew only the seven planets (*graha*) of the ancients—Sun (*Sūrya*, *Ravi*), Moon (*Candra*, *Soma*), Mercury (*Budha*), Venus (*Śukra*), Mars (*Maṅgala*), Jupiter (*Bṛhaspati*) and Satum (*Śani*);† to these *grahas* two more were added, *Rāhu* and *Ketu*, the ascending and descending nodes of the moon.‡ At the beginning of each æon all the planets were believed to commence their revolutions in line, and to return to the same position at the end of it. The apparently irregular course of the planets was explained on the hypothesis of epicycles, as in classical and medieval astronomy. Unlike the Greeks, the Indians believed that the planets had equal real motion, and

---

*The naksatras were: (1) *Aśvini* (β and γ Arietis), (2) *Bharaṇī* (35, 39, and 41 Arietis), (3) *Kṛttikā* (Pleiades), (4) *Rohiṇī* (Aldebaran), (5) *Mṛgaśiras* (λ, φ[1], and φ[2] Orionis), (6) *Ārdrā* (α Orionis), (7) *Punarvasū* (α and β Geminorum), (8) *Puṣyā* (γ, δ, and θ Cancri), (9) *Āileṣā* (δ, ε, η, ρ and σ Hydrae), (10) *Maghā* (α, γ, ε, ζ, η, and μ Leonis), (11) *Pūrva-phalguni* (δ and θ Leonis), (12) *Uttara-phalguni* (β and 93 Leonis), (l3) *Hastā* (α, β, γ, δ, and ε Corvi), (14) *Citrā* (Spica, α Virginis), (15) *Svāti* (Arcturus), (16) *Viśākhā* α, β, γ, and ι Libra;), (17) *Anurādhā* (β, δ, and π Scorpionis), (18) *Jyeṣṭhā* (α, σ, and τ Scorpionis), (19) *Mūlā* (ε, ζ, η, θ, ι, κ, λ, μ, and ν Scorpionis), (20) *Pūrvāṣāḍhā* (δ and ε Sagittarii), (21) *Uttarāṣāḍhā* ζ and σ Sagittarii), (22) *Śravaṇā* (α, β, and γ Aquilae), (23) *Dhaniṣṭhā* or *Śraviṣṭila* α, β, γ and δ Delphinis), (24) *Śatabhiṣaj* (γ Aquarii etc.), (25) *Pūrva-bhadrapadā* (α and β Pegasi), (26) *Uttarabhadrapadā* (γ Pegasi and α Andromedae), and (27) *Revatī* (ζ Piscium, etc). The 28th nakṣatra was *Abhijit* (α, ε, and ζ Lyrae), which was placed between *Uttarāṣāḍhā* and *Śravaṇā.* It will be seen from this list that the ancient Indian system of constellations differed widely from that of the West.

†The names of the planets had many synonyms, some of which were evidently borrowed from the Greek, e.g. *Ara,* Ares, or Mars.

‡At the "Churning of the Ocean" (p. 265f) a demon named Rāhu stole some of the *amṛta.* Viṣṇu destroyed his body, but as he had tasted of the divine drink he had become immortal. His head and tail survive for ever in the heavens, as Rāhu and Ketu, and the head causes eclipses by trying to swallow the planets. Of course the astronomers did not believe this myth, and some texts explicitly reject it.

that their apparently different angular motion was due to their different distances from the earth.

For purposes of calculation the planetary system was taken as geocentric, though Āryabhaṭa in the 5th century suggested that the earth revolved round the sun and rotated on its axis; this theory was also known to later astronomers, but it never affected astronomical practice. The precession of the equinoxes was known, and calculated with some accuracy by medieval astronomers, as were the lengths of the year, the lunar month, and other astronomical constants. These calculations were reliable for most practical purposes, and in many cases more exact than those of the Greco-Roman world. Eclipses were forecast with accuracy and their true cause understood.

APPENDIX III

THE CALENDAR

In recording dates the basic unit was not the solar day, but the *tithi* or lunar day, approximately thirty of which formed a lunar month (i.e. the four phases of the moon) of about 29½ solar days. The month was divided into two halves (*pakṣa*) of fifteen tithis each, beginning with the full (*pūrṇimāvāsyā*) and new (*amāvāsyā* or *bahulāvāsyā*) moons respectively. The fortnight beginning with the new moon was called the bright half (*śuklapakṣa*) and the other the dark half (*kṛṣṇapakṣa*). According to the system followed in Northern India and much of the Deccan the month began and ended with the full moon, while in the Tamil country the month generally began with the new moon. The Hindu calendar is still in use throughout India for religious purposes.

The tithi might begin at any time of the solar day. For the practical purpose of recording dates that tithi current at sunrise was supposed to prevail for the whole day and gave that day its number in the pakṣa. If a tithi began just after sunrise and ended before the sunrise of the next day it was expunged, and there was a break in the numerical sequence of days.

The year normally contained twelve lunar months:

Caitra (March-April), *Vaiśākha* (April–May), *Jyaiṣṭha* (May–June), *Āṣāḍha* (June–July), *Śrāvaṇa* (July–Āugust), *Bhādrapada* or *Prauṣṭhapada* (August–September), *Āśvina* or *Āśvayuja* (September–October), *Kārttika* (October–November), *Mārgaśīrṣa* or *Agrahāyaṣa* (November–December), *Pauṣa* or *Taiṣa* (December–January), *Māgha* (January–February) and *Phālguna* (February–March).* According to the usual systems of reckoning the year began with Caitra, but it was sometimes taken as beginning with Kārttika or another month.

A group of two months formed a season (*ṛtu*). The six seasons of the Indian year were: *Vasanta* (Spring, March-May), *Grīṣma* (Summer, May-July), *Varṣā* (The Rains, July-September), *Śarad* (Autumn, September-November), *Hemanta* (Winter, November-January) and *Śiśira* (the Cool Season, January-March).

Twelve lunar months make only about 354 days, and the problem of the discrepancy between the lunar and solar years was solved very early; sixty-two

---

[0] The names of the months in early times were as follows: *Madhu, Mādhava, Śukra, Śuci, Nabhas, Nabhasya, Iṣa, Ürja, Sahas, Sahasya, Tapas, Tapasya.* These Vedic names are sometimes found in later poetry.

lunar months are approximately equal to sixty solar months, and so every thirty months an extra month was added to the year, as in Babylonia. This leap-month was generally inserted after Āṣādha or Śrāvaṇa and called second (*dvitīya*) Āṣādha or Śrāvaṇa. Thus every second or third year contains thirteen months, and is some twenty-nine days longer than the others. The Hindu calendar, though quite efficient, is thus rather cumbrous, and is so different from the solar calendar that it is impossible to reduce dates from one to the other without very complicated calculations or lengthy tables. It is even impossible to establish at a glance the month in which a given Hindu date falls with any certainty.

Indian dates are usually given in the order—month, paksa, tithi, the abbreviations *śndi* and *badi* being used for the bright and dark halves of the month; e.g. *Caitra śudi* 7 means the seventh day from the new moon of the month Caitra.

The solar calendar, imported with Western astronomy, was also known from Gupta times onwards though it did not oust the old luni-solar calendar until recent years. Where solar dates are given in early records they are usually mentioned for extra accuracy, with the prevailing nakṣatra of the day in question, after the regular luni-solar date. In the solar calendar the months are named after the signs of the zodiac, which are literal or nearly exact translations of their Greek originals: *Meṣa* (Aries), *Vṛṣabha* (Taurus), *Mithuna* (Gemini), *Karkaṭa* (Cancer), *Siṃha* (Leo), *Kaṇyā* (Virgo), *Tuia* (Libra), *Vṛścika* (Scorpio), *Dhanus* (Sagittarius), *Makara* (Capricornus), *Kumbha* (Aquarius) and *Mīna* (Pisces). With the solar calendar the seven-day week was also introduced, the days being named after their presiding planets as in the Greco-Roman system: *Ravivāra* (Sunday), *Somavāra* (Monday), *Maṅgalavāra* (Tuesday), *Budhavāra* (Wednesday), *Bṛhaspativāra* (Thursday), *Śukravāra* (Friday) and *Śanivāra* (Saturday).

ERAS

Until the lst century B.C. there is no good evidence that India had any regular system of recording the year of an event by dating in a definite era like the *A.U.C.* of Rome or the Christian era of medieval and modern Europe. Early inscriptions are dated if at all in the regnal year of the ruling king. The idea of dating over a long period of time from a fixed year was almost certainly introduced into India by the invaders of the North-West, who have left the earliest inscriptions thus dated in India. Unfortunately the Indians did not adopt a uniform era, and a number of systems of dating were in use from that time onwards, the chief of which, in order of importance, are as follows:

The Vikrama Era (58 B.C.), traditionally founded by a king called Vikramāditya, who drove the Śakas out of Ujjayinī and founded the era to celebrate his victory. The only king who both took the title Vikramāditya and drove the Śakas from Ujjayinī was Candra Gupta II, who lived over 400 years later than the beginning of the Vikrama era, and so the legend is certainly false. In the earliest inscriptions using this era, all from Western India, it is called simply

Kṛta ("established"), or "handed down by the Mālava tribe". Some authorities believe that many inscriptions of the Śakas and Pāhlavas of North-West India are to be read in this era, and that it was founded by Azes, one of their early kings; but this is by no means certain. This era was most popular in North India. Its year began originally with the month Kārttika, but by medieval times Vikrama years began in the bright half of Caitra in the North, and in the dark half of the same month in the Peninsula.

The Śaka Era (A.D. 78) was, according to tradition, founded by a Śaka king who occupied Ujjayinī 137 years after Vikramāditya. This era may in fact have been founded by Kaniṣka, and was certainly used early in the 2nd century A.D. by the "Western Satraps", who ruled Mālwā and Gujarāt. Thence the use of the era spread through the Deccan and it was exported to South-East Asia.

The Gupta Era (A.D. 320) was probably founded by Candra Gupta I, and its use was continued by the Maitraka dynasty of Gujarāt for some centuries after the Gupta empire fell.

The Harsa Era (A.D. 606), founded by Harsavardhana of Kānyakubja, was popular in Northern India for a century or two after his death.

The Kalacuri Era (A.D. 248), perhaps founded by a small dynasty called the Traikūṭaka, was current in Central India down to the Muslim invasion.

Other eras of local or temporary importance were the *Lakṣmaṇa Era* of Bengal (A.D. 1119), wrongly said to have been founded by King Lakṣmaṇa Sena; the *Saptarṣi* or *Laukika Era*, current in Kashmīr in the Middle Ages, and recorded in cycles of one hundred years, each cycle commencing seventy-six years after each Christian century; the *Nevār Era* of Nepāl (A.D. 878); the *Kollam Era* of Kerala (A.D. 825); and the *Era of Vikramāditya VI Cālukya* (a.D. 1075). The *Era of the Kaliyuga* (3102 B.C., v. p. 39) was often used for religious dates and rarely for political. In Ceylon a *Buddha Era* from 544 B.C. was in use from an uncertain date, when it probably replaced an earlier reckoning from 483 B.C. The Jainas used an *Era of Mahāvīra*, reckoned from 528 B.C. The two latter eras, together with the *Vikrama* and *Śaka Eras*, are still in use for religious purposes, but the others are extinct.

In reducing dates in Indian eras to the Christian era it must be remembered that the year, according to most reckonings, begins with the month of Caitra, which usually commences in the middle of March. Thus the months Māgha and Phālguna, and generally the second half of Pauṣa, occur in the Christian year after that in which the Hindu year began. Dates were usually given in expired years; this was sometimes explicitly stated (e.g. "when 493 years had passed from the establishment of the tribe of the Mālavas"), but more often taken for granted. In medieval dates it is best to assume an expired year, even when this is not specified, unless there is special reason to believe otherwise.

The following table will be useful for reducing Indian dates to the Christian era:

Era			First 9½ months approx. (assuming the year to begin with Caitra)	Second (usually dark) half of Pauṣa, and the whole of Māgha and Phālguna
Vikrama	current	subtract	58	57
	expired	"	57	56
Śaka	current	add	77	78
	expired	"	78	79
Kalacuri	current	add	247	248
	expired	"	248	249
Gupta	current	add	319	320
	expired	"	320	321
Harṣa	current	add	605	606
	expired	"	606	607

APPENDIX IV

MATHEMATICS

THROUGH the necessity of accurately laying out the open-air site of a sacrifice Indians very early evolved a simple system of geometry, but in the sphere of practical knowledge the world owes most to India in the realm of mathematics, which were developed in Gupta times to a stage more advanced than that reached by any other nation of antiquity. The success of Indian mathematics was mainly due to the fact that the Indians had a clear conception of abstract number, as distinct from numerical quantity of objects or spatial extension. While Greek mathematical science was largely based on mensuration and geometry, India transcended these conceptions quite early, and, with the aid of a simple numeral notation, devised a rudimentary algebra which allowed more complicated calculations than were possible to the Greeks, and led to the study of number for its own sake.

In the earlier inscriptions of India dates and other numerals are written in a notation not unlike that of the Romans, Greeks and Hebrews, with separate symbols for the tens and hundreds. The earliest inscription recording the date by a system of nine digits and a zero, with place notation for the tens and hundreds, comes from Gujarāt, and is dated A.D. 595.* Soon after this however, the new system had been heard of in Syria (p. vi),† and was being used as far afield as Vietnam. Evidently the system was known to mathematicians some centuries before it was employed in inscriptions, the scribes of which tended to be conservative in their methods of recording dates; in modern Europe the cumbrous Roman system is still sometimes used for the same purpose. The name of the mathematician who devised the simplified system of writing numerals is unknown, but the earliest surviving mathematical texts—the anonymous "Bakshālī Manuscript", which is a copy of a text of the 4th century A.D., and the terse *Āryabhaṭīya* of Āryabhaṭa, written in A.D. 499—presuppose it.

For long it was thought that the decimal system of numerals was invented by the Arabs, but this is certainly not the case. The Ārabs themselves called mathematics "the Indian (art)" (*hindisat*), and it appears that the decimal notation, with other

---

* *Epigraphia Indica,* ii, 20.

† Some earlier authorities, disinclined to give India her due, have declared that none of these sources gives certain evidence of the existence of a sign for zero. But Āryabhaṭa's text implies a knowledge of it, and Severus Sebokht's "nine symbols" would be quite useless for expressing quantities over nine without a zero sign and place notation. The Maya of Central America had a vigesimal numeral system with positional notation long before this time, but it had, of course, no effect on the world at large (S. G. Morley, *The Ancient Maya,* London, 1946, p. 274).

mathematical lore, was learnt by the Muslim world either through merchants trading with the west coast of India or through the Arabs who conquered Sind in A.D. 712.

The debt of the Western world to India in this respect cannot be overestimated. Most of the great discoveries and inventions of which Europe is so proud would have been impossible without a developed system of mathematics, and this in turn would have been impossible if Europe had been shackled by the unwieldy system of Roman numerals. The unknown man who devised the new system was from the world's point of view, after the Buddha, the most important son of India. His achievement, though easily taken for granted, was the work of an analytical mind of the first order, and he deserves much more honour than he has so far received.

Medieval Indian mathematicians, such as Brahmagupta (7th century), Mahāvīra (9th century) and Bhāskara (12th century), made several discoveries which in Europe were not known until the Renaissance or later. They understood the import of positive and negative quantities, evolved sound systems of extracting square and cube roots, and could solve quadratic and certain types of indeterminate equations. For π Āryabhaṭa gave the usual modern approximate value of 3.1416, expressed in the form of a fraction ${}^{6}/_{2}\,{}^{2}/_{0}\,{}^{8}/_{0}\,{}^{3}/_{0}\,{}^{2}/_{0}$. This value of π, much more accurate than that of the Greeks, was improved to nine places of decimals by later Indian mathematicians. Some steps were made in trigonometry, spherical geometry and calculus, chiefly in connexion with astronomy. The mathematical implications of zero (*śunya*) and infinity, never more than vaguely realized by classical authorities, were fully understood in medieval India. Earlier mathematicians had taught that ${}^{x}/_{0}=x$, but Bhāskara proved that it was infinity. He also established mathematically what had been recognized in Indian theology at least a millenium earlier, that infinity, however divided, remains infinite, represented by the equation ¥/x = ¥.

APPENDIX V

PHYSICS AND CHEMISTRY

ANCIENT Indian ideas of physics were closely linked with religion and theology, and differed somewhat from sect to sect. As early as the time of the Buddha, if not before, the universe was classified by elements, of which all schools admitted at least four—earth, air, fire and water. To these orthodox Hindu schools and Jainism added a fifth, *ākāśa*, which is generally translated "ether". It was recognized that air was not of infinite extension, and the Indian mind, with its abhorrence of a vacuum, found it hard to conceive of empty space. The five elements were thought of as the mediums of sense impressions—earth of smell, air of feeling, fire of vision, water of taste, and ether of sound. Buddhists and Ājīvikas rejected ether, but the latter added life, joy and sorrow, which were thought of as in some way material, making a total of seven elements.

Most schools believed that the elements other than ether were atomic. Indian atomism was certainly independent of Greek influence, for an atomic theory was taught by Pakudha Kātyāyana, an older contemporary of the Buddha, and was therefore earlier than that of Democritus. The Jainas believed that all atoms (*aṇu*) were identical, and that differences of the character of the elements were due to the manner in which the atoms were combined. Most schools, however, maintained that there were as many types of atom as there were elements.

The atom was generally thought to be eternal, but some Buddhists conceived of it not only as the minutest object capable of occupying space, but also as occupying the minutest possible duration of time, coming into being and vanishing almost in an instant, only to be succeeded by another atom, caused by the first. Thus the atom of Buddhism in some measure resembles the quantum of Planck. The atom was quite invisible to the human eye; the orthodox Vaiśeṣika school believed the single atom to be a mere point in space, completely without magnitude.

A single atom had no qualities, but only potentialities, which came into play when the atom combined with others. The Vaiśeṣika school, which specially elaborated its atomic doctrines and was the school of atomism *par excellence*, maintained that, before combining to form material objects, atoms made primary combinations of diads and triads. This doctrine of molecules was developed differently by Buddhists and Ajivikas, who taught that in normal conditions no atoms existed in a pure state, but only combined in different proportions in a molecule (*saṃghāṭa*, *kalāpa*). Every molecule contained at least one atom of all four types, and obtained its character from the predominance of a given element. This hypothesis accounted for the fact that matter might show characteristics of more than one element; thus wax might melt and also burn, because its molecules contained proportions of water and fire. According to the Buddhists the molecules cohered by virtue of the atoms of water in each, which acted as an adhesive.

Indian atomic theories were not based on experiment but on intuition and logic. They were not universally held. The great theologian Śaṅkara (p. 287) did not believe in atoms and argued strongly against their existence. But the atomic theories of ancient India are brilliant imaginative explanations of the physical structure of the world; though it is probably mere coincidence that they agree in part with the discoveries of modern physics, they are nevertheless much to the credit of the intellect and imagination of early Indian thinkers.

Beyond this ancient Indian physics developed little. Without knowledge of an all-embracing law of gravity it remained in a rudimentary state, like all the physical systems of the ancient world. It was generally believed that the elements of earth and water tended to fall, and fire to rise, and it was recognized that solids and fluids alike generally expanded on heating, but no serious effort was made to study such phenomena experimentally. In the science of acoustics, however, India made real discoveries based on experiment, and the ear, highly trained by the phonetic study necessary for the correct recitation of the Vedas, learned to distinguish musical tones far closer than those of other ancient musical systems. Very early the octave was divided into twenty-two *śrutis*, or quarter-tones (p. 310) and their proportions were measured with great accuracy. It was recognized that differences of timbre were caused by overtones (*anuraṇana*), which varied with different instruments.

We know from the evidence of the Iron Pillar of Delhi (p. 190f) and other sources that Indian metallurgists gained great proficiency in the extraction of metal from ore and in metal-casting, and their products were known and valued in the Roman Empire and the Middle East; but their knowledge appears to have been largely pragmatic, and had no counterpart in a highly developed science of metallurgy. Chemistry in ancient India was the handmaid not of technology but of medicine; her chemists did not share the interest of medieval Europe in transmuting base metal into gold, but apparently devoted most of their attention to making medicines, drugs to promote longevity, aphrodisiacs, and poisons and their antidotes. These medical chemists did succeed in producing many important alkalis, acids and metallic salts by simple processes of calcination and distillation, and it has even been suggested, without good basis, that they discovered a form of gunpowder.

In the Middle Ages Indian chemists, like their counterparts in China, the Muslim World and Europe, became engrossed in the study of mercury, perhaps through contact with the Arabs. A school of alchemists arose, who experimented with the wonderful fluid metal and decided that it was the specific for all diseases, the source of perpetual youth, and even the surest means to salvation. In this infatuation with mercury Indian chemistry foundered, but not before it had passed many ideas on to the Arabs, who gave them to medieval Europe.

APPENDIX VI

PHYSIOLOGY AND MEDICINE

THE Vedas show a very primitive stage of medical and physiological lore, but the basic textbooks of Indian medicine—the compendia of Caraka (1st–2nd centuries A.D.) and Susruta (*c.* 4th century A.D.)—are the products of a fully evolved system which resembled those of Hippocrates and Galen in some respects, and in others had developed beyond them. There is little doubt that two factors encouraged medical knowledge—the growth of interest in physiology through the phenomena of yoga and mystical experience, and Buddhism. Like the Christian missionary of later times the Buddhist monk often served as a doctor among the lay folk from whom he begged his food; moreover he was encouraged to care for his own health and that of his fellow-monks, and his creed tended towards rationalism and a distrust of the medical magic of earlier times. The development of medicine was also probably stimulated by contact with Hellenistic physicians, and the resemblances between Indian and classical medicine suggest borrowing on both sides. After Susruta Indian medicine developed little, except in the growing use of mercurial drugs, and of others, such as opium and sarsaparilla, which were introduced by the Arabs. In its essentials the system practised by the *ayurvedic* physician of present day India remains the same.

The basic conception of Indian medicine, like that of ancient and medieval Europe, was the doctrine of the humours (*doṣa*). Most authorities taught that health was maintained through the even balance of the three vital fluids of the body—wind, gall and mucus, to which some added blood as a fourth humour. The three primary humours were connected with the scheme of the three *guṇas*, or universal qualities (p. 285), and associated with virtue, passion and dullness respectively.

The bodily functions were maintained by the five "winds" (*vāyu*): *udāna*, emanating from the throat, and causing speech; *prāṇa*, in the heart, and responsible for breathing and the swallowing of food; *samāna*, fanning the fire in the stomach which "cooked" or digested the food, and dividing it into its digestible and indigestible parts; *apāna* in the abdomen, responsible for excretion and procreation; and *vyāna*, a generally diffused wind, causing the motion of the blood and of the body generally. The food digested by the *samāna* became chyle, which proceeded to the heart, and thence to the liver, where its essence was converted into blood. The blood in turn was in part converted into flesh and the process was continued through the series fat, bone, marrow and semen; the latter, when not expelled, produced energy (*ojas*), which returned to the heart and was thence diffused over the body. This process of metabolism was believed to take place in thirty days.

Ancient Indian doctors had no clear knowledge of the function of the brain, and believed with many ancient peoples that the heart was the seat of intelligence. They realized, however, the importance of the spinal cord (p. 287), and knew of the existence of the nervous system, though it was not properly understood. The progress of physiology and biology was impeded by the taboo on contact with dead bodies, which much discouraged dissection and the study of anatomy, although such practices were not completely unknown.

Despite their inaccurate knowledge of physiology, which was by no means inferior to that of most ancient peoples, India evolved a developed empirical surgery. The caesarian section was known, bone-setting reached a high degree of skill, and plastic surgery was developed far beyond anything known elsewhere at the time. Ancient Indian surgeons were expert at the repair of noses, ears and lips, lost or injured in battle or by judicial mutilation. In this respect Indian surgery remained ahead of European until the 18th century, when the surgeons of the East Indian Company were not ashamed to learn the art of rhinoplasty from the Indians.

Though Indians very early conceived of the existence of microscopic forms of life, it was never realized that these might cause diseases; but if Indian surgeons had no true idea of antisepsis or asepsis they encouraged scrupulous cleanliness as they understood it, and recognized the therapeutic value of fresh air and light. The pharmacopceia of ancient India was very large, and comprised animal, vegetable and mineral products. Many Asian drugs were known and used long before their introduction into Europe, notably the oil of the *chaulmugra* tree, traditionally prescribed as a specific for leprosy, and still the basis of the modern treatment of the disease.

The physician was a highly respected member of society, and the *vaidyas* rank high in the caste hierarchy to this day. The rules of professional behaviour laid down in medical texts remind us of those of Hippocrates and are not unworthy of the conscientious doctor of any place or time. We quote part of the sermon which Caraka instructs a physician to preach to his pupils at a solemn religious ceremony to be performed on the completion of their apprenticeship.

> "If you want success in your practice, wealth and fame, and heaven after your death, you must pray every day on rising and going to bed for the welfare of all beings, especially of cows and brāhmaṇs, and you must strive with all your soul for the health of the sick. You must not betray your patients, even at the cost of your own life. ... You must not get drunk, or commit evil, or have evil companions. ... You must be pleasant of speech ... and thoughtful, always striving to improve your knowledge.
>
> "When you go to the home of a patient you should direct your words, mind, intellect and senses nowhere but to your patient and his treatment. ... Nothing that happens in the house of the sick man must be told outside, nor

must the patient's condition be told to anyone who might do harm by that knowledge to the patient or to another."*

Under the patronage of the more benevolent kings and religious foundations free medical aid was given to the poor. Asoka took pride in the fact that he had provided medicines for man and beast, and the traveller Fa-hsien, in the early 5th century A.D., made special note of the free hospitals maintained by the donations of pious citizens. Unfortunately we have no detailed descriptions of such establishments.

Veterinary medicine was also practised. The doctrine of non-violence encouraged the endowment of animal refuges and homes for sick and aged animals, and such charities are still maintained in many cities of India. The horse and elephant doctors were members of skilled and respected professions, much in demand at court, and texts on veterinary science survive from the Middle Ages.

* *Caraka Saṃhitā,* iii, 8, 7.

APPENDIX VII

LOGIC AND EPISTEMOLOGY

WITH such an intense interest in metaphysical problems and a tradition of lively debate and discussion it is not surprising that India developed her own distinctive system of logic. The basic logical text is the *Nyāya Sūtras* of Gautama, perhaps composed in the early centuries of the Christian era, a series of brief aphorisms much commented on by later writers, and the foundation-text of the Nyāya, one of the six schools of orthodox philosophy (p. 283). Logic was not, however, confined to this one school, but was utilized and adapted by Hindu, Buddhist and Jaina alike.

One of the most important topics of Indian thought in this field was the question of *pramāṇa*, which may be translated "means of reliable knowledge". According to the later Nyaya schools there were four pramāṇas, perception (*pratyakṣa*), inference (*anumāna*), inference by analogy or comparison (*upamāna*), and "word" (*śabda*), the pronouncement of a reliable authority, such as the Vedas. The Vedānta school added intuition or presumption (*arthāpatti*) and non-perception (*anupalabdhi*), the latter an unnecessary scholastic refinement. The six categories overlapped somewhat, and the Buddhists generally included all forms of knowledge under the first two categories, while the Jainas usually allowed only three, perception, inference and revelation. The materialists allowed only perception, and their opponents made short work of their efforts at proving by inference that inference could not give reliable knowledge.

It was probably in the study of the process of inference that schools of true logic arose. From the necessities of metaphysical discussion false arguments were analysed and classified; of these logicians recognized the chief fallacies of classical logic, such as *reductio ad absurdum* (*arthaprasaṅga*), circular argument (*cakra*), infinite regression (*anavasthā*), dilemma (*anyonyāśraya*), and *ignoratio elenchi* (*ātmāsraya*).

A correct inference was established by syllogism, of which the Indian form (*pañcāvayava*) was somewhat more cumbrous than the Aristotelian. Its five members were known as proposition (*pratijñā*), reason (*hetu*), example (*udāharaṇa*), application (*upanaya*) and conclusion (*nigamana*). The classical Indian example may be paraphrased as follows:

(1) There is fire on the mountain,
(2) because there is smoke above it,
(3) and where there is smoke there is fire, as, for instance, in a kitchen;
(4) such is the case with the mountain,
(5) and therefore there is fire on it.

The third term of the Indian syllogism corresponds to the major premiss of that of Aristotle, the second to Aristotle's minor premiss, and the first to his conclusion. Thus the Indian syllogism reversed the order of that of classical logie, the argument being stated in the first and second clauses, established by the general rule and example in the third, and finally clinched by the virtual repetition of the first two clauses. The "example" (in the above syllogism the kitchen) was generally looked on as an essential part of the argument, and helped to strengthen its rhetorical force. Evidently this elaborate system of syllogism is the outcome of much practical experience in discussion. Three-membered syllogisms were admitted by the Buddhists, who rightly rejected the fourth and fifth members of the orthodox syllogism as tautological.

The basis of the generalization (for example "where there is smoke there is fire") on which every inference rests was believed to be the quality of universal concomitance (*vyāpti*). The nature and origin of this quality was much discussed, and its consideration led to theories of universals and particulars, which are too recondite for consideration in this book.

No treatment of Indian thought is complete without a brief reference to the remarkable epistemological relativity of Jainism. Jaina thinkers, and some other heterodox teachers also, explicitly rejected what in classical logic is called the law of the excluded middle. For the Jaina there were not merely the two possiblities of existence and non-existence, but seven. Thus we may affirm (1) that an object, say a knife, exists as a knife. We may further say (2) that it is not something else, say a fork. But it exists as a knife and does not exist as a fork, and so we may declare of it (3) that in one aspect it is and in another it is not. From another point of view (4) it is indescribable; its ultimate essence is unknown to us and we cannot posit anything final about it—it is inexpressible. By combining this fourth possiblity with the three former ones we obtain three further possibilities of predication—(5) it is, but its nature is otherwise indescribable, (6) it is not, but its nature is indescribable, and (7) it both is and is not, but its nature is indescribable. This system of seven aspects of predication is known as *syādvāda* ("the doctrine of 'maybe'"), or *saptabhangi* ("the sevenfold division")*

As well as syādvāda the Jainas had another sevenfold system of predication known as *nayavāda*, the theory of standpoints, or ways of approaching an object of observation or study. The first three of these are connected with the object itself (*dravyārthika*), and the latter four with its modifications and the words used to describe it (*paryāyārthika*). (l) A mango tree may be considered simultaneously as an individual having a definite size and shape and as a member of the species "mango tree"; (2) it may be treated merely as a representative of the "universal" mango tree, and as corresponding to the general concept of a mango tree, without taking its individual qualities into account; or (3) it may be considered merely as an individual, without taking note of its specific qualities. Further it may be thought

*The Sanskrit terms for the seven aspects are: (1) *syādasti,* (2) *syānnāsti,* (3) *syādastināsti,* (4) *syādavaktavya,* (5) *syādastyavaktavya,* (6) *syānnāstyavaktavya,* and (7) *syādastināstyavaktavya.*

of (4) as it is at the present moment, for instance as hearing ripe fruit, without any regard to its past as a sapling or its future as firewood. (5) We may think of it from the point of view of its name "mango", considering all the synonyms of that name, and their implications. These synonyms may be subtly differentiated, and (6) we may consider their nuances and connotations. Finally (7) we may consider an object in its relation to a given epithet; thus by referring to a hero as a "lion" we mentally remove all his unlionlike qualities, and think of him only as a being of strength and courage.* Some Jaina schools rejected the last three standpoints, which are hardly consistent with the first four, being rather semantic than epistemological in character.

Modern logicians might make short work of these rather pedantic systems of ontological and epistemological relativity, but they have a fundamental quality of breadth and realism, implying a full realization that the world is more complex and subtle than we think it, and that what is true of a thing in one of its aspects may at the same time be false in another.

* The Sanskrit names of the seven *nayas* are: (1) *naigama,* (2) *saṅgraha,* (3) *vyavahāra,* (4) *ṛjusūtra,* (5) *śabda,* (6) *samabhirūḍha, and* (7) *evambhūta.*

APPENDIX VIII

WEIGHTS AND MEASURES

MEASURES OF WEIGHT

The basic weight of ancient India was the *raktikā*, the bright red seed of the *guñja* (*abrus precatorius*), which was conventionally reckoned at about 1.83 grains (.118 grams). Many sources give series of weights rising from this, which are not wholly consistent, and show that standards varied very widely with time and place.

The goidsmith's scale given by Manu, which was probably the most widely followed, was:

5 *raktikās*	= 1 *māṣa*,
16 *māṣas*	= 1 *karṣa*, *tolaka*, *or suvarṇa*,
4 *karṣas*	= 1 *pala*,
10 *patos*	= 1 *dharaṇa*.

The weight of the *pala* was thus approximately 1⅓ oz., or 37.76 gms. Of heavier weights the chief were the *prastha*, usually given as of 16 *palas*, and the *droṇa* of 16 *prasthas*. The *prastha* was thus approximately 21 oz. (600 gms.), and the *drona* 21¼ lb. (9–6 kg.).

MEASURES OF LENGTH

The commonest table, omitting microscopic measurements, was:

8 *yava* (barleycorns)	= 1 *aṅgula* (finger's breadth, ¾ in. or approx. 2 cm.)
12 *aṅgulas*	= 1 *vitasti* (span, 9 ins., 23 cm.)
2 *vitastis*	= 1 *hasta* or *aratni* (cubit, 18 ins., 47 cm.)
4 *hastas*	= 1 *daṇḍa* (rod) or *dhanus* (bow, 6 ft., 1.82 m.)
2,000 *dhanus*	= 1 *krośa* (cry) or *goruta* (cow-call, 2J miles, 3.6 km.)
4 *krośas*	= 1 *yojana* (stage, 9 miles approx., 14.5 km.).

Though most sources give the *krośa* (in modern Indian languages *kos*) as 2,000 *daṇdas* the *Arthaśāstra* gives it as only 1,000; the *yojana*, which was the commonest measure of long distances in ancient India, would thus be only 4½ miles (7.2 km.). It is therefore clear that there were at least two yojanas, and distances as given in texts are thus very unreliable. It would seem that for practical purposes the shorter *yojana* was more often used than the longer, especially in earlier times.

MEASURES OF TIME

Ancient Indian learned men devised a detailed terminology for minute intervals of time, which had little relation to everyday life and must be looked on as a flight of fancy. The longer measurements in most general use were:

18 *nimesas* (winks)	= 1 *kāṣṭhā* (3⅕ secs.)
30 *kāṣṭhās*	= 1 *kalā* (1⅗ mins.)
15 *kalās*	= 1 *nāḍikā* or *nālikā* (24 mins.)
30 *kalās* or 2 *nāḍikās*	= 1 *muhūrta* or *kṣaṇa* (48 mins.)
30 *muhūrtas*	= 1 *aho-rātra* (day and night, 24 hours).

A measurement frequently used, but not consistent with this system, was the *yāma* or watch, one-eighth of a day and night, or three hours. In some sources, however, the *yāma* is given as three *muhūrtas*, or one-tenth of a day and night. The hour (*horā*) was introduced from the West in the Gupta period and was used in astronomy, but was not widely employed in everyday life.

For longer measures of time see p. 494 ff.

APPENDIX IX

COINAGE*

EARLY PUNCH MARKED COINS

UNINSCRIBED punchmarked coins were probably minted from the 6th century B.C. onwards, and were in circulation for many centuries. Among the earliest silver specimens are those in the shape of a small bent bar, the largest of which, the *śatamāna*, weighed 180 grains (11.66 gms.). Half, quarter and half-quarter *śatamānas* are attested.

The basic silver punchmarked coin of the usual type was the *kāriāpana* or *paṇa*, of 57.8 grains (3.76 gms.). The *māṣa* or *māṣika* weighed one-sixteenth of this, or 3.6 grains (0.25 gms.). Various intermediate weights are attested, as well as large silver coins of 30 and 20 *māṣas* and small half-*māṣa* pieces.

Punchmarked copper coins were generally based on a different standard— a *māṣa* of 9 grains (0.58 gms.) and a *kārṣāpaṇa* of 144 grains (9.33 gms.). Quarter-*māṣas* in copper, or *kākiṇīs* (2.25 grains or 0.13 gms.) are attested, as well as large coins of 20, 30 and 45 copper *māṣas*.

Only one gold punchmarked coin is known, and it must be assumed that gold was very rarely minted before the beginning of the Christian era.

INDO-GREEK COINS

The earlier Greek kings minted coins according to the Attic standard, based on the drachm of 67.2 grains (4.34 gms.) and the obol (⅙ drachm) of 11.2 grains (0.71 gms.). Silver coinage of this type ranges from hemiobols to the very large double decadrachms, struck by a king Amyntas, which have recently been found in Afghānistān. After their southward expansion the Greeks adopted a reduced weight, with silver coins of 152 and 38 grains (9.85 and 2.46 gms.).

The Greek kings issued numerous copper coins, but their metrology is not clear. Gold coins must have been very rare. There exist a very large 20 stater piece of the Bactrian usurper Eucratides and rare staters of a few other kings.

Śaka and Pahlava coins in silver and copper follow the reduced Indo- Greek standard.

* We are much indebted to Professor A. K. Narain, of Banāras Hindu University, for providing the material for this appendix.

KUṢĀṆA COINS

These were minted in gold and copper. The gold *dīnāras* or *suvarnas* were based on the Roman denarius and were of 124 grains (8.04 gms.). Double and quarter *dināras* were also issued. The copper coins were large, of from 26 to 28 *māṣas*, or 240 to 260 grains (15.55 to 16.85 gms.).

PRE-GUPTAN AND GUPTAN COINS

A large range of coins in silver and copper, of very varied weight and character, was issued by the indigenous kings, tribes and cities of Northern India in the centuries immediately preceding and following the beginning of the Christian era. The Sātavāhanas of the Deccan also issued coins of lead and potin (base silver), while the Śakas of Gujarāt, Mālwā and the Western Deccan issued a distinctive series of coins in silver.

The gold coins of the Guptas (*dīnāra*) originally approximated to the Kuṣāṇa standard, but in the middle of the 5th century rose in weight to 144 grains (9.33 gms.), thus retuming to the Indian standard of the copper *kārṣāpaṇa*. Gupta silver coins (*rūpaka*), based on those of the Śakas of Ujjayinī, weighed 32.36 grains (2.07-2.33 gms.). The metrology of Gupta copper coinage is obscure, and weights of from 3.3 to 101 grains (0.19-6.54 gms.) are attested.

MEDIEVAL COINS

Gold coins (*suvarṇa*, *ṭahka*) were minted by only a few dynasties in the 11th century. These approximated to the Greek drachm standard of 67 grains (4-34 gms.). Silver coins (*dramma*, *tanka*) also conformed to this standard, and coins of ¾, ½ and ¼ *dramma* are attested. Numerous types of copper coin were issued, of diverse metrology. The coinage of the medieval dynasties of the Peninsula was very varied and a full study of its metrology is yet to be made.

APPENDIX X

THE ALPHABET AND ITS PRONUNCIATION

THE alphabet devised by ancient Indian phoneticians and adapted to all the chief Indian languages except Urdū is as follows:

I. VOWELS

(a) *simple*

	short	long
guttural . . .	(1) *a*	(2) *ā*
palatal . . .	(3) *i*	(4) *ī*
labial . . .	(5) *u*	(6) *ū*
retroflex . . .	(7) *ṛ*	(8) *ṝ*
dental . . .	(9) *ḷ*	(10) *ḹ**

(b) *diphthongs*

palatal . .	(11) *e*
	(12) *ai*
labial . .	(13) *o*
	(14) *au*

II. CONSONANTS

(a) *visarga* (15) *ḥ*

(b) *anusvāra* (16) *ṃ*

(c) *stopped consonants*

	unvoiced	unvoiced aspirate	voiced	voiced aspirate	nasal
guttural . . .	(17) *k*	(18) *kh*	(19) *g*	(20) *gh*	(21) *ṅ*
palatal . . .	(22) *c*	(23) *ch*	(24) *j*	(25) *jh*	(26) *ñ*
retroflex . . .	(27) *ṭ*	(28) *ṭh*	(29) *ḍ*	(30) *ḍh*	(31) *ṇ*
dental . . .	(32) *t*	(33) *th*	(34) *d*	(35) *dh*	(36) *n*
labial . . .	(37) *p*	(38) *ph*	(39) *b*	(40) *bh*	(41) *m*

* This vowel is the invention of the paṇḍits, and never occurs in practice. The short vocalic *ḷ* occurs only in the root *kḷp* and its derivatives.

(d) *semivowels*

alatal • • (42) *y*
retroflex • • (43) *r*
dental • • (44) *l*
labial • • (45) *v*

(e) *sibilants*

palatal • • (46) *ś*
retroflex • • (47) *ṣ*
dental • • (48) *s*

(f) *aspiration* (49) *h*

To these letters the Dravidian languages and Sinhalese add the short vowels *ĕ* (between *ḷ* and *e*) and *ŏ* (between *e* and *o*). Sinhalese has also the additional vowels *ä* and *ǟ* (between ā and *i*). Tamil adds the consonants *l*, *ḷ* (not the same as the vocalic *ḷ* of Sanskrit), *r*, and *n* at the end of the alphabet; these letters cannot stand at the beginning of a word. The Tamil alphabet omits the aspirate letters and several others, and the unvoiced letters serve to express the sound of the voiced. The system of transliteration used for Tamil words and quotations in this book does not show this peculiarity.

It will be seen that this alphabet is methodical and scientific, its elements classified first into vowels and consonants, and then, within each section, according to the manner in which the sound is formed. The gutturals are formed by the constriction of the throat at the back of the tongue, the palatals by pressing the tongue flat against the palate, the retroflexes by tuming up the tip of the tongue to touch the hard palate, the dentals by touching the upper teeth with the tongue, and the labials by pursing the lips.

The vowels *ā*, *i*, *ī*, *u*, *ū*, *e*, *ai*, *o*, and *au* are pronounced approximately as in German or Italian, *e* and *o* being "close "sounds, as in German *beten* and *boten*, but short *a* has the dull sound of the English *shut*. In very early times r and the vocalic *ḷ* were pronounced approximately as are the second syllables of the words *water* ánd *bottle* by Americans, but before the Christian era they were sounded as *ri* and *lri*. The Sinhalese *ä* and *ǟ* are pronounced approximately as the vowels in the English *hat* and *hair* respectively. According to traditional phonetics *e* and *o* are classed as diphthongs and in Sanskrit are invariably long.

Of the two first consonants *ḥ*, occurring only at the end of words or syllables, is a rough breathing, replacing an original *s* or *r*. It is a distinct emission of breath, often followed by a faint continuation of the preceding vowel. *Anusvāra*, or *ṃ*, written in Indian scripts as a dot, is in part a mere abbreviation, representing a nasal sound before a stopped consonant. Thus *saṃdhi* is pronounced as *sandhi*, and *aṃga* as *aṅga*. Before semi-vowels, sibilants or *h* it had the effect of nasalizing the preceding vowel, as in French or Portuguese; thus *aṃśu* was pronounced very approximately as the French *un chou*. By many modern speakers *ṃ* in this context is pronounced as the English *ng* in *sing*.

The distinction between the aspirate and unaspirate consonants is not immediately recognized by the Westerner, but it is clear to the Indian. *K*, for instance, is pronounced without any noticeable emission of breath, and *kh* (written as one letter in Indian scripts) with a strong emission, as in the usual pronunciation of the English *c* in *come*. Thus the reader should avoid the temptation to pronounce *th* and *ph* as the initial sounds of the English *thing* and *phial*; they approximate to the sounds in *pothook* and *shepherd*. *C* is pronounced approximately as the second consonantal sound in the English *church*, and *eh* as the first sound in the same word, i.e. with a stronger emission of breath. *J* is pronounced as in English, and not as in German or French. A clear distinction is made between the retroflex or cerebral consonants and the dental, though it is not very evident to the untrained ear. The English *t* and *d* are nearer to the Indian retroflex *ṭ* and *ḍ* than to the Indian dentals *t* and *d*, which approximate to the corresponding sounds in Italian.

Modern Indians do not generally differentiate in speaking between *ś* and *ṣ*, and inscriptions show that the two sounds began to be confused at an early date. Both resemble *sh* in the English *shut*. Originally *ṣ* was pronounced, like the other retroflex consonants, with the tip of the tongue touching the top of the hard palate.

Of the special Tamil letters *ḷ* has the sound of an *l* with the tongue turned as far back as possible. Many modern Tamil speakers pronounce this letter rather like the *s* in the English *measure* or the French *j*, but more harshly. The consonantal *ḷ* (which also occurs in Vedic and some Prākrits) is pronounced by placing the tongue on the top of the hard palate and flapping it forward; *ṟ* at the end of a syllable is often pronounced as *t*; between two vowels it is approximately *dr*, and when doubled *tr*, while *ṉṟ* is usually pronounced as *ndr*; though a distinction formerly existed, Tamil, *ṉ* is in modern speech indistinguishable from *n*.

We have seen that Vedic Sanskrit, like Greek, had a tonic accent, but this, again as in Greek, disappeared very early from ordinary speech, its place being taken by a stress accent, as in most European languages. The stress is placed on the last prosodically long syllable of a word (i.e. a syllable containing either a long vowel or a short vowel followed by two consonants) other than the final syllable, which never has the accent. In a word with no long syllables the accent is on the first syllable. E.g. *sábhā*, *Himālaya*, *Śakūntalā*, *ávayava*. The stress is not as marked as in English.

APPENDIX XI

PROSODY

LIKE those of classical Europe the metres of Indian poetry are quantitative, based on the order of long and short syllables, and not, as in English, on stress. As in classical European languages a syllable was counted as long if it contained a long vowel (*ā*, *ī*, *ū*, *ṝ*, *e*, *o*, *ai* or *au*) or a short vowel followed by two consonants. The favourite stanza form at all times was of four lines or "quarters" (*pāda*), usually equal, and varying in length from eight to over twenty syllables each, with a full caesura between the the second and third quarters. Most of the metres of classical poetry were set in rigid pattems, and not divided into feet but broken only by one or two cæsuræ in each quarter. The metres of the Veda, however, and the epic *śloka* metre, allowed considerable variation.

Though most of the Vedic hymns are in stanzas of four quarters there are some with three or five divisions. Of these one, called *Gāyatrī*, is common, and is that of the famous Gāyatrī verse quoted on p. 163. It consists of three sections of eight syllables each, the first four of which are free while the last four have the cadence ⏑ – ⏑ ⏓.

The commonest Vedic stanza is *Tristubh*, consisting of four quarters of eleven syllables each. The quarter normally has a cæsura after the fourth or fifth syllable, and is prevailingly iambic. The last four syllables of each quarter have the cadence – ⏑ – ⏓. For example:

> *Índrasya nu víriāṇi prá vocam*
> *yáni cakára prathamáni vajrí.*
> *Áhann Áhim, anu apás tatarda,*
> *pra vakṣáṇā abhinat párvatānām.**

Similar to this, but with an extra syllable in each quarter, was the twelve-syllabled *Jagatī*, with the cadence – ⏑ – ⏑ ⏓.

In the later hymns of the *Ṛg Veda* a stanza of four eight-syllable quarters, called *Anuṣṭubh*, became popular. This was much the same as *Gāyatri*, with a fourth line added, but there was considerable variation in the final cadence. For example:

> *Sahásra-śīrsā Pūruṣaḥ,*
> *sahasrākṣáḥ, sahásrapāt.*
> *Sá bhúmiṃ viśváto vrtvá*
> *áty atiṣṭhad daśāṅgulám.*†

* The first verse of the hymb to Indra (*R.V.* i. 32) translated on p. 353.

† The first verse of the "Hymn of the Primeval Man" (R.V. x. 90), in part translated on p. 210.

From the *Anuṣṭubh* of the Vedas developed the *Śloka*, the chief epic metre of later times. This consisted of four quarters of eight syllables each, the first and third normally ending with the cadence ⏑ – – ⏓, and the and fourth with ⏑ – ⏑ ⏓. Certain specified variations were allowed. As an example we quote the first verse of the account of Damayantī's svayamvara, translated on p. 362.

Atha kāle śubhe prāpte,
tithau puṇye kṣaṇe tathā,
ājuhāva mahīpālān
Bhīmo rājā svayaṃvare.

The *śloka* metre was widely used for poetry of all kinds, especially for didactic and narrative verse. The courtly poets, however, favoured longer metres, with their quantities rigidly fixed in complicated rhythmic pattems, some with regular caesurae. Textbooks describe over 100 metres of this kind, many with fanciful names, but only some twenty or thirty were popular. Of these we mention a few of the most common.

Indravajra ("Indra's Thunderbolt"):

4 × 11: – – ⏑ – – ⏑ ⏑ – ⏑ – ⏓

Bhāgīrathi-nirjhara-sikarāṇāṃ
voḍhā muhuḥ kampita-devadāruḥ
yad vāyur anviṣṭamrgaih kirātair
*āsevyate bhinna-śikhaṇḍi-barhaḥ.**

Upendravajra (Secondary *Indravajra*), a variant of the above, with the first syllable short:

4 × 11: ⏑ – ⏑ – – ⏑ ⏑ – ⏑ – ⏓.

Quarter lines of *Indravajra* and *Upendravajra* were often combined in mixed stanzas. Such stanzas of varying metres were called *Upajāti*.

Vaṃśastha:

4 × 12: ⏑ – ⏑ – – ⏑ ⏑ – ⏑ – ⏑ ⏓.

Indravaṃśa: like *Vaṃśastha*, but with a long first syllable:

4 × 12: – – ⏑ – – ⏑ ⏑ – ⏑ – ⏑ ⏓.

Vaṃśastha and *Indravaṃśa* were often combined in an *Upajāti* metre, e.g. the verses of Kālidāsa quoted on p. 376, n.

Vasantatilakā ("The Ornament of Spring"):

4 × 14: – – ⏑ ⏑ ⏑ – ⏑ ⏑ – ⏑ – ⏓.

---

* *Kumarā Sambhava*, i. 15, translated on p. 373 — "And the wind forever..."

Adyāpi tām praṇayinīṃ mṛgaśāvakākṣīṃ
pīyūṣa-varṇa-kuca-kumbha-yugaṃ vahantīm
paśyāmy ahaṃ yadi punar divasāvasāne
*svargāpavarga-vara-rājya-sukhaṃ tyajāmi.**

Mālinī ("The Girl wearing a Garland "):

4 × 15: ⏑ ⏑ ⏑ ⏑ ⏑ – – / – ⏑ – – ⏑ – ⏓.

Kim iha bahubhir uktair yukti-śūnyaiḥ pralāpair?
Dvayam api puruṣāṇām sarvadā sevaniyam—
abhinava-mada-lili-lālasaṃ sundarīṇāṃ
stana-bhara-parikhinnaṃ yauvanaṃ va vanam vā.†

Pṛthvi ("The Earth"):

4 × 17: ⏑ – ⏑ ⏑ ⏑ – ⏑ – ⏑ ⏑ ⏑ – ⏑ – – ⏑ ⏓.

Labheta sikatāsu tailam api yatnataḥ pīḍayan
pibec ca mṛgatṛṣṇikāsu salilaṃ pipāsārditaḥ
kadācid api paryaṭañ chaśa-viṣāṇam āsādayen,
na tu pratīniviṣṭa-mūrkha-jana-cittam ārādhayet.‡

Mandākrāntā ("The Slow-stepper"):

4 × 17: – – – – / ⏑ ⏑ ⏑ ⏑ ⏑ – / – ⏑ – – ⏑ – ⏓.

An example of this metre is given on p. 371, n.

Śikhariṇī ("The Excellent Lady"):

4 × 17: ⏑ – – – – – / ⏑ ⏑ ⏑ ⏑ ⏑ – – ⏑ ⏑ ⏑ ⏓.

Yad' āsīd ajñānaṃ smara-timira-saṃskāra-janitaṃ
tadā dṛṣṭaṃ nārī-mayam idam aśeṣaṃ jagad api.
Idānīm asmākaṃ paṭutara-vivekāñjana-juṣāṃ
samibhūtā dṛṣṭis tribhuvanam api Brahmā manute.§

Hariṇī ("The Doe"):

4 × 17: ⏑ ⏑ ⏑ ⏑ ⏑ – / – – – – / ⏑ – ⏑ ⏑ – ⏑ ⏓.

Apara-jaladher Lakṣmīṃ yasmin Purīṃ Purabhit-prabhe
mada-gaja-ghaṭākārair nāvāṃ śatair avamṛdnati

---

* Bilhaṇa, *Caurapañcāśikā,* 45, translated on p. 380: "Even today, if this evening ..."

† Bhartṛhari, *Śṛṅgāraśataka,* 53, translated on p. 378: "What is the use ...?"

‡ Bhartṛhari, *Nitiśataka,* 5, translated on p. 377: "You *may* if you squeeze hard enough ..."

§ Bhartṛhari, *Vairāgyaśataka,* 82, translated on p. 378: "When I was ignorant ..."

jalada-patalānīkākīrṇaṃ navotpala-mecakaṃ
*jalanidhir iva vyoma vyomnaḥ santo 'bhavad ambudhiḥ.**

Śārdūla-vikriḍita ("The Tiger's Sport"):

4 × 19: — — — ⏑ ⏑ — ⏑ — ⏑ ⏑ ⏑ — / — — ⏑ — — ⏑ ⏓.

Keśāḥ saṃyaminaḥ, śruter api paraṃ pāraṃgate locane,
cāntarvaktram api svabhāva-sucibhiḥ kīrṇaṃ dvijānāṃ gaṇaiḥ,
muktānāṃ satatādhivāsa-ruciraṃ vakṣoja-kumbhadvayaṃ
cetthaṃ tanvi vapuḥ praśāntam api te kṣobham karoty ēva naḥ†

Sragdharā ("The Girl with a Garland"):

4 × 21: — — — — ⏑ — — / ⏑ ⏑ ⏑ ⏑ ⏑ ⏑ — / — ⏑ — — ⏑ — ⏓.

The verses of Bāṇa quoted on p. 379, n. are in this metre.

In a few rather rare metres the first and third quarters differ in length from the second and fourth. The commonest of these is *Puṣpitāgrā*:

2 × (12 + 13): ⏑ ⏑ ⏑ ⏑ ⏑ ⏑ — ⏑ — ⏑ — ⏓ /
⏑ ⏑ ⏑ ⏑ — ⏑ ⏑ — ⏑ — ⏑ — ⏓.

"*Aham iha nivasāmi. Yāhi Rādhām,*
anunaya madvacanena c' ānayethāḥ".
Iti Madhuripuṇā sakhi niyuktā,
svayam idam etyapunar jagāda Rādhām.‡

As well as metres of this type there are others, the scansion of which is based on the number of syllabic instants (*mātrā*) in each quarter-verse. The most common of these is *Āryā* ("The Lady"). This is divided into feet, each containing four instants, counting a prosodically short syllable as one and a long syllable as two instants (i.e. — —, — ⏑ ⏑, ⏑ — ⏑, ⏑ ⏑ —, or ⏑ ⏑ ⏑ ⏑). The first quarter of the *Āryā* stanza contains three such feet; the second, four and a half; the third, three, and the fourth three and a half, with an extra short syllable after the second foot. The whole of Hāla's *Saptaśataka* is written in this metre; for example:

Bhaṇḍantia taṇāiṃ
suttuṃ diṇṇāi jāi pahiassa.

*"Radiant as the god Śiva, he besieged Purī, the fortune of the Western Sea,
with hundreds of ships, like elephants in rut,
the dark blue sky, scattered with hosts of heavy clouds,
looked like the sea, and the sea looked like the sky."

From a panegyric of King Pulakeśīn II Cālukya in an inscription at Aihoḷe, Mysore, composed by Ravikīrti and dated A.D. 634 (*EI* vi, 8ff.).

† Bhartṛhari, *Śṛṅgāraśataka,* 12, translated on p. 377: "Your hair well combed ..."

‡ The introductory verse to the lyric of Jayadeva's *Gīta Govinda,* translated on p. 380.

Tāi ccea pahāe
*ajjā āaḍḍhaī ruantī**

This verse is to be scanned as follows:

– – / – ⏑ ⏑ / – – /
– – / – – / ⏑ – – ⏑ / ⏑ ⏑ – / –
– – / – ⏑ ⏑ / – – /
– – / – – / ⏑ / ⏑ ⏑ – / –.

The metres employed by Jayadeva in his *Gīta Govinda* are exceptional, although imitated by later poets. They are no doubt borrowed from popular song. The stanzas of the lyric quoted on p. 381, excluding the refrain, consist of four quarters of nine, eight, nine and ten syllables respectively, all of which are short except the last rhyming syllable in the first and third quarters and the penultimate in the second and fourth.

The prosody of Tamil poetry differs considerably from that of Sanskrit. In Tamil the basic unit is the "metrical syllable" (*aśai*), which may be a single syllable or a long syllable preceded by a short one. Two, three or four of these form a foot, of which a line of poetry may contain from two to six or occasionally more. Complicated rules, which cannot be discussed here, much restrict the order of syllables and feet in the line.

* *Saptaśataka,* 379, translated on p. 412: "Last night with scorn …."

APPENDIX XII

THE GYPSIES

AMONG India's many gifts to the world we must include the Gypsies, who, with their music and dancing, have formed a romantic and colourful element in European life for over five centuries.

The European Gypsies have no recollection of their Indian origin, but have generally claimed to be Egyptians. The Russian Gypsies, it is said, even declare that their ancestors were a single soldier of the army of Pharaoh and a young girl, who escaped drowning when Moses led the Israelites over the Red Sea. This tradition of the Gypsies' Egyptian origin was for long taken at its face value, until in 1763 a Hungarian protestant theological student, Stefan Vályi, published a brief paper pointing to the close similarity between the language of the Gypsies of his native plains and that of three Indians whom he had met at the University of Leyden. It was long before the true significance of this fact was recognized, but it is now universally agreed that the Gypsy language or Romani is an Indo-Āryan one, and that the fact can only be accounted for by postulating that the Gypsies came from India. The relationship of Romani to the languages of Northern India is very obvious, even to those with no linguistic training, for many of the commonest words of Romani are little different from those of India. Thus:

Romani*	***Indo-Aryan***	***English***
Ek	Sanskrit *eka*, Hindi *ek*	one
dui	Skt. *dva*, H. *do*	two
trin	Skt. *tri*, H. *tin*	three
śtar	Skt. *catvār*, H. *cār*	four
pañci	Skt. *pañca*, H. *pāṃc*	five
śo	Skt. *ṣaṣ*	six
efta	(Greek, ἑπτά)	seven
ohto	(Greek, οκτώ)	eight
īnea	(Greek, ἐννέά)	nine
deś	Skt. *daśa*	ten
biś	H. *bīs*	twenty
śel	Skt. *śata*	hundred
manuś	Skt. *manuṣya*	man

* These words are taken from Serboianu's grammar and glossary of Rumanian Romani *(Les Tsiganes,* Paris, 1930). His rather unscientific system of transliteration has been modified in accordance with the usual Indo-Āryan system.

bal	Skt. *bāla*, H. *bāl*	hair
kan	Skt. *karṇa*, H. *kān*	ear
nak	*H. nāk*	nose
yak	Skt. *akṣa*	eye
kalo	Skt. *kāla*	black
caco	Skt. *satya*, H. *sac*	true, etc., etc.

Philologists have shown by the comparison of Romani with the Prākrits and modern Indian languages that the Gypsies originated in the Gangā basin, which they left before the time of Aśoka (3rd century B.C.), to reside for several centuries in North-Western India. Probably even at this time they were wandering musicians and entertainers. In modern India there is a lowly caste of such people called *Doms*, attested since the early Middle Ages, and with this word the word *Rom*, by which the Gypsies universally designate themselves, is probably connected. In Syrian Romani it occurs as *Doum*, very close to the Indian form.

According to the 11th c. Persian poet Firdūsi, who collected many legends and traditions of pre-Muslim Persia in his "Book of Kings" (*Shāh-nāmah*), the 5th-century Sāsānian king Bahrām Gūr invited ten thousand Indian musicians to his realm, and gave them cattle, corn and asses, so that they might settle in the land and entertain his poorer subjects, who had been complaining that the pleasures of music and dance were reserved for the rich. But the musicians refused to settle; they ate the cattle and seed-corn which the king had given them, and wandered about the land like wolves or wild dogs.

Though Firdūsī's story may not be wholly accurate, it shows that low caste Indian musicians were well known in the Middle East at a very early time. With the Arab conquest of Sind in the early 8th century further groups of Indian entertainers must have found their way westwards and later have moved on to Africa and Europe. Folk called Athinganoi are recorded as living in Constantinople in A.D. 810, and later Byzantine records refer to these Athinganoi or Azinganoi as magicians and conjurors. These were probably the forerunners of the Tsigany bands who appeared in Central and Western Europe in the late Middle Ages. The earliest evidence of Gypsies in Europe other than in the Balkans comes from the German city of Hildesheim, where a passing band is recorded in 1407. A great horde of Gypsies passed through Basel in 1422, under a chief who called himself Michael, Prince of Egypt. Within a few decades they had overrun all Europe; the earliest records show that they had all the characteristics of their descendants—they were careless, lazy, dirty and cheerful, skilled in metal work and tinkering, splendid musicians and dancers, their bodies bedecked with bright garments and jewellery, their menfolk cunning horse-dealers, their womenfolk telling fortunes, and both sexes losing no opportunity to pilfer from the unsuspecting *gorjo*. It was not long before the Gypsies began to feel the fierce persecution which they were to suffer in most parts of Europe down to recent times, when many Gypsies perished in the gas-chambers of the Third Reich.

From numerous loan-words in the various dialects of Romani we may roughly trace the course of their migrations. All the Romani dialects of West and Central Europe contain many Greek and South Slavonic words, which prove that the ancestors of our western Gypsies dwelt long in the Balkans. The Spanish Gypsies appear to have arrived in their new homeland from two directions, a first immigration coming via Egypt and the north coast of Africa, no doubt during the Moorish occupation of southern Spain, and a second, later, over the Pyrenees.

Little but their language remains to connect the Gypsies with their original home, and even their speech is full of borrowings from almost every tongue of Europe and many of Asia. Though the Gypsies have always tended to marry their own kind, centuries of wandering have left their mark on the Gypsy type and there are now many fair Gypsies, though others, if suitably attired, would not seem out of place in a modern North Indian city. On analysis their music is that of the lands in which they dwell. Whether in Hungary, Rumania or Spain, it is based on local folk-song and dance. Unfortunately the English Gypsies have largely forgotten their traditional art, but when they sing they sing folk-songs and music-hall ballads; in Ireland the tinkers sing Irish folk-songs. Yet, wherever the Gypsies go, their musicians tend to give their music a character of its own. A predilection for ornamentation of the melody, especially with quarter-tones, a preference for the minor mode, a tendency to introduce progressions by augmented whole tones into their melodies, and a love of complex rhythm, are perhaps survivals of the Indian musical tradition which the first Romanis brought with them from their homeland. Some Gypsy folktales resemble those of India, but the same may be said of the traditional tales of every country of Europe. A few Gypsy customs and beliefs may be genuine Indian survivals. Though by no means a hygienically inclined people, the Gypsies have ideas of ritual purity and birth and death taboos which remind us of those of Hinduism. Thus a woman in childbirth is impure, and must bear her child outside her caravan or tent lest she pollute it Gypsy midwives are impure throughout their lives, and are taboo to all respectable Gypsies, like the outcast village midwives of India. Corpses are also impure, and dying Gypsies are carried from their caravans to end their lives in the open air, for fear of pollution. The Gypsy taboo on horse-slaughterers may have an Indian origin. But all these resemblances might well be accounted for otherwise.

The Gypsies have, in fact, forgotten their ancestry. In one respect, however, they have kept to the traditions of their homeland. Though they have adapted their ways to time and place, and have always been open to new influences, they are still governed by their own laws and their own code of morality. They have doggedly retained their individuality against persecution and persuasion alike—an indepedent social group, transcending regional and national boundaries, knit together by common customs, common means of livelihood, and common blood. In this respect they are Indian. They are a caste, as their Indian counterparts, the Doms, are a caste, and even the innovations of the Twentieth Century have not been able to destroy their caste solidarity.

BIBLIOGRAPHY AND REFERENCES

The following standard abbreviations are used:

AI	*Ancient India* (the Journal of the Archaeological Department). Delhi.
AL	*Art and Letters* (Journal of the Royal India, Pākistān and Ceylon Society). London.
ARSIE	*Annual Reports of South Indian Epigraphy*. Delhi.
ASIAR	*Archaeological Survey of India Annual Reports*. Delhi.
AV	*Atharva Veda*.
BhG	*Bhagavad Gita*.
Br.	*Brāhmaṇa*.
BSOAS	*Bulletin of the School of Oriental and African Studies*, London.
CHI	*Cambridge History of India*, *6* vols. (voi. ii not yet published). Cambridge, 1922-
CII	*Corpus Inscriptionum Indicarum*, 4 vols. London and Ootacamund, 1888-1955.
DN	*Dīgha Nikāya* of the Pāli Canon.
ed.	Edited by, edition.
EI	*Epigraphia Indica*. Calcutta and Delhi.
IA	*Indian Antiquary*. Calcutta.
IC	*Indian Culture*. Calcutta.
IHQ	*Indian Historical Quarterly*. Calcutta.
J	*Jātaka*.
JA	*Journal Asiatique*. Paris.
JAHRS	*Journal of the Āndhra Historical Research Society*. Rājamundry.
JAOS	*Journal of the American Oriental Society*. Baltimore.
JESHO	*Journal of the Economic and Social History of the Orient*. Leiden.
JIH	*Journal of Indian History*. Trivandrum.
JNSI	*Journal of the Numismatic Society of India*. Calcutta.
JRAI	*Journal of the Royal Anthropological Institute*. London.
JRAS	*Journal of the Royal Asiatic Society*. London.
Mbh.	*Mahābhārata* (Poona edition unless otherwise stated).
P.E.	Pillar Edict of Aśoka.
PHAI	*PoliticalHistory of Ancient India*, H. C. Raychaudhuri. 6th ed. Calcutta, 1953.
R.E.	Rock Edict of Aśoka.

RV	*Ṛg Veda.*
SBE	*Sacred Books of the East*, 50 vols. Ed. F. Max Miiller, Oxford, 1879-1900.
tr.	Translated by, translation.
Up.	*Upaniṣad.*
ZDMG	*Zeitschrift der deutschen morgenländischen Gesellschaft*. Berlin.

A NOTE FOR THOSE WHO WISH TO READ FURTHER

This book is primarily intended for those who know no Sanskrit; hence editions of original texts are not generally mentioned, but reference is made to translations wherever possible. As many Indian readers of this book will have little or no knowledge of European languages, English translations of works by Continental scholars are referred to wherever they exist and only a few very important untranslated works are mentioned. Few of the books mentioned will be found in the ordinary western libraries, but most can be obtained on request by local librarians. Many of the older works, for long unobtainable, have recently been reprinted in India.

CHAPTER I: INTRODUCTION

BIBLIOGRAPHY

Geography, etc.

L. Dudley Stamp. *Asia*. 8th ed., London, 1950.

O. H. K. Spate. *India and Pakistan*. London, 1954.

Sir A. Cunningham, ed. S. Majumdār. *The Ancient Geography of India* Calcutta, 1924.

B. C. Law. *Historical Geography of Ancient India*. Paris, 1954.

B. S. Guha. *Outline of the linciai History of India*. Calcutta, 1937.

The Discovery of Ancient India

A. J. Arberry. *Asiatic Jones*. London, 1946.

Sir J. Cumming and others. *Revealing India's Past*. London, 1939.

R. Schwab. *La Renaissance Orientale*. Paris, 1950.

General Works on Ancient Indian Culture

G. T. Garratt and others. *The Legacy of India*. Oxford, 1937.

P. Masson-Oursel and others. *Ancient India and Indian Civilization*. London, 1934.

A. A. Macdonell. *India's Past*. Oxford, 1927.

L. D. Barnett. *Antiquities of India*. London, 1913.

R. C. Majumdār. *Ancient India*. Banāras, 1952.

——— and *others*. *History and Culture of the Indian People*, voi.*i*, *The Vedic Age*. London, 1950; voi. ii, *The Age of Imperial Unity*. Bombay, 1951; voi.

iii, *The Classical Age*. Bombay 1954; voi. iv, *The Age of Imperial Kanauj*. Bombay 1955; voi. v, *The Struggle for Empire*, Bombay 1957; voi. vi. *The Delhi Sultanate*. Bombay, I960.

L. Renou. *La Civilisation de VInde Ancienne*. Paris, 1950.

——— and others. *L'Inde Classique*, voi. i. Paris,1947; voi.ii, Paris, 1953. 1 vol. to follow.

CHAPTER II: PREHISTORY

BIBLIOGRAPHY

General Works

S. Piggott. *Prehistoric India*. Harmondsworth, 1950.

B. Subbarao. *The Personality of India*. 2nd ed., Baroda, 1958.

D. H. Gordon. *The Prehistoric Background of Indian Culture*. Bombay, 1958.

Sir R. E. Mortimer Wheeler. *The Indus Civilization* (Supplement to *CHI*). Cambridge, 1953.

——— *Early Indiaand* Pakistan.

H. D. Sankalia. *Indian Archaology Today*. London, 1962.

——— *Prehistory and Protohistory in India and Pakistan*. Bombay, 1962.

V. Gordon Childe. *New Light on the Most Ancient East*. 4th ed., London, 1952.

——— *The Āryans*. London, 1926.

L. de la Vallée Poussin. *Indo-Européens et Indo-Iraniens*. 2nd ed., Paris, 1936.

A. A. Macdonell and A. B. Keith. *A Vedic Index*. 2 vols., London, 1912.

W. Rau. *Staat und Gesellschaft im alten Indien nach den Brāhmaṇa-texten dargestellt*. Wiesbaden, 1957.

Chief Archaelogical Reports

Sir J. Marshall and others. *Mohenjo Daro and the Indus Civilization*. 3 vols., London, 1931.

E. Mackay and others. *Further Excavations at Mohenjo Daro*. Delhi, 1938.

——— *Chanhu Daro Excavations*. New Haven, Conn., 1943.

M. S. Vats and others. *Excavations at Harappā*. 2 vols., Delhi, 1940.

Sir R. E. M. Wheeler. *Harappā*, 1946 ... *AI*, 3, 1947, p. 58 ff.

B. B. Lal. *Excavations at Hastināpura* ... *AI* 10-11, 1954-5.

G. R. Sharma. *Excavations at Kauśāmbī*, 1957-59. Allahabad, 1960.

F. A. Khan. *Kot Diji*, 1957-8. Preliminary Report. Karachi, n.d.

For progress reports of other recent excavations, the reader is referred to the annual publication of the Indian Archaeological Department, *Ancient India*.

Sources

For translations of Vedic literature see Bibliography to Chapter VII, p. 532.

REFERENCES

1. D. H. Gordon. *The Early Use of Metals in India and Pākistān*. *JRAI*, lxxx, pp. 55 ff.
2. *Prehistoric India*, p. 155
3. G. de Hevesy. *Bulletin de la Soditi Préhistorique Francaise*. 7-8, 1933
4. F. O. Schrader, *ZDMG*. 1934, pp. 185ff.
5. W. Koppers. *Geographica Helvetica*. 1946, voi. ii, pp. 165 ff.
6. C. von Fürer Haimendorf. *Illustrated London News*. 1.7.1950, pp. 24ff.
7. M. A. Murray. *The Splendour that was Egypt*. London, 1949, p. 318 26
8. *RV*. viii, 46, 32 33
9. This conclusion is based on the unpublished thesis of Dr J. P. Sharma (*Republican and Quasi-Republican Institutions in Ancient India*, University of London, 1962).
10. *RV*. x, 97, 6
11. *Job*, 39, 19-25
12. *RV*. iv, 38, 5-6
13. Gordon (n.l above). p. 67
14. B. B. Lai. *Illustrated London News*. 4.10.1952, pp. 55lff.
15. *PHAI*. pp. 27 ff.
16. *Satapatha Br*., i, 4, 1
17. Rau, *Staat und Gesellschaft*, pp. 109-111.
18. S. D. Singh, *JESHO* v, 1962, pp. 212-16; D. D. Kosambi, ibid., vi, 1963, pp. 309-18. 43

CHAPTER III: HISTORY

BIBLIOGRAPHY

General Histories of India

R. C. Majumdār and others. *Advanced History of India*. 2nd ed., London, 1950.

V. A. Smith, ed. T. G. P. Spear. *The Oxford History of India*, 3rd ed., Oxford, 1958.

H. G. Rawlinson. *India, a Short Cultural History*. London, 1937.

Various Authors. *The Cambridge History of India*. 6 vols. (voi. ii not yet published). Cambridge, 1922- .

R. C. Majumdār and others. *History and Culture of the Indian People* (see p. 519).

Histories of Pre-Muslim India

H. C. Raychaudhurī. *Political History of Ancient India*. 6th ed., Calcutta, 1953.

E. J. Rapson. *Ancient India*. Cambridge, 1916.

V. A. Smith. *Early History of India*. 4th ed., Oxford, 1924.

K. A. NIlakanta Sāstrī. *History of India*. Part i. Madras, 1950.

L. de la Vallēe Poussin. *L'Inde aux Temps des Mauryas* ... Paris, 1930.

——— *Dynasties et Histoire de l'Inde* ... Paris, 1935.

D. D. Kosambi. *The Culture and Civilisation of Ancient India*. London, 1965.

Specialized Textbooks

T. W. Rhys Davids. *Buddhist India*. London, 1903.

R. Thāpar. *Aśoka and the Decline of the Mauryas.* Oxford, 1961.

K. A. Nīlakanta Sāstrī and others. *A Comprehensive History of India*, voi. ii, *The Mauryas and Satavahanas*. Calcutta, 1957.

Sm W. W. Tarn. *The Greeks in Bactria and India*, 2nd ed., Cambridge, 1951.

A. K. Nārāin. *The Indo-Greeks* Oxford, 1957.

Sir J. Marshall and others. *Taxila*. 3 vols., Cambridge, 1951.

J. E. van Lohuizen de Leeuw. *The"Scythian" Period.* ... Leiden, 1949.

R. Ghirshman. *Bégram, Recherches Archéologiques et Historiques sur les Kouchans*. Cairo, 1946.

R. C. Majumdār and others. *The Gupta-Vākātaka Age*. Lahore, 1946.

——— *History of Bengal*. vol. i. Dacca, 1943.

R. K. Mookerjī. *The Gupta Empire*. Bombay, 1947.

——— *Harsha*. London, 1926.

R. S. TripāthI. *History of Kanauj*. Benares, 1937.

H. C. Ray. *Dynastic History of Northern India*. 2 vols., Calcutta, 1931-36.

B. N. Puri. *History of the Gurjara-Pratihāras*. Bombay, 1957.

G. Yazdānī (ed.). *Early History of the Deccan*. 2 vols. Oxford, 1960.

K. A. NIlakanta SāstrI. *History of South India*. O.U.P., Indian Branch, 1955.

A. K. Majumdār. *The Chaulukyas of Gujarāt*. Bombay, 1955.

P. T. S. Iyengar. *History of the Tamils to* 600 A.D. Madras, 1929.

K. N. Sivarāja Pillai. *Chronology of the Early Tamils*. Madras, 1932.

R. Gopālan. *History of the Pallavas of Kānchī*. Madras, 1928.

K. A. NIlakanta SāstrI. *The Colas*. 2nd. ed., Madras, 1955.

J. D. M. Derrett. *The Hoysalas*. O.U.P., Indian Branch, 1955.

R. Sewell. *A Forgotten Empire* (*Vijayanagar*). London, 1900.

B. A. Saletore. *Social and Political Life in the Vijayanagar Empire*. 2 vols., Madras, 1934.

G. C. Mendis. *The Early History of Ceylon*. 9th impression, Calcutta, 1948.

H. W. Codrington. *A Short History of Ceylon*. Revised ed., London, 1939.

H. C. Rāy and S. Paranvitāna (ed.). *History of Ceylon*. Voi. i (two parts). Colombo, 1960. 2 vols. to follow.

C. W. Nicholas and S. Paranavitāna. *A Concise History of Ceylon*. Colombo, 1961.

Sources*—(a) *Inscriptions

Corpus Inscriptionum Indicarum

E. Hultzsch (ed.). I. *Inscriptions of Aśoka*. London, 1925.

S. Konow (ed.). II. *Kharoṣṭhī Inscriptions*. London, 1929.

J. F. Fleet (ed.). III. *Inscriptions of the Early Gupta Kings*. London, 1888.

V. V. Mirāshī (ed.). IV. *Inscriptions of the Kalachuri-Chedi Era*. 2 parts. Ootacamund, 1955.

Various Editors. *Epigraphia Indica*. Calcutta and Delhi, 1892- (in progress).

L. Rice (ed.). *Epigraphia Carnatica*. 12 vols., Bangalore, 1886-1904.

Various Editors. *South Indian Inscriptions*. Madras, 1890-(inprogress).

——— *Annual Reportof South Indian Epigraphy*. Madras, replaced by: *Annual Report of Indian Epigraphy*. New Delhi, 1952- (in progress).

D. de Z. Wickremasinghe and S. Paranavitāna (ed.). *Epigraphia Zeylanica*. 5 vols., London, 1904-55.

J. Bloch. *Les Inscriptions d'Asoka*. Paris, 1950.

D. C. Sircār. *Select Inscriptions Bearing on Indian History and Civilization*. Voi. i. Calcutta, 1942.

(b) *Literary Sources*

F. E. Pargiter. *The Purāṇa Text of the Dynasties of the Kali Age*. London, 1931.

J. Przyluski (tr.). *La Legende de l'Empereur Acoka*. ... Paris, 1923.

Sir M. A. Stein (tr.). *Kalhaṇa's Chronicle of the Kings of Kashmīr*. 2 vols. Westminster, 1900.

E. B. Cowell and F. W. Thomas (tr.). *The Harṣacarita of Bāṇa*. London, 1897.

W. Geiger (tr.). *Mahāvamsa*. 2nd impression with addendum by G. C. Mendis, Colombo, 1950.

——— (*tr*.). *Cūlavaṃsa*. 2 vols., London,

(c) *Classical References to India*

J. W. McCrindle (tr.). *The Invasion of India by Alexander the Great*. ... 2nd ed., Westminster, 1896.

—— *Ancient India as Described by Megasthenesand Arrian*. Calcutta, 1877

—— *Ancient India as Described in Classical Literature*. Westminster, 1901.

—— *Ancient India as Described by Ptolemy*. 2nd ed., ed. S. N. Majumdār, Calcutta, 1927.

R. C. Majumdār. (ed.) *Classical Accounts of India*. Calcutta, 1960.

W. H. Schoff (tr.). *The Periplus of the Erythrean Sea*. London, 1912.

(d) *Chinese Travellers*

S. Beal (tr.). *Si Yu Ki. Buddhist Records of the Western World*. 2 vols., London, 1883.

—— *Life of Hiuen-Tsiangby the Shamans Hwui Li and Yen Tsung*. 2nd ed., London, 1911.

T. Watters. *On Yuan Chwang's Travels in India*. 2 vols., London, 1904-05.

REFERENCES

1. De la Vallēe Poussin, *L'Inde aux Temps des Mauryas*, pp. 58-9
2. 13th R. E., Bloch, *Les Inscriptions d'Asoka*, p. 125. Professor Bloch's translation of *na ca haṃñeyasu* as "et cessent de tuer" is incorrect. The verb is certainly passive.
3. 4th R. E., Bloch, p. 93, de la Vallée Poussin, pp. 109ff.
4. *PHAI*, pp. 354 ff.

5. Przyluski, *La Légende de l'Empereur Acoka*, pp. 296ff.
6. H. Kern, quoted de la Vallée Poussin, p. 115
7. *EI*, xx, p. 57
8. van Lohuizen de Leeuw, *the "Scythian" Period*. pp. 352ff.
9. *Pattuppāṭṭu*, *Maduraikkāñji*. Ed. U. V. Sāminātha Aiyar, Madras, 1918, p. 212
10. P. L. Gupta, A. S. Altekar and A. K. Narain, *JNSI*, xii, pt. ii, 1950
11. R. Ghirshman, *Les Chionites-Hephthalites*. Cairo, 1948. Especially ch, v.
12. Tr. R. Sewell, *A Forgotten Empire*, p. 247

CHAPTER IV: THE STATE

BIBLIOGRAPHY

Monographs and Textbooks

A. S. Alterar. *State and Government in Ancient India*. 3rd ed., Delhi, 1958.
Benī Prasād. *The State in Ancient India*. Allahābad. 1928.
—— *Theory of Government in Ancient India*. Allahābad, 1927.
K. V. R. Aiyangar. *Rājadharma*. Adyar, 1941.
J. W. Spellman. *Political Theory of Ancient India*. Oxford, 1963.
C. Drekmeier. *Kingship and Community in Early India*. Stanford, Cal., 1962.
R. S. Sharma. *Aspects of Political Ideas and Institutions in Ancient India*. Delhi, 1959.
—— *Indian Feudalism*, Calcutta, 1965.
J. Gonda. *Ancient Indian Kingship from the Religious Point of View*. *Numen* (Leiden) iii, 36-71, 122-155, iv, 23-58, 127-164.
J. J. Anjariā. *The Nature and Grounds of Political Obligation in the Hindu State*. London, 1935.
H. N. Sinha. *Sovereignty in Ancient Indian Polity*. London, 1938.
R. C. Majumdār. *Corporate Life in Ancient India*. 2nd ed., Poona, 1922.
A. S. Alterar. *Village Communities in Western India*. Oxford, 1929.
U. N. Ghoshal. *Contributions to the History of the Hindu Revenue System*. Calcutta, 1929.
—— *The Agrarian Systemin Ancient India*. Calcutta 1930.
— *Historyof Indian Political Ideas*. O.U.P., Indian Branch, 1959.
— *History of Hindu Public Life*. Calcutta, 1945.
T. V. Mahālingam. *South Indian Polity*. Madras, 1955.
B. C. Law. *Some Kshatriya Tribes of Ancient India*. Calcutta, 1924.
—— *Ancient Mid-Indian Kshatriya Tribes*. Calcutta, 1924.
—— *Tribes in Ancient India*. Poona, 1945.
N. N. Law. *Aspects of Ancient Indian Policy*. Oxford, 1921.
—— *Inter-state Relationsin Ancient India*. Calcutta, 1920.
P. V. Kāne. *History of Dharmaśāstra*. 6 vols., Poona, 1930-62.
J. Jolly. *Hindu Law and Custom*, tr. B. K. Ghosh. Calcutta, 1928. (Original title

Recht und Sitte. ... Strassburg, 1896.)
N. C. Sen-Gupta. *Evolution of Ancient Indian Law*. Calcutta, 1953.
S. D. Singh. *Ancient Indian Warfare*. Leiden, 1965.
G. T. Date. *The Art of War in Ancient India*. London, 1929.

Sources

R. P. Kangle (ed. and tr.). *The Kauṭilīya Arthaśāstra*. 3 vols. Bombay. Pt. i (text), 1960; pt. ii (translation), 1963; pt. iii (critical study), 1965.
G. Bühler (tr.). *The Laws of Manu*. *SBE* xxv, Oxford, 1886.
—— *Sacred Laws of the Āryas*. (The Dharmasūtras of Āpastamba, Gautama, Vasiṣṭha and Baudhāyana.) *SBE* ii, xiv. Oxford, 1879-82.
J. Jolly (tr.). *The Institutes of Vishnu*. *SBE* vii, Oxford, 1880.
— *The Minor Law-books* (Nārada and *Bṛhaspati*). SBE xxxiii, Oxford, 1889.

REFERENCES

1. *Manu*, viii, 271
2. *Aitareya Br.*, i, 14.
3. *Taittrīya Up*, i. 5
4. *Satapatha Br.*, v. 4, 3, 4
5. Ibid., v, 2, 1, 24
6. Ibid., v, 2, 2, 15
7. *DN* vol. iii, pp. 92–3. Cf., *Mahādeva*, i, 347-8
8. Benī Prasād, *Theory of Government in Ancient India*, pp. 220ff.
9. *Arthaśāstra*, i, 13.
10. Ibid., x, 3.
11. Ibid., xiii, 1
12. *Manu*, vii, 3–5, 8
13. K. A. N. Sāstri, *The Colas*, vol. ii, p. 220
14. *Rāmāyaṇa*, ii, 57
15. *Mbh.*, xii, 67
16. Ibid., xii, 59, 14
17. Bāṇa, *Kādambarī* (tr. C. M. Ridding, London, 1896), p. 82
18. *Mbh.* (Kumbakonam ed.), xiii, 96, 34-5
19. *ARSIE*, no. 387 of 1904
20. *Mbh.*, xii, 57,
21. *Arthaśāstra*, i, 19
22. Ibid., i, 17
23. Ibid.
24. *EI*, ii, no. 27, p. 343ff.
25. *Arthaśāstra*, xi, 1
26. *CII*, iii, p. 252
27. *EI*, xxvii, p. 265
28. *Arthaśāstra*, i, 7

29. *Yājñavalkya*, i, 312
30. *Arthaśāstra*, ii, 9
31. Ibid., v, 3
32. Ibid., ii, 24
33. *EI*, xv, pp. 130ff.
34. *CU*, iii, pp. 58ff.
35. *Yājrtavalkya*, ii, 30
36. *Manu*, viii, 39
37. to *Arthaśāstra*, ii, 24
38. Śabarasvāmin to *Pūrvamīmāṃsā Sūtras*, vi, 7, 3
39. *Vyavahāramayūkha*, *Svatvāvagama*, quoted Altekar, *State and Government*, p. 200, n. 4
40. The conclusion of Dr. U. N. Ghoshal (*The Beginnings of Indian Historiography and Other Essays*. Calcutta, 1944, p. 166)
41. *Arthaśāstra*, lv, 1. *Nārada*, i, 10
42. *Manu*, vii, 39
43. Kane, *History of Dharmaśāstra*, voi. iii, pp. 288 ff.
44. Przyluski, *La Légende de l'Empereur Acoka*, pp. 120ff.
45. *Mbh*., xii, 259
46. 4th P.E., Bloch, p. 164
47. *Dhammapada*, 201
48. *Mbh*., xii, 97, 1–2
49. *Arthaśāstra*, vii, 1
50. Ibid., xii, 1
51. Ibid., vi, 2
52. *Kāmandaka*, xiii, 69; cf., xvi, 29

CHAPTER V: SOCIETY

BIBLIOGRAPHY

Monographs and Textbooks

P. V. Kāne. *History of Dharmaśāstra* (p. 479 above).

J. Jolly. *Hindu Law and Custom* (p. 479 above).

E. Senart, tr. Sir E. Denison Ross, *Caste in India*. London, 1930. (Original ed., *Les Castes dans l'Inde*. Paris, 1896.)

J. H. Hutton. *Caste in India*. 3rd ed., O.U.P., Indian Branch, 1961.

R. S. Sharma. *Śūdras in Ancient India*. Delhi, 1958.

J. Brough. *The Early Brāhmaṇical System of Gotra and Pravara*. Cambridge, 1953.

K. M. Kapādiā. *Hindu Kinship*. Bombay, 1947.

R. Gopal. *India of Vedic Kalpasūtras*. Delhi, 1959.

R. K. Mookerjī. *Ancient Indian Education*. London, 1947.

J. J. Meyer. *Sexual Life in Ancient India*. 2nd ed., London, 1952. (Original ed., *Dos Weib im altindischen Epos*. Leipzig, 1915.)

A. S. Altekar. *The Position of Women in Hindu Civilization*. 2nd ed., Banāras, 1956.
N. Sengupta. *Evolution of Hindu Marriage*. Bombay, 1965.
R. Fick, tr. S. K. Maitra, *Social Organization in North East India in Buddha's Time*. Calcutta, 1920. (Original ed., *Die soziale Gliederung*. ... Kiel, 1897.)
P. H. Valavalkar. *Hindu Social Institutions*. 2nd ed., Barodā, 1942.
B. K. Ghosh. *The Hindu Ideal of Life*. Calcutta, 1947.
D. R. Chanana. *Slavery in Ancient India*. Delhi, 1960. (Originally *L'Esclavage dans l'Inde ancienne*. Pondichéry, 1957.)

Sources

See Bibliography to Chapter IV, p. 525 above. Vatsyāyana. *The Kāma Sūtra*. The paraphrase by Sir Richard Burton and F. F. Arbuthnot, for long a "banned book", has recently been published in a British and American edition. (London, 1963; New York, 1962.) The most recent annotated translation is that of S. C. Upadhyaya (Bombay 1961).

REFERENCES

1. *Manu*, i, 88 ff.
2. Ibid., x, 97
3. Ibid., ix, 317
4. Ibid., x, 107
5. Ibid., iv, 192; ix, 319
6. *RV*, vii, 103
7. *Chāndogya* Up., i, 12
8. *Aitareya Br.*, vii, 29
9. *Manu*, x, 44
10. Ibid., ix, S26ff.
11. *Arthaśāstra*, iii, 13
12. *Manu*, x, 41
13. Ibid., x, 129
14. Ibid., xi, 132.
15. *Arthaśāstra*, ii, 1
16. *BhG*, ix, 32
17. *Manu*, x, 39
18. *Parāśara*, i, 4, 11
19. *CII*, iii, pp. 46ff.
20. *Mbh.*, iii, 256, 11
21. *Āpastamba*, ii, 4, 9, il
22. *Manu*, viii, 299f.
23. *Atharva Veda*, *v*, 21, 3
24. *Baudhāyana Śrauta Sūtra*, *Pravarādhyaya*, 54
25. Jolly, *Hindu Law of Partition*. …, p. 81. *Vasiṣṭha*, xv, 2; xvii, 31 f. *Gautama*, xxviii, 33

26. E.g. *Āpastamba*, ii, 6, 13, 10
27. *Yājñavalkya*, ii, 135
28. *Manu*, viii, 416
29. *Śakuntalā*, vii, 17
30. *RV*, iii, 62, 10
31. *Manu*, ii, 140f.
32. *Baudhāyana*, iv, 1, 12
33. *Manu*, ix, 94
34. *Suśruta Saṃhitā*, iii, 10, 54f.
35. *Kāmasūtra*, iii, 2
36. *Manu*, viii, 371
37. *Arthaśāstra*, iii, 3
38. Ibid., iii, 4
39. *Āpastamba*, ii, 5, 11f.
40. *Nārada*, i, 190
41. *Arthaśāstra*, iii, 2
42. M6A. (Bombay ed.), ii, 68, 81ff. The Poona ed. (ii. 61, 73ff.) rejects the fifth and sixth lines of our translation
43. *Bṛhaspati*, quoted *Smṛticandrikā*, i, 10. Ed. Aiyangar, Barodā, 1941, p. 495
44. *Manu*, vi, 23,
45. Ibid., vi, 45 ff.
46. *Bṛhadāraṇyaka Up*., iii, 6; iii, 8
47. *Puranānūru*, *66*
48. *Arthaśāstra*, ii, 23
49. *Manu*, v, 147ff.
50. *Bhojaprabandha* (ed. Vidyāsāgara, p. 90)
51. *Mbh*. (Bombay ed.), i, 74, 40ff. The verses are somewhat rearranged in the Poona ed. (i., 68, 40ff.)
52. *Mbh*., *v*, 30, 6
53. *Kāmasūtra*, i, 3
54. *Arthaśāstra*, ii, 27
55. *ASIAR*, 1903-04, p. 122
56. *EI*, xiii, *36*
57. *Gautama*, xxii, 27
58. *Nārada*, xii, 97; *Parāśara*, iv, 30; *Agni Purāṇa*, cliv, 51
59. *Manu*, v, 162
60. *RV*, x, 18, 8
61. *CII*, iii, p. 92

CHAPTER VI: EVERYDAY LIFE

BIBLIOGRAPHY

Prān Nāth. *A Study in the Economic Condition of Ancient India*. London, 1929.

A. Bose. *Social and Rural Economy of Northern India* ... 2 vols., Calcutta, 1942–45.

G. L. Adhya. *Economics of Early India* (*c.* 200 B.C.–A.D. 300). Bombay, 1965.

S. K. Maity. *Economic Life of Northern India in the Gupta Period*. Calcutta, 1958.

L. Gopal. *Economic Life of Northern India*. Delhi, 1965.

P. Niyogi. *Economic History of Northern India* (l0th–12th centuries). Calcutta, 1962.

A. Appādorai. *Economic Conditions in South India*. 2 vols., Madras, 1936.

B. A. Saletore. *The Wild Tribes in Indian History*. Lahore, 1935.

B. B. Lāl. *Śiśupālgarh*, 1948. *AI*, v, 1949, pp. 62 ff.

J. Auboyer. *Daily Life in Ancient India*. London, 1965. (Originally *La Vie Quotidienne dans l'Inde ancienne*. Paris, 1961.)

R. N. Saletore. *Life in the Gupta Age*. Bombay, 1943.

H. Luders. *Dos Würfelspiel im alteri Indien*. Berlin, 1907.

G. S. Ghurye. *Indian Costume*. Bombay, 1951.

H. G. Rawlinson. *Intercourse between India and the Western World*. Cambridge, 1916.

E. H. Warmington. *Commerce between the Roman Empire and India*. Cambridge, 1928.

J. Kennedy. *Early Commerce of Babylon and India*. *JRAS*, 1898, pp. 241ff.

R. K. Moorerjī. *History of Indian Shipping* ... London, 1912.

A. L. Basham. *Notes on Seafaring in Ancient India*. *AL*, xxiii, pp. 60ff., 1949.

Sir W. W. Tarn. *The Greeks in Bactria and India* (above, p. 522), ch. ix.

G. N. Banerjee. *Hellenism in Ancient India*. Calcutta, 1920.

R. A. Jairazbhoy. *Foreign Influence in Ancient India*. Bombay, 1963.

Sir R. E. M. Wheeler and others. *Arikamedu*: *an Indo-Roman Trading Station*. *AI*, ii, 1946.

REFERENCES

1. Prān Nāth (p. 484 above), p. 122
2. *J*, no. 31
3. *Arthaśāstra*, ii, 24
4. Ibid., ii, 1
5. *IA*, xvii, pp. 350ff.
6. *Arthaśāstra*, ii, 29
7. 1st R. E., Bloch, p. 92
8. Saletore, *The Wild Tribes*..., pp. 10ff.
9. *Arthaśāstra*, li, 29

10. *AI*, *v*, pp. 62 ff.
11. *Mālavikāgnimitra*, ii, 12
12. *Raghuvaṃśa*, xix, 9
13. *Arthaśāstra*, ii, 36
14. *Pattuppāṭṭu*, *Maduraikkāñji*
15. *CII*, iii, pp. 81ff., line 22
16. *Kāmasūtra*, i, 4
17. Ibid.
18. *Arthaśāstra*, iii, 20
19. Sewell, *A Forgotten Empire*, p. 383
20. *Kalittogai*, iv, 3
21. J. Fergusson, *Tree and Serpent Worship*, London, 1873, pp. 102-3
22. Altekar, *The Position of Women in Hindu Civilization*, pp. 334ff.
23. *Arthaśāstra*, ii, 26
24. Ibid., ii, 25
25. *Uvāsaga Dasāo* (Ed. Hoemle, Calcutta, 1889), voi. i, p. 105
26. *Arthaśāstra*, ii, 16
27. J. C. Hudson, *Nature*, 12, ix, 53, p. 499
28. *Manu*, viii, 141 f.
29. *Arthaśāstra*, iii, 11
30. *J*, no. 339
31. *Daśakumāracarita* i, tr. Ryder, p. 14
32. *Rājāvaliya* (Codrington, *Short History of Ceylon*, p. 23)
SS. E. Hultzsch, *JRAS*, 1904, p. 399
34. *AI*, ii, 1946, pp. 17ff.
35. Pliny, xii, 18
36. *I Kings*, *x*, 22
37. Ibid., x, 11
38. Hemādri's *Caturvarga-cintāmaṇi* (Calcutta, 1895), voi. iii, pt. 2, p. 667

CHAPTER VII: RELIGION

BIBLIOGRAPHY

Textbooks and Monographs—(a) General

L. Renou. *Religions of Ancient India*. London, 1953.
J. N. Farquhar. *Outline of the Religious Literature of India*. Oxford, 1920.
Sir C. Eliot. *Hinduism and Buddhism*. 3 vols., London, 1922.
S. N. Dās Gupta. *History of Indian Philosophy*. 4 vols., Cambridge, 1923-49.
Sir S. Rādhākrishnan. *Indian Philosophy*. 2 vols., London, 1923-27.
—— (ed.), *History of Philosophy, Eastern and Western*. 2 vols., London, 1952-53.
H. Zimmer. *Philosophies of India*. New York, 1951.

(b) Vedic Religion

A. B. Keith. *The Religion and Philosophy of the Vedas and Upaniṣads*. Cambridge, Mass., 1925.

M. Bloomfield. *The Religion of the Veda*. New York, 1908.

A. A. Macdonell. *Vedic Mythology*. Strassburg, 1897.

(c) Buddhism

T. W. Rhys Davids. *Buddhism, its History and Literature*. 2nd ed., London, 1926.

E. J. Thomas. *The Life of the Buddha as Legend and History*. London, 1927.

—— *History of Buddhist Thought*. London, 1933.

E. Lamotte. *Histoire du Bouddhisme Indien*. Voi. i, Louvain, 1958.

L. de la Vallēe Poussin. *Le Bouddhisme*. 3rd ed., Paris, 1925.

A. B. Keith. *Buddhist Philosophy in India and Ceylon*. Oxford, 1923.

E. Conze. *Buddhism, its Essence and Development*. 2nd ed., Oxford, 1953.

- *Buddhist Thought in India*. London, 1962.

T. R. V. Murti. *The Central Philosophy of Buddhism*. London, 1955.

S. B. Dasgupta. *Introduction to Tantric Buddhism*. 2nd ed. Calcutta, 1958.

(d) Jainism, etc.

Mrs. S. Stevenson. *The Heart of Jainism*. Oxford, 1915.

H. von Glasenapp. *Der Jainismus*. Berlin, 1926.

W. Schubring. *The Doctrine of the Jainas*. Delhi, 1962. (Originally *Die Lehre der Jainas*. Gottingen, 1926.)

A. Guérinot. *La Religion Djāina*. Paris, 1926.

A. L. Basham. *History and Doctrines of the Ājīvikas*. London, 1951.

D. P. Chattopadhay. *Lokāyata*: *A Study in Ancient Indian Materialism*. New Delhi, 1959.

(e) Hinduism

J. N. Farquhar. *A Printer of Hinduism*. London, 1912.

L. D. Barnett. *The Heart of India*. London, 1908.

J. Dowson. *A Classical Dictionary of Hindu Mythology and Religion*. 7th ed., London, 1950.

E. Washburn Hopkins. *Epic Mythology*. Strassburg, 1915.

J. E. Carpenter. *Theism in Medieval India*. London, 1921.

H. C. Raychaudhurī. *Early History of the Vaiṣṇava Sect*. 2nd ed., Calcutta, 1926.

Sir R. G. Bhāndārkar. *Vaishṇavism, Śaivism and Minor Religious Sects*. Strassburg, 1913.

M. Éliade. *Yoga*: *Immortality and Freedom*. London, 1958.

H. W. Schomerus. *Der Çaiva Siddhānta*. Leipzig, 1912.

Arthur Avalon. *Shakti and Shākta*. Madras, 1929.

J. N. Banerjea. *Development of Hindu Iconography*. Calcutta, 1946.

T. A. GopInāth Rao. *Elements of Indian Iconography*. 2 vols., Madras, 1914.

(f) Christianity

A. E. Medlycott. *India and the Apostle Thomas*. London, 1905.

L. W. Brown. *The Indian Christians of St. Thomas*. Cambridge, 1956.

G. M. Moraes. *A History of Christianity in India*. Bombay, 1964.

Translations— (a) General

Lin Yutang and others. *The Wisdom of India*. London, 1949 (translations of both religious and secular literature, by various hands).

W. Th. De Bary (ed.). *Sources of Indian Tradition*. New York, 1958.

S. Radhakrishnan and C. A. Moore (ed.). *A Source Book of Indian Philosophy*. Princeton, 1957.

(b) Vedic

N. Macnicol and others. *Hindu Scriptures*. London (Everyman), 1938.

R. T. H. Griffith (tr.). *The Rig Veda*. 2nd ed., 2 vols., Benares, 1896-7.

F. Max Muller and H. Oldenberg (tr.). *Vedic Hymns*. 2 vols., *SBE* xxxii, xlvi, Oxford, 1891–7.

F. Geldner (tr.). *Der Rig-veda*. 3 vols. Cambridge, Mass., 1951.

W. D. Whitney and C. R. Lanman (tr.). *The Atharva Veda*. 2 vols. Cambridge, Mass., 1905.

J. Eggeling (tr.). *The Śatapatha Brāhmaṇa*. 5 vols., *SBE* xii, xxvi, xii, xliii, xliv. Oxford, 1882-1900.

F. Max Muller (tr.). *The Upaniṣads*. 2 vols., *SBE* i, xv, Oxford, 1879-82.

R. A. Hume (tr.). *Thirteen Principal Upanishads*. Oxford, 1921.

(c) Buddhist

Al the more important texts of the Pāli Scriptures have been translated by various hands and published by the Pāli Text Society, London, with the exception of the following:

E. B. Cowell and others (tr.). *The Jātaka*. 6 vols., Cambridge, 1895-1907.

T. W. Rhys Davids (tr.). *The Questions of King Milinda*. 2 vols., *SBE* xxxv-vi, Oxford, 1890-94.

Selectїons from Buddhist Scriptures

F. L. Woodward (tr.). *Some Sayings of the Buddha*. Oxford (World's Classics), 1938.

E. J. Thomas (tr.). *Early Buddhist Scriptures*. London, 1935.

H. C. Warren (tr.). *Buddhism in Translations*. Cambridge, Mass., 1915.

E. Conze (tr.). *Buddhist Scriptures*. Harmondsworth, 1959.

—— (ed.). *Buddhist Texts through the Ages*. Oxford, 1954.

Mahāyāna Texts

E. B. Cowell and others (tr.). *Buddhist Mahāyāna Sūtras*. *SBE* xlix, Oxford, 1894.

H. Kern (tr.). *Saddharma-puṇḍarika*. *SBE* xxi, Oxford, 1884.

C. Bendall and W. H. D. Rouse (tr.). *Śikshā-samuccaya ... compiled by Śāntideva, chieflyfrom earlier Mahāyāna Sūtras*. London, 1922.
D. T. Suzuki (tr.). *The Laṅkavatāra Sūtra*. London, 1932.
D. L. Snellgrove (tr.). *The Hevajra Tantra*. 2 vols., Oxford, 1959.

(d) Jaina

H. Jacobi (tr.). *Jaina Sūtras*. 2 vols., *SBE* xxii, xlv. Oxford, 1884-95.
L. D. Barnett (tr.). *Antagaḍa Dasāo*. London, 1907.

(e) Hindu

For translations of Smṛti Literature, see p. 525.

The Epics

P. C. Roy (tr.). *The Mahābhārata*. 2nd ed., 11 vols., Calcutta, 1919-35.
C. V. Narasimhan (tr.). *The Mahābhārata* (abridged). New York, 1964.
R. T. H. Griffith (tr.). *The Rāmāyaṇa*. Benares, 1915.
H. P. Shastri (tr.). *The Rāmāyaṇa of Vālmīki*. 3 vols., London, 1952-59.
R. C. Dutt (tr.). *The Mahābhārata and Rāmāyaṇa* (abridged versions). London (Everyman), 1917.
Sir E. Arnold (tr.). *Indian Idylls*. (Episodes of the *Mahābhārata*.) London, 1883.

The Bhagavad Gita

This has been translated by many hands. Perhaps the best versions for the general reader are those of L. D. Barnett (in Macnicols' *Hindu Scriptures*, London, 1938) and W. D. P. Hill (Oxford, 1928). The scholarly version of F. Edgerton (2 vols., Cambridge, Mass., 1946) includes the original text, interpretation, and Sir Edwin Amold's verse translation entitled *The Song Celestial*.

Later Religious Literature

H. H. Wilson (tr.). *The Viṣṇu Purāṇa*. 5 vols., London, 1864-70. (Reprinted, Calcutta, 1961.)
E. Burnouf and others (tr.). *Bhāgavata Purāṇa*. 5 vols., Paris, 1840-98.
G. Thibaut (tr.). *The Vedānta-Sūtras with the Commentary of Śankarācārya*. 2 vols., *SBE* xxxiv, xxxviii, 1890-96.
—— *The Vedānta-Sūtras with Rāmānuja's Commentary Śrībhāṣya*. *SBE* xlviii, Oxford, 1904.
F. Kingsbury and G. E. Philips (tr.). *Hymns of the Tamil Śaivite Saints*. Calcutta, 1921.
J. S. M. Hooper (tr.). *Hymns of the Ālvārs*. Calcutta, 1929.
J. M. NallaswāmI Pillai (tr.). *Śivajñāna Siddhiyār of Aruṇandi*. Madras, 1913.
G. Matthews (tr.). *Sivañāna Bodham* of Meykaṇḍa. Oxford, 1948.

REFERENCES

1. *RV*, x, 119, 2-9
2. *Atharva Veda*, iv, 16, 2
3. *RV*, vii, 89
4. Ibid., x, 121
5. Ibid., x, 90
6. Ibid., x, 16
7. *Bṛhadāraṇyaka Up*., vi, 2, 16
8. *RV*, x, 136
9. *Atharva Veda*, xv
10. *Maitrāyaṇī Up*., i, 1
11. *RV*, x, 129, 4-5
12. Ibid., x, 121
13. Ibid., x, 129
14. *Bṛhadāraṇyaka Up*., i, 1
15. Ibid., i, 4
16. *Chāndogya Up*., vi, 13.
17. Ibid., cf. *Bṛhadāraṇyaka Up*., ii, 4, 12
18. *Bṛhadāraṇyaka Up*., iv., 4, 22
19. Ibid.
20. *Īśa Up*., 8
21. *Kaṭha Up*., ii, 6, 2-3
22. *Śvetāśvatara Up*., iii, 2-11
23. *Chāndogya Up*., ii, 23
24. *Bṛhadāraṇyaka Up*., iv, 4, 26ff.
25. *Kaṭha Up*., ii, 6, 14f.
26. Ibid., i, 2, 1
27. *Chāndogya Up*., vi, 4
28. T. S. Eliot, *The Waste Land*, 395ff.
29. *Bṛhadāraṇyaka Up*., *v*, 2
30. Ibid., iv, 5, 5; cf. ii, 4.
31. Mrs. C. A. F. Rhys Davids, *Outlines of Buddhism* (London, 1934), ch. iii; *What was the Original Gospel in Buddhism?* (London, 1938), ch. xiii and *passim*
32. J. G. Jennings, *The Vedāntic Buddhism of the Buddha* (Oxford, 1947), p. xxxviff.
33. *DN*, ii, *99* 262n
34. A. Waley, *Mélanges Chinois et Bouddhiques*, Brussels, voi. i, 1931–32, p. 343ff.
35. E. J. Thomas, *IC*, xv, 1948-49, p. 1 ff.
36. 12th R.E., Bloch, p. 121 ff.
37. P. Pāi in *JRAS*, 1965, pp. 103, 268ff.
38. *Saṃyutta Nikāya*, v, 421–23

39. *Vinaya Piṭaka*, i, 239
40. *Majjhima Nikāya*, i, 431
41. *Milinda Pañha*, v, 6
42. *Majjhima Nikāya*, i, 142; cf. *DN* ii, 140ff.
43. *Vajradhvaja Sūtra* quoted in Śāntideva's *Śikṣāsamuccaya*, tr. Bendali and Rouse, p. 256 f.
44. Nāgārjuna, *Mādhyamika Kārikā*, xxv, 19-20 28
45. *Sutta Nipāta*, 143 ff.
46. *Khuddaka Pātha*, viii
47. *Vinaya Piṭaka*, Mahāvagga, viii, 26
48. *DN* iii, 181 ff.
49. *Ācārāṅga Sūtra*, i, 2, 3, 1–4
50. *Uttarādhyayana Sūtra*, 10
51. *Iṣṭopadeśa* (ed. C. R. Jain, Hardoi, 1925), 8, 9, 29, 30 and 50
52. *DN, i*, 53-4
53. Ibid., i, 55
54. *Sarva-darśana-saṃgraha* (Poona, 1924), p. 14
55. Ibid., p. 4
56. Ibid., p. 14
57. *BhG., x*, 20-H
58. Ibid., iv, 6-8
59. *Chāndogya Up.*, iii, 17, 6
60. *Gīta Govinda*, i, 1, 13
61. *Revelation*, xix, 11–13
62. *BhG.*, vii, 21–2
63. *Kumārasambhava*, ii, 4ff.
64. *CU*, iii, p. 72 ff.
65. Ibid., iii, p. 79ff.
66. *BhG.*, xi, 43-5
67. *Pattuppāṭṭu*, *Tirumuruganarrupadai*, 285-90
68. Apparsvāmī, Kingsbury and Philips, p. 48
69. Apparsvāmī, *ibid.*, p. 62
70. Sundarar, *ibid.*, p. 74 334
71. Māṇikka Vāsagar, *ibid.*, pp. 93-4
72. Māṇikka Vāsagar, *ibid.*, p. 124
73. *BhG.*, vii, 18
74. *Śivarñānasiddhiyar*, i, 47
75. Ibid., ii, 15, 23
76. Ibid., ii, 25
77. Ibid., ii, 26-7
78. *Mānasollāsa*, i, I4ff.
79. *Gautama*, viii, 24
80. *Tirukkuraḷ*, 72, 101, 156, 160, 203
81. *Viṣṇu Purāṇa*, iii, 821 ff.

82. *BhG.*, ii 19-33
83. Ibid., iii, 22-35

CHAPTER VIII: THE ARTS

BIBLIOGRAPHY

V. A. Smith. *History of Fine Art in India and Ceylon*. 3rd ed., revised by K. Khandlawala. Bombay, 1962.
A. K. Coomāraswāmı. *History of Indian and Indonesian Art*. London 1927.
B. Rowland. *The Art and Architecture of India*. London, 1953.
Sir Leigh Ashton and others. *The Art of India and Pākistān*. London, 1950.
H. Goetz. *India*. (Art of the World, voi. i.) London, 1959.
H. Zimmer. *The Art of Indian Asia*. 2 vols. New York, 1955.
J. Auboyer. *Arts et Styles de l'Inde*. Paris, 1951.
S. Paranavitana. *Art and Architecture of Ceylon*. Colombo, 1954.
J. Fergusson. *History of Indian and Eastern Architecture*. 2nd ed., London, 1910.
P. Brown. *Indian Architecture, Buddhist and Hindu*. 2nd ed., Bombay, 1949.
S. Kramrisch. *The Hindu Temple*. 2 vols., Calcutta, 1946.
C. Frederic. *Indian Temples and Sculpture*. London, 1959.
Sir J. Marshall. *Taxila* (above, p. 522).
Sir J. Marshall and A. Foucher. *Monuments of Sānchī*. 3 vols., Calcutta, 1940.
P. K. Āchārya. *Indian Architecture According to Mānasāra*. Oxford, 1921.
—— *A Dictionary of Hindu Architecture*. London, 1927.
D. N. Shukla. *Vāstu-Śāstra*. 2 vols. Lucknow n.d. (?1962).
S. Kramrisch. *Indian Sculpture*. Calcutta, 1933.
L. Bachhofer. *Early Indian Sculpture*. 2 vols., Paris, 1929.
D. Barrett. *Sculpture from Amarāvati in the British Museum*. London, 1954.
A. Foucher. *L'Art Gréco-bouddhique du Gandhāra*. 2 vols., Paris, 1905-18.
Sir J. Marshall. *A Guide to Taxila*. 4th ed. Cambridge, i960.
—— *Buddhist Art of Gandhāra*. Cambridge, 1960.
C. Kar. *Classical Indian Sculpture*. London, 1950.
—— *Indian Metal Sculpture*. London, 1950.
D. R. Thapar. *Icons in Bronze*. Bombay, 1961.
J. N. Banerjea. *The Development of Hindu Iconography*. 2nd ed., Calcutta, 1956.
S. Kramrisch. *A Survey of Painting in the Deccan*. London, 1937.
N. Mehtā. *Studies in Indian Painting*. Bombay, 1926.
G. Yazdānī. *Ajantā*. 3 vols., London, 1930.
Sir J. Marshall and others. *The Bāgh Caves*. London, 1927.
B. Rowland. *The Wall Paintings of India, Central Asia and Ceylon*. Boston, Mass., 1938.
E. Clements. *Introduction to the Study of Indian Music*. London, 1913.
A. H. Fox Strangways. *The Music of Hindostān*. Oxford, 1914.
C. Marcel-Dubois. *Les Instruments de Musique de l'Inde Antique*. Paris, 1941.

A. Coomāraswāmy. *The Mirror of Gesture* (annotated translation of Nandikeśvara's *Abhinaya-darpaṇa*). 2nd ed., New York, 1936.

La Meri. *The Gesture of the Hindu Dance*. New York, 1941.

Beryl de Zoete. *The Other Mind. A Study of Dance in South India*. London, 1953.

P. BanerjI. *Dance of India*. 2nd ed., Allahābād, 1947.

F. Bowers. *The Dance in India*. New York, 1953.

REFERENCES

1. Coomāraswāmy, *Indian and Indonesian Art*, pp. 90-1
2. Kramrisch, *The Hindu Temple, passim.*
3. Brown, *Indian Architecture*, p. 3 and pl. i
4. Ibid., p. 90
5. The chief is the medieval *Mānasāra*. V. Āchārya, *Indian Architecture* according to Mānasāra (Oxford, 1921)
6. Brown, op. cit., p. 123f. and pl. Ixxv
7. The unpublished view of my colleague, Mr. P. Rawson
8. Kramrisch, op. cit., pp. 346-7
9. Brown, op. cit., p. 127
10. Rowland, *The Art and Architecture of India*, p. 155

CHAPTER IX: LANGUAGE AND LITERATURE

BIBLIOGRAPHY

Textbooks and Monographs

T. Burrow. *The Sanskrit Language*. London, 1955.

W. D. Whitney. *A Sanskrit Grammar*. Leipzig and London, 1879.

A. A. Macdonell. *A Vedic Grammar*. Oxford, 1916.

W. S. Allen. *Phonetics in Ancient India*. London, 1953.

S. K. Belvalkar. *Systems of Sanskrit Grammar*. Poona, 1915.

W. Geiger, tr. B. K. Ghosh, *Pāli Literature and Language*. Calcutta, 1943. (Original ed. *Pāli Literatur und Sprache*. Strassburg, 1916.)

R. Caldwell. *A Comparative Grammar of the Dravidian Languages*. 2nd ed., London, 1875.

J. Vinson. *Manuel de la Langue Tamoule*. Paris, 1903.

G. Buhler. *Indian Palaeography*. Bombay, 1904. (Original ed. *Indische Palāographie*. Strassburg, 1896.)

G. S. Ojhā. *Bhāratīya Lipimālā* (in Hindi). Ajmer, 1918,

A. H. Dani. *Indian Palaeography*. Oxford, 1963.

A. C. Burnell. *Elements of South Indian Epigraphy*. 2nd ed., London, 1878.

A. A. Macdonell. *History of Sanskrit Literature*. London, 1900.

M. Winternitz, tr. S. Ketkar, *History of Indian Literature*. 2 vols. Calcutta, 1927-33. (Originaied. *Geschichte der indischen Litteratur*. 3 vols. Leipzig, 1909-20.)

A. B. Keith, *History of Sanskrit Literature*. Oxford, 1928.
—— *Sanskrit Drama*. Oxford,1924.
H. W. Wells. *The Classical Drama of India*. Bombay, 1963.
S. Lévi. *Le Théâtre Indien*. Paris, 1890.
S. N. Dās Gupta and S. K. De. *History of Sanskrit Literature*. Voi. i, 2nd ed., Calcutta, 1962.
S. K. De. *History of Sanskrit Poetics*. 2nd ed., Calcutta, 1960.
E. Washburn Hopkins. *The Great Epic of India*. New York, 1901.
M. S. Pūrnalingam Pillai. *Tamil Literature*. Tinnevelly, 1929.
P. T. S. Iyengar. *History of the Tamils ...* (above, p. 522).
V. R. R. Dīkshitar. *Studies in Tamil Literature and History*. London 1930.

Translations

There are many translations of early Indian literature, but most have been produced in India, and are in the nature of "cribs", with no pretensions to literary merit. We mention a few only of the best literary translations in English.* For translations of religious and legal literature see the bibliographies to chapters iv and vii.

Lin Yutang. *The Wisdom of India* (above, p. 532).
J. Brough (tr.). *Selections from Classical Sanskrit Literature*. London, 1951.
H. H. Wilson (tr.). *Select Specimens of the Theatre of the Hindus*. 2nd ed., 2 vols., London, 1835.
H.W. Wells (ed.). *Sanskrit Plays in English Translation*. Bombay, 1963.
A. Ryder (tr.). *Shakuntala and Other Writings of Kalidasa*. London (Everyman), 1912.
—— *The Little Clay Cart* (Śūdraka's *Mṛcchakaṭika*). 1905.
A. Ryder (tr.) *The Ten Princes* (Daṇḍin's *Daśakumāracarita*). Chicago, 1927.
E. B. Cowell and F. W. Thomas (tr.). *The Harṣacarita of Bāṇa*. London, 1897.
C. M. Ridding (tr.). *Kādambarī* (*of Bāṇa*). London, 1896.
Dixon Scott (tr.). "*Bhartrihari Says*." London, 1940.
Sir E. Arnold (tr.). *The Chaurapanchāśikā* (of Bilhaṇa). London, 1896.
G. Keyt (tr.). *Shrī Jayadeva's Gīta Govinda*. Bombay, 1947.
C. H. Tawney (tr.). Ed. N. Penzer, *The Ocean of Story* (Somadeva's *Kathāsaritsāgara*). 10 vols., London, 1925-8.
J. A. Bivan Buitenen. *Tales of Ancient India*. New York, 1961.
A. Williams (tr.). *Tales from the Pancatantra*. Oxford, 1930.
N. R. B. Mudaliyar. *The Golden Anthology of Ancient Tamil Literature*. 3 vols., Madras, 1959-60.
J. V. Chelliah (tr.). *Ten Tamil Idylls* (*Pattuppāṭṭu*). Colombo, 1947.
V. R. R. DIkshitar (tr.). *The Lay of the Anklet* (*Śilāppadigāram*). Oxford, 1939.
K. Aiyangar (tr.). *Maṇimekalai in its Historical Setting*. London, 1928.

* Exceptional among translations from Sanskrit into Western languages are the numerous works of the great German poet Friedrich Ruckert, whose version of Jayadeva's *Gīta Govinda* especially is among the greatest masterpieces of the translator's art.

G. U. Pope (tr.). *The Sacred Kuṛaḷ*. London, 1886.
—— *Nālaḍiyār*. Oxford, 1893.

REFERENCES

1. *CII*, iii, p. 8
2. Caldwell, *Comparative Grammar of the Dravidian Languages*, p. 64ff.; T. Burrow, *Dravidian Studies IV*, *BSOAS*, xi, p. 328f.
3. In Marshall, *Mohenjo Daro and the Indus Civilization*, voi. ii, p. 423 ff.
4. Biihler, *Indische Palāographie*, p. 10ff.
5. Dani, *Indian Palaeography*, pp. 8-9. For the *boustrophedon* inscription of Aśoka at Yerragudi, *IHQ*, vii, p. 817ff.
6. R. B. Pāndey, *Indian Palaeography* (Banāras, 1952), p. 70
7. *RV*., i, 32
8. Ibid., x, 127
9. Ibid., X, 146
10. Ibid., x, 34
11. Ibid., X, 95
12. *Śatapatha Br*., xi, 5, 1
13. *Mbh*., iii, 54
14. *Rāmāyaṇa*, vi, 108
15. S. N. Dās Gupta, *History of Sanskrit Literature*, p. xx 418
16. S. K. De in the above, p. 37
17. *Meghadūta*, 19, 21
18. Ibid., 31–2
19. Ibid., 66
20. Ibid., 101
21. *Kumārasambhava*, i, 1, 5, 8, 10, 15
22. Ibid., XV, 14-24
23. *Śiśupāla-vadha*, xix, 114
24. Ibid., xix, 104
25. *Śiśupāla-vadha*, xix, 27
26. Ibid., xix, 88
27. *Nītiśataka*, 4-5
28. *Śṛṅgāraśataka*, 12
29. Ibid., 53
30. *Vairāgyaiataka*, 82
31. Ibid., 85
32. *Amaruśataka* (ed. R. Simon, Kiel, 1893), 22, 45, 51
33. *Harṣacarita*, iii
34. *Caurapañcāśikā*, 27, 45
35. Gīta Govinda, v
36. *Kathāsaritsāgara*, xii, 88, 33-44
37. *Hammīramahākāvya* (ed. N. J. Klrtane, Bombay, 1879), xiii, 13-32

38. *Śakuntalā*, v
39. *Daśakumāracarita*, xi
40. *Harṣacarita*, vii
41. *Hitopadeśa*, iv, 9-10
42. *Nidānakathā*, the introduction to the Jātakas. Ed Fausböll, voi. i, pp. 61–62
43. *J*, 360
44. *Therīgāthā*, 252-70
45. *Theragāthā*, 522-4
46. do. 308-10
47. *Mahāvaṃsa*, xxv, 28-38
48. *Sūtrakṛtāṅga*, i, 4,2. Our translation has been revised in the light of an important study of this passage by Professor L. Alsdorf (*Itthīparinnā*: *Indo-Iranian Journal* ii, pp. 249-70)
49. *Saptaśataka* (ed. Weber, Leipzig, 1881), 379, 381, 385, 484, 445
50. *Nāladiyār*, 194
51. *History of the Tamils to 600 A.D.*, Madras, 1929, passim
52. *Puranānūru*, 86
53. Ibid., 92
54. Ibid., 94
55. Ibid., 95
56. *Kuruntogai*, 2
57. Ibid., 4
58. Ibid., 6
59. *Kalittogai*, *Pālaikkali*, 9, 12-17
60. Ibid., 51
61. *Kuruntogai*, 167
62. *Puranānūru*, 2
63. Ibid., 3
64. *Narriṇai*, 111
65. Ibid., 120
66. *Puranānūru*, 24
67. Ibid., 164
68. *Narriṇai*, 380
69. *Tirukkuraḷ*, 740, 1036, 1040, 1065, 1166, 1201, 1330
70. Nāladiyār, 219, 271,345, 356, 386, 392
71. *Śilāppaḍigāram*, cento from cantos xvii-xxii. The translation owes much to the literal prose version of Professor V. R. R. Dīkshitar (above, p. 539)

CHAPTER X: CONCLUSION

BIBLIOGRAPHY

For general histories of India in later times, see bibliography to chapter iii, p. 521.

Expansion of Indian Culture

D. G. E. Hall. *History of South East Asia*. London, 1955.

H. G. Quaritch Wales. *The Making of Greater India*. London, 1951.

R. le May. *The Culture of South East Asia*. London, 1954.

G. C. Coëdes. *Les États Hindouisés d'Indochine et d'Indonēsie*. Paris, 1948

R. C. Majumdār. *Ancient Indian Colonies in the Far East*. 2 vols. in 4 parts, Lāhore, Daccā and Madras, 1927-44.

Indian Influence on Modern Europe

R. Schwab. *La Renaissance Orientale*. Paris, 1950.

REFERENCE

1. Interesting and stimulating, but often fantastic, is A. Lillie, *India in Primitive Christianity* (2nd ed., London, 1909); also A. J. Edmunds, *Buddhist and Christian Gospels* (Tokyo, 1905)

APPENDICES

BIBLIOGRAPHY

I. Cosmology and Geography

L. D. Barnett. *Antiquities of India*. London, 1913, eh. vi.

L. Renou. *L'Inde Classique* voi. i. Paris, 1947, pp. SS2ff., 546ff.

II. Astronomy

L. D. Barnett. Op. dt, eh. vi.

G. Thibaut. *Indisene Astronomie, Astrologie, und Mathematik*. Strassburg, 1899.

III. Calendar

L. D. Barnett. Op. cit., ch. vi and pp. 94-5.

R. Sewell and S. B. Dikshit. *The Indian Calendar*. London, 1896.

L. D. Swāmikannu Pillai. *Indian Chronology*. Madras, 1911.

Sir A. Cunningham. *A Book of Indian Eras*. Calcutta, 1883.

IV. Mathematics

B. B. Datta and A. N. Singh. *History of Hindu Mathematics*. Voi. i, Lahore, 1935.

G. R. Kaye. *Indian Mathematics*. Calcutta, 1915.

D. E. Smith and L. C. Karpinski. *The Hindu-Arabic Numerals*. Boston, 1911.

V. Physics and Chemistry

A. B. Keith. *Indian Logic and Atomism*. Oxford, 1921, ch. viii.

H. Ui. The Vais'esika Philosophy. London, 1917.

P. R. and P. C. Rāy. *History of Chemistry in Ancient and Medieval India*. Calcutta, 1956.

VI. Physiology and Medicine

L. D. Barnett. Op. cit., ch. viii.

J. Jolly. *Indian Medicine*. Poona, 1951. (Original ed. *Indische Medizin*. Strassburg, 1901).

J. Filliozat. *La Doctrine Classique de la Médicine Indienne*. Paris, 1949.

H. R. Zimmer. *Hindu Medicine*. Baltimore, 1948.

VII. Logic and Epistemology

A. B. Keith. Op. cit. above.

T. Stoherbatsky. *Buddhist Logic*. 2 vols. New York, 1962. (Originally published in Leningrad, 1932.)

S. Mookerjee. *The Jaina Philosophy of Non-Absolutism*. Calcutta, 1944. (For Jaina epistemology and ontology see also bibliography to ch. vii, p. 531.)

VIII. Weights and Measures

L. D. Barnett. Op. cit., ch. vii.

A. Bose. Op. cit. above, p. 529, voi. ii, ch. iii.

IX. Coinage

E. J. Rapson. *Indian Coins*. Strassburg, 1897.

Sir A. Cunningham. *Coins of Ancient India*. London, 1891.

C. J. Brown. *The Coins of India*. Calcutta, 1922.

A. S. Alterar. *The Coinage of the Gupta Empire*. Corpus of Indian Coins, voi. iv. Banaras, 1957.

Catalogues of Indian Coins in the British Museum

J. Allan. *Ancient India*. London, 1936.

P. Gardner. *Greek and Scythic Kings*. London, 1886.

E. J. Rapson. *Āndhras, Western Kṣatrapas, etc*. London, 1908.

J. Allan. *Gupta Dynasties*. London, 1914.

V. A. Smith. *Catalogne of Coins in the Indian Museum, Calcutta. Pt. i, Early Foreign Dynasties and the Guptas*. Oxford, 1906.

R. B. Whitehead. *Catalogue of Coins in the Panjāb Museum, Lahore. Vol. i, Indo-Greek Coins*. Oxford, 1914.

X. The Alphabet

See bibliography to eh. ix, above.

XI. Prosody

A. B. Keith. *History of Sanskrit Literature*. Oxford, 1928, p. 417ff.
V. S. Apte. *Sanskrit-English Dictionary*. 2nd ed., Bombay, 1912. App. I.
J. Vinson. *Manuel de la Langue Tamoule*. Paris, 1903, p. 225ff.

XII. The Gypsies

D. Macritchie. *Accounts of the Gypsies in India*. London, 1886.
Sir R. L. Turner. *The Position of Romani in Indo-Aryan*. London, 1927.
C. J. P. Serboianu. *Les Tsiganes*. Paris, 1930.
M. Block. *Zigeuner*. Leipzig. 1936.
J. Bloch. *Les Tsiganes*. Paris, 1953.

INDEX AND GLOSSARY

NOTE. The following abbreviations are used: arch., archæological; c. city; dyn., dynasty; H., Hindī; k., king; leg., legendary; n., proper name; Pkt., Prākrit; pl., place-name; reg., region; Skt., Sanskrit; Tam., Tamil.

B

N

U

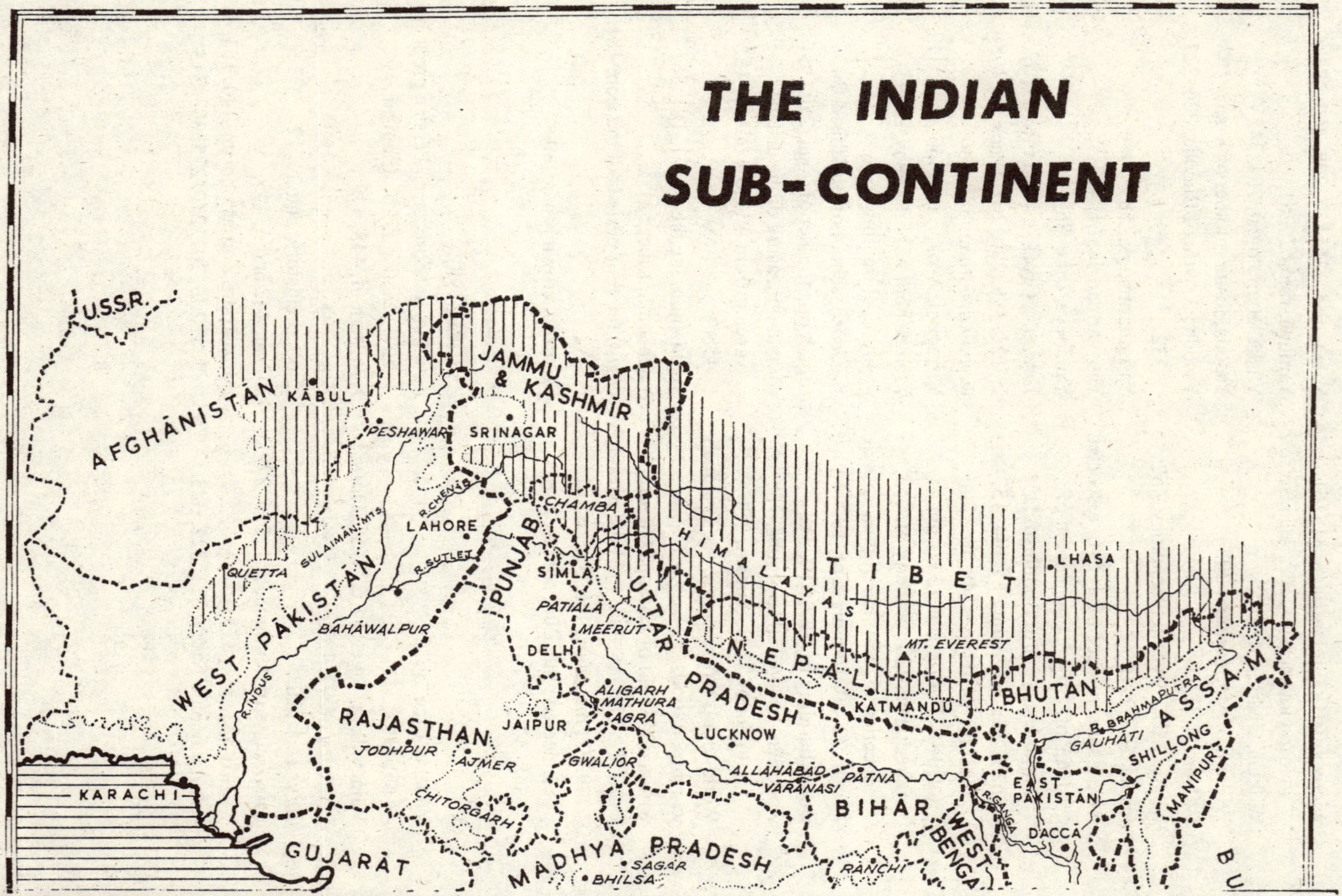
THE INDIAN
SUB-CONTINENT
U.S.S.R.
AFGHĀNISTĀN
KĀBUL
PESHAWAR
JAMMU & KASHMĪR
SRINAGAR
R. CHENAB
LAHORE
SULAIMĀN MTS.
QUETTA
R. SUTLEJ
CHAMBA
PUNJAB
SIMLA
PATIĀLĀ
HIMALAYAS
TIBET
LHASA
WEST PĀKISTĀN
BAHĀWALPUR
R. INDUS
KARACHI
MEERUT
DELHI
UTTAR PRADESH
NEPAL
MT. EVEREST
KATMANDU
BHUTĀN
ASSAM
R. BRAHMAPUTRA
GAUHĀTI
SHILLONG
MANIPUR
ALIGARH
MATHURA
AGRA
LUCKNOW
JAIPUR
RAJASTHAN
JODHPUR
AJMER
CHITORGARH
GWALIOR
ALLĀHĀBĀD
VARANASI
PATNA
BIHĀR
R. GANGA
EAST PĀKISTĀN
DACCĀ
WEST BENGA
RĀNCHI
GUJARĀT
MADHYA PRADESH
SAGAR
BHILSA
BU

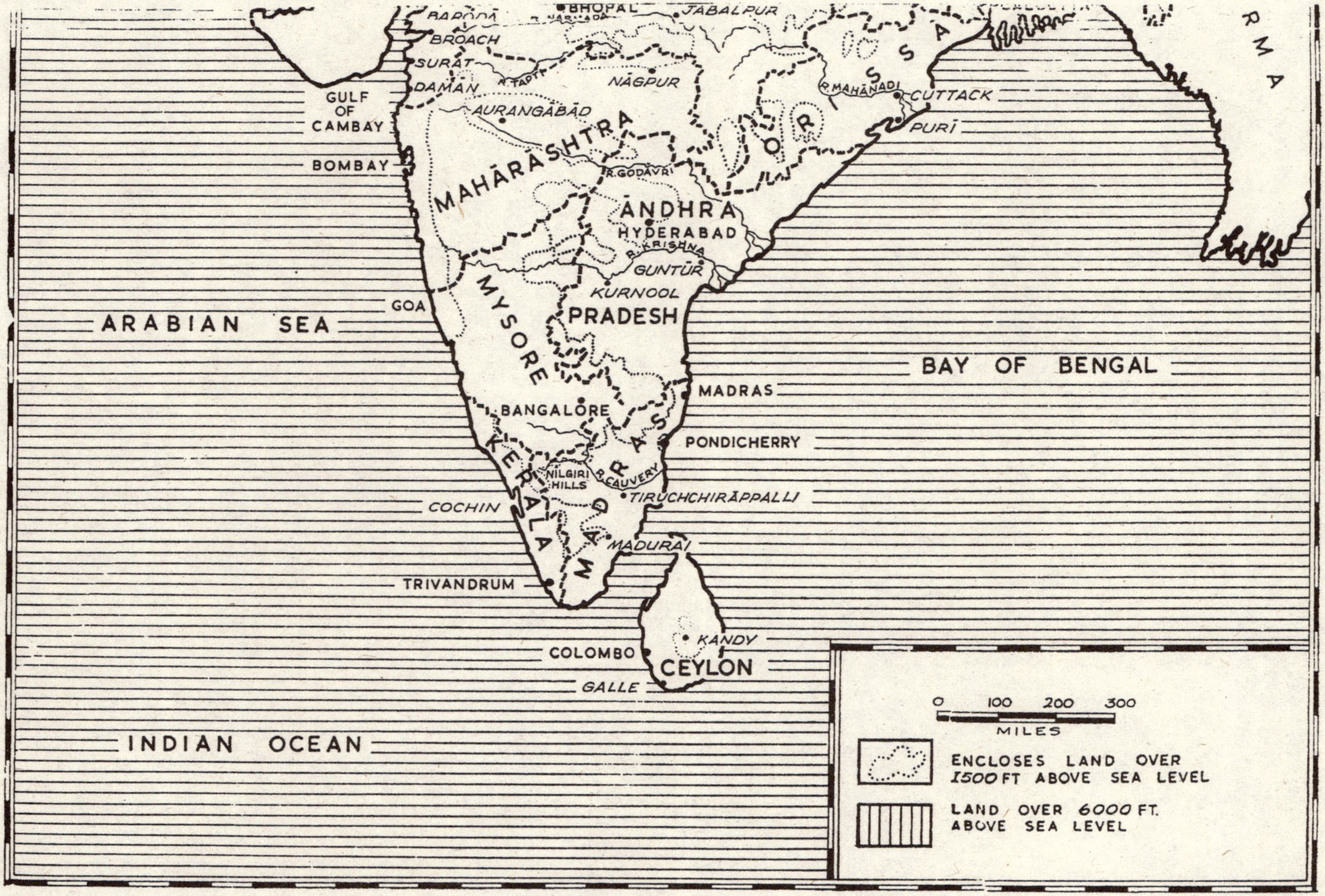

BHOPAL
JABALPUR
BARODA
BROACH
SURAT
DAMAN
R. TAPTI
NĀGPUR
GULF OF CAMBAY
AURANGĀBĀD
MAHĀRĀSHTRA
BOMBAY
R. GODĀVRI
ĀNDHRA
HYDERABAD
R. KRISHNA
GUNTŪR
KURNOOL
PRADESH
GOA
ARABIAN SEA
MYSORE
BAY OF BENGAL
MADRAS
BANGALORE
PONDICHERRY
KERALA
NILGIRI HILLS
R. CAUVERY
TIRUCHCHIRĀPPALLI
COCHIN
MADRAS
MADURAI
TRIVANDRUM
KANDY
COLOMBO
CEYLON
GALLE
INDIAN OCEAN
ORISSA
R. MAHĀNADI
CUTTACK
PURĪ
RMA
0 100 200 300
MILES
ENCLOSES LAND OVER 1500 FT ABOVE SEA LEVEL
LAND OVER 6000 FT. ABOVE SEA LEVEL